ANIMAL RIGHTS

A BEGINNER'S GUIDE

Animal Rights Updates

Resource information changes quickly!
To receive a FREE copy of the most recent updates, send a long, self-addressed, stamped envelope to:

Animal Rights Updates
P.O. Box 51 • Yellow Springs, OH 45387

ANIMAL RIGHTS

A BEGINNER'S GUIDE

A Handbook of Issues,
Organizations, Actions, and Resources

AMY BLOUNT ACHOR

Excerpts from *Animal Farm* by George Orwell, copyright 1946 by Harcourt Brace & Company and renewed 1974 by Sonia Orwell, reprinted by permission of Harcourt Brace & Company. The author gratefully acknowledges and thanks all authors and publishers who extended permission to use quotes.

Typesetting by April E. Wilson and Amy Blount Achor.

Cover design by Lisa Wolters.

Front cover photograph by Linda Leas.

Published by WriteWare, Inc.
P.O. Box 51, Yellow Springs, Ohio 45387

Printed in the United States of America.

ISBN 0-9631865-1-5

Library of Congress Catalog No. 96-090093

Printed on paper that is 85% recycled with 10% post-consumer waste. Printed with soy-based ink.

A portion of the proceeds from this book will be donated to animal rights causes.

In loving memory of my sister,
Lucy Ellen Blount,
whose rebellious spirit and
determined sense of justice live on.

This second edition is also dedicated to
all of you — human and nonhuman,
in body and in spirit — who have helped me
see, feel, and express who I am, and thus have
enabled me to move beyond myself.

Acknowledgements

Extra special thanks to the following friends and extended family:

- *Berniece E. Blount* and *Henry C. Blount, Jr.*, my parents, whose support made this book possible. I could never have done it without you.
- *April E. Wilson*, for your diligence, patience, and enthusiasm in the initial typesetting of this book.
- *Victor A. C. Mickunas*, for your keen eye and literary know-how.
- Each of you who wrote a supportive note, spoke a kind word, or otherwise offered encouragement for this book. Never underestimate the power of kindness.
- The animal rights advocates and organizations across the country, and across the planet, whose courage and determination have helped bring us closer to an era of compassion. The information presented in this book is largely a compilation of facts from these dedicated rights advocates.
- *Agnes, Ann, Brownie, Buster, Clancy, Cody, Dinah, F.M., Hank, Heather, Hershell, Kate, Lily, Max, Molly, Ms. Brown, Nicky, Pearson, Sarah, Sunshine*, and the many other named and unnamed spirits who continue to touch my life.

Photograph and Illustration Credits

Amy Blount Achor (back cover, pages 127, 135, 145, 165, 169, 173)

The American Anti-Vivisection Society (back cover, pages 93, 103, 121, Chapter 6 insert)

Coalition of Municipalities to Ban Animal Trafficking (page 43)

Farm Animal Reform Movement (pages 19, 77, 81, 83, 86, 87, 185 [S. Behm])

Glorious Graphics, Gloria Reich (Chapter 4 insert)

Stephanie Haythe (page 3)

Jeff Hiles (page 33)

Linda Leas (front cover, page 36)

William McCuddy (back cover)

People for the Ethical Treatment of Animals (pages 15, 97, 110, 111, 132, 151, Chapter 6 insert)

People/Animals Network (page 44)

Randy Shields (back cover, pages 37, 48, 169, 193, 204)

Sabrina Simon (page 156)

Lisa Wolters (cover design)

Woodstock Animal Rights Movement (page 194)

A Note From the Author

This was not an easy book to write and it is not an easy book to read. It deals with the truth about animals in American society today. By its very nature, the subject is a serious one that requires examining the darker side of human behavior — the side that is able to turn a blind eye and a deaf ear toward suffering. That said, this book also points the way out. It is a guide to personal empowerment and practical change. It addresses the problems, but it also provides solutions.

Some argue that selfishness and greed are human nature. I disagree. The human heart, though capable of allowing gross atrocities, has an equal capacity for love and kindness. The human mind is capable of extraordinary insight and creativity. We have the power of choice, and that is a great power indeed. We need only keep our eyes, our minds, and our hearts open, and have the courage to live our convictions. That is enough.

The intent of *Animal Rights: A Beginner's Guide* is to start you on a journey. It offers a glimpse into the lives of animals in our present society, and encourages you to examine yourself and the roles of animals in your own life. It then invites you to explore ways in which you can make a difference, by yourself or with others of like-mind.

This book is designed to meet the needs of a wide range of readers, from those who haven't the faintest idea what animal rights is, to "old-timers" who have been active in the movement for years. Beginners will want to start with Parts One and Two, "Introduction to Animal Rights" and "The Issues." Relatively new activists will find guidance in Part Three, "Personal Action." Seasoned activists will want to turn directly to Part Four, "Resources for Animals."

All of us can and do make a difference in the lives of animals. Whether you know it or not, decisions you make every day impact animals that you have never seen. From the food you eat and the clothing you wear, to the products you buy and the charities you support, your actions can harm or benefit animals. *Animal Rights: A Beginner's Guide* tells you how.

Let this book touch you. The reality is a painful one, but it is not insurmountable. It is a reality that we ourselves collectively create. And we are always free to begin creating anew. Here's to a more compassionate reality...for all of us.

In peace for all beings,

Amy Blount Achor

Table of Contents

PART ONE — INTRODUCTION TO ANIMAL RIGHTS

PART TWO — THE ISSUES

PART FOUR — RESOURCES FOR ANIMALS

Chapter 12: Products and Services 325

Chapter 13: Further Reading 359

Part One

Introduction to Animal Rights

Chapter 1

Animal Rights

A Movement Whose Time Has Come

Stephanie Haythe

Now, comrades, what is the nature of this life of ours? Let us face it: our lives are miserable, laborious, and short. We are born, we are given just so much food as will keep the breath in our bodies, and those of us who are capable of it are forced to work to the last atom of our strength; and the very instant that our usefulness has come to an end we are slaughtered with hideous cruelty...The life of an animal is misery and slavery: that is the plain truth...Man is the only real enemy we have.

— Major, an elder boar, speaking in *Animal Farm* by George Orwell

Like the civil rights and women's rights movements before it, the animal rights movement has mushroomed into a social and political movement of monumental proportions. As never before in history, people of all persuasions are speaking out against practices and institutions that violate animals. Advocates are challenging the furrier, the puppy mill operator, the circus promoter, and the laboratory researcher. They are confronting the zoo keeper, the pet shop owner, the dog track operator, the meat and dairy farmer, and the sport hunter. In every arena where animals are exploited, people are standing up and declaring, "Enough! We won't take it any more! Animals have rights!"

Animal rights can no longer be dismissed as an extremist philosophy spouted by "fringe elements." Leaders of the animal rights movement are educated and well-informed. Their challenges are based on facts, not rhetoric.

Many victories have been achieved for animals in recent years. Animal advocates have successfully intervened to reduce the needless suffering and untimely deaths of countless animals. But that's just the tiniest tip of the iceberg. There is still a long, long way to go.*

Why Is Animal Rights Important?

I am in favor of animal rights as well as human rights.
That is the way of a whole human being.

— Abraham Lincoln

It has been said that "no one is free until everyone is free." This ideology has been the cornerstone of much social and political change throughout the centuries. It embodies in it the implication that we humans are by nature sensitive beings who are affected not only by what goes on inside of us as individuals, but also what goes on outside of us.

The animal rights movement is as much about people as it is about animals. Civil rights movements have always included members outside of the oppressed group; the abolition of human slavery in the U.S. was orchestrated by "free" whites, and the women's rights movement has always included supporters of both genders. It is incorrect to assume that just because we are not the direct target of an action, that we are not oppressed by it. We do not ourselves need to personally experience torture or imprisonment to be affected by it. The knowledge that such a thing exists is enough to affect our own happiness, our own sense of freedom.

By addressing the atrocities inflicted upon nonhuman animals by humans, we are certainly helping those less fortunate than ourselves. We are also, however, helping *ourselves* in the process. By eradicating oppression in all its forms, we speed the creation of a compassionate society that respects each of us as individuals and all of us as a whole. As we move away from oppressive systems that perpetuate suffering, we move toward the safety of a community that protects us all. As long as any segment of the society is oppressed, all are candidates for oppression. What happens to my neighbor today, can happen to me tomorrow.

On a more concrete level, there are literally billions of living, breathing reasons why people are willing to put themselves on the line for animal rights. Every year in the United States, almost *seven billion* animals die at the hands of people:[1]

- 6 billion are slaughtered as food
- 365 million are hit and killed on roads and highways

---

* The author uses the term "animals" to distinguish nonhuman animals from human animals. This choice of convention is intended to facilitate reader comprehension and should not be interpreted as implying an "us and them" relationship of superiority/inferiority.

- 200 million are murdered by sport hunters
- 50 million die in laboratories
- 25 million are murdered for their fur
- 15 million "surplus" dogs and cats are killed in pounds and shelters

Many of these animals not only die hideous deaths, but suffer through equally tragic lives. As the perpetrators of this suffering, the responsibility for the pain returns to us. Perhaps more to the point: "The blood is on our hands."

So, Why Do Animals Have Rights?

What "qualifies" animals as beings with rights? Some people point to the fact that animals are capable of suffering. Others propose that animals, like humans, have a special awareness of their lives that differentiates them from the plant and mineral kingdoms. Still others base their support of animal rights on simple observation of animals. The next few sections take a closer look at these ideas.

Animal Sentience

All the arguments to prove man's superiority cannot shatter this hard fact: in suffering the animals are our equals.

— Peter Singer (*Animal Liberation*)

Most of us agree that there are certain basic rights to which all humans have a claim. These human rights reflect our belief that, despite outward appearances, humans are more alike than different. Our system of human rights stems from a belief that central to every person's being is a potential physical and psychological experience of the world. Depending on what happens to us, we experience safety and comfort, or fear and discomfort. In this way, all humans are "created equal."

Humans, however, aren't the only ones who experience the world. Like humans, animals possess *sentience,* the capacity to experience the world through senses. Like humans, animals feel comfort and discomfort. They are conscious of their existence, in the sense that they seek to avoid pain and maximize comfort. Even fish share this trait with us. As Alex Pacheco, co-founder of People for the Ethical Treatment of Animals, told an interviewer, "You and I are equal to lobsters when it comes to being boiled alive."[2]

A well-known philosopher of the late eighteenth and early nineteenth centuries, Jeremy Bentham, recognized the sentient quality of animals when he expressed the now much-quoted thought:

the question is not, Can they *reason?* nor, Can they *talk?* but, Can they *suffer?* [3]

A contemporary animal rights philosopher, Dr. Tom Regan, says:

> [Animals] have a life of their own that is of importance to them apart from their utility to us. They are not only *in* the world, they are *aware* of it. What happens to them *matters* to them. Each has a life that fares better or worse for the one whose life it is.[4]

Animals have their own lives and their own realities. Although species vary in terms of characteristics, needs, and outward expression, they share one thing in common: they are capable of *experiencing* their lives. An animal is not an *it;* an animal is a *he* or *she,* an individual with his or her own distinct character. In this way all animal species, human and nonhuman, are "created equal."

Intrinsic Value

A man is really ethical only when he obeys the constraint laid on him to aid all life which he is able to help, and when he goes out of his way to avoid injuring anything living. He does not ask how far this or that life deserves sympathy as valuable in itself, not how far it is capable of feeling. To him life as such is sacred...

— Dr. Albert Schweitzer

Many people agree that there is an even more subtle justification than sentience for both human rights and animal rights. It is the concept of *intrinsic value* or what animal rights philosopher Dr. Tom Regan calls "independent value of the individual." Dr. Regan says:

> At its deepest level, human ethics is based on the independent value of the individual: The moral worth of any one human being is not to be measured by how useful that person is in advancing the interests of other human beings...The philosophy of animal rights demands only that logic be respected. For any argument that plausibly explains the independent value of human beings implies that other animals have this same value, and have it equally. And any argument that plausibly explains the rights of humans to be treated with respect also implies that these other animals have this same right, and have it equally, too.[5]

Humans and animals have value in and of themselves, not because they are useful in some way, but simply because they exist. Humans do not exist *for* other humans, but rather *with* other humans. Similarly, animals do not exist *for* humans, but *with* them. Animals are not playthings or tools for human use; they are individuals who share the Earth with us. If you accept the intrinsic value of human beings, then you must also consider the intrinsic value of other animal beings.

Experiences and Observations of Animals

Our mistake in the past has been to assume that because other forms of life perceive things differently from us, they are necessarily, inferior: they are not. Pioneering scientific work is now opening up the immense diversity of sensory worlds experienced by other creatures: extraordinary worlds which we may never be able to enter, but which we can at least start to appreciate through our awareness of animal "supersenses." [6]

— John Downer, wildlife photographer and zoologist

Much of our mistreatment of animals stems from our lack of knowledge about them or from our misbeliefs about them. Whereas we historically think of them as "dumb animals," studies show animals to be intelligent, sensitive, and communicative, not unlike humans.

Anyone who has ever had a companion animal knows that animals are individuals with distinct characters. They think, feel, and express themselves. They are capable of affection, aggression, depression, and elation.

People who see animals as stupid or as "just animals" either have not interacted closely with animals, have not made an attempt to know them, or are so blinded by their culturally ingrained ideas about animals that they fail to observe them accurately. When there is a communication breakdown between a person and an animal, why is it that the animal is assumed to be "stupid"? Is a human infant "stupid" because I fail to understand the meaning of his cry? Is a dog stupid because I fail to understand the meaning of her bark?

Many people who have had close associations with animals confirm the existence of this communicative bond between animals and humans — and also our habit of ignoring it. Alice Walker, author of the book *The Color Purple* , observes in her essay "Am I Blue?" that children who are raised around animals quite naturally communicate with them, but unfortunately seem to forget this ability as they approach adulthood.[7] Through his association with Strongheart, the first canine to become the star of his own films, caretaker J. Allen Boone's perceptions of animals changed dramatically. He relates:

> Without being aware of the unfair thing I had been doing, I had mentally assigned myself to the upper part of the relationship of ours, because I happened to be "a human," and had mentally assigned [Strongheart] to the lower part, because he was "a dog"...[T]he more I stopped treating Strongheart like "a dog" in the conventional meaning of the term, the more he stopped acting like "a dog," at least as far as I was concerned. And the more this fascinating thing happened, the more we began functioning as rational companions and the more the kinship barriers between us came tumbling down.[8]

Contrary to popular belief, many researchers observe that animals have sophisticated systems of communication. The more publicized studies are of whales and dolphins, but scientists have also identified detailed systems of communication in animals as diverse as squirrels and elephants. You know all that tail twitching, leaf rustling, chasing, and chattering that squirrels do? It's part of a dialogue. And elephants possess an intricate communication system which includes deep rumbling noises and sounds that fall below the frequencies audible to humans.

While we humans have done a relatively poor job of learning the languages of other species, other animals have made truly amazing strides at learning to communicate with us in a way that we can understand. Almost two decades ago, a chimpanzee named Washoe became the first of her species to learn and use American Sign Language (ASL)* to communicate with humans. She has since taught ASL to another chimpanzee. Gorillas have also learned to communicate with humans through ASL, and have invented their own gestures, which they've used to communicate with each other and with humans.[9] Dolphins are another species who has learned to communicate with humans through human-devised symbols. It appears that communication between species is not so much a matter of intelligence, but rather a matter of finding a common language.

Even less understood than the languages of animals are the extraordinary abilities that they display. As one author states:

> [T]hose who are in close contact with animals for any length of time, and who are able to observe them constantly at close quarters, know how much animals do and know which cannot be explained.[10]

Scientists report that many animal species possess senses, means of communication, and means of orientation that humans lack. For example:

- Dogs have sensed the onset of their caretakers' epileptic seizures — before they occur.
- Bats have five times the hearing range of humans.
- English sheep dogs can read hand signals from a mile away.
- Birds and marine animals such as horseshoe crabs use celestial navigation.
- Many fish emit electrical impulses and are highly sensitive to changes in electrical fields.
- A snake, by flicking her tongue, can pick up chemical particles from the air and ground, and follow the trail of an animal better than a bloodhound can.
- A pit viper (a type of snake) can sense a living being by the difference in temperature between the being and his immediate environment.

The more we learn about animals, the more remarkable we find them to be. Don't they at least deserve our respect?

---

* American Sign Language (ASL) is a language consisting of manual gestures developed for deaf people.

What Rights Do Animals Have?

The goal of the human rights movement is to uniformly apply the same ethical code of treatment to all human beings. The animal rights movement has a similar goal, to establish a basic code of ethics which guides the treatment of all animal beings. Both the human rights movement and the animal rights movement seek the same end — a code of behavior that optimally benefits all members of the society. Like all rights movements, the animal rights movement asks that society broaden its definition of itself to include members previously excluded due their "inferior" status.

The animal rights movement asks for more than *kindness* towards animals; it asks for, in the words of philosopher Peter Singer, *equal consideration* of animals. That is, animal rights requests that the interests of the being be taken into account, whoever that being might be, and whatever those interests might be.[11]

From the animal rights perspective, all animals have the same basic inalienable rights which embody as much as possible the simple maxim "Live and let live." Humans, as members of the animal kingdom, are also entitled to these rights. Animal rights include:

- The right to be treated with respect.
- The right to physical, psychological, and emotional health.
- The right to not be exploited.
- The right to live in a suitable habitat.
- The right to be valued for who we are, not for how we can be used.
- The right to cooperatively share the Earth with other species.
- The right to live as much as possible according to our natures and to express our individual characters.

Obviously, circumstances are not always black and white; there are many shades of gray. Peaceful coexistence between humans is often complicated. Where one person's rights end and another person's rights begin is not always clear. The same is true for coexistence between humans and animals. Do companion animals have the "right" to breed haphazardly? By belling my cat, am I denying her a "right" to kill birds? It is possible that in fulfilling the rights of one species, there may appear to be a conflict with the rights of another species. That is why, while we are feeling our way through these transitions, we must be guided by the single question: "What best serves all parties involved?" By approaching situations in this manner, we consider the rights of all beings, as well as those of the collective community. By pursuing solutions from this perspective, we are more likely to develop creative resolutions that mutually benefit everyone involved.

What Animal Rights Is Not

Until he extends the circle of his compassion to all living things, man will not himself find peace.

— Dr. Albert Schweitzer

Some Misconceptions About Animal Rights

Some people have the wrong idea about animal rights. Before continuing, let's clear up some popular misconceptions.

◆ ***Misconception 1* — Animal rights means valuing animals over humans.**

Animal rights does not value animals over humans. Rather, it broadens the "circle of compassion" which humans reserve for themselves to include other animal beings. Animal rights recognizes both people and other animals as valuable in and of themselves. It does not take any rights away from people, but extends the basic rights enjoyed by people to the other members of the animal kingdom.

◆ ***Misconception 2* — Animal rights advocates are "animal-loving sentimentalists."**

While many individuals in the animal rights movement undoubtedly do love animals, animal rights is not about *loving* animals any more than human rights is about *loving* people. Animal rights is about respecting animal beings for who they are, and extending basic rights to all members of the animal kingdom. It has nothing to do with how lovable or unlovable an animal is. Rather, it has to do with an animal's right to live a quality life.

◆ ***Misconception 3* — Animal rights implies that there's no difference between humans and other animals.**

There are differences between all species, and between individuals within species. Animal rights simply claims that humans do not have the right to exploit other species, based on those differences. In other words, simply because humans have the ability to dominate other species doesn't make it right for us to do so.

◆ ***Misconception 4* — Giving animals rights means letting them take over the world.**

Recognizing the basic rights of animals does not mean letting them "take over." Human societies have rules. So do the societies of other species. In the same respect, some rules need to govern the cooperative living of humans and nonhumans. The crucial point for humans to remember is that we need to live in partnership with other species, not dominate and exploit them.

◆ ***Misconception 5* — Animal rights advocates are terrorists.**

A favorite claim of industries that make money off of animals is that animal rights activists are nothing less than "terrorists." Portraying activists as terrorists is intended to discredit all members of the animal rights movement, and to sway public opinion against the movement, particularly in the area of using animals in scientific research.

It's true that there is a small, organized faction of animal rights advocates that engages in the destruction of property related to animal exploitation, particularly research laboratories. These activists, who call themselves the Animal Liberation Front (ALF), readily take credit for breaking into research laboratories and "neutralizing" them by destroying equipment, stealing research records (such as videotapes), and relocating laboratory animals to safe havens. While these individuals unquestionably break the law, they can hardly be considered terrorists. In fact, they have stated that they operate by a strict code of ethics which allows them to destroy property directly linked to animal suffering, but forbids them from threatening the life of any living creature, human or otherwise.*

Very simply, these "animal liberators" feel that drastic circumstances call for drastic measures, and that destruction of property is justified when it relieves suffering. Moved by the horrors of animal research, they feel compelled to relieve suffering in the most direct way possible — by doing away with the laboratory. In at least one case, published evidence acquired from a break-in resulted in a halt to the research when, after examining the research records, funding officials withdrew the funding. The evidence also led to an animal cruelty charge against the researcher.

While laboratory break-ins make sensational headlines, those who participate in them are simply a few scattered individuals who do not represent the hundreds of thousands of other animal advocates in the movement. The vast majority of advocates in the animal rights movement stick to lawful methods to accomplish their goals. In fact, many animal rights groups and individuals have condemned the use of unlawful tactics such as break-ins. Judging the entire animal rights movement on the actions of a few "animal liberators" is like discrediting the entire civil rights movement because of the militant actions of the Black Panthers.

The intent behind continually publicizing laboratory break-ins is to shift attention away from the actions of the animal exploiters and to turn public opinion against all animal rights activities. Animal rights advocates in general *do* threaten animal exploiters — but they threaten them with exposure, not with physical harm. By investigating and publicizing what exploiters do to animals, animal rights advocates naturally put exploiters on the defensive. Portraying all activists as terrorists stems from a rising fear within the research industry that animal rights proponents are having a tremendous impact.

---

* Recently, individuals identifying themselves as the "Justice Department" or "Animal Rights Militia" have claimed responsibility for letter bombs that *have* harmed people in Europe. These individuals are *not* the same as the ALF and *should* be considered terrorists. There is speculation that the true purpose of these activities may be to discredit the animal rights movement in the public's mind.

On the other side of the coin are the animal rights advocates who have suffered serious injury and death at the hands of their opposition. These instances of violence are rarely publicized. Injuries range from black eyes, broken noses, and broken legs to broken backs, scalp lacerations, gunshot wounds, a fractured skull, and death. Animal advocates have been gunned down on the street and killed by explosives.[12] Advocates have had their homes broken into and vandalized, and have been the target of death threats and other direct harassment which local police and the FBI have chosen to ignore, failing to even file reports. Sometimes the harassment is from local and federal law officials themselves. In some cases the harassment has been so extreme that advocates have been forced to withdraw from the movement.

So next time you hear something about an animal rights "terrorist," think twice before jumping to conclusions. Think about who is reporting the story and what they may have to gain from it. After all, animal rights activists invest time, energy, heart, and money into trying to help individuals who don't even know they're being helped; animal activists are working to put themselves out of business. Those who exploit animals do so because they have a vested interest in doing so; they are acting out of selfishness. Who do you think is more likely to tell the truth?

Animal Rights, Welfare, and Conservation

What's in a name? According to Shakespeare, "that which we call a rose by any other name would smell as sweet," but when it comes to animal rights, names can make a difference. Technically, *animal rights* differs from *animal welfare* and from *wildlife conservation* in significant ways. The following definitions indicate the meaning of these terms as used in this book.

■ Animal Rights

We've already discussed animal rights pretty thoroughly. To summarize, animal rights recognizes the inherent right of all animals to lives that are free from exploitation and undue interference. In addition to addressing individual instances of cruelty, animal rights advocates work to institute laws, customs, and practices that grant animals their basic rights.

■ Animal Welfare

Animal welfare historically differs from animal rights in important ways. Animal welfare insists on certain minimal standards for the treatment of animals, but it does not necessarily recognize the rights of animals to not be exploited by humans; animal welfare is more concerned with kindness than with rights. For example, animal welfare historically has not been concerned with whether or not animals are used for food, clothing, or in research; it has been concerned with whether or not the animals used for these purposes have adequate food, water, and shelter. By way of analogy, think of the welfare advocate as working for the humane treatment of slaves, and the rights advocate as working for the abolition of slavery.

Lately, the lines between animal welfare and animal rights have become blurry. Some animal welfare organizations are advocating for animal rights. This reflects the growing awareness that the true welfare of animals intrinsically implies recognition of animal rights. Still, while some welfare organizations have updated their thinking to include rights, others cling to the old definition. Don't get hung up on the words, but do recognize that animal rights and animal welfare are two different concepts.

■ Wildlife Conservation

Wildlife conservation is a different matter altogether. Most of us think of conservation as implying protection or preservation. Ironically, a great number of so-called wildlife conservation groups exist to protect and preserve *hunting*. Groups such as Ducks Unlimited do put some effort into conserving selected species — conserving them for the hunter's bullet.

The Wildlife Conservation Fund of America sounds like an animal protection group, but part of its stated purpose is "to protect the heritage of the American sportsman to hunt, fish, and trap."[13] They, like many other wildlife conservation groups, work to preserve wildlife so that there is a steady supply for the hunter, fisher, and trapper. Many conservation groups do not advertise the fact that they support hunting or that a large percentage of their membership are hunters.

Other groups don't openly support hunting, but neither do they oppose it. They may advocate or condone hunting in certain instances, as long as the species as a whole isn't threatened. Their concern is not for individual animals, but for preserving species. Members of the very visible World Wildlife Fund might be surprised to discover that it is headed by Prince Philip, an avid hunter throughout his lifetime. This doesn't mean that these organizations don't do some good things for animals and habitats, but their overall philosophies may merit consideration by potential or current supporters.

A handful of wildlife conservation groups, such as the Sea Shepherd Conservation Society, do live up to the true meaning of conservation. These groups work vigorously to protect animals for the animals' sake, sometimes putting themselves at risk in the process.

In general, it is wise to err on the side of caution when it comes to conservation groups. How can you tell the difference between the organizations that work for animals and the ones that work for hunters? See Chapter 7 for a list of groups that support hunting and trapping.

Conclusion

Animal rights is a moral position based on the following assertion:

> All animals, human and nonhuman, are unique expressions of life that have inherent value, for no reason other than the fact that they exist. Animals are sentient beings, capable of feeling pain and of suffering. As such, they have the right to not be intentionally subjected to unnecessary pain. They have the

right to live their lives without exploitation or undue interference.

Might does not make right! Just because humans have the ability to exploit animals does not make it right to do so, any more than the ability to dominate a particular race or social class of people makes it right to do so. Like humans, animals are unique individuals. They experience their lives, and the quality of their lives matters to them.

One aim of the animal rights movement is to motivate human society to recognize itself as part of a larger society. By identifying ourselves as part of this larger society, we can begin to see ourselves not as a be-all end and-all, but as members of a vast, complex community of which we are but one part. This perspective ceases to see animals as things to be used and begins to view them instead as beings with which to interact.

Animal Rights

At a Glance

Did you know:

- Over seven billion animals die at the hands of humans in the U.S. every year.
- Like humans, animals feel emotions such as pain, anxiety, and affection.
- Animals are different from, not inferior to, people. Both humans and animals have value not because they are useful in some way, but simply because they exist.
- Many animals have abilities far superior to human abilities.
- The animal rights movement is very similar to the humans rights movement, asking only that a common basic code of ethics be applied to all animal beings.

Chapter 2

Violence Towards Animals

So, What's All the Fuss About?

People for the Ethical Treatment of Animals

You and I want to love and be loved; we really don't want to hurt, or violate, or kill. We used to believe that we had to do that to live; we were trained to accept violence as normal. Now we know there are alternatives. Now we can leave behind our inherited patterns of brutality and domination, creating together a better world for all beings.

— Billy Ray Boyd (*For the Vegetarian in You)*

When you think of animal cruelty, what do you think of? Someone beating a dog? Or starving a horse? These are unquestionably cruel acts, but they don't begin to scratch the surface of cruelty to animals in our society.

Do you support cruelty towards animals? Of course not! Yet, you may be surprised at the number of ways you unwittingly *do* contribute to cruelty. For example, do you:

- Eat meat?
- Drink milk?
- Wear leather?
- Wear fur?
- Use down pillows?
- Use a shampoo produced by a major corporation?

- Go to the circus or rodeo?
- Attend dog races or horse races?
- Donate money to a charity that conducts animal research?

If you answered "yes" to any of those questions, you are probably an indirect contributor to violence towards animals. How? Violence is built into products you use every day and entertainment you pay to attend. Let's take a closer look.

Institutionalized Cruelty

Most of the violence towards animals in our society is not perpetrated by individuals acting on impulse. Most violence is in the form of calculated actions administered by industries that exploit animals for profits. Very simply, the vast majority of animal cruelty in our society exists because of economics. This cruelty is part of many of our societal institutions, part of our way of life. For example:

- **In the food industry...**
  Billions of animals suffer painful, unnatural lives, confined to cramped quarters and subjected to stressful living conditions and invasive procedures. Modern factory farming methods treat animals as if they were machines, denying them even basic needs. The reason? Humane farming methods would cut too deeply into profits. This industry also provides us with leather and pet food ingredients.

- **In the fur industry...**
  Animals spend unnatural lives crammed into cages on fur farms, or are snared by painful steel-jaw leghold traps and subsequently clubbed or crushed to death. All of this for the "luxury" of a fur coat or fur-lined gloves.

- **In the personal care and household product industries...**
  Millions of unanesthetized animals suffer through painful, unnecessary procedures designed solely to protect the financial interests of companies against consumer lawsuits. These tests are not required by law and do not protect consumers.

- **In the scientific community...**
  Animals suffer horribly in psychological, military, and biomedical tests that have no relevance for humankind. Our tax dollars fund much of the torment.

- **In the entertainment industries...**
  In television programs, movies, rodeos, and animal acts of all kinds, pain and fear coerce animals into performing actions unnatural to them. Wild animals are "tamed," while tame animals are provoked into acting out of control (such as so-called "bucking" broncos). These animals suffer for the admission fees paid by curious patrons.

- **In classrooms...**
  Animals are unnecessarily killed and dissected so that companies who sell animals for this purpose can prosper.

- **In horse and dog racing...**
  Animals are disposable commodities that exist for the sole purpose of turning a profit. The thousands of animals bred for this industry who don't make the grade are destroyed or sold to laboratories to undergo painful experiments.

- **In the pet industry...**
  Puppy mill operators subject animals to starvation, filth, disease, and outright physical abuse for a few dollars of profit. Unscrupulous animal dealers steal animals from backyards and streets, and sell them to breeders for a quick buck.

- **In hunting circles...**
  Animals are gunned down or pierced with arrows for "fun." Many wounded animals die slow, painful deaths so that weekend "sportsmen" can enjoy the art of killing and so that state fish and game agencies can prosper.

Meat, fur, meaningless product tests, useless experiments, exploitive entertainment, animal overpopulation, killing for fun — none of these things are necessary for our well-being. They are all perpetrated for economic gain.

As a society, we openly condemn individual acts of cruelty, yet we silently condone institutionalized cruelty such as that described above. We condone the cruelty that has become a part of the way we do business, solve problems, and have fun.

The Foundations of Cruelty

It is safe to state that for someone to inflict pain, suffering, and death on sentient beings, there has to be a considerable denial of the heart. The heart would sense the suffering and reflect this to the vivisector. Those who practice cruelty must split their awareness from their feeling nature.

— Louis J. Marx, M.D. (*Vivisection: Science or Science Fiction*)

There are many reasons why animal cruelty persists. Our culture, our individual characters, and our insulation from the abuse all contribute to its continuance. Here are some of the influences that affect our perceptions of animals and our treatment of them.

A Heritage of Violence

Ours is a violent society, based on a heritage of violence. The so-called "settling" of this country involved the virtual annihilation of entire societies of native peoples, animal species, and everything else that got in the way. This consciousness of violence persists today.

In his book *On An Average Day*, Tom Heymann reports that on a given day in the United States:[1]

- 3,786 people are assaulted, 175 of those assaults being rape or murder
- 1,849 children are abused
- 5,556 schoolchildren are spanked in schools
- Children witness 33 acts of violence for every 3-1/2 hours of television watched

Is it any wonder that our violence extends to animals? Our actions towards animals are simply an extension of what we do to ourselves. The mistaken ideas about animals that underlie abuse — that they are unfeeling, morally inferior, exist only for our use, etc. — are the same ideas people in power have used to condone the enslavement and exploitation of various human subgroups throughout history. The target changes, but the nature of the abuse remains the same.

Economics

Most people who make money off of animal suffering don't do it in order to hurt animals; they do it to make a profit. The fact that animals suffer in the course of making money is just an unfortunate circumstance.

Most businesses that involve animals are inherently cruel. They require confining animals to cages in unnatural environments, subjecting them to less than humane conditions, and in most cases, killing them. Whether it's farms, circuses, zoos, classrooms, or laboratories, when money is involved, animals become just so much merchandise. Animal suffering is simply a requirement of the business.

Treating animals humanely requires shifts in the job market. But such shifts have always been a part of life. New trends make old ways of doing things obsolete. We've seen it time and again as we've evolved technologically and socially. Automobiles replaced carriages, light bulbs replaced oil lamps, refrigerators replaced ice boxes. The abolition of human slavery put slave traders out of business. Change is inevitable. Job security is a genuine concern, but it is not a justification for continuing cruelty.

As we incorporate the principles of animal rights into our society, we can and must be creative about the economic realities that such a shift demands. For example, the organization Food Animal Concerns Trust (FACT), promotes more humane treatment of farm animals by providing packaging, point-of-sale materials, publicity, and other marketing assistance to farmers who employ more humane farming methods. While FACT can't be considered an animal rights group, their approach is one that goes right to the heart of the matter — practical assistance. It is by encouraging alternatives to abuse, and offering assistance to those who pursue the alternatives, that the most progress can be made.

Speciesism: The Us and Them Mentality

All of the rationalizations that allow us to exploit animals, or that allow us to let others exploit animals, can be summed up in one attitude: speciesism (pronounced SPEE-sheez-izm). Speciesism is "prejudice or discrimination based on species."[2]

Like racism and sexism, speciesism is a belief in the superiority of one group over another group. It creates distance between two groups, separating them into divergent camps of *us* and *them*.

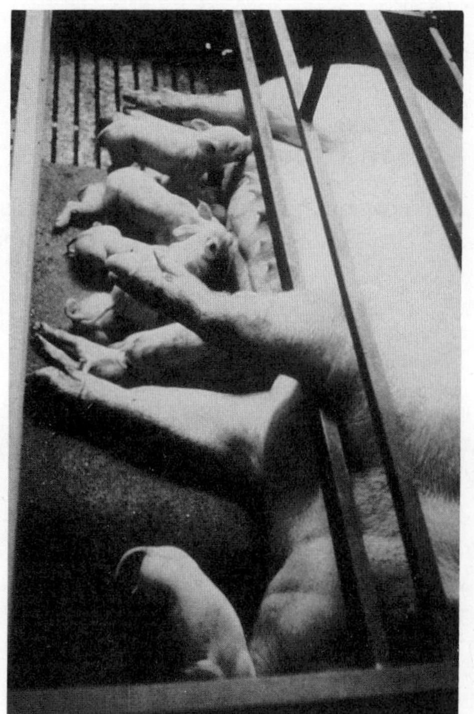

Farm Animal Reform Movement

Speciesism allows us to treat animals as property, instead of as beings.

Like all prejudices, speciesism focuses on the differences, rather than the similarities, between *us* and *them*. By mentally placing humans into one group and all other animals into another group, we emotionally separate ourselves from *them*. This emotional distancing is essential to any exploitive relationship; it is difficult to exploit those with whom we identify and empathize. Maintaining the attitude that they are "just animals" allows us to rationalize our self-centered treatment of animals.

Our language reflects the depth of speciesism in our culture. Although we ourselves are animals, when we say "animal," we mean *them*. We use a completely different word, "human," to refer to ourselves. This strengthens the *us* and *them* mentality. The Cruelty Clichés box on the next page contains other examples of speciesist language.

The roots of speciesism are anchored in the various myths and misconceptions about animals passed through the ages. The influence of these ancient myths persists even to this day. Here are some of the surviving myths that continue to influence the way many people regard animals.

Cruelty Clichés

Are you responsible for spreading negative images of animals? Here are some common phrases that contain references to animals. We often use these expressions without thinking of their meaning. As you read them, think about what we are really saying. When we use these "cruelty clichés," we promote a mode of thinking that endorses cruelty towards animals and negative images of them.

"Killing two birds with one stone."
"More than one way to skin a cat."
"Taking the bull by the horns."
"I'm a dead duck."
"Bringing home the bacon."
"Bleeding like a stuck pig."
"Living high on the hog."
"My goose is cooked."
"Beating a dead horse."
"Eating crow."

We also promote negative images of animals by attributing negative characteristics to them. Think about what it means to call someone:

An animal. (a brute or beast)
A pig. (a slob)
A jackass. (an idiot)
A dog. (lazy, no-good, or ugly)
A turkey. (an idiot)
A snake in the grass. (deceptive, sleazy)

Avoid using such stereotypic phrases that convey false, negative images of animals. Remember, if someone calls you a "pig," they are actually calling you an intelligent, social being!

◆ ***MYTH 1* — Unlike people, animals lack souls.**

The assertion that humans have souls, which live on after the body dies, and that animals lack souls is a centuries-old justification for doing whatever we like to animals. Low spiritual status is equated with low moral status. If animals do not have souls, the reasoning goes, then humans have no moral obligation towards them.[3] Not surprisingly, women and slaves have also been branded as beings without souls, and therefore unentitled to the same rights as white men.

No one can absolutely say if either people or animals have souls, or whether having a soul places one in a position of moral superiority. These are moral arguments for which no proof exists. What we do know for certain is that both humans and animals possess life, and that both experience comfort and discomfort. We know that for animals, as for humans, what happens to them makes a difference to them. That fact in itself is enough reason to treat all humans and animals with common respect.

For the sake of argument, though, let's suppose that we know without doubt that humans have souls and animals don't. This would mean that an animal's existence is limited solely to his or her immediate life on Earth. If this is the case, the argument for animal rights is actually strengthened. As Cardinal Bellarmine contended, the very fact of animals lacking souls would be all the more reason to treat them kindly in this, their only, lifetime.[4]

◆ ***MYTH 2* — Animals don't feel; they're machines.**

Back in the 1600's, René Descartes, the well-respected French philosopher, scientist, and mathematician of "I think; therefore I am" fame, concluded that animals were merely mechanical systems, bodies without consciousness. He claimed that, unlike humans, animals do not think. Asserting that a lack of "consciousness" precludes the experience of pain, he theorized that animals do not feel either emotional or physical pain. When an animal cries out in seeming pain, he said, it is simply an automatic response from a mechanical system, much like a clock striking.

As ridiculous as Descartes' "reasoning" sounds today, it was widely accepted in his day and long thereafter. Many scientists used Descartes' reasoning to justify brutal surgery without anesthesia on live, screaming animals. Today, we know without question that animals do indeed experience pain. Unfortunately, old ways of thinking die hard. Even as recently as 1966, theologians were speaking out in agreement with Descartes,[5] and remnants of Descartes' philosophy are still alive in modern-day laboratories and other societal institutions. A pigeon shooter at the annual Hegins, Pennsylvania Pigeon Shoot summed it up as follows: "I don't think a bird has any feeling. You can shoot them three-quarters dead out there and they'll just go on over to some corn and go on eating."[6]

◆ ***MYTH 3* — Dominance is power. Anything I can conquer, I am superior to.**

Those who feel powerless often dominate others in an attempt to gain a sense of personal power. A familiar illustration of this is the old story about the boss who yells at the supervisor, who in turn yells at the worker, who then yells at the spouse, who yells at the child, who mistreats the dog. It's also evident in the bully who picks on those who are weaker.

The philosophy of "might makes right" is a long tradition in our society. Europeans who invaded the North American continent slaughtered both human and animal natives. The phrase "conquering nature" reveals an attitude about survival as a contest between ourselves and the world outside ourselves. The emphasis is on competition, not cooperation.

In modern times, "sports" such as hunting and fishing and spectacles such as rodeos and bullfights are all arenas where people test their abilities to dominate nature. These "contests" are hardly fair, of course, given the equipment employed and the constraints on the animals involved. Still, these traditionally male activities are regarded as arenas where men can "prove" themselves. They are activities that supposedly "separate the men from the boys."

Violent domination is not the same as power. The truly powerful person does not have to dominate or resort to violence. The real man does not have to prove his "manliness." True personal power lies in the ability to know oneself, to empathize, and to respond. Unfortunately, violent domination is an American tradition that still inhabits the consciousness (and unconscious) of many people.

◆ ***MYTH 4*** **— Human intelligence proves the moral superiority of humans.***

Our society places a high value on intelligence. We admire the intellectual. We even use the word "smart" to describe the attractiveness of inanimate objects as in, "What a smart outfit!"

Consciously or not, we link intelligence to worth. "Worthless" actually appears as a dictionary definition for the word "stupid."[7] Calling someone stupid is, in essence, calling them worthless.

This is a revealing glimpse into a strong prejudice. For centuries, humans have assumed that nonhumans are "dumb animals," implying inferiority based on a lack of intelligence (and perhaps on an inability to speak our language, the original meaning of "dumb" being "lacking the power of speech"). This implied inferior status has been used to justify the cruel treatment of both animals and humans who were considered "stupid."

For the supposedly intelligent creatures we claim to be, we have made a grave error. We have incorrectly assumed that intelligence is somehow a virtue, a reason for moral elevation. But as author and columnist Jeff Cox observes:

> Mental intelligence alone is value-neutral. It can function for evil or good. Intelligent minds carefully planned the extermination of millions of people in the bloody excesses of the 20th Century — proving in the most extreme way that intellect alone can be horrifyingly cold...The mind is a great tool, capable of astounding leaps of comprehension and calculation. But like any tool, the service to which it's put is determined by the intent of the user. For optimum mental health, intelligence must be tempered with compassion, and set to the service of a good and kind heart.[8]

Intelligence by itself is not a moral virtue; it does not make humans morally superior to animals. Then why do humans have their particular brand of intelligence? Perhaps for the same reason that the panther has speed or the turtle has a hard shell. Intelligence is our survival mechanism. Compared to other species, we don't excel at speed, strength, agility, camouflage, hearing, smell, or sight. We don't have sharp quills or threatening venom to repel those who might bother us. What else is there besides our wits to keep us alive?

As one animal behaviorist observes:

> Every animal is the smartest for the ecological niche in which it lives — if it were not, it would not be there.[9]

---

* Although intelligence is not a valid criterion for determining "worth," it is interesting to note that several scientific studies confirm the conceptual abilities of a variety of nonhuman species, including gorillas and chimpanzees who use sign language, chimpanzees who count and add, horses who demonstrate logic, and an African gray parrot who counts, selects objects with particular characteristics when verbally asked to do so (for example, "Which object is the blue, wooden circle?") and verbalizes the differences or similarities between objects.

◆ ***MYTH 5* — Humans are natural predators; it's natural for humans to kill other animals.**

Nature is a balancing act. The predator/prey scheme works because it is part of the entire web of life. Humankind's place in this scheme of life is less clear than for other animals because we have an opportunity that other animals don't have — choice. We can choose to be predators or to forego predation. In this way we are unique.

Like all life, humankind is continually evolving. There was a time in our history when killing and using animals meant the difference between life and death. This is no longer the case. Our survival does not depend on our predation of other species. Today, we do not *need* to kill; we *choose* to kill. Far from keeping a natural balance, the human obsession with killing animals has led to the near and actual extinction of many species.

Many animals are vegetarian, killing other animals only in self-defense. A close look at the human body reveals that it is well-suited to a vegetarian diet (see Chapter 4 for more on vegetarianism and the human body). We no longer need to kill to feed ourselves, clothe ourselves, house ourselves, or protect ourselves. Killing is a preference, not a necessity. For people, killing is no more natural than not killing. The "natural predator" argument just doesn't hold water.

Are You a Closet Speciesist?

You may want to pause here to examine your own speciesist attitude. Consider the following statements:

The Speciesist Believes...	Animals are inferior to humans.	Animals are here merely to serve humankind.	Humans can treat animals any way they choose.
The Non-Speciesist Believes...	Animals are different from, not inferior to, humans. Many animals demonstrate abilities that far out-perform human abilities.	Animals are here for themselves, as part of the vast animal kingdom of which humans are but one part. Humans are not the center of the universe around which all other life evolves.	Humans are obligated to treat animals with the same respect they would extend to any sentient being.

Speciesism is so pervasive that most of us are "born and bred" speciesists. If you identify with the speciesist beliefs, take a minute to think about why you feel that way. Have you ever thought about or questioned those beliefs before? Did you grow up in an environment that taught you those beliefs? Fortunately, we can unlearn speciesism by acknowledging our prejudice and opening up ourselves to conscious re-education.

Selfishness: The "Me First" Mentality

After having lunch with a group of acquaintances, a friend reported the following incident: One woman in the party ordered veal as her main course. The man sitting across from her (who, by the way, was not an animal activist) said, "How can you order veal? Don't you know how horribly veal calves are treated?" In response the woman laughed and blithely answered, "Oh, I know all about veal calves, but, well, it just tastes so darn good! I can't resist!"

This attitude is not uncommon. When it comes to food — or anything else for that matter — it's hard to give up old favorites. But there comes a time to weigh our actions against the "greatest good," a time to look beyond our present actions to the effects of those actions. Is the taste of a favorite food really worth a sentient being's misery? Likewise, is personal vanity more important than the suffering of dozens of sentient, fur-bearing beings for a fur coat?

Yes, it is a "free country" and we each have the right to choose what we eat and wear, within contemporary legal parameters. But might not the "free choice" argument merely be a thinly-disguised attempt to justify personal selfishness?

What we want as individuals *does* matter, but our personal desires aren't the only factor to consider. Just because I want a sports car doesn't give me license to steal one. My dislike of waiting in long lines at the check-out counter doesn't justify my barging in at the front of the line. Selfishness denies other beings consideration, and those denied consideration are likely to suffer as a result.

The Law of Inertia

In physics, inertia is the tendency of a body at rest to remain at rest or a body in motion to stay in motion, unless some outside influence comes into play. This law of physics aptly describes the human tendency toward habit — our tendency to follow a particular course of action simply because it is familiar. Sometimes our lives can become a series of habits where we go through motions without really thinking about them. Eating is a good example of this; we even refer to our patterns of eating as our "eating habits."

Because animal exploitation is so thoroughly integrated into our society, many of our personal habits — what we eat, wear, buy, and do — may be linked to animal suffering. We're not accustomed to questioning these choices. We don't think of a chicken sandwich as the muscle of a dead animal.

It requires an outside influence — such as a new insight about the consequences of our choices — to overcome the inertia of habits. Within us, we have the power not only to change the inertia of our personal habits, but also the power to change the inertia of societal habits. Consumers have significant influence over the marketplace. If we stop supporting products that hurt animals and instead demand animal-friendly products, you can bet that the marketplace will respond.

Misplaced Trust

The pervasiveness of animal cruelty in our society escapes some of us because of a naive faith in authority figures. Authority figures include government agencies, corporations, and other so-called "experts."

This innocent but misplaced trust in authority figures is sometimes so complete that it is blind. When told the truth, some people don't believe it because their faith in the "experts" is so unshakeable. For example, when questioned about allegations against the Moscow Circus, a patron attending the Circus said he believed that cruelty might happen in small circuses, but certainly not in a famous circus such as this. The circus-goer based his opinion solely on the fact that this was an internationally-renowned circus. In other words, he looked up to this circus as an authority. The fact is, the Moscow Circus *has* been accused of various instances and degrees of cruelty. The same is true of laboratories that use animals. The "authority" of scientists and doctors is so strong in our minds that we tend to believe everything they say without question, refusing to acknowledge the cruelties that exist behind many laboratory doors. The sad truth is that our faith in authority figures is often misplaced. We need to always "question authority."

Selective Compassion: The Double Standard

Selective compassion is a mechanism that allows us to manage our emotions when they are too overwhelming or in conflict. It is an emotional distancing that lets us reserve our empathy for a select few. For example, it's what keeps us from eating a dog, but allows us to eat a cow, and what compels us to help out a neighbor in trouble, but allows us to ignore a stranger in the same situation.

What determines whether or not we feel compassion for another being? Our emotional connection to a being, our identification with him, and our ability to respond may all be factors. For example, an acquaintance of mine was acutely disturbed to see a deer, who had been shot dead by a hunter, tied to the top of her neighbor's car, yet she experiences no distress over eating a hamburger. The emotional connection to the deer is clearly present, while the emotional connection to hamburger is nonexistent. After all, how many of us look at hamburger and see a dead cow? Even if we did, how many of us have enough of an emotional connection with cows to actually respect them as sentient beings?

Another acquaintance told me that when it comes to eating habits, he draws the line at animals with whom he can "communicate." He respects and refuses to eat animals with whom he feels he can "communicate," such as dogs, but he has no hesitation eating animals with whom he feels a lack of communication, such as cows. Of course, what he really means is that he finds it difficult to eat animals with whom he feels rapport. To make his life easier, he reserves his compassion for certain "deserving" animals (that is, those with whom he can "communicate") and places all other animals in a distinctly separate category.

Having a personal, one-on-one experience with an animal can forever change the way a person regards animals in general. After "close encounters" with animals, hunters have put down their guns, trappers have abandoned trapping, and meat eaters have become vegetarians. All of these experiences have one element in common — an awakened identification with the animal, resulting in new-found empathy and compassion.

Another reason we may choose to be selective in our compassion is to avoid emotional "overload." For some of us, acknowledging the pain of another may put us in touch with our own pain. Too many of us have acquired a habit of numbing ourselves in order to escape the pain of hurtful events in our lives, and witnessing the pain of another can awaken that hurt in us. Closing our hearts is a way we protect ourselves. Conversely, a willingness to feel the pain in ourselves will open the way to compassion for others. By feeling and accepting emotions, they become integrated, and we're thus able to think more clearly and respond more effectively.

Insulation: Hear No Evil, See No Evil, Speak No Evil

Cruelty is easy to ignore when we don't have a personal experience of it. "Out of sight, out of mind," as the saying goes. Most cruelty takes place behind closed doors in laboratories, on factory farms, in slaughterhouses, in puppy mills, and on fur farms. It takes place behind the scenes at dog races, horse races, circuses, rodeos, night clubs, and movie sets. And it takes place out in the wild, where animals are trapped, poisoned, wounded, and killed.

If it happened next door or down the street, we'd probably take notice. If we heard the cries of frightened animals being hurt, we'd react. Seeing or hearing *is* believing. But businesses that exploit animals take precautions to make sure the public doesn't see what goes on.

The "closed door" policy of industries that exploit animals means it's hard to get accurate information as to what actually goes on inside. Since their purpose is to protect their own interests, the information we get from industries that exploit animals is usually from their public relations offices or their advertising firms. We hear what they want us to hear. And what they want us to hear are those things that will make us want to buy their products, attend their shows, or fund their research projects.

For example, in egg factories newborn male chicks are tossed into plastic garbage bags, where they slowly suffocate by being buried under the bodies of other live chicks thrown in on top of them. Male chicks are not useful to the egg industry, and this is considered an acceptable method for "disposing" of them. What would the general public think of the egg industry if this practice appeared in a television commercial?

Another example is the rodeo. When you think of a rodeo, chances are you don't think of horses being jabbed with electric prods to make them bolt out of the chutes, or having belts cinched tightly around their genitals so they will buck in response to the pain. You may also be unaware that calf roping is a terrifying and brutal experience for a calf, often resulting in severe injuries. This is the type of information the ticket sellers don't include in the program.

Sometimes, it isn't the exploitive industry that insulates us from the truth. Sometimes, we employ our own self-imposed "perceptual blinders." That is, we don't *want* to know, so we simply ignore the issue.

Toward a More Compassionate Ethic

Peace and the survival of life on Earth as we know it are threatened by human activities that lack a commitment to humanitarian values. Destruction of nature and natural resources results from ignorance, greed, and lack of respect for the Earth's living things.

— The Dalai Lama (*Greenpeace*)

Animal rights is part of a broader ethic that challenges us to regard all life as sacred. It teaches us to look and feel beyond ourselves. This ethic benefits us by moving us toward greater peace within ourselves, with others, and with our planet.

The ultimate goals of the animal rights movement can teach us:

- Respect for all life forms.
- Nonviolence towards all beings.
- A humane regard for all beings.
- An acceptance of our role in the vast network of life.
- Personal responsibility through an awareness of our actions and their consequences.

Overcoming our speciesist attitude means opening up our hearts as well as our minds. It means questioning both our personal attitudes and the prevailing societal attitudes towards animals. It means admitting that our life is a series of choices and realizing that we have power over our personal choices.

We may not be able to totally abandon our self-centeredness, but we can continue to expand our conscious awareness and create space for the other beings with whom we share the planet. As Albert Einstein has stated:

> A human being is part of the whole, called by us the "Universe," a part limited in time and space. He experiences himself, his thoughts and feelings, as something separate from the rest — a kind of optical delusion of his consciousness. This delusion is a kind of prison for us, restricting us to our personal desires and to affection for a few persons nearest to us. Our task must be to free ourselves from this prison by widening our circle of compassion to embrace all living creatures and the whole of nature in its beauty. Nobody is able to achieve this completely, but the striving for such achievement is in itself a part of the liberation and a foundation for inner security.[10]

Where Do You Go From Here?

There are many things you can do to better the plights of animals in the world today. Some of these things involve the personal choices you make regarding your own lifestyle. Others involve speaking out for animals.

The first step is to educate yourself. *Part Two* tells you about specific animal rights issues and how you can make a difference on whatever level you wish to participate. If there is a particular topic that interests you, turn right to that chapter. You don't have to read the chapters in sequence. The last two sections of the book help you get started making a difference for animals. *Part Three* gives pointers to beginning activists and activist wanna-bes. *Part Four* contains resource listings to help you get the support, products, and information you need.

Part Two

- **Companion Animals**
  Companion animals are those animals who live with us in our homes, mostly cats and dogs. This chapter examines our special relationships with these animals.

- **Vegetarianism**
  The vast majority of animals killed by humans die so that we can eat them. This chapter explores reasons for adopting a vegetarian lifestyle.

- **Factory Farms**
  Factory farm is a phrase that describes the modern replacement for what was once the family farm. This chapter looks at the treatment of animals we raise to eat.

- **Research, Education, and Testing**
  Perhaps the most sensationalized of the animal rights issues is the use of animals in laboratories and classrooms. This chapter questions this controversial practice.

- **Wildlife**
  Wildlife conservation and management are shams that benefit hunters and animal exploiters, not animals. This chapter tells you about this and other ways humans hurt and destroy wildlife.

- **Entertainment**
  Animals are not toys. This chapter tells you what happens to animals behind the scenes at rodeos, circuses, and similar spectacles.

Part Three

- **Getting into the Act**
  Helping animals is as easy as changing the shampoo you use. This chapter tells you some things you can do for animals.

Part Four

- **Animal Advocacy Organizations**
  You are not alone! This chapter tells you where you can find others who care about animals.

- **Vegetarian Organizations**
  It's more fun when you do it with other people! This chapter tells you where to find people who support vegetarianism.

- **Products and Services**
  Money talks. This chapter tells you how to spend yours wisely.

- **Further Reading**
  Knowledge is power. This chapter tells you where to learn more about the subjects introduced in this book.

Conclusion

Many of our societal institutions use animals in ways that are physically and psychologically painful. We contribute to animal suffering when we support these institutions and their activities, such as animal agriculture, animal acts, and the use of animals in laboratories. While some of our mistreatment of animals stems from our ignorance about them, much of it is due to our own greed and selfishness.

Abolishing animal cruelty is as easy as examining our own lifestyle habits, exercising our power as consumers, and fulfilling our obligation as voters. Animal rights doesn't just benefit animals; it also benefits humans by moving us toward a more compassionate way of thinking and living that includes all living beings.

Homo sap[ien], that creature who believes his purpose is to control and conquer Nature, is just now beginning to remember the obvious — that he is a part of Nature himself.

He has fought his way to the top of the planetary spinal cord, inflicting damage every step of the way. Now, bewildered, he looks around: "What am I doing here?"

"Assuming responsibility," answers a still, small voice all around him.

— Paul Williams (*Das Energi*)

Violence Towards Animals

At a Glance

Did you know:

- Most violence towards animals in our society is not by individuals, but by industries that exploit animals for profit.
- Our societal treatment of animals stems from a prejudice called *speciesism* which, like racism and sexism, excuses discrimination toward those we perceive as "inferior."
- Things that contribute to animal cruelty in our society include a societal history of violence, misbeliefs about animals, personal selfishness, habit, misplaced trust in authority figures, and insulation from the abuse.
- We have the power as individuals and as a society to choose compassion over cruelty and to upgrade the status of animals in our society.

Cowardice asks the question, "Is it safe?"
Expediency asks the question, "Is it polite?"
Vanity asks the question, "Is it popular?"
But conscience asks the question, "Is it right?"
And there comes a point when one must take
a position that is neither safe, nor polite, nor popular,
but he must take it because his conscience
tells him that it is right...

— Martin Luther King, Jr.

Part Two

The Issues

Chapter 3

Companion Animals

Is That Any Way to Treat Your Best Friend?

Jeff Hiles

Heaven is by favor; if it were by merit your dog would go in and you would stay out.

— Mark Twain

Companion animals are those animals who live in our homes and share our lives. Whether they are cats, dogs, guinea pigs, hamsters, birds, fish, or any other animal, companion animals play a vital role in our lives. Studies show that animals who live with us not only ease our loneliness, but can relax us and even help us live longer.[1]

Some of us consider our animal friends to be family members. As a nation, we spend twice as much money on food for our companion animals than we do on baby food.[2] Add on toys, pillows, bowls, carriers, grooming costs, and medical care, and we're talking about a substantial investment.

But not all companion animals are pampered friends. Millions of cats and dogs end up in animal shelters or pounds every year, willingly surrendered by their caretakers. Most of these healthy animals die simply because they've been abandoned and can't find new homes. Some companion animals end up in research laboratories as experimental subjects, or suffer other ill treatment at the hands of humans.

There are some tough questions we need to ask ourselves about the animals we keep as companions:

- Can we keep animals as companions and still address their needs?
- Is our keeping companion animals in their best interest, or are we exploiting them?
- Is it fair to continue to raise domesticated animals to act as our companions?

The answers to these questions may lie in the attitudes of the human caretakers and their abilities to provide suitable environments for companion animals. Animal rights doesn't mean that humans and animals can't be friends, or that they can't exist in symbiotic relationships. What it does mean is that the needs of *both* the human and the nonhuman animals be considered.

The discussions in this chapter focus on our two most prevalent animal companions — cats and dogs. However, the ideas presented may be generalized to all companion animals, no matter how large or small.

Attitudes Toward Companion Animals

...the hope for the animals of tomorrow is to be found in a human culture which learns to feel beyond itself. We must learn empathy, we must learn to see into the eyes of an animal and feel that its life has value because it is alive. Nothing else will do.

— Kenneth White, Deputy Director, San Francisco Department of Animal Care and Control (*The Animals' Voice Magazine*)

Treating Companion Animals as "Things"

As individuals, we may relate to animals as the sentient beings they are. According to law, however, companion animals are personal property; a companion animal's life is worth only the dollar amount required to "replace" her. When the death of a companion animal results from another person's negligence, a few states also recognize a person's right to recover damages for suffering.[3] The law, however, does not recognize the rights of the animal who died; it merely compensates the "owner" for his or her emotional attachment to the animal.

Perceiving companion animals as property turns them into things. It values them only in as far as they are useful to us. Dictionaries specifically define the word "murder" as the unlawful killing of a *person*. Killing an animal is not considered murder, no matter the circumstances. After all, how can you murder "property"?

The perception of animals as property underlies much of our cultural treatment of animals. Like speciesism (prejudice towards other species), regarding companion animals as property is largely an unconscious attitude. It's a belief that permeates our society to such an extent that we accept it without question.

Language as a Reinforcement

Our attitudes toward companion animals are evident in the ways we refer to them and to ourselves in relation to them. When we think of ourselves as "owners" or of animal friends as "pets," we reinforce a superior/inferior, master/slave attitude. The language we use not only conveys our attitudes but reinforces them. Consider these examples.

Common Term	What It Implies	Better Term
Pet	Plaything, toy	Companion, friend
Master	Superiority, control	Caretaker, friend, human, guardian
Owner	An animal is property, an object we possess	Caretaker, friend, human, guardian
It	An animal is an object	He or she

Changing our language is one step in changing our attitudes. Use words that acknowledge animals as beings, not words that imply that they are things.

The societal attitude of animals as things is evidenced in many ways:

- Laws protecting companion animals are generally inadequate, nonexistent, or unenforced. The National Society for the Protection of Animals finds that many enforcement officials and courts consider it "beneath their dignity" to respond to reported instances of animal abuse, and that county attorneys seem to lack interest when it comes to animal welfare cases.[4]
- More than we like to know, companion animals are victims of severe abuse. They are shot, viciously beaten, burned, kicked, scalded, and thrown out of moving cars. Live animals have been found tied up in plastic bags, discarded in dumpsters, left in a sealed box on active railroad tracks, and just tied up and left to starve.[5]
- Discarding unwanted animals is a common, even socially acceptable, behavior. When people who regard companion animals as possessions decide that they don't want them any more, what happens? They do what all of us do with an unwanted possession: give it away, sell it, or sometimes just throw it out. A no-kill shelter, Animal Friends of Connecticut, Inc., reports that callers often say they're just going to kill or abandon their dogs or cats if the shelter won't take them.

An estimated 25 million animals become homeless every year. As many as 27% of purebred dogs are among the homeless.[6] Of the 25 million homeless animals, an average of 9 million die on the streets from disease, starvation, exposure, injury, or some other hazard of street life. The remaining 16 million die in pounds or shelters that have no room for them and kill them.[7] Almost 50% of the animals brought to shelters are turned in by their caretakers.[8] Many others are strays, some of whom presumably were dumped in the streets by their caretakers.

This lack of regard for animals as living beings is tragic, and is only possible because we perceive them as things rather than as beings.

Perceiving Companion Animals as Beings

Valuing companion animals as beings means recognizing them as individuals. It means valuing them for *who* they are, not for *what* they are.

As domesticated animals, our companion animals rely on us for their safety, comfort, and well-being — indeed, for their very survival. We've created a caretaker position for ourselves which means no less than taking responsibility for the condi-tions under which companion animals are born, the environments in which they live, and the circumstances in which they die.

Linda Leas

Katie Leas relaxes in the security of a loving home.

As individuals, some of us do an extraordinary job of caretaking. As a society, however, we have failed in this obligation. As a society, we condone behaviors that we would never tolerate as individuals. For change to occur, we have to educate ourselves about the realities. Let's take a look at some questionable treatment of companion animals in our society today.

Life-Threatening Realities

Our animal companions may be our "best friends," but are we theirs? Some of the things we do, or neglect to do, for our companion animals endanger their very lives.

Uncontrolled Breeding

The millions of cats and dogs killed as "surplus" each year are mostly victims of overpopulation due to unwanted pregnancies. In terms of sheer numbers of animals affected, overpopulation is the gravest threat companion animals face.

Randy Shields

People who allow companion animals to breed are responsible for the deaths of millions of animals every year.

In regard to animal overpopulation, "an ounce of prevention is worth a pound of cure." But let's face it; our companion animals aren't going to go to the drug store and get birth control. That's why it's up to humans to take the measures necessary to prevent pregnancies. By spaying or neutering our companion animals before they have the opportunity to reproduce, we may literally save hundreds of lives. How? Let's assume that a cat in our care has a litter of four. Where there was once one cat, now there are five. Now suppose that each one of those kittens grows up to populate the world with a litter of four. Now we've gone from five cats to 21 (assuming that the original mama cat hasn't gotten pregnant again). Another season of unspayed/unneutered cats brings our extended family to 85 (again, leaving out the reproductive potential of the cats who previously generated offspring). In the short span of four generations, the cat population has increased by 84 cats! Graphically, it looks like this:

That is why literally millions of healthy but homeless companion animals are killed every year as surplus.

Some individuals think that finding a home for each of those kittens or puppies absolves them from contributing to the overpopulation problem. But a survey conducted by an animal shelter revealed that 80% of the caretakers surrendering unwanted animals had obtained the animals from a neighbor or friend.[9] The implication is that the new caretakers didn't really want the animals in the first place, or weren't prepared to handle them, but took them anyway, only to later abandon them. This is no solution.

■ Addressing the Overpopulation Crisis

Companion animal overpopulation is not an animal problem, it's a people problem. Caretakers must accept the blame for this atrocity. Local, state, and federal governments must also share the blame for failing to respond to the crisis.

Every community should have a responsible birth control program in place for companion animals. The state of Louisiana has instituted a mandatory spay/neuter policy for all animals adopted from public or private shelters. The county of San Mateo, California has gone a step further in requiring a countywide ban on all dog/cat breeding for at least five months. (Professional and hobby breeders can apply for exemption to the ban.) The county adopted this policy to prevent the deaths of the 10,000 "surplus" dogs and cats the humane society is forced to kill every year. Realistically addressing the overpopulation problem means instituting a ban such as the one in San Mateo County on a nationwide level.

Spaying/Neutering Benefits Companion Animals

In addition to preventing unneeded pregnancies, spaying or neutering a companion animal has positive effects for your friend and for you:

Spaying a female cat or dog:

- Eliminates the risk of uterine and ovarian cancer.
- Reduces the chances of breast cancer.
- Prevents males from hanging around.
- Can increase her life span an average of two years.

Neutering a male cat or dog:

- Reduces the risk of prostate cancer.
- Reduces the urge to "mark" territory.
- Reduces the urge to roam.
- Can increase his lifespan an average of two years.

An alternative to spaying/neutering is chemical birth control for females. Various synthetic hormones have been developed and successfully field-tested in the U.S. as well as in other countries such as the Netherlands and Mexico. Who or what is preventing large-scale implementation of chemical birth control? Perhaps the answer lies in another question: Who would "lose" if companion animal overpopulation were curtailed? Possibly those whose services or products depend on these animals, such as pet food/product manufacturers and veterinarians. Or perhaps these drugs aren't considered profitable enough for drug companies to develop and market. In any case, it is the animals who lose.

The Misery of Puppy Mills

Puppy mills are low-budget, backyard breeding factories that churn out puppies for profit. Most puppy mills are located in the Midwest with Missouri leading as the number one puppy mill state. Approximately 5,000 puppy mills are believed to exist. Pinning down the exact number is hard, since most of these operations aren't licensed.

Puppy mills are the factory farms of the companion animal industry. (See Chapter 5 if you are unfamiliar with factory farms.) What are you likely to find in a puppy mill? Overcrowding, filth, malnourishment, exposure to extreme elements, females serving as breeding machines, and lots of unhealthy, starving, neglected puppies. The American Humane Association reports:

> Undercover visits to puppy mills have revealed what some have termed "canine concentration camps." Puppies were found to be living in wire cages scattered with animal carcasses, piled with feces, and unprotected from snow, rain, freezing, or blazing hot weather. Few were allowed to exercise. Food and water were scarce, and often contaminated. In fact, an investigator at one puppy mill found a breeder feeding dogs the heads of slaughtered animals.[10]

Animals that come from puppy mills are unhealthy due to many factors:

- Removal from their mother at too young an age results in impaired natural immunity to disease.
- Puppy mills subject the animals to filthy conditions.
- Overcrowding contributes to the spread of disease.
- Animals receive little or no veterinary care.

These animals not only have physical problems, but also suffer from behavioral problems. Their lack of contact with people and early removal from their mother often results in unsocial behaviors which surface only as the pups grow into dogs.

Who ends up with these puppies? Approximately 360,000 puppies from puppy mills are sold to pet shops across the nation annually,[11] the largest market being franchise pet stores, such as Docktor Pet Center. California is a large market for Midwest puppy mills, as is the East Coast. The Massachusetts Society for the Prevention of Cruelty to Animals (MSPCA) reports that "at least 90 percent of the half million purebred puppies sold in pet stores" are from puppy mills.[12]

The American Society for the Prevention of Cruelty to Animals (ASPCA) says that the problem of sick animals from pet stores is so prevalent that many states, including New York and New Jersey, now require the stores to compensate people who buy animals that are sick at the time of purchase. The store may be liable for veterinary bills (up to the purchase price of the animal) or may have to allow an exchange or refund.[13]

Animals also suffer in kennels licensed by the U.S. Department of Agriculture (USDA), which is responsible for inspecting them. The USDA admits that as many as 25% of licensed kennels have substandard conditions. The USDA just doesn't have enough staff available to stay on top of the problem.[14]

Stricter laws and stricter enforcement of those laws would go a long way toward helping close down inhumane puppy mill operations. Unfortunately, local law enforcement is often lacking, and even when kennel owners are charged with cruelty, they too often get off with a warning or a laughable "penalty." One kennel owner was given the "choice of selling her dogs within 60 days or facing charges of cruelty."[15] What kind of deterrent is that? One major puppy mill state, Kansas, even went so far as to make it a felony to photograph the goings-on at a puppy mill. This makes investigation difficult, if not impossible.

The Tragedy of Pet Shops

Pet shops support the puppy mill industry by buying their "goods," which as you've just read are not so good. Today's pet shops are often just like any other business, not owned by someone who values animals, but by someone whose motivation is profit. Pet shops, especially the large franchises, are another example of how animals are regarded as commodities, valued only as merchandise. Docktor Pet Center, a popular chain pet store seen in malls across the country, has had 812 animal cruelty charges brought against its stores in five different states since 1987.[16]

What happens to surplus or unwanted animals at pet shops? The following account from *The Animals' Voice Magazine* is a sworn statement made by a former Northern California pet store manager:

> In my presence, the pet shop owner picked up one of the kittens in one hand, picked up a wooden dowel in the other hand, and struck the kitten in the front of the head...He then instructed me to kill the remaining eight kittens the same way. I did as I was told.[17]

This is not the isolated act of a sadistic individual. This is part of business as usual.

Socialization is another problem for pet shop animals. According to the Monks of New Skete, who are professional dog trainers:

> Because of the conditions under which dogs live in pet shops, proper socialization often does not take place. Given that dogs are pack animals, the row on row of caged puppies does not seem an acceptable environment and substitute for early growth in a litter/family. Our experience suggests that behavior disorders in later life can result from improper socialization and suggest that pet shops be avoided in your search for a pup.[18]

Retail outlets that sell animals also hold a more subtle danger to animals — the impulse purchase. Who can resist that adorable puppy or kitten in the window? Too often passers-by purchase animals on a whim, without knowing or thinking about the responsibilities involved. Too often purchases stem from a momentary emotional attachment, not from a rational knowledge of the care an animal requires.

Keeping Exotic and Wild Animals as Companions

Some people like to own unusual or wild animals, such as lions, wolves, or rare birds. Why? Perhaps it's because these animals are out-of-the-ordinary or because they help us feel closer to the natural world from which we've strayed. For some, novelty pets are simply an ego trip, a way for owners to feel special.

But does a lion, a monkey, or a large lizard really belong in the terribly unnatural environment of a cage in someone's home? Are average people prepared to provide for the needs of an animal they know practically nothing about? And what happens when the novelty wears off, or a baby animal grows up? As is true of many domesticated companion animals, most exotic animals are discarded after the thrill is gone. Those donated to zoos — a common dumping ground — often end up not in the zoo but as a rug on someone's floor or as a specimen in a research lab.

The Wildlife Director for the Animal Welfare Association says that many exotic pets never make it that far, though; many die of malnutrition and stress.[19] A former wolf hybrid breeder and zoo employee says that the majority of exotic pets, including hybrids, are dead before they reach their third birthdays.[20] And for every exotic, wild bird that survives being smuggled or transported into this country, there are three or four who die in transit. This is in addition to the percentage of captured birds who die before exportation is even attempted — an astounding 60%, according to the United States Fish and Wildlife Service.[21]

Keeping wild animals captive is not in the best interest of the animals, whether they're exotic animals from other countries or native wildlife such as raccoons. Domestic animals are the result of thousands of years of special breeding and socialization. Wild animals are wild. Even if they are born in captivity, they are still wild animals. As one zoo employee reports:

> Frequently we receive requests for information about how to handle a difficult situation with a wolf hybrid. More often it is a desperate plea for a home for an animal that has turned out to be nothing like the owner expected, more like a wild animal than he/she is prepared to handle, and a big problem the owners need to unload.[22]

Taking an animal out of the wild does not take the wild out of the animal. Exotic and wild animals are dangerous to humans and are not good "pets." Although wild animals may be tamed, they are not domesticated, and can easily revert to natural, wild, unpredictable behaviors. Just because an animal is captive-born and hand-raised, doesn't make her "domesticated."

We'll do both the animals and ourselves a favor by outlawing the sale or ownership of exotic or wild animals.

Free to a Good...Research Laboratory?

Sometimes life circumstances dictate that we locate a new home for our own dog or cat friend or for a stray animal. We sincerely want and look for a home that will benefit our friend. One tactic for finding a new home is to advertise in the newspaper. The ad might read something like this:

> Playful, friendly, two-year old beagle. Loves affection. Good with children. Free to a good home. Call xxx-xxxx.

One woman placed a similar ad for her dog. The man who responded was friendly, personable, and said that he'd take the dog to his country ranch. The dog took to him immediately, so the woman gave the friendly stranger her dog. He in exchange gave her the telephone number to his ranch, the dog's new home. End of story? Unfortunately not.

When the woman called the telephone number the man had given her, the line was always busy. She became suspicious and notified authorities. Four months later, her dog and five others were turned over to animal regulation authorities by a medical laboratory. The friendly, personable man had sold the woman's dog to a kennel that in turn sold her to the laboratory. When the laboratory learned that the kennel was involved in criminal actions, it turned over to authorities six dogs it had purchased from the kennel.[23]

Do you find this story shocking? It happens all the time, every day. The only part of the story that is a bit extraordinary is the recovery of the dog. That's not the usual ending. In addition to answering "free to good home" ads, unscrupulous people also obtain dogs by answering "found" ads in papers and posing as the dog's family.

■ Pet Theft

Here's an equally shocking reality: Every day, cats and dogs are stolen out of cars, out of their own backyards, and off of streets. As many as four million companion animals disappear annually.[24] Most of these are not purebreds or expensive animals; they are the typical family friend.

An acquaintance who grew up in a rural community in Ohio told me that a van routinely pulls into their neighborhood and a man starts loading dogs into the van. This has been going on for years. Law enforcement officers are unresponsive.

Where do these stolen animals end up? Some end up with breeders, some end up with dog fighters (either as fighters or as bait), and some end up with attack trainers.[25] Most thieves, however, are part of a network that reaches from your neighborhood to research laboratories. A group called the Coalition of Municipalities to Ban Animal Trafficking (COMBAT) explains the network this way:

> The United States Department of Agriculture (USDA) licenses Class B dealers, giving them the legal sanction to purchase "random source" animals for re-sale to research laboratories. Although the dealer may have other clientele, such as dogfighters and guard dog companies, their main source of income is selling to research facilities that pay up to $500 for dogs and $75 for cats. This is a

> fairly good profit for the dealer, who pays his sources $35 to $50 for dogs, and $12 to $15 for cats.
>
> The dealer buys random source dogs and cats from "bunchers," middlemen who obtain them from a variety of sources. This is where the problem comes in. Often, these bunchers are unscrupulous individuals who will resort to pet theft...
>
> [An] important point is that federal agencies such as the National Institutes of Health, award billions of federal tax dollars each year to researchers for projects involving dogs and cats. So, in a roundabout way, our tax dollars are financing the theft of our pets from our own back yards.[26]

Coalition of Municipalities to Ban Animal Trafficking

A buncher (who later became a USDA-licensed animal dealer) deals dogs at the Poplar Bluff, Missouri dog and gun auction.

The dealer-laboratory network is successful for a number of reasons. First, animals are easily transported across state lines where they are then sold. Second, falsifying papers is easy and papers are rarely scrutinized. Third, laboratories prefer friendly, trusting animals (such as previous companions) and can obtain such animals at a reduced price from Class B dealers. Fourth, there is little law enforcement to prevent these dealings. Many transactions between bunchers and dealers take place at dog and gun auctions, and are easily observed. Witnesses claim that some of the animals that dealers buy are still wearing collars. Dealers ask no questions as to where the animals came from. Certainly, law enforcement officials could easily intervene if they chose to.

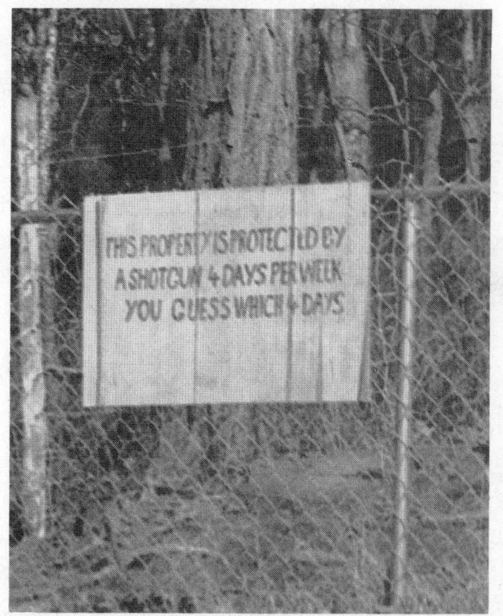

Coalition of Municipalities to Ban Animal Trafficking

This sign greeted visitors to a USDA-licensed animal dealer's property in West Fork, Arkansas.

In at least one instance, a local law enforcement officer was actually identified as a buncher. His ex-wife reported that for several years, her husband, who was a sheriff's deputy, got animals through "free to good home" ads, from an animal shelter, and from local pounds.[27]

■ Pound Seizure

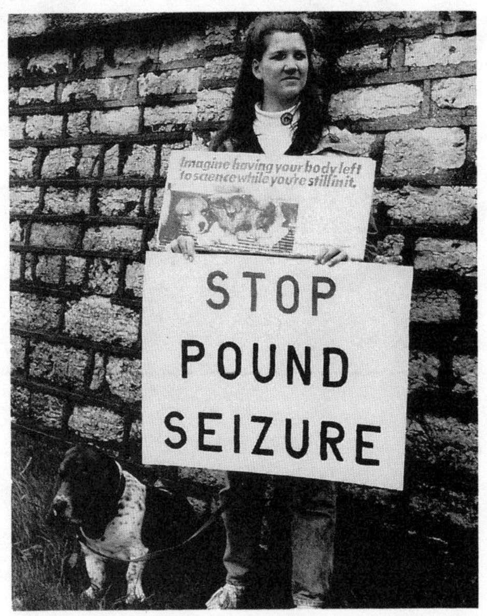

Imagine having your body left
to science while you're still in it.
STOP
POUND
SEIZURE

Peolple/Animals Network

Pound seizure allows research facilities to take live animals from pounds and shelters for experimentation.

Some communities allow their animal shelters to sell dogs and cats directly to research or testing labs, a practice called *pound seizure*. The friendlier the animal, the better suited for this purpose, since friendly animals are more cooperative.

While laboratories regard pounds as a cheap and convenient source of laboratory specimens, many people feel that subjecting animals to research or testing is a fate worse than death. Shelters are intended to be protective havens for animals, not commodities brokers for laboratory resources.

Eleven states and many local communities have banned the sale of shelter animals to laboratories. The National Institutes of Health, the largest funder of biomedical research in this country, stopped using shelter animals in its own in-house research over 10 years ago because they consider such animals unsuitable as research subjects. Experience shows that people stop bringing stray animals to the pound when they believe that the animals might go to research laboratories. This compounds animal control problems in the community.

Pound seizure is unfair to companion animals and unfair to communities. Shelters should function as shelters. All communities should push to outlaw pound seizure at the local, state, or national level.

■ Breeding Research Specimens

While some people steal animals to sell as laboratory specimens, others deliberately breed dogs, cats, and other animals for this purpose. Their clients include high schools, colleges, veterinary schools, medical schools, biomedical research laboratories, psychological research laboratories, veterinary research laboratories, product testing laboratories, and military bases. Animals are also used as sales tools. U.S. Surgical Corporation uses live dogs to train sales people in the use of its product, a surgical stapler. All of these activities, in which live, healthy animals are used and then discarded, are legally sanctioned.

Perhaps the most shocking clients of animal dealers are veterinary schools. It's logical to assume that "animal doctors" would be the last people to advocate the unnecessary killing of healthy animals. But logic does not always prevail. All but a handful of veterinary schools kill healthy dogs and cats in the name of "education." The fact that some veterinary schools have implemented alternatives to killing healthy animals shows that this use of animals is an unnecessary waste of life.

The Steel-Jaw Leghold Trap

A lesser-known threat to companion animals is the steel-jaw leghold trap. Designed to catch fur-bearing wildlife, these traps also catch unsuspecting dogs and cats unlucky enough to wander into them. The steel-jaw leghold trap is a spring-loaded trap that snaps shut on an animal's leg as he steps into the trap. Imagine an oversized mousetrap and you have the picture. These cruel traps should be outlawed in all communities. See the trapping section of Chapter 7 for further discussion of the steel-jaw leghold trap.

The Plight of Purebreds

Purebreds are animals whose ancestry is confined to a single breed. Purebred dogs and cats are often regarded as status symbols that owners show in competitions or sell for profit. Bred to obtain certain physical characteristics, purebreds end up with much more — genetic defects such as hip dysplasia, kidney failure, deafness, eye disorders, and gastric problems.

Besides these physical afflictions, purebred breeding has other effects. Some dog breeds have had natural abilities, such as the ability to herd, bred right out of them. Other breeds, such as Irish setters, have lost their natural intelligence.[28]

Certain physical traits are deliberately bred into purebreds. For example, bulldogs are purposely bred to have large heads. Unfortunately for the dog, the abnormally large head prevents the poor mother from giving birth naturally; the pups must be delivered by cesarean section.

The health and temperament problems that afflict some breeds, or some individuals within a breed, are unintentional. They are the result of haphazard breeding orchestrated by people who don't understand the possible consequences of breeding for outward appearance alone. Healthy animals with healthy temperaments are the result of careful, selective breeding of healthy animals with known histories and temperaments. Most purebreds are bred through indiscriminate match-ups that don't take the individual traits of an animal into account.

Many people believe that a purebred with American Kennel Club (AKC) papers has somehow met criteria guaranteeing her physical and psychological health. In fact, AKC papers identify only the parents of a puppy and her birth date. AKC registration has nothing to do with the health or well-being of a dog. One author reports, "AKC reportedly derives 80% of its $15,000,000 annual income from registering puppy-mill progeny."[29] This is a shocking statistic, given the blatant abuse, neglect, and resulting ill-health rampant in puppy mills, as discussed earlier in the chapter.

AKC also sets the standards for "show" dogs. For some breeds, standards require mutilation of the ears (cropping) and/or amputation of the tail (docking) for over 300 breeds of dogs.[30] These unnecessary mutilations serve no purpose except to conform with guidelines for show dogs, and they are both psychologically and physically painful to the pups.

Cats as well as dogs are bred to obtain certain characteristics. Says one cat breeder, "Artists work in paints; I work in genetics."[31] This meddling with genetics is not for the benefit of the cats, but for the satisfaction, prestige, and enrichment of the breeder. The following excerpt from an article on rare cat breeding conveys how these animals are regarded:

> Show-quality Bengals can go for as high as three thousand dollars; pet-stock cats are more commonly priced between six hundred and a thousand. If that seems like a lot, perhaps some would-be Bengal owners will be enticed by the fact that the *Los Angeles Times* recently placed the Bengal on its list of "New Status Seekers" — along with Bogner ski wear and personal dog trainers.[32]

Treating animals as status symbols reduces them to things. Animals should be valued as living beings, not because they are unusual and expensive toys.

One breeder — who does not crop the ears or tails of her dogs, and who thoroughly scrutinizes all potential homes for her pups — cautions against lumping all breeders into a single category. She admits that most purebreds come from backyard breeders who don't have the expertise to breed for health and temperament as well as appearance. However, she says, knowledgeable breeders who are able to address the complexities of proper breeding produce healthy animals. Combine this with a genuine concern for animals and there is nothing "dirty" about the word "purebred."

Is the breeding of purebreds ever justified? Until the time when all companion animals have homes, with no killing of "surplus" animals, there is no justification for the breeding of any companion animals, purebred or not.

Companion Animals as Servants

Throughout history, humankind has utilized "working dogs" to perform services other than companionship. The services fulfilled by dogs range from assisting the blind, deaf, or physically challenged to herding sheep to guarding homes. In a fairly recent trend, both cats and dogs are used in "pet-facilitated therapy" programs with lonely or emotionally disturbed people.

There is no question that these animals provide an important service for humans. What is not so clear is the impact of the training methods and the programs themselves on the animals. As in so many other instances, when the emphasis is on the benefits to humans, often the quality of the animal's life suffers.

This does not mean that animals should never be "put to service." What it means is that we have to be careful to guarantee a beneficial partnership between service animals and humankind. For some animals, being put to service is not in their best interest. For other animals, being put to work is exactly what they need. Naturally, animals become frustrated when they have natural tendencies they are unable to fulfill. Denial of certain breeds' instincts can result in destructive behavior, as the Monks of New Skete relate in this example of a dog brought to them because of behavior problems:

> We once had a Labrador retriever with serious chewing and house-soiling problems. While the dog was with us, we took it into the woods. Immediately, a light went on in the dog's eyes, and when the dog returned from an outing, he was quiet and mellow...Chewing and house-soiling ceased after the dog became a field dog, and he continued to live in the house.[33]

Just as certain people are most suited to certain jobs, so must animals be correctly matched with tasks for which they are suited. This means paying attention not only to an animal's breed, but to the individual character of the animal as well.

"Pet-facilitated therapy" programs, where animals are taken to visit shut-ins, are a recent use of animals that many animal shelters not only endorse but actively operate. However, the MSPCA is less than enthusiastic about this recent trend. Because "the animals involved in some therapy programs are subjected to neglect, stress, and/or abuse," the MSPCA "does not support the use of temporary shelter residents in pet-facilitated therapy programs, nor the maintenance of companion animals by institutions exclusively for visitation or in-home therapy programs."[34] Clearly, some animals may be well-suited to such visitations, but not every animal will be. The job requires an animal who is comfortable being handled by many people, and is not adversely affected by strange surroundings and noises. As in all cases of service animals, we need to examine what will most benefit all parties involved.

Perhaps the most reprehensible use of service animals is the training of dogs as guard dogs. This industry not only specially breeds dogs for viciousness, but "trains" them through teasing and torment. This is totally unacceptable, no matter how "useful" the animals are after suffering this conditioning. No living being deserves this kind of treatment, for any reason.

Nor should wild animals be used to perform services for humans. A case in point is the recent use of capuchin monkeys to assist quadriplegics. Monkeys are wild, not domesticated, animals. To keep the monkeys in the program from biting humans, all of their teeth are permanently removed, prohibiting not only consumption of a normal diet, but also any hope of return to a normal life with other monkeys. The training method used with the monkeys is electric shock. The former training director for this program, a primate behavior consultant, says:

> These animals (and their human patients) are being totally exploited for a futile and dangerous program. It became very obvious that, given the first chance, every one of the monkeys I've ever worked with would escape or eventually attack someone. No matter how much training you give them, they will always remain wild and unpredictable. If monkeys are appropriate for this type of program, why are their teeth removed and shock packs used on them?[35]

Under no circumstances should wild animals be used as pets or as service animals.

When "Humane" Services Aren't So Humane

This discussion wouldn't be complete without a word of caution about humane societies, animal shelters, pounds, and other adoption centers for companion animals. They can, and do, vary widely from community to community.

Some adoption centers are truly dedicated to animal rights principles and do all they can to promote humane treatment of animals. They rescue animals, treat them humanely, screen people who want to adopt animals, and work to educate the community about humane caretaking.

Randy Shields

Shelters and pounds sometimes voluntarily turn over animals to research facilities, such as Wright State University in Dayton, Ohio, where these cats were photographed.

Other adoption centers...well, it's another story. Animal rights publications have cited a number of examples. Here are a few.

- A volunteer from the group Sav-A-Pet found neglect and sub-standard conditions at a Lancaster, California shelter, where employees left promptly at quitting time whether or not all the animals had been fed, watered, and their cages cleaned. At this writing, the shelter was under investigation.[36]
- An animal rights group in Louisiana, Legislation in Support of Animals, reports that animals at a city animal shelter there routinely go without food, water, or clean cages and are left entirely alone on weekends.[37]
- A Fort Worth, Texas animal shelter reportedly gave unwanted animals to research facilities, and neglected and abused shelter animals.[38]
- The manager and assistant manager of a north Florida animal shelter were unseated following an investigation revealing that shelter employees drowned puppies and kittens and routinely over-crowded the facility's carbon monoxide chamber.[39]
- The North Shore Animal League of New York, a no-kill shelter which has assets of over $33 million, reportedly buys purebred dogs for resale.[40]
- A no-kill shelter called Love & Care For God's Animalife, Inc. has been investigated by the states of Alabama and Georgia, the Internal Revenue Service, and local health authorities. Alleged wrongs are unethical business practices, tax evasion, and keeping animals in crowded, unsanitary conditions.[41]

People close to the animal rights movement have also told me their own stories of battling humane societies who continued to use inhumane decompression or carbon monoxide chambers to kill animals, although the more humane method of fatal injection was available. The humane societies changed to the injection method only after courts declared the other methods inhumane.

Complaints have also been lodged against some of the more prestigious humane societies, but for a different reason. The Connecticut Humane Society and the Humane Society of Missouri reportedly hold millions of dollars worth of stock in companies that use animals in product testing. The Humane Society of Missouri is also a stockholder in Ralston-Purina, notorious for sponsoring "coon hunts" in which dogs chase terrorized raccoons.[42] These humane societies apparently do not see a conflict of interest in these investments. The Connecticut Humane Society has the further distinction of having a director who is also a vice-president of the American Cancer Society, which supports the use of animals in biomedical research.[43]

Instances of neglect and abuse are no doubt the exceptions, not the rules. Still, the rule to go by is "better safe than sorry." Shelters are not all "created equal." Take a tour of your local animal facilities. A little investigative work can pay off. If you find conditions or circumstances that you don't like, don't hesitate to report them. If local authorities aren't responsive, contact your local animal rights group or the news media.

On the other hand, don't forget to commend and support those shelters that are doing a good job. Caring for animals is hard, expensive work. It's emotionally and financially draining. See if you can offer a word of thanks, an extra donation, or a day or two of volunteer help.

Dog and Horse Racing

Greyhound racing, dog sled racing, and horse racing all treat companion animals as means to an end—the end being sizable profits at the expense of the animals' comfort and lives. For a discussion of these abusive industries, see Chapter 8, "Animals in Entertainment."

The Horse Slaughter Trade

Next to dogs and cats, horses are perhaps the most beloved of companion animals. Unfortunately, their popularity exceeds the number of knowledgeable and competent caretakers. According to the President of H.O.R.S.E. of Connecticut, an organization that rescues and rehabilitates abused equines, many instances of horse abuse are the backyard variety — caretakers who have acquired horses for pleasure and simply neglect to provide proper care. Like the impulse pet store purchase, horse purchases are often based more on whim than on working knowledge of the time, effort, and expense involved in proper care. When reality hits and the animal proves to be too much of a burden, too often caretakers simply sell the horse to someone else who also lacks the knowledge to provide proper care.

For companion horses, as well as for former racing and work horses, the "end of the line" is often less than ideal. Instead of a quiet, natural death or, when necessary, a humanely-induced death, horses frequently suffer violence, pain, and severe abuse at the hands of the horse slaughter trade. This industry buys, transports, and kills horses for their meat, which is most often sold to foreign countries. According to the Coalition Against the Horse Slaughter Trade, horses transported for slaughter are starved, beaten, whipped, shocked with electric prods, and stuffed into double-decker trucks or bullwagons designed for cattle and unsuitable for horses. Horses in transport often lose their footing on urine- and feces-smeared floors and are trampled by other horses. Injured horses are whipped and shocked to make them stand and move on their own accord. Those too injured to get up, even with the incentive of beatings, are dragged on the ground. Transport trucks stuffed with horses on their way to slaughter houses in the U.S. or Canada can be seen on highways and interstates in all parts of the country, from coast to coast and border to border. For more information on horse slaughter, see the horse organizations listed in the Resources section at the end of the chapter.

Being a Responsible Caretaker

Even those of us with the best intentions can too often give too little attention to the needs of our companion animals. Here are some things to think about.

Declawing

Whether it's for convenience or out of not knowing any better, many people declaw cats, even though it is a physically and psychologically painful procedure. Cats use their claws in stretching and exercising, and for balance and protection. According to one veterinarian, declawing is "the equivalent to cutting off the tips of all the fingers and thumbs of a human at the last joint."[44] Is protecting furniture upholstery really worth this? There are other alternatives, such as having your vet trim the cat's nails and providing a scratching post scented with catnip.

Loneliness and Boredom

Another common problem companion animals face is loneliness and boredom. Many of us leave companion animals alone for long periods of time, often shut up in apartments or rooms. Sometimes we leave them in cages. Natural pack animals such as puppies are especially affected by being left alone and often develop behavior problems such as chewing, biting, or barking in response to isolation. And what about the rabbit or gerbil who spends his entire life in a small cage with nothing to look forward to and no other pals of his own species with whom to interact? Why do we assume that a small cage is all these animals need? Animals are conscious beings with real emotional needs.

We need to provide our companion animals with company and stimulation. Sometimes, adopting a second companion animal of the same species can be a great help. An animal of a different species may also provide company. Many cats and dogs get along well. Or how about providing another human companion in the form of a dog or cat sitter who comes over and spends an hour or so with your friend in the middle of the day? If we can't provide another living being, sometimes we can provide toys or a stimulating environment, such as an obstacle course to challenge a dog.

As a society, we hardly ever think in terms of the needs of our nonhuman companions. How does "daycare" for dogs of working caretakers sound? Such facilities could exercise and play with our dog friends. How about setting aside spaces in community parks where caretakers can let dogs safely run free for awhile? There are all kinds of ways we could improve the lives of our companion animals; we just need to care enough to do it.

The Pet Food and Pet Product Industries

"Dinner time. Let's see, here you go Kitty — some rotten meat, a little cancerous tissue, some worm-infested liver, and, oh, here's some plastic wrap and Styrofoam." Wait a minute! Who would ever feed their companion animal such trash? Believe it or not, *you* might. There's a high probability that these very things you'd never knowingly feed your companion animals are in the commercial food you buy for them.

Pet food manufacturers spend millions of advertising dollars to assure us of the high-quality of their products, but evidence exists to the contrary. The meat and poultry "by-products," "meal," and "fat" shown on the labels of animal food aren't what most of us think they are. An investigative journalist who observed first-hand a veterinary meat-inspector at a slaughterhouse, reported that animal organs unfit for human consumption were thrown into a drum marked "Dog Food." These organs included a beef liver infested with worms and a beef lung blotchy with pneumonia. Another writer was told by a meat inspector with the Meat and Poultry Inspection Program of the USDA that "a good number of cancerous cows go into pet foods."[45] In addition to diseased organs, animal carcasses and unsold supermarket meats still in their plastic wrappers and foam trays may find their way into animal foods. Thoughtful caretakers should also be aware that salmonella bacteria thrives on meat and bone meal, common ingredients in dog food.[46]

Other products for animals should also be approached with caution. Chemical flea collars and sprays can poison animals, causing liver damage, kidney damage, nerve damage, cancer, or death. Hartz Mountain Blockade Flea and Tick Repellent has been implicated in the poisoning and deaths of dogs and cats, and consequently Hartz Mountain has had 18 charges filed against it by the Environmental Protection Agency.

So, what's a caring human to do? The best thing is to use only natural foods and safe products. Some animals are allergic to the dyes and additives in foods and develop skin disorders or other reactions. Veterinarians interested in nutrition have found that switching a companion animal from an off-the-shelf commercial food to a natural diet can have remarkable, in fact almost unbelievable, effects. Animals for whom there was "no hope" have recovered to live many additional, healthy years. In many cases, improved nutrition has alleviated so-called "incurable" diseases such as arthritis and hip dysplasia. In fact, veterinarians who have administered vitamin C to canine patients since puppyhood claim that these patients do not develop hip dysplasia. For health supplies and books on how to keep companion animals happy and healthy, see Chapter 12, "Products and Services" and Chapter 13, "Further Reading."

How You Can Help

Here are some ways you can further care for your own companion animals and help change the tragedies that all of our companion animals face.

Protect Your Friend From the Research Laboratory

The surest way to make sure that your friend doesn't end up in a research or testing laboratory is to outlaw the use of dogs and cats as laboratory subjects. In the meantime, you can do the following things:

- Outlaw pound seizure in your community. For more information on pound seizure, contact one or more of the organizations listed under Pound Seizure in the Resources section at the end of the chapter.
- Laboratories that use companion animals and Class B animal dealers should allow access to their facilities in order to look for lost or stolen companion animals. Push for such laws.
- Find out if the animal rights and humane organizations in your area monitor animal dealers, dog auctions, or research laboratories. Encourage them to do so and volunteer your services toward this effort. For advice, contact the groups listed under Pet Theft in the Resources section at the end of the chapter.
- Call "free to good home" ads and warn advertisers about the unscrupulous bunchers who obtain animals this way. Urge the current caretakers to scrutinize interested parties and charge a nominal fee to discourage animal dealers. Encourage them to accompany the animal to her new prospective home for a visit. This way they can verify that the new caretakers are legitimately interested and can verify that the new home is suitable.
- Tattoo and register your companion animals. It is a quick, painless procedure that may deter thieves and help in the recovery of a lost or stolen animal. See the Companion Animal section of Chapter 12 for businesses that provide this service.
- Always supervise your animal friend. Don't let her run loose.
- Keep an eye out for suspicious vans or trucks cruising your neighborhood. Take down the license number and a description. Report their presence to the police.

Keep Your Friend Healthy and Happy

- Think of your companion animal's needs for exercise, companionship, and stimulation. Don't leave her alone for long periods of time. Set aside some time each day for interacting with your friend. Providing a second companion of the same species, or even a different species, may help alleviate some loneliness and boredom.
- Buy only safe, cruelty-free toys and products for your companion animals. Don't buy rawhide, which is a slaughterhouse by-product and often contains formaldehyde. Chemical flea collars and sprays are poisonous. Use herbal, citrus, or other natural flea

repellents. Also, many household cleansers are poisonous, such as toilet bowl cleaners and disinfectant sprays. For mail-order sources of safe products, see the Companion Animal Products & Services section and the Cruelty-Free Home, Beauty, & Personal Care Products section of Chapter 12.

- Avoid off-the-shelf "grocery store" food. Instead, buy a "health store" pet food or make food yourself. For further reading on this subject and sources of do-it-yourself recipes, see Chapter 13. You'll find mail-order sources for natural animal foods in Chapter 12.
- Declawing is the equivalent of amputation. Instead of declawing your cat, regularly trim his nails (ask your vet how) and/or provide a good scratching post occasionally scented with catnip tea. You can obtain information and alternatives to declawing from the International Society for Animal Rights, Inc. or the Association of Veterinarians for Animal Rights.
- Learn about your friend and his/her needs, instincts, and natural behaviors by reading up on his/her species and/or consulting an interspecies communicator. You might be surprised to find out the motivation behind some behaviors.

More Dos and Don'ts for Companion Animals

- DO adopt animals from animal shelters or breed rescue clubs, not from retail stores. If you're looking for a particular breed of dog, see the Companion Animals section of Chapter 13 for breed rescue directories. And don't forget the so-called "unadoptables" — old or handicapped animals. They make wonderful friends.
- DO support a ban on breeding in your community. For information on how to do it, see the guide *Killing the Crisis, Not the Animals* in the Companion Animals section of Chapter 13 and/or contact the Vacaville, CA office of The Fund for Animals, Inc.
- DO always have your companion animal wear a collar with an I.D. tag.
- DO support federal, state, and local legislation for low-cost spay/neuter programs and the strengthening of animal protection laws for companion animals. Support the outlawing of pound seizure, puppy mills, the sale of exotic animals, steel-jaw leghold traps, and any inhumane treatment of companion animals. Push for the enforcement of existing laws concerning companion animals.
- DO report any abuse you witness or suspect to your local humane society. If your complaint is against the humane society, contact the closest animal rights group or the police. If necessary, contact a national animal rights group for advice.
- DO provide for your companion animals in your will. Make sure you entrust them to caretakers who really want them and who are able to care for them. See the Companion Animals section of Chater 13 for publications on this subject.
- DO treat *all* companion animals with the respect due autonomous, feeling, intelligent creatures.
- DON'T let companion animals breed. Always spay and neuter before it's too late. For low-cost spay/neuter services, call your local animal shelter or see the Companion

Animal Products & Services section of Chapter 12 for referrals.

- DON'T adopt an animal into your home unless you can make a lifelong commitment.
- DON'T ever give your nonhuman friend to a stranger unless you've thoroughly checked out the person and the proposed new home.
- DON'T expect your veterinarian to be informed about or sympathetic to animal rights. Most aren't. To find out if there is a veterinarian in your area who belongs to the organization Association of Veterinarians for Animal Rights (AVAR), contact AVAR at P.O. Box 6269, Vacaville, CA 95696-6269, (707) 451-1391.

Resources for Companion Animals

For products and services that benefit companion animals, see the following sections of Chapter 12: Audio Tapes & CDs, Companion Animal Products & Services, Hotlines, Humane Education, Radio & Television Programming, and Videos & Films.

For books and periodicals related to companion animal health, behavior, overpopulation, and rescue, see Chapter 13.

Here are just a few of the organizations of special interest that work on behalf of companion animals. For addresses and descriptions, see Chapter 10. See also the Resources section at the end of Chapter 8, "Entertainment." *Note: See the state listings in Chapter 10 for additional organizations and for shelters and rescue organizations that serve local regions.*

- **General**
  American Humane Association (CO), American Society for the Prevention of Cruelty to Animals (NY), Animal Protection Institute of America (CA), Association of Veterinarians for Animal Rights (CA), Massachusetts Society for the Prevention of Cruelty to Animals (MA)

- **Breed Rescue**
  Humane Animal Rescue Team (CA), Project BREED, Inc. (MD)

- **Feral Cat Assistance**
  Alley Cat Allies (MD), Alliance for Animals (MA), Animal Unbrella (MA), Every Creature Counts (CO), Forgotten Felines of Sonoma County (CA), Streetcat Rescue Team (CA)

- **Ferret Rescue**
  American Ferret Association, Inc. (MD), Central Illinois Friends of Ferrets (IL), Ferret Adoption, Information, and Rescue Society (IL), Ferret Family Services (KS), Ferret Sense/ Shelter (OH), Ferrets of Pet Pals/Ferret Rescue & Adoption Service (VA), Fran's Ferret Rescue (PA), Just A Business of Ferrets (VA), Kansas City Ferret Hotline Association (MO), New York Ferret's Rights Advocacy (NY), Sanders Ferret Halfway House (MD), STAR (Shelters That Adopt & Rescue) Ferrets—national referral (VA), Save Our Critters (OK)

◆ **Greyhound Adoption**

Fort Myers Greyhound Adoption Center (FL), Friends for Life (CA), Greyhound Club of America (CA), Greyhound Friends, Inc. (MA), Greyhound Friends for Life (CA), Greyhound Life Line (MA), Greyhound Pets of America (TX), Greyhound Protection League (CA, TX), Greyhound Racers Recycled, Inc. (TX), Greyhound Rescue, Inc. (FL, MD), Greyhound Rescue and Adoption (IL, IN), Greyhound Rescue League (FL), Greyhounds As Pets (CO, MT, NV, NM, WY), Make Peace With Animals, Inc. (PA), National Greyhound Adoption Program (PA), National Greyhound Adoption Network (GA, NH), National Greyhound Network (CA), Northern California Sighthound Rescue (CA), Oregon Greyhound Rescue (OR), Retired Greyhounds As Pets/REGAP (FL, CT, IN, IA, NH), Save The Greyhound Dogs! (VT), Second Chance for Greyhounds (FL), Tampa Greyhound Adoption Center (FL), USA Defenders of Greyhounds, Inc. (IN)

◆ **Horses (Domesticated)**

Coalition Against the Horse Slaughter Trade (CA), Brighter Days Horse Refuge, Inc. (TX), Colorado Horse Rescue (CO), Days End Farm Horse Sanctuary (MD), Equestrian Training Center/Horse Rescue (FL), Equine Rescue and Education (WV), Equine Rescue League (VA), EQUUS Horse Rescue Network and Sanctuary (CA), Harness Horse Retirement and Youth Association, Inc. (PA), Hooved Animal Welfare Society (IL), (MI), HorseAid (CA), Horse Power Projects & Horse Power International, Inc. (CA), HorseSafe! (CA), Horse Welfare Committee (CA), Humane Organization for Retired and Standardbred Equines (CA), Humane Organization Representing Suffering Equines/H.O.R.S.E. (CT, MI), Maryland Horse Rescue Center, Inc./HorseNet (MD), New Hampshire Equine Services, Inc. (NH), Noah's Ark/The Horse Rescue Group (NY), Panorama Horse Sanctuary (NY), Redwings Horse Sanctuary (CA), Retirement Home for Horses, Inc. (FL), Ryers Farm for Aged Equines (PA), Southern West Virginia Equine Education and Protection, Inc. (WV), Standardbred Retirement Foundation (WI), Thoroughbred Retirement Foundation (NJ)

◆ **Pet Theft**

See the Resources section of Chapter 6, "Research, Education, and Testing."

◆ **Pound Seizure**

See the Resources section of Chapter 6, "Research, Education, and Testing."

◆ **Rabbits**

Adopt-A-Rabbit Program (NC), Fund for Animals Rabbit Sanctuary (SC), House Rabbit Sanctuary (CA), North Texas Rabbit Sanctuary (TX)

◆ **Spay/Neuter Assistance**

Animal Alliance (NM), DJ&T Foundation (CA), Friends of Animals (CT), Mercy Crusade, Inc. (CA), Pet Savers Foundation, Inc. /SPAY/USA (NY), United Humanitarians (PA)

◆ **Miscellaneous**

Dogs for the Deaf, Inc. (OR), Home for Unwanted and Abandoned Guinea Pigs (GA), Potbellied Pig Interest Group & Shelter (WV)

Conclusion

Companion animals are those animals who live in our homes and share our lives. Too often, people treat them as property or as playthings, forgetting that they are living beings with needs and preferences. Many companion animals face homelessness because caretakers neglect to spay or neuter animals in their care, or because caretakers discard animals on streets or at animal shelters when it is no longer convenient to keep them. Millions of animals are killed as "surplus" each year as more are deliberately bred for profit.

Animals sold at pet shops are often victims of inhumane treatment. Most pet shops buy animals from *puppy mills,* breeders who regard animals only as merchandise and treat them accordingly. Some people keep wild or exotic animals as companions. Keeping these animals in our homes does a great disservice to them. Domesticated animals also suffer from neglect or from being kept in unsuitable environments.

In some communities, pounds and shelters sell companion animals to research laboratories. Companion animals also end up in laboratories after they are stolen by unscrupulous people who answer "free to good home" ads or steal animals out of cars and backyards.

Often, animals are bred for profit or status. Many purebreds suffer both physical and psychological abnormalities caused by improper breeding. In order to "beautify" dogs, people sometimes mutilate them by cutting off their ears or tails, a custom which is of no benefit to the animals.

It's time for us to reexamine our relationship with companion animals, including their legal status in our society and the ways we meet, or don't meet, their needs. We can help companion animals by finding out what's going on in our own community, boycotting businesses that exploit animals, and supporting local, state, and federal legislation to protect companion animals and to create a proper sense of responsibility on the part of humans.

The fact that man knows right from wrong
proves his intellectual superiority to the other creatures;
but the fact that he can do wrong proves his moral inferiority
to any creature that cannot.

— Mark Twain

Companion Animals

At a Glance

Did you know:

- Legally, companion animals are regarded as nothing more than property.
- Mandatory birth control measures could save millions of "surplus" dogs and cats who are killed every year due to a lack of available homes.
- Pet stores often sell puppy mill progeny with hidden physical and emotional problems.
- Purebreds suffer physically and emotionally from improper breeding.
- Universities and other research laboratories sometimes use former pets taken from pounds as research specimens, a practice called "pound seizure."
- Companion animals have real emotional needs for companionship and stimulation.

Very little of the great cruelty shown by men can really be attributed to cruel instinct.
Most of it comes from thoughtlessness or inherited habit.
The roots of cruelty, therefore, are not so much strong as widespread.
But the thoughtlessness will succumb before humanity championed by thought.
Let us work that this time may come.

— Albert Schweitzer

What If...

What if we adopt the radical notion that companion animals are individuals, not property, and that sharing a home with an animal is a privilege, not a right? What if we require competency tests, proof of financial responsibility, and permits for those wishing to adopt companion animals, like we do for driving? What if we provide the same safeguards for the adoption of companion animals as we do for the adoption of children?

What if we outlaw the buying and selling of companion animals, as we have the buying and selling of people? What if there was no profit to be made by puppy mills, backyard breeders, and others who breed companion animals for profit? How would this affect the "surplus" crisis?

What if we stop killing for convenience? What if we make it a crime to kill companion animals simply because they are "surplus"? Ban the killing of homeless animals and we will very quickly rise to the challenge. It is amazing how creative we can be when it is required of us.

Killing "surplus" animals does nothing to solve the homeless problem. In fact, it perpetuates the problem by continuously "making room" for more and more outcasts. "Excess" animals is not the problem; the problem is in people's heads and hearts, in the ways they think and feel—or fail to.

It's time for a radical change.

Chapter 4

Vegetarianism

Guess Who You're Having for Dinner?

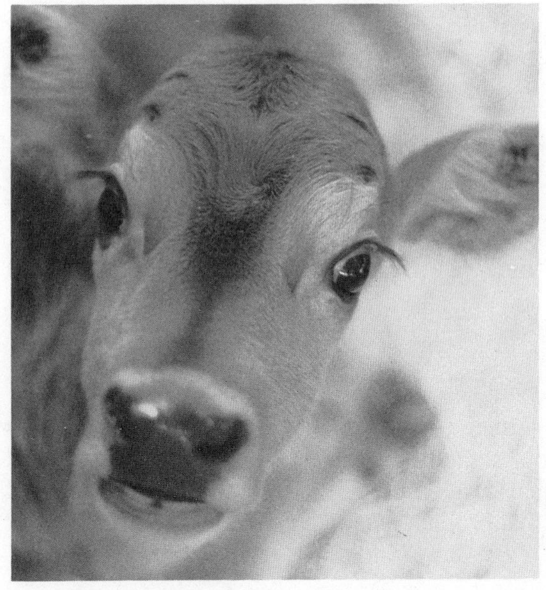

Name Withheld By Request

Does your food have a face?

— *PETA News*

One evening while cruising the local supermarket, a friend of mine was startled by a pig's head sticking out of the meat case. Knowing that I cared about animals, she reported her disgust to me. "It was so gross!" she exclaimed. "I told the butcher to get that pig's head out of there!"

The interesting point of the story is that my friend eats meat without hesitation. Why, then, did she react so strongly to the sight of a butchered pig's head? It's simple. The butcher violated an unspoken agreement between those who supply meat and those who eat it — he showed that meat has a face. When we eat meat, it's not a matter of *what* we're eating, but *whom*.

If you see yourself in the above story, you're not alone. Many people who wouldn't dream of harming an animal don't think twice about eating meat. In fact, we only remotely associate meat with living animals. It's only in rare cases that we realize the true nature of our "food."

Times are changing fast, though. A recent Gallup Poll commissioned by the National Restaurant Association discovered that 20% of the restaurant-going public bases their restaurant choices on whether or not an establishment offers nonmeat main dishes.[1] More and more people are becoming aware of the inherent cruelty in their past food choices. The result is that more people are becoming vegetarian.

What Is a Vegetarian?

Animals are my friends...and I don't eat my friends.

— George Bernard Shaw

Vegetarians are people who abstain from eating animal flesh. Animal flesh includes all animals — mammals, fish, and fowl. People who refrain from eating "red meat," but still eat fish or fowl, are not vegetarians!

A true vegetarian also avoids all food ingredients obtained from dead animals. This includes products such as gelatin (obtained from boiling animal tissues) and lard (animal fat), among many others. Vegetarians substitute plant-based ingredients for these items.

Approximately 15 million people in the U.S. are vegetarian.[2] Within this group, there are many different types of vegetarians. Some of them are:

◆ **lacto-ovo vegetarian**
(Pronounced lack-toe-OH-voe.) A lacto-ovo vegetarian doesn't eat any form of animal flesh, but may eat dairy products (lacto) and eggs (ovo). The general term "vegetarian" most often refers to lacto-ovo vegetarians.

◆ **vegan**
(VEE-gun.) Sometimes incorrectly pronounced VAY-gun, who is someone from Las Vegas.) Vegans avoid all animal products, including animal flesh, dairy products, and eggs. Vegans also avoid using other animal-derived products, such as leather, wool, and silk. Some vegans consider honey an animal product and therefore do not eat it. Vegans are sometimes called "total vegetarians," "pure vegetarians," or "strict vegetarians."

◆ **ethical vegetarian**
There are many different reasons why people choose vegetarianism. An ethical vegetarian refuses to eat animal flesh because s/he believes it is morally wrong to kill animals for consumption.

There are also many other specialized categories of vegetarians. For example, *fruitarians* eat only the fruit a plant produces. *Natural hygienists* emphasize a diet of uncooked, seasonal foods, and many *macrobiotic* eaters are vegetarian. See the Glossary at the back of the book for a fuller explanation of these terms.

Some Types of Vegetarians			
Type of Vegetarian	**Eats animal flesh (including fish or fowl)**	**Eats dairy or eggs**	**Uses animal-derived products (leather, silk, etc.)**
lacto-ovo vegetarian	no	yes	maybe
vegan	no	no	no
ethical vegetarian	no	maybe	maybe

Why Is Vegetarianism Important to Animal Rights?

Vegetarianism is important to animal rights because as many as 95% of the animals killed by humans are killed as food.[3] That's more than the total number of animals killed on roads and highways, killed by sport hunters, killed in laboratories, killed for their fur, and killed in pounds and shelters combined!

Even more distressing is the fact that we do not need to eat animals to be healthy. Animal flesh is nonessential to our diets. Meat-eating is a preference, a matter of taste and habit.

Ten Good Reasons to Adopt a Vegetarian Diet

I'm a vegetarian because
I know when animals are killed, they scream.

— Howard Jones, musician

There are many reasons why a growing number of people choose to adopt a flesh-free diet (vegetarian) or a diet totally free of animal-derived foods (vegan). A vegetarian diet, and particularly a vegan diet, benefits you, the animals, and the planet.

Here are ten reasons why it pays to "eat vegetarian."

Reason 1 — Body Design

Some animals have bodies that are specifically designed for meat-eating. Evidence indicates that humans are not one of those animals. One theory suggests that we were originally herbivores (vegetarians), but were forced to start eating meat when the Ice Age made plant food scarce.

Today, our reasons for eating meat are primarily psychological. First, meat-eating is simply a habit; it is readily accessible, familiar, and socially acceptable. We consume meat without even thinking. Second, meat is historically associated with affluence; it is more expensive than plant food and was once even reserved for nobility. This mindset persists, not only in our country but across the world. Finally, we are constantly bombarded with propaganda from a meat industry (with a multi-million dollar advertising budget) that implores us to believe that eating meat is "good," "smart," and "healthy." How about the beef industry's slogan, "Beef. Real Food For Real People." Are they implying that I'm less than a real person if I don't eat beef? It sure sounds like it. This type of programming works exceedingly well.

Many who have studied the subject conclude that humans are plant eaters by both physical and chemical design. Here are some reasons why.

- **Claws**
  The sharp claws of flesh-eaters help them tear flesh. Humans do not have claws.

- **Teeth**
  Our teeth are designed for grinding food, not tearing flesh. Flesh-eaters have long, pointed teeth. Adult humans have 20 pre-molars and molars, ideal for grinding grains, versus only four canines, which are pointed. We can only chew flesh that has been ground up or cooked. One theory suggests that the pointed canines of vegetarians are not for food consumption at all, but rather solely for a show of defense.

- **Chewing**
  Flesh-eaters chew in an up and down motion, swallowing large chunks of food. Humans and other herbivores chew in a slightly circular motion, which grinds the food.

- **Saliva**
  Flesh-eaters have acidic saliva, while humans have alkaline saliva. Unlike flesh-eaters, human saliva contains digestive enzymes that start digesting grains while they're still in the mouth.

- **Stomach**
  The stomachs of flesh-eaters contain 10 times the amount of hydrochloric acid as the stomachs of humans and other natural herbivores.

- **Intestines**
  Unlike humans, flesh-eaters have intestines that are straight and short, allowing flesh to pass through without putrefying. Humans have long, convoluted intestines, designed to digest foods through a process of fermentation. Flesh introduced into human intestines putrefies, releasing toxins, before it passes all the way through.

- **Metabolism**
  Flesh-eaters are designed to eat high-cholesterol, high-fat, low-fiber diets without harm. This type of diet is harmful to humans.

Many other differences between humans and natural carnivores also exist. Two of them are the ways in which we ingest water and the ways in which we cool ourselves. Flesh-eaters drink through lapping and cool themselves through panting. Vegetarians (including humans) drink through sucking and sweat to lower their body temperatures.

After studying data on diet and its effects from 6,500 Chinese subjects, a nutritional biochemist from Cornell University, Dr. T. Colin Campbell, concluded: "We're basically a vegetarian species and should be eating a wide variety of plant foods and minimizing our intake of animal foods."[4]

Reason 2 — Degenerative Diseases

The tally's in and the vegetarians won by a landslide! Studies show that a vegetarian diet can significantly reduce the instances of the most common degenerative diseases. On the other hand, meat, dairy products, and eggs contribute to a number of degenerative diseases, as shown in the table on the next page.[5]

Vegetarians, particularly vegans (no dairy or eggs), have been shown to have lower instances of the following ailments:

- uterine cancer
- colon cancer
- lung cancer
- breast cancer
- ovarian cancer
- peptic ulcers
- diabetes
- osteoporosis
- heart disease
- strokes
- kidney stones
- anemia

Additionally, low-fat diets, such as those that exclude animal products, are credited with dramatically improving symptoms in those who suffer from:

- gallstones
- rheumatoid arthritis
- diabetes
- bronchial asthma
- multiple sclerosis

A study that looked at vegetarian and meat-based diets in relation to elderly women found that a vegetarian diet was of benefit to the elderly not only because it helped reduce atherosclerosis, but also because the vegetarians had a higher intake of health-promoting vitamins and minerals.[6]

Some Effects of Animal Products

People who eat meat, dairy products, and eggs are susceptible to a variety of health risks

Characteristic of meat, dairy, eggs	**Linked to These Health Risks**	
High in saturated fat	• breast cancer • uterine caner • prostate cancer • hypoglycemia • heavier, more painful menstrual periods	• cervical cancer • ovarian cancer • heart disease • dental cavities
The only sources of dietary cholesterol	• atherosclerosis, which leads to heart disease and stroke	
The most acid-forming of all foods	• peptic ulcers	
Contain excessive amounts of protein	• osteoporosis* • kidney hypertrophy • breast cancer • pancreatic cancer	• kidney stones • kidney inflammation • prostate cancer • colon cancer
Provide no dietary fiber	• colon cancer • hemorrhoids	• rectal cancer • constipation

* The widely-held belief that calcium from dairy products helps prevent osteoporosis is now believed to be wrong. Excessive protein from dairy products may actually *contribute* to osteoporosis.

Reason 3 — Chemical Poisoning

More and more, we're learning how the artificial chemicals in our foods can adversely affect our health. You might be surprised at the array of chemicals present in today's commercial meat, dairy products, and eggs. They include (but are not limited to) antibiotics, insecticides, herbicides, larvicides, chemicals from synthetic fertilizers, hormones, growth stimulants, tranquilizers, and appetite stimulants.

Here's a closer look at some of the chemicals fed to animals who are raised for food — chemicals that can end up in our bodies if we eat animal products.

◆ **Antibiotics**

Nearly half of the antibiotics produced in the U.S. end up in animal feed. That's $435 million worth of antibiotics per year.[7] "Milk-fed" veal contains as much as 500 times the legal tolerance levels of antibiotics.[8] The antibiotics promote weight gain in animals who ordinarily would have trouble gaining weight in stressful, overcrowded living quarters.

Penicillin and tetracycline are the most common antibiotics used in animal feed. Over-use of these antibiotics has fostered the development of antibiotic-resistant bacteria. That is, there are now new strains of bacteria against which these antibiotics have no effect.

◆ **Pesticides and Insecticides**

Many pesticides, such as DDT, stay in the environment for decades, or even centuries, after all use of them has stopped. Farm animals ingest pesticides from pesticide-saturated grains and ground-up fish from pesticide-contaminated waters. Animals store pesticide residues in their tissues, passing them on to consumers who eat flesh, eggs, or milk from contaminated animals.[9] According to the U.S. Department of Agriculture (USDA), illegal levels of pesticides and drugs occur most often in pork, followed by beef, and then poultry.[10]

◆ **Hormones**

Animals are flooded with artificial hormones designed to increase milk production, litter size or frequency, or egg-laying. These hormones are passed to consumers through the animals. Mounting evidence relates the intake of these hormones to the extremely premature onset of puberty in children. There are documented cases of breast development and pubic hair in children as young as one year of age! Fortunately, removal of the hormone-laced foods usually results in a reversal of the symptoms.[11]

The European Community is so concerned about the health aspects of hormone-laden meat that it has banned imports of U.S. meat from cows fed hormones, as well as hormone-laden meat from other sources. Still, U.S. farmers persist in using hormones.

◆ **Artificial Colors**

Eggs from healthy hens have dark yellow yolks. To improve the yolk color of commercial eggs, the feed of commercial egg-laying hens contains artificial color to enrich the pale color of their egg yolks.[12] Of course, this doesn't improve the quality of the eggs, it just makes them look healthier!

Reason 4 — Food Poisoning

Many times, what we think of as gastric flu is actually food poisoning, a condition that kills around 9,000 people in the U.S. every year.[13] An official for the Centers for Disease Control says that only one-tenth to one-hundredth of salmonella food poisoning cases are even reported, the actual number of cases being between 40,000 and 4 million per year in the United States.[14] The Centers for Disease Control also estimates that chicken is responsible for up to half of all salmonella poisoning cases, as well as for an even higher incidence of food poisoning from campylobacter, another type of bacteria.[15] The USDA reports that about one-third of all raw poultry in the U.S. is contaminated with salmonella bacteria.[16]

According to USDA inspectors, chickens that pass inspection for human consumption include those stained with feces, those visibly dripping pus, and those that contain cancerous tumors. Said one USDA chicken plant inspector, "You know the USDA seal of approval we put on the chicken? Well, it's meaningless." Said another inspector, "I'm ashamed to even let people know I'm a USDA inspector. There are thousands of diseased and unwholesome birds going right on down the lines that we can't catch."[17] How does this happen? Chicken plants use automated equipment to slaughter and process chicken carcasses at top speed. Government inspectors have less than two seconds to examine each chicken on the production line. The equipment itself increases contamination by spreading bacteria. Stopping contaminated chicken from reaching the consumer market means slower processing, resulting in higher prices, fewer buyers, and therefore reduced profits. End of story.

Reason 5 — Economics

Meat is much more costly to produce than grains. People for the Ethical Treatment of Animals (PETA) reports that the same plot of land that produces enough plants to feed 12 people can feed only one person if the plants are first fed to an animal.[18]

The price paid for meat in the supermarket is not a realistic cost. When considering meat prices, we forget to figure the hidden cost of price supports paid for with our tax dollars. If you tag on the tax money that comes out of our pockets to subsidize meat farmers, the price of meat rises astronomically. One estimate puts the real price of a pound of hamburger at about $35! And this figure doesn't include the money spent on medical care as a direct result of eating meat, or the money spent to counter the adverse consequences to the environment caused by raising and slaughtering food animals.[19]

The same is true for dairy products. Taxpayer-backed subsidies to the dairy industry total almost $3 billion annually.[20]

Reason 6 — Ecology

Meat, dairy, and egg production hurt the environment by polluting water, polluting the atmosphere, and contributing to rainforest destruction. They also consume an astounding one-third share of the raw materials used for any purpose in the United States.[21]

◆ **Water**

Livestock production and slaughter are the main sources of water pollution in the United States. Run-off from dairy farms also pollutes water.

Livestock production uses approximately one-half of the water used for any purpose in the U.S. per year.[22] The amount of water used to produce a pound of wheat is one one-hundredth of the amount of water used to produce one pound of meat:

- Producing one steak uses 2,607 gallons of water.
- Producing one serving of chicken uses 408 gallons of water.
- Producing one pat of butter uses 100 gallons of water.[23]

◆ **Topsoil Erosion**
Overgrazing and modern methods of growing animal feed have contributed to a one-third loss in topsoil from U.S agricultural lands.[24]

◆ **Global Warming (The Greenhouse Effect)**
Chemical fertilizers produced for livestock feed crops contribute nitrous oxide to the atmosphere, a major cause of global warming. The elimination of forests to increase feed crop and pasture land for livestock contributes to increased carbon dioxide in the atmosphere, another major contributor to global warming.[25]

◆ **The Ozone Layer**
Through the process of rumination, cows produce as much as 60 million metric tons of methane, which is implicated in the reduction of the ozone layer.[26]

◆ **Rainforest Destruction**
The Rainforest Action Network reports that humans are deliberately destroying 100 acres of tropical rainforests per minute.[27] About one-third of that destruction is to provide grazing land for cattle.[28] The cattle provide cheaper meat for U.S. fastfood burgers. How much cheaper? Five cents per burger![29] Is this "savings" worth the extinction of one plant or animal species each day? That's one result of clearing rainforests for grazing.

Reason 7 — Wildlife Displacement and Death

More and more land is being turned into grazing pasture for cattle and sheep. This means that there is less and less land for displaced wildlife. Coyotes, mountain lions, wolves, wild horses, and bears are all victims of encroachment. The barbed wire fencing that surrounds grazing land has become a leading cause of death for deer and pronghorn antelope, second only to hunting.[30] Angry ranchers do not hesitate to kill wild animals, viewing them merely as a nuisance and a threat to livestock. The U.S. government sanctions the killings, sponsoring many mass exterminations. In 1989, the federal Animal Damage Control program spent $25.6 million in tax dollars to kill 133,000 mammals and two million birds to "protect" agricultural interests.[31]

Reason 8 — World Hunger

Feeding grain to animals is an inefficient use of food. Food animals raised in the U.S. consume an amount of grain that could feed five times the U.S. human population. Reducing the U.S. consumption of meat by just 10% would make 12 million more tons of grain available per year. That's enough to feed all people in the world who starve to death.[32]

Livestock consume over 80% of the corn and over 95% of the oats grown in the United States.[33] An acre of these grains can feed 12 times more people if fed directly to people, rather than being fed to an animal that is then slaughtered for food.

In the first edition of her book *Diet for A Small Planet*, Frances Moore Lappé compares the amount of protein an acre of land can yield for different food sources. If we take the amount of protein that can be produced by an acre used for meat production, we find that:

- One acre of cereals = five times more protein.
- One acre of legumes = 10 times more protein.
- One acre of leafy vegetables = 15 times more protein.[34]

You might think that food exports from the U.S. go a long way to reducing world hunger. The truth is that two-thirds of our agricultural exports go to livestock, not people.[35]

Reason 9 — Compassion

An astounding 95% of the animals deliberately killed in the U.S. every year are killed for food. If everyone in the U.S. were vegetarian, it would prevent the suffering of approximately 6 billion animals every year.[36]

Food animals suffer terribly during their confinement in factory farms, in their transport to stockyards or slaughterhouses, and at the stockyards and slaughterhouses themselves. If we each reduced our meat intake by just 1%, 60 million animals would be spared these agonies. McDonald's hamburgers alone account for the slaughter of over 16,000 cattle per week. That's more than 2,000 cattle per day.[37]

Slaughterhouses are not humane for people, either. They have the highest rates of both employee turnovers and injuries of any occupation.

Some of us justify eating meat by reassuring ourselves that "at least the animals had happy lives before they were killed." Nothing could be further from the truth. *Factory farms,* the most common method of raising animals for consumption, use a method called *intensive confinement* to raise the most animals possible in the smallest space possible. Animals lead miserable lives, confined to filthy, cramped quarters, unable to move. Some spend their entire lives indoors, never feeling fresh air or sunshine. Some are kept in almost total darkness. None are allowed to exercise or to engage in natural behaviors. All are fed chemicals and artificial foods designed to fatten them to abnormal degrees. These poor animals get sick and literally go crazy. Factory farms also hurt family farmers and consumers. See Chapter 5 for more on this modern method of food production.

Reason 10 — Nonviolence

Any way you look at it, meat is murder. It involves taking the life of a sentient being. Many people who support nonviolence embrace vegetarianism on these grounds. If you think of yourself as a peaceful person and you eat meat, it's time to rethink your eating habits.

There's more to a burger

than meets the eye . . .

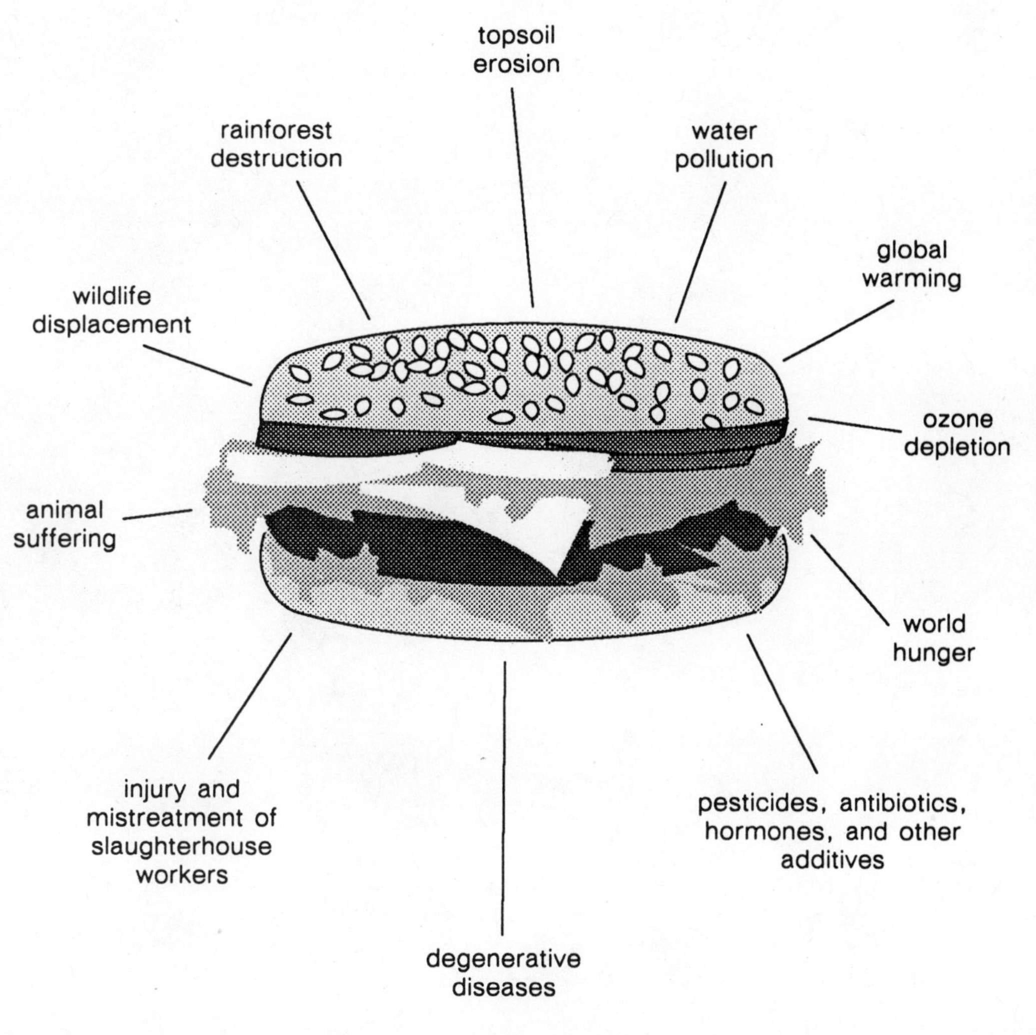

Gloria Reich, Glorious Graphics

Common Doubts and Questions

It is nearly fifty years since I was assured by a conclave of doctors that if I did not eat meat I should die of starvation.

— George Bernard Shaw

By now, you probably have a pretty good idea how eliminating animal foods from your diet will benefit your health, the animals, and the environment. But there are always those nagging doubts. Here are some common questions asked by people exploring vegetarianism.

What about the four food groups I learned about in school?

The "four food groups" idea was conceived not by health experts but by the food industry, which sponsored and distributed "educational" materials on foods to school children. The materials were slanted toward the products sold by the sponsoring food industry and taught children, teachers, and parents alike that these foods were essential to good health. The four categories of foods deemed "essential" for good health were: meat, dairy, grains, and fruits/vegetables.

Today, instead of the four food groups, the Department of Agriculture and the Department of Health and Human Services recommend these seven nutritional guidelines:

1. Eat a variety of foods.
2. Maintain a desirable weight.
3. Avoid too much fat, saturated fat, and cholesterol.
4. Eat foods with adequate starch and fiber.
5. Avoid too much sugar.
6. Avoid too much sodium.
7. If you drink alcohol, do so in moderation.[38]

For those of us still stuck on the "four food groups" concept, Physicians Committee for Responsible Medicine has developed a New Four Food Groups for health. The New Four Food Groups consist of the following categories: grains, legumes, vegetables, and fruits.[39] If you'd like more information on these revised food groups, contact Physicians Committee for Responsible Medicine, P.O. Box 6322, Washington, D.C. 20015, (202) 686-2210.

Isn't it okay to eat fish?

Fish feel pain, fear, and anxiety. They have sensitive nerve endings around their mouths. When out of water, they slowly suffocate. Don't they have a right to the same consideration as anyone else?

Remember, too, fishing doesn't stop with the suffering of the fish. In their attempts to catch tuna, fishers kill a dolphin every 11 minutes. The fishers deliberately set their nets on dolphins to catch the tuna that swim below them. The dolphins become trapped in the nets and drown. The majority of dolphins killed in this fashion are mothers and babies. When the babies get caught in the nets, the mothers stay with them, even though it costs them their lives, too. Even though we're now seeing some progress in this area, dolphin deaths still occur.[40]

Sea turtles also suffer from fishing practices. They become caught in shrimp trawl nets and drown. About 30 sea turtles meet this fate daily.[41] Many other marine mammals and birds become entangled and die in discarded fishing nets. Chapter 7 talks more about the destructiveness of fishing to marine animals.

Isn't it better to eat fowl than to eat red meat?

Does a turkey or chicken feel less pain and fear than a cow? The answer is no. Birds are sentient beings with emotional as well as physical lives. They are entitled to the same respect and humane treatment as any other animal.

But why not eat milk products and eggs?

There are lots of reasons.

From a health perspective, studies show that vegetarians who bypass dairy products and eggs are healthier than both meat-eaters and vegetarians who continue to eat dairy products. Also, many people are allergic to cow's milk and don't know it. Twenty percent of Caucasians and 90% of Blacks and Asians lack the enzyme needed to digest cow's milk (lactase).[42] Allergic reactions can show up as fatigue, mood swings, or sleep disorders. Another consideration is that most milk and eggs consumed today are from large-scale manufacturing operations, and contain an array of artificial chemicals. Also, dairy products are very high in protein, which in excess is detrimental to health. Says one researcher, "Ironically, osteoporosis tends to occur in countries where calcium intake is highest and [where] most of it comes from protein-rich dairy products."[43]

From an ethical perspective, most milk and eggs are from factory farm animals, who suffer inhumane treatment. Laying hens live in deplorable conditions and are "spent" after only two years, at which time they are slaughtered. Dairy cows also suffer from crowded, artificial conditions in factory farms, which treat them as "milk machines" rather than as living beings. Dairy cows wear out after a fraction of their normal life span. Although cows don't have to die in order for us to have cheese, most commercial cheese contains *rennet*, which includes enzymes from the stomachs of dead veal calves or pigs. In general, using dairy products supports both the slaughterhouse and inhumane factory farming.

From an environmental perspective, dairy farm run-off pollutes water supplies, and the gasses from cows and their excrement contribute to depletion of the ozone.

Remember, we don't need milk or eggs in our diets. They are something we choose to eat, not something we need to eat.

How will I get enough protein and calcium?

A vegetarian who eats healthy foods gets plenty of protein without even trying. It was once believed that vegetarians had to be careful to combine foods in a particular way to fill protein requirements, but this is no longer accepted as true. In fact, most of us, vegetarians and meat eaters alike, eat too much protein.[44] Excess protein is linked to various cancers, kidney problems, and loss of calcium from our bones, which contributes to osteoporosis.

Loss of calcium is also linked to overconsumption of acid-forming foods, of which animal flesh, dairy products, and eggs are the highest. We once believed that eating dairy products was a good prevention of osteoporosis, but studies now indicate that dairy products do not prevent osteoporosis. In fact, excessive protein from sources such as dairy products may actually contribute to osteoporosis.[45] A recent study confirms that calcium from plant sources is perfectly adequate.[46] Plenty of vegetables contain calcium, and the calcium is more readily available to our bodies than the calcium in animal foods. If you're concerned about getting enough calcium, just eat dark green leafy vegetables, broccoli, and acorn squash, or take a calcium supplement.

Will a vegetarian diet make me feel weak?

To the contrary, the word vegetarian comes from a Latin word meaning "to be lively." Unless you load up on vegetarian "junk food," you will feel lighter and have more energy on the vegetarian diet than you did on a meat-based diet. Many outstanding athletes, including Olympic champions, are vegetarian.

Note that when you first change your diet, you may experience a temporary adjustment period. This is because your body goes through a cleansing period, getting rid of stored-up impurities. That is, once you provide a healthier environment for your body, it begins to "clean house."

What if I'm pregnant or lactating? What about my children?

No problem. There are lots of vegan mothers and lots of kids who have been vegetarian or vegan since conception. Studies confirm that vegetarian kids suffer no ill-effects from their diets.

If you have any questions about vegetarian pregnancy or raising vegetarian children, see Chapter 13 for suggested reading or contact the vegetarian groups in Chapter 11 for more information.

How will I learn all of this?

Learning to eat differently is a process, not an overnight occurrence. You can learn about healthy vegetarian eating through books, magazines, video tapes, and from other vegetarians. For specific resources, see Chapters 11-13.

Say It Like It Is

It's easier to eat animals if we use euphemisms to soften the reality.

What We're Really Eating:	What We Call It:
• Cow flesh	beef, hamburger, steak, roast
• Pig flesh	pork, ham, bacon
• Baby cow flesh	veal
• Sheep flesh	mutton

The fact is, when you order a hamburger, you're ordering ground-up cow flesh. Let's just say it like it is.

Excuses, Excuses

It is easier with delicious-tasting animals like lobster to chew first and ask questions later. Unless you happen to be a lobster.

— Wiley A. Hall III, columnist

Your food choices are entirely up to you. Base your food choices on a growing consciousness that how you eat makes a difference to yourself, to animals, to the environment, and to those who don't have enough to eat. Choose to eat nonanimal foods because you support nonviolence, health, and a system of eating that supports life rather than death. And don't forget to congratulate yourself each time you make a food choice that furthers peace and kindness in the world. Each time you choose vegetarian food, you choose to support compassion for all beings.

At first, you may find yourself creating a variety of excuses for sticking to your familiar meat-based eating pattern. After all, you are changing a mindset. Recognize these for what they are — excuses. Here are some common ones.

I don't know what else to eat.

It's true, you may not know what to eat. As with any diet change, you need to educate yourself and experiment a little bit — or a lot! See Chapter 13 for some good books that talk about whole foods and contain vegetarian recipes. Also, talking with other vegetarians can help. If you're lucky enough to have a whole foods store in your area, talk to the people who run the store. They can offer suggestions.

Vegetarians eat a wide variety of foods, including grains, beans, pasta, legumes, cereals, nuts, seeds, vegetables, and fruits. There are dozens of excellent vegetarian dishes, including soups, sandwiches, "burgers," pizzas, stir-fries, burritos, pasta dishes, salads, casseroles, and vegetable pies. In addition to more traditional foods, health food stores contain a number of frozen and off-the-shelf vegetarian convenience foods.

If you're not familiar with vegetarian foods, there are a variety of good books that describe vegetarian eating. If you live near a natural foods store, go there and browse through the food items on their shelves. But you don't have to go to a special store to purchase vegetarian foods. You'll find many of them in your local grocery store.

For me, one of the exciting things about becoming vegetarian was that I discovered all kinds of foods that I never knew existed! For example, yummy grains such as brown rice, bulgur (cracked wheat), millet, and couscous; a variety of beans, legumes, nuts, seeds, fruits, and vegetables; and speciality foods such as nut milks (nuts blended into a liquid), soy milk, rice milk, soy cheese, tofu (soybean curd), tempeh (cultured soybeans, a good meat substitute), seitan (wheat gluten, a good meat substitute), textured vegetable protein (soy granules, a good meat substitute), meatless "hot dogs," and meatless "burgers."

It's too much work/too inconvenient to not eat meat.

Realize that you are embarking upon an adventure, a totally new way of approaching your eating habits. You are changing a major component of your lifestyle. It's going to take some thought, some effort, and some exploration. Any change always does. But it's exciting and fun! And once you learn new patterns of eating, it's no effort at all.

The only real challenge I've encountered is restricted choices at some restaurants. Even so, most restaurants offer salad and baked potatoes, and many offer vegetables, rice, pasta, breads, and other vegetarian foods. I often tell the restaurant personnel that I'm vegetarian and let them tell me what they have to offer. In this way, I let them know that there is a demand for vegetarian food. Restaurants want your business and are happy to accommodate "special" diets.

People will think I'm weird.

If you know why you are choosing a vegetarian diet, then you have no reason to feel weird; you are being true to yourself. You are not alone in choosing a flesh-free diet. There is a vast community of vegetarians. Once I became vegetarian, I discovered two other vegetarians in my office. I just never noticed that they were vegetarian until I became one.

Anyway, how can "Mister" (Fred) Rogers be wrong? How about Albert Einstein? Or Benjamin Franklin? Or Leonardo da Vinci? They were all vegetarians.

I need meat.

The meat and poultry industries spend millions of dollars every year to convince you of this! There is no basis in fact for the assertion that you need meat. In fact, empirical evidence supports the contrary. Vegetarians who eat whole food diets, especially those who minimize their intake of dairy products, are healthier than their meat-eating counterparts.

Do you perhaps have a psychological addiction to meat? Your belief that you need meat may be so strong that you think you are hurting yourself by not eating it. Or your habit of eating meat may be so ingrained that you have a difficult time weaning yourself. To combat this psychological addiction, change your food habits gradually. Recondition your thinking by reading about the studies that support vegetarianism. John Robbins' book *Diet for a New America* and the magazine *Vegetarian Times* are good places to start.

Tips to Help You Take the Plunge

Here are some tips to help you make the change to a healthy vegetarian diet.

- **Contact your local vegetarian society for support.**

  It's much easier to change your eating habits if you have support from others who understand and can teach you. See Chapter 11 for a list of vegetarian groups.

- **Read vegetarian magazines.**
  Vegetarian Journal contains recipes, book reviews, product descriptions, and articles on food, nutrition, and well-being. It will link you to a national support group of vegetarians. See the ordering information for this and other vegetarian magazines in the Vegetarianism & Whole Foods section of Chapter 13.

- **Read vegetarian cookbooks.**
  There is an abundance of good vegetarian cookbooks. Consult your local library if you want to "try before you buy." You'll find a list of selected cookbooks in Chapter 13.

- **Don't just stop eating meat. Learn about and eat healthy foods!**
  Eat whole grains, fruits, and vegetables. Whole foods are hearty and nutritious. They contain more nutrients and fiber than highly refined, processed foods. There are many good books about whole foods. See Chapter 13 for some recommendations.

- **Don't substitute dairy products for meat.**
  Dairy products are associated with many degenerative diseases. Also, because dairy products are high in protein, overconsumption can cause calcium loss. Many people are unwittingly allergic to dairy products, experiencing symptoms such as fatigue.

- **Take it in steps.**
  For example, you might stop eating the flesh of mammals first, then fowl, then fish, then all foods with an ingredient that requires killing an animal. Then focus on dairy products and eggs. Try reducing the number of times you eat meat during the week. For example, start out being vegetarian three days a week, then increase it until you are vegetarian seven days a week.

- **Remember that adopting vegetarianism is not about denial, but rather about choice.**
  You are not denying yourself animal flesh, you are choosing to not eat it. You have good reasons for the choices you make. When you're faced with a food choice, it might help to say to yourself, "I choose to eat vegetarian (vegan) food because I care about myself, about other beings, and about the Earth. By choosing this food, I am choosing life for myself and others. I am making a responsible choice."

- **Be kind to yourself.**
  You are changing a lifelong, culturally-ingrained habit. Give yourself positive reinforcement. Acknowledge and be proud of whatever progress you make. Don't beat yourself up. If you feel resistance from yourself, simply examine the reasons. Be patient. Each time you choose a nonflesh meal, congratulate yourself on your compassionate choice.

How You Can Help

- **Go veggie.**
  Start the change to a whole food, vegetarian diet. Join national and local vegetarian groups for information and support. See Chapter 11 for a list of groups.

- **Request veggie food.**
  Ask your school or office cafeteria to offer vegetarian food. If you attend meetings where food will be served (such as professional workshops), request ahead of time that they provide vegetarian food for you. Be specific about what constitutes "vegetarian" — many people don't know. See the Vegetarian Supplies & Services section of Chapter 12 for sources of vegetarian "quantity recipes" for institutions.

- **Advertise.**
  Encourage others to become vegetarian by wearing a veggie button or T-shirt and providing information to those who request it.

- **Celebrate.**
  Participate in the annual Great American Meatout (March 20), sponsored by the Farm Animal Reform Movement (FARM), and World Vegetarian Day (October 1), sponsored by the North American Vegetarian Society (NAVS).

Resources for Vegetarians

I have from an early age abjured the use of meat, and the time will come
when men such as I will look upon the murder of animals
as they now look upon the murder of men.

— Leonardo da Vinci

For products and services related to vegetarianism, see the following sections of Chapter 12: Audio Tapes & CDs, Clothing, Clubs for Kids & Young Adults, Computer-Based Communication & Products, Leather Alternatives, Radio & Television Programming, Stamps & Stickers, Travel Services, Vegetarian Supplies & Services, and Videos & Films.

For books, cookbooks, and periodicals on whole foods and the benefits of a vegetarian diet, see the Vegetarianism & Whole Foods section of Chapter 13.

See Chapter 11 for a list of vegetarian organizations. Many of the animal advocacy groups listed in Chapter 10 also provide support and information on vegetarianism. See also the Resources section of Chapter 5, "Factory Farms."

Conclusion

Now I can look at you in peace; I don't eat you any more.

— Franz Kafka

A vegetarian lifestyle is better for your own health, for animals, for the health of the planet, and for world hunger. A flesh-based diet is cruel to animals and detrimental to health, ecology, and humanity.

Vegetarians eat a variety of delicious whole foods, and experience more energy and health as a result. There is a lot of easily-accessible information on vegetarianism, and vegetarian support groups have sprung up all over the country. There's probably one near you. By joining the growing movement toward vegetarianism, you help not only yourself; you say no to cruelty, world hunger, pollution, and disease. A vegetarian diet helps the Earth and all of her inhabitants.

Vegetarianism

At a Glance

Did you know:

- The human body is designed for vegetarianism.
- Ninety-five percent of the animals killed in this country are killed as food.
- Studies indicate that vegetarians, especially those who refrain from dairy products and eggs, are healthier than meat eaters.
- Animal agriculture wreaks devastation on the environment, contributing to water pollution, topsoil depletion, rainforest destruction, global warming, and destruction of the ozone layer.

Chapter 5

Factory Farms

Old MacDonald's Ain't What it Used to Be

Farm Animal Reform Movement

Riddle: *What has billions of legs but still can't run away?*

Answer: *The six billion animals raised and killed for food every year in the U.S.*

Life on the farm. Cattle grazing in fields. Chicken scratching the ground. Hogs wallowing in mud.

Now consider this scene. A calf chained inside a tiny crate, a crate so small he can't even turn around. Chickens crammed four to a wire cage the size of a record album cover, their upper beaks cut off, patches of skin rubbed raw from constant contact with each other or the sides of the cage. Newborn chicks tossed on top of each other into plastic garbage bags to slowly suffocate. A sow isolated in a concrete stall too small to turn around in, or strapped to a concrete floor. An outlandish nightmare? A living hell. Welcome to the factory farm.

What Are "Factory Farms"?

You have just dined, and however scrupulously the slaughterhouse is concealed in the graceful distance of miles, there is complicity.

— Ralph Waldo Emerson

Gone is the family farm. In its place is the factory farm, a large-scale food production factory. Factory farms are responsible for 90% of the eggs,[1] 98% of the poultry, and 70% of the cattle, pigs, and veal calves consumed today.[2]

Like any efficient factory, a factory farm aims to maximize profits and minimize costs. To achieve this, factory farms employ a method of production called *intensive confinement.* Intensive confinement is exactly what its name implies — extreme restriction. Land is expensive, so factory farmers utilize space as efficiently as possible. Instead of barns and open fields, the factory farm consists of huge metal warehouses. Wasted space is wasted money, so farmers crowd the warehouses to absolute capacity, cramming as many animals as possible into the limited space. Most animals spend their entire lives inside small cages or pens that they never leave. Sometimes they exist in nearly constant darkness. The only time the animals go outside or feel sunshine is when workers load them onto trucks headed for the auction block or the slaughterhouse.

While proponents of factory farming claim that animals "benefit" from the rigidly controlled environment, the reality is that factory farms benefit only one group — the owners. The environment is designed solely to maximize profits. No thought is given to an animal's needs, feelings, instincts, or comfort. The animals are just so much meat.

Within the confines of factory farms, animals understandably suffer extreme stress. Overcrowding and the inability to fulfill even basic instincts result in stress-induced behaviors such as cannibalism and self-mutilation. Since these behaviors hurt profits, factory farmers must address them. Their solutions reflect their attitudes towards the animals:

- To prevent cannibalism in frustrated chickens, farmers instituted the practice of *debeaking*, cutting off the chickens' upper beaks. The chickens still peck at each other, but the damage isn't severe enough to cut into profits.
- To prevent crazed pigs from biting off each others' tails — a stress-induced behavior — farmers eliminated the target; they simply cut off the pigs' tails.

Viewed purely from an economic perspective, factory farming seems to make sense. It maximizes profits and minimizes costs by automating or eliminating maintenance. It keeps labor to a minimum; often, the only contact farm animals may have with their "caretakers" is when the animals are initially shoved into the cages in which they spend their lives and when they are pulled from their cages for transport to the slaughterhouse. Feeding, watering, and waste removal in many instances are entirely automated. Handling animals takes time, and time is money. This is "modern" animal agriculture.

The Costs of Factory Farms

Despite the economic justification for factory farms, the non-dollar costs of factory farms is great. The animals are not the only ones paying a great price. The cost to consumers and family farms is also high.

The Cost to Family Farms

According to The Humane Society of the United States, three multi-million dollar conglomerates control the majority of factory farms. These corporations own all aspects of the food production system, from the feed companies to the farms themselves to the slaughterhouses.[3]

How can family farms compete? They can't. Small-scale farming is economically unfeasible, particularly if animals are treated as living beings with their own natures and needs. Family farmers cannot survive against the competition of factory farms. Thus, family farms are giving way to factory farms. A former editor of the magazine *Farm Journal* warns family farmers:

> If large-scale animal factories continue to have their way, you will be slowly pushed out of the hog and beef business just as has happened to 95 percent of the chicken farmers.[4]

The Cost to Consumers

What happens to people forced to live in crowded, stressful environments, with no access to sunshine or fresh air, and no outlets for their natural feelings and instincts? They typically get sick, become depressed, and/or go crazy. The same is true of animals. The inhumane conditions of factory farms result in a high susceptibility to disease. The factory farm solution? Drugs.

Drugs are a major component in factory farming methods, providing millions of dollars in profits for pharmaceutical companies each year. Factory farmers reportedly buy over 15 million pounds of antibiotics annually. Evidence shows that drugs used on factory farms affect not only the animals, but the people who consume the animal-derived products.[5] Through meat, eggs, and milk, consumers unwittingly ingest an array of drugs including antibiotics, hormones, and artificial colors.

Do drugs guarantee that animals are disease-free? No. A farmer at one stockyard felt that many cattle brought to the auction showed signs of having cancer. He went on to say that the meat from those cows would probably end up in cheap hamburgers, and that he never let his family eat fast food hamburgers.[6] Dozens of U.S. Department of Agriculture (USDA) chicken inspectors have stated that they personally no longer eat chicken because they don't trust that it is safe.[7]

The Cost to the Environment

The environment pays dearly for large-scale animal production:

- **Water**
  Livestock production operations and slaughterhouses are the single largest users and polluters of water in the U.S. today.

- **Rainforests**
  About half of rainforest destruction occurs expressly to provide additional grazing land for cattle.

- **Topsoil**
  Methods used to grow animal feed have contributed to a one-third loss of topsoil from our farmland.

- **Atmosphere**
  Cows and their excrement release gasses that contribute to the greenhouse effect and depletion of the ozone layer.

- **Resources**
  Feeding grain to animals instead of directly to humans is inefficient and wastes resources. Grain grown for human consumption feeds more people. To provide meat for one person at one meal, a cow has to eat as much grain as would be eaten by 12 people at one meal. The bottom line is that one person can eat meat or 12 people can eat grain. Meat is a poor return on the investment.

The Cost to Animals

The federal law that sets minimum conditions for animal care, the Animal Welfare Act, specifically excludes animals raised for food or fiber. Farm animals have no protection under the Animal Welfare Act. Existing regulations for farm animals are controlled and enforced by the U.S. Department of Agriculture (USDA). The USDA exists to assist people in the agriculture business, not to protect animals.

The best way to understand factory farming is to look at the treatment received by specific types of animals. The horrors of factory farming are well-documented, most notably by John Robbins in *Diet for a New America* and by Jim Mason and Peter Singer in *Animal Factories*. These authors provide thorough, first-hand observations of factory farms, along with revealing photographs and statements from the industry itself. These books are highly recommended for the reader who wants a more substantial insight into factory farming.[8]

Here is a brief look at the conditions that some animals endure on factory farms.

■ Laying Hens

The next time you reach for a carton of eggs, consider these facts. Then reconsider that carton of eggs.

Factory farm chickens suffer overcrowded, unnatural lives of confinement.

◆ **Out of the Egg**
From the time they first break through the shell till their throats are slit at the slaughterhouse hens live in a mechanized world that ignores their needs and instincts. Far from the idyllic scene of a mother hen hatching her eggs by sitting on them, baby chicks never know their mothers. They hatch in incubators, far away from any nurturing hen.

◆ **Sorting the Males from the Females**
The first step in egg production is to sort freshly-hatched baby chicks according to gender. Female chicks, useful as future egg-layers, are allowed to live. Male chicks, useless to the egg-laying industry, are discarded. A person called a *puller* or *sexer* picks the males out of a crowded tray of chicks and tosses them into plastic garbage bags. There they eventually suffocate from the other chick bodies piling up on top of them, or they are later crushed, drowned, or ground up for chicken feed, fertilizer, pet foods, or food for minks on mink farms. Over 200 million male chicks meet this fate every year.[9]

◆ **Debeaking**
Female chicks survive the gender-sorting only to be mutilated by *debeaking*, intended to reduce the harm chickens can inflict on each other in the crowded conditions. During debeaking, a person holds the chick and inserts her beak into a machine that slices off about one-third of the chick's sensitive upper beak, without anesthetic. The shock of this procedure kills some chicks.

◆ **Growing Up**
Future egg-layers spend the next phase of their lives in a large warehouse with as many as 60,000 to 250,000 other chicks. By the time they reach adult size, the building provides an average of only six square inches per hen. The grossly abnormal flock size frustrates the hens' strong drive to establish a pecking order. To help prevent fighting among the frustrated birds, farmers may keep the birds in darkness except at feeding times.

◆ **Battery Cages**

When they reach egg-laying age, the hens get a new home — the laying warehouse. Here they spend the remainder of their lives crammed four or five to a wire cage the size of a record album cover. Reportedly, at the Hainsworth Farm in Mt. Morris, New York, the cage size is one square foot.[10] These cages, called *battery cages*, are outlawed in some European countries, but are still legal in the United States. A single building may hold as many as 80,000 hens, with cages jammed side-by-side. Sometimes cages sit on top of each other in tier fashion, with chicken excrement falling through the bottom of each cage onto the chickens in the cages below.

The suffering for these animals is unrelenting; it is a way of life. The floors of the wire cages, slanted so that eggs will roll forward, cut into the hens' feet. Many hens lose their feathers and develop sores because they are constantly rubbing against the wire cage and each other. Crowding prevents the hens from ever spreading their wings. Although their beaks are severed, they attempt to peck at each other. The hens cannot even fulfill minimal natural instincts.

After two years of this confinement, hens that would normally live 15 to 20 years in a natural setting are "spent." Having exhausted their usefulness as laying hens, they are shipped to the slaughterhouse where they become ingredients in chicken soups and pet foods.

■ Broilers

◆ **A Chick is Born**

Chickens raised to be eaten start out the same way that laying hens do, hatched by incubators and debeaked by a hot blade. Unlike chickens targeted for egg-laying, both males and females serve as "broilers."

◆ **Into the Warehouse**

Because consumers demand that chicken skin be free of bruises, broiler chickens are spared from confinement in wire battery cages. Instead, they are crowded together in a huge warehouse with up to 60,000 other birds, where they are fattened as quickly as possible. By the time they reach adult size, there is barely room to move. Overwhelmed by the overcrowding, which makes it impossible to establish a "pecking order," the birds experience extreme anxiety. Like egg-layers, chickens destined for the oven never experience sunshine or the outdoors. Lighting is artificially controlled to make them eat more or quiet down. This unnatural environment, coupled with unsanitary conditions, breeds disease.

◆ **To the Slaughterhouse**

Before they are two months old, the broiler chickens are stuffed into crates, sometimes suffering broken wings in the process, and are shipped off to the slaughterhouse.

■ Pigs

Pigs are extremely intelligent, highly social beings. We commonly think of them as dirty because they wallow in mud to keep cool and discourage insects. The truth is, pigs are very clean animals when they are in a clean environment. Here's how factory farm pigs spend their entire lives.

Farm Animal Reform Movement

Pigs suffer psychological as well as physical distress in factory farms.

◆ **Breeding Machines**
Sows in factory farms are breeding machines. Kept continuously pregnant by means of artificial insemination, they are immobilized in tiny crates the size of their bodies while pregnant. For the birthing and nursing processes, sows are often strapped to the floor.

◆ **Weaning Piglets**
Piglets are weaned early so that their mother can be reimpregnated as soon as possible. Some piglets are removed from their mothers as soon as a few days after birth, even though natural weaning would normally occur at 12 weeks. A few piglets die from the shock of early weaning.

◆ **Physical Distress**
After weaning, piglets reside in wire cages similar to those that house chickens, or in small, cement holding pens in warehouses. At 50 pounds they are confined to individual stalls in warehouses or to a crowded pen shared with other pigs. Due to costs, no straw bedding is provided. The concrete or metal warehouse floor is unsuited to the pigs' cloven hooves. As a natural response to this unnatural "ground," the pigs' feet develop painful sores and become deformed.

Pigs also suffer from the effects of breathing ammonia and other poisonous gases from their own excrement, from which they are unable to escape. Breathing the gases damages the pigs' lungs and they become ill. A study conducted by the Eli Lily Company and Elanco Products Company revealed that 71% of factory farm pigs show symptoms of atrophic rhinitis and 70% show symptoms of pneumonia.[11] The USDA reports that 23%, or 24 million pigs per year, die before they can be slaughtered, largely due to respiratory diseases.[12] The pigs are not the only ones to suffer, however. Many of the people who work in these facilities also experience acute respiratory problems.

Male pigs suffer the additional pain and trauma of castration done without anesthetic. It isn't hard to empathize with the excruciating pain the pig must experience from this mutilation.

◆ Psychological Distress

Perhaps worse than the physical suffering is the psychological distress experienced by pigs. Overcrowding, living in their own excrement, and other built-in stresses of the factory farm cause unnatural reactions in pigs. The pig industry itself reports a condition called Porcine Stress Syndrome, in which pigs unexpectedly die from experiencing shock such as early weaning or being placed with strange pigs.[13] More common is an aggressive reaction to stress called *tail-biting,* in which one pig bites off another pig's tail. The evident solution would be more room, but instead the factory farmer "prevents" tail-biting by simply cutting off all pigs' tails, a practice called *tail-docking*.

Boredom is another problem for highly intelligent beings who are forced to stand around in the same spot day after day. Reactions to boredom and stress include repetitive actions such as head rocking, swaying, and bar biting. In the book *Animal Factories,* Jim Mason and Peter Singer observed the following:

> At one pig farm we visited, we watched one young pig methodically bite the large-gauge wire on the gate of her nursery pen. Starting at one side of the gate, she would bite at each square, work her way across, and then continue back and forth. Occasionally she would break this routine to run to the rear of her pen, then return and begin the pattern all over again.[14]

◆ To the Slaughterhouse

As is true for all animals transported to the slaughterhouse, the journey is no joy ride for pigs. First, they may be transported to stockyards where they are herded off the truck to undergo the trauma of being auctioned off. They then go back onto a truck and head to the slaughterhouse. Handlers use electric cattle prods to drive pigs onto and off of trucks. Observers report seeing trucks so overcrowded that pigs were on top of one another. Witnesses also report pigs being kicked by the handlers, and saw one of the handlers "hit a pig over its head with a huge iron mallet simply because it did not move fast enough into the holding pen."[15] In winter, young pigs have reportedly become frozen to the sides of transport trucks.[16] These occurrences are just part of the normal routine in an industry that regards animals as nothing more than products.

■ Beef Cattle

◆ Starting Out

Beef cattle typically begin life in the pasture, but are then sold to factory farmers. In transport, animals receive rough handling by people who regard them only as things. No matter how long the trip, the animals are denied food and water, and must endure extreme temperatures. As John Robbins reports:

> Today's cattlemen regard it as a normal part of the business that some of the animals will die in transit. It's a calculated loss. They find it more profitable to absorb the loss due to deaths and injuries than to handle the

animals differently.[17]

◆ **Living Accommodations**

Animals surviving the journey are crowded into fenced feedlots or confined to warehouses with automated feed and waste removal systems. As with other factory farm animals, exercise is minimized because it burns calories, which is contrary to the goal of fattening the animals as quickly as possible. Anyway, there simply isn't room for it.

◆ **Castration and Dehorning**

Castrated bulls produce a more fatty, expensive grade of meat. Castration is done without anesthetic Cattle are also subjected to dehorning, a painful procedure that is only necessary because of excessive overcrowding in feedlots.

◆ **To the Slaughterhouse**

Transportation to the slaughterhouse is no better than was the transportation to the factory farm. After all, at this point the animals are already fatted and are heading for their deaths. Why waste time or money on their comfort or safety?

■ Dairy Cows

◆ **Short But Not Sweet**

The natural lives of cows is from 20 to 25 years. Dairy cows in factory farms often do not live more than four years.[18] Once their milk output drops, dairy cows are shipped off to the slaughterhouse.

As with other factory farm animals, cows are confined to the smallest space possible. The dairy cow spends her life moving between a crowded, automated feedlot and a mechanized milking parlor. Ever on the lookout for ways to increase milk production, agricultural scientists have developed a growth hormone that produces oversized udders on cows. The pain this "improvement" may inflict on the cows is inconsequential.

◆ **Separated at Birth**

To give as much milk as possible, the dairy cow is impregnated every year. As in many species, calves and their mothers are strongly bonded; the mother recognizes and cares about her calf. Factory farming does not acknowledge this emotional bond. Calves are taken from their mothers shortly after birth and the milk intended for the calf is instead given to people. Female offspring suffer the fates of their mothers and become milk machines. Male offspring become sources for veal.

■ Veal Calves

Thanks to nationwide campaigns by animal rights advocates, the plight of veal calves has gained much public attention. Unfortunately, at this writing, there are still no improvements in U.S. regulations regarding veal calves, despite attempts at legislation.

◆ **Solitary Confinement**

After being taken from his mother a day or two after his birth, the calf is isolated in a stall called a *veal crate,* which is just big enough for him to stand up in; there isn't even enough room for him to comfortably lie down. The calf is then chained by the neck so that he cannot turn around or groom himself.

This severe restriction of his movement is necessary in order to produce the desired color and texture of muscle. The slightest exercise, even walking around, would develop his muscles and change the "veal." These veal crates, though still legal in the U.S., have been banned in Great Britain as inhumane.

Farm Animal Reform Movement

Calves, isolated in tiny stalls and fed iron-deficient diets, end up as "veal" before their first birthday.

◆ **The Myth of Milk-Fed Veal**

Milk-fed veal is valued for its tenderness and white color. However, so-called milk-fed veal would more accurately be called "anemic veal." The desired white color of the muscle results from keeping the calf on an iron-deficient liquid diet. In response to this deficiency, calves have been observed licking the iron railing of their crates in attempts to ingest some iron. The farmer's response has been to replace the iron railings with wooden ones, since it's possible that licking the metal could affect the color of the veal.[19] Another reason that milk-fed veal is misnamed is because the largest U.S. producer of the formula fed to the calves does not include any cow's milk in the formula.[20]

Besides anemia, there are other side effects of the liquid diet. One is chronic diarrhea. Another is denial of a basic instinct, that of rumination or "chewing the cud"; there can be no cud without solid food.

◆ **No Comforts**

In addition to solid food, calves are denied bedding, water, and light:

- Bedding is denied because, were it present, the calves would eat it. Due to the lack of bedding, the calves develop serious leg injuries from standing on the hard floor.
- Water is denied because it was found that if deprived of water, a calf attempts to quench his thirst by drinking more of the liquid formula, thus gaining weight that much faster.

- Light is denied because keeping the calves in darkness reduces restlessness. For many calves, a side effect of living in darkness is permanent blindness.

After four months of this miserable existence, the calves are slaughtered for their white, tender muscles.

■ Other Unfortunates

Although less publicized, factory farming methods are now employed to raise sheep, rabbits, and other "food" animals. Similar methods are also used on fur farms, which raise animals for their pelts. For a closer look at fur farms, see Chapter 7.

A Word About Stockyards

Stockyards are temporary stopovers for animals who are on their way to slaughter. Animals brought to the stockyard are put in holding pens and auctioned off to buyers who then ship them to slaughter. Like farms, stockyards are exempt from federal humane laws, which exclude "food" animals, including horses destined for meat packing plants.

Interestingly, Webster's dictionary defines *stock* as "something without life or consciousness." This aptly describes stockyards, where animals are treated as inanimate objects. As a matter of routine, animals too injured or too sick to move under their own power are left to die in heaps appropriately called *dead piles*.

Farm Animal Reform Movement

Pigs left in a "dead pile."

Animals healthy enough to be auctioned off are really no better off than those left in dead piles. From the stockyard, the next stop is the slaughterhouse.

At the Slaughterhouse

As long as there are slaughterhouses, there will be battlefields.

— Leo Tolstoy

Slaughterhouses are truly places of horror, for both the people who work in them and the animals killed there. Slaughterhouse workers suffer the highest rate of on-the-job injuries of any occupation. They are continuously surrounded by death. Some slaughterhouses are undoubtedly worse than others. A former employee at a Perdue chicken plant reported to National Public Radio that she witnessed women urinating and vomiting on the work line because they were not allowed to visit the bathroom.[21]

You can imagine what the slaughterhouse is like for the animals awaiting their murder. They can smell the blood, hear the cries, and feel the terror of the animals ahead of them in line. At the same time, they are forced to move forward into this panic.

Regardless of the species of animals, the general slaughtering procedure is the same: they are hung upside-down, stunned, and their throats are slit. Kosher slaughter stipulates that the animals must be fully conscious when killed, so they are suspended and have their throats slit without being stunned. The suspension itself can be terrifying and painful. Just imagine a steer being hoisted up by one leg and left to hang upside down for many minutes until his throat is cut and he bleeds to death. Many more animals than we know of suffer this fate; much meat that is sold today is from animals killed according to the kosher method, even though it is not labeled as kosher.[22]

On the Bright Side

I have no doubt that it is part of the destiny of the human race,
in its gradual improvement, to leave off eating animals,
as surely as the savage tribes have left off eating each other
when they came in contact with the more civilized.

— Henry David Thoreau

While the factory farm industry is a grim reminder of how callous people can be, there are increasing bright spots in the fight to improve the conditions of farm animals. Here are a few of them.

◆ **Global Progress**

While the United States continues to largely ignore the humane issues of farm animals, elsewhere in the world farm animals are winning rights. Great Britain has outlawed veal crates, and the American Society for the Prevention of Cruelty to Animals reports that a new program for farm animals in Sweden:

> ...gives cattle grazing rights and grants pigs separate bedding and feeding places and forbids their tethering. Both cows and pigs must have access to straw and litter, chickens must be let out of their cramped cages and no drugs or hormones may be used on farm animals, except those needed to treat disease.[23]

◆ **A Change of Heart**

Dr. Eldon Keinholz, a tenured professor of animal science at Colorado State University, has had a change of heart after 25 years of teaching ways to breed poultry for profit. He is quoted by People for the Ethical Treatment of Animals as saying, "My decisions from the heart have turned me from a noncaring animal exploiter to a person who wants freedom for all animals. I have become a vegetarian in an animal science department."[24]

◆ **Proposals for Change**

The National Academy of Sciences has released an extensive report in support of a national food production system called Humane Sustainable Agriculture (HSA). HSA by design eliminates the abuses of factory farming while benefiting the environment and consumers.[25]

◆ **Firsts**

Pressure from Farm Sanctuary resulted in the first time ever that a livestock facility adopted regulations and procedures to reduce animal suffering at auctions and stockyards. Farm Sanctuary is also responsible for the successful cruelty conviction of a vealer who abandoned 64 calves, leaving them chained to their crates to starve to death (Farm Sanctuary rescued the calves), and with persuading a hatchery to implement a more humane method for killing unwanted male chicks.

◆ **More Support for Farm Animals**

There are now groups that specialize in farm animal issues, and animal sanctuaries specifically for farm animals. For the names of these groups, see the Resources section at the end of the chapter.

◆ **Boycott Success**

More and more restaurants refuse to sell milk-fed (anemic) veal due to pressure from consumers. The Humane Farming Association reports that sales of anemic veal nationwide are down by 10%, and down by 13% in the largest anemic veal-producing county in the nation. This translates into 100,000 calves.[26] A large restaurant chain, The Olive Garden, now assures diners that its "naturally-raised" calves are fed mother's milk and other natural food, graze in open pastures, and are given no drugs. They have a flyer with this information designed specifically to address the concerns of animal rights advocates.

How You Can Help

Due to the campaigns of many animal rights organizations, the number of people learning about factory farming grows daily. More and more consumers are refusing to support the inherent cruelty of this industry. Here are some things that you can do for farm animals.

◆ **Don't buy factory farm products, including milk, eggs, or animal flesh.**
If you do buy dairy products or flesh, buy only locally-produced items that you know are from more humane sources.

◆ **Ask your school and office cafeterias to serve non-flesh/non-dairy meals.**
For quantity recipes suitable for institutions, see the Vegetarian Supplies & Services section of Chapter 12.

◆ **Request that your local grocery stores sell humanely-raised brands of eggs and veal.**
For details, contact Food Animal Concerns Trust, P.O. Box 14599, Chicago, IL 60614-9966, (312) 525-4952.

◆ **Ask your local restaurants to stop serving milk-fed veal.**
Better yet, ask them to stop serving veal altogether.

◆ **Sponsor an Easter Eggless Hunt, instead of the usual Easter egg hunt.**
For details, contact the Animal Protection Institute of America (API), P.O. Box 22505, Sacramento, CA 95822, (916) 731-5521 or 422-1921.

◆ **Educate yourself.**
Read books and articles on factory farming. See Chapter 13 for suggestions.

◆ **Spread the word.**
Educate your friends and your community. Write a letter to the editor of your local newspaper. Set up an information table at a mall or street fair. Some of the organizations that help farm animals can provide you with literature.

◆ **Visit your local factory farm, stockyard, or slaughterhouse.**
Take photographs and document what you witness. Then publicize what you discover.

Resources for Factory Farms

For products and services related to Factory Farming, see the following sections of Chapter 12: Activist Aids, Audio Tapes & CDs, Clothing, Computer-Based Communications and Products, Stamps & Stickers, Vegetarian Supplies & Services, and Videos & Films.

For additional reading on factory farming, see Chapter 13.

The following organizations work on behalf of animals raised for consumption. See Chapter 10 for a description of these and other organizations that help the animals we raise to eat and wear. *Note: See the state listings in Chapter 10 for additional organizations.*

- **General**
  Animal Liberation Action (AZ), Animal Liberation Front Support Group (TN), Animal Rights International/Coalition for Nonviolent Food (NY), Coalition Against Fur Farms (OR), Coalition Against the Horse Slaughter Trade (CA), Farm Animal Reform Movement (MD), Food Animal Concerns Trust, Inc. (IL), EarthSave (CA), The Humane Farming Association (CA), International Society for Cow Protection (NC), People for the Ethical Treatment of Animals (VA), Ranching Task Force—grazing on public lands (AZ), United Poultry Concerns (MD)

- **Sanctuaries**
  Adopt-A-Cow (PA), Animal Place (CA), Aspin Hill Memorial Park and Sanctuary (MD), Community of Compassion for Animals (CA), Farm Sanctuary (NY, CA), Green Acres Sanctuary (PA), Hemlock Hill Farm Sanctuary (ME), Heron Run Refuge, Inc. (MD), Purple Cow & Friends (CA), Wilderness Ranch Sanctuary for Farm Animals (CO)

Conclusion

Most animals raised for consumption today live in giant, crowded warehouses. Unlike the "family farm" that so readily comes to mind, these animals may live their entire lives indoors in tiny stalls or cages under artificial light. Denied fulfillment of even their most basic instincts, many animals go crazy or get sick. Instead of providing better conditions for animals, and thus reducing disease, factory farmers instead use drugs and mutilation to "solve" the problems stemming directly from these intensive confinement methods of animal agriculture. Stockyards and slaughterhouses are also places where animals suffer needlessly.

Factory farming means suffering for animals and unhealthy products for consumers. You can start helping these animals by refusing to buy factory farm products and by supporting organizations that work to improve conditions for farm animals. Ultimately, however, "humane" farming can only be achieved by eliminating animal products from our diets. As long as we continue to demand animal products, animals will continue to be regarded as things rather than as the sentient beings that they are.

Factory Farms

At a Glance

Did you know:

- The federal Animal Welfare Act does not apply to farm animals.
- Ninety percent of the eggs, 98% of the poultry, and 70% of the cattle, pigs, and veal calves consumed today are from factory farms.
- Factory farms are large-scale food production factories that deny animals even basic needs and instincts. Factory farm animals suffer severe physical and psychological distress.
- The meat, dairy products, and eggs from factory farm animals are full of antibiotics, hormones, and other chemicals, which are passed on to consumers.
- Slaughterhouses have the highest on-the-job injury rate of any occupation.
- You can help factory farm animals by refusing to buy factory farm products.

A man can live and be healthy without killing animals for food; therefore, if he eats meat, he participates in taking animal life for the sake of his appetite. And to act so is immoral.

— Leo Tolstoy

Chapter 6

Research, Education, and Testing

The Unkindest Cut of All

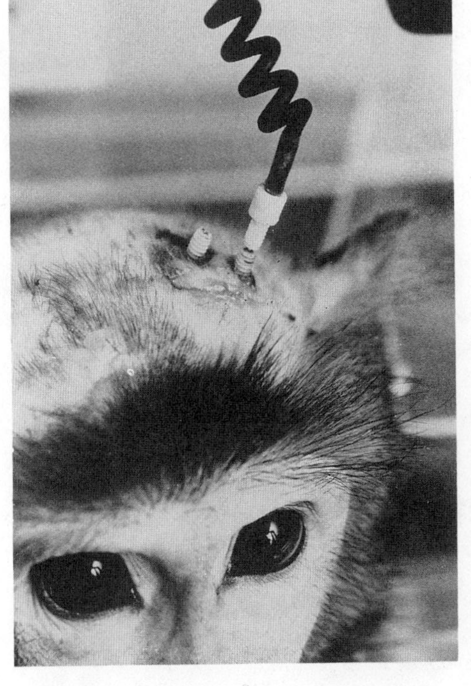

The American Anit-Vivisection Society

During my medical education at the University of Basle I found vivisection horrible, barbarous and above all unnecessary.

— C.G. Jung (as quoted in *The Extended Circle*)

The use of animals in research, testing, and education is perhaps the most controversial of all animal rights issues. After all, what is a feeling human being to do when posed with the question, "Whose life is more important? A child's or a dog's?"

The problem, of course, is with the question itself. Animal research is not about choosing between humans and animals, as researchers would have us believe. Animal research is a choice between humanity and inhumanity, between good science and bad science, and between health and sickness — but it is not a choice between people and animals. In this chapter, we'll see how animal research hurts people as well as animals.

What is "Vivisection"?

Traditionally, *vivisection* meant cutting into living tissue. Today, vivisection means all injurious use of animals in laboratories and classrooms, whether for experimentation, product testing, training, or demonstration. In this book, *vivisection, animal research,* and *animal experimentation* are synonymous.

Modern day animal research includes a lot more than the search for cures to diseases. Today, live animals are used in:

- cosmetic and personal care product tests
- household product tests
- toxicity tests by chemical industries
- product tests by toy companies
- safety tests by auto manufacturers
- psychological experiments
- demonstrations in elementary, junior high, senior high, and college-level biology classes
- agricultural research
- veterinary research
- biomedical research
- drug addiction studies
- veterinary training
- medical training
- practice for sales people who sell surgical staplers

Do any of these laboratory and classroom endeavors have merit? Aren't at least some of these uses of animals justified? Yes and no. Yes, some of the endeavors are worthwhile. No, use of animals is not justified nor is it necessary, as we'll see.

Who Are the Anti-Vivisectionists?

> *I would not want to promote research on animals — fortunately, only my back is twisted, not my mind.*
>
> — Linn Pulis, polio victim (*PCRM Update, Special Edition*)

The first formal anti-vivisection society was formed in England in 1875. Anti-vivisectionists in the U.S. followed suit a few years later. The goal of the anti-vivisection movement is the abolition of animals as experimental "tools." From the animal rights perspective, a procedure is justified only when it serves the animal on whom it is performed.

Most animal advocates realize that the nature of change is such that it does not happen overnight, and that animal research and testing will be phased out gradually. However, improvements in the treatment of research animals is not a substitute for abolition of the practice itself. As Ingrid Newkirk, co-founder of People for the Ethical Treatment of Animals (PETA) has stated, the goal is not larger, cleaner cages for laboratory animals, but rather *empty* cages.[1]

In its beginnings, the anti-vivisection movement focused primarily on the inhumanity of hurting and killing living beings for experimental discovery. This is still a valid claim, but the last few decades of animal research have provided further objections to vivisection — scientific invalidity.

Today, those who question the scientific merits of animal research include scientists, medical doctors, psychiatrists, nurses, veterinarians, and other medical professionals. These experts claim that animal research is an outdated, inefficient mode of research that has failed to give us the answers we need. Says Robert S. Mendelsohn, M.D., "The reason why I am against animal research is because it doesn't work, it has no scientific value, and every good scientist knows that."[2]

Who Are the Pro-Vivisectionists?

Few persons seem to realize that vivisection is a business.
Men enter this business for the same reason they enter any other business:
to make money and to further their own interests.

— Dr. Arthur V. Allen, surgeon
(1000 Doctors (and Many More) Against Vivisection)

Animal research continues for two main reasons: habit and money.

Animal research is a habit that continues not because it has merit but because it is the status quo. The belief that animal experimentation is valuable is nothing more than a well-accepted bias. Its acceptance is so deeply ingrained that it's hard for some researchers of the "old school" to get used to the idea of not using animals. The following scientist's view reflects this mindset:

> Physicians hoping to alleviate the pain and suffering these [accidental human] tragedies cause have but three choices: create an animal model of the injury or disease...experiment on human beings...or finally, leave medical knowledge static, hoping that accidental discoveries will lead us to the advances.[3]

This scientist fails to consider that science can advance without animal research. To him, science *is* animal research; thus, his perception is that without animal research, there is no science. This scientist and many others are wearing perceptual blinders that prevent them from seeing other possibilities that are faster, cheaper, and more reliable than reliance on animal research. Vivisectionists would have us believe that an end to animal experimentation means an end to cures for the diseases of humankind. Not true.

Opposition to new ideas is a tradition in the conservative medical community. As Murry Cohen, M.D. points out, the American Medical Association (AMA) opposed "use of the newly introduced electrocardiograph, the idea that smoking was bad for the health, the preventative-health oriented and successful discipline of chiropractic, and the development of nuclear magnetic imaging techniques."[4] The traditional medical community also found the idea that diet could influence cancer to be absurd. It took decades for the cancer-diet connection to become widely accepted by medical doctors.

Those with vested interests in animal research use scare tactics such as the illogical "your child versus your dog" argument to convince the public that animal research is essential. Since the general public perceives researchers as "experts," whatever researchers say is regarded as truth. An uninformed and unsuspecting public believes that by supporting animal research, they are supporting wellness. This is an unfortunate misconception.

Many careers are based on animal research and people in those careers understandably are reluctant to lose their livelihoods. According to the U.S. Office of Management and Budget, approximately 70% of the millions of dollars allocated for research grants goes towards salaries.[5] An estimated 100 million animals are used in research every year. That translates into a lot of dollars for suppliers. Vested interests such as animal breeders, animal dealers, equipment suppliers, and animal food suppliers obviously have a lot to lose when animal research goes the way of the horse and buggy.

The saga of the now famous Silver Spring monkeys is an example of just how far the medical community will go to protect what they see as their own interests. These 17 monkeys, who had previously lived in the wild in the Philippines, were victims of experiments that involved severing the sensory nerves in one arm to numb it without disturbing the motor functions in the arm. The purpose of the experiments was to test for nerve regeneration and the relationship between numbness and arm movement. To encourage the monkeys to use their numbed arms, the animals were burned, shocked, and thrown against the walls of their cages.[6] The experiments were performed at the Institute for Behavioral Research in Silver Spring, Maryland, thus the name "Silver Spring monkeys."

When Alex Pacheco, co-founder of PETA, secured a volunteer position at the lab, he discovered gross violations of federal and state animal welfare laws which led to 17 state animal cruelty charges against the researcher, psychologist Edward Taub (federal law does not have a provision for prosecuting animal cruelty, so no federal charges could be filed).

The National Institutes of Health (NIH), a federal agency that uses tax money to fund research, withdrew the grant that funded the research. That was the end of those particular experiments, but it is just the begining of the story.

People for the Ethical Treatment of Animals

One of the Silver Spring monkeys that NIH refused to release to a primate sanctuary.

When animal rights organizations sued for custody of the monkeys in order to transfer them to a primate sanctuary for rehabilitation, the scientific community rallied in opposition. Although there were no plans to use the monkeys for further experimentation, a number of scientific organizations signed a letter opposing relocation of the monkeys to a sanctuary. Why? Because it wouldn't look good if animal rights advocates won custody of former research animals. Said a representative from the Pharmaceutical Manufacturers Association, "The major reason [we opposed release of the monkeys] was the problem of standing that these [animal rights] groups might obtain if they win the court case on these animals. That's our primary concern." In the words of a representative from the American Society for Microbiology, "The concern is for the precedent. This could set a precedent for animal activists to make demands."[7]

Consequently, although over 300 members of Congress requested that NIH release the monkeys to a sanctuary, NIH refused to do so. Despite intense public outcry, the monkeys have remained incarcerated for years in small, taxpayer-subsidized cages at a cost of over $200,000. And one-by-one, researchers have systematically killed them.

There is a lot more to the story, but throughout the long, sad saga the scientific community has let one unwavering concern take precedence over all others, including the welfare of the animals: the scientific/medical community must maintain its absolute power to dictate the fates of animals, without interference from animal rights activists, animal welfare advocates, or even Congressional interests. It is clear that those with vested interests in vivisection are out to protect their own interests, whatever the cost.

Biomedical Research

There will come a time when the world will look back to modern vivisection in the name of Science, as they do now to burning at the stake in the name of religion.

— Henry J. Bigelow, M.D. (as quoted in *The Extended Circle*)

Members of the biomedical research community, such as the researcher-funded Foundation for Biomedical Research, have put a lot of time and money into public relations campaigns designed to convince the general public that animal research is not only essential but well-regulated. These claims sound convincing — until you hear the whole story.

Here are some common claims made by researchers and the real facts behind the claims.

***MYTH*:** **Strict laws protect animals used in research, testing, and education.**

***FACT*:** **Laws and regulations designed to protect laboratory animals are grossly inadequate and favor the laboratories rather than the laboratory animals.**

When questioned about their treatment of laboratory animals, the research industry points to the federal Animal Welfare Act as proof that laboratory animals are well cared for. Passed by Congress in 1966, this law sets standards for the care of animals by animal dealers, research facilities, and animal exhibitors. The Act, however, is not what it may seem.

The Animal Welfare Act is far from a panacea for the mistreatment of laboratory animals. Specifics of the Animal Welfare Act are left up to the Secretary of the U.S. Department of Agriculture (USDA), who is charged with administering the Act. In 1985, when Congress amended the Animal Welfare Act and instructed the USDA to establish stricter rules for animal care, the USDA did nothing for three years. Only when the Animal Legal Defense Fund sued them did the USDA begin to make some moves toward new regulations.[8] This is how much the USDA cares about protecting animals.

The Animal Welfare Act, though well-intentioned, is woefully lacking in practical application. Laboratory animals receive little protection under this law. Don't let researchers tell you any different. Here are some facts about the Animal Welfare Act.

- **Exclusions**

  Animals specifically excluded from the Act include mice, rats, birds, fish, and all other cold-blooded animals used for research purposes — approximately 70% of all research animals, according to the USDA.[9] (Some sources estimate that rats and mice make up as much as 90% of research animals.) In the opinion of the U.S. government's Office of Technology Assessment (OTA), excluding these animals was not the original intent of the Act, but merely reflects the preference of the USDA Secretary. In OTA's opinion, the USDA Secretary overstepped his statutory authority in excluding these animals.[10]

There is no reason for excluding rats and mice or any other animals from the Animal Welfare Act. Though smaller and perhaps held in less esteem than other animals, rodents are still conscious, feeling beings who deserve protection. As Henry Spira of Animal Rights International points out, "Rodents have feeling. They try to avoid pain. That's the reason they are used in psychology experiments."[11]

◆ Pain

The Animal Welfare Act applies only to the care and handling of animals before and after experiments. It does not limit what is done to an animal during an experiment, including how much or what type of pain may be inflicted. There is no federal law that regulates what an experimenter may do to an animal during an experiment. According to USDA figures for 1987, 130,373 animals underwent painful procedures without pain relief. This figure includes only animals covered by the Act. It does not include the 70% to 90% of mice, rats, and other animals specifically excluded from the Act.[12]

The following sample experiments, reported by United Action for Animals, Inc., were allowed by the Animal Welfare Act:[13]

> Burning dogs on over 30% of their bodies by pressing a hot plate to their skin for over five minutes, to observe the effects of burns on metabolism. (Cost: Over $100,000)
>
> Shocking the eyelids of cats up to 100 times per day, paired with a tone, to observe how quickly the cats could learn to blink when the tone sounded without the shock. (Cost: Over $287,000)
>
> Injecting sheep with a bacteria and then burning them on up to 50% of their bodies with scalding water to observe the increased death rate from the bacteria. (Cost: Over $183,000)

◆ Provisions

The Act covers only minimum maintenance standards for items such as cage size, lighting, ventilation, food, water, temperature, sanitation, veterinary care, and transportation. For example, the cage size for nonhuman primates need only be three times the area occupied by a primate when standing on four feet. Cats are only entitled to two and one-half square feet per adult cat. Except for primates, no provisions are made for the psychological or emotional well-being of any animals.

◆ Inspections

Inspection of research facilities is required only once a year, and the visit may be announced ahead of time. A study by the U.S. government General Accounting Office (GAO) found that inspectors were too few in number, were inadequately trained or not trained at all, and that there was no consistent quality-control of inspections.[14] According to GAO findings, because of the inadequate number of inspectors, many research sites were never inspected during the fiscal year GAO examined. In California and New York, where the highest number of research facilities in the country are located, approximately half of the laboratories received no inspection whatsoever.[15] Despite the starkly minimal standards set forth by the Animal Welfare Act, 114 institutions that inspectors did visit during the year had serious violations of the Animal Welfare Act.[16]

Those who have been found in violation of the Animal Welfare Act include prestigious institutions such as Harvard University's New England Primate Center (multiple violations, including caked excreta on resting boards, inadequate cage space, empty water bottles, and unsanitary nest boxes), the Mayo Foundation in Rochester, Minnesota (multiple deficiencies, including housing, ventilation, and sanitation),[17] and the University of California at Berkeley (60 violations, including death and neglect, severely substandard housing, and lack of veterinary care).[18]

- **Prosecutions**

  No criminal prosecution of violators is provided for under the Act. Although violators of state anti-cruelty laws may be prosecuted under state law, in at least one case an appellate court overturned a state's cruelty conviction of a researcher, exempting him from state laws because his research was federally funded.[19]

- **Animal Care and Use Committees**

  Although the Act requires each research facility to convene an Animal Care and Use Committee to conduct semi-annual reviews of laboratory animal use, these committees serve little real purpose except to give the public a false sense of security. Members of this committee are hand-picked by the Chief Executive Officer of the research institute. Says an anesthesiologist of his experience on one such committee at a Topeka, Kansas medical center, "I was truly appalled by what impressed me as an extremely cold disregard for the value, comfort, and welfare of animals."[20]

***MYTH*: Animal rights advocates are anti-science.**

***FACT*: Far from being anti-science, animal rights advocates believe that a continued focus on animal research impedes scientific progress, keeping us from the development of faster, cheaper, and better research methods.**

Claiming that anti-vivisectionists are anti-science is ridiculous given the fact that many anti-vivisectionists are medical professionals. The emergence of groups such as Physicians Committee for Responsible Medicine, Psychologists for the Ethical Treatment of Animals, and the International League of Doctors for the Abolition of Vivisection indicates a growing awareness that animal research hurts not only animals, but people. Some of the greatest scientists in history have opposed animal research, including Albert Einstein, Hippocrates, Galileo, and Sir Isaac Newton.

Labeling animal rights advocates as anti-science is a clever tactic cooked up by the AMA to thwart anti-vivisection efforts. This is evidenced by the *Animal Research Action Plan*, sent by the AMA to each of its U.S. members in June of 1989. This plan is an organized strategy to counter what the AMA calls the "problem" of "animal rights groups who are dedicated to the elimination of the use of animals in biomedical and other scientific research." The fourth item in the General Strategy section of the *Animal Research Action Plan* reads as follows: "Identify animal rights activists as anti-science and against medical progress."[21]

Anti-vivisectionists are not anti-science; they are simply against bad scientific methods that retard scientific progress.

***MYTH*: Animal research is necessary for human well-being.**

***FACT*: To the contrary, after studying the recent history of animal research, many medical doctors and scientists conclude that animal research has not only failed to provide the answers we need, but actually threatens our well-being.**

Those with a vested interest in animal research would like for the public to believe that such research is responsible for all of the medical breakthroughs of the last few decades. That simply is not true. The benefits of animal research are greatly exaggerated. Here are some facts animal researchers don't publicize.

◆ **Animal research doesn't provide the answers**

The National Cancer Institute has publicly admitted that after 35 years, its animal experiments have contributed little to finding cancer cures. They are switching from animals to automated devices and computers to test potential cancer-fighting drugs on real human cancer cells.[22]

The New England Anti-Vivisection Society reports that many major medical discoveries originate from nonanimal sources, among them the discovery of antibiotics, sulfa drugs, anesthetics, x-rays, aspirin, digitalis, radium and mercury therapy disinfectants, opium, morphine, and bacteriology as well as CAT scans, magnetic resonance, and the Ames cancer test.[23]

Pro-vivisectionists often refer to the polio vaccine when defending animal research. The truth is that polio was already on the decline by the time the vaccine was introduced. The decline of many infectious diseases for which vaccines were produced is largely attributable to improved sanitation and standards of living, rather than to vaccines. In fact, many people experienced severe reactions, and in some cases death, from polio, rabies, rubella, or smallpox vaccines.[24] Other people who had been vaccinated became infected with the disease anyway.

In *The Argument for Abolition,* published by the International Society for Animal Rights, Inc., Steven Tiger, a Physician Assistant-Certified (PA-C) accurately sums up the "pay off" of animal research as follows:

> Medical research is like a slot machine that pays off once every thousand plays. So after a million plays, yes, you can point to a thousand payoffs. Its payoffs are splashy and they make headlines, but they have almost no impact on our national level of health.[25]

◆ **Animal research ignores prevention**

Despite decades of research on animals, cancer and heart disease remain epidemics in this country. According to the National Cancer Institute, 80% of cancer is preventable — it is caused by environmental pollutants and lifestyle choices such as diet, tobacco, alcohol, stress, and lack of exercise. Heart disease, which is virtually 100% preventable, is also a result of lifestyle choices. Yet, we pour billions of dollars into animal research to find wonder cures for diseases we know how to prevent in the first place. A better use of funds would be to prevent people from getting sick, rather than subjecting them to costly and uncomfortable procedures after their health has deteriorated. The only obstacle to prevention is that there is no profit to be made from keeping people healthy; profits are generated from treating sick people. That, paired with the scientific fascination and excitement of finding a "cure," has kept us from pursuing prevention.

◆ **Animal research diverts attention away from more reliable research methods**

By concentrating our efforts on animal research, we fail to pursue more advanced research methods. Only in recent years, because of the pressure applied by animal advocates, has any concerted effort been made to look at other technologies. Since very little attention has been given to nonanimal methods of research, we have no way of knowing what could have been achieved without animals. How do we know that the same, or better, knowledge couldn't have been acquired through nonanimal methods? Very simply, we don't. We do know, however, that recently-devised nonanimal methods are far superior to animal research. One example is the Ames test, which is used to test whether or not substances are likely to be carcinogens. The test works by introducing a suspected carcinogen to salmonella bacteria. If the substance causes genetic changes in salmonella bacteria, then the substance is very likely carcinogenic. This test takes a few days to complete, compared to years for tests using animals, and costs a fraction of what animal tests cost.[26] For example, the modified Ames test, used by Mobil Oil Company to test petroleum-based products, takes 48 hours and costs $600, compared to two-and-one-half years and up to $50,000 for traditional animal tests. But money and time aren't the only savings; Mobil's implementation of the Ames alternative spares 30,000 animals per year from animal testing.[27]

The Ames test is an example of a micro-organism culture. Other alternatives to using and killing healthy animals are:

- In-vitro studies (cell and tissue cultures grown in test tubes or glass dishes). John Hopkins Center for Alternatives to Animal Testing reports that we can now even grow human brain cells (neurons) in the laboratory. Human cancer cells are also duplicated in labs.
- Mathematical models which describe a biological system and are used to predict novel results.
- Physio-chemical studies. For example, analyzing the properties of drugs.
- Human studies (clinical, epidemiological, and preventive medicine).
- Image-scanning devices.
- Behavioral studies (studying organisms in their natural environment).
- Postmortem studies on humans.

For publications that describe specific alternatives to animals, see the Research, Education, & Product Testing section of Chapter 13.

◆ **Animal research misdirects funds**

Animal research provides a very low return for the investment. The billions of dollars put into animal research have yielded few results. Congress spends more than $4.5 billion per year on animal research, 60% to 75% of which is estimated to duplicate previous studies.[28] Drug addiction studies are a good example of waste. While people seeking help from drug addiction are turned away from treatment programs for lack of funds, hundreds of thousands of dollars are funneled into experiments such as these cited by In Defense of Animals: [29]

- $500,000 to study ervet monkeys' acute physical dependence on morphine and Valium.
- $100,000 to study rats' tolerance of Valium and librium.
- Approximately $200,000 annually to study biochemicals in the brains of opiate-addicted rats.
- $801,811 to study the effects of PCP, footshock, and LSD on the brains of rats.
- $239,009 to study the effects of pain in combination with cocaine, amphetamines, nicotine, and caffeine on the central nervous systems of nonhuman primates.
- More than $394,000 to study drug dependence and "noxious" stimuli, such as electric shock.

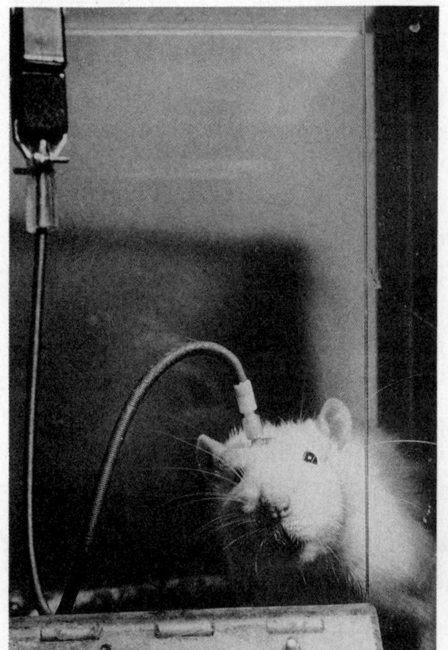

The American Anti-Vivisection Society

Millions of dollars are spent to addict animals such as this rat to drugs, while thousands of human drug addicts are turned away from treatment programs for lack of funds.

Are these studies helping human drug addicts? Not in the opinions of many people who work with drug addicts. Says one M.D.: "These studies seem aimed at experimenting simply for the sake of experimenting."[30]

Some grant money for animal research is being used for projects that do not involve animals — but not in ways you may think. In the spring of 1991, a federal investigation named 13 universities that had fraudulently bilked the government out of hundreds of thousands of dollars of research funds. The universities are Stanford, Dartmouth, Yale, Rutgers, Johns Hopkins, University of Pennsylvania, University of Pittsburgh, Duke, Emory, University of Chicago, University of Texas Southwest Medical Center at Dallas, Washington University (St. Louis), and University of Southern California. In Defense of Animals reports that overcharges at Stanford may be as high as $175 million, according to a federal investigator. A sample of expenditures billed to research include:

- $184,286 for depreciation on the University's yacht.
- $2,000 per month for President Donald Kennedy's florist bill.
- $9,000 for antiques for Kennedy's home.
- $3,000 for a cedar closet for Mrs. Kennedy.

- $18,500 for the Kennedy's wedding reception.
- $44,000 for miscellaneous expenses.

Dartmouth, which is accused of misusing $1.1 million, has so far admitted guilt to the tune of $111,785.[31]

◆ **Animal research has actually harmed people**

Time and time again, history has shown that animal studies cannot accurately predict the effects of drugs on humans. Roy Kupsinel, M.D., says:

> Animal experimentation produces a lot of misleading and confusing data which poses hazards to human health. For example, 4 million patients per year are hospitalized for side effects caused by "thoroughly tested" drugs, and of those 50,000 die of the "cures," not the disease.[32]

One of the most famous, and tragic, examples of the failure of animal testing to discern harmful side effects from drugs is the thalidomide disaster. After being confirmed as safe by extensive animal tests, this drug caused birth defects such as missing limbs in thousands of babies whose mothers were prescribed the drug while pregnant. The accompanying box, The Unreliability of Animal Tests, shows many more instances of people harmed by dependence on animal tests. As already discussed, animal research has also harmed people in less direct ways by misdirecting funds and attention away from prevention and research methods that are more reliable than those utilizing animals.

***MYTH*: Animals are good research tools for human maladies.**

***FACT*: Studying rats to find out about humans is like studying apples to find out about oranges.**

Because living systems differ in significant ways, data obtained by studying one species can't reliably predict reactions in another species. There are great differences between rats and mice, let alone between rats and humans. Yet, rats and mice are the animals most commonly used to attempt to study human disease. It is likely that rodents are so prevalent in research not because they reliably emulate the human condition, but because they are cheaper to buy, easier to maintain, and are exempt from federal regulations.

The American Anti-Vivisection Society reports that Pzifer, a major pharmaceutical company, compared human records against experimental data from animal tests to see whether or not animal tests had correctly identified cancer-causing substances. They found that most of the animal tests were so unreliable that tossing a coin would have been a better predictor of which substances were carcinogens.[33]

In instance after instance, results from animal research have differed from actual occurrences in human beings. Says one recipient of an animal-tested drug:

> My deafness was caused by an antibiotic, Streptomycin, which was tested on dogs, guinea pigs, and mice, and was considered safe enough for use on human babies. I was one of those thousands of babies who received the drug

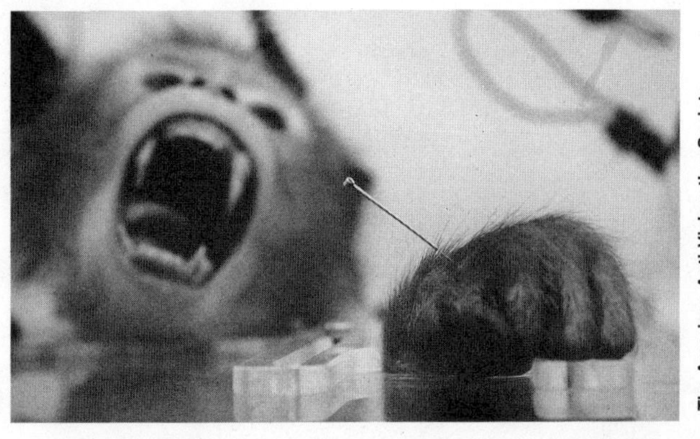

The American Anti-Vivisection Society

The Animal Welfare Act does not regulate the amount or type of pain that may be inflicted on animals during experiments.

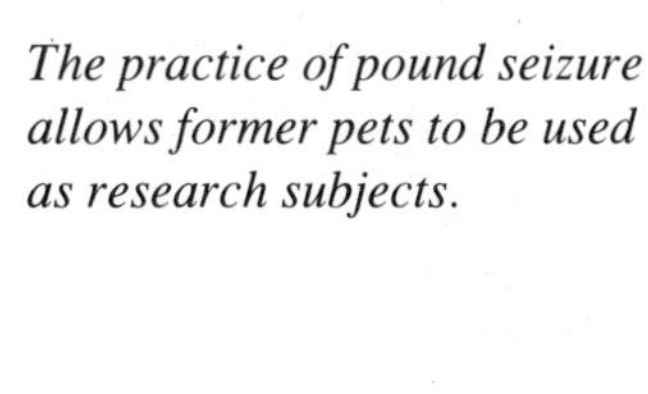

The practice of pound seizure allows former pets to be used as research subjects.

The American Anti-Vivisection Society

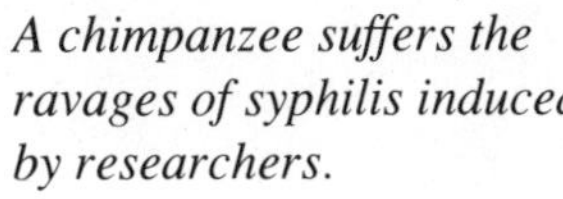

A chimpanzee suffers the ravages of syphilis induced by researchers.

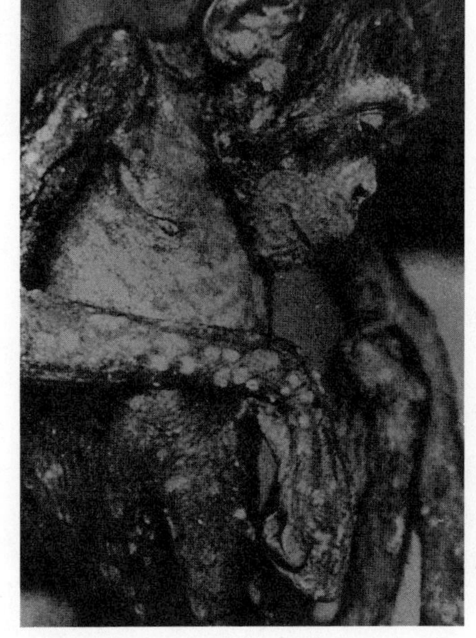

The American Anti-Vivisection Society

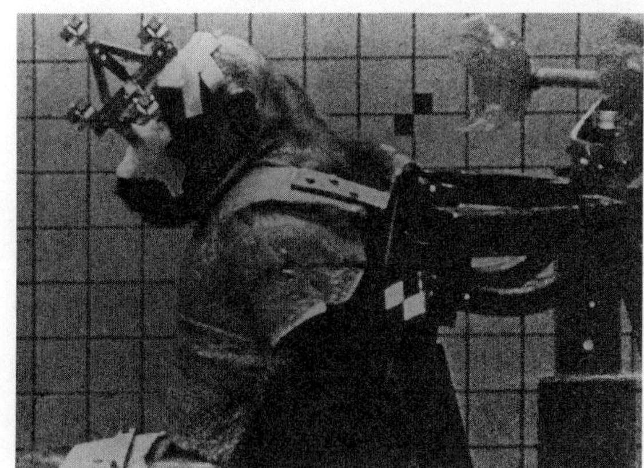

The American Anti-Vivisection Society

This baboon served as a living "dummy" in crash test experiments.

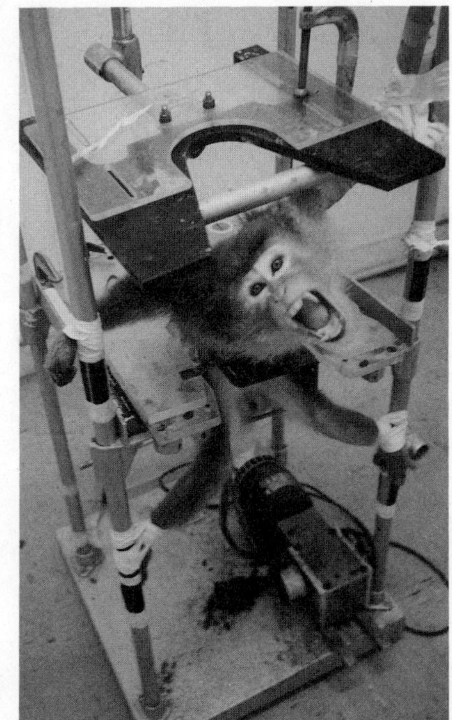

People for the Ethical Treatment of Animals

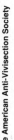

Monkeys are sometimes confined to restraining chairs for long periods of time, a practice one veterinarian calls "cruel and unusual punishment."

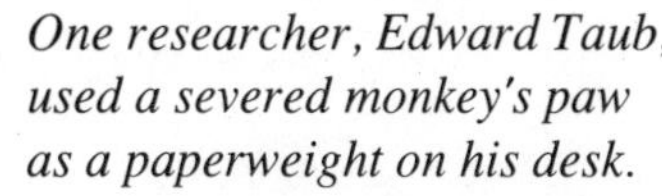

One researcher, Edward Taub, used a severed monkey's paw as a paperweight on his desk.

The American Anti-Vivisection Society

WARNING

The photographs on these pages depict disturbing realities of animal experimentation.

> to fight a fever. My side effect was deafness. Many other babies were worse off — they were blind[ed] or brain damaged, and some even died.[34]

In the opinion of the Director of AIDS Activities at San Francisco General Hospital, Dr. Paul Volberding, "Clearly the chimpanzee work (with AIDS) has no necessary relevance to what we can find in humans."[35]

The courts also seem to agree. In one case, a judge ruled that pouring shampoo into rabbits' eyes was not a sufficient test of the shampoo's effect on human eyes.[36] In a product liability lawsuit brought by Vietnam veterans against the manufacturer of Agent Orange, the court ruled that data from animal tests was inadmissible because extrapolation of data between different species is misleading.[37] And another court examining possible toxic effects of lead on humans called the use of animal data "speculative and unconvincing," and instead demanded epidemiological evidence from humans.[38]

Many factors influence animals and can alter the outcomes of experiments. One striking example occurred during an experiment with rabbits to determine the effect of a high-fat diet on arteriosclerosis. Two groups of rabbits were fed identical diets, yet one group showed 60% less damage than the other group. After the experiment was repeated with the same results, the baffled researchers discovered the influential factor. As reported in *SelfCare Journal*, "a graduate assistant assigned to one group of rabbits took them out of their cages regularly and petted them tenderly before he fed them."[39] That was the only factor that was found to influence the varying outcomes of the study. If love can have such a radical effect on animals, it makes sense that the stress to which most laboratory animals are subjected would have an equally influential effect.

***MYTH*:** **Researchers care about the laboratory animals they use and treat them compassionately.**

***FACT*:** **Researchers show virtually no regard for laboratory animals as beings capable of suffering. When animals enter the laboratory, they lose their status as beings and become tools with one purpose — to serve the experimenter.**

Andrew Rowan, director of Tufts University Center for Animal and Public Policy, is quoted by author Patrick Cooke in *In Health* magazine as follows: "You don't see much moral questioning from researchers about the pain they inflict. There are scientists who don't view the way in which they treat animals as a moral issue at all."[40] Former researcher Donald Barnes refers to cruelty in research labs as "conditioned ethical blindness," learned as part of the trade.[41]

The Unreliability of Animal Tests

Animals are unreliable indicators of how drugs will react in humans. Animal tests do not protect people from harmful drug side effects. Many drugs that are harmful to various animal species are still marketed to humans — a fact that shows even animal researchers believe animal tests to be unreliable indicators of human reactions.

The information in this table was extracted from *The Cruel Deception* by Dr. Robert Sharpe. See Chapter 13 for information on ordering *The Cruel Deception*.

Drug	Effect on Animals	Effect on Humans
aspirin	birth defects (rats and mice), poison (cats), no effect on fever (horses)	pain killer and fever reducer
Azauracil (anti-cancer drug)	no evidence of toxicity to nervous system (dogs and monkeys)	coma, lethargy, mental deterioration, twitching, muscle weakness, hallucinations
benzene	no leukemia	leukemia
captopril (for high blood pressure)	none	skin and kidney problems
chloramphenicol (antibiotic)	no harmful effects detected	aplastic anemia (a fatal blood disease)
clindamycin (antibiotic)	can tolerate 20 times the maximum dose every day for one year (rats and dogs)	fatal intestinal disease
clioquinol (an ingredient in two anti-diarrhea drugs)	no harm (cats, rats, beagles, and rabbits)	numbness, leg weakness, paralysis, and eye problems including blindness
Eraldin (for heart conditions)	no harmful effects detected	serious eye damage, blindness, and death
Fenclozic acid (for arthritis)	no evidence of liver damage (rats, mice, dogs, monkeys, rabbits, guinea pigs, ferrets, cats, pigs, and horses)	liver toxicity

continued...

Drug	Effect on Animals	Effect on Humans
halothane (anesthetic)	no evidence of liver damage	liver damage and 150 reported deaths
Ibufenac (for arthritis)	no harm	12 deaths, mainly from liver damage
insulin	deformities in lab animals	no deformities
isoprenaline (for asthma)	cats tolerate 175 times the dose found dangerous to asthmatics (also tested on rats, guinea pigs, dogs, and monkeys)	3,500 deaths
ketoconazole (anti-fungal drug)	no liver toxicity	serious liver damage
Mitoxantrone (anti-cancer drug)	no evidence of heart failure (beagles)	heart failure
morphine	stimulant (cats)	sedative
nitrophenol	cataracts in ducks and chicks, but not in other animals	cataracts
Opren (for arthritis)	no harm (rhesus monkeys)	61 deaths, mainly from liver damage in elderly people
oral contraceptives	in some species, no effect on blood clotting; in other species, difficulty in blood clotting	increased risk of blood clots, causing heart attacks, lung disorders, and strokes
penicillin	highly toxic (guinea pigs and hamsters)	not toxic to most people
phenylbutazone and oxyphenbutazone (anti-inflammatory drugs)	considered safe (rhesus monkeys, dogs, rats, and rabbits)	10,000 deaths worldwide
thalidomide (sedative)	no birth defects (rats and mice)	birth defects
Zelmid (anti-depressant)	no harm (rats and dogs)	convulsions, liver damage, neuropathies, Gullain-Barre syndrome
Zipeprol (cough suppressant)	none	seizures and coma

Testimony from other researchers and former researchers confirms this attitude. Toxicologist Oscar Marino uses animals to test the ingredients of household and personal care products such as colognes and cleansers. As Marino told CBS News Correspondent Bob Faw during a segment of the television program *48 Hours*:

> Sometimes, you know, I'll be riding along the road and if a rabbit comes along, I'll practically kill myself to avoid hitting the rabbit, but out here [in the lab], you know, it's kind of different. There's no feeling for these animals here in the laboratory. You know, they're a tool and that's about it.[42]

Bobbie Jean Kennedy, a former lab worker, states in a *PCRM Update*:

> When I was 16 I began working in a medical research department...I spent hours bashing in the heads of rats, and thinking about it today makes me nauseated. At the time I was so enthusiastic about learning something and being helpful, that I never until today tuned into my feelings about what animals and I were subjected to...In order for me to survive in that kind of environment I had to totally dissociate myself from what was really happening and it obviously was so painful that I am only today able to take a look at it.[43]

Let's face it. "Treating research animals compassionately" is a contradiction in terms. To treat animals compassionately is to get them out of the laboratory.

Say It Like It Is

It's easier to think of animals as things if we call them something other than what they really are.

What They Really Are: animals, individuals, beings

What The Researcher Calls Them: models, specimens, tools, subjects

•*Distress* is the word researchers use instead of *pain* or *suffering*.

•*Apply noxious stimuli* is the phrase researchers use instead of *shock*, *burn*, etc.

•*Sacrifice* or *euthanize* are the words researchers use instead of *kill*.

The reality is that researchers do not "sacrifice specimens," they kill animals.

Let's just say it like it is.

Product Testing

At present scientists do not look for alternatives simply because they do not care enough about the animals they are using.

— Peter Singer (*Animal Liberation*)

The next time you reach for your shampoo, remember this — it may have been cruelly tested on innocent animals. Prominent personal care and household product manufacturers such as Procter & Gamble and Gillette, among many others, have been pouring shampoos, toilet cleaners, cosmetics, and virtually every other personal care and household substance into the eyes, into the mouths, and onto the raw, scraped skins of millions of rabbits, guinea pigs, rats, mice, cats, dogs, and other animals for years.

No law requires that products be tested on animals. Hundreds of companies produce cosmetics, personal care products, and household products that are not tested on animals. Under pressure from caring consumers, many major corporations, such as Revlon, Inc. and Amway Corporation, have modernized their operations and stopped animal tests.

Other major producers, however, have made no real effort to move away from animal testing. Some have even put up smoke screens to woo the public into thinking they care about animals, when in fact their compassionate claims appear to be more public relations than anything else. Procter & Gamble Corporation, though claiming to be an industry leader in advancing alternatives to animal tests, not only continues to unnecessarily use animals in product tests, but has formed a coalition with a $17.5 million budget to defend animal testing to the public and to legislators. An internal memorandum from Procter & Gamble, made public by the Doris Day Animal League, revealed that the three-year plan included an educational brochure and film, a National Speaker's Bureau, a legislative defense package, a plan for coalition building with like-minded groups, media advertising, and teaching materials supporting the continuance of animal tests designed for students from kindergarten through high school. The $17.5 million budgeted to defend animal testing would go a long way if applied instead to switching over to nonanimal methods of testing.

What types of animal tests do cosmetic and household product companies perform? Two of the most popular are the Draize Eye Irritancy Test and the LD50 Test.

◆ **Draize Eye Irritancy Test**

The Draize test, named after its inventor, involves introducing substances into the eyes of an animal to observe the degree of irritation caused by the substance. White albino rabbits are the animal of choice because their eyes are very sensitive and because the structure of their tear ducts prevents tears from washing away the foreign substance.

Placed into stocks so that only their heads stick out (like the old punishment device of the Pilgrims), rabbits have anything from shampoo to oven cleaner to lipstick to lawn care products placed into their eyes with no pain relief. Some rabbits have reportedly broken their necks while struggling to free themselves from the painful procedure.[44] The degree of irritation is then recorded over a period of time and the rabbit is eventually killed.

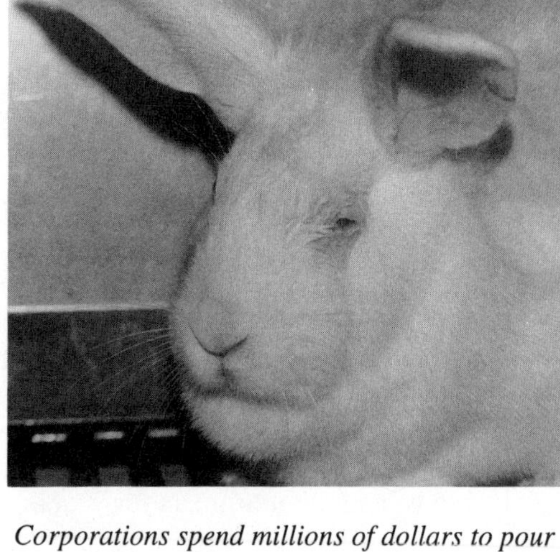

People for the Ethical Treatment of Animals

Corporations spend millions of dollars to pour caustic substances into the eyes of animals. No law requires that products be tested on animals.

The Draize test is inhumane, painful, cumbersome, and expensive. Is it at least scientific? Not according to a study conducted at Carnegie-Mellon University, which revealed broad discrepancies in lab reports for the same substance.[45] Because the Draize test relies on the subjective judgment of the observer, findings for the same substance vary widely from one laboratory to the next, resulting in contradictory evaluations of the same substance. In addition to questions about the scientific validity of the test itself, there is also a question about the difference between a rabbit's eye and a human's eye. In a 1974 Ohio court case, a judge ruled that just because a shampoo irritated a rabbit's eye didn't mean that the information was meaningful in regard to a human eye.[46] Says Stephen Kaufman, M.D.: "As an ophthalmologist in the New York University I am surprised that the Draize eye irritation test is done at all...I know of no case in which an ophthalmologist found Draize data useful." [47]

◆ LD50 Test

Just as inhumane and pointless as the Draize test is the Lethal Dose 50 (LD50) test, which gets its name from its purpose of discovering how much of a substance it takes to kill 50% of the test group. As many as 200 animals may be force-fed a toxic substance for a single test, which may last from two weeks to several years, depending on the material being tested. This poisoning causes a great deal of suffering; symptoms may include pain, convulsions, weakness, and vomiting.

Variations of the LD50 test include the Acute Dermal Toxicity Test and the Acute Inhalation Test. The Acute Dermal Toxicity Test involves scraping the skin until raw, smearing a substance on the raw skin, covering the "treated" area with a bandage to protect the experiment, and then removing the bandage a few hours later to observe the degree of irritancy. The Acute Inhalation Test consists of repeatedly exposing test animals to spray products.

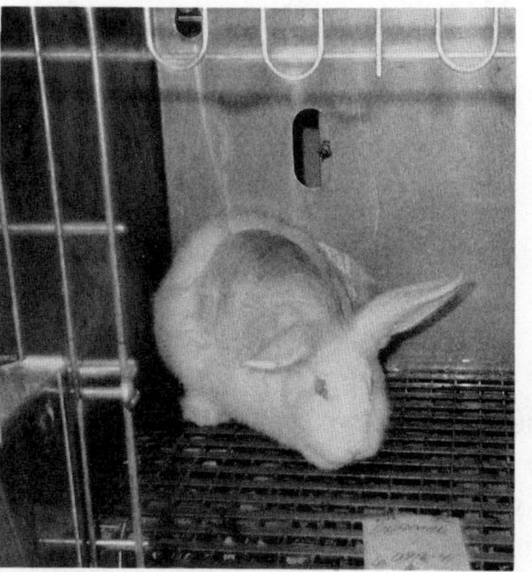

People for the Ethical Treatment of Animals

The skin of this rabbit was scraped raw and smeared with Kenner Dress 'n Dazzle Lipstick. Product tests do not guarantee consumer safety.

Is the LD50 test scientifically valid? Many medical doctors don't think so. As with the Draize test, they point to the difficulty in extrapolating data from animals to humans and to the scientific invalidity of the experiments themselves. Lynda Dickinson, author of the book *Victims of Vanity,* contends that some deaths are caused not by the poisonous nature of the tested substance, but from the sheer volumes of the doses administered, which result in blocked internal organs and subsequent death.[48] Says one medical doctor, Donald Doll:

> As a practicing physician who is board certified in internal medicine and oncology, I can find *no* evidence that the Draize test, LD50 test, or any other tests using animals to support the "safety" of chemicals and cosmetics have any relevance to the human species. Such tests are outdated, insensitive, cruel, and provide no useful data for humans. I strongly support legislation that prohibits the use of such animal tests by industry...[49]

Humane alternatives to the animal tests for both eye and skin irritancy are already in use by many companies. However, the cosmetics industry, which has extensive resources to fund any needed research into alternatives, has invested only a token amount toward nonanimal testing. Proposals for nonanimal methods are going unfunded as a result of this lack of interest by the industry. Additionally, money is being spent on research methods that simply reduce, rather than eliminate, the use of animals.

Why do companies such as Procter & Gamble continue with outmoded, expensive animal tests? It's anyone's guess. It may be that companies are waiting for the federal government to officially endorse an alternative to animal tests, so that companies can use this endorsement as a defense in case of consumer lawsuits for product-related injury or harm. The most influential factor may simply be a conservatism that resists change. Whatever the reason, exposing animals to suffering and death to test yet another new deodorant or hairspray is unjustifiable on any count.

Military Research

If you cannot attain knowledge without torturing a dog, you must do without knowledge.

— George Bernard Shaw

The military's use of animals is notoriously horrific. According to Physicians Committee for Responsible Medicine (PCRM), a 1986 report by the federal Office of Technology Assessment (OTA) stated that the military subjected 84% of its experimental animals to painful or noxious experiments. Over 540,000 animals — more than half a million — die in Department of Defense laboratories every year, their deaths paid for by approximately $110 million in taxpayer money. This head count does not include the animals used in experiments contracted out to civilian labs — in 1985, 66% of the Army's research, 64% of the Navy's, and 15% of the Air Force's, according to the OTA report.[50]

The military uses a variety of animals in its experiments, including nonhuman primates, dogs, cats, rats, guinea pigs, hamsters, opossums, rabbits, sheep, goats, pigs, and chickens, as well as marine mammals such as dolphins and whales. Experiments focus largely on weapons of war and their effects, including firearms, explosives, chemical and biological warfare, and radiation. The military also conducts experiments related to conditions that may influence the performance of soldiers in wartime, such as heat, cold, oxygen deprivation, and various injuries. In addition, the military trains some animals to perform life-threatening tasks, such as training dolphins to place mines on enemy submarines or attack enemy divers. In direct contradiction of the Marine Mammal Protection Act of 1972, the Navy is allowed to capture and use 25 marine mammals every year. A former dolphin trainer for the Navy says that the animals have been punished by being clobbered on the head with dead fish, kicked, and starved. He also reports that several sea lions were negligently drowned by drunken trainers.[51]

Military researchers are supposed to abide by the rules and regulations of the federal Animal Welfare Act, but military labs are off-limits to USDA inspectors. Who inspects military labs? The military itself; it is totally self-policing. Some military bases try to soothe public objections to their "closed-lab policy" by claiming accreditation by the American Association for Accreditation of Laboratory Animal Care (AAALAC). What the public does not know is that AAALAC is funded by the research community itself. Passing AAALAC's inspection is no guarantee of anything. PCRM quotes a former member of the Animal Care and Use Committee at Letterman Army Institute of Research (LAIR) as referring to "the horrible conditions in which the animals were housed" at LAIR, although LAIR was certified by the AAALAC.[52]

Military experiments are criticized for being cruel, poorly conducted, unnecessary, hidden from public scrutiny (although paid for by public monies), and for exhibiting gross negligence and callousness towards animals. For example:

- In experiments for Letterman Army Institute for Research (LAIR), Louisiana State University shot 700 cats in the head at a cost of $2.1 million, to learn how to return brain-injured soldiers to active duty. The conclusion of the researcher was that breathing stops upon brain wounding, a fact that has been known since 1894. Congress put a stop to the experiments after a General Accounting Office report highlighted sloppy techniques leading to questionable results.[53]
- Again at LAIR, monkeys have been confined to restraining chairs for as long as 12 years.[54] In the words of one veterinarian, "Confining any normally gregarious, inquisitive, and social animal to a restraining chair for extended periods is cruel and unusual punishment..."[55]
- Necropsy (postmortem) reports on primates at the Armstrong Aerospace Medical Research Laboratory at Wright Patterson Air Force Base in Dayton, Ohio revealed neglect and abuse of primates. Animals died from severe intestinal blockage, internal bleeding, choking on their own vomit, gradual debilitation and emaciation (starvation), and unknown causes, all due to inattention and inadequate care. At least one primate was dead for 15 hours before anyone noticed. Said one veterinarian who examined the reports, "These findings indicate neglect, animal abuse, poor experimental technique, and grotesquely inadequate medical practices."[56] The Air Force base's response has been to issue a statement that they are "committed to providing exceptional care" for their laboratory animals.[57]
- At the Armed Forces Radiobiology Research Institute, experimenters soaked mice with alcohol on 30% of their body surface, set them on fire, and let them burn for 12 seconds. For another group of mice, experimenters used a metal punch to cut away the skin and underlying tissue on 30% of their body surfaces. These mice were part of an experiment that measured how radiation affected recovery from the injuries. Besides the blatant cruelty of the experiment, the researchers also have been criticized for exercising poor experimental controls and for duplicating what we already know from observing humans.[58]

Of the hundreds of animal experiments conducted by the military, a rare few come to public attention. The military hides its experiments behind a cloak of "classified information" and "national security." The public is likely to learn of the military's uses of animals only when conscientious "insiders" come forward.

Military experiments are funded by tax dollars. It's time for the U.S. Congress to stop funding these military experiments and to begin funding nonanimal alternatives. A former military researcher, Donald Barnes, agrees. After 16 years as a primate researcher for the Air Force, he is now convinced not only of the inhumanity of animal research but also of its invalidity for humans. He left the research laboratory to become director of the National Anti-Vivisection Society, a group that works to end all use of animals in research.

Psychological Research

As a scientist, I have witnessed at first hand the increasing sufferings of animals here and abroad, so often doubtfully justified as being for the betterment of mankind when frequently the real motive is petty academic ambition.

— Richard D. Ryder

Psychology experiments involving animals are close contenders with military experiments in terms of their brutality. In psychology experiments, live animals become tools for exploring everything from maternal deprivation, aggression, and sexual behavior to alcohol addiction and color blindness. Experimental subjects range in species from goldfish to primates.

Although the American Psychological Association has a Committee on Animal Research and Ethics (the acronym is, ironically, CARE), the committee chairs are all researchers who reportedly "conduct painful and harmful research on animals."[59]

A psychologist writing in *The Psychological Record* relates the attitudes of his colleagues towards animals:

> Animals in psychological experiments are simply complex research tools. Thus a significant work on research methods in psychology can refer to the deaths of several hundred monkeys from perforated ulcers after many days of exposure to a shock-avoidance schedule as "an annoying feature of these experiments."[60]

As with other experiments that utilize animals, there are serious doubts as to the usefulness of animal-based psychology experiments and their practical applications to humans. Much research appears to be solely for the sake of research or for the sake of research grants. Funds would be better applied elsewhere. Here are some examples of common psychological studies.

◆ **Maternal Deprivation and Isolation**

Begun in the late 1950's and repeated in one form or another for year after year since then, maternal deprivation and isolation studies explore the effects of separating infants from their mothers. The most popular victims for these experiments traditionally have been primates.

The experiments study various aspects of what happens to infants taken from their mothers at or shortly after birth. Not surprisingly, repeated studies have shown that infants reared in isolation are depressed and exhibit abnormal behavior, such as self-mutilation. Infant monkeys who are kept in total isolation for two years are, in the words of one experimenter, "totally destroyed." These experiments have used over a thousand primates, hundreds of dogs, and millions of taxpayer dollars.[61]

◆ Substance Abuse

While thousands of people are turned away from drug rehabilitation centers because there aren't enough services available, over $500 million in federal money is poured into research laboratories that addict animals to drugs. Animal addiction studies have been going on for years and have not helped drug addicts. Making cocaine addicts out of squirrel monkeys and testing their lever-pressing responses to electric shock does nothing to help human cocaine addicts. Forcing pregnant monkeys to ingest alcohol to the point where they give birth to deformed babies does not prevent human alcoholics from drinking. Nor does addicting cats and chimpanzees to morphine and cocaine and then forcing them into sudden withdrawal help ease the pain of human addicts.[62]

Addiction is a complex process with social, mental, emotional, and physical components. Information derived from one species is not necessarily applicable to another species. Animal experiments on addiction may be of academic interest, but they do little to address the real needs of human addicts.

◆ Learned Helplessness

A common type of psychological experiment involves negative conditioning, or administering pain to an animal in order to make him not do something or to encourage him to do something. For example, an animal may be given an electric shock until he presses a lever, at which time the shock ceases. In this way the animal learns to press the lever in response to the shock.

A variation of this scene is learned helplessness, or placing an animal in a "no win" situation. For example, after teaching the animal to press a lever to turn off a shock, the experimenter continues to administer the shock, even when the animal presses the lever. The idea is to then observe the reactions of the animal to the situation. This type of experiment is based on inflicting pain and/or fear. Again, such observations may satisfy some academic curiosity, but they are of no value to solving human problems and are intensely cruel to the research "subjects."

◆ Sexual Behavior

Sexual dysfunction in people is a genuine problem and worthy of study. It is unlikely, however, that the following experimental findings, reported by United Action for Animals, Inc., will help alleviate any human sexual problems. The studies took place between 1982 and 1986 and cost a total of $514,600: [63]

- Female rhesus monkeys who have been sprayed with a sex scent have more frequent sexual contact than unsprayed females. (Cost: $164,000)
- Female stump-tailed macaques achieve human-like orgasmic responses in both heterosexual and homosexual encounters. (Cost: $133,200)
- Burning particular portions of a cat's brain results in reduced sexual activity for females, but has no effect on male sexuality. (Cost: $141,400)
- Male beagles exhibit strong dominance over female beagles, but they exhibit only slight dominance over female beagles who have been surgically altered to resemble males. (Cost: $38,000)

- Treatment with male hormones and manual stimulation cause erections in both male beagles who were castrated at birth and female beagles who were surgically altered to resemble males. (Cost: $38,000)

The way to learn about people is to study people. Redirecting our financial and creative resources into programs and studies that focus on people will directly benefit both those who are in need and the animals who suffer in inconsequential experimentation.

Animals in Classrooms

Vivisection is a social evil because if it advances human knowledge, it does so at the expense of human character...

— George Bernard Shaw

Although the harmful use of animals in medical education has been banned in Great Britain for over 100 years, in the U.S. five to six million healthy animals still die every year for the sake of "education."[64] Some U.S. schools have adopted nonanimal teaching methods, but many more refuse to offer students the choice of a humane alternative to killing healthy animals.

Forcing students to participate in classroom procedures that harm animals is not just an animal rights issue, it is a student rights issue. Students have the right to follow their consciences and say, "No!" to dissection. It is students who are leading the movement to abolish dissection in classrooms.

Where Do the Animals Come From?

I once spoke with a college student who had just come from a class where she was required to dissect a cat. She was upset and apologetic about cutting into a dead cat, but told me it was all right because the cat had been accidentally killed when it was hit by a car.

This student evidently believed the "cat hit by a car" story not because it was plausible, but because she *wanted* to believe it. It was a way she could console herself for what was an otherwise intolerable circumstance. Despite what this student was told (or what she wanted to believe), the animals used in classrooms are not the victims of accidental death. They come from a variety of sources, among them:

- **Local Pounds and Shelters**

  Many communities allow schools and laboratories to purchase dogs and cats from animal shelters for use in research experiments and classroom demonstrations, a practice called *pound seizure*. Even in communities where pound seizure is outlawed, unscrupulous animal dealers or their helpers (people called *bunchers* who supply animals to licensed dealers), may obtain animals from pounds and shelters and later sell them to schools and laboratories.

- **Streets, Backyards, and Cars**

  Bunchers collect animals from a variety of sources, including from backyards, inside of cars, off of streets, and by answering "free to good home" ads. Bunchers then sell these stolen companions to animal dealers, who in turn sell them directly to laboratories or sometimes to animal supply houses, who then sell to schools and laboratories. Over a million animals are believed to meet this fate every year.[65]

- **Animal Supply Houses**

  Over 4,000 animal dealers licensed by the USDA sell animals to large supply houses who then prepare them for shipment to schools and laboratories.[66] "Preparation" more often than not means killing the animals and replacing their blood with formaldehyde, so they arrive at schools ready for dissection. The "specimens" supplied by these companies include, but are not limited to, cats, dogs, rabbits, rats, frogs, horse heads, and crayfish.

  Undercover investigators for the animal rights group PETA recently infiltrated Carolina Biological Supply Company (CBS), the leading dissection supply house in the country. CBS fills as many as 3,000 orders per day. The investigators observed firsthand what animals undergo at these facilities — live cats crammed together so tightly into cages that they couldn't even stand up; animals being drowned; cats being embalmed while still alive; live rats being cut into; cats being beaten and jabbed in the face with a metal hook; crates of live animals being dropped from elevations of up to five feet; workers callously tormenting animals for the fun of it...in all 13 pages of violations of the Animal Welfare Act, which PETA has filed with the USDA.[67]

Elementary School Classrooms

Students in elementary schools do not usually dissect animals. Often, however, live animals are kept in cages in classrooms so that children can observe or interact with them. Animals kept in classrooms are frequently victims of neglect and cruelty, treated only as objects of curiosity and frequently ignored after the initial novelty wears off. Over weekends and school vacations, animals may be uncared for over a period of days or may go home with a student for an unsupervised visit.

PETA reports that they are often called to investigate animal cruelty at schools. One case involved rabbits used in a "responsible pet ownership" project for Future Farmers of America. In the words of PETA:

> ...82 rabbits were being held in a public school basement in filthy, dark, rusting cages...Some of the rabbits' teeth had grown so long it was difficult for them to eat, and others had suffered burns from months of lying in their own and other animals' urine. Toenails on some were so long that they curled upwards and had caught in the cage floor wires.[68]

Caged animals in classrooms characteristically do not receive the care they require. Instead of learning about the true natures of animals, children learn to regard animals as playthings. Animals do not belong in classrooms.

Biology Classrooms

For many years, dissecting frogs and fetal pigs has been standard practice in biology classrooms. Not any more. The National Association of Biology Teachers (NABT) published a policy which states that "all biology teachers should foster a respect for life" and that "NABT is committed to providing teachers' materials that offer alternatives to the more traditional practices involving dissection and vivisection."[69]

Even so, educators and school administrations are not always cooperative when it comes to respecting a student's right to refuse dissection. Although there are many commercial alternatives to dissection available, some students have been forced to use the courts to persuade educators to provide humane alternatives to needlessly killing healthy animals.

As many students and educators are now learning, it is not necessary to harm animals in order to learn about them. California has a state law protecting students who refuse to kill animals, when students state religious or moral reasons.[70] The most prestigious science competition in the country, the Westinghouse Science Talent Search, refuses to consider any animal-based projects, except those that are purely observational.[71]

Says one student, Mary Pacheco of Portsmouth, Ohio:

> I passed geography without leaving my home state, and geology without seeing planets collide. It's insulting to argue that students can't understand anatomy unless they stick scissors into a frog's brain.[72]

Classroom dissection will only stop completely when students and teachers refuse to participate in it. Across the country, students have been standing up and winning their rights to refuse dissection. There is now a dissection hotline students can call for advice on how to best approach their right to refuse: 1-800-922-FROG. Other helpful contacts are listed in the Resources section at the end of the chapter.

Veterinary Classrooms

You might think that of all professions, veterinary medicine would be the leader in advocating for animals. Unbelievably, the traditional animal medicine community parallels the traditional biomedical community in its callous disregard for animals as research and teaching tools.

In 1990, only one-third of this country's 27 colleges of veterinary medicine offered humane alternatives to students who elected to bypass killing healthy animals in classroom exercises.[73] In recent years, the list has grown. but is still not complete. Many of these schools agreed to honor student requests for alternatives only after students took them to court. Note that the schools who do offer humane alternatives did not necessarily change their inhumane curriculum; they simply added on humane alternatives for students who insist on having them.

Animals, students, and faculty members are all victims of traditionally-minded veterinary schools. Students who have requested their right to humane alternatives have faced opposition from faculty, administrators, and even fellow students. Often they are told they must participate in the traditional inhumane practices or face a failing grade. At Ohio State University, a veterinary student who requested humane alternatives received hate mail, had a petition against her circulated by fellow veterinary students, and even found a dead mouse taped to her locker. Although she won the right to not kill healthy animals (after filing a lawsuit), other students who preferred the humane options confided that they were too afraid of being ostracized to take advantage of the alternatives.

Faculty members have also been "punished" for advocating humane alternatives. A professor at the School of Veterinary Medicine at the University of California at Davis who spoke out in favor of offering students humane alternatives, Nedim Buyukmihci, was subsequently relieved of some duties, threatened with being fired, and denied a pay increase. When Dr. Buyukmihci sued the University for violating his civil rights, the University admitted its wrongdoing and paid punitive damages.[74]

What's the alternative to killing healthy dogs, cats, sheep, horses, and other animals? Using models, simulators, cadavers, and animals who will benefit from the surgery or treatment. One model in use at New York State College of Veterinary Medicine, Resusci-Dog, is a plastic mannequin linked to a computer. The model simulates an arterial pulse and is used to teach students cardiac massage and cardiopulmonary resuscitation. While students are learning to save lives, Resusci-Dog is also saving lives — approximately 100 dogs per year at New York State College.[75]

Does implementing humane alternatives mean sacrificing quality education? To the contrary, first-year students who used a model to learn how to tie-off (ligate) bleeding vessels were found to perform the actual procedure on live animals faster and more accurately than third-year students who had learned to ligate blood vessels using live animals.[76] Nonanimal alternatives are not only humane, they are cost-effective, are readily available to students, can be used over and over again, allow students to take their time and concentrate on what they are trying to learn, and remove the emotional trauma and guilt many students experience from unnecessarily wasting animal lives. This results in superior education.

Medical Classrooms

Do medical doctors need to kill animals to learn about treating human patients? Not according to at least 34 medical schools in the U.S. that use only nonanimal teaching methods to train doctors. Medical schools with humane curriculum include:[77]

Albert Einstein College (NY)
Baylor University (TX)
Columbia University (NY)
Creighton University (NE)
Dartmouth Medical School (NH)
Eastern Virginia Medical School
George Washington University (D.C.)
Hahnemann University (PA)
Harvard University (MA)
Marshall University (WY)

Mayo Medical School (MN)
Medical University of South Carolina
Mercer University (GA)
Michigan State University, 5 of 6 campuses
New York University
Northwestern University (IL)
Rush Medical College (IL)
Stanford University (CA)
Texas A & M University (TX)
Thomas Jefferson University (PA)
University of Arizona
University of Chicago Pritzker School of Medicine
University of Hawaii
University of Iowa
University of Louisville (KY)
University of Maryland
University of Michigan
University of Oklahoma
University of Southern California
University of Washington
Vanderbilt University (TN)
Wayne State University (MI)
West Virginia University
Yale University (CT)

If medical education doesn't require killing animals, then why continue to use animals to train doctors, nurses, and other health professionals? Again, the only answer seems to be indoctrination into the traditional mindset. That and the fact that many researchers who use animals are threatened by any attempts to reduce or eliminate animals from instructional institutions. Their fear is that if animals are respected as inappropriate training tools, then the next step may be regarding animals as inappropriate research tools. That, in turn, would threaten their job security.

Many physicians have gone on record in support of nonanimal teaching methods. They do so not only because using animals in classrooms is inhumane and unnecessary, but because they believe that the alternatives offer superior education to future physicians. Says Dr. Donald Doll, a physician at a Phoenix, Arizona hospital:

> I certainly would not want my infant son to be the first infant subject of one who had trained in intubation [insertion of a tube down the throat] on a kitten. This kind of training does not prepare a health care professional to handle the delicate physiology of a human infant. In my own medical training, intubation was done on human cadavers. Some medical schools now use mannequins for this kind of training.[78]

Says another Arizona physician:

> I did many experiments on live animals during medical school. I would say they had nothing to do with what I later had to know about or do to humans.[79]

Many excellent nonanimal teaching devices exist, among them:

- Life-like mechanical models, such as the plastic model infant Baby AirIn, which replaces the use of cats to teach endotracheal intubation (insertion of a tube into the trachea by way of the nose or mouth). Some advantages of mechanical models over animal models are that they are anatomically correct and can be practiced on repeatedly until the student is proficient.

- State-of-the-art computer models and simulations.
- Surgical training boards with simulated intestine, skin, and vascular tissue.
- Films and videos.
- Postmortem studies on humans.
- Observation of surgical techniques, followed by closely supervised hands-on work.

The American Anti-Vivisection Society

Cats and dogs are often the animals of choice for medical research and training.

Medicine is supposed to be a healing profession. Isn't it time for all medical schools to modernize their curricula and stop unnecessarily killing animals in the name of healing?

How You Can Help

Animals Used in Product Testing...

- Use only cruelty-free products. See Chapter 12 for lists of cruelty-free companies and sources for cruelty-free products.
- If you are a college student, persuade your university bookstore to stop selling products by companies that continue to test on animals (such as Gillette and Procter & Gamble).
- Write or call companies that continue to use animals in product testing, and tell them that as a caring consumer, you have chosen to boycott their products.
- Introduce legislation to ban the Draize test in your state. New Jersey Animal Rights Alliance has an information packet on how they introduced legislation in New Jersey.

Animals Used by the Military...

- Investigate and publicize the animal research taking place at military facilities in your area. See Chapter 9, "Getting into the Act," and the activist publications in Chapter 13 for pointers on how to conduct investigations.
- Write to your senators and representatives about your concerns. Ask them to make military facilities accountable for the animals they use by making this information public. Let them know you don't want your tax dollars to go for research that involves animals.
- For help in investigating military research on college campuses, contact the War Research

Information Service (WRIS), P.O. Box 748, Cambridge, MA 02142, (617) 354-9363 (voice/FAX). Ask for information packet #2 (August-September 1991). This packet contains "how to" instructions and resource information useful in requesting information on military research.

Animals Used in Biomedical Research...

- Use your state "open meetings" law to open up Animal Care and Use Committee meetings at your local state-funded universities. These meetings are required by the federal Animal Welfare Act and are supposed to provide a forum for discussing research protocols. Groups in Ohio, Washington, Florida, Minnesota, and Vermont have already opened up meetings in their states. For further information, have your attorney contact the Animal Legal Defense Fund. Contact the Progressive Animal Welfare Society (WA) for information on how they opened up meetings at the University of Washington, or SPARE (OH) for how they opened up meetings at Wright State University.
- Save your donations for organizations that do not use animals in research, such as Easter Seals. Withhold donations to foundations and organizations that use animals in research. When I receive requests for money, I write on the slip enclosed for return, "Please note that I do not contribute money to organizations that use animals in research or testing. If you do not use animals in research or testing, please let me know and I will be happy to send a donation." I then send it back in the postage-paid envelope accompanying the request. If you plan to contribute to any charity, be sure to ask them about animal research before handing over any money to them. According to Physicians Committee for Responsible Medicine, the following private health foundations do and do not fund animal research.[80]

Foundations That *Do Not* Fund Animal Research

American Kidney Fund (MD)

Arthritis Research Institute of America (FL)

Association of Birth Defect Children (FL)

Cancer Care, Inc. (NY)

Cancer Fund of America, Inc. (TN)

Designer Institute Foundation for AIDS (NY)

Disabled American Veterans (OH)

Easter Seals (IL)

The Green Foundation, Inc. (TX)

Heimlich Foundation (OH)

International Child Health Foundation (MD)

International Eye Foundation (MD)

Multiple Sclerosis Association of America (NJ)

National Burn Victim Foundation (NJ)

National Federation of the Blind (MD)

National Head Injury Foundation (Washington, D.C.)

Quest Cancer Test (England)

Rheumatoid Disease Foundation (also known as The Arthritis Fund) (TN)

Foundations That Fund Animal Research

Alzheimer's Disease and Related Disorders Association (IL)

American Cancer Society (GA)

American Diabetes Association (VA)

American Heart Association (TX)

American Institute for Cancer Research (Washington, D.C.)

American Lung Association National Headquarters (NY)

American Parkinson Disease Association (NY)

Arthritis Foundation (GA)

Cancer Prevention Project (Washington, D.C.)

City of Hope (NY)

Cystic Fibrosis Foundation (MD)

Epilepsy Foundation of America (MD)

The Foundation Fighting Blindness (formerly Retinitis Pigmentosa Foundation) (MD)

Joslin Diabetes Center (MA)

Leukemia Society of America (NY)

March of Dimes Birth Defects Foundation (NY)

Muscular Dystrophy Association (AZ)

National Foundation for Cancer Research (MD)

National Kidney Foundation (NY)

National Multiple Sclerosis Society (NY)

National Parkinson Foundation (FL)

National Psoriasis Foundation (OR)

Nina Hyde Center for Breast Cancer Research (Washington, D.C.)

Parkinson's Disease Foundation (NY)

Shriners Burn Institute (MA)

St. Jude Children's Research Hospital (TN)

United Parkinson Foundation (IL)

University of Texas MD Anderson Cancer Center (TX)

- Physicians Committee for Responsible Medicine (PCRM) suggests that you talk to your doctor and hospital operating room manager about U.S. Surgical Corporation's practice of killing 1,000 dogs per year to train sales representatives in surgical stapling. Urge them to register their disapproval of this practice with their U.S. Surgical representative. Contact PCRM for free brochures on this subject.
- Avoid all products by Bausch and Lomb, which owns Charles River Breeding Labs, the largest breeder of lab animals in the United States. For cruelty-free contact lens solution, contact Lobob Labs, 1440 Atteberry Lane, San Jose, CA 95131, (408) 432-0580.
- Let your alma mater know that you won't contribute money to them until they stop using animals for experimentation and training. The group In Defense of Animals requests that you send them a copy of the letter you send to the university for their Alumni Campaign Against Animal Experimentation.
- If animals from your local pound are sold to biomedical research facilities, approach the dog warden about stopping this practice. For help, see the organizations listed under Pound Seizure in the Resources section at the end of the chapter.
- Obtain a Humane Research Donor Card from the American Anti-Vivisection Society. The purpose of the card is to spare animals from suffering in scientific and medical research by providing actual human organs for study. The donor card states: "I request that after my death any part of my body be used for medical and scientific research." You can also specify any organs you do not want to donate to research.

Animals Used in Classrooms...

- Choose to refuse dissection and help your children refuse dissection. If you need help, call the Dissection Hotline, 1-800-922-FROG. For additional help, see the Resources section at the end of the chapter, and the books on dissection in Chapter 13.
- Provide biology teachers in your community with one or more catalogs of alternatives to dissection. See the guides and directories in the Research, Education, & Product Testing section of Chapter 13 for ordering information.
- If you live near a medical or veterinary school, find out whether or not animals are used in classroom training. If they are, approach the administration and faculty about modernizing their curriculum to exclude animal labs. Educate students about the alternatives to using animals in their training. For help, see the organizations listed in the Resources section of this chapter.
- Pass laws in your community that outlaw the harmful use of animals at science fairs and in classrooms. Find out what's happening in your own community, then speak out and educate others.

Resources for Animals in Education, Research, and Testing

For products and services related to animals in research, education, and product testing, see the following sections of Chapter 12: Activist Aids, Audio Tapes & CDs, Clothing, Cruelty-Free Home, Beauty, & Personal Care Products, Clubs for Kids & Young Adults, Hotlines, Letter-Writing Services, Paints & Stains, Radio & Television Programming, Stamps & Stickers, and Videos & Films.

For more information on animals in research, education, and testing, and for publications that can help you conduct investigations of institutions that use animals in these capacities, see Chapter 13.

The following organizations can provide you with assistance and information on topics related to vivisection. See Chapter 10 for a description of these and other organizations that work to eradicate the harmful use of animals for research, testing, or education. *Note: See the state listings in Chapter 10 for additional organizations.*

- **General (see other categories for specific interests)**

  American Anti-Vivisection Society (PA), Animal Emancipation, Inc. (CA), Animal Liberation Front Support Group (TN), Association of Veterinarians for Animal Rights (CA), Citizens Committee for Laboratory Animal Liberation (NY), CIVIS/Civitas (NY), In Defense of Animals (CA), International Foundation for Ethical Research (IL), International League of Doctors for the Abolition of Vivisection (NY), International Society for Animal Rights, Inc. (PA), Last Chance for Animals (CA), Medical Research Modernization Committee (NY), National Anti-Vivisection Society (IL), New England Anti-Vivisection Society (MA), People for Reason in Science and Medicine (CA), People for the Ethical Treatment of Animals (VA), Physicians Committee for Responsible Medicine (D.C.), Psychologists for the Ethical Treatment of Animals (MD), Scientists Group for Reform of Animal Experimentation (MD), Society in Opposition to Human-Animal Hybridization (NJ), SUPRESS, Inc. (CA), United Action for Animals, Inc. (NY), University Students Against Vivisection (CA)

◆ **Alternatives**
Alternatives Research & Development Foundation (PA), American Fund for Alternatives to Animal Research (NY)

◆ **Dissection**
Animal Rights International/Coalition to Abolish Classroom Dissection (NY), American Anti-Vivisection Society (PA), Animal Legal Defense Fund (CA), Association of Veterinarians for Animal Rights (CA), Classrooms for Ethical Labs in the Life Sciences (NJ), Ethical Science Coalition (MA), National Anti-Vivisection Society (IL), Physicians Committee for Responsible Medicine (D.C.), People for the Ethical Treatment of Animals (VA), Student Action Corps for Animals (D.C.)

◆ **Pet Theft**
Action 81, Inc. (VA), Coalition of Municipalities to Ban Animal Trafficking (AR), Last Chance for Animals (CA)

◆ **Pound Seizure**
American Society for the Prevention of Cruelty to Animals (NY), Animal Allies (CA), Animal Connection of Texas (TX), Animal Protection Association (TN), Defenders of Animal Rights, Inc. (MD), Eliminate All Suffering and Exploitation (CA), For Animals, Inc. (MI), International Society for Animal Rights, Inc. (PA), Kanawha Action for Animals, Inc. (WV), New England Anti-Vivisection Society (MA), Sangre de Cristo Animal Protection, Inc. (NM), SPARE (OH), Tennessee Network for Animals (TN), Women's Humane Society (PA)

◆ **Product Testing**
American Anti-Vivisection Society (PA), Animal Rights International/Coalition to Abolish the LD50 and Draize Tests (NY), Animal Welfare Alliance—Draize test ban (NY), Beauty Without Cruelty USA—cruelty-free living (NY), Committee for a Cruelty Free California—Draize bill (CA), Fashion With Compassion—cruelty-free living (WA), National Anti-Vivisection Society (IL), New England Anti-Vivisection Society (MA), New Jersey Animal Rights—Draize test ban (NJ), People for the Ethical Treatment of Animals (VA)

Conclusion

Vivisection, the injurious use of animals in classrooms and laboratories, is a tradition that hurts people as well as animals. After decades of animal research, medical professionals conclude that animal research has failed to give us the answers we need. It has wasted not only countless animal lives, but human lives as well.

Testing products on animals does not guarantee their safety for humans. To the contrary, because living systems differ in significant ways, data obtained by studying one species cannot reliably predict reactions in another species. The tragic case of thalidomide, a drug which was "proven" safe in animal tests but caused severe birth defects in humans, is just one of many examples where dependence on animal tests has harmed humans.

No laws protect animals from painful experiments. The experimenters themselves determine what types of things may be done to animals during experimentation. In many instances, painful experiments produce useless information that has no practical application. In other instances, experiments simply tell us the obvious or duplicate experiments that have already been conducted many times before.

Using animals to teach medical students and veterinary students is a waste of life. A number of veterinary and medical schools in this and other countries offer humane alternatives to the traditional classroom exercises that kill healthy animals. Killing animals does not make for better education.

Animals are not good research "tools." Animal experimentation has not helped us get healthy or stay healthy. It has diverted our financial and creative resources away from prevention and from state-of-the-art nonanimal research methods that are faster, cheaper, and more reliable than animal tests. It's time to recognize vivisection for what it is — a waste of money and lives, and an impediment to scientific progress.

Research, Education, and Testing

At a Glance

Did you know:

- Vivisection — the injurious use of animals in laboratories and classrooms — is an outdated practice opposed not only on the grounds that it is cruel and unnecessary, but also because it retards scientific progress, misdirects funds, and doesn't provide the answers we need.
- The Animal Welfare Act does not prohibit the amounts or types of pain that may be administered to animals during experimentation.
- People who oppose vivisection include medical doctors, nurses, medical technicians, people who have disabilities and incurable diseases, and former animal researchers.
- Many products you use every day, such as soaps and shampoos, may have been needlessly and painfully tested on animals. Many companies now offer "cruelty-free" products that involve no cruelty to animals.
- Vivisection is big business for researchers, universities, and animal suppliers, who make large profits off of animal suffering.

Chapter 7

Wildlife in Crisis

Hunting, Trapping, and Other Human Interference

A. Achor

The rhino is a homely beast,
For human eyes he's not a feast.
Farewell, farewell, you old rhinoceros,
I'll stare at something less prepoceros.

— Ogden Nash

Like poet Ogden Nash, you may conclude that the rhinoceros is no feast for your eyes. But what if one day there were no more rhinoceros, anywhere, to look at — ever again? That idea isn't as "prepoceros" as it sounds. Rhinos are one of almost 800 known species of endangered and threatened wildlife — animals in danger of extinction. Some of the animals officially listed by the U.S. Fish and Wildlife Service as endangered and/or threatened include various species of:

albatross
alligator
armadillo
bat
bear
beaver
bobcat
camel
catfish
cheetah
chinchilla
clam
condor
cougar
crocodile
curlew
deer
duck
eagle
elephant
falcon
finch
fox
frog
gazelle
gibbon
goose
gorilla
hawk
hyena
iguana
jaguar
kangaroo
kangaroo rat
kestrel
leopard
lion
lizard
lynx
macaque
manatee
monkey
mouse
ocelot
orangutan
otter
owl
panda
panther
parrot
pheasant
pigeon
prairie dog
pronghorn sheep
python
quail
rhinoceros
salamander
seal
sloth
snail
sparrow
squirrel
stork
tamarin
tapir
tiger
toad
tortoise
trout
vole
wallaby
warbler
whale
whooping crane
wolf
woodpecker
zebra

Tragically, many species of plants and animals disappear forever while awaiting inclusion on the official list of endangered or threatened species.

Why this crisis in wildlife populations? There are many threats to wildlife, but they can all be summed up with one word — people. People with guns, people with bows, people with traps, people buying fur, people throwing litter along roadways, people polluting lakes and oceans, people building houses and shopping centers, people doing the things that people do, with little regard for the consequences.

The world's wildlife is dying at an astounding rate — and we're the reason why. Some wildlife dies because we are shortsighted and uninformed, not realizing the consequences of our actions. We don't understand that spraying a pesticide on a field or filling in a marsh can forever alter the future of a species. Other times, both individual wildlife and entire species of wildlife die as a result of sheer human selfishness. Anyway you look at it, one thing is clear: wildlife destruction is a *human* problem. And it is a monumental one. This chapter looks at some of the many ways we have failed wildlife, and have thus failed ourselves and our planet.

Federal Laws and Endangered Species

In the early 1970's, Congress passed two significant pieces of legislation to protect endangered animals, the Marine Mammal Protection Act of 1972 and the Endangered Species Act of 1973. Many people believe that these laws protect wildlife, and that is their intent. The problem is that a law is only as good as those who enforce it. Getting the federal government to enforce these laws as intended has been a problem. And lately, efforts are being made to gut the laws altogether.

The Marine Mammal Protection Act

The Marine Mammal Protection Act of 1972 is designed to protect depleted populations of marine mammals. Congress passed the Act largely in response to the slaughter of dolphins by tuna fishers.

Tuna fishers have long known that where there are dolphins, there are likely to be tuna swimming beneath them. The old-fashioned method of catching tuna by rod fishing was harmless to the dolphins. Problems began when a method of fishing called *purse seining* was introduced in the early 1960's. A seine is a large net that hangs vertically in the water with floats along the upper edge and sinks along the bottom edge. Fishers encircle the tuna (and dolphins) with this net and then pull the bottom edge of the net together, to form a bag or purse; thus the name "purse" seining. The trapped animals are then hauled onto the boat.

Purse seining proved tragic to dolphins. Every year, 250,000 to 500,000 dolphins died as a result of the practice.[1] One of the intents of the Marine Mammal Protection Act was to stop this dolphin massacre, with the Act specifying "it shall be the immediate goal that the incidental kill or incidental serious injury of marine mammals permitted in the course of commercial fishing operations be reduced to insignificant levels approaching a zero mortality and serious injury rate."[2]

The tuna industry didn't like this proposal. When they complained, the agency responsible for administering the Act, the National Marine Fisheries Service (NMFS), granted them a "grace period" to reduce the incidental kills of dolphins from tuna fishing. A year passed. Then two years. Then five years, and still dolphins were dying in purse seines. Only when threatened with a lawsuit from 13 environmental groups did the NMFS pressure tuna fishers to comply with the law. Even then, although the law calls for reducing the number to "levels approaching a zero mortality and serious injury rate," NMFS allowed a limit of 20,500 "incidental" dolphin deaths per year to become the accepted number.

The tuna fishers have also found other ways to circumvent the Act. When the NMFS banned setting nets at night, due to the increased dolphin kill rate compared to daytime netting, tuna industry lobbyists successfully pressed for the withdrawal of the prohibition just eight days after its proposal. They also kept NMFS observers off of tuna boats for three years, until an appellate court ruled in favor of the observers.[3] And when all else fails, as the tuna industry discovered, just register your ships with foreign countries, which are not bound by the Act. U.S. ships that have done so are reportedly responsible for 100,000 dolphin deaths per year.[4]

Driftnets are another issue that many people think the NMFS should be addressing under the Marine Mammal Protection Act. Driftnets are monofilament nets, mostly used to catch salmon or squid. They also catch and kill tens of thousands of marine mammals, including sharks, whales, seals, and porpoises, and an estimated 800,000 sea birds every year.[5] Friends of the Earth reports that "everyone, including the Japanese, admits that it is impossible to use driftnets and not kill marine mammals." They also report that 639 miles of these non-biodegradable nets are lost or abandoned in oceans each year, killing marine mammals, fish, and sea birds who become entangled in them.[6] The Marine Mammal Protection Act allows restriction of "fishing techniques which have been found to cause undue fatalities to any species of marine mammal." The NMFS has chosen to exclude driftnets from this category.*

The NMFS has also come under fire for failure to protect marine mammals captured and confined for display in amusement parks and hotels. Under the Marine Mammal Protection Act, permits for public display of marine mammals may be issued only to applicants whose displays have educational or conservation purposes. Many marine mammals, however, are little more than circus performers for paying audiences. Their captivity teaches nothing about the natural lives of marine mammals. Richard (Ric) O'Barry, a former dolphin trainer for the television show "Flipper," contends that current displays of marine mammals teach only cruelty, domination, and humiliation.[7] Speaking of the merit of such shows, he says, "If that is educational, then a boxing kangaroo is also educational. And so is a dancing bear chained to a tree."[8] The Animal Legal Defense Fund has brought suit against the NMFS for allowing facilities without permits to receive marine mammals, thereby side-

---

* In 1992, Japan announced some good news for animals: a long-awaited agreement to end all driftnet fishing by the beginning of 1993.

stepping requirements outlined in the Marine Mammal Protection Act.

As if all of this wasn't enough, the conservatives who have taken over the 104th U.S. Congress are working to demolish the Marine Mammal Protection Act. The International Dolphin Conservancy Program Act (SB 1420) has been introduced to lift restrictions on "dolphin safe" tuna and on dolphin deaths by purse seining. The General Agreement on Tariffs and Trade (GATT), an international trade agreement adopted in 1994, further undermines protective measures by barring members from regulating tuna caught in a dolphin-safe manner from tuna caught at the expense of dolphin lives. It also invalidates protections to other species, such as sea turtles. Current U.S. law protects sea turtles from shrimp fishers by requiring the use of "turtle extruder devices (TEDs), which allow turtles to escape from shrimp nets. GATT effectively removes this safeguard, claiming that a country can't restrict imports based on one method of fishing over another. The only recourse is for the U.S. to stop importing shrimp altogether, an unlikely proposition.

The Endangered Species Act

The Endangered Species Act of 1973 is landmark legislation that protects plant and animal species threatened with extinction. Initially, the Act was a significant victory for wildlife. It mandated a system for listing species or populations of species as endangered or threatened, protections for those species, and recovery programs for reviving the species.

Perhaps the most significant thing about this legislation is that it recognizes species for their "esthetic, ecological, educational, historical, recreational, and scientific value,"[9] aside from their economic value. The Act implores us to protect species simply because they exist, not because they are known to benefit humans.

Another important part of the law is its provisions for protecting ecosystems on which endangered and threatened species depend. It specifically forbids federal agencies to authorize, fund, or carry out any action "likely to jeopardize the continued existence of any endangered species or threatened species or result in the destruction or adverse modification of habitat of such species."[10]

The Act sounded great on paper; at last fragile animal and plant species were to receive federal protection. Then construction of a Tennessee Valley Authority dam came face-to-face with an endangered fish called a snail darter. This became the test case for the Endangered Species Act. Although the snail darter won the battle, the Endangered Species Act lost the war. From then on, the battle lines were drawn.

Wildlife once again started taking a backseat to economic interests. One method for achieving this was to keep species from being listed as endangered or threatened. Amendments to the Endangered Species Act succeeded in greatly encumbering the process for listing species. During the first year of the Reagan Administration, not a single species was added to the list. Today, a backlog of 6,012 applications await examination, while another 3,000 species are suspected as endangered.[11] In the meantime, species on the waiting list receive no federal protection. Perhaps not coincidentally, certain species were added to the list only *after* projects threatening their survival were completed.

Even those species that receive endangered status are not guaranteed protection. Applications for exemption from the Act (essentially, "licenses to kill") may be submitted to the Endangered Species Committee, nicknamed the "God Squad" because of its power to grant life or death to a species. This committee has seven members, including the Secretary of the Army, the Secretary of Agriculture, and the Secretary of the Interior. What can be expected from this committee? In the opinion of former Interior Secretary Manuel Lujan, the Endangered Species Act is a threat to jobs and economic development and therefore should be weakened.[12] In the years following amendments to the Act, endangered animals have taken a backseat to such things as a residential subdivision, a golf course, waterways and dams, and telescopes for the University of Arizona. As one writer aptly observes, "We all recognize the Endangered Species Act hardly exists in this nation today in situations where a species is in conflict with awesomely financed developmental forces."[13]

Again, conservative forces in the 104th Congress are hard at work to undermine this law entirely. A bill titled the Endangered Species Reauthorization Act (HB 2275) is backed by the Ringling Brothers Circus, animal breeders, and others who benefit from "animal acts" or exotic animal sales. This bill eliminates or reduces restrictions on habitat destruction, recovery programs, importation of endangered species, etc. The 1994 GATT agreement may also be used to further reverse efforts to protect endangered species.

Federal Lands – Havens for Animals?

Many people are under the mistaken impression that federal lands, particularly the National Wildlife Refuge System and the National Parks, are havens for wildlife. Unfortunately, this isn't the case.

The National Wildlife Refuge System

In 1903, President Theodore Roosevelt created the National Wildlife Refuge System explicitly to set aside safe habitat for this country's wildlife. Today the System consists of over 450 different refuges that total over 90 million acres spanning every state except West Virginia. Animals living on the refuges include approximately 70 species of endangered wildlife.[14]

If there is any last hope for our country's wildlife, it should be these national refuges. But don't relax just yet. They are not what they seem.

The U.S. Congress passes the laws that govern the refuge system. The U.S. Fish and Wildlife Service (USFWS), a division of the Department of the Interior, manages the refuge system. Although originally established to protect wildlife, the National Wildlife Refuge System has become what The Humane Society of the United States calls "a national disgrace."[15] Here's why.

- **Hunting**
  Sport hunting is allowed on over half of the refuges, despite the fact that 96% of people visiting the refuges don't hunt. Kills by hunters include some endangered species.

Hunting proponents argue that hunters are entitled to hunt on wildlife refuges because much of the land was purchased with revenues from duck stamps (which all waterfowl hunters are required to buy). In fact, only 3.4% of refuge land was purchased with revenues from these stamps.[16] Additionally, the maintenance costs of the refuges comes from the general tax fund, not specifically from hunters.

◆ **Trapping**
Commercial and sport trapping are allowed on over one-quarter of the refuges. Trapping is a barbaric practice that causes great suffering for animals. Millions of additional untargeted animals are caught in the traps and discarded as "trash." Such "trash" animals include birds, endangered species, cats, and dogs. See Killing for Profit later in the chapter for more on trapping.

People for the Ethical Treatment of Animals

Predators are the targeted victims of many government-sponsored exterminations.

◆ **Predator Control**
To provide more waterfowl for hunters, USFWS officials kill natural waterfowl predators such as coyote and fox by poisoning, shooting, and trapping them. Although this artificial manipulation of predator populations is called "predator control," it would more accurately be termed "eliminating the sport hunter's competition."

◆ **Water Pollution**
Road salt, agricultural run-off, irrigation drainage, industrial contaminants, lawn-care chemicals, pesticides, and sewage from nearby communities all contribute to the poison waters now found in some wildlife refuges. Contaminated waters are responsible for massive die-offs of fish, snakes, frogs, and birds, and for grotesque birth defects in birds on refuges. One refuge in California is officially closed because of water poisoning; duties of wildlife officials now include scaring birds away from the toxic water.[17]

◆ **Recreational Pursuits**
Originally intended as sanctuaries for wildlife, some National Wildlife Refuges have become recreation centers for people. Besides the relatively harmless pursuits of hiking and bird-watching, recreational activities include camping, sunbathing on beaches, speed boating, water skiing, fishing, hunting, trapping, and off-road jeep riding. Such invasive activities not only pollute and destroy habitat, but also create noise, confusion, and crowding.

◆ **Commercial Pursuits**
Are cows wildlife? From their presence on wildlife refuges, you might think so. The reality is that many National Wildlife Refuges are open to a host of commercial interests, including farming, ranching, commercial fishing, bee keeping, mining, logging, oil drilling, and fur trapping. These vested interests don't give a fig for the wildlife; they are there solely for their own economic benefit.

◆ **Military Use**
Believe it or not, even the military has a presence on some wildlife refuges — more correctly, above them. In at least 36 refuges, wildlife are disrupted by sonic booms and explosions from jet fighters practicing overhead maneuvers and target practice.[18]

◆ **Habitat Destruction**
Permitting secondary uses of refuges for commercial, recreational, and military purposes results in habitat destruction and disruption. Almost all refuges in the system, 92%, allow secondary use.[19] That leaves only 8% that function according to the original intent — as true wildlife preserves.

In response to the fiasco that the National Wildlife Refuge System has become, a number of organizations have banded together to form the Wildlife Refuge Reform Coalition. This coalition is backing a federal bill that would end sport hunting and trapping in National Wildlife Refuges. (For more on this coalition, see their description in Chapter 10, "Animal Advocacy Organizations.") In contrast, an Arkansas congressman is trying to pass the Wildlife Refuge Improvement Act (HB 1675), which would redefine the primary purpose of the National Wildlife Refuge System as a "refuge" for hunters and fishers.

National Parks

If you think of National Parks as havens for wildlife, think again:

- National Parks are subjected to many of the same commercial and recreational uses discussed above for Refuges — from mining and oil drilling to snowmobiling.
- Sport hunting, fishing, and trapping are allowed in some National Parks. In fact, hunting and trapping are specifically mandated by federal statute in some parks.
- Wildlife managers kill park animals when they deem it necessary for "management" purposes. Methods include poisons which contaminate the surrounding environment.[20]
- Illegal poaching is rampant in many parks. Poachers range from trophy hunters and collectors to profiteers who sell animals and animal parts on the black market. They use everything from semi-automatic weapons to airplanes to dogs in pursuit of their victims.

  Wildlife officials estimate that poachers kill two or three animals to every one animal killed by legal hunters.[21] Why is poaching so prevalent? Poachers have little to lose and a lot to gain. The USFWS has approximately 200 wildlife agents to patrol more than 270 million acres of parks and forests spread across the nation.[22] With too few law enforcement officials and too many lenient judges, poachers rarely get caught or get off with light fines. On the other hand, there are hundreds of thousands of dollars to be made in the poaching business.

Killing by Encroachment

...most people have forgotten how to live with living creatures, with living systems, and that, in turn, is the reason why man, whenever he comes into contact with nature, threatens to kill the natural system in which and from which he lives.

— Konrad Lorenz, naturalist

People don't need to hunt or trap to be a threat to wild animals. We threaten wildlife by our very existence.

Human Overpopulation

The human population explosion of the last 40 years has more than doubled the number of people inhabiting the Earth. The U.S. population has steadily expanded by about 1% each year for the last 10 years. Accompanying this mass of "civilization" are a host of by-products — overcrowding, resource consumption, habitat destruction, pollution, and other serious threats to wildlife. The single best thing we could do for wildlife is to curb human population.

Habitat Destruction

As people spread over the face of the Earth, we occupy more and more of the land that once sustained wildlife. As we bulldoze forests for shopping malls and erect beachfront condos, we displace and destroy wildlife. Less than 2% of the Earth's land mass is set aside specifically for wildlife.[23]

Habitat destruction ranks right up next to hunting as the major cause of species extinction.[24] Tropical biologist John Terborgh estimates that the number of migratory land birds in the United States is now one-fourth of what it once was, due mostly to deforestation.[25] All six species of area sea turtles are officially listed as endangered or threatened due largely to people disturbing their beach nesting sites and stealing their eggs. And crowding is forcing Florida's endangered panthers onto highways and into the paths of cars.[26]

Habitat destruction isn't strictly a consequence of needing homes for people. A large part of it is rooted in commercialism and consumption. Livestock grazing is responsible for crowding wildlife off of nearly 70% of western range land.[27] Clearing rainforests for cattle grazing annually kills 17,500 animal and plant species.[28] Over half of the wetlands, which are home to nearly half of the officially-recognized endangered or threatened animal species, are already gone and continue to disappear at a rate of about 450,000 acres per year, again due to agricultural practices.[29] The logging industry is contributing to the near-extinction of the spotted owl, and proposed dams threaten the existence of sandhill cranes. Nor does our encroachment stop at the water's edge. Oil drilling and mining in oceans, recreational boating, destruction of coral reefs by divers, and military weapons testing all interfere with ocean wildlife habitat.

Pollution

The more people, the more waste that makes its way into the forests, onto the beaches, and into the oceans. By now, we're well acquainted with the all too familiar devastation that oil spills wreak on wildlife. Oil not only means death for the animals in its path, but ruins the habitat for future generations. Less publicized but just as deadly is the pollution from industrial waste, toxic waste, and agricultural run-off. Poisoned water is responsible for many wildlife deaths, including massive die-offs in National Wildlife Refuges, the near-extinction of the peregrine falcon and brown pelican,[30] and the deaths of 10,000 striped dolphins in the Mediterranean Sea who died from liver damage.[31]

A. Achor

Pollution threatens many species of wildlife, including pelicans.

Like water pollution, solid waste is not only unsightly, it's deadly. Plastic bags, helium balloons, Styrofoam, and six-pack rings all spell disaster for sea birds, whales, dolphins, seals, turtles, and other wildlife who either ingest the litter or become entangled in it:

- Plastic bags, balloons, pellets, and other plastics ingested by animals lodge in their guts, resulting in slow starvation. A starving leatherback turtle was found to have enough plastic in his gut to "make a ball several feet in diameter."[32]

- Plastic six-pack holders and discarded fish netting pose a strangulation danger. Young animals, particularly seals, stick their heads through openings in the plastic and end up "wearing" it around their necks. The young animals grow, but the plastic does not. It becomes tighter and tighter, cutting into their skin and, eventually and painfully, choking them to death.

- Birds who poke their beaks into portions of plastic six-pack rings or similar debris find themselves in the fatal situation of being unable to remove the plastic from around their closed beaks.

- Marine mammals who become entangled in discarded netting and rope drown. A study of Alaskan fur seals determined that 30,000 seals annually die from entanglement.[33]

Killing for Fun

The squirrel that you kill in jest, dies in earnest.

— Henry David Thoreau

Besides loss of habitat, hunting is the number one threat to wildlife today. Hunters kill over 200 million animals every year.[34] Deer, rabbits, and squirrels top the list of desirable targets. Why do people hunt? Is hunting justified? Do animals actually benefit from hunting? These are some of the questions we'll attempt to answer.

Murder by Number

According to the U.S. Fish and Wildlife Service and state fish and game agencies, licensed hunters killed the following numbers of animals during the 1988-89 hunting season. (*Note*: The totals do not include animals killed by unlicensed hunters, those killed on "pay to shoot" game ranches, or the additional 25% of animals who are wounded, but are never retrieved.)[35]

111,850,000 birds
52,139,740 mammals
163,989,740 total animals in one season

The Hunter's Mystique

Hunting is traditionally a male activity; over 99% of hunters are male.[36] Note the word "sports*man*," commonly applied to hunters. The hunter's mystique is that of a rugged traditionalist and outdoorsman, squaring off against nature to prove his manhood.

Are hunters beer-guzzling, red-necked, backwoods yahoos? Some of them are. Others are wealthy trophy hunters who pay large sums to "bag" an endangered species of animal without ever getting their hands dirty. Most recreational hunters fall somewhere between the two types.

Why do men hunt? Most hunt for one or more of the following reasons:

- **Tradition.**
  In many parts of the country, hunting is a tradition that boys enter into without ever

questioning. Their fathers do it, their peers do it, so they do it, too. One hunter has gone so far as to say, "Hunting is one of the most time-honored activities of the human species."[37]

◆ **To be in the club.**
For many men, hunting is a fraternity, a "boy's club" full of rituals. Hunting gives men an excuse to get out in the woods and hang out with "the boys." For many kids, hunting is a chance to be with and win the approval of their fathers.

◆ **Recreation.**
Some hunters are simply after entertainment. Hunting is an outlet for their energy, a way to challenge themselves. They enjoy the "chase." Hunting lets them play "Davy Crockett," frontiersman. One former hunter said that he hunted because there was simply nothing else to do in the rural community in which he grew up.

◆ **To be close to nature.**
Some men use hunting as an opportunity to get away from city life and into a natural environment. They like the solitude of the woods and the chance to "commune with nature," a chance to recapture a part of themselves that they've lost touch with in modern life.

◆ **To feel "like a man."**
Many men perceive hunting as a sign of masculinity, a way to prove themselves. This is perhaps a holdover from the days when survival was more closely tied to "the wild." Characteristically, men who feel insecure about their masculinity seek out activities they identify as masculine. In some communities, hunting is a sort of rite of passage that signifies a move from boyhood to manhood. For some men, conquering another being provides a sense of control and compensates for feelings of inadequacy in other parts of their lives.

◆ **To experience the thrill of the kill.**
For some hunters, the awesome power of destroying a life is appealing. Rock musician Ted Nugent is a fervent bowhunter for whom slaughtering scores of deer is a distinct pleasure. For this type of hunter, domination and control is the name of the game. Becoming the master of the animal by killing her is a thrill.

Ironically, many hunters claim that they do not hunt to kill. Consider the following statements from hunters, both of which appeared in *Deer and Deer Hunting* magazine:[38]

> The pleasure I personally receive from hunting is a mixture of intellectual, emotional, and spiritual experiences that renews my sense of being a small part of the natural order of things...All of these pleasures considered, the kill becomes truly anticlimactic. (G. Thomas Morgan)

> To the non-hunter, hunting is just walking out in the woods and killing something. It's so easy to do that such an activity must only appeal to some baser element of humanity who enjoys killing animals for the sole sake of killing. (Linné Hansen)

If killing is not the main point of hunting, as these hunters claim, then the obvious question is, "Why kill at all?" Can't an outdoorsman experience the same sense of adventure and exhibit as much skill, if not more, by shooting a deer with a camera instead of with a gun or bow?

The Hunting Bias

...I'll be a great conservation and environmental President. I plan to fish and hunt as much as possible.

— George Bush, former President of the U.S. (Copyright 1990, *U.S. News & World Report,* February 5, 1990)

A study conducted by a Yale professor concluded that 60% of Americans disapprove of sport hunting and about one-third of Americans favor a total ban on hunting.[39] Hunters are a distinct minority, yet billions of dollars are spent to promote hunting. Hunting is allowed on over half of all refuges in the National Wildlife Refuge System, even though 96% of the visitors to the refuges don't hunt. Why? One reason is that there are hunters in high places.

The President and Vice President are the top executives in this country. Consider this:

- President Bill Clinton hunts, as did former President Bush, and many other former presidents and vice presidents. (Former Vice President Dan Quayle is a member of Safari Club International, which describes itself as "the world's largest and fastest-growing hunting organization.")[40]

The U.S. Department of the Interior is the executive department charged with overseeing public lands and natural resources, including wildlife:

- A former Assistant Secretary of the Interior for Fish, Wildlife, and Parks, G. Ray Arnett, not only "fixed things" for a friend who was caught illegally importing endangered species, but went on to form the Wildlife Legislative Fund of America, a national lobbying group for hunters and trappers.[41]

- A pamphlet distributed by the Department of the Interior calls the trapping of furbearing animals "wholesome outdoor recreation."[42]

- The Department of the Interior allows hunting on over half of the refuges in the National Wildlife Refuge System, land originally set aside as inviolate sanctuaries for wildlife. It also allows trapping in over a quarter of the refuges.

- The Department of the Interior uses taxpayer money to hire individuals to kill predators of waterfowl, for the sole purpose of guaranteeing enough waterfowl for "sportsmen."

- The Department of the Interior engineers the annual slaughter of bison who wander across the protective border of Yellowstone National Park every winter in search of food.

The United States Fish and Wildlife Service (USFWS) is the agency of the U.S.

Department of the Interior charged with the "conservation" of wildlife:

- John Turner, head of the USFWS in February 1990, said that doing away with hunters would mean doing away "with a vital cultural and historical aspect of American life."[43]
- The USFWS permits Exotic Game Ranches to stock enclosed areas with endangered species that trophy hunters pay a fee to kill.
- In a book published by USFWS, one of the wildlife manager's duties is stated as "keeping hunters satisfied."[44]

Say It Like It Is

To impersonalize killing and reinforce the idea that animals are things, we create euphemisms to describe both the act of killing and the animals who fall victim to it.

- Instead of "killing" or "murdering" an animal, we "cull," "take," or "harvest" her.
- The "thing" that we kill is not an animal, it is a "renewable resource," "game," "quarry," or "catch."
- The organized murder of animals by government agencies is called "wildlife management," "predator control," or "conservation."

By using such euphemisms, we soften the reality.
Let's say it like it is: murdering animals for fun and profit.

Do state and local fish and "game" officials take wildlife's side any more than federal officials do? You decide:

- The Massachusetts State Fisheries and Wildlife Board is composed entirely of hunters, fishers, and trappers. In fact, Massachusetts law requires that five of the seven board members have sporting licenses for five consecutive years.[45]
- To increase the pronghorn antelope herds for sport hunters, the Arizona Fish and Game Commission trapped and poisoned natural predators in a 17,000 square mile area, also unintentionally killing birds and domesticated animals who ate the carcasses.[46]
- New York State spent more one year on ringneck pheasants, a non-native bird raised in captivity specifically for hunters, than it spent on all endangered and nongame species combined.[47]
- The state of Florida sponsors youth hunts that consist of kids shooting deer from deer stands.[48]
- The Montana Department of Fish, Wildlife, and Parks maintained an 8-week trapping season for lynx at the same time that the state tried to import lynx from Canada to bolster the Montana lynx population.[49]

- A Massachusetts game warden has had charges filed against him for setting a padded leghold trap. Such traps are illegal in Massachusetts.[50]
- The California Department of Fish and Game distributes a pamphlet titled *Get Set to Trap*, which instructs kids on how to trap animals and then kill the animals they have trapped by bludgeoning them to death, drowning them, or suffocating them.[51]
- The more hunters there are, the more money there is for state wildlife agencies. State agencies receive money from the sale of hunting, fishing, and trapping licenses, as well as from matching funds from federal excise taxes on guns, ammunition, and archery equipment.[52]

Hunters also have a friend in the big-moneyed National Rifle Association (NRA). Any proposal to limit hunting is soundly quashed by the NRA lobby. The hunting lobby also gets help from other organizations, some of which are listed later in this chapter.

Common Misconceptions About Hunting

When I feel like destroying something,
I put a golf ball on a tee and try to kill it.

— Clint Eastwood, actor

MYTH: **Hunters are filling a niche left by natural predators.**

FACT: **Hunters are not anything like natural predators. While natural predators cull the weak, the old, and the sick members of the species, human hunters kill the strong, large, healthy animals. This weakens the overall gene pool. Because of heavy hunting of the palm-antlered moose in Europe, the antlers of the male now resemble the thinner antlers of a deer.**[53]

Additionally, unlike natural predators, hunters wound an estimated 600,000 deer every season who escape. These crippled deer die slow, painful deaths from gangrene and, because they are often too weak to eat, from starvation.[54] Around 50% of the deer hit by bowhunters escape to die slow deaths from wound infections.[55]

Sometimes hunters are the *cause* of predator shortages. As previously mentioned, hunting interests purposely kill natural predators such as coyotes and foxes to "eliminate the competition."

MYTH: **Hunting is wholesome recreation.**

FACT: **Hunting trivializes killing and glorifies it as "fun." It has a desensitizing effect on kids, teaching them to distance themselves from animals and relate to animals as things rather than as living, autonomous beings.**

Testimony from former hunters indicates that once a person "connects" with an animal as an individual, that person's relationship to animals in general often changes. A former hunter who quit his job killing "nuisance" animals such as coyotes, wolves, mountain lions, and bears for the U.S. Fish and Wildlife Service says of his conversion:

> Animals became individuals. They're extremely intelligent and very adaptable. I developed relationships with them, and...well...I think that's probably what turned me.[56]

Says another former hunter:

> For 25 years, I hunted, trapped, and fished with a passion. I killed thousands of animals throughout the United States, Canada, and Mexico. But, ultimately, seeing the life drain from an innocent creature became unbearable...I quit bloodsports.[57]

Hunting hurts people in more blatant ways as well. Approximately 200 hunters and innocent passersby die and between 1,500 and 1,700 are injured in hunting accidents each year.[58] In one much-publicized case, a mother of one-year-old twins was shot while standing in her own backyard. Interestingly, the word *recreation* has as its root the word *create,* which means "to bring into existence." Hunting does exactly the opposite; it destroys an existing being.

MYTH: **Hunters kill for food.**

FACT: **Only 1%-2% of hunters hunt for food.[59] Other hunters may eat what they kill, but they hunt for sport, not food.**

Hunting is not a cheap source of food. Says one hunter, "You could live on filet mignon for what shooting a deer costs."[60] Hunters spend money on weapons (which must be kept in good working condition), ammunition, licenses, blinds, treestands, mobile stands, scents, lures, camouflage clothing, products to camouflage human scent, and an array of other equipment. Hunters annually shell out $10 billion in supplies, equipment, motels, restaurants, and other expenses related to hunting trips.[61]

MYTH: **Hunters make important contributions to wildlife conservation.**

FACT: **Hunters are a self-interest group who limit their so-called conservation efforts to animals who make good hunting targets. This is done at the expense of the environment and of other animal species. As writer Joy Williams so aptly observes, "A hunter is a conservationist in the same way a farmer or a rancher is: He's not."[62] The "conservation" programs that hunters contribute to are programs that perpetuate hunting. Hunters perceive no contradiction in saving animals in order to kill them.**

Hunters claim that without the revenues from their hunting licenses and the taxes they pay on guns, ammunition, and archery equipment there would be no wildlife conservation. But very little hunting money is spent to acquire wildlife habitat, which is true conservation. The money that does go for habitat acquisition is limited to land that supports favored hunting targets. Such "donations" are totally self-serving.

Tax money from nonhunters makes up the bulk of conservation programs. Unfortunately, even many of these programs are nothing more than "game management" projects that support hunting. Money targeted for wildlife is spent to build roads, trails, hunting blinds, and buildings for hunters to use. Some of it is used to create habitat for deer at the expense of less-huntable species who are burned, poisoned, and displaced in the process. Much of the tax revenue from handgun and archery equipment sales goes toward hunter education and shooting ranges. An underlying motive for hunter education is to encourage hunting. In the words of USFWS hunt educators, informed hunters have "the best chance of being successful and will probably continue to hunt."[63]

How much do hunters care about conservation? They cared so much they refused to replace poisonous lead shot with steel shot, despite USFWS's claims that the millions of birds who were ingesting lead pellets from lake bottoms were dying slow, painful deaths from lead poisoning. Up to 15% of Minnesota's trumpeter swan population died as a result of ingesting lead shot. And because it lasts for decades, lead shot continues to kill waterfowl for many years after its use is discontinued.[64] This is "conservation"?

There are also many instances of licensed hunters killing more animals than allowed by law. *Newsweek* reports that limit violations were found in 25% of hunters examined at roadblocks in Utah and in 40% of hunters examined in Idaho. Forty-one of 42 Texas hunting clubs examined by federal investigators were found to be in violation of waterfowl hunting laws.[65]

Many species have been hunted into extinction or near-extinction. These include the now-extinct eastern elk, Merriam elk, badlands bighorn, passenger pigeon, heath hen, California parakeet, Eskimo curlew, and ivory billed woodpecker.[66] The grizzly (or brown) bear, leopard, jaguar, Florida panther, key deer, Columbian white-tailed deer, woodland caribou, red wolf, San Joaquin kit fox, ocelot, Utah prairie dog, Sonoran Pronghorn, Lower Keys rabbit, American crocodile, American alligator, whooping crane, and Mississippi Sandhill crane are among those now endangered or threatened.[67] Hunters are many things, but they are not wildlife conservationists.

What About Bowhunting?

Because of the limitations of the bow as a humane weapon
I would have given it up years ago in favor of the camera
except for my [archery] business.

— Fred Bear, bowhunter and President of Bear Archery
(as quoted in *The Bowhunting Alternative*
by Adrian Benke)

The latest craze to hit deer hunting circles in recent years is replacing the hunting rifle with the bow and arrow. Game management officials encourage bowhunting (and the additional revenues from special bowhunting license sales) by offering bowhunting seasons that start earlier and last longer than the gun season.

Bowhunting offers a new form of entertainment to deer hunters. It gives grown men permission to dress up in costumes of full camouflage clothing and black face paint and play "the stealth hunter." For others, the appeal is the new challenge of learning archery, a more demanding skill than shooting firearms. And let's face it, for some reason bowhunting seems more "macho" than blasting a deer with a gun. It's more like killing the deer with your own hands.

While bowhunting may be more fun for hunters, it is grossly more inhumane than firearms for animals:

- **Bowhunting has a higher crippling rate.**
  According to *U.S. News and World Report,* studies over a 15-year period indicate that bowhunters retrieve only 50% of the deer they hit, while gunners retrieve 90% of their hits.[68] *Deer and Deer Hunting* magazine, a magazine by and for deer hunters, reports an even bleaker figure, approximately 67%.[69] Says one bowhunter, "I know many people who took to the bow for hunting but gave it up after crippling losses without any take."[70]

  Bowhunting is so inefficient, it is not advocated as a deer population tool. An Illinois wildlife biologist says, "...bowhunting has never been an effective tool for deer control."[71]

- **Bowhunting kills more wounded animals that get away.**
  Due to the design of the multi-bladed broadhead arrow, most animals wounded by bowhunters eventually die from their wounds. This is because, unlike bullets, the arrowhead clips the animal's hair as it pierces the skin, carrying bacteria into the wound. Wounded animals then die from infection. Deer hit in the abdominal cavity also get infections from lacerated digestive organs.

- **Wounding deaths from bowhunting take longer and are more painful.**
  Deer wounded by arrows rarely bleed to death. They die instead from infections, most commonly a type of gangrene called peritonitis which takes two to five *days* to kill the deer, and a septic infection which takes one to two *weeks* to kill the deer.[72] Says one deer hunter in an article written for other deer hunters:

  > I do not have to tell you what happens in the end when death occurs from wounding. Most of you know. It is, to say the least, a very terrible, suffering death. Gangrene in the wild is the worst of all worlds to a wounded animal.[73]

- **The better shot you are, the higher your crippling rate is.**
  Experience and training do not lower the rate of crippling losses. In *The Bowhunting Alternative,* hunter Adrian Benke says:

  > ...two published studies document *increased* wounding rates for more experienced and successful bowhunters. And another suggests that "crippling is not correctable by increased training or field experience and is a by-product of the sport." In other words, the problem is the weapon itself. It is so inefficient that better hunters wound more deer.[74]

Trophy Hunting

We have never understood why men mount the heads of animals and hang them up to look down on their conquerors. Possibly it feels good to these men to be superior to animals, but does it not seem that if they were sure of it they would not have to prove it? Often a man who is afraid must constantly demonstrate his courage and, in the case of the hunter, must keep a tangible record of his courage.

— John Steinbeck (as quoted in *The Extended Circle*)

A "trophy" is a symbol of victory or achievement. Trophy hunters kill animals and then display their heads, skins, or sometimes the entire stuffed body. Trophy hunters collect and display animal remains much like someone else may collect and display salt and pepper shakers. They also compete with each other to win awards from trophy hunting clubs such as Safari Club International or Game Conservation International. For example, a trophy hunter who kills all 29 animals defined as North American "big game" is honored as having achieved a "Grand Slam."

The purpose of trophy hunting is to obtain an impressive collection, so the rarer an animal, the more desirable it is. Animals on the federal endangered or threatened list are most attractive. Investigative reporter Ted Williams reports that undercover agents broke up a $100 million poaching ring of trophy hunters that spanned at least 19 states. He further details how hunters are killing endangered species under the guise of "science." Federal agents recently caught up with a former curator of a Museum of Natural Sciences who was essentially selling museum "associate curator" licenses to trophy hunters. This allowed the hunters to legally hunt endangered species in other countries. Special agents also discovered someone within their own ranks, an official of Fish and Wildlife's Office of Scientific Authority, who allegedly helped trophy hunters get permits to bring endangered species into the country under the guise of being museum curators. Many other improprieties by trophy hunters were also discovered, such as shooting endangered animals from airplanes, which is illegal.[75]

Trophy hunters don't always have to resort to illegal means to acquire specimens for their collections. One legal way is to obtain permits for special hunts offered by wildlife agencies from time to time. Sometimes these special permits are awarded by lottery and sometimes they go to the highest bidder. One Utah hunter "bagged" a desert bighorn sheep by paying $20,000 for a special permit.[76]

Exotic Game Ranches

Monied trophy hunters can also take their pick of endangered species living on *exotic game ranches*. Perhaps the most perverse of hunting operations, these ranches are exactly what their name implies — enclosed areas where animals native to other continents are shot for sport.

Game ranches are anything but sporting, however. They are little more than shooting galleries for trophy hunters who pay exorbitant fees to add the head or skin of a tame, captive animal to their collections. Many of the animals on game ranches — jaguars, leopards, antelope, giraffes, gazelle, and other "exotic" animals — are former zoo animals or their offspring. Many are prodded out of cages and herded toward waiting "hunters."

A. Achor

At exotic game ranches, hunters can kill tame and endangered animals for a fee.

Hunters are allowed to kill endangered species because ranch operators obtain special permits from the USFWS. It is doubtful that this is what drafters of the Endangered Species Act had in mind when they included the power to issue special permits in exception to the Act.

How many exotic game ranches are there in this country? They are perhaps hunting's best kept secret. The Exotic Wildlife Association, which heads the exotic game ranch industry, places the number at 10,000 nationwide, with approximately 1,000 of them in Texas.[77]

It's Time to Stop Killing for Fun

...the MSPCA has serious concerns that cultural approval of sport hunting as an acceptable recreational activity may have the effect of desensitizing people, particularly the young, to the needless suffering and killing of animals.

— Massachusetts Society for the Prevention of Cruelty to Animals (*Statements of Belief*)

The arguments that hunters put forth to try to justify their bloodsport — conservation, curbing overpopulation, etc. — have no merit. Hunting benefits only the hunter — and those who make money from servicing hunters. Hunting is recreation, done for pleasure.

There are numerous arguments against hunting, all of which were discussed earlier in the chapter:

- Hunting causes needless human injury and death.
- Hunting glorifies violence and teaches insensitivity.
- Hunting is one of two main reasons for the extinction and decline of species.
- Hunting interferes with real conservation efforts.
- Hunting causes undue suffering for animals.
- Hunting does not contribute to human welfare.

It's time to move out of the Dark Ages and outlaw killing for sport.

Killing for Profit

...as long as men massacre animals, they will kill each other.
Indeed, he who sows the seed of murder and pain cannot reap joy and love.

— Pythagoras, 6th Century B.C.

People hunt and kill animals not only for sport, but for the profits to be made from animal skins, body parts, fat, and muscles. In the pursuit of one species, profiteers may kill incidental victims from other species who just happen to be in the way.

Satisfying the Demand for Body Parts

Hunters kill millions of animals every year to satisfy consumer demands for products, none of which are vital to our well-being. Many of the animals killed are in danger of extinction, their scarcity making them even more desirable. Some animals are killed with the blessing of the law, while others are illegally poached.

Here is a sampling of wildlife killed to meet commercial demands:

- **Kangaroos**
  Approximately four million kangaroos, including three species listed as threatened under the U.S. Endangered Species Act, are killed each year for commercial purposes. The United States continues to import kangaroo products.[78]

- **Elephants**
  According to the African Wildlife Foundation, hunters killed over 90,000 African elephants for their ivory tusks in 1989 and an additional 10,000 died as a direct result (mostly orphaned calves). The elephant population has been cut in half over the last

decade.[79]

- **Rhinoceros**
  The rhinoceros population in Kenya has been reduced by 98% in the last 20 years. Rhinos are killed for their horns, which are worth up to $27,000 each, and for their skins, toenails, and genitals, which are regarded by some Asian cultures as necessary ingredients in medicines.[80]

- **Elk**
  Elk antlers are valued as an aphrodisiac in some Asian cultures and can be worth $400 an ounce.[81]

- **Bears**
  Fresh bear gallbladders, used in Asian medical practices, have a reported market value of up to $500.[82] Bearskins are used for rugs.

- **Seals**
  Seals are clubbed to death not only for their fur, but for their penises, the bone of which is used to "treat" impotence in Japan and China.[83]

- **Sea Turtles**
  In Japan, the shells of endangered turtles are used for such "necessities" as eyeglass frames, jewelry, and cigarette lighters.[84]

- **Crocodiles and Snakes**
  The United States buys $200-$250 million in crocodile, snake, and other reptile skin products every year.[85]

Such senseless slaughter of wildlife occurs because a market exists for these products. The United States imports 200 million products manufactured from animals every year.[86] We also legally import hundreds of millions of live animals, mostly exotic birds and tropical fish.

The Endangered Species Act prohibits the import or export of endangered species or products made from endangered species. Still, USFWS confiscates a wide assortment of illegal wildlife products, and it is likely that the majority of illegal products are never discovered by enforcement officers. A trophy hunter unwittingly talking to an undercover agent said that to smuggle body parts of endangered species into the U.S., he relies on the general incompetence of the USFWS.[87] In some cases, falsified papers are used to get live endangered species into the United States. For example, Paraguay, in one reporter's words, "has long been recognized as a sieve through which legally protected animals flow out of South America into the pet trade in Europe, Asia, and North America" with forged papers.[88]

The unnecessary killing of wildlife for trinkets and other superfluous products can only be stopped by (1) outlawing the import of such animal products, (2) cracking down on poachers, exporters, and importers, and (3) providing other economic incentives to countries where the wildlife lives. Addressing the economic realities of countries where wildlife is poached and/or legally killed is critical to saving wildlife. Wealthier nations such as the United States must take some responsibility for redistributing the world's wealth to the benefit of all.

If properly implemented and supervised, *eco-tourism* can in some instances be a viable economic alternative to slaughter. Eco-tourism refers to ecologically-sound travel ventures, such as viewing wildlife in natural habitat. This encourages the formation of wilderness parks and preserves which protect wildlife. In 1989, Prince Edward Island and Nova Scotia made about 20% more money from tourists who came to view baby harp seals in their natural habitat than they ever made from hunters who came to kill the seals.[89] In Kenya, a live elephant is worth around $3,000 per year to the local economy in tourism.[90]

Eco-tourism must be strictly regulated, however, to guarantee that it doesn't become what it's trying to prevent. Visits by too many people can destroy natural environments and greatly disturb wildlife. The strictest of cautions must be exercised and these programs must be operated by people who are experts on animals and habitat.

Commercial Fishing and Whaling

Many people who eat fish think of it as a "kinder" form of meat, one that doesn't involve as much cruelty as devouring, say, a chicken or pig. This way of thinking is wrong on not one, but two, counts.

Fish are not at all what most of us think they are. They are sensitive creatures who respond to pain, perceived danger, and safety. They have been observed caring for injured companions and have exhibited behavior that indicates psychological states such as depression in response to loss. Experimenters who have deliberately threatened fish conclude that fish do indeed experience what can only be interpreted as fear.[91]

In addition, fishing affects more than fish. The well-publicized fate of dolphins caught in tuna nets is by now a familiar story. Because some tuna swim underneath dolphin, tuna fishers look for dolphin and cast their nets over them in efforts to catch the tuna swimming beneath. Here's how the Sea Shepherd Conservation Society, which has witnessed firsthand accounts of tuna fishing, recently described this practice, called "fishing on porpoise":

> After locating the dolphins with a helicopter, the seiner dispatches speed boats to encircle the dolphins. Using small explosive discharges, the fishermen cause the dolphins to panic and herd them into a tight circle. The ponga boat then encircles the frightened cetaceans with the one mile long purse seine net, so-called because it can be closed at the bottom like a purse. Once the net is set, the bottom is closed and the tuna are caught. The dolphins are just incidental victims. They are soon released — excepting those who have drowned in the net or have had a flipper or a tail amputated by the net and

cables or have been crushed in the power blocks.[92]

The captain of one tuna vessel told Sea Shepherd that he had killed about a thousand dolphins during a single trip. Annually, from 100,000 to 250,000 dolphins die in nets set to catch tuna.

Sea birds, seals, turtles, sharks, whales, and other animals are also victims of fishing nets. Annually, 100,000 sea mammals and one million sea birds become entangled in driftnets and take up to 45 minutes to die. As many as 50,000 Northern fur seals accidentally die in discarded driftnets each year.[93] Approximately 11,000 sea turtles die in trawls (nets) used to catch shrimp, and for every pound of shrimp caught, nine pounds of fish are inadvertently killed and dumped back into the ocean.[94]

Although commercial whaling has been prohibited by the International Whaling Commission (IWC) since 1985, many countries including Iceland, Norway, Spain, Chile, and Japan have continued to kill whales for their "exotic" meat. Since the prohibition, 13,650 commercial whale kills have been recorded. Residents of the Faeroe Islands (Danish islands that lie between Iceland and Scotland) annually kill one to three thousand pilot whales by driving them onto the shore and sawing through the still-conscious whales with knives.[95] Other whalers, including Japanese whalers, use painful exploding harpoons to kill whales.[96]

Fur – The Skin Off Their Backs

Don't buy fur. Get a Rolex or a life.

— Sign at the March for the Animals, June 1990

Anyone who doubts the effectiveness of the animal rights movement need only look to the fur industry for proof. Since anti-fur campaigns began, the billion-dollar fur industry in this country has shrunk to a mere shadow of itself. Fur salons across the country and the world have closed their doors. Prestigious department stores, such as Harrod's of London, have phased out their fur departments. Popular mail-order catalogs, such as Spiegel and Sears, no longer offer fur items. And over 500 New York fur manufacturers have vanished in the last 12 years.[97]

Aspen, Colorado even had a proposed ban on fur sales before the voters recently. Although 75% of residents polled said they disapproved of wearing fur, the ban was voted down, reportedly because residents feared expensive lawsuits from furriers if the ban passed.[98]

What's put a damper on the thirst for fur? The truth. Animal advocates have merely told the public the facts about fur, facts such as these:

- Over 100 million wild animals are killed for their pelts every year.[99]
- Many animals killed for their pelts have become endangered or have vanished altogether from some locales.
- According to the International Society for Animal Rights, Inc., to make one fur garment, it takes:[100]

400 squirrels	80 sables	30 raccoons
240 ermine	70 skunks	26 fishers
200 chinchillas	50 martens	22 bobcats
160 hamsters	45 broadtail lambs	12 lynx
120 muskrats	40 opossums	5 wolves

- Fur trapping is a horribly inhumane practice that Great Britain has outlawed (see The Trappings of "Glamour," below).
- The lives and deaths of animals raised for their pelts is far from pretty (see Fur Farms, below).

Unfortunately, legislators have not been as responsive to public opinion as has the private sector. Hunting, trapping, and gun lobbies have joined efforts to keep fur hunting, trapping, and ranching legal. Despite public pressure, these hideous practices continue.

■ Hunting for a Fur

Many of us remember the graphic clubbing to death of white-furred baby harp seals that set off a flurry of public outcry a few years ago. As a result, the killing of baby seals was banned. But what most of us don't realize is that it is still legal to kill seal pups who are only a few days older than the white-coated babies.

In Canada, Alaska, South Africa, South America, and elsewhere, the slaughter of seals continues. The Ministry of Fisheries and Oceans in Canada reported that in the 1988 season, hunters legally killed more than 80,000 seals.[101] The Sea Shepherd Conservation Society reports 1990's figure for Canada at 60,000 pups. In African Namibia, hunters have killed 11,700 seals in the last year, many on a so-called Seal Reserve.[102] Seals as young as 25 days old are clubbed to death while on shore or shot while in the water. Who's buying the pelts of these babies? Mostly Japan and Taiwan. Unfortunately, Asian countries have become the new market for furs, with Japan leading the way.

■ The Trappings of "Glamour"

Trapping is a barbaric practice that causes intense suffering for millions of animals each year. Although outlawed in Great Britain, trapping continues to receive government approval and support in the United States and many other countries. Trapping is allowed in over 90 "refuges" in our federal National Wildlife Refuge System.

Trappers sometimes try to justify their cruelty by claiming that trapping is a way to control rabies or wildlife overpopulation. According to the National Academy of Sciences, trapping reduces neither rabies incidence nor wildlife reservoirs.[103]

Eighty-seven percent of animals trapped in the U.S.[104] —approximately 40 million per year according to the Association of Veterinarians for Animal Rights[105] — are victims of the steel-jaw leghold trap. The steel-jaw leghold trap is a spring-loaded trap designed to clamp around the leg of an animal who steps into it. Sometimes multiple traps are set in the same area to entrap more than one appendage. What does a leghold trap feel like? Friends of Animals suggests that you can get a "feel for fur" by slamming your fingers in a car door.

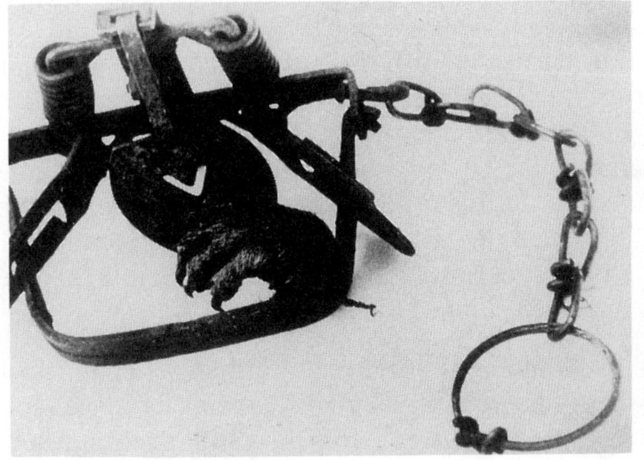
People for the Ethical Treatment of Animals

The steel-jaw leghold trap.

Painful as leghold traps are, they aren't designed to kill their victims. Their purpose is to snare and hold the animal until the trapper can return to finish him or her off. By law, trappers are supposed to check traps every 48 hours, but there is little enforcement of this rule. Trapped animals may experience thirst, hunger, exposure to elements, and attack by other animals while waiting for the trapper to return to club or suffocate them.

Trapped animals also try in vain to free themselves from the trap. Those trapped for even a few minutes try to escape by struggling, gnawing at the trap, or gnawing at their own flesh, attempting to chew off the trapped paw(s). In one of its brochures, the Society for Animal Rights (now called International Society for Animal Rights, Inc.) quotes a Canadian Wildlife Service report as follows:

> The stomachs of (trapped) arctic foxes...often contain parts of their own bodies. They may swallow fragments of their teeth broken off in biting the trap, and sometimes part of a mangled foot; almost every stomach contains some fox fur, and a considerable number contain pieces of skin, claws, or bits of bone.[106]

Otters, ermine, and minks in particular sometimes struggle so violently to free themselves from the leghold trap that they kill themselves in the process. Animals who do succeed in escaping by chewing off their paws — as many as 27% for many species — are likely to suffer blood loss, infection, blood poisoning, or gangrene leading to death.[107]

Animals unable to escape the trap must eventually face the trapper's return. In the booklet *Get Set to Trap,* the California Department of Fish and Game instructs kids who are first-time trappers in the "proper" methods for killing wildlife, as follows:

> Most furbearers can be quickly and humanely killed by first sharply striking them on the skull [with a heavy iron pipe or an axe handle]. It is highly recommended that the animal be struck two times, once to render it unconscious and again to render it either dead or comatose. To ensure death, pin the head with one foot and stand on the chest (area near the heart) of the animal with the other foot for several minutes...Furbearers trapped in the water may also be struck on the head and then drowned.[108]

In addition to the millions of targeted animals snared by leghold traps every year, five million "trash" animals — unintentional catches — also become victims of leghold traps.[109] "Trash" animals include dogs, cats, and birds, among others. In one coyote-trapping program in the United States, leghold traps snared almost 10 times as many "trash" animals as coyotes. In this instance, "trash" animals included bobcat, golden eagles, and sheep.[110] What happens to the "trash" animals unintentionally killed by leghold traps? In one instance, trappers sold cat corpses to a South Dakota man who paid them $2 per animal. The man then skinned the cats.[111]

Due to its inherent cruelty, more than 70 countries have banned the leghold trap. The powerful fur, trapping, and gun lobbies have prevented the passage of similar legislation by the United States government. Still, some states have taken the initiative. New Jersey has banned its use, and other states, including Rhode Island, Massachusetts, Florida, and South Carolina, have placed restrictions on the use of leghold traps.[112]

In addition to the leghold trap, trappers also sometimes employ a Conibear trap, named after its inventor. The Conibear is a "whole body" trap designed to snap shut around an animal's head, neck, or body, much like a conventional mousetrap. Although intended to kill its victim, the Conibear fails to do so in 40% to 60% of cases. Instead, trapped animals suffer slow, agonizing deaths. The Humane Society of the United States reports that a Doberman who wandered into a Conibear trap suffered for as long as 18 hours with the trap clinched around her neck before she finally suffocated. There is nothing humane about these traps.

■ Fur Farms

Most U.S. fur comes from fur farms or ranches. In some people's minds, wearing fur from ranched animals is acceptable since the animals are specifically bred and raised for their pelts. The truth is, animals raised for their skins suffer even more horribly than those who are trapped for theirs. Here are some of the facts that fur wearers would rather not know.

- Fur farming condemns millions of foxes, beavers, minks, sables, ocelots, rabbits, chinchillas, and other animals to lifelong confinement in tiny wire cages with nothing to do and no room to move. Enforced confinement and the lack of privacy are shattering to naturally wild animals, such as fox and mink, who often exhibit neurotic behaviors such as compulsive movements and self-mutilation when caged.[113]
- Like food animals, those raised for their skins receive no protection from the federal Animal Welfare Act.

- Fur farms are a cross between factory farms (discussed in Chapter 5) and puppy mills (discussed in Chapter 3). They are breeding factories that use intensive confinement methods to maximize output. Animals are simply a means to an end; there is no regard for their mental, emotional, or physical well-being.

- Conditions in fur farms are of no consequence unless they affect the fur itself. Farmed animals suffer thirst, disease, deformity, and exposure to extreme elements. Some animals suffer frost-bite while others are victims of heat exhaustion. By U.S. mink farmers' own figures, 45,000 animals died from heat stress in 1987, according to People for the Ethical Treatment of Animals.[114]

- There are many stories of unsuccessful fur farmers simply abandoning the farms, leaving caged animals to starve to death. Some animals found in these predicaments have been rescued; for others, it was too late.

- Genetic tinkering and breeding for fur color leaves many animals with crippling deformities and conditions such as blindness, deafness, neck spasms, painfully contracted uteruses, and susceptibility to disease.

- No laws dictate the killing of animals on fur farms. The least expensive methods are the most appealing. Some common methods are:

  - Carbon monoxide poisoning, often from the exhaust of a running motor vehicle. The unfiltered, uncooled exhaust burns the eyes and lungs of its victims before loss of consciousness sets in.

  - Strychnine poisoning, which causes painful muscle cramping, leading to suffocation because of an inability to breathe.

  - Electrocution, which causes extreme pain for up to 20 seconds because the current does not pass through the brain.

  - Suffocation by crushing the chest. One fur company, Jindo, places a fox between two boards and squeezes the boards together until the fox eventually suffocates.

  - Breaking the neck, particularly with small animals such as mink. An animal advocate conducting an undercover investigation of fur farms reports:

    > One particular farm in Montana where we witnessed and documented the neck-breaking of over one hundred mink was particularly horrific. Being a small operation, the "farmer" felt comfortable literally bending these animals' necks backward, and crushing down until the sound of vertebrae popping was heard over the animals' screams. Sometimes he failed, instead breaking the jaw, only to have the crippled, yet conscious animal try to crawl away to safety.[115]

As the anti-fur campaign of The Humane Society of the United States admonishes, "You should be ashamed to wear fur." Period.

Animal Damage Control – Your Tax Dollars at Work

The real issue with the whole ADC program is public money used to kill public wildlife, often on public land, with no public input — all to benefit a handful of heavily subsidized ranchers and farmers.

— Tom Woods, chairman of Arizona Game and Fish Commission
(Copyright 1990, *U.S. News and World Report*, February 5, 1990)

The Animal Damage Control (ADC) program is a federal program operated by the U.S. Department of Agriculture (USDA). Its purpose is to control "nuisance" wildlife, with most of its budget going to help farmers and ranchers eliminate animals who feed on crops, kill livestock, or otherwise compete with their profits. Critics of ADC claim that it is a waste of money and lives. They have a strong argument.

A former "hired gun" for the ADC program says, "I started questioning why we were having to kill all these animals, and nobody gave me any good answers...It was just a total waste of life."[116] Another ADC employee, a trapper, reportedly "resigned in disgust" at the extreme and senseless massacre of coyotes.[117] Greenpeace reports that in 1990, the USDA spent $26 million on the ADC program. A portion of that budget went to poison, trap, shoot, burn, blow up, club, and sic dogs on:[118]

86,626 coyotes	3,675 raccoons	506 mountain lions	80 wolves
9,703 beavers	1,300 badgers	500 prairie dogs	
7,151 foxes	1,200 bobcats	236 black bears	

Kills were as high as 133,000 mammals and two million birds in 1989, and 123,000 mammals and four million birds in 1988.[119] Incidental kills of nontargeted animals is also frequent. In 1988, kills included 400 domestic dogs and 100 domestic cats.[120]

States also add their own money to ADC funds to assist with killings in their jurisdictions. In 1988, California paid $3.2 million to exterminate 32,368 mammals believed responsible for causing $1.4 million in damage.[121] It would have been cheaper and more humane to simply reimburse farmers and ranchers for their losses.

Predators do kill livestock; after all, livestock grazing has taken over almost 70% of rangeland previously home to wild animals.[122] One expert, a former coyote trapper, says that predators can play a positive role, pointing out that coyotes help keep the rodent population in check and mostly prey on sick or dying cattle or deer.[123]

Other than killing the predators, what can be done? Plenty. Dogs, llamas, and donkeys are all proven deterrents to predation. Dogs have successfully guarded livestock for over 1,000 years. Llamas are fearless animals who are now being utilized by sheep farmers to successfully ward off coyotes. Similarly, donkeys, known for their "stubbornness," intimidate predators. Other nonlethal methods for discouraging livestock kills are physical barriers such as predator-proof fencing, noise, and strobe devices. Contraception is also a viable method for controlling predator populations. However, one author reports, "The USDA's National Advisory Committee on Animal Damage Control has not permitted even the mention of fertility control, chemosterilization, or other nonlethal techniques in their recommendations to the Secretary of Agriculture."[124]

In the past, at least a fraction of ADC funds have been budgeted for nonlethal remedies, but according to The Humane Society of the United States, the USDA funneled almost the entire 1991 through 1994 research budget into poisons, a method lethal not only to predators but to other animals and to the environment.[125] It appears that the USDA cares about ensuring the safety of livestock regardless of the cost to anyone or anything else. An acting deputy administrator for the ADC program says, "We serve agriculture. We want to see more meat, wool, sunflowers, and catfish reach the market."[126]

Backyard Wildlife

The wildlife familiar to most of us is the backyard variety — birds, squirrels, chipmunks, rabbits, and other fuzzy creatures. Most of these critters are a welcome addition to our yards, but sometimes they are unwelcome visitors to our attics, gardens, and yards.

Peaceful coexistence with wildlife is a combination of knowledge, willingness, and creativity. For example, officials of the University of Florida in Gainesville, plagued with bats roosting in their sports stadiums, have built a "bat house" next to a wildlife sanctuary that adjoins the campus. The University has also hired an expert to humanely relocate the bats from the stadiums to the bat house. This kind of concern and ingenuity is to be applauded.

Here are some things to keep in mind about coexisting with our nonhuman neighbors:*

- **Lawn Care Can Be Poisonous**
  Chemical lawn care products threaten not only wildlife, but companion animals, ground water, and people. Avoid them at all costs. Use natural products instead of poisonous chemicals.

- **Physical Barriers**
  Fences, screens, nets, and similar barriers are often effective in keeping wildlife out of "off limits" areas. Keeping unwelcomed animals out of your house or garage is always easier than evicting them after they have settled in.

---

* *The Pocket Guide to the Humane Control of Wildlife in Cities and Towns,* published by The Humane Society of the United States, offers more suggestions for specific situations. See the Hunting & Wildlife section of Chapter 13, "Further Reading," for ordering information.

Squirrels and other "backyard wild-life" enrich our lives.

- **Sights, Sounds, and Scents**
  A harmless and clever way to deter unwanted visitors is to employ a commercial or homemade product to which animals have a natural aversion. Human or dog hair sprinkled around a garden will ward off some nibblers. Balloons or plastic "predators" are effective scarecrows for some birds and mammals. If deer nibbling on ornamental plants is a problem, plant foliage that is less tasty to deer, such as holly, boxwood, English ivy, barberry, daffodil, iris, spruce, fir, or cactus.[127]

- **Relocation**
  When all else fails, using a humane trap to capture an animal and then releasing him in a safe, distant location can be an answer. This should only be a last resort, though, since it so severely disrupts the animal's life and that of his family. For humane traps, see the Wildlife Traps, Deterrents, & Attractors section of Chapter 12, "Products and Services."

- **Professional "Pest" Control**
  If you feel it necessary to hire a professional to help with your wildlife problems, keep in mind that while some professionals are now oriented toward humane disposition of animals, others still employ poisons or inhumane traps. Be sure to ask about their methods and the eventual destination of trapped animals. Check around till you find someone who meets your humane standards.

Pro-Hunting/Trapping Organizations

Have you ever wondered about an organization's stance on hunting or trapping? Here's a list of organizations that support these activities. There's also a list containing organizations that play the middle ground by neither openly supporting nor opposing hunting and/or trapping.

If you wonder about a group that's not on the list, contact the group in question and ask them for their stance.

Organizations That Support Hunting/Trapping (In All or Some Instances)

The following organizations condone hunting and/or trapping some or all of the time:

AFL-CIO (pro-trapping)

American Fur Resources Institute

American Fur Resources Foundation

Atlantic Waterfowl Council

Boone and Crockett Club

Deer Unlimited

Ducks Unlimited

Exotic Wildlife Association (exotic game ranches)

Foundation for North American Wild Sheep

Game Conservation International

Izaak Walton League of America, Inc.

Max McGraw Wildlife Foundation

National Audubon Society

National Rifle Association

National Trappers Association

National Waterfowl Council

National Wild Turkey Association

National Wildlife Federation (affiliates include hunting and trapping organizations)

The Nature Conservancy (has used both hunting and trapping to "manage" wildlife on some of its preserves)

Quail Unlimited

Ruffed Grouse Society (big-game hunting group)

Safari Club International (big-game hunting group)

Sierra Club (supports "regulated periodic hunting or fishing" to promote "optimum diversity and numbers of wildlife")

Society for the Conservation of Bighorn Sheep (the president of this group placed hunt saboteurs under citizen's arrest for disrupting a bighorn hunt)

Stripers Unlimited

Trout Unlimited

Whitetails Unlimited

The Wilderness Society

Wildlife Conservation Fund of America (legal defense, research, and education arm of the National Rifle Association)

Wildlife Legislative Fund of America (legislative and political arm of the National Rifle Association)

World Wildlife Fund and World Wide Fund for Animals (its president, Prince Philip, has been an avid hunter throughout his lifetime)

Organizations That Do Not Take a Stand on Hunting/Trapping

The following organizations neither support nor oppose hunting and/or trapping. If you oppose hunting, you may want to redirect contributions to groups that openly work to stop hunting and/or trapping. If you do this, let the organizations listed here know why you have chosen to send your money elsewhere.

American Forestry Association

American Wildlife Institute

Campfire Club

Defenders of Wildlife (opposes hurtful trapping but evaluates hunting on a case-by-case basis, sometimes opposing it and sometimes taking no position on it)

National Geographic Society

Wildlife Conservation International (New York Zoological Society)

The Wildlife Society

Corporate Sponsors of Hunting

Be on the lookout for corporations that sponsor hunting-related events and let them know how you feel. Here are a couple of examples:

- *Vegetarian Times* reports that Northeast Michigan McDonald's restaurants have offered free drinks to licensed hunters and free meals to those who can produce a dead deer.
- Ralston Purina has sponsored a United Kennel Clubs Nite Hunt Coonhound Award. This raccoon ("coon") hunt involves luring raccoons with bait and siccing dogs on them.

How You Can Help

◆ **Clean up your act.**
If you live near a beach, organize a "beach clean-up" party to remove plastic and other life-threatening debris from shorelines. If you don't live near water, organize a "roadside clean-up" party. Invite the media to participate.

◆ **Don't get hooked.**
Fishing practices result in the deaths of numerous marine mammals. Avoiding fish saves not only the fish's life, but may save that of a turtle, porpoise, seal, or other unfortunate creature. Even tuna marked "dolphin safe" is no guarantee. Also, according to the Sea Shepherd Conservation Society, there's been a "dangerous decline in tuna populations."[128] Tuna also need your protection.

◆ **Be a compassionate shopper.**
Refuse to buy products made from animal parts, skins, feathers, shells, etc. Don't buy parrots or other "exotic" animals as pets.

◆ **Give them the coat off your back.**
Donate all fur items to animal rights groups for use in protests, or ask your local wildlife shelter if the fur could be useful in rehabilitating animals (such as giving orphaned babies something furry to cuddle up next to). If you donate a fur coat to the wildlife shelter, cut it up into pieces to guarantee that it is used as intended.

◆ **Get some field experience.**
Try following in the footsteps of hunt saboteurs (literally). Hunt saboteurs use nonviolent, direct action tactics to intervene in the field between the hunter and the hunted. For example, one "weapon" of choice for hunt saboteurs is the airhorn, which chases potential victims away from hunters. Sabotaging hunts is not a new concept. For centuries, people who opposed animal cruelty, including the Archbishop of Canterbury and many saints, have reportedly rescued animals from hunters.[129]

Are hunt saboteurs effective? Yes, so much so that a majority of states have quickly passed "hunter harassment" laws, designed to "protect" hunters from anyone who "interferes" with a hunter's "right" to kill animals. This includes scaring animals away from hunters or quietly talking with hunters on public lands. Conceivably, these laws could make it unlawful to peacefully walk in the woods and rustle leaves anytime during hunting season.

The unconstitutionality of these laws, which protect the interests of hunters while violating the first amendment rights of nonhunters, have been challenged and overturned in Wisconsin, Connecticut, and Idaho Still, the hunting and gun lobbies are very strong, and the fight is far from over. Animal advocates need to continue to challenge these laws.

- **Make refuges live up to their names.**
  Support the Wildlife Refuge Reform Coalition, a collection of animal protection groups working to pass legislation to make sport hunting and trapping illegal in our National Wildlife Refuges. To help or for information, contact the Wildlife Refuge Reform Coalition, P.O. Box 18414, Washington, D.C. 20036-8414, (202) 778-6145.

- **Give 'em both barrels.**
  Write a card or letter to magazines, commercial sponsors, and television shows that advertise, glamorize, or otherwise promote fur, hunting, or trapping.

- **Let them know Nugent is "no gent."**
  Join Friends of Animals (FoA) in a nationwide boycott against Ted Nugent, rock musician and crazed "blower away" of countless animals. Nugent has made a video of his gruesome hunting exploits, and publishes a magazine titled *Bow Hunter.* Write to Epic Records (a subsidiary of Columbia Record Company) to let them know you are boycotting any Nugent recording. Also write or call radio stations and music stores, and ask them to join the boycott.

Resources for Helping Wildlife

For products and services related to wildlife, see the following sections of Chapter 12: Activist Aids, Clubs for Kids & Young Adults, Hotlines, Radio & Television Programming, Stamps & Stickers, Toys, Travel Services, Videos & Films, and Wildlife Traps, Deterrents, & Attractors.

For additional reading on endangered species, hunting, trapping, and wildlife, see the Hunting & Wildlife section of Chapter 13.

The following organizations work to protect, rehabilitate, or provide sanctuary for wildlife. See Chapter 10 for a description of these and other organizations that help wildlife. *Note: See the state listings in Chapter 10 for additional organizations.*

- **General (see other categories for specific species or interests)**
  African Wildlife Foundation (D.C.), Alaska Wildlife Alliance (AK), Biodiversity Legal Foundation (CO), Elsa Wild Animal Appeal (IL), Environmental Investigation Agency U.S. (D.C.), Friends of Animals (CT), Fund for Animals, Inc. (NY), International Fund for Animal Welfare (MA), International Wildlife Coalition (MA), National Institute for Urban Wildlife

(WV), Predator Project (MT), Sierra Club Legal Defense Fund (CA), Wildlife Preservation Trust International (PA), World Pets Society (CA)

- **Birds**

  See also the wildlife rehabilitators listed under each state in Chapter 10.

  Bird Rescue/York County (PA), The Bird Sanctuary (CA), Bird Treatment and Learning Center (AK), Cascades Raptor Center (OR), Coalition to Protect the Destruction of Canada Geese (NY), Delaware Valley Raptor Center (PA), Florida Keys Wild Bird Center (FL), Free Flight Bird and Marine Mammal Rehabilitation (OR), Hawk Watch International (UT), International Crane Foundation (WI), Ironside Bird Rescue—raptors & others (WY), National Foundation to Protect America's Eagles (TN), Northlook Wild Bird Rescue (OH), Pelican Man's Bird Sanctuary (FL), Pembina Hills Wildlife Rehabilitation Center—raptors, especially owls, & others (ND), Safe Harbor Rehabilitation—raptors, owls (FL), Suncoast Seabird Sanctuary, Inc. (FL), Westlake Bird Sanctuary and Rehabilitation Center (LA), West Virginia Raptor Rehabilitation Center (WV), Wild Bird Care and Rehabilitation Fund (CA), World Bird Sanctuary (MO)

- **Fur (Trapping and Fur Farms)**

  Animal Emancipation, Inc. (CA), Aspen Society for Animal Rights (CO), Coalition to Abolish the Fur Trade (TN), Coalition to Protect Animals in Parks and Refuges (NY), Fund for Animals, Inc. (NY), Fur-Bearer Defenders (CA), Help Abolish Leghold Traps (AZ), Lynx Educational Fund for Animal Welfare (CA), Noah's Friends Unlimited (VA), People for the Ethical Treatment of Animals (VA), Santa Cruz Society for the Prevention of Cruelty to Animals—steel-jaw leghold trap ban (CA), Wildlife Damage Review—ADC program (AZ), Wildlife Refuge Reform Coalition (D.C.)

- **Hunting**

  Coalition to Protect Animals in Parks and Refuges (NY), Committee to Abolish Sport Hunting (NY), Fund for Animals, Inc. (NY), Fur-Bearer Defenders (CA), Hunt Saboteurs (CA), Lifeforce (CA), Non-Hunters Rights Alliance (CT), Wildlife Refuge Reform Coalition (D.C.)

- **Marine Animals**

  Alaska Wildlife Alliance (AK), American Cetacean Society (CA), Animal Alliance—sea turtles (NM), California Marine Mammal Center (CA), CCAW, Inc. (FL), Center for Marine Conservation (D.C.), Cetacean Society International (CT), Cousteau Society, Inc. (VA), Dolphin Alliance (FL), Dolphin Freedom Foundation (FL), Dolphin Network (CA), Earth Island Institute/Dolphin Project (CA), Earthtrust (HI), Eco-Solar, Inc.—sea turtles (MA), Free Flight Bird and Marine Mammal Rehabilitation (OR), Friends of the Sea Lion (CA), Friends of the Sea Otter (CA), Friends of Whales (FL), Greenpeace (D.C.), International Dolphin Project (CA), International Wildlife Coalition (MA), Into the Blue—dolphins (FL), Lifeforce (CA), Marine and Wildlife Rescue Station (CA), Monitor Consortium (D.C.), Ocean Impact Foundation/Marine-Wildlife Care Center (FL), Preservation of Amazon River Dolphins (CA), Save Our Sealife Committee (FL), Save the Whales (CA), Save the Manatee Club, Inc. (FL), Sea Shepherd Conservation Society (CA), Sea Turtle Survival League (FL), South Carolina Association for Marine Mammal Protection (SC), Whale Rescue Team (CA)

- **Miscellaneous Species (not mentioned in other categories)**

  Advocates for Forgotten Wildlife—invertebrates (NJ), Bat Conservation International, Inc.

(TX), Desert Tortoise Preserve Committee, Inc. (CA), Friends of Beaversprite—beavers (NY), Great Bear Foundation (MT), Grizzly Bear Task Force (MT), International Crane Foundation (WI), International Snow Leopard Trust (WA), Kentucky Wildlife-Line, Inc.—bobcats (KY), Leave It to the Beavers (NH), Live Elephant, Inc. (MA), Mountain Lion Foundation (CA), National Opossum Society (CA), New York Turtle and Tortoise Society (NJ), Opossum Society of California (CA), Prairie Dog Rescue, Inc. (CO), Reptile Rescue (TX), The Rhino Trust (OR), Save the Florida Panther (FL), San Diego Bat Conservation (CA), Society of Kind Understanding for Not Killing Skunks (CA), Unexpected Wildlife Refuge—beavers (NY)

- **Primates**
  African Wildlife Foundation (D.C.), Friends of the Silver River Monkeys (FL), Gorilla Foundation (CA), International Primate Protection League (SC), Jane Goodall Institute (CT), Orangutan Foundation (CA), Primarily Primates, Inc. (TX)

- **Wild Horses or Burros**
  Amberwood—wild burros (GA), American Mustang and Burro Association, Inc. (CA), Colorado Horse Rescue (CO), Corolla Wild Horse Fund (NC), International Society for the Protection of Mustangs and Burros (AZ), PHARM, Inc.—mustangs (MA), Wild Horse and Burro Sanctuary (CA), Wild Horse Discovery Center (CA), Wild Horse Organized Assistance (NV)

- **Wildlife Rehabilitation (not mentioned elsewhere)**
  See also the wildlife rehabilitators and sanctuaries listed under each state in Chapter 10, the sanctuaries listed in the Resources section of Chapter 8, "Entertainment," and the other categories in this section (Birds, Primates, etc.).
  American Wildlife Rescue Service, Inc. (CA), Animal Rehabilitation Center, Inc. (TX), Associated Humane Societies, Inc. (NJ), The Association Of Sanctuaries, Inc. (CA, TX), International Wildlife Rehabilitation Council (CA), National Gneiser Wildlife Rehabilitation Center (CO), National Wildlife Rehabilitators Association (MN), North American Wildlife Association (CT), Wildlife Rescue and Rehabilitation, Inc. (TX), Wildlife Waystation (CA)

- **Wolf Hybrids**
  Coalition of All-Breed Rescue of Arizona (AZ), Where Wolves Rescue (AZ)

- **Wolves**
  Clem and Jethro Lecture Service (NM), Help Our Wolves Live (MN), International Foundation for the Protection of the Wolf (WA), International Wolf Center (MN), Mission: Wolf (CO), Preserve Arizona's Wolves (AZ), Project Wolf USA (WA), Sinapu (CO), Timber Wolf Preservation Society (WI), Wolf Action Group (MT), Wolf Haven International (WA), Wolf Lifeline, Inc. (CA), Wolf Mountain Sanctuary (CA), Wolf Park (IN), Wolf Sanctuary/Wild Canid Survival and Research Center (MO), Wolf Song of Alaska (AK)

Conclusion

Wildlife in this country and around the world is in serious trouble. Human overpopulation, pollution, modern fishing practices, hunting, trapping, and the demand for products made from animals are all contributing to the demise of wild animals. Laws designed to protect animals are often fraught with loopholes. State and federal agencies and departments are not only ineffective in protecting wildlife, but often contribute to their demise. Tax dollars subsidize hunting, trapping, and other lethal "wildlife management" practices on public lands, including the National Wildlife Refuges. Marine mammals and endangered species continue to die at an alarming rate, due largely to hunting and commercial fishing. Sport hunters and trappers kill millions of animals every year, teaching youngsters that inflicting pain and suffering for fun is acceptable "recreation."

It doesn't have to be this way. With proper enforcement of existing legislation and the introduction of new legislation, wildlife still has a chance. But once it's gone, it's gone. As we're hearing more and more these days, "extinct is forever."

Wildlife in Crisis

At a Glance

Did you know:

- There are almost 800 known species of endangered and threatened wildlife. Habitat destruction and hunting are the two main reasons for the extinction and decline of wildlife species.
- Sport hunting is allowed on over half of the refuges in our National Wildlife Refuge System, and trapping is allowed in over a quarter of the refuges. Many of our National Parks also allow hunting and trapping.
- Hunting is a purely recreational activity that interferes with real conservation efforts, causes undue suffering for animals, causes needless human injury and death, and glorifies violence.
- Commercial fishing and pollution kill countless marine mammals and birds every year.
- Over 100 million animals die horrible deaths in traps or in fur farms every year to supply fur products to consumers.
- Millions of tax dollars fund the extermination of hundreds of thousands of mammals and millions of birds every year for a USDA program designed to help farmers and ranchers.
- Wildlife protection laws such as the Endangered Species Act and the Marine Mammal Protection Act look good on paper but are ineffectively enforced and offer little real protection to animals.

Chapter 8

Animals in Entertainment

Are We Having Fun Yet?

A. Achor

No animal should suffer just to make an audience smile.

— Casey Kasem, radio personality

Animals fascinate us. Not surprisingly, many forms of entertainment involve animals — circuses, rodeos, zoos, aquariums, racing, and movies, to name a few. But when animals are part of the entertainment, the admission fee isn't the only price paid. Performing animals pay a high price for our "entertainment."

Unlike human performers, animal performers don't choose their profession; they don't thrill at the roar of the crowd or dream of fame and fortune. Animal performers are captives. The arenas in which they are forced to spend their lives are as unnatural to them as their natural environment would be to us.

In this chapter, we'll look at some of the ways humans use animals for amusement, and what's in it for the animals.

When the Circus (or Other Act) Comes to Town

We traditionally think of the circus as a happy place, full of excitement and pageantry. This may be true on the outside, but a look behind the scenes reveals a different world.

The "Two-By-Four" Training Method

Remember going to the circus and seeing tigers jump through flaming hoops? How about elephants balancing on one foot? Stop for a moment and consider: What incites an animal do something unnatural, even dangerous, such as jumping through flames? Animal trainers would like for the public to believe that animals are coaxed into such behaviors with the promise of rewards. The truth is that animals perform because they fear punishment.

Dominance, subservience, and pain are integral parts of the training process. In one former trainer's words:

> A minimum of intelligence and a maximum of force are employed in order to compel blind obedience. In professional circles this is known as the "make 'em or break 'em" technique. The animal's resistance is so broken down and its spontaneity and initiative so dulled that it supinely does whatever the trainer demands. With its thinking and natural impulses walled off, it becomes a four-legged slave, submissively serving the moods and whims of the human ego that is playing God to it.[1]

Primatologist Dr. Roger S. Fouts calls the circus tradition in training the "two-by-four technique." In other words, the animal is beaten into submission.[2] Eye-witness reports of animal trainers include the following:

- In Yellow Springs, Ohio, a circus-goer witnessed a performer with the Kelly Miller Brothers Circus (based in Hugo, Oklahoma) repeatedly and forcefully strike an elephant in the face with a large rod for no apparent reason. The elephant and performer had just emerged from performing in the Big Top, and the trainer was unaware that anyone was watching. When confronted with the action, the trainer denied it.
- Eye-witnesses report that the training tools at the Ringling Brothers Circus include whips and electric prods.[3] The Washington D.C. Humane Society observed animals traveling with the Ringling Brothers Circus being unloaded and report "callousness and beatings given for no apparent reason," "elephants with fresh sores and old scarring apparently from hook punctures," "several handlers using their elephant hooks to repeatedly and forcefully beat elephants who were merely walking in line," and animals "appearing frantic for food and water."[4]
- One of the Ringling Bothers' world-famous animal trainers, Gunther Gebel-Williams, was videotaped in Cincinnati, Ohio beating a camel in the face with a whip.[5]
- A former animal trainer who worked in the television and motion picture industry for over 20 years witnessed elephants being electroshocked in the ears, mouth, and anus,

and bears having their noses broken and feet burned by trainers who were establishing "dominance."[6]

- Las Vegas nightclub performer Bobby Berosini has been videotaped along with his "helpers" holding and beating the orangutans in his nightclub act. Witnesses claim that this is the prelude to every performance.
- During a British performance of the Moscow Circus school children witnessed horses being whipped and a bear being tied to a stool and a metal wheel.[7]

Unnatural Lives

Aside from violent training methods, even the most famous circuses and traveling acts subject animals to less than ideal living conditions. Circuses condemn animals who are wild by nature to live out their days isolated in tiny, barren cages or, in the case of elephants, shackled in chains for up to 95% of their lives. Fed unnatural diets on irregular schedules, subjected to sometimes life-threatening temperature extremes, denied normal exercise and socialization, and shuttled around from place to place, these animals lack any semblance of natural lives.

For every animal that appears in a prestigious circus, many more appear in roadside carnivals and fairs, or at special events such as car dealership grand openings. One such act was Tyrone the Terrible, a captive of a small traveling circus. Tyrone was a caged chimpanzee. By banging on his cage, rattling the cage door, screaming at him, and throwing water in his face, his handlers incited Tyrone into stomping his feet and hitting his arms against the sides of the

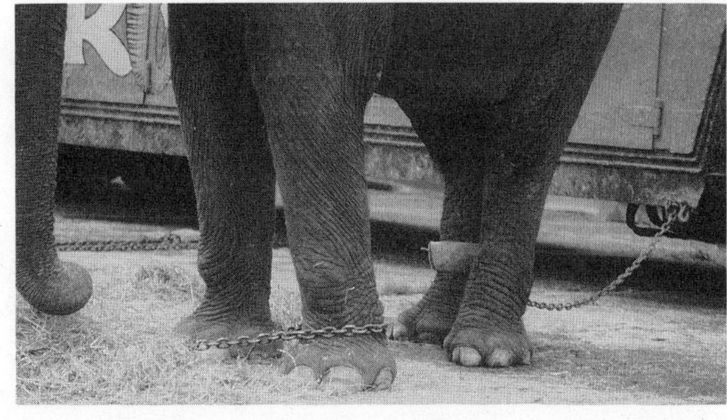

A. Achor

Circus elephants, forced to spend desolate lives in chains, become depressed and listless, totally unlike the gregarious creatures they are in the wild.

cage. This "uncontrolled fury" was what spectators paid one dollar apiece to see. Fortunately, the Michigan Humane Society confiscated Tyrone and he now resides with others of his species at Primarily Primates, a sanctuary for primates.[8]

Other traveling animal acts include a wrestling bear, a mule who is forced to dive into a tub of water from a highdive, and chimpanzee "jockeys" who are tied to miniature horses. The absurdity, and cruelty, of these acts is limited only by the imaginations of the promoters.

Getting Out of the Act

Animals feel fear, loneliness, and pain, just like you do. What animal would choose to spend her entire life in captivity if she had a choice? Human performers may thrive on the attention of the audience, but animal performers don't enjoy the circus. It is something they are forced to endure.

Why expose animals to these trials and abuses? Promoters of animal acts make money by exploiting animals. If we refuse to attend these performances and if we educate others and encourage them to boycott the acts, promoters will have no choice but to stop using animals in this "entertainment."

Does doing away with animal acts mean the end of the circus? Not in the least! Top-rated circuses such as the Cirque de Soleil from Quebec, the Peking Acrobats, and the Pickle Family Circus offer exciting alternatives to shows that rely on animal acts.

The use of animals in entertainment has already been restricted or banned in Switzerland, Sweden, Denmark, and parts of England, as well as in certain municipalities in the United States. Just as the "entertainment" of feeding Christians to lions came to pass, so should we lay to rest the "tradition" of animal acts.

Television and Movies

I don't think you should hurt or kill animals just to entertain an audience. Animals should have some rights. But there are a lot of directors, including Ingmar Bergman, who will injure animals to further a plot. I will have none of it.

— Actor James Mason, explaining why he refused a role in a film containing a cockfighting sequence

Animals are popular performers in movies, television shows, and commercials. Are these animals treated any better on the sets than they are in traveling animal acts? The answer is: maybe. The American Federation of Television and Radio Artists (AFTRA), AFL-CIO, recently stated that "the occurrence of animal abuse on union sets is becoming more and more apparent" and passed a resolution requiring their members to immediately report to the nearest union office any incidence of animal abuse witnessed on the set. Even so, some actors have stated off-the-record that reporting animal cruelty during commercial or movie production could result in their being blacklisted, which would ruin their careers.[9]

The harm that animals suffer from television programming, commercials, and movies takes three forms: mistreatment by trainers, harm or death during production, and depiction of abusive situations. Let's take a closer look at each of these areas.

Mistreatment by Trainers

The most severe abuse of animal performers undoubtedly occurs as a result of their "training." Animals performing in films are subjected to the same "two-by-four" methods used on circus animals.

In sworn statements, six people testified about abuse of chimpanzees used in the movie "Project X," starring Matthew Broderick. This was all the more shocking in light of the fact that "Project X" is a movie with a strong pro-animal message; it portrays the rescue of chimps from a military research laboratory. A special effects worker connected with the movie stated that he witnessed trainers beat the chimps with clubs, blackjacks, and fists. When confronted by concerned people on the set, the animal trainers retorted that they were professionals and knew what they were doing.[10]

Harm or Death During Production

Thanks to technological advances — and the momentum of the animal protection movement — creative camera work and special effects are beginning to replace cruelty on the screen. Where an old western may have used rope to trip a running horse and make him fall, such a method would not be tolerated today. We're even beginning to see statements such as "No animals were hurt or killed in the making of this film" included in the credits of some films. Hopefully, these statements are true and subsequent filmmakers will follow suit.

Still, when a scene shows live fish from a shattered fish tank flopping helplessly on the floor, out of water, amid glass shards, it raises the question, "How much has the industry really improved?" If you see something questionable, contact the studio that produced the film. See the Resources section of Chapter 9, "Getting Into the Act," for whom to contact.

Depiction of Abusive Situations

Depicting animal abuse on television or in movies conveys the message that animal abuse is acceptable. Movies like "Problem Child," which shows a child mistreating a cat, link animal abuse with humor. Other filmmakers use abuse for shock value, to "gross out" audiences.

Depictions of animal abuse do not help animals. In fact, they may serve to desensitize people toward abuse or even encourage such behavior. People, especially children, are highly suggestible and often mimic what they see.

When you see animals or references to animals in movies, pay attention to the message being sent. If you don't like what you see, voice your concerns to the producers.

Violent Spectacles

Of all the creatures ever made he (man) is the most detestable...
He is the only creature that inflicts pain for sport, knowing it to be pain.

— Mark Twain (as quoted in *The Extended Circle*)

Not all violence towards animals occurs behind the scenes. Sometimes, the violence is legally sanctioned or even cherished as an American tradition. Such is the case with the all-American rodeo.

Rodeo: Cruelty for a Buck

Rodeo is, as many activists' signs have portrayed, "Cruelty for a Buck." While spectators imagine a wild west being "tamed" by cowboys, the rodeo is a much different scene. Far from its romanticized image, rodeo is actually a contrived spectacle of cruelty that exists for one reason — to make money. Are animals hurt during rodeos? You bet they are.

"Bucking" broncos don't buck because they're wild; they buck because they're in pain. A belt, called a *flank strap* or *bucking strap,* is secured around the horse's body, over the sensitive genital area. As the horse leaves the chute, a tight jerk on the belt is enough to start the horse bucking in response to the pain. To further excite the audience, the horse is worked up by being slapped, teased, and otherwise tormented for as much as half an hour before his release from the chute. Electric prods called "hot shots" are then used to administer shocks to the horse so he will bolt out of the chute in a seeming frenzy of wildness.

Calf or steer roping, another popular rodeo event, involves throwing a rope around the neck of a frightened animal who is running at full speed, jerking him to a halt, and slamming him to the ground. By stunning and knocking the air out of the animal in this manner, the rodeo contestant has sufficient time to tie the animal's legs together. It isn't hard to imagine the pain and injury likely to occur when a rope suddenly jerks to a halt an animal who is running at 25 miles per hour. Animals who are too injured to continue in the rodeo circuit are simply shipped to the slaughterhouse. Said one veterinarian of calf roping:

> I have personally seen calves that were purchased for the sole purpose of being used for calf roping. These calves were roped in a home arena day after day until they finally appeared dead on the manure pile. They were discarded there after they succumbed to the mental and physical stress that was their daily lot.[11]

Steer wresting, another rodeo crowd-pleaser, consists of grabbing a steer by his horns and violently twisting his head so as to wrestle him to the ground. This can cause not only torn neck ligaments, but broken bones.

In addition to the treatment animals receive in the rodeo arena, like other performing animals they're confined to small trailers and hauled around the country, exposed to unregulated temperatures and feeding schedules, and denied any semblance of a natural life. They are used over and over again, in rodeo after rodeo, or in training sessions for potential rodeo contestants.

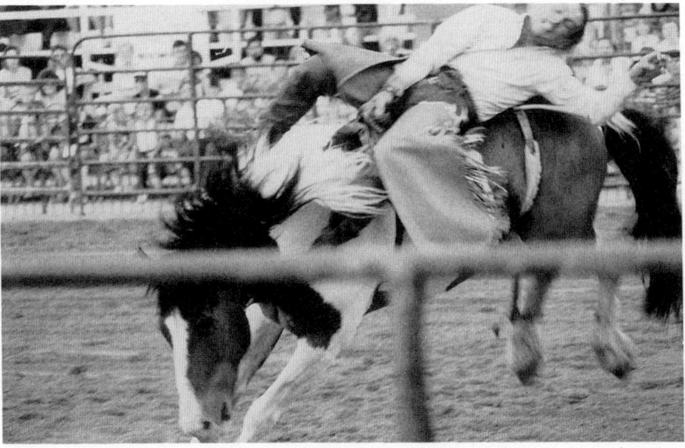
Randy Shields

Horses buck in response to pain. Notice the "bucking strap" cinched around the horse's genital region.

What do rodeo promoters have to say about all this? Paul Hoffman of Five Star Rodeo, Pembroke Pines, Florida says, "These are the best cared-for animals on the planet. They only have to work eight seconds a day."[12] Such comments give the term "rodeo bull" new meaning.

Fights to the Finish

Other violent spectacles of animal cruelty include cockfights and dog fights. These "entertainments" reveal a grotesque side of human beings.

Cockfighting — still legal in Arizona, Louisiana, Missouri, New Mexico, and Oklahoma — pits two roosters against each other in a fight to the death. What's the point in such a fight? As Kentucky's cockfighting bill used to read, individuals may "cause fowl to fight for fun or profit."* *The Animals' Voice Magazine* reported one Kentucky cockfighter's motivation: "I don't do it for the money. It's the personal satisfaction of knowing that I can do it better than anybody else can. At the moment I turn one loose, he's going to whip the guy. I know he is."[13] Dog fighting provides a similar "high." Watching dogs tear each other apart is a real hoot.

It's a Blast

Wondering how to raise money to maintain your town park? Residents of Hegins, Pennsylvania have the answer — a pigeon shoot, with participants paying to shoot birds released one-at-a-time from cages. That's been the fiscal solution for Hegins residents for over 57 years. In 1991, shooters killed over 5,000 birds, despite protesters' attempts to free the birds.[14] It's fun for the kids, too. After birds are shot, boys run onto the field to retrieve them. The kids also take care of wounded birds who survived being shot — they

---

* Cockfighting was just recently outlawed in Kentucky. Although Missouri doesn't specifically outlaw cockfighting, some individuals have been prosecuted under existing anti-cruelty statutes.

finish them off by wringing the birds' necks or pulling their heads off. It's fun for the whole family. What better way to spend Labor Day weekend?

If shooting pigeons doesn't appeal to you, how about a fund-raising suggestion from the Central Florida Council of the Boy Scouts of America — a dove shoot. You can also attend a "championship" prairie dog shoot in Colorado, or the annual gopher shoot in Minnesota, where a 16-year old champion killed 385 gophers. These "contests" are all legal and they are going on all over the country.

At the Races

When we see horses or dogs running on a racetrack, what often catches our eye is the sleekness and beauty of the animals. What we don't realize is that these animals are literally running for their lives. Like any other business, dog racing and horse racing are industries motivated by a common denominator: profit. The animals used in these "sports" are simply disposable commodities. Here are some of the things that racing promoters don't tell you.

Greyhound Racing

The Doris Day Animal League reports that an estimated 50,000 greyhounds were killed as surplus in the U.S. in 1988.* Tens of thousands of them were pups, killed before they were one year old because they didn't have winning potential. Another 30,000 were between the ages of two and five, and were killed because they weren't winning enough races or were injured in trying.[15]

An alternative to killing unwanted greyhounds is selling them to research laboratories. This use of greyhounds came to public attention when an anonymous worker told a local humane society that Letterman Army Institute for Research in San Francisco planned to use former racing greyhounds in painful bone-grafting experiments. Thanks to a number of animal protection groups and U.S. Representative Barbara Boxer, the experiments were halted.

A particularly interesting footnote to the story is that none of the dogs' owners, who were traced using numbers tattooed on the dogs, knew that their dogs had been sold for research. Owners had been told various stories by trainers to whom the dogs had been entrusted — that their dogs had been placed in adoptive homes, that their dogs were still racing, or that their dogs had been humanely euthanized — but not a single owner had been told the truth about the fate of their dogs. The dogs had been sold to research by the dog trainers and by animal dealers licensed by the U.S. Department of Agriculture.[16] The group In Defense of Animals reports that this network of greyhound dealers sold as many as 600 greyhounds to various laboratories in California and Arizona.[17] Neither greyhound owners nor the public realize that thousands of greyhounds still end up in research laboratories each year.

---

* Greyhound racing is legal in 16 states. It is banned in Maine, Virginia, Vermont, and Idaho.

Perhaps just as bad as the eventual fate awaiting racing greyhounds are the conditions under which they live. They spend their lives muzzled in tiny cages, without the attention or affection given to dogs who are companion animals. Forced to exert themselves on command in all types of weather, the dogs suffer many injuries inherent to the "sport" of dog racing. Investigators for The Humane Society of the United States (HSUS) have found greyhounds literally starving to death, neglected, and living in deplorable, filthy conditions. Many animals were so bad off that they had to be euthanized.[18]

Another shocking aspect of the dog racing industry is the use of live animals such as rabbits, cats, guinea pigs, and chickens in the training of greyhounds. The animals serve as live "lures," hung by their legs from a mechanical arm that spins around the track, or set loose to run in an enclosed field from which there is no escape. Greyhound trainers have been known to break the front legs of rabbits before releasing the dogs on them. The use of live animals as bait is reportedly standard practice; HSUS estimates that 90% of greyhound trainers do it.[19] These "training methods" are supported by a lucrative animal trafficking underground that obtains "bait" animals from the Southwest and delivers them to greyhound racers in the Southeast.

Sled Dog Racing

Using dogs to pull sleds—"mushing"—is an Alaskan tradition, once providing a necessary means of travel over frozen ground. But what was once a necessity has become a sport. Every year, a gruelling, competitive, high-stakes dog sled race called the Iditarod takes place in Alaska—and every year, at least one dog dies and several others are unable to finish the race.[20] Some animals are simply pushed beyond their endurance levels.

The harsh conditions of the race itself are only part of the danger racing sled dogs face. Like the greyhound and horse racing industries, many excess potential racers are bred in the hopes of producing a winner. Those unable to make the grade join the overflowing pool of surplus dogs needing homes, or are sometimes killed outright by breeders.

Exposure by animal activists of Iditarod cruelties has prompted many sponsors to withdraw financial support. Money talks—race officials are now paying more attention to the treatment of the dogs. Still, there are many more improvements to be made, short of stopping the race altogether. Even one preventable death or injury "for fun and profit" is too many.

Horse Racing

As in dog racing, horse racing is an industry that treats animals simply as a means for making money. These beautiful animals are not appreciated for who they are, but rather for what they can earn. Horses who don't make the grade — the majority — are sold to slaughter as horse meat.

A special type of abuse permeates the horse racing industry — drug abuse. Drugs play a major role in making horses run faster and in making them run when they shouldn't be running at all. Veterinarians administer drugs to mask the pain of injuries that would normally keep a horse from running fast, injuries that need time to heal. They may also administer drugs to mask the presence of other drugs which would disqualify the horse if detected. The side effects of these drugs, such as bleeding in the lungs, and the aggravated injuries that get worse instead of better because they were never given the chance to heal, are of no consequence to the trainers. All that matters is the immediate, winning performance of the horse. If the horse turns up lame as a result of running a race it shouldn't have run in the first place, so be it. There are plenty of other horses to take his place.

Another problem in horse racing is the use of young horses whose bones are still developing. To prevent fractures, horses should be at least four or five years old before they begin race training. Currently, training begins when they're one year old, so they can be racing by age two or three. The result is increased fractures and lameness for as many as 60% to 90% of race horses,[21] resulting in more drug abuse, resulting in more lameness, resulting in a nightmarish trip to the slaughterhouse.

Zoos and Aquariums

As a kid, I loved the zoo. I watched animals for hours, mesmerized by them. In those days, I filtered everything I saw through the belief that the animals were well cared for by knowledgeable people who really cared about them. I trusted the "experts." I actually believed that zoo animals were there for their own good. I never thought to question what I saw.

Most people who visit zoos and aquariums have the same "blind spots" that I used to have. Let's shed light on some of the realities of these "attractions."

The Real Purpose of Zoos

Are zoos valuable educational and conservation institutions? That's what they would like for us to believe, but in reality zoos have two basic purposes: (1) to entertain people and (2) to make money.

■ The Myth of Education

Zoos may be interesting, but they are educational only in the sense that they teach a disregard for the natures of other living beings. What can we learn about wild animals by viewing them in captivity? Zoo animals are very little like their wild relatives.

Zoos exist because we are intrigued by "exotic" things, and to zoo-goers, zoo animals are just that — things. Says a curator for the National Zoo, "Going to the zoo seems to be some sort of ritualistic social event, but this ritual doesn't seem to include much appreciation, contemplation, and learning."[22]

How, then, will our children learn about non-native animals? The same way they learn about non-native peoples — through films, books, and other media. We may want our child to learn about Australian bushmen, but we don't capture bushmen, put them in cages, and display them in public exhibits. We should show the same regard for nonhumans.

■ The Myth of Conservation

A current trend in zoo public relations is to emphasize the role of zoos in conservation. But in reality, zoos have little impact on the conservation of endangered species.

True conservation requires the preservation of an animal's habitat, so that he can thrive in his natural environment. Zoo "conservation" programs consist of breeding captive animals and then reintroducing them to the wild. These captive-breeding programs are exorbitantly expensive; the money spent on them far exceeds that spent on habitat conservation efforts. One author observes, "Every year zoos around the world spend many times over the combined incomes of all conservation organizations, but their contribution to the saving of endangered species is negligible by comparison."[23] In addition, some captive-bred animals have difficulty adjusting to life in the wild or are rejected by wild members of their species.

Captive breeding is effective for a zoo's public image, but does relatively little in terms of conservation. And it does nothing to justify the large number of nonendangered species confined in zoos.

The Lives of Zoo Animals

■ Imprisonment

A. Achor

The lives of zoo animals are unnatural, tedious, and lonely.

Animals in zoos and aquariums are no less than prisoners serving a life sentence with no chance of parole. Their crime? Being beautiful animals who attract paying customers. Born in captivity, or captured in the wild and caged, zoo and aquarium inmates suffer totally unnatural lives that deny their innate instincts — food gathering, mating, interacting with members of their own and other species, establishing a social order, and so on. In their natural environments, elephants live in herds of up to 100 members, roaming great distances to gather food. In the zoo, elephants spend their days confined to a small exhibition area and their nights in ankle chains. Elephants at the Cleveland Metroparks Zoo reportedly spend 16 hours a day in leg chains.[24] Marine mammals, whose natural behavior includes diving into the ocean depths and swimming many miles each day, are confined to small, concrete tanks. There is virtually no similarity between the natural lives of animals and the routine of imprisonment.

Captivity takes its toll on animals. Deprived of outlets for their natural behaviors, animals adopt neurotic behaviors such as pacing, swaying, and repetitive head bobbing or weaving, as well as self-mutilation, over-eating, and misplaced or exaggerated aggression. With all the stimulation of survival removed from their lives, zoo animals are bored, lonely, and only a shadow of their wild ancestors.

■ Neglect

"At least," some argue, "zoo animals are well-cared for." Unfortunately, this isn't true. Zoo animals commonly suffer from neglect and poor care.

In the book *Living Trophies,* Peter Batten reports what he found when he traveled the country and documented the conditions of America's zoos. In his words, "Four months of depressing zoo viewing and photography confirmed that the majority of American zoos are badly run, their direction incompetent, and animal husbandry inept and in some cases nonexistent."[25] Among Batten's findings were these:

- foot and hoof deformities due to improper floor surfaces and neglect
- illness and death due to improperly prepared food and unnatural diet
- illness and death from exposure to extreme temperatures, precipitation, and dampness due to improper housing and care
- injury and death from poorly designed exhibits and restraints, most commonly from drowning and falls
- a variety of stress-induced and boredom-induced abnormal behaviors
- small, filthy, barren cages
- excessive noise and improper lighting
- mutilation and death from harassment and vandalism by zoo spectators due to improper security measures
- stress, injury, and death due to mixing incompatible species in the same or adjoining displays
- death due to neglect and lack of veterinary care

The 1,300 marine mammals in captivity have a particularly poor record of survival. A study conducted by the ecology organization Lifeforce found that premature death is the norm rather than the exception for captive whales and dolphins, as high as 72.4% in one aquarium.[26] The Mystic Marinelife Aquarium in Connecticut alone has lost 50 animals since 1983, the equivalent of one death every six weeks.[27] Nearly half of the orca whales captured for Sea World since 1965 have died in captivity. This is due in part to the inherent stress of captivity. As Animal Rights Front of Connecticut explains:

> ...marine mammals in aquariums live frustrated, stressful lives, which, just as in humans, leads to disease and early death. Captive dolphins and whales, for example, are unable to dive into deep, cold waters, something they do frequently in the wild. Prevented by the Aquarium's shallow pools from ever

meeting this basic need, they develop low levels of hemoglobin, which affects their immune systems and lowers their resistance to infection and disease.[28]

Additional hazards to marine mammals include their contact with humans, which fosters disease, and the bright paint, chlorine, and unsalted water in the artificial pools, which causes the animals to go blind. Also, keep in mind that dolphins and other marine mammals use sonar to orient themselves; in other words, they send out sound waves. When these waves hit the walls of the concrete tanks, they bounce back. Says a former dolphin trainer for the "Flipper" television show, "The concrete tanks to the acoustical dolphin are what a blinding house of mirrors would be to us."[29]

■ Abuse

Some zoo animals also suffer from outright abuse, ranging from beatings to killings. For example, the Cleveland Metroparks Zoo drains a manmade lake every few years, deliberately leaving the fish who live in the lake to slowly die of suffocation as the water disappears.[30]

Zoo elephants are abused by their "caretakers" as a matter of routine. San Francisco Zoo Director David Anderson maintains that beating is acceptable in elephant management.[31] Trainers at the San Diego Wild Animal Park admit chaining a 19-year-old elephant by all four legs, pulling her to the ground, and beating her in the head with axe handles over a two day period when she arrived at the Park from the San Diego Zoo. This "discipline" was performed to establish dominance.[32]

■ Where Do the Animals Come From?

There are two sources for zoo animals: animal dealers and captive breeding programs. Animal dealers sometimes obtain animals, including endangered species, from the animals' native countries.

Every animal delivered to a zoo represents many others who died. It is well known that in order to capture a baby primate, poachers shoot the entire family. They then retrieve the terrified baby as she clings to the dead mother. The International Primate Protection League reports that for gibbons and gorillas, as many as 20 mothers and babies die for each one shipped. Ten chimpanzees may die for each one shipped, and for orangutans the ratio is eight deaths for every animal shipped.[33] Many more captured animals never survive the journey to the zoo or die shortly after arrival. Others are injured during capture.

Another source of animals is captive breeding. Some people feel that because an animal is born in captivity, it automatically adjusts to life in captivity. But wild animals are still wild animals, regardless of where they are born. They retain the same instincts as their wild-born ancestors. Too often, captive breeding is done for the wrong reasons. Sometimes "baby" zoo animals are used to attract patrons to the zoo. Other times, keepers simply fail to control breeding, resulting in unwanted additions to the zoo. (Despite what the public believes, additional animals are not always welcomed by zoos, which have limited space and resources.)

What Happens to Surplus Animals?

Zoos do not house animals out of compassion; they house them because they are "goods" that can be sold to the public. When a zoo's "inventory" becomes unmanageable, it must clear out some of its "merchandise." What happens to surplus animals at the zoo, those who aren't profitable to keep? Depending on the type of animal:

- Some end up in research laboratories as victims of biomedical, veterinary, psychological, or military experiments. Zoos themselves also conduct animal experiments. One such experiment at the Detroit Zoo, reported by *The Animals Voice Magazine,* involved keeping 17 North African sheep for two years in what a former zoo keeper and several current keepers called "inhumane" conditions.[34]
- Some become "big game" on hunting ranches in the U.S., where hunters pay large fees to shoot trophy animals.
- Some are condemned for life to circuses or small roadside zoos. HSUS estimates that 50% to 80% of all large animals in roadside zoos are the result of breeding programs in larger zoos.[35]
- Some are sold or traded to other zoos.
- Some surplus zoo animals — those with no redeeming value in the marketplace — are simply put to death at the zoo.

Roadside Zoos

As bad as the large city zoos are for animals, they don't come close to the hundreds of small roadside zoos and "museums" that dot highways all across the country. These rundown menageries typically consist of small, barren, filthy cages where isolated animals do nothing but sit day in and day out, year after year, without veterinary care or any hope of relief from their stark existence.

Primarily Primates, a sanctuary in Texas, reported on one such roadside zoo in Louisiana called Snake Farm, which, among other animals, housed five primates who had been discarded by previous owners. These primates were isolated in deteriorating concrete and rusty wire cages for 20 years, until, after negotiations with Friends of Animals and other animal advocates, the owner of Snake Farm voluntarily released the primates to Primarily Primates' sanctuary.[36] This rescue is the exception, not the rule. Most animals in roadside zoos are condemned for life.

But This Zoo Is a Member of AAZPA...

The American Association of Zoological Parks and Aquariums (AAZPA) is the accreditation organization for zoos and aquariums which sets standards for zoos. Certification by AAZPA is not a requirement. Fewer than 10% of licensed and registered animal exhibitors are accredited by AAZPA.[37]

AAZPA approval is no guarantee of humane or competent supervision of animals. The Network for Ohio Animal Action reports that Steve Taylor is now president of AAZPA.

Taylor is director of Cleveland Metroparks Zoo, an AAZPA-approved facility. This is the zoo mentioned earlier that regularly drains a pond and lets the fish living therein slowly suffocate as the water disappears.

Here are some more standards being set by that particular zoo:[38]

- The zoo was recently cited by the USDA for violation of the Animal Welfare Act in the preventable deaths of three sea lions who died in transit from Cleveland to Memphis, Tennessee.
- Dogs managed to penetrate the zoos exterior fence and kill zoo inmates.
- Elephants are forced to wear leg chains 16 hours a day.
- An auto mechanic, without any animal experience or education, was hired as the elephant keeper.

This gives you an idea of what "AAZPA-approved" really means.

The Final Word on Zoos and Aquariums

Some of the abuses of zoos and aquariums, such as poor maintenance, can be corrected. Others cannot. The very nature of a zoo involves confinement of sentient beings. No matter how "natural" the habitat appears to the zoo patron, the fact is that zoos and aquariums force animals to live in confined areas, in unnatural climates, on unnatural diets, in unnatural social groups, and prohibits their natural interaction with other animals. Zoos and aquariums, by their very nature, fail to address the complex social, psychological, and biological needs of wild animals.

The Massachusetts Society for the Prevention of Cruelty to Animals (MSPCA) states what should be the final word on zoos and aquariums:

> ...the only valid goal of zoological institutions is to promote and effect the preservation and welfare of wild animals in their natural habitat.[39]

Carriage Rides

Horse-drawn carriages conjure up romantic images of leisurely rides in the moonlight. For carriage horses, however, the ride is somewhat less than romantic.

Carriage horses often work long hours without breaks in excessive heat on busy, noisy, exhaust-filled, paved roads. Horses collapse and die from heat exhaustion while on the job, and they've injured people by bolting in response to loud traffic noise. An investigation of New Orleans carriage horses revealed, as reported by the National Society for the Protection of Animals, "improper nutrition, no veterinary attention, no drinking water, and harness sores all over their bodies."[40] According to a representative from People for the Ethical Treatment of Animals, carriage horses in Covington, Kentucky "were tethered on hard concrete all night, never allowed to sit down."[41]

Another problem with horse-drawn carriages is the type of horse used. While draft horses have the required strength to pull a heavy load, carriage operators sometimes use inappropriate horses to pull carriages, horses who don't have the natural strength needed to haul the required load. Temperament can also be a problem. Some horses are nervous and are easily spooked by the commotion on city streets.

In response to recent publicity about carriage horse abuse, some cities have enacted laws to regulate the treatment of these horses. Still, we need to ask ourselves whether or not regulation is really enough. Is the price these horses pay really worth the momentary enjoyment of a carriage ride?

Animals as Prizes

County fairs and school fairs sometimes offer animals as prizes for games of chance. By tossing a ping-pong ball into a goldfish bowl or winning at a ring toss game, you can go home with a live animal.

At the 1991 Greene County (Ohio) Fair, fairgoers could walk away with goldfish, canaries, or rabbits. Obviously, animals impulsively won at such fairs don't have a great chance of survival. Prize winners who suddenly find themselves in possession of a living animal are unprepared to take proper care of their new charge. At events where goldfish are awarded as prizes, dead fish are often found littering the ground after the event. Other animals are likely to meet similar fates.

Caring for any animal requires knowledge, time, and financial commitment. Being a caretaker is a commitment that shouldn't be left to chance; it is a privilege, not a right. Offering animals as prizes reinforces the concept that they are merely things to be passed around and discarded at a whim. It's way past time to outlaw such obviously abusive situations.

Animals in "Scrambles"

Another popular feature of local fairs is the animal "scramble." These events consist of children or adults chasing and trying to grab onto animals. The 1991 Clark County (Ohio) Fair featured scrambles with rabbits, pigs, and calves — something for everyone.

Is it fun? Not for the animals. Perhaps the promoters of these events should let screaming people chase and grab at *them* instead of subjecting frightened animals to this spectacle. These and similar events should be outlawed.

Pulling Contests

Another event that needn't be abusive, but often is, is animal-pulling contests. These events pit draft horses or oxen against each other to see who can pull the heaviest load.

Pulling contests are common in New England, and, reportedly, so are the abuses of draft animals. Concealed nails or other sharp devices are used to "urge" the animals to pull harder. The Maine Animal Coalition reported the following:

> Last June, a state humane agent filed written complaints after observing "welts, swelling, and presence of blood" on oxen as they left a pulling arena in Farmington. Superintendent Richard Allingford (also president of the Maine Draft Horse & Ox Association and a long-time teamster himself) made no effort to stop the abuse, explaining that the men involved weren't as abusive as they used to be.[42]

Need more be said?

Greeting Cards and Posters

Next time you shop for a greeting card, be conscious of animals. Take a close look at the cards that contain photographs of animals and try to see behind the picture. Is dressing up chimps in clothes and photographing them under hot lights really appropriate? Does the photograph depict the animal in a setting natural to his or her nature? What do you think happens to the animals when they are not being used for photographs?

If consumers refuse to buy cards, posters, and other products that require placing animals in unnatural situations, then manufacturers will stop producing them.

How You Can Help

Here are some specific things you can do to help stop the exploitation of animals used for entertainment.

- **Don't buy into it.**
  Put your money where your heart is. Don't attend events or buy products that exploit animals. Urge others to join the boycott.

- **Educate others.**
  Write a letter to the editor of your local newspaper, pass out flyers, organize a demonstration, talk to classes of school children — do whatever you can to educate others about the realities of animals in entertainment.

- **Legislate.**
  Ask your local government officials about the procedure for introducing a city or county ordinance. Then find sympathetic citizens and officials to back you. Many individuals have made changes on the local level. The cities of Pittsburgh (PA) and Baltimore (MD), and the state of Rhode Island are among those who have passed laws to protect rodeo animals. An individual activist in a rural Ohio community convinced the health department to outlaw bear wrestling in her county. If they can do it, so can you.

- **Speak up.**
  Next time you see an animal being exploited, say something. If the event has a local sponsor, talk to the sponsor. If you are questioning something you see on television or in a movie, contact the producers.

Resources for Animals in Entertainment

For products and services related to animals used in entertainment, see the following sections of Chapter 12: Radio & Television Programming, Stamps & Stickers, and Videos & Films.

For further reading on animals used in entertainment, see Chapter 13.

The following organizations work on behalf of performing animals. See Chapter 10 for a description of these and other state organizations that help animals who are victims of the entertainment industries.

- **Aquariums, Zoos, Circuses, and Rodeos**
  Action For Animals (CA), Animal Rights Mobilization (CO), Animals and the Environment (NY), Citizens Lobbying for Animals in Zoos (CA), Dolphin Alliance (FL), Dolphin Freedom Foundation (FL), Dolphin Network (CA), Elephant Alliance (CA), Fund for Animals, Inc. (NY), International Dolphin Project (CA), International Society for Animal Rights, Inc. (PA), People for the Ethical Treatment of Animals (VA), South Carolina Association for Marine Mammal Protection (SC), United Activists for Animals—Coalition to Protect Animals in Entertainment (CA)

- **Bull Fights/Blood Fiestas**
  Fight Against Animal Cruelty in Europe (NY)

- **Carriage Horse Legislation**
  These organizations are among those successful in passing legislation to help protect carriage horses:
  Animal Rights Foundation of Florida (FL), Carriage Horse Action Committee (NY), Sarasota In Defense of Animals (FL)

- **Greyhound Racing**
  See also the Greyhound Adoption groups listed in the Resources section of Chapter 3, "Companion Animals."
  Greyhound Friends, Inc. (MA), Greyhound Protection League (CA), Make Peace With Animals, Inc. (PA), No More Victims (PA), Retired Greyhounds As Pets (FL), USA Defenders of Greyhounds, Inc. (IN)

- **Horse Racing**
  Humane Organization for Retired and Standardbred Equines (VA), Humane Society of the United States (D.C.)

- **Rehabilitation/Sanctuaries for Captive Exotic Animals**
  See also the organizations listed in the Resources section of Chapter 7, "Wildlife in Crisis."
  Animal Education, Protection, and Information Foundation—elephants & others (MO), Cedarhill Animal Sanctuary, Inc.—exotic cats (MS), The Elephant Sanctuary (TN), JES Exotics Sanctuary—exotic cats (WI), Performing Animal Welfare Society (CA), Primarily Primates, Inc. (TX), Protective Association of World Species (WI), Roar Foundation/Shambala Preserve—exotic cats & elephants (CA), Walden's Puddle (TN), Wildlife Waystation (CA)

- **Shooting Contests**
  Fund for Animals, Inc. (NY), People for the Ethical Treatment of Animals (VA)

- **Sled Dog Racing**
  International Society for Animal Rights (PA), Massachusetts Society for the Prevention of Cruelty to Animals (MA), United Coalition of Iditarod Animal Rights Volunteers (AK)

Conclusion

The time will come when public opinion will no longer tolerate amusements based on the mistreatment and killing of animals. The time will come, but when?

— Albert Schweitzer

There is nothing fun about using animals for entertainment. Whenever an animal is removed from her native habitat and forced to live an unnatural life, she suffers. Whips, chains, clubs, and electric shock are all "training tools" employed to break an animal's spirit and make her perform tricks. Captive animals spend lonely, boring, dismal lives confined to barren cages with nothing to look forward to. In dog and horse racing, animals are disposable objects, cast aside if they don't make the grade. From county fairs to movie sets, from rodeos to carriage rides, animals suffer neglect and abuse for a few dollars of profit. There is nothing entertaining about that.

Animals in Entertainment

At a Glance

Did you know:

- Behind the scenes, trainers commonly use a "two-by-four" method to beat performing animals into submission and gain "dominance" over them.
- The circus is no fun for animals. Traveling animals in circuses and other acts live unnatural lives in barren cages or trailers, exposed to temperature extremes, unnatural diets, and irregular schedules, without normal exercise, socialization, or even the semblance of a natural life.
- Rodeos are contrived performances that use pain to make horses buck and subject frightened animals to severe injuries.
- The purpose of zoos is to entertain people and make money. Zoos do little if anything to benefit the animals imprisoned in them.
- You can help performing animals by refusing to attend places and spectacles that feature animal acts or imprison animals for entertainment.

We would consider it cruel to confine a dog permanently in a kennel. Yet we visit zoos where hundreds of wild animals are kept permanently in the equivalent of a kennel. It is as if we, like the animals, become trapped within the zoo concept and we cannot see beyond the bars. We forget that wildlife in zoos is still wildlife.

— Virginia McKenna (*Beyond the Bars*)

Part Three

Personal Action

Chapter 9

Getting into the Act

What, Me an Activist?

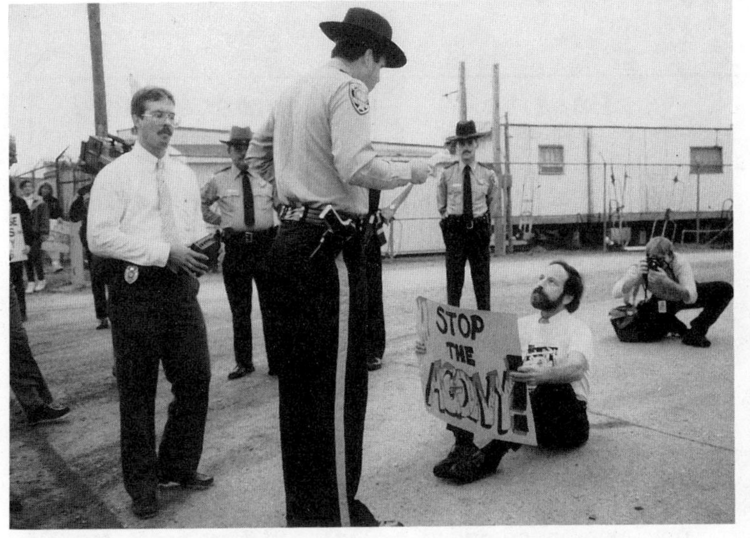

S. Behm, Farm Animal Reform Movement

Whatever you can do, or dream you can do, begin it. Boldness has genius, power and magic in it.

— Goethe

By now you've read most of this book and you're acquainted with the major animal rights issues. Now what?

No matter who you are, there's a place for you in the animal rights movement. It's a wonderful forum for expressing your talents and developing your skills. You don't have to stand in picket lines or face off with hunters to be an advocate. There are plenty of things you can do right from your own home, all by yourself.

The only requirements for becoming an animal activist are a genuine concern for the rights of animals and a willingness to get involved. It doesn't matter whether or not you've ever done something like this before; you can learn as you go.

Looking at Yourself

The first thing every advocate needs to do is invest in a little self-examination. As the saying goes, "People who live in glass houses shouldn't throw stones." Translated, it means, "People who support animal rights should make sure they reflect it in their own lifestyles."

None of us is perfect. We live in a society that makes it very difficult to live our convictions 100% of the time. Sometimes we unknowingly, or even knowingly, support a business or practice that exploits animals.

I call the perpetrators of deliberate animal exploitation *active abusers.* Those of us who either support an exploitive business by buying its products or condone an exploitive behavior by participating in it are *passive abusers.*

Here are some examples of Active Abuse and Passive Abuse. See how many of these activities you identify with. Then consider adopting the Compassionate Alternative. By doing so, you automatically help animals.

Active Abuse	Passive Abuse	Compassionate Alternative
Raising, capturing, or killing an animal for food.	Buying or eating any part of an animal.	Choosing to forego "food" that was once a member of the animal kingdom.
Using intensive confinement (factory farming) methods to confine and abuse animals for use as food.	Buying or eating an animal victimized by factory farming.	Choosing to not buy or eat any factory farm products. Better yet, choosing to not eat any animal products, period.
Testing a product on an animal or using slaughterhouse by-products as ingredients in a product.	Buying or using a product tested on an animal or containing an ingredient from a slaughtered animal.	Choosing to buy only cruelty-free products — those that are not tested on animals and do not contain any ingredients requiring the death or suffering of an animal.
Using an animal in research experiments. Selling animals to laboratories or animal supply houses. Breeding animals for research.	Giving money to an organization that performs animal experimentation.	Choosing to support only universities and charitable organizations that use nonanimal methods of research.

continued...

Active Abuse	Passive Abuse	Compassionate Alternative
Requiring dissection of an animal as part of a school curriculum.	Performing a dissection, or requiring your child to do so.	Choosing to stand up for student rights by insisting on a humane educational alternative to dissection.
Sanctioning the killing of wildlife by hunting, trapping, or other means.	Contributing to a "conservation" organization that supports hunting, trapping, or other means of killing wildlife.	Choosing to support only organizations that support protection of all wildlife and oppose hunting and trapping.
Raising, killing, or trapping an animal for her skin or some other body part.	Buying or wearing an animal skin (fur or leather), or a product made from any body part.	Choosing to not buy, wear, or use the skins of animals.
Capturing or breeding wild animals, including birds, as pets.	Buying or keeping wild animals as pets.	Choosing to leave wild animals in the wild, and supporting efforts to maintain natural habitats for wild animals.
Breeding dogs and cats when pounds and shelters are killing animals for a lack of loving homes.	Buying a dog from a pet store or a breeder.	Choosing to obtain animals only from homeless shelters, and spaying/neutering companion friends before they have a chance to breed.
Deliberately neglecting or abandoning a companion animal.	Contributing to cat and dog overpopulation by neglecting to spay/neuter an animal in your care, or supporting the breeding industry by buying an animal from a pet store or breeder.	Choosing to spay/neuter all animals in your care, before they have a chance to breed. Making a lifetime commitment to all animals you choose to adopt.
Directly exploiting or harming an animal.	Being quiet about abuse or exploitation that you witness or suspect.	Choosing to get involved by calling attention to abuse or exploitation you witness or suspect.

Emotions in Action

The minute I took my focus off of my own problems and focused on reaching out to the needs around me, I discovered a deep sense of inner peace and direction...when people ask, "Why do you do that?" I say, "Well, it's opened my heart."

— Guy Polhemus (Noetic Sciences Review)

Animal rights is a canvas for many emotions. We each have our own personal ways of feeling, expressing, and avoiding our emotions. Here's a brief word about some natural feelings an activist is likely to experience.

◆ **Use Your Anger Constructively**

Anger stems from a sense of powerlessness or betrayal. Used wisely, it can be a great motivator, moving you out of grief or helplessness, and into a state of action.

Acting on anger can be constructive or destructive, depending on what you do with it. Punching the face of an offensive party might provide a moment of satisfaction and will no doubt dispel some of your anger, but the consequences are probably not the ones you're really after. Because anger can cloud your thinking, before you act on your anger, ask yourself the following questions:

- What am I creating with my actions?
- What results do I want to see from my creations?
- How can I modify my behavior to achieve the desired results?

Express anger in constructive ways. Before you act, talk about your anger with someone you trust (that is, "vent" your emotion). After you cool down a bit, direct your anger into a letter, a call, or some other constructive action that will remedy the situation. Let your anger work for you.

◆ **Express Your Grief**

Sadness and grief are normal responses to suffering. Although some of us, especially men, may have been told early in life that it's "inappropriate" to express hurt and sadness, expressing grief is normal and necessary, for both men and women. Sometimes it helps to talk it out or write it out. Other times, there's nothing quite as cathartic as a good cry (men, that means you, too). Movies can be good catalysts for getting us in touch with our grief and giving us an opportunity to express it. When you're feeling grief, be as kind and understanding with yourself as you would be with someone else.

Although none of us likes to feel grief, it is a sign that we are alive. The ability to feel grief carries with it the ability to feel joy. It is when we remain unaffected by accounts of abuse that we should worry. Too much grief is not a good thing, though. Sometimes it's necessary to step back and take a break. We all have limits, and getting to know your own limits is an important part of activism. Becoming overwhelmed can lead to burn out and total withdrawal. Learn to pace yourself and be able to say "No" when you need to.

◆ **Guilt Is Not the Same as Responsibility**

As you begin to gain more awareness of animal rights, you may feel guilty for ways you've treated animals in the past, whether or not you acted deliberately. Or you may feel guilty for present habits directly or indirectly linked to animal suffering.

Shaming and blaming yourself for past or present choices is not the same as admitting your actions and taking responsibility for them. Letting go of shame and blame will allow you to move on. Learn from your mistakes. Take responsibility for who you are and what you do *now*. You can't change the past, but you can do your best in the present. If you feel remorse for things you've done, forgive yourself. Extend the same compassion to yourself that you'd extend to any other animal. You'll be a more effective advocate if you don't waste energy beating up yourself for past behaviors.

◆ **Keep a Positive Focus**

Sometimes it's easy to feel defeated and wonder, "What difference can I make?" It may seem like writing a postcard to a company that tests products on animals just won't make any difference. But what if a hundred people do it? What if a thousand people do it? What if a thousand people each give $1 to an organization that works for animals? Individual actions add up. Your actions do count.

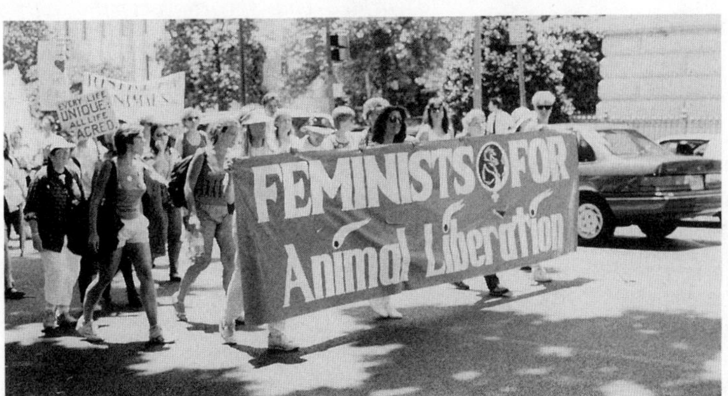

Randy Shields

Advocating for the rights of the less fortunate can be an empowering experience.

Especially when you are feeling powerless, do something, no matter how small it seems. Write a letter, make a phone call, send a donation to a group that is working for animals. As the saying goes, "The journey of a thousand miles begins with one step." You may not be able to do it all, but you can do *something*. You never know the effect that you or your actions may have on someone or something.

Being an activist can be hard. It requires patience, tenacity, and a definite sense of humor. Things are not likely to change overnight — but they do change. Activists have achieved many victories for animals, and continue to do so.

The following prayer, credited to Reinhold Niebuhr, is commonly called The Serenity Prayer. It can be helpful to keep in mind:

> God, grant me the
> Serenity to accept the things I cannot change;
> Courage to change the things I can; and
> Wisdom to know the difference.

Things You Can Do

Only one-third of the colonists supported the American Revolution. The abolitionist movement never numbered more that about 100,000 — a tiny fraction. As one historian points out, "Five percent keep saving the world." That's worth remembering.

— Christian Science Monitor (quoted in *Pax Facts*)

Animal rights is an easy movement to get involved in because animal abuse is so pervasive. The clothes we wear, the food we eat, the products we choose to buy, the entertainment we choose to support — we are constantly faced with everyday decisions that affect the well-being of animals. As individuals, consumers, and voters, we have tremendous personal power when it comes to animal rights. We can easily be animal rights advocates without ever holding a protest sign.

Do you like to write? Do you like to let others know how you feel? Do you like to be out there in the public eye, or do you prefer to work quietly behind the scenes? Whatever your talents and inclinations, there's a place for you in animal rights.

Animal rights can also be an opportunity for you to challenge yourself by venturing into new territory. If you are a person who is shy about standing in a picket line, perhaps you should give it a try with a friend, just to see what it's really like. You may discover something new about yourself.

Chapters 3 through 8 discussed some specific ways you can help animals. Here are some additional things you can do on behalf of animals.

Investigate

The first step to resolving any problem is exposing the problem. Getting the facts is half the battle. Here are some pointers on the who, what, and how of investigations.

■ Whom Should You Investigate?

Investigate anyone who you feel might be exploiting or mistreating animals. This might include:

- Research institutions such as hospitals, universities, and military bases.
- Stockyards, slaughterhouses, and "animal agriculture" setups.
- Animal exhibits such as zoos and traveling animal acts.
- Pet shops.
- Animal dealers.
- Local humane societies, shelters, and pounds.

■ What Should You Look For?

- Violations of local laws or federal regulations.
- Things that might arouse public interest or outcry. Public pressure can sometimes stop things that laws can't.

■ How Should You Conduct an Investigation?

Some investigations involve on-site inspections, such as inspecting conditions at the local pound or pet shop. Other investigations are more of a "paper chase," such as obtaining documents from research facilities about the animals they use in experimentation. Whatever type of investigation you pursue, keep the following things in mind:

◆ **Do preparatory reading.**

The more you know before you start, the easier it will be. Some useful guides are described in the Activism section of Chapter 13. Among them are these:

- *The PETA Guide to Becoming an Activist* by People for the Ethical Treatment of Animals
- *Investigating Animal Abuse Information Packet* from the Animal Legal Defense Fund
- *How to Use the Freedom of Information Act* by the International Society for Animal Rights, Inc.

◆ **Find an attorney.**

An attorney familiar with animal-related laws can be indispensable. If you don't know of one in your area, contact the Animal Legal Defense Fund and see if they can refer you to someone. You can also try recruiting volunteers from local law schools or running an ad in local papers.

- **Know the law.**

  Whether or not you are able to recruit a lawyer, you should know the laws that may apply to your investigation. Here are some laws you may want to look into:

  - *Animal Treatment Laws.* These include state anti-cruelty statutes, the federal Animal Welfare Act, the federal Humane Slaughter Act, the federal Endangered Species Act, and the federal Marine Mammal Protection Act. Some, but not all, libraries carry state and federal codes. Ask your reference librarian for help.

    You may also want to consult the regulations mandated by federal laws. The regulations contain the details of how the laws are applied. The *Code of Federal Regulations* contains regulations for the Animal Welfare Act and Humane Slaughter Act. A free copy of the Animal Welfare Act and its regulations is available from the United States Department of Agriculture (USDA), 6505 Belcrest Road, Room 269, Hyattsville, MD 20782, (301) 436-7833.

  - *Local Health Codes.* These may apply in some cases. In one instance, health codes were used to ban a wrestling bear act from establishments that serve food.

  - *State "Search and Seizure" Laws.* You don't want to end up breaking the law during your investigation.

  - *The Freedom of Information Act (FOIA).* Often pronounced FOY-ya, FOIA allows access to certain documents from federal institutions, for example, from the U.S. Department of Agriculture or National Institutes of Health. There is a certain format you must follow when making a FOIA request, so be sure to read up on it before making the request (see the previously mentioned activist guides for help). For low cost or free legal advice on using FOIA, contact: Freedom of Information Act Clearinghouse, 2000 P Street NW, P.O. Box 19367, Washington, D.C. 20036, (202) 785-3704 (a Ralph Nader group) or American Civil Liberties Union, 122 Maryland Avenue NE, Washington, D.C. 20002, (202) 544-1681.

  - *Your State "Sunshine" (Public Records and Meetings) Laws.* These laws allow access to public documents and meetings of state institutions. The public meetings law may help you gain access to the Animal Care and Use Committee meetings at state universities (you may have to file a lawsuit to gain access to these meetings). The public records law allows you to request information on the numbers and types of animals used in research, and on the types of research being conducted. Documents you may want to request include invoices of animals bought or sold, contracts or agreements with animal dealers or pounds, minutes of Animal Care and Use Committee meetings, and reports filed with the National Institutes of Health or USDA.

    If you make a records request, ask to inspect the records and reserve the right to ask for photocopies of any records you may want copies of. (Be sure to find out what they'll charge you in photocopy costs.) When you inspect records obtained through a records request, be sure to examine them carefully. Make a list of each record provided. Note information that may have been deleted ("redacted") from existing pages or that may be missing altogether (for example, a page with a staple in it obviously had something attached to it at one time). By keeping a precise list of the provided records, you can discover what requested documents may be missing. If copies contain deletions, or if requested documents are missing, follow-up with a letter requesting that the institution provide complete, unredacted copies or that they list specifically what information they are withholding and the specific part of the law that allows them to withhold it.

◆ **Keep excellent records.**
Include dates, times, names, places, and observations. If possible, take photographs or video footage and get eyewitness reports in writing. Leave a "paper trail" of letters and other documents that record the progress of the investigation. That is, make written requests and responses, and keep a copy of all incoming and outgoing correspondence.

◆ **Recruit law enforcement and/or the media.**
If your investigation uncovers violations of law, recruit the involvement of humane, animal control, or law enforcement officers. Again, if you have the services of an attorney at your disposal, all the better. Even if your investigation doesn't uncover illegal activities, you may have discovered information of interest to the general public. Use the media to publicize such information when it's to your advantage.

◆ **Ask for help.**
Don't be afraid to ask for help from more experienced investigators. Call some of the groups listed in Chapter 10 if you need advice.

◆ **Go the extra mile.**
Some investigations require more than others. The group Last Chance for Animals used 24-hour surveillance to bust an operation in Bakersfield, California that was illegally obtaining animals by answering "found" ads and posing as a placement service (Puppy Pavilion), but was actually selling the animals to medical labs. Undercover investigators of People for the Ethical Treatment of Animals regularly uncover and expose cruelty by obtaining jobs at companies that exploit animals, recording what they witness, and making the information public.

Educate

In the words of Mark Glover, founder of the anti-fur organization Lynx, "...public support is the key to fundamental change...It is the pressure created by the public that effects change of a lasting nature."[1] Public education is vital to change. People need to hear about issues — and hear about them often — in order for public opinion to shift. Here are some ways you can tell others about the cause.

■ Cheap and Easy Things You Can Do

- Educate yourself. Keep up on what's happening by joining local and national organizations and reading animal rights publications.
- Use stamps and stickers on envelopes. Place them immediately above the name and address block so they'll be noticed by anyone handling the letter. See Chapter 12 for sources of stamps and stickers.

- Be a "living billboard" — wear a button or T-shirt with an animal rights message. Put a bumper sticker on your car.
- Post animal rights information in your office or school.
- Set up an information table at a street fair or mall, or hand leaflets to passersby.
- Leave animal rights flyers in library books when you return them, in waiting areas at airports, in public restrooms — be creative! Ask your doctor, dentist, and hair dresser if you can leave animal rights literature in their waiting rooms. Free literature is available from many groups.

Woodstock Animal Rights Movement

An information table, such as this one by Woodstock Animal Rights Movement, is an effective way to reach the public.

- Slip anti-fur cards or pamphlets into the pockets of fur coats hanging on racks in stores.
- Write a letter on an animal issue to the editor of your local newspaper.
- Volunteer to create an animal rights display for your local library.
- Put an animal rights message on your telephone answering machine.
- Request that your library carry animal rights and vegetarian periodicals, books, and videos.
- Give animal rights or vegetarian books, magazine subscriptions, and merchandise as gifts during holidays.
- Host a letter-writing get together. If you don't know who to write, get on the mailing list of Joan W. Jenrich. Joan provides monthly samples of who to write and what to say. You can reach her at P.O. Box 7251, St. Petersburg, FL 33734-7251.
- Participate in protests that attract attention. Dress up in costumes. Use humor and creativity. Have fun! The wilder the better! PETA once sponsored a "Barf-In" against L'Oreal, sending letters to them enclosed in barf bags containing the message "What L'Oreal Does to Animals Makes Us Sick." You can bet that got attention!

■ Actions That Require More Investment of Time or Money

- Speak to grade school classes on animal rights and vegetarianism. Help interested kids get a club going.
- Donate vegetarian and animal rights books, magazine subscriptions, and videos to public

and school libraries.

- Donate animal rights and vegetarian videos to a local video store.
- Sponsor a message on a billboard, a bench, or the side of a bus. Contact People for the Ethical Treatment of Animals or another large group for help. For an effective anti-fur billboard, contact Noah's Friends Unlimited, P.O. Box 36197, Richmond, VA 23235, (804) 320-7090.
- Run an ad in your local newspaper. Some national groups can provide you with camera-ready ads.
- Air animal rights programs on your local cable access station, or arrange to broadcast animal rights Public Service Announcements on local channels. See the Radio & Television Programming section of Chapter 12 for resources.

Litigate

Don't be afraid to go to court to get what you want. Many victories for animals have resulted from lawsuits. Many students exercising their right to refuse dissection have seen uncooperative administrations become quite accommodating as soon as a lawsuit was filed.

Filing a lawsuit requires the assistance of an attorney. Again, the Animal Legal Defense Fund may be able to refer you to a legal animal advocate in your community. You should also contact animal organizations that specialize in the issue you're pursuing, or who have pursued similar lawsuits. Browse through Chapter 10 for leads.

Legislate

It's important to communicate with elected officials on the local, state, and federal levels. Enacting legislation is a formidable task that takes political savvy. But your voice can make a difference. Legislators do pay attention to letters, calls, and visits, particularly when they receive a large volume of requests on a particular bill. Here are some tips for communicating your wishes to your legislators.

- To find out the names and addresses of your state and federal representatives and senators, contact your local League of Women Voters, board of elections, or your reference librarian. In addition to telling you the names of your representatives over the phone, the League offers a booklet called *Tell It to Washington*, which contains names and telephone numbers for members of the federal government as well as tips for communicating effectively with officials (for ordering information, see the Activism section of Chapter 13). One useful reference book your library might have is Congressional Quarterly's *Politics in America,* which contains for each state a district map, a photograph and description of each federal senator and representative, and their voting records on major bills.
- To find out what animal-related bills are before your state legislature, call the League of Women Voters. They can tell you where to call or write for that information. Ohio's state legislature has a toll-free number that Ohioans can call for daily updates on legislative items (1-800-282-0253). Your state may have a similar service.

Some states have political action committees (PACs) that keep track of legislation affecting animals. Check the state listings in Chapter 10 to see if there is such a group in your state.

Once you know the number of a state bill, you can request a free copy of house bills from your state representative's office or copies of senate bills from your state senator's office. Bills preceded by the letter "S" are senate bills, and those preceded by "H" are house bills. Proposed wording changes to bills appear in all uppercase letters within the text of the bill.

- To find out about proposed federal legislation affecting animals, follow these steps:

  1. Call Federal Legislative Information at (202) 225-1772. Ask for the bill numbers of pending legislation related to animals. (Remember, bills that begin with "S" are senate bills and those that begin with "H" are house bills. Proposed wording changes to existing bills appear in all uppercase letters within the text of the bill.)

  2. For house bills, call the House Documents Room at (202) 225-3456. You may request a free copy of no more than six bills per day over the phone. If you want copies for more than six house bills, have someone else call or wait and call back the next day.

  3. For senate bills, send a written request to Senate Documents Room, Hart Building, Room SHB04, Washington, D.C. 20510 (the telephone number is (202) 224-7860, in case you have questions). Include a self-addressed label with your request. Again, you may order a maximum of six senate bills per request (they're free and you get one copy of each bill requested). If you want copies of more than six senate bills, you must wait and send an additional request on a different day.

  You can also find out about proposed federal legislation by contacting organizations concerned with federal legislation on behalf of animals. Some of these organizations are listed at the end of this chapter.

- Be aware that there are organized efforts for and against animals in Congress. The Congressional Friends of Animals (CFA) is a group of congressional members who support legislation benefiting animals. They face-off with members of the Sportsmen's Caucus and the Animal Welfare Caucus (AWC) that, despite its name, represents the interests of the farming and research communities. Political information goes out of date quickly, but as of this writing, Congressional Friends of Animals consisted of the members shown in the box on the next page. For updates on members, contact Winthrop Wulsin c/o Tom Lantos' office, 2217 Rayburn, House Office Building, Washington, D.C. 20515, (202) 225-3531.

- Question political candidates on relevant animal rights issues, such as mandatory spay/neuter laws, pound seizure, etc. Try to do this at public forums such as "Meet the Candidates Night."

- For help on passing specific legislation, such as stopping pound seizure, it may be helpful to contact others who have tried a similar measure. Check the Resources sections at the end of previous chapters and browse the group descriptions in Chapter 10 for organizations that may have dealt directly with the issue of interest.

Congressional Friends of Animals 104th Congress	
Co-Chairs: Tom Lantos (D-CA) Charlie Rose, Senator (D-NC) **Members:** Robert Borski (D-PA) George Brown, Jr. (D-CA) William Clay (D-MO) Ronald V. Dellums (D-CA) Peter Deutsch (D-FL) Elliot Engel (D-NY) Sam Gibbons (D-FL)	William Hughes (D-NJ) John Lewis (D-GA) Carolyn Maloney (D-NY) Patsy Mink (D-HI) Frank Pallone (D-NH) Illeana Ros-Lehtinen (R-FL) Pat Schroeder (D-CO) Charles Schumer (D-NY) Robert G. Torricelli (D-NJ) Edolphus Towns (D-NY) Charles Wilson (D-TX), who is also a member of the Sportsmen's Caucus

- Letter-writing is an easy and important way to let your legislators know how you feel. According to the League of Women Voters, some Congressional members base their vote on a bill solely on their "mail count."[2] When writing letters, keep the following points in mind:
  - Don't write as an animal activist; simply write as a concerned citizen.
  - Confine letters to one topic. Keep them short and to the point. Ask for something specific, such as support of or opposition to a specific bill.
  - Address correspondence to federal legislators as follows:

Senators:

The Honorable (name)
U.S. Senate
Washington, D.C. 20510

Dear Senator (name):

Representatives:

The Honorable (name)
U.S. House of Representatives
Washington, D.C. 20515

Dear (Mr. or Ms.) (name):

Be a Consumer Advocate

As a consumer, you have a strong voice in the marketplace. Thanks to consumer pressure, many companies have stopped carrying furs and others have stopped testing their products on animals. Three of the big-name canned tuna sellers now offer "dolphin-free" tuna. These are just a handful of the victories consumers have won for animals. As a consumer, here's how you can be a positive influence for animals:

- Offended by the use of furs or the sport hunting shown on your favorite sitcom? Don't like the way a story was handled on the evening news? Let them know! You don't even have to leave your spot in front of the television. Just keep a stack of stamped postcards next to you, and when you see a program or commercial that exploits animals, write a quick paragraph to the offending program or company. Also tell them that you are registering a complaint with their sponsors, then do so. See the Resources section at the end of the chapter for addresses and telephone numbers of the leading commercial television broadcasters. You'll find the addresses and phone numbers for many sponsors in the *Consumer's Resource Handbook*, free from the Consumer Information Center, Pueblo, Colorado, 81009.

The same goes for local stations. If you don't like the way your local newscasters ignored the animal rights advocates at the pork convention, let them know with a phone call and/or a letter. For addresses and telephone numbers of your local stations, look under Television Stations and Broadcasting Companies in the Yellow Pages of your local telephone directory.

Also be sure to let television producers and companies know when they air something you especially like. Positive reinforcement works!

- Buy a share of stock in companies that exploit animals. This entitles you to attend shareholders meetings and ask questions such as, "Why does this company continue to needlessly test its products on animals?"
- American Express is not a friend to animals. They sell furs through their catalog and support the Moscow Circus. If you have an American Express Card, cut it up and send it back to them with a note. If you get an application for an American Express Card, write on the application that you will be happy to apply for a card as soon as American Express starts showing respect for animals by refusing to support exploitive activities. Or you can call AmEx Headquarters, 1-800-THE-CARD.
- Boycott mail order companies that support the exploitation of animals, including companies that sell animal skins or down products, and those that support hunting or fishing. Write them a friendly but firm letter that explains why you will no longer buy from them. Such companies include The Company Store (sells sheepskin and down) and L.L. Bean (sells fur and glorifies hunting).

Guidelines for Being Out in the Field

Here are some pointers for those who like being on the front lines.

◆ **Find out about the opposition.**
There are many groups who find animal rights principles threatening, among them farmers and organizations that support biomedical research. Some people have recently formed groups with the sole purpose of countering animal rights efforts. One such group is Putting People First (PPF), which offers a sweatshirt that reads, "Save an animal; eat an activist" and other such slogans. This group's stance is that animals are here to serve humans, in whatever capacity humans choose. By requesting their literature, you cost them money in printing and mailing expenses. Don't let on that you are an animal rights supporter or they probably won't respond. You can contact the

national office at: Putting People First (PPF), 4401 Connecticut Avenue NW, Suite 310-A, Washington, D.C. 20008, (202) 364-7277. (*Note:* They may not give you a referral to a local chapter unless you become a PPF member, but you can request it anyway.)

◆ **Attack the behavior, not the person.**

While it's tempting to see animal exploiters as the "enemy," try to remember that it's not the people you object to, it's the behavior of the people. Target the behavior, not the individuals. Of course, you may need to name names in order to pressure individuals into changing their behavior, but that isn't the same as attacking the person.

Paul Obis, speaking as editor of *Vegetarian Times* magazine, said:

> When we come into contact with people whose views differ from our own, we can become angry and resentful or we can reach for the understanding and compassion that dwell within each of us. It is a case of learning to love the hunter, but not the hunting.[3]

Apply the same principles to other people that you would apply to other animals: tolerance, understanding, and compassion. Show the same respect to others that you want them to show you. Respect the right to disagree. In the words of Michael Klaper, M.D.:

> No matter what passionate feelings or beliefs we may hold about anything, including the eating of animal products, Love is more important...all of us are emerging from a deep sleep of non-understanding...We can most help others on their journey of increasing understanding by giving them a most wonderful and powerful gift: a loving example of respectful listening, of compassionate consideration of their point of view, and of forgiveness if hurtful words are said from anger or non-seeing.[4]

◆ **You're in the spotlight, so shine.**

When you are a representative for animal rights, people view you as an "example." Be sure that your appearance and demeanor are appropriate. For example, don't wear animal products (such as leather, fur, or feathers) during animal rights activities. Model the behaviors you want from others. Be polite, even when someone is rude to you. Also, better to dress conservatively and profession-

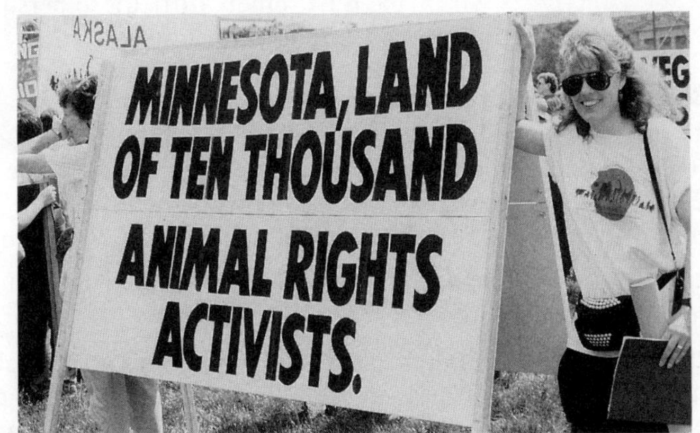

Thousands of animal rights activists found strength in numbers at the 1990 March for the Animals in Washington, D.C.

ally. People do make judgments based on appearance.

- **Be prepared for the "third degree."**

People who are angry about your cause (or are just angry in general) sometimes look for any excuse to ridicule you. No matter what you are demonstrating for or against, many people will try to discredit you as an animal activist by inquiring whether or not you eat meat and whether or not you wear leather. G. Thomas Morgan, a deer hunter, levels this criticism against animal activists:

> The same people who raise their hackles over the killing of animals by hunters acquiesce the killing that provides for their fast-food burgers, and they never even flinch when purchasing fish, meat, and poultry at the local grocery store.[5]

If you are a vegetarian who refrains from wearing leather, you have nothing to worry about. If you do eat animals or wear animal skins, then you may need to look at whether or not the criticism you're receiving is warranted. Is it hypocritical to eat meat and demonstrate against using animals in product testing? Many people think so. Yet, you may feel strongly about certain issues, such as product testing, but not as strongly about others, such as vegetarianism. One way to answer someone who questions you about such things is to bring the conversation back to the issue at hand. For example, you can say, "I'm here today because I feel that using animals to test products is cruel, unnecessary, and unjustifiable. That is the focus of this demonstration and that is the sole reason why I am here. Eating meat is a separate topic which I'll be happy to discuss with you at some other time."

But keep in mind the following point, made by The American Anti-Vivisection Society in their booklet *Point/Counterpoint* :

> ...vivisection is cruel in and of itself, and this fact remains true regardless of the habits of the person making the statement...It should be remembered, however, that inconsistency on the part of animal activists will make it extremely difficult to persuade others to accept their arguments concerning animal rights.[6]

- **Be prepared for rudeness.**

It is the rare animal rights advocate who, while standing on a sidewalk holding a sign against rodeo, fur, or some other animal rights issue, has not had one or more passersby shout something derogatory as they whiz by in a car. I've heard everything from "Mind your own business!" to "What about human rights?" to a string of profanities.

Why do people say such things? There are many reasons, few of which have anything to do with animal rights.

Protesters are convenient targets. People who are unable to express their emotions appropriately often vent their emotions on strangers, such as store clerks. Protesters are safe targets because the person can remain anonymous and can simply drive or walk away without allowing even the slightest chance for recourse.

Sometimes the protester's message is perceived as a threat. Some people take your message as personal criticism. In this case, anger covers guilt. The person doesn't want to be reminded that they are part of the problem. Their anger at their own internal struggle is misdirected at you.

Some people just like to pick fights. No matter what you're protesting, some people will take exception simply for the sake of argument. Don't get sucked into arguing with them; it's a no-win situation. Acknowledge that you each have a right to your respective opinions. If someone is downright obnoxious, it's okay to call them on it. You might tell them that there's no need to be rude, or say something to this effect: "I'll be happy to talk with you about this in a calm, civilized manner, but if you are going to insult me then this conversation is finished!" One of the most unexpected things you can do with an argumentative person is to not get defensive. Staying open and friendly and showing respect for them is really disarming!

- **Let the facts speak for themselves.**
  It's okay to say how you feel about something, but don't make emotion-laden accusations that could result in a defamation or libel lawsuit against you. For example, don't use terms such as "monster" or "torturer" to describe a particular researcher. Instead, concentrate on what s/he does to animals. More and more often these days, those who make money from animal exploitation are using the courts to stall animal activists. Even if they have no real case against you, the hassle, expense, and intimidation of a court case can effectively throw a wrench into the works. Don't give them the opportunity.

Resources for Activists

Helpful Addresses and Telephone Numbers

For numbers other than the ones listed here, ask the reference librarian at your local library for help. Also, the periodical *Bunny Hugger's Gazette* regularly includes a list of addresses for newspapers, networks, television and radio programs, and government offices and officials. See the Activism section of Chapter 13 for information on subscribing to *Bunny Hugger's Gazette* .

FEDERAL GOVERNMENT

The President

The White House, 1600 Pennsylvania Ave. NW, Washington, D.C. 20500, (202) 456-1414, FAX: (202) 456-2461, Comment Line: (202) 456-1111 (M-F, 9-5 EST, allows you to answer a survey of current issues which is presented to the President each day, or to leave a message of your own)

E-mail: president@whitehouse.gov
Internet: http://www.whitehouse.gov

The Vice President

The Old Executive Office Building, Washington, D.C. 20500, (202) 456-1414, FAX: (202) 456-2326, E-mail: vice.president@whitehouse.gov

U.S. Senators

The Honorable (name), U.S. Senate, Washington, D.C. 20510, (202) 224-2115

U.S. Representatives

The Honorable (name), U.S. House of Representatives, Washington, D.C. 20515, (202) 225-7000

Animal and Plant Health Inspection Service (APHIS)

Note: APHIS is responsible for the inspection of animal research facilities and dealers. This office can refer you to the regional office for your area. Contact them for copies of the latest inspection reports for facilities or dealers in your area.

Federal Center Building, Hyattsville, MD 20782, FAX: (202) 720-3982

TELEVISION NETWORKS

ABC Television

Audience Information, 77 West 66th Street, New York, NY 10023-6298, (212) 456-7477 (Programming Dept.)

or

2040 Avenue of the Stars, 7th Floor, Century City, CA 90067, (310) 557-7777

CBS Audience Services

524 West 57th Street, New York, NY 1001, (212) 975-3166, ext. 3247

or

7800 Beverly Blvd., Los Angeles, CA 90036, (213) 852-2345

NBC Audience Services

30 Rockefeller Plaza, New York, NY 10112, (212) 664-2333

or

3000 W. Alameda, Burbank, CA 91523, (818) 840-4444

Fox Television Stations, Inc.

10201 West Pico Blvd., Los Angeles, CA 90035, (310) 203-3553

or

205 East 67th Street, New York, NY 10021, (212) 452-5555

PBS Television

1320 Braddock Place, Alexandria, VA 22314, (703) 739-5068

MTV Networks, Inc.

(A subsidiary of Viacom International, Inc.), 1775 Broadway, New York, NY 10019, (212) 713-6400

Turner Broadcasting System, Inc.

One CNN Center, Box 105366, Atlanta, GA 30348, (404) 827-1700

MOTION PICTURE COMPANIES

Columbia Pictures Entertainment, Inc.

(A subsidiary of Sony Corporation), 711 Fifth Avenue, New York, NY 1002, (212) 751-4400

Four Star International, Inc.

2813 West Alameda Avenue, Burbank, CA 91505, (818) 840-7186

MCA, Inc.

100 Universal City Plaza, Universal City, CA 91608, (818) 777-1000

MGM/UA Communications Company

10000 West Washington Blvd., Culver City, CA 90230, (213) 280-6000

Orion Pictures Corporation

1323 Avenue of the Americas, New York, NY 10019, (212) 956-3800

Paramount Pictures Corporation

(A subsidiary of Paramount Communications, Inc.), 5555 Melrose Avenue, Hollywood, CA 90038, (213) 956-5000

Twentieth Century-Fox Film Corporation

P.O. Box 900, Beverly Hills, CA 90213, (213) 277-2211

The Walt Disney Company
500 South Buena Vista Street, Burbank, CA 91521, (818) 560-1000

Warner Brothers, Inc.
(A subsidiary of Time Warner, Inc.), 4000 Warner Blvd., Burbank, CA 91522, (818) 954-6000

Other Resources

For products and services that will help you "walk your talk," see all of Chapter 12.

For publications that will keep you up-to-date on animal rights issues and help you with activism, see Chapter 13.

The following organizations may be of particular interest to activists. For organizations that specialize in specific animal rights issues, see the Resources sections of Chapters 3-8 and the index at the back of the book. See Chapters 10 and 11 for a description of these and other activist organizations.

- **Law**
  American Bar Association Young Lawyers Division/Committee for Animal Protection (TX), Animal Legal Defense Fund (CA), Rutgers Law School/Animal Rights Law Center (NJ), Sierra Club Legal Defense Fund (CA)

- **Legislation & Political Action**
  For PACs and organizations that work on a state or local level, see the state listings in Chapter 10.
  Humane Society of the United States (D.C.), Animal Legislative Action Network (CA), Committee for Humane Legislation (D.C.), Doris Day Animal League (D.C.), Humane Farming Action Fund (CA), Humane Political Action Committee (IL), Society for Animal Protective Legislation (D.C.)

- **Media**
  Animal News Network—television (NY), Animal Rights Information Service—television (NY), Animal Rights Network—magazine (CT), Animal Watch—radio program (NJ), Ark Trust, Inc.—media watch, awards presentation (CA), Arts Activist—artists, photographers, and writers (CA), Compassion for Animals Foundation, Inc.—magazine (CA), Culture and Animals Foundation—original artistic and literary works (NC), Earth! Educate!—printed material (AR), Focus on Animals—film (CT), Gaia Institute—television (MA), Institute for the Development of Earth Awareness—photography and printed material (NY), Nine Lives Productions—television (NY), San Francisco Bay Institute—journal (CA), True Nature Network—television (NY)

- **Special Interest & Professional Groups**
  American Bar Association Young Lawyers Division/Committee for Animal Protection (TX), Animal Legal Defense Fund (CA), Arts Activist (CA), Association of Veterinarians for Animal Rights (CA), Culture and Animals Foundation—original art and literary works (NC), Engineers and Scientists for Animal Rights (TX), Feminists for Animal Rights (NC), International League of Doctors for the Abolition of Vivisection (NY), Medical Research Modernization Committee—health care professionals (NY), National Wildlife Rehabilitators Association

(MN), Physicians Committee for Responsible Medicine (D.C.), Psychologists for the Ethical Treatment of Animals (MD), Society for the Study of Ethics and Animals—philosophers, writers, etc. (VA), Vegetarian Dietitians and Nutrition Educators (NY)

◆ **Spiritual & Religious Organizations**

Christians Helping Animals and People, Inc. (NY), Friends Vegetarian Society of North America—Quakers (KY), Interbeing Partnerships (NJ), Interfaith Council for the Protection of Animals and Nature (GA), International Network for Religion and Animals (MD), Jehovah's Witnesses for Animal Rights (CA), Jewish Vegetarian Society International (NY), Jewish Vegetarians of North America (MD), Jews for Animal Rights/Micah Publications (MA), Ministries for Animals (CA), Prevention of Cruelty to Animals and Plants—Ananda Marga (NY), Unitarian Universalists for the Ethical Treatment of Animals (NY), Universal Great Brotherhood (MO), World Mission for Animals (OR)

◆ **Student & Campus-Based Organizations**

Note: Student groups often come and go with the school year, and tend to be inactive during the summer months. Student/campus-based groups are organized by state.

AR—Students for the Ethical Treatment of Animals (University of Arkansas); CA—Animal Emancipation (USCB Student Chapter), SUPRESS, Inc. (national), University Students Against Vivisection; D.C.—Student Action Corps for Animals (national); FL—Students for the Ethical Treatment of Animals (University of Florida); IA—Iowa State University Humane Society (Iowa State University), University of Iowa Animal Coalition; LA—Students in Defense of Animals (University of New Orleans); MD—Animal Rights Coalition (University of Maryland); MA—Animal Rights Coalition (University of Massachusetts at Amherst), University Conversion Project/Center for Campus Organizing (national); MI—People for Animal Welfare (Western Michigan University), Students Concerned About Animal Welfare (Michigan State University), United Students for Animals; MN—Animal Rights Coalition (University of Minnesota Chapter), Student Organization for Animal Rights (CMU); NV—United Students for Animals; NY—Binghamton Animal Rights Coalition (State University of New York), Cornell Students for the Ethical Treatment of Animals (Cornell University), Students for the Ethical Treatment of Animals (New York University); OH—Students for Animals (Wright State University), Students for Animal Rights (University of Dayton), Students for the Ethical Treatment of Animals/S.O.A.R. (Ohio State University), Wittenberg University Animal Rights Club; PA—Penn State Alliance for Animal Rights; TX—Students for the Welfare of Animals (San Antonio College); VT—Students Organized for Animal Rights (University of Vermont); WI—Alliance for Animals, Inc. (contact for UW-Madison, UW-Milwaukee, and UW-Oshkosh), Students for Animals (UW-Green Bay)

It is not only what we do, but also what we do not do, for which we are accountable.

— Moliére

Conclusion

You don't have to hold a protest sign to be an animal advocate. There are plenty of things each of us can do for animals. Very simply:

- Don't contribute to animal exploitation yourself. Avoid products, events, and charities that involve animal suffering.
- Let animal exploiters know that you know who they are and what they're doing. When you witness exploitation, speak up. Publicize local exploitation by staffing information tables and writing letters to the editor of your local newspaper.
- Support those who are helping animals by donating money or services to deserving organizations.

Remember, your actions do make a difference. Live your convictions.

Activism

At a Glance

Did you know:

- Many of us are unwitting "passive abusers" who unintentionally support animal cruelty by supporting the industries that abuse animals.
- Voicing your concerns to elected representatives does make a difference. According to the League of Women Voters, some Congressional members base their vote on a bill on their "mail count."
- As a consumer, you wield tremendous power over the marketplace. Helping animals is as simple as changing your buying habits.
- Things you can do to help animals include investigating abusive practices and industries, using the courts to stop animal abusers, advocating for humane laws, educating others by speaking out for animals, and being a conscious, caring consumer.

Never doubt that a small group of thoughtful, committed citizens can change the world; indeed, it's the only thing that ever has.

— Margaret Mead

Quick and Easy Guide to Activism

WRITE...	companies, store managers, restaurants, filmmakers, legislators, and letters to the editor of newspapers and magazines to address animal rights concerns.
BOYCOTT...	all products, events, and companies that exploit animals (and let them know why).
PROTEST...	at events and companies that hurt animals.
INFORM...	yourself and others about animal rights issues, national campaigns, and pending legislation.
JOIN...	animal rights and vegetarian organizations.
LIVE...	your convictions.

Nothing is more powerful than an individual acting out of his conscience, thus helping to bring the collective conscience to life.

— Norman Cousins (as quoted in *The Extended Circle*)

Part Four

Resources for Animals

Chapter 10

Animal Advocacy Organizations

The groups listed here represent a broad spectrum of animal helpers—welfare groups, humane societies, wildlife rehabilitators, and specialized rescue organizations as well as national, international, and local animal rights groups.* Not all of these groups have an animal "rights" orientation, but all serve animals in some capacity. The main intent of this resource list is to help you find the advice or help you may need to assist individual animals, as well as to further animal rights in general.

The vast majority of grassroots groups are staffed entirely by volunteers who receive no financial compensation. Many are operated out of people's homes (when you call, in many instances, you're calling a residence, not an office). Larger groups usually have paid staff. All groups are, to my knowledge, not-for-profit, although some of the largest groups have plush offices and pay exceedingly large salaries to their executives (more on this in a page or two).

All groups play an important role in the animal rights movement and need your help. Grassroots groups especially depend on your support. They don't have advertising budgets that allow them the luxury of mass mailings. It's a pretty sure bet that every penny you give to a grassroots group goes directly to helping animals. And don't forget to check with your employer's personnel office to see if they sponsor a matching gift program. If they do, they may match your donation to tax-exempt organizations.

Joining an organization has many benefits. It allows you to:

- **Contribute to the animal rights movement.**
  Whether your support is purely financial or includes active participation, every little bit helps.

- **Stay informed.**
  Many groups keep members updated on issues through newsletters and special alerts. By joining a variety of groups, including different grassroots groups, you can keep current on animals rights information from different parts of the country.

- **Gain moral support.**
  It's nice to connect with people who think like you do.

---

* This listing is confined to organizations with offices in the United States of America. For organizations in other countries, contact *Bunny Hugger's Gazette*, P.O. Box 601, Temple, TX 76503-0601 for information on how to purchase their annual *Animal Organizations Directory*.

Finding What You Want

If you know the name of a group but you're not sure where it's located, look under "Animal Advocacy Organizations" in the index at the back of the book for an alphabetical list of all organizations. To locate groups with special areas of interest, check under the appropriate heading (for example, Factory Farming, Sanctuaries, etc).

The list in this book is by no means complete. Several groups politely requested they not be included, and a few were downright hostile (one wildlife rehabilitator in Wautoma, WI threatened to sue me if I listed his center, and a greyhound adoption group in Houston, TX was quite sharp in their insistence that I remove them from my mailing list). Some groups were sympathetic to "the cause," but felt that being listed in an animal rights book could somehow hamper their efforts. Then there were some groups that I chose to omit. If you don't see what you need, check with the resources listed in the next section, "Keeping Up-To-Date," or contact this publisher for help (see the order form at the back of the book).

Keeping Up-To-Date

Information on organizations changes frequently. Groups disband or change locations, and new groups form. For updated information, try the following sources:

- *Bunny Hugger's Gazette* prints an annual directory of animal rights/vegetarian organizations, published every February. Contact *BHG Directory,* P.O. Box 601, Temple, TX 76503-0601.
- The *No-Kill Directory* lists 250 "no-kill" humane organizations that provide rescue, sanctuary, and rehabilitation to animals in 38 states. Contact Doing Things for Animals, Inc., P.O. Box 2165, Sun City, AZ 85372-2165.
- The *Project BREED (Breed Rescue Efforts & EDucation) Directory, Volumes 1 & 2,* contains nearly 3,000 volunteers rescuing over 100 breeds of dogs, as well as rabbits, ferrets, and wild bats nationwide (including Hawaii and Alaska) and in Canada. Contact Project BREED, Inc., P.O. Box 15888, Chevy Chase, MD 20825-5888.
- STAR Ferrets (Shelters That Adopt & Rescue Ferrets) is an organization that maintains an international database of ferret-related contacts. For free information on shelters, rescue groups, vets, etc. in your state, send a self-addressed, stamped envelope to STAR Ferrets, P.O. Box 1714, Springfield, VA 22151-0714, (703) 354-5073.
- The International Wildlife Rehabilitation Council is a network of professional wildlife rehabilitators. Contact IWRC, 4437 Central Place, Suite B-4, Suisun, CA 94585, (707) 864-1761, FAX: (707) 864-3106. The National Wildlife Rehabilitator's Association is another network of wildlife professionals. Contact NWRA, 14 N. 7th Avenue, St. Cloud, MN 56303-4766, (612) 259-4086. (*Note*: Animal rehabilitators are frequently *not* animal rights people, so don't be surprised.) You can also call local veterinarians, your state wildlife agency (they go by different names—Department of Wildlife, Department of Natural Resources, Department of Fish and Game, etc.) to see who is licensed to handle wildlife in your area, or check your library for the book *Living with Wildlife* by

The California Center for Wildlife, which contains a list of wildlife rehabilitators by state.

- The Association Of Sanctuaries is developing a national database of existing sanctuaries. Contact TAOS, P.O. Box 22428, Sacramento, CA 95822, (916) 448-5588 or Route 1, Box 33A, Comfort, TX 78013, (512) 995-3680.
- For welfare/humane agencies in your area, check the Yellow Pages of your telephone directory under the heading "Humane Societies" or "Animal Welfare."

Some Things to Consider: Is Bigger Better?

Animal advocacy groups include everything from local groups consisting of one or two very active volunteers to large, million-dollar national and international organizations. Is one better than the other?

The Big Guys

Some large groups have been criticized for the size of their budgets and the ways they choose to spend contributors' money. Critics claim that too much is spent on executive salaries and on generating additional contributions instead of on direct actions for animals.* For example, the president of The Humane Society of the United States, John Hoyt, drew over $226,000 in compensation in 1994.[1] Some activists have commented on the big difference that sum of money could make if applied elsewhere, such as to spay/neuter services. Some nationally-known groups have also been accused of routinely grabbing the spotlight (and thus monetary contributions) for rescues or actions in which they have invested minimal effort. The grassroots groups who initiated the efforts then receive no credit—or money. Additional criticism has been leveled against groups accused of working to save only "high profile" animals, those with the most public appeal.

Is such criticism warranted? In some cases, yes. Large and small groups alike must be judged on their own merits. Some groups seem to invest more in plush offices and salaries than in true actions for animals. On the other hand, some national/international organizations have furthered the cause of animal rights dramatically in a very short time, accomplishing things that only groups with large budgets and high profiles can accomplish. People for the Ethical Treatment of Animals (PETA) is almost synonymous with animal rights in many people's minds, and must receive much of the credit for bringing animal rights into the living rooms of Americans. High-visibility public campaigns and professionally-produced literature bring a lot of public attention to animal rights and rouse people into action. Many large groups work with legislators to pass animal protection laws. A national movement

---

* *Animal People* annually publishes a list of the budgets and executive salaries for top-money animal protection groups. Contact *Animal People*, P.O. Box 205, Shushan, NY 12873. You can also find out about a group's finances by asking them for a copy of their annual report (which tells how it spends contributions) and form IRS 990 (which reveals the salaries of the highest paid executives).

such as the one happening now would not have been possible without the big-budget organizers.

Grassroots groups often look to the larger groups for support and guidance. Depending on the nature of the request, help is often forthcoming. Many large groups are able to supply literature, merchandise, and advice, although they are not always able to become directly involved with the local effort.

The Little Guys

Always remember, though, that for every organization with a large budget, there are dozens of grassroots organizations working on shoestring budgets to change things on community, state, national, and even international levels. Most grassroots organizations can't afford to produce slick literature, nor can they afford to send mailings many times a year asking for support. Virtually all grassroots organizations are staffed by volunteers who receive no money for their efforts. In fact, many grassroots activists end up covering expenses with their own money. Often, it's the unrelenting efforts of one or two individuals that make things happen.

Grassroots organizing is vital to the animal rights movement; as the saying goes, "Change begins at home." While large and small organizations alike need your support, don't forget that a few dollars can play a significant role in what small groups are able to accomplish.* And there's no substitute for participation. Whether you like to work in the background or out in front, there's plenty of work to be done. Support the grassroots groups.

Question Authority—Even in the Animal Rights Movement

Just because the subject is animal rights doesn't mean that everyone involved is an angel. As in any other movement, business, or circumstance where egos and money are involved, there are always a few individuals who take advantage or don't live up to their images. The animal protection community has its share of squabbles, infiltrators, government informers, and even fraud. This shouldn't, however, discredit the 99% of activists who sincerely dedicate themselves to creating a more compassionate society.

Please Note: A listing is not necessarily an endorsement. The author makes no claims as to the organizations listed herein. All groups listed are believed to work for animals in good faith, but in the final analysis, the investigative work is up to you. Don't be afraid to ask a group about its finances and how the funds are applied. They should be happy to tell you

* A simple way you can help is by including a self-addressed, stamped envelope whenever you write to grassroots groups for information or literature.

exactly how the money is spent, and what they have specifically accomplished for animals.

This list is not complete. Some changes may have occurred since this writing, and some groups were omitted by their request or at my discretion. For additional organizations, see Keeping Up-To-Date, earlier in this chapter.

A Note About Area Codes: A shortage of telephone numbers has prompted the creation of additional area codes for many parts of the country. Because area codes are still changing, some area codes may be outdated. If you get a "wrong number," check to see whether the area code could be the culprit.

National & International Organizations

The organizations listed here describe themselves as having a national and/or international scope. Some are big-money operations, while others are essentially grassroots groups doing wonders on relatively small budgets. For more information, contact the groups that interest you. If you know of a group missing from the list that should be included, please contact this publisher.

800 For Animals, Inc.
(Animal Referral Hotline)
P.O. Box 2082, Ashland, VA 23005,
1-800-8-ANIMAL (outside Richmond, VA),
(804) 798-5957 (inside Richmond, VA)
A national, toll-free hotline for referrals and information on animal-related services.

Action 81, Inc.
Route 3, Box 6000, Berryville, VA 22611,
(703) 955-1278
Operates as a national network to prevent, monitor, and expose the theft of dogs and cats within the dealer-laboratory system. Has contacts and/or co-workers in every state, and in parts of Canada and England. Can tell you what you can do in your own community.

Adopt-A-Cow
RD1, Box 839, Port Royal, PA 17082,
(717) 527-2476
Provides a cruelty-free life for cows, bulls, and oxen at Gita-nagari Farm. Funded entirely by donations. Adoptions and contributions are tax-deductible.

African Wildlife Foundation
1717 Massachusetts Avenue NW, Suite 202,
Washington, D.C. 20036, (202) 265-8394
Works to protect African wildlife, including the mountain gorillas who are threatened with extinction from hunters, wildlife dealers, and loss of habitat due to mining, logging, and development.

Alley Cat Allies
P.O. Box 397, Mount Rainier, MD 20712
National feral cat network. Advice and literature available.

Alternatives Research & Development Foundation (ARDF)
801 Old York Road, Suite 204, Jenkintown, PA 19046-1685, (215) 887-0816, FAX: (215) 887-2088, E-mail: aavsonline@aol.com
Affiliated with the American Anti-Vivisection Society. Funds projects that develop alternatives to the use of animals in biomedical research, testing, and education. Also promotes the expanded use of alternatives to animals through education, television programming, awards, etc. (See the listing for American Anti-Vivisection Society elsewhere in this section).

Amberwood Sanctuary
Route 2, Box 300, Baker County,
Leary, GA 31762, (912) 792-6246
Provides a peaceful, permanent home to burros. Involved in all areas of concern for donkeys worldwide through direct action, education, and legislation. Supported in part

by a vegan mail-order business.

The American Anti-Vivisection Society (AAVS)

801 Old York Road, Suite 204, Jenkintown, PA 19046-1685, (215) 887-0816, FAX: (215) 887-2088, E-mail: aavsonline@aol.com
Dedicated to the elimination of animal use in research, testing, and education.

American Bar Association Young Lawyer Division, Committee for Animal Protection

700 N. Pearl, #2001, LB317, Dallas, TX 75201-2847, (214) 965-0202, FAX: (214) 965-0201

American Cetacean Society (ACS)

National Headquarters: P.O. Box 2639, San Pedro, CA 90731-0943, (213) 548-6279, FAX: (213) 548-6950
International, with a total of nine chapters. Concentrates its efforts on the protection of whales and dolphins. Membership includes many scientists and educators, as well as lay persons.

American Ferret Association, Inc. (AFA)

P.O. Box 3986, Frederick, MD 21705-3986, (301) 663-6616
Promotes the domestic ferret as a companion animal. Protects the domestic ferret against anti-ferret legislation, mistreatment, unsound breeding practices, overpopulation, needless scientific research, and any practice deemed to lower the health standards or survivability of the animal. Provides constant and up-to-date information on vets, research, rescue shelters, and other information of interest to ferret owners. Please include a self-addressed, stamped envelope with inquiry.

American Fund for Alternatives to Animal Research (AFAAR)

175 West 12th Street, Suite 16G, New York, NY 10011, (212) 989-8073
Finances the development, evaluation, validation, and promotion of alternatives to animal research. Awards scientific grants to scientists interested in developing and promoting nonanimal research methods. Finances CELLSERV, successful laboratory kits for beginning high school and college biology classes. Also funds summer classes with lab studies in alternatives for high school teachers and pre-med students.

American Horse Protection Association

1000-29th Street NW, Suite T-100, Washington, D.C. 20007, (202) 965-0500
Works to end abuses of horses and burros.

American Humane Association (AHA)

Headquarters: 63 Inverness Drive East, Englewood, CO 80112, (303) 792-9900
Works to prevent neglect, abuse, cruelty, and exploitation of animals.

American Mustang and Burro Association, Inc. (AMBA)

P.O. Box 788, Lincoln, CA 95648-0788, (509) 588-6336
Dedicated to the protection and preservation of wild equine, to public education and awareness, and to adopter support. Maintains a comprehensive registry for wild equine and their descendants. Sponsors the nation's only wild horse and burro Information Hotline and Abuse/Neglect Hotline. Operates a rescue, rehabilitation, and relocation service.

American Society for the Prevention of Cruelty to Animals (ASPCA)

- National Office: 424 East 92nd Street, New York, NY 10128, (212) 876-7700
- National Legislative Office: 1755 Massachusetts Avenue NW, Washington, D.C. 20036, (202) 232-5020

Shelters and hospitals in New York City and Brooklyn. Pet receiving centers in the Bronx, Rego Park, and Staten Island. The first humane society in the U.S. In NYC, provides animal rescue work and operates animal shelters, veterinary hospitals, and spay/neuter clinics. Nationally, provides education, consultation, investigation, and legislative initiatives.

Animal Alliance

P.O. Box 8031, Santa Fe, NM 87504-8031
A small group creating model spay/neuter programs for the "Third World," focusing on Central and South America.

Animal Legal Defense Fund (ALDF)

National Office: 1363 Lincoln Avenue, San Rafael, CA 94901, (415) 459-0885
A nationwide network of more than 300 attorneys dedicated to protecting and promoting animal rights.

Animal Legislative Action Network (ALAN)

2379 Panorama Terrace, Los Angeles, CA 90039, (213) 662-6728

A grassroots, Political Action Committee (PAC) of animal advocates. "Our intention is to produce for animals the same legal protections we enjoy as human beings." Vigorously campaigns for candidates who will work on behalf of animals or those facing an opponent with a clear history of opposition to animal protection legislation. Offers an *Animals Under the Law* packet for $5 postpaid for those who wish to form their own local PAC. Also a quarterly newsletter which reviews significant animal legislation nationwide for $5.

Animal Liberation Action (ALA)

726 N. Palo Verde, Tucson, AZ 85716, (602) 795-8258 (Jack Norris, National Coordinator)

Regional contacts in Ohio, Pennsylvania, and Wisconsin. Focuses on animals raised and slaughtered for food, but works to stop the exploitation of all animals.

Animal Liberation Front Support Group (ALFSG)

- North American ALF Support Group: P.O. Box 8673, Victoria, BC, Canada, V8X 3S2
- Merchandise & Literature Distribution: NA-ALFSG DISTRO, P.O. Box 241532, Memphis, TN 38124

Supports the Animal Liberation Front (ALF) by all lawful means possible. The ALF consists of small, autonomous groups of individuals nationwide who carry out "direct action" according to ALF Guidelines. The support group is a completely separate entity, which supports the ALF without breaking the law.

The Animal News Network (ANN)

P.O. Box 439, Old Albany Post Road, Garrison, NY 10524, (914) 424-3005, FAX: (914) 424-4132

"A new concept in television programming." A loose confederation of individuals and organizations consisting of producers, directors, and writers of environmental video materials with a special emphasis on animal issues. Formed by a group of public access producers for the purpose of gaining improved nationwide exposure for animal-related issues.

Animal Place

3448 Laguna Creek Trail, Vacaville, CA 95688-9724, (707) 449-4814, E-mail: Porcilina@ad.com Internet: http://envirolink.org/arrs/animal_place/ap_www.htm

A sanctuary for abused and discarded "farm" animals—chickens, ducks, geese, pea and guinea fowl, pigs, goats, and cattle. Founded and operated by Kim Sturla and Nedim Buyukmihci, co-founder and president of The Association of Veterinarians for Animal Rights (see their listing elsewhere in this section).

Animal Protection Educators (APE)

8503 East Davies Avenue, Englewood, CO 80112, (303) 773-2571

Works to educate the public, especially youth, as to the basic intrinsic rights and value of all living beings. Prepares and disseminates curricula, video and audio tapes, slides, and literature to other animal rights groups, schools, individuals, and the community at large. Conducts lectures and classes, and trains educators.

Animal Protection Institute of America (API)

- Street Address: 2831 Fruitridge Road
- Mailing Address: P.O. Box 22505, Sacramento, CA 95822, (916) 731-5521 or 422-1921

Works to stop animal abuse. Members collaborate on such diverse campaigns as stopping cat poisoners in the cities, reckless ranchers starving horses out on the range, and gorilla poachers threatening the last survivors of a remarkable species.

Animal Referral Hotline

See 800 For Animals, Inc.

Animal Rehabilitation Center, Inc.

P.O. Box 629, Midlothian, TX 76065, (214) 775-6228

Provides a permanent home for unwanted/confiscated exotic, native, or domestic animals. Rescues, rehabilitates, and releases over 500 wild animals per year.

Animal Rights International (ARI)

P.O. Box 214, Planetarium Station, New York, NY 10024, (212) 873-3674

The umbrella group for the Coalition to Abolish the LD50 and Draize Tests, the Coalition to Abolish Classroom Dissection, and the Coalition for Non-Violent Food. Works to promote non-violent foods, and reduce and eliminate the use of lab animals without compromising human safety.

Animal Rights Kinship, Inc. (ARK)

P.O. Box 200789, Austin, TX 78720-0789, (512) 335-6346

Strives to eliminate animal exploitation and suffering through a concerted program of public education. Works directly with most of the large groups, but is independent of them.

Animal Rights Mobilization (ARM!)

National Office: P.O. Box 6989, Denver, CO 80206, (303) 388-7120, 1-800-CALL-ARM (Hotline)

A grassroots, multi-issue organization with affiliated local groups nationwide.

Animal Rights Network

456 Monroe Turnpike, Monroe, CT 06468, (203) 452-0446

Publishes *The Animals' Agenda* magazine. See the Activism: Periodicals section of Chapter 13 for information on *The Animals' Agenda.*

Animal Welfare Associates, Inc. (AWA, Inc.)

P.O. Box 10752, Stamford, CT 06904, (203) 322-8283 or 968-8282

Works to prevent suffering (abuse, exploitation, trauma, stress) of animals in any form or location, for any purpose.

Animal Welfare Institute (AWI)

P.O. Box 3650, Washington, D.C. 20007, (202) 337-2332

Seeks to reduce the pain and fear inflicted on animals by man. Areas of interest include laboratory animals, humane science teaching, trapping, importation of wild-caught exotic birds for the commercial pet trade, shipping conditions for all animals, species threatened by extinction and their habitats, and food animals. Awards the Albert Schweitzer Medal for outstanding achievement in the advancement of animal welfare.

The Ark Trust, Inc.

5461 Noble Ave., Sherman Oaks, CA, (818) 786-9990, FAX: (818) 786-9070

Promotes extensive and positive coverage of animal topics by the major media. Sponsors the annual Genesis Awards, which honors outstanding individuals whose creative output has helped educate and sensitize the public to the rights and needs of animals.

Arts Activist

P.O. Box 4271, Chico, CA 95927, (916) 345-2729

Networks artists, writers, and photographers in six major rights movements—animal, civil, environmental, gay, human, and "womyn's." Primary focus is the animal rights movement.

Associated Humane Societies, Inc.

124 Evergreen Avenue, Newark, NJ 07114, (201) 824-7084

Dedicated to safeguarding the humane treatment of homeless, abandoned, and injured animals, both domesticated and wild. Maintains Popcorn Park Zoo, a federally licensed zoo for handicapped and exploited wildlife and exotics. Actively engages in humane education and runs a low-cost spay/neuter clinic. Maintains three Animal Care Centers in New Jersey, the Animal Haven Cemetery, and Animal Haven Farm, a retirement home for pets.

The Association Of Sanctuaries, Inc. (TAOS)

P.O. Box 22428, Sacramento, CA 95822, (916) 448-5588

- and -

Route 1, Box 33A, Comfort, TX 78013, (512) 995-3680

Assists sanctuaries in providing rescue and care to wild animals in captivity. A primary goal is to establish a national database that provides information on existing sanctuaries. Also concerned with addressing the causes of "surplus" wild, captive animals. No breeding or commercial use of animals allowed by member sanctuaries.

Association of Veterinarians for Animal Rights (AVAR)

P.O. Box 6269, Vacaville, CA 95696-6269, (707) 451-1391

"Committed to balancing the needs of nonhuman animals with those of human animals." Operates under the premise that all animals have value and interests individual of the values and interests of other animals, including people.

Bat Conservation International, Inc. (BCI)

P.O. Box 162603, Austin, TX 78716-2603, (512) 327-9721

International leader in conservation and education initiatives that protect bats and their habitats. Efforts have resulted in the protection of many bat caves in North America, the banning of pesticide use against bats in several states, and the setting aside of land in American Samoa that will protect flying foxes.

Beauty Without Cruelty USA

175 West 12th Street, Suite 16G, New York, NY 10011, (212) 989-8073

Informs the public about the massive suffering imposed on animals by the fashion, cosmetic, and household product industries.

The Beaver Defenders

See Unexpected Wildlife Refuge elsewhere in this section.

Biodiversity Legal Foundation (BLF)

P.O. Box 18327, Boulder, CO 80308-1327, (303) 442-3037

Dedicated to the preservation of all native wild plants and animals, communities of species, ecosystems, and natural landscapes in this country, no matter how small or seemingly trivial.

Black Beauty Ranch

P.O. Box 367, Murchison, TX 75778, (903) 469-3811

A sanctuary for 600 formerly abused, abandoned, or orphaned animals of various species. Run by The Fund for Animals, Inc. (see their listing elsewhere in this section).

Center for Campus Organizing (CCO)

See University Conversion Project.

Center for Marine Conservation (CMC)

Headquarters: 1735 DeSales Street NW, Washington, D.C. 20036

Dedicated to protecting marine wildlife and their habitats, and to conserving coastal and ocean resources. Works with individual industries, other conservation groups, government, and private citizens. Supports major international efforts to protect all wildlife species threatened by international trade.

Center for Respect for Life and the Environment (CRLE)

A humane education division of The Humane Society of the United States (see their listing elsewhere in this section).

Cetacean Society International

P.O. Box 953, Georgetown, CT 06828-0953

Chicago Animal Rights Coalition

Yorkville, IL

This is a local group, but their methods are so innovative and their campaigns so successful that they deserve national recognition and support. See Illinois for a description.

Christians Helping Animals and People, Inc. (C.H.A.P.)

P.O. Box 272, Selden, NY 11784, (516) 732-3138

Primary goals are to preach the Gospel of Jesus Christ, educate church leaders, comfort those grieving lost pets, and pray for all creatures, human and nonhuman.

Citizens Committee for Laboratory Animal Liberation (CCLAL)

2686 Broadway, #446, New York, NY 10025

Exposes and protests the waste of billions of taxpayer dollars on duplicative, redundant, and useless animal experiments. Publishes reports of recently-published experiments on maternal deprivation, electric shock, starvation, blinding, hind limb beating, chemical warfare, etc. from academic journals and technical reports, translated into lay terminology.

Citizens Lobbying for Animals in Zoos (CLAZ)

Elkgrove, CA

See the description for this group under California.

Citizens to End Animal Suffering and Exploitation (CEASE)

P.O. Box 44-456, Somerville, MA 02144, (617) 628-9030

An educational and activist animal rights group that seeks to raise public consciousness and to act on institutionalized forms of animal suffering and exploitation.

CIVIS / Civitas

P.O. Box 26, Swain, NY 14884

Civitas is the American branch of Centro Informazione Vivisezionista Internzionale Scientifica (Center for Scientific Information on Vivisection) with headquarters in Switzerland. Publishes information showing how results obtained from animal experimentation are unreliable when extrapolated to humans and impede progress in human medical practice. Exposes practices of chemical and pharmaceutical conglomerates that harm human health with direct chemical assault and poisoning of the environment. Founded by Hans Ruesch (author of many books, including *Slaughter of the Innocent*, *Naked Empress*, and *1000 Doctors (and Many More) Against Vivisection*).

Classrooms for Ethical Labs in the Life Sciences (CELLS)

68 Mill Road Extension, Woodcliff Lake, NJ 07675, (201) 930-9026 or 930-9432

A grassroots group working to abolish dissection in the classroom. Campaign starter pack available for a self-addressed, stamped envelope and $3 optional donation for costs.

Clem and Jethro Lecture Service (C&JLS)

Pamela Brown, P.O. Box 5817, Santa Fe, NM 87502, (505) 983-8602

Travels across the country, teaching school children and others about wolves and respect for the connectedness of life, and encouraging environmental involvement. Intent is to heighten the public's awareness and thus help the survival of wolves. Program includes a film, a live wolf "ambassador" (when available), and a question and answer period. Geared to all age levels. Fee negotiable.

Coalition Against The Horse Slaughter Trade

P.O. Box 907, Penngrove, CA 94951, (707) 762-3644

A subsidiary of the Horse Welfare Committee. Addresses the extreme atrocities inflicted on equines destined for slaughter, both in the U.S. and abroad. Has initiated, supported, and helped pass legislation to better the lot of horses. Rescues horses, monitors and exposes abuses, and offers expertise and help in horse abuse situations.

Coalition of Municipalities to Ban Animal Trafficking (COMBAT)

P.O. Box 3189, Fayetteville, AR 72749, (501) 848-3678, (501) 824-4353 (24-hour Hotline)

A pet theft clearinghouse and investigation team, which operates primarily in the Midwest. Investigates licensed animal dealers and their suppliers (called *bunchers*). Focus is primarily the Midwest, but the network stretches across the country. Attends dog auctions and collects license plate numbers and photographs of individuals who go there to sell animals to research dealers. Helps others across the country set up similar programs.

Coalition to Abolish the Fur Trade (CAFT)

P.O. Box 40641, Memphis, TN 38174

Coordinates grassroots activism "all over." Acts as a clearinghouse on the fur trade. Offers an *Activists Guide to Defeating the Fur Trade* for $2.

Coalition to Protect Animals in Parks and Refuges (CPAPR)

Bina Robinson, Coordinator, P.O. Box 26, Swain, NY 14884, (607) 545-6213

Works to eliminate hunting in parks and National Wildlife Refuges so that natural population balances will be maintained.

Committee for Humane Legislation (CHL)

1623 Connecticut, NW, Washington, D.C. 20009, (202) 483-8998

The lobbying arm of Friends of Animals (see their listing elsewhere in this section). Works for legislation to protect all animals, including marine mammals, wildlife, laboratory animals, and farm animals.

The Committee to Abolish Sport Hunting, Inc. (CASH)

P.O. Box 44, Tomkins Cove, NY 10986-0044, (914) 429-8733, FAX: (914) 429-1545

Referred to by the National Rifle Association (NRA) as "the most aggressive and dangerous anti-hunting group in America." Uses legal means to actively oppose sport hunting. Encourages supporters to become "CASH Affiliates" (there is no fee or legal obligation with affiliation). Contact them for details.

Compassion for Animals Foundation, Inc.

3960 Landmark Street, Culver City, CA 90232, (213) 204-2323

Publishes *The Animals' Voice Magazine*. See the Activism: Periodicals section of Chapter 13 for information on *The Animals' Voice*.

Concern for Helping Animals in Israel (CHAI)

P.O. Box 3341, Alexandria, VA 22302, (703) 658-9650

Assists the Israeli animal welfare community in their efforts to improve the condition and treatment of Israel's animals.

The Cousteau Society, Inc.

870 Greenbrier Circle, Suite 402, Chesapeake, VA 23320-2641, (804) 523-9335, Telefax: (804) 523-2747

Does not consider itself to be an animal rights group per se. Produces television films, newspaper columns, and books, and conducts research and lectures addressing issues of humanity's interaction with natural ecosystems.

Culture and Animals Foundation (CAF)

3509 Eden Croft Drive Raleigh, NC 27612, (919) 782-3739

Fosters the growth of intellectual and artistic endeavors united by a positive concern for animals. Strives to expand our understanding and appreciation of animals—improving the ways in which they are treated and their standing in human society. Founded by philosopher Tom Regan (author of many books, among them *The Case for Animal Rights* and *The Struggle for Animal Rights*).

Dedication & Everlasting Love To Animals (D.E.L.T.A.)

P.O. Box 9, Glendale, CA 91209, (818) 241-6282, FAX: (805) 269-5049

Rescues, shelters, and places animals abandoned in the wilderness, mainly dogs and cats. Operates a 25-acre super-shelter (over 750 rescued dogs and cats currently). Free booklet, *How to Find a Loving Home for Your Pet or Rescued Animal.*

DJ&T Foundation

9201 Wilshire Blvd., Beverly Hills, CA 90210, (310) 278-1160

Funds grants for low-cost or free spay/neuter clinics.

Dogs for the Deaf, Inc.

10175 Wheeler Road, Central Point, OR 97502, (503) 826-9220 (voice/TDD), FAX: (503) 826-6696

Rescues dogs from shelters and trains them through praise and affection to help hearing impaired caretakers. Careful screening and ongoing follow-up.

The Dolphin Network

524 San Anselmo Avenue, #218, San Anselmo, CA 94960, (415) 454-7964, FAX: (415) 457-6079 EcoNet Electronic Mail: dolphin

Provides education on dolphin captivity and ecology issues, and on the importance of studying whales and dolphins as related to long-term survival and cooperation. Publishes a 30-page quarterly educational newsletter *Dolphin Net.*

Doris Day Animal League (DDAL)

227 Massachusetts Avenue NE, Suite 100, Washington, D.C. 20002, (202) 546-1761, FAX: (202) 546-2193, E-mail: ddal@aol.com

A legislative organization focusing on bills that will increase animal protection at the state and federal levels. Assists grassroots activists in drafting bills and lobbying for legislation at the state and local levels. Primary focus has been in the areas of toxicity testing legislation and pet overpopulation.

Earth! Educate!

Marianne Beasley, 327 West Meadow, Fayetteville, AR 72701, (501) 521-1998

Works to keep animal rights, vegetarian, and ecology issues before the thinking public. Produces and distributes educational publications at no charge. Focuses on the most blatant of cruelties, such as fur, ivory, and gourmet veal, in order to not alienate "mainstream America." Contributions not accepted. Publications funded by advertising sold to mainstream businesses (which may sell animal-derived products).

Earth Island Institute / Dolphin Project

ATTN: Brenda Killian, 300 Broadway, Suite 28, San Francisco, CA 94133, (415) 788-3666

Works to protect marine mammals, with a specific focus on the dolphin slaughter by the tuna industry and other fisheries.

EarthSave

See the National & International Organizations section of Chapter 11.

Earthtrust

Aikahi Park, Garden Court, 25 Kaneohe Bay Drive, Suite 205, Kailua, HI 96734, (808) 254-2866, FAX: (808) 254-6409

International, with support groups in Auckland, Geneva, Maui, New York, San Francisco, Taipei, and Toronto. Helps endangered wildlife, particularly marine mammals and Asian wildlife killed and sold for "medicinal" use. Many projects in the works, including an adopt-a-dolphin or whale program, a driftnet campaign, and a campaign to end the killing of dolphins by the tuna industry.

Eco-Solar, Inc.

294 South Street, Jamaica Plain, MA 02130, (617) 522-6430

Working to stop the slaughter of sea turtles in Latin America. Develops training projects to help local people stop deforestation and learn organic farming, vegetarian nutrition, recycling, and water management.

Elect! For Animals

1832 Wisconsin Avenue NW, Suite 23, Washington, D.C. 20007, (202) 337-3123

Supports candidates who support pro-animal legislation.

The Elephant Alliance (EA)

6265 Cardeno Drive, La Jolla, CA 92037, (619) 454-4959, FAX: (619) 454-7989

Works on behalf of captive elephants by investigating and documenting abuse, providing materials for demonstrations, educating the public, and supporting legislation. Working to establish a permanent sanctuary where abused and unwanted elephants can live, unchained and free. Send a self-addressed, stamped envelope for information.

The Elephant Sanctuary

P.O. Box 393, Hohenwald, TN 38462, (615) 796-6500, 1-800-98-TRUNK, FAX: (615) 796-4810

A natural-habitat refuge 65 miles southwest of Nashville where "sick, old, and needy elephants can once more walk the earth in peace and dignity." A new sanctuary designed expressly to meet the specific needs of Asian elephants who have been retired from zoos and circuses across the country. The 112-acre property will support a family group of 8 elephants. The Phase I facility is 98% complete at this writing, but must be funded and finished before the state will license them to receive their second, third, and fourth elephants. Also operates an outreach program to educate children, and an interactive telephone/video/multi-media computer teleconference program called DIANE which has been praised by President Clinton. (The sanctuary is not intended to provide entertainment, but public education represents a key component of the sanctuary's ongoing mission.)

Elsa Wild Animal Appeal

P.O. Box 675, Elmhurst, IL 60126, (708) 833-2560 (voice/FAX)

Founded by Joy Adamson of *Born Free* fame. Work encompasses a range of activities, from supporting wildlife sanctuaries to improving state and national humane laws. Unlike most groups of this scope, this is an all-volunteer organization.

Engineers and Scientists for Animal Rights (ESAR)

P.O. Box 1119, Kyle, TX 78640-1119, (512) 268-2502, E-mail: ESARol@aol.com

Works to extend the animal rights ethic to the scientific and technical communities and to counter the propaganda from animal exploiters portraying animal rights activists as anti-science zealots. Confronts and challenges animal experimentation on scientific as well as ethical grounds.

Environmental Investigation Agency U.S. (EIA)

1611 Connecticut Avenue NW, Suite 3B, Washington, D.C. 20009, (202) 483-6621, FAX: (202) 483-6625

An international organization that conducts several campaigns to help protect the world's animals. Actions include those to protect dolphins, porpoises, and whales from international whaling; wild-caught birds; primates; elephants killed for the ivory trade; rhinos; tigers; bears; and other wildlife. Emphasizes the overwhelming need for a legally-binding global forest convention to halt the large-scale deforestation of the world.

Ethical Science Education Coalition (ESEC)

1647 Milk Street, #423, Boston, MA 02109-4315, (617) 367-9143 or (203) 872-8877

A coalition of educators, students, and concerned citizens working to ensure that a student's right to a quality education need not be compromised by his/her ethical beliefs. Affirms the rights of students who conscientiously object to participating in the dissection of animals, and maintains the responsibility of school officials to provide these students with appropriate learning opportunities. Informs and helps administrators, teachers, and students formulate and implement dissection policies.

Farm Animal Reform Movement (FARM)

P.O. Box 30654, Bethesda, MD 20824, (301) 530-1737, E-mail: farm@gnn.com
Internet: http://members.gnn.com/FARM/

Works to expose and stop animal abuse and other destructive impacts of factory farming. Annually conducts five national campaigns: (1) The Great American Meatout (March 20), (2) World Farm Animals Day (October 2), (3) Veal Ban, an ongoing campaign, (4) Industry Watch, and (5) Development and Training, to recruit and train activists. Sponsors the Vegetarian Information Service.

Farm Sanctuary—East

P.O. Box 150, Watkins Glen, NY 14891-0150, (607) 583-2225, FAX: (607) 583-2041

Works to stop all aspects of abuse in food animal production. Rescues abused and neglected farm animals (over 500 to date), and maintains two sanctuaries for farm animals (see "Farm Sanctuary-West," below). Investigates and exposes abuse. Provides public education and outreach.

Farm Sanctuary—West

P.O. Box 1065, Orland, CA 95963-1065, (916) 865-4617, FAX: (916) 865-4622

Shelter for farm animals. See "Farm Sanctuary-East," above.

Fashion With Compassion (FWC)

P.O. Box 13303, Burton, WA 98013

Promotes a vegan lifestyle through Fashion With Compassion fashion shows, where the audience is exposed to cruelty-free clothing and cosmetics. Also educates others through tabling, mailings, and demonstrations. Founder/director is Marcia Claire Pearson, an ex-fashion model who refused to model furs and other items dangerous to animals and humans.

Feminists for Animal Rights (FAR)

- National Headquarters: P.O. Box 16425, Chapel Hill, NC 27516, (919) 286-7333 (voice/FAX)
- Editorial Office: P.O. Box 694, Cathedral Station, New York, NY 10025-0694, (212) 866-6422 (voice/FAX)

Feminist, vegetarian women with a vegan orientation, dedicated to ending all forms of abuse against women and animals. Works to raise the consciousness of the feminist community, the animal rights community, and the general public about the connections between the objectification, exploitation, and abuse of women and animals in patriarchal society. Activities include coordinating foster care for the companion animals of battered women in shelters, and providing presentations to schools and community organizations.

Ferret Family Services (FFS)

P.O. Box 186, Manhattan, KS 66502-0186, (913) 456-8FFS

Domestic ferret information and education. A no-kill organization unconditionally dedicated to domestic ferrets. All ferrets are spayed/neutered. Services offered to members and the general public include behavior modification, cruelty/welfare investigations, foster homes, grief counseling, grooming, legislative and litigation activities, lost and found/wanted/for sale lists, rescue, telephone help, and therapy. *Ferret News* offers medical tips, recipes, stories, and national updates on ferret-related issues.

Fight Against Animal Cruelty in Europe (FAACE)—USA

Old Albany Post Road, RR2, Box 111, Garrison, NY 10524

Works against bullfighting and Spain's cruel "blood fiestas."

Focus on Animals

The Marian Rosenthal Koch Fund, P.O. Box 150, Trumbull, CT 06611, (203) 377-1116

An educational clearinghouse specializing in the production and distribution of broadcast-quality films and video tapes about animal issues to increase awareness of and encourage empathy for the animals in our society. Illustrated catalog that describes each videotape. See the Videos & Films section of Chapter 12 for more information.

Food Animal Concerns Trust, Inc. (FACT)

P.O. Box 14599, Chicago, IL 60614-9966, (312) 525-4952

Promotes humane farming by providing packaging, point-of-sale materials, publicity, and other marketing assistance to humane-farmers. Sponsors NEST EGGS® brand eggs from uncaged hens and RAMBLING ROSE BRAND® free-range veal.

Friends of Animals (FoA)

National Headquarters: 777 Post Road, Suite 205, Darien, CT 06820, (203) 656-1522, FAX: (203) 656-0267, National spay/neuter referral: 1-800-321-PETS

Works to reduce and eliminate animal suffering. Identifies and investigates inhumane practices, vigorously exposes them to public view, and implements programs of action to bring them to an end. Sponsors a national spay/neuter program (1-800-321-PETS). Successfully banned leghold traps in New Jersey. Spearheaded the Marine Mammal Protection Act of 1972.

Friends of Beaversprite

P.O. Box 591, Little Falls, NY 13365, (518) 568-2077

Carries on the work of Dorothy Richards, the "Beaver Woman," an environmentalist and wildlife advocate. Specializes in wildlife—and especially beaver—issues. Provides nonlethal, effective solutions to beaver/human conflicts.

Friends of the Sea Otter (FSO)

2150 Garden Road, Suite B-4, Monterey, CA 93940, (408) 373-2747, FAX: (408) 373-2749

Works for the welfare of the sea otter along the California Coast and all sea otter habitat.

Friends of Washoe

Chimpanzee and Human Communication, Central Washington University, 400 E. 8th Avenue, Ellensburg, WA 98926-7573, (509) 963-2244

International. Supports the first and longest running research project on the study of chimpanzees who live together as a social group and use American Sign Language (ASL) in their interactions with humans and with each other. "Our philosophy is that they [the chimpanzees] did not apply for immigration status; they were, and still are, incarcerated against their wills. We, as researchers and more importantly as friends and caring human beings, do as much as possible to better the lives of chimpanzees." "As Jane Goodall has said, 'Only when we understand can we care. Only when we care will we help. Only if we help shall they be saved.'"

The Fund for Animals, Inc.

National Headquarters: 200 West 57th Street, New York, NY 10019, (212) 246-2096

Works to protect wildlife and eliminate cruelty to animals wherever, however, and whenever it occurs. Operates a rabbit sanctuary in South Carolina and Black Beauty Ranch in Texas. Many regional offices throughout the country.

Fur-Bearer Defenders (FBD)

- Sacramento Office: P.O. Box 188950, Sacramento, CA 95818, (916) 391-4617
- Home Office: The Fur-Bearers, 2235 Commercial Drive, Vancouver, British Columbia, Canada V5N 4B6, (604) 255-0411, (604) 888-5817 (after hours), FAX: (604) 255-1491

Works to abolish cruel trapping by raising public awareness.

Gaia Institute

P.O. Box 852, South Lynfield, MA 01940, (508) 535-8980

Produces television programming on the issues of animal rights, deep ecology, and the environment. See the Radio & Television Programming section of Chapter 12 for more information.

The Gorilla Foundation

Box 620-530, Woodside, CA 94062, (415) 851-8505, Internet: http://www.gorilla.org

Dedicated to the protection, preservation, and propagation of gorillas and other endangered primate species. Primary program involves teaching American Sign Language to two lowland gorillas—the longest continuous interspecies communication of its kind in the world—with the hopes that the study will lead to improved treatment and protection of gorillas. Developing a 70-acre gorilla preserve on Maui, Hawaii, the first such preserve outside of Africa. Speakers available for presentations.

The Great Ape Project

P.O. Box 87, Watertown, MA 02272-0087, (617) 325-3851

International organization working for the removal of non-human great apes from the category of "property," and for their immediate inclusion within the category of "persons," granted the basic moral and legal protection that only human beings currently enjoy. The book by the same name is a collection of scientific and scholarly thought against the unthinking denial of fundamental rights to beings who are not of our own species, but who quite evidently possess many of the characteristics we consider morally important.

Great Bear Foundation (GBF)

P.O. Box 2699, Missoula, MT 59806-2699, (406) 721-3009, FAX: (406) 728-2881

- and -

P.O. Box 1289, Bozeman, MT 59771, (406) 596-5533, FAX: (406) 586-6103

Seeks to save wild populations of bears and their natural habitats. Works to promote coexistence of bears and humans, and to reduce conflict between bears and humans.

Greenpeace

1436 U Street NW, Washington, D.C. 20009, (202) 462-1177

An environmental organization whose actions sometimes benefit animals.

Greyhound Friends, Inc.

167 Saddle Hill Road, Hopkinton, MA 01748, (508) 435-5969

Works to save as many racing greyhounds from death as possible, to prevent inhumane disposition of any animal, to educate the public as to the true nature of the greyhound breed, and to insist that the organizations and individuals who profit enormously from greyhounds be made responsible for their appropriate, or at least humane, disposition. Maintains a kennel from which retired greyhounds are placed to adoptive homes. Shelters in Hopkinton, Falmouth, Great Barrington, and in Skillman, NJ.

Greyhound Friends for Life

9728 Tenaya Way, Kelseyville, CA 95451, (707) 277-91647

A national network of volunteers who rescue greyhounds from the track, research, or any other form of abuse, and find adoptive homes for them. Offers the book, *My Greyhound Friend* (see the Children & Young Adults section of Chapter 13 for ordering information).

Hawk Watch International

P.O. Box 660, Salt Lake City, UT 84110, (801) 524-8511

Conservation organization working to protect and monitor populations of eagles, hawks, falcons, and other birds of prey through migration research and environmental education. Adopt-A-Hawk program.

Help Abolish Leghold Traps (HALT)

Phoenix, AZ

See Arizona for a description of this group.

Help Our Wolves Live (HOWL)

4600 Emerson Avenue South, Minneapolis, MN 55409, (612) 827-3402

Works to protect and preserve the timberwolf and other endangered species, and to discourage the misuse of any species by humans. Focuses on the wolf as a species, not on individual animals. Challenges state and federal government policies. Opposes keeping wolves as pets and breeding hybrids.

Hemlock Hill Farm Sanctuary

Karen O'Donoghue, RFD #2, Box 474, North Lebanon, ME 04027, (207) 457-1371

Formed in November 1990 by an animal rights activist who in the course of 10 years has worked to ban leghold traps, sport hunting, and factory farming. The sanctuary takes unwanted and abused animals, cares for them, rehabilitates them, and offers healthy, emotionally stable animals for adoption under strict guidelines.

The Home for Unwanted and Abandoned Guinea Pigs

699 Creekview Drive, Lawrenceville, GA 30244, (404) 963-4755

Advocates rights for guinea pigs as a species and provides advice, support, adoptions, rescue, and follow-up.

Honey Foundation

5778 Commercial Street SE, Salem, OR 97306, (503) 588-1175

Works in concert with the local SPCA to improve the health conditions of domesticated animals on the Cook Islands by providing a veterinarian and technicians on a continuing basis on the island. (The Cook Islands are in the middle of the South Pacific, south of Hawaii and 700 miles west of Tahiti.)

Horse Power Projects & Horse Power International, Inc.

P.O. Box 1965, Monterey, CA 93942, (408) 648-1965 (voice/FAX)

Works for the humane treatment of the greatest number of horses, through education, networking, and legislative action.

House Rabbit Sanctuary (HRS)

P.O. Box 1201, Alameda, CA 94501, (415) 521-4631

Rescues abandoned rabbits from animal shelters and provides them with foster homes until permanent adoptive homes can be found. Spays/neuters all incoming rabbits. Provides educational materials to humane societies. Helps with behavior and health problems.

Humane Education Committee (HEC)

P.O. Box 445, New York, NY 10028, (212) 410-3095

- and -

P.O. Box 384, Allendale, NJ 07401, (201) 934-7749

Works to bring balanced educational materials concerning pets, wild animals, and farm animals into classrooms, changing the fact that children and their families are often not exposed to options for coping or given support in solving animal-related problems humanely. Participated in the development of the NYC Board of Education *Humane Education Resource Guide*.

The Humane Farming Action Fund (HFAF)

76 Belvedere Street, Suite B, San Rafael, CA 94901

The legislative arm of the Humane Farming Association (see their listing below). Addresses state and federal legislation related to farm animals, from cockfighting to rodeo horse tripping to agribusiness.

The Humane Farming Association (HFA)

1550 California Street, Suite 6, San Francisco, CA 94109, (415) 485-1495

Actively campaigns to protect consumers from the dangerous misuse of chemicals in food production and to eliminate the severe and senseless suffering to which farm animals are subjected. Members include public health specialists, veterinarians, consumer advocates, family farmers, and others.

Humane Organization for Retired and Standardbred Equines (H.O.R.S.E.)

Box 88, Church Road, VA 23833, (804) 265-5257

Places retired standardbreds (who can no longer race or are no longer competitive) in loving, lifetime homes. Chapters in many areas and volunteers in many states. Offers advice, support, and guidelines for those interested in starting local chapters.

Humane Political Action Committee

Chicago, IL

See Illinois for a description of this group.

The Humane Society of the United States (HSUS)

National Office: 21001 L Street NW, Washington, D.C. 20037

The nation's largest animal protection organization. Dedicated to improving the lives of animals, both wild and domesticated. Provides support to local humane organizations, animal control agencies, officials, educators, media, and the general public through legislative, investigative, educational, and legal activities on behalf of animals. Also serves as a resource of humane education for educators.

In Defense of Animals (IDA)

- Home Office: 816 West Francisco Blvd., San Rafael, CA 94901, (415) 453-9984, FAX: (415) 453-0510
- South Bay Chapter: 6560 Ashfield Court, San Jose, CA 95120, (408) 268-4577, FAX: (408) 927-9281

Opposes the use of animals for medical or scientific research and teaching, product testing, fur, and other areas of exploitation. Stresses nonviolent actions. Acts as national coordinator for the U.S. activities of World Lab Animal Liberation Week.

The Institute for the Development of Earth Awareness (I.D.E.A.)

P.O. Box 124, Prince Street Station, New York, NY 10012, (212) 741-0338

An educational organization which takes a multi-issue approach to the world's problems. Believes that issues affecting the environment, animals, and humans are complexly interconnected and deeply rooted; that only by addressing the actual causes of these problems will they be solved; and only by recognizing the interconnectedness of all life will we realize that the fate of all life is also intertwined. Projects include publishing, land preservation and habitat revitalization, and bio-sustainable building. Founded by Marjorie Spiegel, author of *The Dreaded Comparison: Human and Animal Slavery* (see Chapter 13 for a description of this book). Currently working on an in-depth photo-documentary of slaughterhouses, which chronicles the experiences of animals in cattle, calf, chicken, and pig slaughterhouses.

Interbeing Partnerships

Summit, NJ
See New Jersey for a description of this group.

Interfaith Council for the Protection of Animals and Nature (ICPAN)

4290 Raintree Lane, NW, Atlanta, GA 30327

International Crane Foundation

E-11276 Shady Lane Road, Baraboo, WI 53913

International Dolphin Project

Civic Center Plaza, 1200 Third Avenue, Suite 1624, San Diego, CA 92101-4112, (619) 530-2672, FAX: (805) 648-1610, E-mail: idp@rain.org
"Restoring Freedom." Dedicated to abolishing the dolphin slave trade by banning the capture of dolphins. Also works to expose the Dolphin Amusement Park industry. Headed by Ric O'Barry, a former dolphin trainer for the television show "Flipper."

International Foundation for Ethical Research (IFER)

53 West Jackson Blvd., Suite 1552, Chicago, IL 60604, (312) 427-6025
This group does not define itself as an animal "rights" organization, but rather as advocates who want to see an end to animal use in biomedical research, product testing, and education. Promotes the development, validation, and implementation of scientifically valid, viable alternatives to the use of live animals in research, testing, and education. Has provided over $200,000 in research grants for researchers working to develop alternatives. Sponsored by the National Anti-Vivisection Society (see their listing elsewhere in this section).

International Foundation for the Protection of the Wolf

3517-1/2 Fremont North, #7, Seattle, WA 98103

International Fund for Animal Welfare (IFAW)

Headquarters: P.O. Box 193, Yarmouth Port, MA 02675-0193, (508) 362-4944, FAX: (508) 362-5841
Promotes and ensures the just and kind treatment of animals as sentient beings. Born over 20 years ago out of the founder's successful campaign to end the clubbing of baby seals for their furs. Has expanded its campaigns to include the whole spectrum of animal life, from bees to whales. Conducts direct rescues and works closely with governments who have the power to save animals. Programs include a Pet Rescue program that gives financial support to local shelters.

International League of Doctors for the Abolition of Vivisection (ILDAV)

c/o CIVIS/Civitas, P.O. Box 491, Hartsdale, NY 10530, (607) 545-6213
An anti-vivisection league composed exclusively of doctors, surgeons, pharmacists, veterinarians, and scientists in medical fields. Holds congresses at which members present papers illustrating how vivisection misleads medical practice and is therefore detrimental to human health.

International Network for Religion and Animals (INRA)

Rev. Dr. Marc A. Wessels, Executive Director, P.O. Box 1335, North Wales, PA 19454-0335, (215) 721-1908
Educates the religious community as to the important role religion plays in improving the treatment of animals. Acts as a network rather than as an activist organization. Sponsors the World Week of Prayer for Animals.

International Primate Protection League (IPPL)

P.O. Box 766, Summerville, SC 29484, (803) 871-2280, FAX: (803) 871-7988, E-mail: ippl@sc.net
Has members in 65 countries and field representatives in 33 countries. Works to conserve and protect all apes and monkeys. Helped jail the world's largest gorilla smuggler

in February 1990. Has influenced the banning of monkey exports in many countries. Operates a sanctuary for gibbon apes.

International Snow Leopard Trust (ISLT)

4649 Sunnyside Avenue North, Suite 325, Seattle, WA 98103-6900, (202) 632-2421, FAX: (206) 632-3967

"Dedicated to the conservation of the snow leopard and its mountain habitat through a balanced approach that considers the needs of the people and the environment." Works closely with village associations, wildlife agencies, governmental organizations, and individuals throughout Central Asia. Encourages local people to find ways to sustain their communities in harmony with nature. Provides supplies, training, support, and education for environmental education programs and scientific field research.

International Society for Animal Rights, Inc. (ISAR)

421 South State Street, Clarks Summit, PA 18411, (717) 586-2200, FAX: (717) 586-9580

Seeks to expose and prevent all forms of exploitation and abuse of animals. The first organization in the world to use the term "Animal Rights" in a corporate name. Initiated the campaign to stop the use of animals for cosmetic tests worldwide and the campaign to prevent the use of animals from pounds and shelters for scientific purposes ("pound seizure"). Sponsored the first National Conference on Animal Rights Law.

The International Society for Cow Protection (ISCOWP)

Box 4607, Timberwood Trail, Efland, NC 27243, (919) 563-3643

Primary concern is to present alternatives to present agricultural practices that support and depend upon the meat industry and industrialized petroleum powered machinery.

International Society for the Protection of Mustangs & Burros (ISPMB)

6212 E. Sweetwater Avenue, Scottsdale, AZ 85254-4461, (602) 991-0273, FAX: (602) 991-2920

The oldest and largest wild horse and burro protection organization in the U.S. Assisted in passing legislation in 1971 to protect wild horses and burros on public lands. Has a national agreement to check on the welfare of untitled wild horses and burros in adoptive homes. "Operation rescue" places titled animals in good homes to prevent them from going to "killer" buyers.

International Wildlife Coalition

- Street Address: 634 North Falmouth Highway
- Mailing Address: P.O. Box 388, North Falmouth, MA 02556, (508) 564-9980

Works to end cruel and abusive treatment and senseless killing of all animals. Main focus is the protection of marine life and endangered species. Created the Whale Adoption Project. Maintains the 600-member Cape Cod Volunteer Stranding Network.

International Wildlife Rehabilitation Council (IWRC)

4437 Central Place, Suite B-4, Suisun, CA 94585, (707) 864-1761, FAX: (707) 864-3106

A network of professionals involved in wildlife rehabilitation. Membership open to individuals actively working in wildlife rehab in administration, conservation, management, education, research, humane work, or veterinary or allied professional practice. Offers a 24-hour hotline for access to expert answers to tough rehab questions, a certification program, skills seminars, an annual conference, a membership directory, and literature discounts.

Intra-movement Coalition for Animal Rights and the Environment (I CARE)

3516 Casey Key Road, Nokomis, FL 34275, (813) 966-4075

A coalition of activists and those who would like to do more to help animals. Dedicated to helping people help animals and to enlightening those who care about the future of all life on this planet. Information available on a wide range of topics. Referrals to local and national animal protection groups.

The Jane Goodall Institute (JGI-USA)

P.O. Box 599, Ridgefield, CT 06877, (203) 431-2099 or 1-800-592-JANE, FAX: (203) 431-4387

Also offices in England, Tanzania, and Canada. Dedicated to researching and publicizing the unique status and special needs of chimpanzees—now an endangered species—to insure both their long-term preservation in the wild and their physical and psychological well-being in captive settings. Actively campaigns on behalf of chimpanzees. Maintains a field research team in Tanzania and is developing a project in Burundi. Supports sanctuaries for orphaned chimpanzees in many African countries. Assists zoos to improve habitats and conditions for captive chimpanzees. Worldwide educational program for youngsters.

Jews for Animal Rights (JAR) / Micah Publications, Inc.

255 Humphrey Street, Marblehead, MA 01945, (617) 631-7601

Educates the general public and informs Jewish people about the tradition of *tsa'ar balei chaim*, which means that you may not cause suffering to any creature. Provides publications, ritual material, and other information on Judaism and animal rights, and on vegetarianism.

Last Chance for Animals (LCA)

18653 Ventura Blvd., Suite 356, Tarzana, CA 91356, (818) 760-2075

Works against vivisection in laboratories by actively protesting and distributing information.

Lifeforce

- Los Angeles Branch: P.O. Box 825, North Hollywood, CA 91603, (818) 985-LIFE
- San Francisco Branch: P.O. Box 210354, San Francisco, CA 94121, (415) 441-3339
- Home Office: Box 3117, Main Post Office, Vancouver, B.C., Canada V6B 3X6, (604) 699-HOPE

An ecology organization formed to raise public awareness of human, animal, and environmental issues, particularly marine ecosystems.

Live Elephant, Inc.

P.O. Box 10, Canton, MA 02021, (617) 821-1512

An all-volunteer organization that works to preserve and protect the African elephant, which has been poached to the brink of extinction. Most activities aimed at reducing the market for ivory worldwide. Offers a teacher program called *The Live Elephant Book*. See the Humane Education section of Chapter 12 for details on this program.

LivingEarth Learning Project

P.O. Box 2160, Boston, MA 02106, (617) 367-8687

Instructors who present a series of dynamic, interactive educational programs about animal and environmental issues for grades 3 through college throughout New England and New York. Programs combine informative presentations with lively classroom discussions, short videos, and group activities. Also offers speakers for teacher in-service training and conferences, a video loaning library, and lesson plans. All presentations are free of charge thanks to the financial support of the New England Anti-Vivisection Society (see their listing elsewhere in this section).

Lynx Educational Fund for Animal Welfare

10573 West Pico Blvd., Suite 155, Los Angeles, CA 90064, (818) 883-3722

Works nonviolently for the protection of fur-bearing animals in the wild and in captivity.

Make Peace With Animals, Inc.

P.O. Box 488 New Hope, PA 18938, (215) 862-0605, FAX: (215) 862-2733

A peace organization with an emphasis on animal protection. Considers the protection of animals part of a whole in terms of general respect for (and appreciation of) life. Runs an adoption service for retired racing greyhounds and equines, and has a weekly humane education radio program, "Animal Talk." Through its Racing Dog Rescue Project, finds homes for "retired" greyhounds, rescues them from laboratories, and educates the public and legislators about the plight of these animals. Their motto is: "Make Peace With Yourself, Make Peace With Each Other, Make Peace With Animals."

Massachusetts Society for the Prevention of Cruelty to Animals (MSPCA)

Boston, MA

See Massachusetts for a description of this group.

Medical Research Modernization Committee (MRMC)

P.O. Box 2751, Grand Central Station, New York, NY 10163-2751, (212) 832-3904

This group does not consider itself to be an animal rights organization. Health care professionals who lend their training, experience, and expertise to evaluate the medical and/or scientific merit of research modalities, in order to identify archaic methods and to promote sensible, reliable, and efficient methods of research.

Mercy Crusade, Inc.

P.O. Box 3265, Van Nuys, CA 91407, (818) 782-1485

Established in 1949. Led the Los Angeles City fight for the first public spay/neuter clinic. Major programs include animal breeding control, cruelty investigations, rescue and placement, animal medical assistance to needy caretakers, humane education, and legislation involving companion animals, food animals, and wildlife.

Mission Wolf

P.O. Box 211, Silver Cliff, CO 81249, (719) 746-2919 (message machine)

Maintains a 36-acre refuge for captive wolves and hybrids, an educational center, and a traveling wolf program. Works to aid wild wolf recovery through education. Maintains that while captive wolves may interact with humans, they are not pets.

Monitor Consortium

1506-19th Street NW, Washington, D.C. 20036, (202) 234-6576

A consortium of over 30 U.S. conservation, environmental, and animal welfare organizations. Acts as an information clearinghouse and as action coordinator for member groups and other conservationists around the world for the protection of marine mammals and endangered species and their habitats.

The National Activist Network

National Office: P.O. Box 19515, Sacramento, CA 95819, (916) 452-7179

Supports direct action by grassroots animal rights activists, including those incarcerated for their actions or beliefs. Refuses assistance from large, national animal rights organizations, which they feel are not being effective enough.

National Alliance for Animals (NAA)

P.O. Box 77196, Washington, D.C. 20013-7196, (703) 810-1085, FAX: (703) 810-1089

Organizer of the historic 1990 and 1996 March for Animals in Washington, D.C. and of an annual symposium on animal rights which brings together grassroots and national groups to help establish a unified animal rights movement.

National Animal Rights, Inc.

P.O. Box 3241, Brandon, FL 33509
- and -
116 Barbados Avenue, Tampa, FL 33606

National Anti-Vivisection Society (NAVS)

53 West Jackson Blvd., Suite 1550, Chicago, IL 60604-3795, (312) 427-6065

Strives to eliminate the practice of using animals in any way for the purposes of medical research, medical testing, or medical training. Educates the public about the evils of vivisection on animals. Teaches associations, societies, and individuals methods and means of combating vivisection and inhumane treatment of animals. Aids the formation of new anti-vivisection societies.

National Association for Humane and Environmental Education (NAHEE)

The humane education division of the Humane Society of the United States (see their listing elsewhere in this section).

National Cat Protection Society

6904 West Pacific Coast Highway, Newport Beach, CA 92663
- and -
9031 Birch Street, Spring Valley, CA 91977

Operates two adoption shelters and retirement centers for owner-relinquished cats. The retirement centers provide a home for life for cats whose human caretakers pay a fee to keep them there. Shelters mainly serve the local area, but cats come to the retirement center from all over the U.S.

National Foundation to Protect America's Eagles (NFPAE)

P.O. Box 333, Pigeon Forge, TN 37868, 1-800-2EAGLES

National Greyhound Adoption Program

ATTN: David Wolfe, 8301 Torresdale Avenue, Philadelphia, PA 19136, 1-800-348-2517

Greyhound rescue and placement.

National Greyhound Network

(415) 851-7812 (Northern CA)

Represents independent greyhound rescue and adoption groups. Call for a referral near you.

National Humane Education Society

Administrative Headquarters: 521-A East Market Street, Leesburg, VA 22075, (703) 777-8319, FAX: (703) 771-4048

Works to foster kindness towards animals and to oppose and prevent cruelty to them. Distributes educational materials. Operates Peace Plantation, a no-kill animal sanctuary in Walton, New York.

National Institute for Urban Wildlife

P.O. Box 3015, Shepherdstown, WV 25443, (304) 876-6146, FAX: (304) 876-3769

A scientific and educational organization dedicated to the conservation of wildlife in urban, suburban, and developing areas. Programs include research, providing technical assistance to urban planners and others, urban conservation education, urban wildlife sanctuaries, publications, etc.

The National Opossum Society

Anita M. Henness, DVM, President, P.O. Box 3091, Orange, CA 92665, (714) 539-3896 (president's number)

With emphasis on nationwide coordination of work, policies, etc., this group is dedicated to the education of everyone about the benefits of North America's only marsupial — the opossum. Concerned with national, regional, and local efforts. Provides information on the care of captive or companion opossums, as well as information on wild opossums. (Does not advocate that the average person have an opossum as a companion, since most people are unwilling to provide proper care.)

National Society for the Protection of Animals (NSPA)

ATTN: Ann Martin-Gonnerman 7611 State Line, Suite 235, Kansas City, MO 64114, (816) 523-0500

Works aggressively to prevent cruelty, neglect, and abuse to all animals. Actively pursues animal protection in the greater Kansas City area. Helped draft and engineer the passage of a Missouri law on the treatment of animals that has become a national model. Gives people the guidance and tools they need to solve problems in their own communities. Has provided assistance to communities in a variety of states.

National Wildlife Rehabilitators Association

14 North 7th Avenue, St. Cloud, MN 56303-4766, (612) 259-4086

Committed to promoting and improving the integrity and professionalism of wildlife rehabilitation (the treatment and temporary care of injured, diseased, and displaced indigenous wildlife), and to the preservation of natural ecosystems. Nationwide *Membership Directory* of wildlife rehabilitators. (*Note*: Members are not necessarily animal rights people.)

New England Anti-Vivisection Society (NEAVS)

333 Washington Street, Suite 850, Boston, MA 02108-5100, (617) 523-6020, TDD/TTY (617) 523-0181, FAX: (617) 523-7925

"Research Modernization and Animal Rights." Established in 1895. Maintains many projects to counter vivisection. Presents over 100 free classes each month in 12 different programs to schools throughout New England. Provides free books and materials to more than 3,000 school libraries nationwide. Supports the development of grassroots activism through professional and financial support nationwide. Continues to fight in the courts, the legislatures, and the marketplace on behalf of animals. Successful in repealing the Massachusetts pound seizure bill.

New York Turtle and Tortoise Society (NYTTS)

P.O. Box 878, Orange, NJ 07051-0878, (212) 459-4803

"Dedicated to the conservation and preservation of habitat and to the promotion of proper husbandry and captive propagation of turtles and tortoises." Maintains an adoption program, annual seminar, public education program, and a national phone directory of veterinarians and members with particular areas of expertise who can answer questions related to turtles and tortoises. *Note:* This organization includes "hobbyists" among its members, those who keep/raise turtles or tortoises for personal enjoyment.

Noah's Friends Unlimited

P.O. Box 36197, Richmond, VA 23235, (804) 320-7090

See Virginia for a description of this group.

North American Wildlife Association (NAWA)

P.O. Box 263, East Lyme, CT 06333, (203) 447-9567

Dedicated to the rescue, rehabilitation, and release of distressed wild animals. Accepts sick, injured, or orphaned wild animals from "anyone and everyone." Maintains a rehabilitation center and a 24-hour telephone line for emergency service.

Opossum Society of the U.S.

P.O. Box 16724, Irvine, CA 92713, (714) 536-3538

Dedicated to understanding, protecting, and preserving 'possums. Care for injured and orphaned opossums.

Orangutan Foundation

822 So. Wellesley Ave., Los Angeles, CA 90049, (213) 207-1655, FAX: (213) 207-1556

Supports the study, understanding, and conservation of orangutans in their principal native habitat, the tropical rain forests of Indonesia.

Peaceable Kingdom

P.O. Box 8756, Greenville, SC 29604, (803) 271-7304

Devoted to the advancement of lifestyles and practices mindful of animal rights, non-violence, and the welfare of our planet.

Peace Plantation Animal Sanctuary

RD 3, Box 84, Walton, NY 13856, (607) 865-5759

No-kill animal sanctuary owned and operated by the National Humane Education Society (see their listing elsewhere in this section).

People for the Ethical Treatment of Animals (PETA)

501 Front Street, Norfolk, VA 23501, Internet: http://www.envirolink.org/arrs/peta/index.html

Note: PETA is pronounced "PEA-ta," with a long "e" sound. Establishes and defends the rights of all animals. Primary focus is on the areas in which the largest number of animals suffer the most for long periods of time—on factory farms, in laboratories, and in the fur trade—but also works on other issues. Request PETA's *Annual Review* for an extensive list of activities conducted over the last year.

Performing Animal Welfare Society (PAWS)

P.O. Box 849, Galt, CA 95632-9979, (209) 745-2606 (Shelter), (916) 393-PAWS (Office), FAX: (209) 745-1809, E-mail: paws@capacess.org

Works to protect performing animals, provide shelter for retired performing animals and unwanted exotics in need of permanent housing, and to enhance the lives of captive wildlife. Conducts lobbying, litigation, and public education. Maintains a shelter. In 1995, filed suit against the USDA on behalf of captive elephants.

Pet Pride

P.O. Box 1055, Pacific Palisades, CA 90272

Operates a "model" no-kill shelter for cats. Promotes cats and their proper care.

The Pet Savers Foundation, Inc.—SPAY/USA

14 Vanderventer Avenue, Port Washington, NY 11050, 1-800-248-SPAY (7729)

Clearinghouse for affordable spay/neuter services nationwide. Can help you start a low-cost spay/neuter program in your community. A program of the North Shore Animal League (see their listing under New York).

Physicians Committee for Responsible Medicine (PCRM)

P.O. Box 6322, Washington, D.C. 20015, (202) 686-2210

Promotes nutrition, preventive medicine, ethical research practices, and compassionate medical policy. Dedicated to stopping the inhumane use of animals in labs. Membership open to non-physicians as well as physicians.

Potbellied Pig Interest Group and Shelter (PIGS)

Director: Dale Raffle, P.O. Box 629, 10 Sanctuary Lane, Charles Town, WV 25414, (304) 725-PIGS (voice/FAX)

A sanctuary and placement service for potbellied pigs. Has a waiting list of over 40 pigs who need homes. Please contact them for adoption information.

The Predator Project

P.O. Box 6733, Bozeman, MT 59771-6733, (406) 587-3389 (voice/FAX)

Endeavors to unite efforts on behalf of predators, whether they are grizzly bears, wolves, coyotes, eagles, great blue herons, ferrets, bluefin tuna, or any other predator. Includes the Wolf Action Network, the Grizzly Bear Task Force, and the All the Dead Critters (ADC) campaign. Welcomes all volunteers who want to defend the vast array of predators.

Preservation of Amazon River Dolphins (PARD)

3302 North Burton, Rosemead, CA 91770, (818) 572-7273

Focus is on saving the Amazon Pink River Dolphins. A project of the International Society for Preservation of Tropical Rainforests. Works with Vegetarian Society, Inc. of California.

Prevention of Cruelty to Animals and Plants (PCAP)

- North American Office: 97-38 42nd Avenue, Corona, NY 11368, (718) 898-1604
- Global Office: V.I.P. Nagar, Tiljala, Calcutta , 700039, India

PCAP, pronounced Pea-Cap, is affiliated with Ananda Marga, a global spiritual and social service network. Works to prevent acts of cruelty to and destruction of the animals and plants whose planet we share. Works to popularize vegetarianism.

Primarily Primates, Inc.

P.O. Box 15306, San Antonio, TX 78212
(210) 755-4616 or 755-8868, FAX: (210) 755-2435

Provides sanctuary, rehabilitation, lifetime care, and shelter to nonnative species of primates, birds, mammals, and reptiles that come from abusive situations, and otherwise would die prematurely by abandonment or euthanasia. Many were subjects of laboratory experiments, were exotic pets that were discarded by owners, or were circus animals. Seeks ways in which some of these animals may be returned to their native habitats. Cares for over 300 primates, 150 birds, and varying numbers of small mammals and reptiles at a nine-acre sanctuary. Rehabilitates animals suffering from severe physical or psychological problems. Provides lifetime care in a large natural-habitat enclosure with companions of the same species.

Progressive Animal Welfare Society (PAWS)

P.O. Box 1037, Lynnwood, WA 98046, (206) 743-PAWS

See Washington for a description of this group.

Project BREED, Inc. (Breed Rescue Efforts and EDucation)

(formerly Network for Ani-males and Females)

- P.O. Box 15888, Chevy Chase, MD 202825-5888, Hotline & FAX: (202) 244-0065
- Information requests, please send a long self-addressed, stamped envelope to: Project Breed, Inc., 5103 Chevy Chase Parkway NW, Washington, D.C. 20008-2920

A national coalition that facilitates public access to breed rescue groups (groups that concentrate on saving homeless dogs of a particular breed), and also some rabbit, ferret, and wild bat rescue groups Publishes the *Project Breed Directory*, with nearly 3,000 sources for rescue assistance nationwide and in Canada. An additional 7,000 contacts are available through Hotline assistance to *Project Breed Directory* owners for listings not yet published in the series (new directory volumes will be added as funding permits). See the Companion Animals: Guides & Directories section of Chapter 13 for ordering information.

Project Wolf USA

168 Galer, Seattle, WA 98109, (206) 283-1957

Works to end the wolf kills in British Columbia, Alberta, and Alaska.

Protective Association of World Species (P.A.W.S.)

P.O. Box 121, New Berlin, WI 53151, (414) 679-3742

A sanctuary where captive-born animals live out their lives in protection and peace.

Psychologists for the Ethical Treatment of Animals (PSYeta)

P.O. Box 1297, Washington Grove, MD 20880-1297, (301) 963-4751 (voice/FAX)

An independent association of psychologists dedicated to the promotion of animal welfare within the science and profession of psychology and within the community at large. *Student Rights Option* brochure and alternative curricula for undergraduate psychology students available on request.

The Pure Food Campaign (formerly Beyond Beef)

See the National & International Organizations section of Chapter 11.

Puerto Rico Street Dog Project

210 So. 24th Avenue, Hattiesburg, MS 39401
- and -
2706 Sherwood Lane, Austin, TX 78704, (512) 445-2841

Works to help homeless dogs in Puerto Rico.

Ranching Task Force

P.O. Box 5784, Tucson, AZ 85703, (602) 578-3173

Works to stop "livestock" grazing on public lands.

Retired Greyhounds As Pets (REGAP)

Ron Walsek, President, P.O. Box 41307, St. Petersburg, FL 33743, (813) 343-4824

Informs the public that greyhounds make great pets and finds loving, responsible homes for retired greyhounds, thus rescuing from death dogs who have passed their racing prime, are injured, or just don't "make the grade." Most dogs are two years old, though some are older.

The Rhino Trust

4045 N. Massachusetts, Portland, OR 97227

Supports efforts to protect and preserve the world's five rhinoceros species within their native habitats. Objectives include fund-raising, public awareness, and education. Currently supports two reserves which protect rhinos in their native habitats—Ngare Sergoi Rhino Sanctuary in Kenya (home to both black and white rhinos) and Ujung Kulon Reserve in Indonesia (home to Javan rhinos).

The Roar Foundation—Shambala Preserve

P.O. Box 189, 6867 Soledad Canyon Road, Acton, CA 93510, (805) 268-0380, FAX: (805) 268-8809

An authentic 60-acre re-creation of African wildlife habitat which serves as a safe haven for over 70 large animals, including lions, tigers, leopards, cougars, and elephants. All inhabitants were captive-born and would not survive in "the wild." Most were orphans or are cast-offs from private owners. Open to the public on special "safari days." "Adopt A Wild One" program. Donations should be made payable to the Roar Foundation.

Rutgers Law School—Animal Rights Law Center

1500 Washington, Newark, NJ 07102, (201) 648-1087, FAX: (201) 645-6119

San Francisco Bay Institute

Schweitzer Center, P.O. Box 8496, Berkeley, CA 94707, (510) 526-5346

Publishes a quarterly journal called *Between the Species*, which provides a forum for the discussion of animal ethics issues. (See the Animals, Rights, & Ethics section of Chapter 13 for more information on *Between the Species*.) Organizes conferences and vegan/vegetarian food events. Maintains a humane education program and hosts an Urban Wildlife Group. Organized the Walk to Rome for Animal Rights and the Souls of Animals.

Save the Manatee Club, Inc. (SMC)

500 N. Maitland Avenue, Suite 210, Maitland, FL 32751, 1-800-432-JOIN or (407) 539-0990

Formed in 1981 by former Florida Governor Bob Graham and singer Jimmy Buffett to save manatees from extinction. Operates the Adopt-A-Manatee program and annually produces about 2,000 waterway signs alerting boaters to the presence of manatees. Provides free education packets. Funds international manatee research, rescue, and rehabilitation. Active in lobbying and grassroots efforts.

Save the Whales

P.O. Box 2397, 1842 Washington Way, Venice, CA 90291, (310) 230-9995

Works to educate children and adults about marine mammals, their environment, and their preservation. Intervened to successfully halt detonations by the U.S. Navy that would have killed or injured an estimated 10,000 marine mammals off the Ventura County, CA coast. Obtained a public hearing on and helped postpone a project that would broadcast sound underwater from California to Hawaii. Many other activities, including working for legislation to stop dolphin capture and end marine mammal captivity, a hands-on Whale On Wheels (WOW) educational program, and an Adopt-A-Whale program.

Scientists Group for Reform of Animal Experimentation (SGRAE)

P.O. Box 1297, Washington Grove, MD 20880-1297

An organization of scientists concerned with ethical problems of animal experimentation, and interested in promoting humane approaches to biological research, testing, and education. Physicians, veterinarians, and research scientists in fields in which experimental animals are used may become voting members. Graduate students in these fields may become non-voting members. Opposes pound seizure and supports the phasing out of purpose-bred animals as quickly as possible. Considers invasive or distressing experiments on animals by high school or college students to be damaging to students. Urges the development and use of alternatives to animals in research and testing.

Sea Shepherd Conservation Society

International Headquarters: 3107A Washington Blvd., Marina Del Ray, CA 90292, (310) 301-SEAL (7325), FAX: (310) 574-3161

Contact the International Headquarters for addresses of international offices. A policing agency that directly intervenes to enforce international laws, regulations, and treaties that protect marine animals and marine ecosystems. Operates a Navy that serves and protects life in the oceans. Has saved hundreds of thousands of seals, whales, dolphins, sea birds, turtles, and fish, without causing a single injury to any person. Aggressive and effective while maintaining that "The Sanctity of Life must be respected at all times and in all encounters."

Sea Turtle Survival League

P.O. Box 2866, Gainesville, FL 32602-2866, 1-800-6478-7853

The membership and advocacy program of the Caribbean Conservation Corporation, continuing the mission of Dr. Archie Carr since 1959. Works to enact protective laws, establish sanctuaries for sea turtles, monitor and intervene as needed, conduct scientific studies of endangered species and their habitats, and increase awareness for the purpose of protection. Notes that loss and disturbance of nesting habitat caused by inappropriate coastal development is one of the biggest threats to sea turtle survival."

Shambala Preserve

See The Roar Foundation elsewhere in this section.

Sierra Club Legal Defense Fund

180 Montgomery Street, Suite 1400, San Francisco, CA 94104-4209, (415) 627-6700, FAX: (415) 627-64740

(*Note*: This Legal Defense Fund is not part of the Sierra Club.) A law firm for the environmental movement whose cases often protect wildlife directly or indirectly by protecting their habitats. No membership.

The Society for Animal Protective Legislation

P.O. Box 3719, Georgetown Station, Washington, D.C. 20007, (202) 337-2334, FAX: (202) 338-9478

Founded by the Animal Welfare Institute (see their listing elsewhere in this section). Works for passage of national animal protection legislation. Prepares information for members of Congress and their staffs, and sends letters urging support of specific legislation to a large mailing list of individuals interested in animal protective legislation.

Society for the Study of Ethics and Animals (SSEA)

c/o Department of Philosophy, VA Polytechnic Institute, Blacksburg, VA 24061-0126, (703) 231-8484

A scholarly organization dedicated to providing a framework for continued discussion of ethical concerns about human treatment of nonhuman animals. About 80% of members are professional philosophers. Other members include psychologists, writers, and animal welfare professionals. Meets three times a year in conjunction with the Eastern, Central, and Pacific divisions of the American Philosophical Association. Many papers delivered at these meetings are later published in *Between the Species* (see the Animals, Rights, & Ethics section of Chapter 13 for subscription information).

Society in Opposition to Human-Animal Hybridization (SOHAH)

23 Alabama Avenue, Lake Hopatcong, NJ 07849, (201) 663-4334

"A society of individuals absolutely opposed to hybridizing humans with animals or plants in any form [i.e. combining animal or plant DNA with human DNA] or for any purpose because it is self-evident that such hybridization is hideously immoral." *Note*: Differentiates humans from other animals ("humans are not animals, and should never be referred to as animals").

STAR Ferrets (Shelters That Adopt & Rescue Ferrets)

P.O. Box 1714, Springfield, VA 22151-0714, (703) 354-5073, E-mail: STARFeret@AOL.com

A network that assists people who own or work with ferrets. Provides education and helps establish private shelters for ferrets. Free international list of ferret-related contacts, including veterinarians, shelters, etc. for a self-addressed, stamped envelope. Paid membership includes the book *Ferret Care and Rescue*, a quarterly newsletter, and other items.

Student Action Corps for Animals (SACA)

P.O. Box 15588, Washington, D.C. 20003-0588, (202) 543-8983

A national advocacy, education, and information organization that specializes in empowering young people in high school and college to work effectively for animal rights and liberation. Provides in-depth individualized counseling on concerns such as dissection refusal, vegetarianism, and student rights. Gives school presentations and workshops. Since most members are non-working junior high and high school students, donations from adults are needed.

SUPRESS, Inc. (Students United Protesting Research on Sentient Subjects) / The Nature of Wellness

- Street Address: 740 East Colorado Blvd., Suite 205
- Mailing Address: P.O. Box 1062, Pasadena, CA 91102, (818) 584-0446 or 1-800-KILL-VIV

This is not an animal rights organization, but rather an anti-vivisection organization which opposes the use of animals on medical and scientific grounds.

The True Nature Network, Inc. (TTNN)

P.O. Box 20672, Columbus Circle Station, New York, NY 10023-1487

"We don't preach to the converted. We reach people who are unaware of these issues." Animal protection/ecology group which produces and actively distributes cable television programs. Also sells and loans videos, and sends educational materials to schools, universities, and libraries. See the Radio & Television Programming section of Chapter 12 for details.

Unexpected Wildlife Refuge, Inc.

The Beaver Defenders

- Street Address: Unexpected Road
- Mailing Address: P.O. Box 765, Newfield, NJ 08344, (609) 697-3541

Provides an inviolate, 400-acre sanctuary for native wild animals and furthers the cause of humane education and animal rights.

Unitarian Universalists For the Ethical Treatment of Animals (UFETA)

P.O. Box 2860, Church Street Station, New York, NY 10008, (212) 724-3842

Dedicated to the recognition of the rights of animals by Unitarians and other denominations.

United Action for Animals, Inc.

P.O. Box 635, Lennox Hill Station, New York, NY 10021, (212) 983-5315

Works to end the waste of billions of animal lives and taxpayer dollars on duplicative, inconclusive, and wasteful animal experiments. Exposes the "research myth" that all animal research is life-saving and necessary. Works to replace live animals in research with currently available alternatives. Introduced the Research Accountability Act in Congress to end wasteful duplication of animal experiments.

United Animal Nations USA (UAN-USA)

- Street Address: 5892A South Land Park Drive
- Mailing Address: P.O. Box 188890, Sacramento, CA 95818, (916) 429-2457, FAX: (916) 429-2456, Emergency Animal Rescue Service Volunteer Info: 1-800-440-EARS

Has several animal protection organizations as members. Provides protection for animals by: (1) uniting the humane movement, (2) providing assistance to organizations and individuals working to help animals, (3) providing emergency assistance to animals in manmade and natural disasters, and (4) prosecuting in the International Court of Justice for Animals individuals, organizations, people, or countries that promote or carry out extreme cruelties upon animals.

United Coalition of Iditarod Animal Rights Volunteers

John Suter, Coordinator, P.O. Box 670144, Chugiak, AK 99567, (907) 688-3103

Working to implement real and meaningful changes in the Iditarod Race, to promote the humane care of sled dogs both on and off the trail. Multiple instances of abuse by mushers are on record, including starving, bludgeoning, and shooting dogs. Since the Iditarod Trail Committee refuses to discuss changes, a national "Dogs Come First!" Campaign has succeeded in convincing major sponsors such as Timberland and Iams to withdraw their sponsorship. (At this writing, only one major sponsor, Alaska Airlines, remained.)

United Humanitarians

P.O. Box 14587, Philadelphia, PA 19115, (215) 750-0171

Operates a low-cost spay and neuter program through branches nationwide. Has given assistance to over 300 animal welfare organizations and committees in the U.S., Canada, Great Britain, and Australia. Supports a system of animal control that places all responsibility on owners rather than impounding and killing pets found at large.

United Poultry Concerns (UPC)

P.O. Box 59367, Potomac, MD 20859, (301) 948-2406

Seeks to show people new ways of relating to chickens, turkeys, and other domestic fowl as companions and fellow beings. Increases public awareness of ways poultry are used and promotes humane alternatives through direct activities (demonstrations, vigils, etc.) and educational efforts (talks, films, literature, etc.).

Universal Great Brotherhood (UGB)

Aquarian Universal Mission, P.O. Box 9154, St. Louis, MO 63117, (213) 839-4247

A Brotherhood of organizations currently working in over 35 countries to promote better health. Opposes killing animals. Promotes positive science, which includes ending medical fraud and vivisection. Seeks to promote respect for life and world peace.

University Conversion Project (UCP)—Center for Campus Organizing (CCO)

P.O. Box 748, Cambridge, MA 02142, (617) 354-9363 (voice/FAX), E-mail: ucp@igc.apc.org

A peace and justice organization that offers campus organizing information and materials useful to animal rights activists as well as other types of activists. See the Activism section of Chapter 13 for more details.

University Students Against Vivisection (USAV)

c/o Roderick Spilman, 2325 El Rancho Vista, Fullerton, CA 92633

A coalition of institutions of higher education that support the complete abolition of vivisection on a medical and scientific basis.

USA Defenders of Greyhounds, Inc.

P.O. Box 111, Camby, IN 46113, (317) 244-0113

Finds good homes for retired greyhound racing dogs and young greyhounds that have not had successful careers.

Wild Horse and Burro Sanctuary

P.O. Box 30, Shingletown, CA 96088, (916) 474-5770, FAX: (916) 474-5728

Provides a permanent home for unwanted wild horses and burros that would otherwise be killed by the government. Educates the public on the threats to the survival of these animals.

Wildlife Damage Review (WDR)

P.O. Box 85218, Tucson, AZ 85754, (602) 884-0883, FAX: (602) 884-0962

Brings public scrutiny to the USDA's Animal Damage Control (ADC) program, which uses over $36 million in tax dollars per year to slaughter thousands of native animals for the purpose of protecting the "livestock" industry.

Wildlife Preservation Trust International (WPTI)

3400 West Girard Avenue, Philadelphia, PA 19104, (215) 222-3636, FAX: (215) 222-2191, E-mail: WPTI@aol.com, Internet: http://www.columbia.edu/cu/cerc/wpti.html

Children's Club (The Wild Ones) Internet Site: http://www.columbia.edu/cu/cerc/WildOnes

"We are a voice on behalf of endangered species...We believe animals are born to be wild, and work to return them to safe natural habitat." Dedicated to protecting species of wildlife from extinction. Works primarily in areas where there are human-wildlife conflicts and where there are highly diverse or unique ecosystems. A high priority is training conservation professionals who are also citizens of the areas where they work. Maintains a "lean management style, with few administrators and contracted field people working on multi-year projects."

Wildlife Refuge Reform Coalition

P.O. Box 18414, Washington, D.C. 20036-8414, (202) 778-6145

A national coalition of over 60 national and local organizations, brought together under the leadership of the Conservation Endowment Fund and The Humane Society of the United States, with strong support from the Massachusetts Society for the Prevention of Cruelty to Animals, American Society for the Prevention of Cruelty to Animals, Friends of

Animals, and the American Humane Association. Overall goal is to restore integrity to the management of the National Wildlife Refuge System.

Wildlife Rescue and Rehabilitation, Inc.

P.O. Box 34FF, San Antonio, TX 78201, (512) 698-1709

Accepts, cares for, and rehabilitates injured, orphaned, abused, and displaced wild animals and returns them to their natural habitats. Maintains a 21-acre sanctuary. Hopes to breed endangered species in captivity and release the offspring back to the wild.

Wildlife Waystation

14831 Little Tujunga Canyon Road, Angeles National Forest, S.F., CA 91342-5999, (818) 899-5201, FAX: (818) 890-1107

A rescue center for abused, injured, and abandoned wild and exotic animals. Home to approximately 800 permanent residents. Provides rehabilitation for an additional 4,000 animals each year.

Wolf Haven International

3111 Offut Lake Road, Terrino, WA 98589, (360) 264-4695, 1-800-448-9653, FAX: (360) 264-4639, Internet: http://www.teleport.com/~wnorton/wolf.shtml

Works for wolf conservation. Objectives include protection of remaining wild wolves and their habitat, promotion of wolf re-establishment in historic ranges, a sanctuary for captive wolves, and public education on the value of all wildlife, including predators.

Women's Humane Society

3839 Richlieu Road, P.O. Box 1470, Ben Salem, PA 19020-5470, (215) 225-4500

One of the oldest humane societies in America. Located in the inner city. Established the first humane veterinary clinic, first animal shelter, and first humane education program in the U.S. Has lost much-needed United Way funding because United Way decided that they "didn't fit their guidelines anymore." Reports to members on national issues, such as leghold trapping and the Hegins, PA Pigeon Shoot.

World Bird Sanctuary (WBS)

P.O. Box 270270, St. Louis, MO 63127, (314) 938-6193, FAX: (314) 938-WING

One of North America's largest conservation facilities for birds, especially birds of prey and parrots. Mission is "to preserve the earth's biological diversity and to secure the future of threatened bird species in their natural environments." Activities include captive breeding and reintroduction, rescue and rehabilitation, habitat management, and public education through the Office of Wildlife Learning (OWL), school education programs, a "Traveling Talons" program, etc. Has commenced construction of a multi-million dollar World Environmental Education Center.

World Mission for Animals (WMA)

P.O. Box 816, Glendale, OR 97442, (541) 832-2665

A worldwide group of like-minded souls who believe that animals have souls and thereby have spiritual as well as physical and moral rights. Mission is to awaken the divine conscience of humans to the fact that "Thou shalt not kill...anything." Establishes sanctuaries for animals worldwide as well as mission schools where they teach natural care and healing techniques.

World Pets Society

P.O. Box 570343, Tarzana, CA 91357, (818) 345-5140

Works to protect the world's wildlife and habitats.

World Society for the Protection of Animals (WSPA)

Western Hemisphere Office:

- Street Address: 29 Perkins Street
- Mailing Address: P.O. Box 190, Boston, MA 02130, (617) 522-7000, FAX: (617) 522-7077

The only international animal protection organization granted nongovernmental, consultative status to the United Nations. Seeks to relieve the suffering of all animal life throughout the world.

Local Animal Organizations

ALABAMA

For additional resources for breed rescue, ferret rescue, wildlife rehabilitation, etc., see "Keeping Up-To-Date" at the front of the chapter.

Alabama Wildlife Rescue Service
Tennessee Valley Chapter: P.O. Box 2305, Huntsville, AL 35804, (205) 830-1170
Wildlife rescue and rehabilitation.

Alabamians Working for Animal Rights and the Environment (AWARE)
ATTN: Patty Blake, P.O. Box 306, Lacey's Spring, AL 35754, (205) 498-5221

The Anelia Animal Sanctuary
P.O. Box 1205, Oneonta, AL 35121
No-kill adoption shelter for dogs.

The Ark, Inc.
P.O. Box 198, Toney, AL 35773

Gulf Coast Ferret Rescue
Ms. Marty Loeffler, 522 Highway 43, Chicksaw, AL 36611, (205) 457-8346
Ferret rescue, adoption, and boarding. Also rescues dogs, cats, etc.

Humane Society of the United States
See Florida for the regional HSUS office that serves this state.

The Humane Society / SPCA
455 Highway 253, Montevallo, AL 35115, (205) 665-4683

PP's Wannabe's Pet Placement Service
P.O. Box 485, Estaboga, AL 36260, (205) 835-0731
A single activist who devotes her time and energy to animal welfare.

Spay/Neuter Action Project (SNAP)
ATTN: Judy Fassina, 2112 Raincreek Trail, Huntsville, AL 35811, (205) 539-8163
Low-cost spay/neuter and financial assistance to those in need.

ALASKA

For additional resources for breed rescue, ferret rescue, wildlife rehabilitation, etc., see "Keeping Up-To-Date" at the front of the chapter.

The Alaska Humane Society
P.O. Box 103567, Anchorage, AK 99510-3567, (907) 274-2422
No-kill adoption shelter for cats. *Note*: Sells gaming permits.

Alaska Wildlife Alliance
P.O. Box 202022, Anchorage, AK 99520, (907) 277-0897
Statewide. Benefits many wild animals in Alaska.

Bird Treatment and Learning Center
1600 E. Tudor Road, Anchorage, AK 99507, (907) 563-3945
Cares for all injured or ill birds.

People and Animals Working Side by Side (PAWS)
P.O. Box 291, Nome, AK 99762
Formed in response to the shooting of loose dogs by local police. Helps companion animals by providing an adoption program. Working on a spay/neuter program.

United Coalition of Iditarod Animal Rights Volunteers
Chugiak, AK
See "National & International Organizations."

Wolf Song of Alaska
P.O. Box 110309, Anchorage, AK 99511-0309, (907) 346-3073
Developing a multi-million dollar, 354-500 acre wolf observation facility in the Anchorage area, which will focus on the educational and scientific aspects of the wolf and will include a major visitor center, museum, theater, lecture hall, guest housing, veterinary care center, predator and prey habitats, and observation facilities.

ARIZONA

For additional resources for breed rescue, ferret rescue, wildlife rehabilitation, etc., see "Keeping Up-To-Date" at the front of the chapter.

The Animal League of Green Valley
P.O. Box 1153, Green Valley, AZ 85622, (602) 625-3170
No-kill adoption shelter.

Animal Liberation Action
National Office: Tucson, AZ
See "National & International Organizations."

Animals Benefit Club of Arizona, Inc. (ABC)
- Office: P.O. Box 26627, Phoenix, AZ 85068, (602) 867-2169, FAX: (602) 867-0630
- Shelter: 3111 E. St John Road, Phoenix

Operates the Pets Are Wonderful Shelter and Educational Center in northeast Phoenix, a no-kill, cageless shelter with runs that lead into a play yard. Live-in caretakers. Founded by a teacher and her Jr. High School students in 1977. Also provides an award-winning educational pet care program and was a driving force behind the county's mandatory spay/neuter program and differential licensing fees.

Animals' Crusaders
P.O. Box 31586, Tucson, AZ 85751-1586, (602) 327-7427
Works to reduce the animal suffering caused by overpopulation. Low-cost spay/neuter and emergency food assistance. Also serves companion animals living on the San Xavier Tohono O'odham Indian Nation.

Arizona Animal Welfare League
30 N. 40 Place, Phoenix, AZ 85034-1802, (602) 273-6852, FAX: (602) 267-7802
No-kill adoption shelter.

Arizona Lobby For Animals (ALFA)
P.O. Box 33093, Phoenix, AZ 85068-6238, (602) 392-2424
Statewide. Volunteer lobbying organization dedicated to animal protection.

Cat Help And Rescue Movement (C.H.A.R.M.)
P.O. Box 62471, Phoenix, AZ 85082-2471, (602) 470-0131
No-kill adoption shelter for cats and a few dogs. Spay/neuter-microchip-release program for cats. Never declaws. Utilizes over 100 foster homes. Volunteers and financial assistance welcome.

Citizens for North Phoenix Strays (CNPS)
P.O. Box 86351, Phoenix, AZ 85080, (602) 375-2428, Spay/neuter Info: 278-6632, 265-SPAY, or 942-SAVE
No-kill adoption service for cats and some dogs. No shelter; depends on foster homes. Emphasizes spay/neuter.

Citizens for Scottsdale Strays
P.O. Box 928, Scottsdale, AZ 85252-0928, (602) 990-4428
No-kill adoption shelter for cats.

Coalition of All-Breed Rescue of Arizona
P.O. Box 7264, Phoenix, AZ 85011-7264, (602) 494-9567
Rescue and adoption of dogs and wolf/dog hybrids.

Concerned Arizonans for Animal Rights and Ethics (CAARE)
- Main Office: P.O. Box 33093, Phoenix, AZ 85067, (602) 241-9778
- CAARE Verde Valley: P.O. Box 580, Cornville, AZ 86325, (602) 634-6233
- CAARE/ASU: Arizona State University, Student Development Office, Box 18, Tempe, AZ 85287-3001, (602) 897-2158

Greater Phoenix area. Educates Arizonans about institutional abuses of animals.

Ferret Friends Club/Shelter
c/o Ginny Childs, 1067 W. Miracle Mile, #4, Tucson, AZ 85705, (520) 622-4940
Ferret information, assistance, rescue, and adoptions.

Friends for Life Animal Sanctuary
(formerly Citizens for Tempe Strays)
715 W. Baseline, #3-178, Tempe, AZ 85283, (602) 893-8858
Rescue and adoption of cats and dogs. Enforces an "intense" spay/neuter policy. Does not practice or condone euthanasia as a means of population control. Also offers help to homeless people and pet adoptions for people with special needs.

Help Abolish Leghold Traps (HALT)
P.O. Box 32714, Phoenix, AZ 85064, (602) 266-5655
Concentrates on animal-related initiatives and legislative efforts. Working on going nationwide.

Helping Animals Live On! (HALO)
P.O. Box 1071, Peoria, AZ 85380-1971, (602) 974-9122
No-kill adoption shelter for cats, dogs, and wildlife.

The Hermitage No-Kill Cat Shelter
P.O. Box 13508, Tucson, AZ 85732-3508, (602) 571-7839
No-kill adoption shelter for cats.

Humane Society of the United States
See Texas for the regional HSUS office that serves this state.

International Society for the Protection of Mustangs & Burros
Scottsdale, AZ
See "National & International Organizations."

Kitty Love
P.O. Box J, Scottsdale, AZ 85252, (602) 481-6920 (24-hour hotline to help abandoned cats)
Short-term focus is on educational and spay/neuter programs. Long-term goal is a permanent adoption facility. Sponsors Sunday adoptions at local PetsMart stores.

Liberty Wildlife Rehabilitation Foundation
11825 N. 70th Street, Scottsdale, AZ 85254, (602) 998-5550
Cares for all injured or orphaned wildlife.

Preserve Arizona's Wolves (P.A.W.S.)
1413 East Dobbins Road, Phoenix, AZ 85040

Ranching Task Force
Tucson, AZ
See "National & International Organizations."

SAFE Humane Society
P.O. Box 347, Pearce, AZ 85625

SPEAK
P.O. Box 143, Tucson, AZ 85702-0143, (520) 883-2488
"Let the smallest cry in the universe be heard." An animal rights speakers bureau.

Sun Cities Animal Rescue, Inc.
P.O. Box 1, Sun City, AZ 85372-0001, (602) 972-8541
No-kill adoption shelter.

Valley Dale Animal Haven, Inc. (VDAH)
Hopewell Mine Road, P.O. Box 70, Clarkdale, AZ 86324, (520) 634-0400
No-kill adoption shelter dedicated to the love and care of elderly, neglected, and homeless pets. Offers pre-planning arrangements for a pet's future through a personal Trust Fund which guarantees a lifelong home at the haven or placement with a loving, responsible family.

Voices for Animals, Inc.
P.O. Box 43026, Tucson, AZ 85733, (602) 623-3101
Statewide. Educates the public on society's abuses of animals.

Where Wolves Rescue
30040 N. 167th Avenue, Sun City, AZ 85373, (602) 546-WOLF (9653)
No-kill adoption shelter for wolf hybrids, coyotes, and related canids. *Note*: Considers wolf hybrids to be "dogs."

Wildlife Damage Review
Tucson, AZ
See "National & International Organizations."

ARKANSAS

For additional resources for breed rescue, ferret rescue, wildlife rehabilitation, etc., see "Keeping Up-To-Date" at the front of the chapter.

Arkansans for Animals
P.O. Box 2918, Little Rock, AR 72203, (501) 375-5848 or 942-3465
Statewide. Promotes state legislation to preserve and protect the rights of animals.

Coalition of Municipalities to Ban Animal Trafficking
Fayetteville, AR
See "National & International Organizations."

Earth! Educate!
Fayetteville, AR
See "National & International Organizations."

Students for the Ethical Treatment of Animals (SETA)
University of Arkansas, 517 Arkansas Union, Fayetteville, AR 72701
Regular activities include tabling, leafletting, and demonstrating.

CALIFORNIA

For additional resources for breed rescue, ferret rescue, wildlife rehabilitation, etc., see "Keeping Up-To-Date" at the front of the chapter.

Abandoned Terrier Rescue Association (ATRA, Inc.)
P.O. Box 824, Somis, CA 93066, (805) 386-3757
Rescues homeless Airedales, Lakeland, Welsh, and wire-haired Fox terriers from shelters or individuals throughout Southern California. Spays/neuters all adoptees. Screens adoptive homes and performs follow-up.

Action For Animals (AFA)
P.O. Box 20184, Oakland, CA 94620, (510) 652-5603
Publishes a monthly calendar of events for San Francisco Bay area activists. Main focus is animals in entertainment—zoos, circuses, and particularly rodeos.

Action For Animals' Rights (AFAR) / North County Humane Society
5935 Traffic Way, Atascadero, CA 93422, (805) 466-5403 or 462-AFAR
Countywide. Working to put themselves and all humane societies out of business.

Activists for Protective Animal Legislation
P.O. Box 11743, Costa Mesa, CA 92627

Actors and Others for Animals (A&O)
11523 Burbank Blvd., North Hollywood, CA 91601, (818) 755-6045, FAX: (818) 755-6048
Promotes the humane treatment of animals. Subsidizes spay/neuter in the Los Angeles area, supports animal protection legislation, conducts humane education in schools, and helps place homeless animals (but does not operate a shelter). Among the original founders were the late Richard Basehart and his wife Diana.

Afghan Hound Rescue of Southern California
(310) 657-8237

A Horse in Miracles
7705 Hampton Avenue, #323, West Hollywood, CA 90046, (213) 850-7027 or 848-8498

American Cetacean Society
National Headquarters: San Pedro, CA
See "National & International Organizations."

American Humane Association (AHA)
Regional Office: Los Angeles, CA
See "National & International Organizations."

American Mustang and Burro Association
Lincoln, CA
See "National & International Organizations."

American Society for the Prevention of Cruelty to Animals (ASPCA)
West Coast Regional Office: 11288 Ventura Blvd., Suite 112B, Studio City, CA 91604, (818) 985-8686
See "National & International Organizations."

American Wildlife Rescue Service, Inc.
1296 Conference Drive, Scotts Valley, CA 95066, (408) 335-3232 or 335-2155, FAX: (408) 438-7516
Provides care for birds, exotic animals, and wild animals in need.

Animal Advocates
1747 Montgomery Drive, Vista, CA 92084-7629, (619) 726-6393

Animal Alternatives
P.O. Box 262396, San Diego, CA 92196-2396
Dedicated to finding alternatives to our dependency on animals for personal lifestyle, beauty care, product testing, and research. Membership is free and open to everyone.

Animal Assistance League of Orange County, Inc.
Ruth Frankel, President, P.O. Box 38, Midway, CA 92655, (714) 978-7387
No-kill adoption shelter.

Animal Emancipation, Inc.
- Corporate Office: 1223 Wilshire Blvd., Suite 856, Santa Monica, CA 90403
- Santa Barbara Chapter: P.O. Box 90658, Santa Barbara, CA 93190
- San Luis Obispo Chapter: P.O. Box 1684, San Luis Obispo, CA 93406
- UCSB Student Chapter: Activities Planning Center, University of California, Santa Barbara, CA 93106

Central/Southern California area, with some national campaigns. A multi-issue animal rights and anti-vivisection organization, focusing on investigations and campaigns.

Animal Freedom Fighters
P.O. Box 5520, Santa Monica, CA 90405

Animal Helpline
P.O. Box 944, Morongo Valley, CA 92256, (619) 363-6511
Telephone aid for lost/found, placement, minor first aid, and referrals. No-kill cat rescue shelter (the founder's home) for older or handicapped cats.

Animal Legal Defense Fund
San Rafael, CA
See "National & International Organizations."

Animal Legislative Action Network
Los Angeles, CA
See "National & International Organizations."

Animal Lovers Unlimited, Inc.
P.O. Box 374, Yuba City, CA 95992-0374

Animal Outreach of Mother Lode
6200 Enterprise Drive, Suite D, Diamond Springs, CA 95619, (916) 642-CATS (2287), FAX: (916) 642-0753
"Helping the companion pets of El Dorado County since 1992." Adoptions, spay/neuter, vaccinations, assistance for seniors and AIDS clients, and trap/alter/release of feral cats.

Animal Place
Vacaville, CA
See "National & International Organizations."

Animal Protection Institute of America
Sacramento, CA
See "National & International Organizations."

Animal Rescue Foundation
P.O. Box 6146, Concord, CA 94524-1146

Animal Rights Connection
P.O. Box 410862, San Francisco, CA 94141, (415) 751-3756

Animal Samaritans / SPCA, Inc.
72-307 Ramon Road, Thousand Palms, CA 92276, (619) 343-3477, FAX: (619) 343-0078
No-kill adoption shelter for cats and dogs.

Animal Watch
P.O. Box 416, Sacramento, CA 95812, (916) 922-0570
Direct, non-violent action for animals while respecting human interests. Works with other community groups in the Greater Sacramento Metropolitan area.

Animals' Lobby
Capitol Plaza Building, 1025 9th Street, Suite 219, Sacramento, CA 95814, (916) 441-1562, (415) 474-4202 (24-hour Animal Rights Action Line)
Statewide. Lobbies for state animal protection legislation.

Animals Unlimited, Inc. (AU, Inc.)
5224 Topanga Canyon Blvd., Woodland Hills, CA 91364, (818) 340-3327

The Ark Trust, Inc.
Sherman Oaks, CA
See "National & International Organizations."

Arts Activist
Chico, CA
See "National & International Organizations."

The Association Of Sanctuaries, Inc.
Sacramento, CA
See "National & International Organizations."

Association of Veterinarians for Animal Rights (AVAR)
Vacaville, CA
See "National & International Organizations."

The Bird Sanctuary
512 Box Canyon Road, Canoga Park, CA 91304

Rescues unwanted or injured birds, and "will take on" birds whose caretakers can't afford veterinary care. Also rescues some dogs.

California Animal Defense and Anti-Vivisection League, Inc.
P.O. Box 3047, Gardena, CA 90247, (310) 549-9196, FAX: (310) 549-9197

California Center for Wildlife
76 Albert Park Lane, P.O. Box 150957, San Rafael, CA 94915-0959, (415) 456-SAVE (7283)

California Equine Retirement Foundation (CERF)
34033 Kooden Road, Winchester, CA 92596, (909) 926-4190

California Federation for Animal Legislation (C.F.A.L.)
c/o Karen Raasch, 3098 Susan Court, W. Sacramento, CA 95691-4817, (916) 641-6059
Statewide. Represents 82 California animal protection organizations. Lobbies for good bills and against animal exploitation.

California Humane Action and Information Network
Marin Humane Society, 171 Bel Marine Keys Blvd., Novato, CA 94949

California Humane Coalition
P.O. Box 60715, Palo Alto, CA 94306

California Marine Mammal Center (CMMC)
Marin Headlands, Golden Gate National Recreation Area, Sausalito, CA 94965
Rescue Line: (415) 331-SEAL
Information: (415) 331-7327
Concerned with marine health and well-being and the conservation of the marine habitat. Focuses on the California coast, but concerned with global as well as local issues.

Californians for the Ethical Treatment of Animals
P.O. Box 13, Morongo Valley, CA 92256, (619) 363-7346, Hotline: (714) 360-9310

Cat Assistance, Referral & Education (C.A.R.E.)
P.O. Box 56631, Sherman Oaks, CA 91403
• East Valley: (818) 982-1473
• West Valley: (818) 347-1323
• West L.A.: (310) 453-8407
Hands-on assistance, equipment, and resource information. Most importantly, provides encouragement and support for others who care about animals. Cats fostered in caring homes.

Cats in Need of Human Care
P.O. Box 431, Pomona, CA 91766, (909) 622-0121
No-kill adoption shelter for cats.

Center for Animal Protection and Education (CAPE)
P.O. Box 67176, Scotts Valley, CA 95067-7176, (408) 426-2214 (24-hour info line)
Actively educates people about the plights of animals. Provides public school programs on vivisection, factory farming, hunting, etc. Rescues, fosters, and adopts animals into permanent homes. Helps with problematic animal behavior.

Center for Marine Conservation (CMC)
Regional Office: San Francisco, CA
See "National & International Organizations."

Citizens Lobbying for Animals in Zoos (CLAZ)
5404 Laguna Park Drive, Elkgrove, CA 95758, (916) 684-3330
(*Note*: CLAZ is pronounced "claws.") Dedicated to improving the quality of life for animals in zoos and the quality of zoos in Sacramento. Works *with* zoos, not against them. Although activities are confined to zoos in the Sacramento area, can answer questions about enrichment.

Coalition Against The Horse Slaughter Trade
Penngrove, CA
See "National & International Organizations."

Coalition for Humane Legislation (CHL)
P.O. Box 8136, San Jose, CA 95155, (408) 993-2255 (voice/FAX)
Works locally for humane legislation, including a breeding ordinance for San Jose.

Committee for a Cruelty Free California
1217 Alpine Trail, Topanga Canyon, CA 90290, (310) 455-2597
Statewide. Established to help the networking effort to pass the California Draize Bill.

Community of Compassion for Animals
19100 Newville Road, Star Rte., Box 20H, Orland, CA 95963, (916) 865-4710
A sanctuary for pigs, dogs, donkeys, cows, cats, sheep, chickens, goats, and others. Accepts farm, feral, companion, or laboratory animals.

Compassion for Animals Foundation, Inc.
Culver City, CA
See "National & International Organizations."

Compassion in Action (CiA)
P.O. Box 5143, Walnut Creek, CA 94596, (510) 671-2413
Performs advocacy on behalf of animals, human health, and environmental health by stressing a vegan lifestyle.

Concerned People for Animals, Inc.
P.O. Box 632, Somis, CA 93066, (805) 482-6587
Ventura County area. Works to improve and protect the lives of animals through education, action, and fellowship.

Dedication & Everlasting Love To Animals
Glendale, CA
See "National & International Organizations."

Desert Tortoise Preserve Committee, Inc.
P.O. Box 2910, Santa Bernardino, CA 92406, 1-800-525-2443

DJ&T Foundation
Beverly Hills, CA
See "National & International Organizations."

The Dolphin Network
San Anselmo, CA
See "National & International Organizations."

Earth Island Institute / Dolphin Project
San Francisco, CA
See "National & International Organizations."

East Bay Animal Referral, Inc.
P.O. Box 13314, Oakland, CA 94661, (510) 841-PAWS
Pound rescues and adoptions.

Education and Action for Animals
P.O. Box 2719, Redondo Beach, CA 90278, (310) 370-8277 (24-hour hotline)
A direct action group that educates the public through demonstrations, leafletting, speaking engagements, and boycotts.

The Elephant Alliance
La Jolla, CA
See "National & International Organizations."

EQUUS Horse Rescue Network and Sanctuary
P.O. Box 3273, Glendale, CA 91221, (818) 768-3469
Rescues horses from stockyards and operates the largest domesticated horse "no-kill" sanctuary in the country.

Farm Sanctuary-West
Orland, CA
See "National & International Organizations."

Film to Liberate Laboratory Animals, Inc.
ATTN: Marie Carosello, 104 Banks Street, San Francisco, CA 94110-5623, (415) 206-0872
The funding, production, and distribution agent for the award-winning documentary "Tools for Research," which exposes the waste and abuse of lab animals, and advocates for alternatives to animals. Soliciting donations to help offset the heavy expenses incurred in the making of this film.

Forgotten Felines of Sonoma County
1275 Fourth St., #366, Santa Rosa, CA 95404, (707) 576-7999
Feral cat control. Offers a manual for $30.

Friends for Life
c/o Susan Netboy, 5 Ranch Road, Woodside, CA 94062, (415) 851-7812
Greyhound rescue and adoption.

Friends for Pets Foundation
7131 Owensmouth, #39A, Canoga Park, CA 91309, (818) 767-5919 or (310) 377-2998, FAX: (818) 767-7805
Breed rescue for the sporting breeds, primarily Weimaraner and Golden Retriever. As space permits (limit is 75), will also accept other sporting breeds. Will take any "Weim"

anytime, no matter the age or medical condition. Certified Tattoo-A-Pet agent.

Friends of Animals Foundation

P.O. Box 34-1230, Los Angeles, CA 90034, (310) 479-5089
No-kill shelter that is special in its acceptance of "difficult-to-place" animals: the old, ill, large, traumatized, etc. Fully investigates potential homes. Animals housed in a rented kennel. All animals spayed/neutered. Assists senior citizens in feeding their companion animals and operates a pet therapy program.

Friends of Cats, Inc.

P.O. Box 1613, Lakeside, CA 92040, (619) 561-0361
No-kill shelter for cats.

Friends of the Long Beach Animal Shelter

3001 E. Willow Street, Long Beach, CA 90806
Dedicated to responsible pet ownership, education, and the humane treatment of all animals. An example of how a handful of volunteers can benefit shelter animals. Welcomes new volunteers.

Friends of the Sea Lion

Marine Mammal Center, 20612 Laguna Canyon Road, Laguna Beach, CA 92651, (714) 494-3050
Rescues and rehabilitates sick or injured sea lions and seals along the Orange County coast, and returns them to their natural environment.

Friends of the Sea Otter

Monterey, CA
See "National & International Organizations."

Friendship for Animals

P.O. Box 7000-226, Alta Loma, CA 91701, (909) 980-7711
Works to help companion animals. No kennel facility.

The Fund for Animals, Inc.

Field Offices: Virginia Handley, California Coordinator, Fort Mason Center, Room 262, San Francisco, CA 94123, (415) 474-4020, FAX: (415) 474-5323
- and -
c/o Kim Sturla, Director of Companion Animal Issues & Education, 808 Alamo Drive, Suite 306, Vacaville, CA 95688, (707) 451-1306
- and -
c/o Joyce Pieper, Los Angeles Area Coordinator, 23128 Bigler Street, Woodland Hills, CA 91364, (818) 222-8485
The Vacaville and Woodland Hills field offices are very active in spay/neuter efforts. For a description of The Fund for Animals, Inc., see "National & International Organizations."

Fur-Bearer Defenders

Sacramento, CA
See "National & International Organizations."

George Whittel Wildlife Rescue and Rehabilitation Center

P.O. Box 264, Monterey, CA 93942, (408) 646-WILD

Good Shepherd Foundation

P.O. Box 1950, Nevada City, CA 95959, (808) 935-5563
Serves Northern California, with national membership and a chapter in Hawaii. Cares for and shelters abused, abandoned, or injured animals, wild or domesticated.

The Gorilla Foundation

Woodside, CA
See "National & International Organizations."

Greyhound Club of America

Cheryl Reynolds, Rescue Chair, 4280 Carpenteria Avenue, Carpenteria, CA 93013, (805) 684-4914
Greyhound rescue and placement.

Greyhound Friends for Life

Kelseyville, CA
See "National & International Organizations."

Greyhound Protection League (GPL)

P.O. Box 620563, Woodside, CA 94062, Contact: Susan Netboy (Media Coordinator) (415) 851-7812, 1-800-446-8637
Protects greyhounds from the exploitation and abuses inherent in the greyhound racing industry.

Happy Tails Pet Sanctuary

P.O. Box 161994, Sacramento, CA 95816-1994, (916) 556-1155
Foster homes for cats.

H.E.A.T. in the Central Valley

5125 E. Lane, #103, Fresno, CA 93727, (209) 251-4056

Helen Woodward Animal Center

- Street Address: 6461 El Apajo Road
- Mailing Address: P.O. Box 64, Rancho Santa Fe, CA 92067, (619) 756-4117

San Diego County. A large, nationally-recognized center for companion animal care, sheltering, and public education. Therapeutic riding, pet encounter therapy, boarding, humane education, and an equine hospital.

HorseAid

P.O. Box 6778, Rancho Palos Verdes, CA 90734-6778, (310) 719-9094 (24-hour line)

Rescue and care of abused, abandoned, or neglected horses and ponies. Closely associated with the International Generic Horse Association.

Horse Power Projects & Horse Power International, Inc.

Monterey, CA

See "National & International Organizations."

HorseSafe!

1354 East Avenue R-252, Chico, CA 95926, (916) 898-1893, FAX: (916) 899-9592

Horse Welfare Committee

P.O. Box 907, Penngrove, CA 94951, (707) 762-3644

House Rabbit Sanctuary

Alameda, CA

See "National & International Organizations."

Humane Animal Rescue Team (H.A.R.T.) & Muttmatchers Messenger

P.O. Box 546, Fillmore, CA 93016, (805) 524-4542

A network of caring people devoted to rescuing animals and bringing compassionate ideals to life by translating them into action. Publishes a quarterly *Breed Rescue List* with the names and numbers of local breed rescuers (people who save dogs of a particular breed), and a bimonthly *Muttmatchers Messenger*, featuring companion animals who need adoption. See the Companion Animals: Periodicals section of Chapter 13 for more on these publications.

Humane Education Network

P.O. Box 7434, Menlo Park, CA 94026, (415) 854-8921

Education and advocacy for the humane treatment of animals, to end unnecessary suffering and the waste of tax dollars. Computerized reference library open to the public.

Humane Farming Action Fund

San Rafael, CA

See "National & International Organizations."

The Humane Farming Association

San Francisco, CA

See "National & International Organizations."

Humane Legislative Network

P.O. Box 171, Jamul, CA 91935, Contact: Bobbie Theodore (619) 669-0434

Statewide. Works to get better legislation for animals through the California legislature.

Humane Society of the United States

West Coast Regional Office:

- Street Address: 5301 Madison Avenue, Suite 202
- Mailing Address: P.O. Box 417220, Sacramento, CA 95841-7220, (916) 344-1710, FAX: (916) 344-1808

Serves CA, ID, OR, NV, and WA. See "National & International Organizations."

Hunt Saboteurs

P.O. Box 2102, Anaheim, CA 92814, (714) 995-4889

Uses whatever nonviolent, direct action tactics are necessary to intervene in the field between the hunter and the hunted, without causing harm to either life or property.

In Defense of Animals

- Home Office: San Rafael, CA
- South Bay Chapter: 6560 Ashfield Court, San Jose, CA 95120, (408) 268-4577, FAX: (408) 927-9281

See "National & International Organizations."

International Dolphin Project

San Diego, CA

See "National & International Organizations."

International Wildlife Rehabilitation Council

Suisun, CA

See "National & International Organizations."

Irish Wolfhound Rescue Trust

16513 Napa Street, Sepulveda, CA 91343, (818) 894-8988

Jehovah's Witnesses for Animal Rights
1362 Kingfisher, #16, Sunnyvale, CA 94087-3553, (408) 737-0935

Last Chance for Animals
Tarzana, CA
See "National & International Organizations."

Latham Foundation
Latham Plaza Building, Clement & Schiller Streets, Alameda, CA 94501, (510) 521-0920
Promotes the concept of compassion for all life.

Lifeforce
Los Angeles and San Francisco
See "National & International Organizations."

Life Is For Everything Foundation
1111 So. Lamb Road, Ridgecrest, CA 93555-9038

Lifeline for Pets
P.O. Box 5812, Pasadena, CA 91117, (818) 286-6390

Lodi Animal Rights Alliance
P.O. Box 2314, Lodi, CA 95241-2314

Lynx Educational Fund for Animal Welfare
Los Angeles, CA
See "National & International Organizations."

Maplewood Farms Wildlife Rescue and Sanctuary
P.O. Box 35665, Monte Sereno, CA 95030, (408) 356-5539

Marine and Wildlife Rescue Station
6112 Bunsall Drive, Malibu, CA 90265-3825

Mercy Crusade, Inc.
Van Nuys, CA
See "National & International Organizations."

Ministries for Animals
1442A Walnut Street, Berkeley, CA 94709

Mountain Lion Foundation (MLF)
P.O. Box 1896, Sacramento, CA 95812, (916) 442-2666
Works to protect California wildlife and habitat. Represents wildlife in the courts, the state legislature, the U.S. Congress, the media, and before voters. Successfully fought to ban trophy hunting of mountain lions.

Mouse Liberation Movement
P.O. Box 2757, Sausalito, CA 94966-2757

The National Activist Network
Sacramento, CA
See "National & International Organizations."

National Cat Protection Society
Long Beach, CA
See "National & International Organizations."

National Greyhound Adoption Network
Northern California
See "National & International Organizations."

The National Opossum Society
Orange, CA
See "National & International Organizations."

Northern California Sighthound Rescue
c/o Sandra Wornum, 570 Riviera Circle, Larkspur, CA 94939, (415) 924-7020
Rescue and placement of sighthounds, including greyhounds.

Opossum Society of California
P.O. Box 3091, Orange, CA 92665, (714) 998-4924 (founder's business phone)
Statewide, with most hands-on work restricted to Southern California. Educates everyone about the benefits of North America's only marsupial—the opossum.

Opossum Society of the U.S.
Irvine, CA
See "National & International Organizations."

Orange County People for Animals (OCPA)
P.O. Box 28918, Santa Ana, CA 92799, (714) 751-OCPA (6272)
An active group that opposes any form of animal exploitation. Supports national groups in statewide efforts when asked.

The Orangutan Foundation
Los Angeles, CA
See "National & International Organizations."

Palo Alto Humane Society (PAHS)

P.O. Box 60715, Palo Alto, CA 94306, (415) 327-0631, FAX: (415) 329-1968

Works to alleviate animal suffering by increasing public sensitivity to animal issues, elevating the status of animals in society, and implementing innovative programs in intervention, education, and advocacy. No shelter. Spay/neuter help, financial assistance to animal rescue efforts, a local hotline for animal questions, obedience training, a pilot program in long-term care for animals bereft of their human companions because of illness or death, etc.

Paradise Animal Shelter Helpers

P.O. Box 1021, Paradise, CA 95967, (916) 872-2341

PAW PAC

California's Political Action Committee for Animals, P.O. Box 2354, San Francisco, CA 94126, (415) 841-7108

Statewide. A nonpartisan Political Action Committee (PAC), unaffiliated with any other organization, that supports the election of candidates to California state offices who favor the enactment of laws to benefit animals.

Pax Animalibus (Peace for the Animals)

c/o Donnelly, P.O. Box 4271, Chico, CA 95927, (916) 345-8493 or 891-4614

Rights activists with an ideology focusing on the interconnection between animals and the environment.

Peninsula Humane Society (PHS), Education Division

12 Airport Blvd., San Mateo, CA 94401-1098, (415) 340-8200 (ext. 344)

Works to ensure the humane treatment of all animals and to improve the quality of life for all animals. Works as the Animal Control agency for San Mateo County.

People for Animal Liberation (PAL)

P.O. Box 2960, Santa Cruz, CA 95063, (408) 426-5072 (Sharon Kaplan, co-founder)

Publishes *Out of the Cages*, which highlights Animal Liberation Front (ALF) activities, as well as those of other groups. See the Activism section of Chapter 13 for ordering information. Send a self-addressed, stamped envelope for all matters requiring a response.

People for Reason in Science and Medicine (PRISM)

P.O. Box 1305, Woodland Hills, CA 91365, Info: (714) 995-4889, Hotline: (818) 345-9654

Los Angeles focus, with members worldwide. An educational, grassroots, environmental and health organization that promotes nontoxic, noninvasive modalities as solutions to health and environmental problems.

Performing Animal Welfare Society

Galt, CA

See "National & International Organizations."

Pet Lovers Protective League

P.O. Box 10088, Canoga Park, CA 91309, (818) 340-8635

A self-help and assistance program for pet owners.

Pet Orphans Fund

7720 Gloria Avenue, Van Nuys, CA 91406, (818) 901-0190

No-kill adoption shelter for approximately 50 dogs and 40 cats in a clean, cheerful facility. Some dogs are rescued from city shelters. Cat "condo" includes screened porches. Carefully screens potential adopters. "Walk-in" program allows those who must give up their dogs to come to the shelter on weekends and offer them for adoption. Foster care volunteers welcome.

Pet Pride

Pacific Palisades, CA

See "National & International Organizations."

Pets & Pals

3739 Balboa St., #206, San Francisco, CA 94121, (415) 221-5733

Works to alleviate the needless suffering of animals in the San Francisco Bay area. The Stop Cat Overpopulation Project (SCOP) focuses on eradicating feral cat overpopulation through humane methods.

Pets In Need, Inc. (PIN)

873-5th Avenue, Redwood City, CA 94063, (415) 367-1405, FAX: (415) 367-1314

San Francisco Bay area. No-kill animal adoption agency and lost/found service for dogs and cats.

Pets Lifeline Animal Shelter

P.O. Box 341, Sonoma, CA 95476, (707) 996-4577

No-kill adoption shelter.

Pets Unlimited
2343 Fillmore Street, San Francisco, CA 94115
A nonprofit veterinary hospital and shelter.

Preservation of Amazon River Dolphins
Rosemead, CA
See "National & International Organizations."

Project Wildlife—A Second Chance
P.O. Box 80696, San Diego, CA 92138-0696, (619) 225-WILD or 692-WILD
Rescues, rehabilitates, and releases San Diego County's native animals, including land and sea birds, and land mammals. Utilizes many volunteers in many capacities—*you* can make a difference by joining!

Purple Cow & Friends
366 N. La Jolla, Los Angeles, CA 90048, (619) 749-4790
Dedicated to saving all living beings from slaughter. Main focus is farm animals, but has rescued dogs, cats, rabbits, rats, fish, and gophers. No-kill adoption shelter (currently full), foster homes, and adoptions.

Redwings Horse Sanctuary
P.O. Box 222705, Carmel, CA 93922, (408) 624-8464, FAX: (408) 622-9451
Educates about the plight of horses, ponies, and donkeys, and protects them from abuse and slaughter.

Respect Our Animals' Rights (ROAR)
915 L Street, Suite 1000, Sacramento, CA 95814, (916) 442-8888
A nonpartisan Political Action Committee (PAC) that supports state legislators who sponsor or support animal legislation in California.

The Roar Foundation—Shambala Preserve
Acton, CA
See "National & International Organizations."

Sacramento Telephone Tree for Animal Rights (STTAR)
P.O. Box 255427-56, Sacramento, CA 95865, (916) 488-4984 (Lavonne Bishop) or (916) 443-4203 (Doris Spiegel), Co-Coordinators
Animal rights information and activity network for the greater Sacramento area.

Sacramento Wildlife Care Association
P.O. Box 60982, Sacramento, CA 95860, (916) 383-7922
Provides emergency and continued care to birds and mammals.

San Diego Bat Conservation
746 Ash Avenue, Chula Vista, CA 91910, San Diego: (619) 426-8987, Mountains: (619) 765-2618

San Diego Humane Society & SPCA
887 Sherman Street, San Diego, CA 92110-4088, (619) 299-7012

San Francisco Bay Institute
San Francisco, CA
See "National & International Organizations."

San Francisco Society for the Prevention of Cruelty to Animals (SPCA)
2500 16th Street, San Francisco, CA 94103-6589, (415) 554-3000, FAX: (415) 552-7041
No-kill shelter. Believes that animals, as living creatures, have value beyond economic measurement, and are entitled to legal, moral, and ethical consideration and protection.

Santa Cruz Society for the Prevention of Cruelty to Animals (SPCA)
2200 7th Avenue, Santa Cruz, CA 95062, (408) 475-6454 (ext. 23)
Shelter serves local area. Involved in local, state, and national issues. Spearheaded a precedent-setting countywide ban on the steel-jaw leghold trap. Very active in supporting humane legislation.

Save a Pet, Inc.
P.O. Box 602, Desert Hot Springs, CA 92240, (619) 329-9847
No-kill adoption shelter.

Save the Whales
Venice, CA
See "National & International Organizations."

Sea Shepherd Conservation Society
Marina Del Ray, CA
See "National & International Organizations."

Society Against Vivisection
P.O. Box 10206, Costa Mesa, CA 92627, (714) 540-0583
Provides rescue and spay/neuter assistance, as well as working to abolish vivisection.

Society for the Preservation of Birds of Prey
P.O. Box 66070, Los Angeles, CA 90066, (310) 636-1662

Society of Kind Understanding for Not Killing Skunks (SKUNKS)
"P.U." Box 82, Topanga, CA 90290, (310) 724-9643
Rescue, release, and research on behalf of skunks. Has developed a network of national alliances fighting for the rights of skunks.

Solano County Friends of Animals
P.O. Box 4081, Vallejo, CA 94590, (707) 552-3323
Adoptions, spay/neuter, and a limited number of foster homes for dogs and cats.

Sonoma People for Animal Rights (S.P.A.R.)
701A Fourth Street, #205, Santa Rosa, CA 95404, (707) 576-1415
A group of citizens who are concerned about the widespread abuse and unnecessary suffering of animals—wild, domesticated, and factory-raised.

Streetcat Rescue Team
136 Marsilly Street, San Francisco, CA 94112, (415) 239-8365

SUPRESS, Inc. / The Nature of Wellness
Pasadena, CA
See "National & International Organizations."

Town and Country Humane Association / SPCA
P.O. Box 1238, Orland, CA 95963, (916) 865-3661
No-kill shelter, spay/neuter services, and cruelty investigations.

United Activists for Animal Rights (Coalition to Protect Animals in Entertainment)
P.O. Box 2448, Riverside, CA 92516, (909) 682-7872

United Animal Nations USA
Sacramento, CA
See "National & International Organizations."

University Students Against Vivisection
Fullerton, CA
See "National & International Organizations."

Valley Animal Rights Alliance
P.O. Box 2314, Lodi, CA 95241-2314

Web of Life / Vegan Resources
P.O. Box 2124, Orange, CA 92669, (714) 639-3791

"We Care" Animal Society, Inc.
P.O. Box 70, St. Helena, CA 94574, (707) 944-0926
No-kill adoption shelter (kenneling) and spay/neuter for dogs and cats.

Western Humane and Environmental Educators' Association
c/o Marin Humane Society, 171 Bell Marin Keys Blvd., Novato, CA 94949, (415) 883-3522

Westside Animal Action Network
1801 Lincoln Blvd., #201, Venice, CA 90291

Whale Rescue Team
115 So. Topanga Canyon Blvd., Suite 129, Topanga Canyon, CA 90290, (310) 455 2579

Wild Bird Care and Rehabilitation Fund
P.O. Box 1336, Studio City, CA 91614, (818) 789-8460

Wild Horse and Burro Sanctuary
Shingletown, CA
See "National & International Organizations."

Wild Horse Discovery Center
295 Del Monte Center, Box 135, Monterey, CA 93940, (408) 625-0166

Wildlife Rehabilitation Center
18740 Highland Road, Ramona, CA 92065, (619) 789-2324
A sanctuary for ill, injured, or orphaned native California wild mammals and birds. The West's largest rehabilitation aviary. Available for incoming wildlife 7 days/week, 24-hours/day. Operated by The Fund for Animals, Inc. (see "National & International Organizations").

Wildlife Waystation
Angeles National Forest, S.F., CA
See "National & International Organizations."

Wolf Lifeline, Inc.
1150 Coddingtown Center, #13, Santa Rosa, CA 95401

Wolf Mountain Sanctuary
Box 385, Lucerne, CA 92356
A sanctuary for rescued wolves. Animal rights orientation.

World Pets Society
Tarzana, CA
See "National & International Organizations."

COLORADO

For additional resources for breed rescue, ferret rescue, wildlife rehabilitation, etc., see "Keeping Up-To-Date" at the front of the chapter.

American Humane Association
Englewood, CO
See "National & International Organizations."

Animal Orphanage (AO)
539 East Mississippi, Denver, CO 80210-1608, (303) 871-8331
Provides rescue, rehabilitation, foster homes, and adoptions for companion animals. Has placed over 600 cats and nearly 400 dogs in qualified homes in the last decade. Help with behavior problems, speakers bureau, referrals for low-cost spay/neuter, and other services.

Animal Protection Educators
Englewood, CO
See "National & International Organizations."

Animal Rescue and Adoption Society
ATTN: Karen Ginaegy, 2390 South Delaware, Denver, CO 80223, (303) 744-6076
No-kill adoption shelter for cats.

Animal Rights Mobilization
Denver, CO
See "National & International Organizations."

Aspen Society for Animal Rights
P.O. Box 2766, Aspen, CO 81612, (303) 925-2547
Local, with national and international support. Concerned with all areas of animal rights, particularly fur and trapping issues. Best known for their widely-publicized efforts to ban the sale of furs in Aspen.

Biodiversity Legal Foundation
Boulder, CO
See "National & International Organizations."

Birds of Prey Rehabilitation Foundation
2290 South 104th Street, Broomfield, CO 80020, (303) 460-0674

Cat Care Society (CCS)
5985 West 11th Avenue, Lakewood, CO 80214-2105, (303) 239-9680
Denver Metropolitan area. A cageless, no-kill shelter and adoption facility for cats. Humane education, animal assisted visitations, spay/neuter assistance, and behavior counseling.

Colorado Horse Rescue
P.O. Box 1510, Arvada, CO 80001, (303) 439-9217, FAX: (303) 439-9259
Statewide. This group does not define itself as an animal "rights" organization. Finds new homes and lives for horses who are no longer needed by their owners, are abandoned, abused and/or neglected, or are in danger of being prematurely sent to slaughter.

Every Creature Counts (ECC)
P.O. Box 1683, Lyons, CO 80540, (303) 823-5941
Works to eliminate feral, stray, abandoned, and unwanted cat and dog populations through spay/neuter, adoptions, and education. Feral cat program. Foster care. Also provides services to those in homeless shelters and in low-income areas, providing transportation to vet clinics. Many volunteers and members are animal rights advocates.

Greyhounds As Pets (GAP)
P.O. Box 6999, Colorado Springs, CO 80934, (719) 633-0171 or (313) 772-1536, Adoptions: 1-800-RITE-PET
Finds good homes for retired racing greyhounds and younger greyhounds who have not had successful racing careers. Representatives serve CO, KS, OK, UT, Southern WY, Northern NM, NV, and MT. Volunteers, ideas, and donations welcome.

Maxfund Animal Adoption Center
P.O. Box 1025 Galapago, Denver, CO 80433, (303) 595-4917, FAX: (303) 595-0665
Aids injured dogs and cats.

Mission Wolf
Silver Cliff, CO
See "National & International Organizations."

National Gneiser Wildlife Rehabilitation Center
2323 55th Street, Boulder, CO 80301, (303) 442-4030
Works with all wildlife, except for raptors and endangered species. Experience includes relocating prairie dogs, raising small mammals such as raccoons and foxes, and some work with bobcats and mountain lions.

Planned Pethood Plus
4170 Tennyson Street, Denver, CO 80212
Operates a full-service spay/neuter facility, with special attention to providing services to low-income and elderly individuals. Also has a large mobile unit (a school bus) that travels throughout Colorado.

Prairie Dog Rescue, Inc. (PDR)
P.O. Box 11164, Englewood, CO 80151, (303) 575-1287
Relocates prairie dogs who have fallen victim to land development and construction in the Denver-Metro area. Rescues endangered prairie dogs and places them in safe areas. Prairie dog information and merchandise.

Rocky Mountain Animal Defense
2525 Arapaho, #E4335, Boulder, CO 80302, (303) 543-0755
An animal rights group.

Sinapu
P.O. Box 3243, Boulder, CO 80307, (303) 447-8655
Named after the Ute word for wolves. Dedicated to restoring a healthy, flourishing population of gray wolves to Colorado.

Urban Wildlife Rescue, Inc.
P.O. Box 201311, Denver, CO 80220, (303) 340-4911
Rescues and rehabilitates bats and small fur-bearing wildlife. Helps with problem-solving.

Western Colorado Wildlife Rehabilitation Center
5945 RD 346, Silt, CO 81652, (303) 876-5489
Cares for all injured and orphaned wildlife, including endangered species. Experience with black bears.

Wilderness Ranch Sanctuary for Farm Animals
P.O. Box 1507, Loveland, CO 80539-1507, (970) 493-7153
A community of people dedicated to teaching respect for all life. Rescues, rehabilitates, and provides permanent sanctuary for abused farm animals. Visitors are welcome, but please call first. Future plans include development of an educational "dude ranch" style vegetarian resort where people can come to learn to live a cruelty-free lifestyle.

CONNECTICUT

For additional resources for breed rescue, ferret rescue, wildlife rehabilitation, etc., see "Keeping Up-To-Date" at the front of the chapter.

Aid to Helpless Animals, Inc. (AHA)
P.O. Box 434, Bloomfield, CT 06002, (203) 232-8317
Statewide. Primarily an animal rescue and placement organization for stray or abandoned cats and dogs. Shelters animals at veterinary clinics. Occasionally becomes involved with animal rights issues.

Animal Friends Of Connecticut, Inc. (AFOC)
Box 307-306, West Hartford, CT 06117, (203) 232-1393
Statewide. No-kill shelter that rescues stray and abused dogs and cats.

Animal Rights Network
Monroe, CT
See "National & International Organizations."

Animal Welfare Associates, Inc.
Stamford, CT
See "National & International Organizations."

A.W.A.R.E. (Animal Welfare And Rights Entity)
P.O. Box 598, Tolland, CT 06084, (203) 871-2315 or (203) 763-0605
Promotes all animal rights issues, including vegetarianism.

Cetacean Society International
Georgetown, CT
See "National & International Organizations."

Connecticut Animal Rights Lobby (C.A.R.L.)
c/o Mumper, 515 Simsbury Road, Bloomfield, CT 06002, (203) 243-2886
Statewide. Works to persuade CT legislators to create new legislation pertaining to animal cruelty, animal welfare, and animal protection.

Focus on Animals
Trumbull, CT
See "National & International Organizations."

Friends of Animals (FoA)
Darien, CT
See "National & International Organizations."

The Fund for Animals, Inc.
Field Office: Julie Lewin (Connecticut Coordinator), 16 Vera Street, West Hartford, CT 06119-1950, (203) 521-7290
See "National & International Organizations."

The Fund for Animals Wildlife Hotline
(203) 393-1050 (Laura Simon, Wildlife Consultant)
Helps solve wildlife problems for residents of Connecticut.

Humane Organization Representing Suffering Equines (H.O.R.S.E.) of Connecticut
311 Bee Brook Rd., Rte. 47, New Preston, CT 06777, (203) 868-1960
Statewide. Dedicated to taking in and caring for neglected, abused, and unwanted horses and ponies. Affiliated with H.O.R.S.E. of MI.

Humane Society of the United States
New England Regional Office:
- Street Address: Norma Terris Center, 67A Salem Road
- Mailing Address: P.O. Box 362, East Haddam, CT 06423, (203) 434-1940, FAX: (203) 434-1790

Serves CT, MA, ME, NH, RI, and VT. See "National & International Organizations."

The Jane Goodall Institute
Ridgefield, CT
See "National & International Organizations."

The Last Post
95 Belden St., Rte. 126, Falls Village, CT 06031, (203) 824-5469 or 824-0831
A 35-acre sanctuary built especially for cats, but home to a variety of domesticated animals. A safe, home-like surrounding for animals whose guardians have died or entered nursing homes.

Meow, Inc. (Make Each Orphan Wanted)
P.O. Box 999, Litchfield, CT 06759-0999, (860) 567-3277
No-kill adoption shelter for approximately 30 cats/kittens. Works to improve the quality of life of abandoned cats and to educate caretakers. Spay/neuter help, animal behavior consulting, humane education, etc.

National Association for Humane and Environmental Education (NAHEE)
647 Salem Road, East Haddam, CT 06423-0362, (203) 434-8666
The educational arm of The Humane Society of the United States (see "National & International Organizations"). For details, see the Humane Education section of Chapter 12.

Non-Hunters Rights Alliance
P.O. Box 101, Wilton, CT 06897, (203) 762-2563

North American Wildlife Association
East Lyme, CT
See "National & International Organizations."

Northeastern Connecticut Animal Rescue, Inc. (NECTAR)
P.O. Box 362, Storrs, CT 06268-0362, (203) 423-0849 or 423-7195 (Linda Wenner, President)
Places pets (especially from pounds) and provides spay/neuter assistance for low-income caretakers.

Quinebaug Valley Animal Welfare Service, Inc. (QVAWS)
P.O. Box 791, Dayville, CT 06241, (203) 974-2541

Rescues abandoned animals, mainly dogs and cats, and places them in good homes. No shelter. Promotes a responsible attitude among pet owners and the general public.

REGAP (Retired Greyhounds As Pets) of CT, Inc.

P.O. Box 76, Bethany, CT 06525, (203) 393-1673
Greyhound rescue and placement.

Save Our Strays, Inc. (SOS)

1677 Post Rd. East, Westport, CT 06880, (203) 255-0514
Statewide. Rescue and adoption of abandoned dogs and cats. Public education.

Wildlife In Crisis

P.O. Box 101, Wilton, CT 06897, (203) 762-2563

DELAWARE

For additional resources for breed rescue, ferret rescue, wildlife rehabilitation, etc., see "Keeping Up-To-Date" at the front of the chapter.

Delaware Action for Animals, Inc. (DAA)

P.O. Box 5885, Newark, DE 19714-5885, (302) 234-1019
Statewide. Multi-issue, including the poultry industry, vivisection, wildlife, fur, rodeos, and companion animal overpopulation.

Delaware Humane Association

701 A Street, Wilmington, DE 19801, (302) 571-0111
No-kill shelter for cats and dogs.

DreamCatcher Ferrets

Steve Krouse and Cindy Sooy, P.O. Box 6201, Wilmington, DE 19804, (302) 633-1090, E-mail: DCFerret@ix.netcom.com
A shelter, rescue, and adoption facility for ferrets. *Note*: Also breeds ferrets.

Humane Society of the United States

See New Jersey for the regional HSUS office that serves this state.

Spay Neuter All Pets, Inc. (SNAP)

See Maryland for a description of this group.

DISTRICT OF COLUMBIA

See Washington, D.C.

FLORIDA

For additional resources for breed rescue, ferret rescue, wildlife rehabilitation, etc., see "Keeping Up-To-Date" at the front of the chapter.

Adopt-A-Pet, Inc.

11900 SW 232nd Street, Miami, FL 33170, (305) 257-2275, FAX: (305) 257-3604
No-kill adoption shelter for cats and dogs. Spay/neuter services.

Animal Activists of Central Florida (AACF)

P.O. Box 26, Winter Park, FL 32790, (407) 657-6222
Dedicated to educating residents about the scope of animal use and abuse in our society.

Animal Defense Coalition of the Treasure Coast

1002 Proctor Lane, Pt. St. Lucie, FL 34983, (407) 879-0991

Animal Protection League (APL) of Hillsborough County, Inc.

P.O. Box 7398, Tampa, FL 33673, (813) 960-4745
Tampa Bay area. A humane society that protects animals and works to make their community a kinder place for people and animals.

Animal Refuge Center, Inc. (ARC)

P.O. Box 6442, Ft. Myers, FL 33911, (941) 731-3535
No-kill shelter for dogs, cats, and the occasional hamster, gerbil, rabbit, etc. Trap/neuter/release program for feral cats, and placement of kittens and cats that are not really feral but are "dump offs."

Animal Rights Foundation of Florida (ARFF)

P.O. Box 841154, Pembroke Pines, FL 33084, (305) 968-7622, FAX: (305) 891-9009
Statewide. Seeks to stop animal abuse and exploitation.

The Animal Shelter and Wildlife Society
5859 County Road 545, P.O. Box 770707, Winter Garden, FL 34777-0707, (407) 877-PETS, FAX: (407) 877-3292
A 60-acre, no-kill adoption facility. Welcomes volunteers to visit the pet residents, assist in the thrift shop, assist in the traveling Petmobile, help sponsor an animal, etc. Also offers boarding and "hog haven," where people can build a pen for their pet pig.

Animal Voice
P.O. Box 3831, Vero Beach, FL 32964

Bradford Friends of Strays
P.O. Box 851, Starke, FL 32091, (904) 964-1457
Conducts humane work and pet theft investigations. Works closely with Last Chance for Animals (see "National & International Organizations").

Brevard Pet Adoption Center (Humane Society of South Brevard)
P.O. Box 2600 Otter Creek Lane, Melbourne, FL 32940-7424, (407) 254-8843
No-kill adoption shelter. Spay/neuter services.

CCAW, Inc. (Committee for Clean Air & Water)
321 East Tarpon Avenue, Tarpon Springs, FL 34689, (813) 938-5303
Statewide. Interests include the environment, marine mammals, and species indigenous to the State of Florida, mainly—but not limited to—the Atlantic bottlenose dolphin.

Center for Marine Conservation (CMC)
Regional Office: St. Petersburg, FL
See "National & International Organizations."

Central Florida Ferret Friends
c/o Debbie Coburn, 1947 Bonneville Drive, Orlando, FL 32826, (407) 380-8712

Citizens Against Pet Overpopulation
1300 NW 31st Avenue, Ft. Lauderdale, FL 33311

CROW, Inc. (Care & Rehabilitation Of Wildlife, Inc.)
P.O. Box 150, Sanibel Island, FL 33957, (813) 472-3644
Provides care for birds, reptiles, mammals, and, recently, dolphins.

The Dolphin Alliance
P.O. Box 510273, Melbourne Beach, FL 32951, (407) 951-1301, FAX: (407) 724-5121
Works to return captive dolphins to their home waters. Successfully campaigned for the release of the first two amusement dolphins ever wrestled away from the captive display industry in America (Bogie and Bacall), and is monitoring their readaptation and release.

Dolphin Freedom Foundation
824 SW 13th Street, Ft. Lauderdale, FL 33315, (305) 462-1817
Works to free captive marine mammals in the "casual entertainment" industry.

Equestrian Training Center—Horse Rescue
P.O. Box 770332, Ocala, FL 34477, (352) 591-1066, Contacts: Mike or Sue Heck
"No horse is ever turned away." Takes in any horse in any condition. Specializes in rehabilitation and retraining, especially of thoroughbred race horses.

The Extended Circle—Animal Protection Alliance, Inc. (TEC-APA, Inc.)
P.O. Box 37279, Tallahassee, FL 32315, (904) 561-4450
Educates the public on animal protection and related issues, raises awareness about steps the public can take to eliminate sources of animal suffering in their daily lives, and assists individuals in defining and pursuing a personal course of activism.

Feed the Pelicans Fund
P.O. Box 65, St. Petersburg, FL 33731-0605

Florida Keys Wild Bird Center
93600 Overseas Highway, Tavernier, FL 33070, (305) 852-4486

Florida Voices for Animals
P.O. Box 17523, Tampa, FL 33682, (813) 977-2585
Primarily Hillsborough and Pinellas Counties. Also works with other Florida organizations. Principal focus is on educating the public about animal rights issues.

Fort Myers Greyhound Adoption Center
c/o Donna Forster, 11511 Deal Road N., Ft. Myers, FL 33905, (813) 731-3187
Greyhound placement.

Foundation For Environmental Awareness (FFEA)
P.O. Box 723, Oklawaha, FL 32179, (904) 288-6754, FAX: (904) 288-2800
Wildlife rescue and protection, pet protection, and community education.

Friends of Animals
Field Office: 724 Northeast, 130th Floor, N. Miami, FL 33161, (305) 891-3613
See "National & International Organizations."

Friends of the Silver River Monkeys
c/o Foundation For Environmental Awareness, P.O. Box 723, Oklawaha, FL 32179, (904) 288-6754, FAX: (904) 288-2800
Working to protect the rhesus monkeys that have peacefully resided on the banks of the Silver River for over 50 years.

The Fund for Animals, Inc.
Field Office: Donna Gregory (Florida Coordinator), 4265 US Highway 948 North
Lakeland, FL 33809, (904) 984-1157
See "National & International Organizations."

Goose Creek Wildlife Sanctuary, Inc.
3337 Homestead Road, Tallahassee, FL 3238, (904) 878-8288
Rehabilitation of all species.

Greyhound Rescue, Inc.
c/o Susan Greenwald, 1833 Rockledge Drive, Rockledge, FL 32955-4909
Greyhound rescue and placement.

Greyhound Rescue League
c/o Paula Johnson, 106 Cayman Lane, Summerland Keys, FL 33042, (305) 872-2749
Greyhound rescue and placement.

Helping Homeless Cats, Inc.
Vaughn Building, MM92, P.O. Box 81, Tavernier, FL 33070, (305) 852-3739
Works to resolve the large feral cat population in the upper Florida Keys with compassion for the animals and respect for the needs of the community. Operates a low-cost spay/neuter facility. Also finds homes for cats and helps sick/injured homeless cats.

Horse Protection Association of FL, Inc.
4510 SW 62nd Avenue, Miami, FL 33155, (305) 880-8268 or 667-3242

Humane Society of the United States
Southeast Regional Office: 1624 Metropolitan Circle, Suite B, Tallahassee, FL 32308, (904) 386-3435, FAX: (904) 386-4534
Serves FL, AL, GA, SC, and MS. See "National & International Organizations."

Into the Blue
3308-29th Avenue, Lighthouse Point, FL 33064
Rehabilitates dolphins and releases them back into the wild.

Intra-movement Coalition for Animal Rights and the Environment
Nokomis, FL
See "National & International Organizations."

K&C (Kindness and Care) Pet Rescue and Adoption Society, Inc.
9160 Commonwealth Avenue, Jacksonville, FL 32220, (904) 781-0936
Dedicated to assisting abused and injured animals, and to speaking for the humane treatment of all animals. Operates a no-kill shelter with limited capacity.

Leesburg Humane Society Inc.
P.O. Box 895334, Leesburg, FL 34789-5334, (904) 669-3312
No-kill adoption shelter that currently cares for over 70 dogs, 85 cats, and assorted other animals. Operates solely on private donations. Spay/neuter assistance. Strict guidelines for adoptive homes.

Lodestar Shelter, Inc.
P.O. Box 2203, Auburndale, FL 33823, (813) 537-5262
No-kill adoption shelter that offers spay/neuter services. Also shelters some horses and "livestock."

National Animal Rights, Inc.
Tampa and Brandon, FL
See "National & International Organizations."

Ocean Impact Foundation (OIF) Marine-Wildlife Care Center
7100 Belvedere Road, West Palm Beach, FL 33411, (407) 471-3403

Operates a wildlife hospital for Palm Beach County. Networks nationally and operates a 24-hour hotline.

Pelican Man's Bird Sanctuary
1708 Ken Thompson Parkway, Sarasota, FL 34236-1000, (941) 388-4444
Rescues and rehabilitates up to 7,000 birds annually—most victims of fishing lines, fish hooks, pollutants, pesticides, and fast boats. Home to more than 200 birds with injuries preventing their return to the wild. Visitors are welcome to view and photograph over 30 species of birds daily.

Planned Pethood of America
13749 NW 7th Avenue, North Miami, FL 33168, (305) 687-SPAY (7729)
Operates a spay/neuter clinic that as of August 1995 had performed 21,376 spays for caretakers from Ft. Lauderdale to Kendall. As of this writing, prices are $20 (male cat), $25 (female cat), $30 (male dog), $40 (female dog), and include "4 in 1" shot.

Retired Greyhounds As Pets
St. Petersburg, FL
See "National & International Organizations."

Retirement Home for Horses, Inc.
Mill Creek Farm, P.O. Box 2100, Alachua, FL 32615-2100, (904) 462-1001
A safe and tranquil equine haven at a wildlife sanctuary. Adopt-A-Horse and other programs. Open to the public every Saturday 11 a.m.-3 p.m.

Sarasota In Defense of Animals (SDA)
P.O. Box 12100, Sarasota, FL 34278, (813) 925-8388
An activist group that emphasizes education. Many members are high school students.

Save Animals From Exploitation, Inc.
P.O. Box 14158, Jacksonville, FL 32238-1158, (904) 781-3304

Save Our Sealife Committee
P.O. Box 4991, Orlando, FL 32802-4991, (407) 649-9850, FAX: (407) 649-9851
Working to add to the state constitution restrictions against the use of entanglement gill nets, etc. in order to stop the resulting destruction of dolphins, turtles, and other marine mammals.

Save the Manatee Club
Maitland, FL
See "National & International Organizations."

Sea Turtle Survival League
Gainesville, FL
See "National & International Organizations."

Second Chance for Greyhounds
c/o Helen Banks, 10826 Dean Street, Bonita Springs, FL 33923, (813) 947-2365
Greyhound rescue and placement.

South Florida Animal Activists (SFAA)
P.O. Box 637, Ft. Lauderdale, FL 33302, (305) 537-3132
A nonviolent, grassroots organization that has been working for animals for the past 10 years.

South Lake Animal League, Inc.
P.O. Box 121504, Clermont, FL 34712-1504, (904) 394-1818
Provides foster homes and spay/neuter services.

Southwest Florida Wildlife Ark
Rt. 15, Box 785-19, N. Ft. Myers, FL 33917, (813) 543-4440
Rehabilitates small mammals, especially raccoons.

Students for the Ethical Treatment of Animals—University of Florida
Box 45 JWRU, University of Florida, Gainesville, FL 32611
A student animal rights organization that is actively involved in coalition-building.

Suncoast Seabird Sanctuary, Inc.
18328 Gulf Blvd., Indian Shores, FL 34635-2097, (813) 391-6211
Provides medical treatment and rehabilitation of wild birds, especially sea birds (pelicans are a specialty).

Tampa Greyhound Adoption Center
c/o Kimberly and Adam Wyler, 5692 E. Chelsea Street, Tampa, FL 33610, (813) 626-1116
Greyhound rescue and placement.

Voices for Animals of Central Florida
P.O. Box 26, Winter Park, FL 32790, (407) 657-6222
Works to educate Central Florida residents (Orlando and surrounding area) about institutional and individual abuses of animals in our society, and to promote lifestyle changes that eliminate such exploitation.

GEORGIA

For additional resources for breed rescue, ferret rescue, wildlife rehabilitation, etc., see "Keeping Up-To-Date" at the front of the chapter.

All Creatures Are Truly Special, Inc. (All CATS, Inc.)
9880 Robinwood Lane, Roswell, GA 30075-4128, (404) 998-9442
No-kill facility for dogs, cats, and some farm animals and wildlife.

Amberwood Sanctuary
Leary, GA
See "National & International Organizations."

Friends of Animals
Field Office: P.O. Box 2929, Atlanta, GA 30359, (404) 662-6006
See "National & International Organizations."

Georgia Earth Alliance (GEA)
P.O. Box 1231, Fayetteville, GA 30214, (404) 416-4500
Dedicated to the protection of all animals as well as the environment we all share.

Good Mews Animal Foundation, Inc.
788 Sandtown Road, Marietta, GA 30060, (404) 499-CATS (2287)
No-kill adoption shelter for cats.

Home for Unwanted and Abandoned Guinea Pigs
Lawrenceville, GA
See "National & International Organizations."

Humane Services, Inc.
1550 Hardeman Avenue, Macon, GA 31201, (912) 745-2273
Works to create a better environment for all creatures through low-cost spay/neuter, public education, legislation, and other programs.

Humane Services of Metro Atlanta, Inc. (HSMA)
4051 Highway 78, Suite C-102-258, Lilburn, GA 30247, (404) 662-4479
Main focus is low-cost spay/neuter program and humane education programs.

Humane Society of the United States
See Florida for the regional HSUS office that serves this state.

Interfaith Council for the Protection of Animals and Nature
Atlanta, GA
See "National & International Organizations."

League for Environmental and Animal Protection
P.O. Box 52105, Atlanta, GA 30355

National Greyhound Adoption Network
Regional Coordinators: Diane and Ken Linthacum, Rte. 2, Box 185-C Thomasville, GA 31792, (912) 226-7632

Paulding Volunteer Animal Rescue
4471 Fairfax Place, Powder Springs, GA 30073, (404) 445-7294
No-kill adoption shelter. Spay/neuter info.

Save-A-Life, Inc.
4 Raintree Lane, Savannah, GA 31411-2605, (912) 598-SPAY
A cageless population control, adoption, and treatment agency that helps abused and neglected animals. Also helps low-income caretakers with emergencies. Public education.

HAWAII

For additional resources for breed rescue, ferret rescue, wildlife rehabilitation, etc., see "Keeping Up-To-Date" at the front of the chapter.

Animal Rights Hawaii
P.O. Box 61386, Honolulu, HI 96839-1386

Earthtrust
Kailua, HI
See "National & International Organizations."

East Maui Animal Refuge (EMAR)

25 Malu 'Aina Place, Haiku, HI 96708, (808) 572-8308

A rehabilitation orphanage for domesticated animals, wildlife, and endangered species. Shelter provides care for as many as 400 sick, abused, and abandoned animals that in most cases would have no other chance for survival.

Good Shepherd Foundation

P.O. Box 1880, Pahoa, HI 96778

Dedicated to the elimination of animal suffering since 1949. See also California for a second chapter.

Hawaiian Humane Society

2700 Waialae Avenue, Honolulu, HI 06826, (808) 955-5122, FAX: (808) 955-6034

Provides a variety of services, including 24-hour emergency services for injured animals, adoptions, humane education, low-cost spay/neuter, a pet bereavement support group, animal assisted therapy, assistance to ill and elderly people having trouble caring for their companion animals, and support to animals coming through the Honolulu airport.

The Sylvester Foundation, Concern for Animals

Mailing Address: 305 Hahani Street, #160, Kailua, HI 96734

No-kill sanctuary helping to save the homeless animals of Hawaii.

IDAHO

For additional resources for breed rescue, ferret rescue, wildlife rehabilitation, etc., see "Keeping Up-To-Date" at the front of the chapter.

Animal Ark

Kooskia, ID 83539

Animals in Distress Association

P.O. Box 3375, Boise, ID 83703-0375, (208) 338-7918

Humane Society of the United States

See Montana for the regional HSUS office that serves this state.

Palouse Voice for Animals, Inc.

P.O. Box 9992, Moscow, ID 83843, (208) 883-4565

Primarily concerned with regional issues of animal care, use, and exploitation, including animal research at the University of Washington State and Idaho, animal-based agriculture, hunting and trapping, and lifestyle choices.

Spokane People for the Ethical Treatment of Animals (SPETA)

P.O. Box 4262, Spokane, WA 99202, (509) 459-8502

Serves Eastern Washington and Northern Idaho. See Washington for a description of this group.

ILLINOIS

For additional resources for breed rescue, ferret rescue, wildlife rehabilitation, etc., see "Keeping Up-To-Date" at the front of the chapter.

A Cause for Paws

Box 64, RR1, Matamora, IL 61548

Action Volunteers for Animals (AVA)

1446 West Argyle, Chicago, IL 60640, (312) 728-7913

Encourages people to actively and visibly get involved in helping animals. Primary goal is public education. Encourages protest letters to legislators and manufacturers.

Advocates for Wild Sanctuary

P.O. Box 573, Woodstock, IL 60098

Animal Legal Defense Fund

Regional Contact: 154 West Hubbard, Suite 300, Chicago, IL 60610

See "National & International Organizations."

Animal Protective Association (APA)

P.O. Box 18098, Chicago, IL 60618, (312) 463-6667

Dedicated to rescuing and placing injured and abandoned cats. Operates a cageless, no-kill shelter for stray cats.

Animal Rights Mobilization (ARM!)

Regional Office: P.O. Box 805859, Chicago, IL 60680, (312) 993-1181

See "National & International Organizations."

Assisi Animal Foundation

P.O. Box 143, Crystal Lake, IL 60039-0143, (815) 455-9411, FAX: (815) 455-9417

Statewide, with representation in 33 states. Shelters dogs and cats in a cageless, no-kill facility until appropriate adoption is made. Also conducts educational outreach, a "Pets for Patients" visiting program, and safari programs traveling to East Africa.

Association for the Protection of Animals (APA)

P.O. Box 1311, Granite City, IL 62040, (618) 931-7030

"We cater to each animal's individual needs and ailments with plenty of TLC." No-kill adoption shelter for cats and dogs. Investigates abuse with licensed animal cruelty officers.

Central Illinois Friends of Ferrets (CIFF)

c/o Kathy Fritz, P.O. Box 3226, Champaign, IL 61826, (217) 356-6063

Rescue, sheltering, and merchandise.

Chicago Animal Rights Coalition (CHARC)

P.O. Box 66, Yorkville, IL 60560, (708) 552-7872, FAX: (708) 552-8559

"An animal abuser's worst nightmare." Fights very aggressively against animal abuse with "in your face" activism. Is successfully innovating the creative widespread use of covert and long-distance video techniques to "bust" animal abusers, as well as "fly overs" in custom flying machines to observe and disrupt hunt activities. Currently seeking funding for these campaigns. Contact them to get on their mailing list.

Citadel Wildlife Orphan Home

1750 Citadel Drive, Naperville, IL 60565-1725

Cares for a variety of birds and mammals.

Citizens for Animal Rights

P.O. Box 5131, Peoria, IL 61601, (309) 446-9772

Educates the public about animal rights issues.

Concerned Citizens for Ethical Research (CCER)

P.O. Box 1334, Evanston, IL 60204-1334, (312) 792-7117

A strictly single-issue group that opposes two specific experiments currently being conducted at Northwestern University. No philosophical statement regarding animal rights.

Elsa Wild Animal Appeal

Elmhurst, IL

See "National & International Organizations."

Felines, Inc.

P.O. Box 60616, Chicago, IL 60626, (312) 465-4132, FAX: (312) 465-6454

No-kill adoption shelter for cats. Low-cost spay/neuter assistance.

Ferret Adoption, Information, and Rescue Society (FAIR)

c/o Mary Van Dahm, 237 S. Lincoln, Westmont, IL 60559, (708) 968-3189

Food Animal Concerns Trust, Inc.

Chicago, IL

See "National & International Organizations."

Greyhound Rescue and Adoption

c/o Beverly Thompson, 116 Mary Street, Washington, IL 61571, (309) 745-5377

Greyhound rescue and placement.

Highland Animal Shelter

Box 307, 1115 Broadway, Highland, IL 62249, (618) 654-6067

No-kill adoption shelter.

Hooved Animal Humane Society (HAHS)

National Headquarters: 10804 McConnell Road, P.O. Box 400, Woodstock, IL 60098, (815) 337-5563; FAX: (815) 337-5569

Animal welfare organization of knowledgeable horse people striving for proper care of animals, whether used for show, work, agriculture, or pleasure.

Humane Political Action Committee (HPAC)

3021 North Clark Street, Chicago, IL 60657, (312) 854-6095 or (708) 258-6077 (voice/FAX)

Works to influence legislation favorable to animals. Teaches political activism to any interested group, anywhere in the country.

Humane Society of Rock Island County
724 West 2nd Avenue, Milan, IL 61264, (309) 787-6830
No-kill adoption shelter for cats, dogs, and other small animals. Low-income spay/neuter and veterinary services.

Humane Society of the United States
North Central Regional Office: 2015 175th Street, Lansing, IL 60438, (708) 474-0906, FAX: (708) 474-9449
Serves ND, SD, IL, MN, and WI. See "National & International Organizations."

Illinois Animal Action, Inc. (IAA)
P.O. Box 507, Warrenville, IL 60555, (708) 393-2935, FAX: (708) 393-2941, E-mail: DLEAHY@delphi.com
A multi-issue, grassroots group that conducts direct actions, public education, and research/investigations.

International Foundation for Ethical Research
Chicago, IL
See "National & International Organizations."

Kindness, Inc.
P.O. Box 7071, Elgin, IL 60121-7071, (847) 888-2750, M-F 9-5
No-kill shelter that handles cat/dog adoptions on a limited basis (utilizes foster homes until a permanent facility is secured). Low-cost spay/neuter service, educational materials, and an animal directory of shelters and wildlife organizations in the Fox Valley and nearby communities.

National Anti-Vivisection Society
Chicago, IL
See "National & International Organizations."

National Greyhound Adoption Network
Regional Coordinator: Ellen Stloukal, P.O. Box 7044, Villa Park, IL 60181, (708) 495-0074

Pets In Need
P.O. Box 58, Ringwood, IL 60072-0058, (815) 728-1462
Provides a no-kill adoption shelter and spay/neuter services.

Save-A-Pet, Inc.
2019 N. Rand Road, Palatine, IL 60074, (708) 934-7788
No-kill adoption shelter for dogs and cats.

Society for the Protection of Animal Rights and Ethics (S.P.A.R.E.)
5238 Stone Crest Street, Loves Park, IL 61111, (815) 877-6833 (Residence)
Brings the unethical treatment of animals to the public's attention.

Society of St. Francis
- Shelter: 12300-116th Street, Kenosha, WI 53142
- Mailing Address: P.O. Box 206, Wadsworth, IL 60083, (414) 857-7260

No-kill adoption shelter for dogs, cats, horses, and other animals. Adoption fee includes spay/neuter, shots, and tattoo. Microchip I.D. also available.

Tree House Animal Foundation, Inc.
1212 West Carmen Avenue, Chicago, IL 60640-2999
- Administrative Office (voice/TDD): (312) 784-5605, FAX: (312) 784-2332
- Pet Info Hotline (free advice for behavior problems): (312) 784-5488
- Adoption Center: (312) 784-5488

No-kill adoption and treatment center for homeless strays who would face immediate death at traditional shelters—the sick, injured, and abused. Conducts rescues, low-cost or free spay/neuter assistance, cruelty investigations, an award-winning pet-facilitated therapy program, and public education.

Treehouse Wildlife Center
RR 1, Box 125E, Brighton, IL 62012, (618) 372-8092

West Suburban Humane Society
P.O. Box 9193, Downers Grove IL 60515, (708) 960-9600, FAX: (708) 960-9604
No-kill adoption shelter. Spay/neuter help.

Will County Humane Society
24109 Seil Road, Shorewood, IL 60436, (815) 741-0695
No-kill adoption shelter for dogs, cats, farm animals, birds, and wildlife.

Willowbrook Wildlife Haven
525 S. Park Blvd., Glen Ellyn, IL 60137, (708) 790-4900
Rehabilitates and releases wildlife.

INDIANA

For additional resources for breed rescue, ferret rescue, wildlife rehabilitation, etc., see "Keeping Up-To-Date" at the front of the chapter.

The Animals' Voice of Indianapolis (AVI)
10245 Churchill, Indianapolis, IN 46229, (317) 894-8601 (Peggy Loise Farrar)
A group of "hardcore" animal rights advocates who stage protests and demonstrations about every issue concerning animal exploitation. Works closely with the Vegetarian Society of Indianapolis.

The Ark Project
ATTN: Sam Chattin, Scottsburg Junior High School, 145 S. Third Street, Scottsburg, IN 47170, (812) 752-8962
Wildlife rehabilitation by supervised 12-13 year olds, specializing in raptors. Animal rights issues.

Fried's Cat Shelter, Inc.
P.O. Box 241, 509 Highway 212, Michigan City, IN 46361-0241, (219) 874-6932
"A port in the storm." No-kill, cageless adoption shelter for cats. Active in promoting spay/neuter of all pets.

Greyhound Rescue and Adoption, Inc.
Ladonna Rea, Director, 8677 So. State Road 243, Clovedale, IN 46120-9696, (317) 653-5690
Greyhound rescue and placement. "Greyhounds are as swift as a ray of light, graceful as a swallow, wise as Solomon. They are poetry and art in motion." Also has a representative in Detroit, MI, as well as other parts of IN.

Humane Society of the United States
See Ohio for the regional HSUS office that serves this state.

Independent Cat Society, Inc. (I.C.S.)
P.O. Box 735, Westville, IN 46391-0735, (219) 759-4936
Rescues abused cats and kittens and houses them in a no-kill adoption shelter. Spay/neuter program. Spends an average of double the amount on each cat than is recovered by the adoption fee.

Indiana Hooved Animal Humane Society
7245 Ippolito Lane, Demotte, IN 46310, (219) 987-3650

Pet Refuge, Inc.
P.O. Box 4534, South Bend, IN 46617, (219) 256-0886
No-kill adoption shelter for cats and dogs. Spay/neuter services.

REGAP (Retired Greyhounds As Pets) of Indiana
c/o Sally Allen, 1306 Bunker Hill Road, Mooresville, IN 46158, (317) 996-2154
Greyhound rescue and placement.

USA Defenders of Greyhounds, Inc.
Camby, IN
See "National & International Organizations."

Wolf Park
North American Wildlife Park Foundation, Battle Ground, IN 47920, (317) 567-2265
Serves Central Indiana with representatives in Minnesota and Michigan, and members nationwide. This group does not define itself as an "animal rights" organization, but rather as a "wolf rights" organization. Studies tame, handraised, free-living wolves in a 75-acre natural setting.

IOWA

For additional resources for breed rescue, ferret rescue, wildlife rehabilitation, etc., see "Keeping Up-To-Date" at the front of the chapter.

Animal Advocates of Iowa
903 Fifth Avenue, Iowa City, IA 52240

Animal Lifeline of Iowa, Inc.
P.O. Box 12, Carlisle, IA 50047, (515) 989-3473 (Ava M. Bothe)
Des Moines area. Dedicated to educating the public as to the abuse, exploitation, and oppression of animals. Works with existing agencies to improve the lives of animals and

to bring animal abuse to the public eye. No-kill shelter for dogs, cats, and birds.

Animal Protection Society of Iowa
P.O. Box 17324, Des Moines, IA 50317

Humane Society of the United States
See Missouri for the regional HSUS office that serves this state.

Iowa Alliance For Animals (IAFA)
P.O. Box 1263, Welch Avenue Station, Ames, IA 50014, (515) 382-3363
Statewide. Provides a network for all organizations and individuals concerned with animal-related issues across the state, and serves as a liaison with activist groups in other midwestern states. Also serves as a clearinghouse for information on both animal welfare and animal rights topics.

Iowa State University Humane Society
P.O. Box 1102, Welch Avenue Station, Ames, IA 50014, (515) 382-3363
Based on Iowa State University (ISU) campus and open to non-university persons in addition to ISU students, faculty, and staff. Although conservatively named, actively addresses and pursues all animal rights issues.

Noah's Ark Foundation, Inc.
P.O. Box 748, Fairfield, IA 52556, (515) 472-6080
No-kill shelter and humane society.

Orphaned and Injured Wildlife
RR Box 5650, Spirit Lake, IA 51360

People for Animal Welfare Society
P.O. Box 135, Jefferson, IA 50129

Protect Our Pets of Iowa
P.O. Box 704, West Branch, IA 52358
Committed to ending pet theft.

REGAP (Retired Greyhounds As Pets) of Waterloo
All Pets Animal Clinic, 3257 W. 4th Street, Waterloo, IA 50701, (319) 234-7511
Greyhound rescue and placement.

University of Iowa Animal Coalition
Student Activities Center—IMU, Iowa City, IA 52242
A student organization.

KANSAS

For additional resources for breed rescue, ferret rescue, wildlife rehabilitation, etc., see "Keeping Up-To-Date" at the front of the chapter.

Ferret Family Services
Manhattan, KS
See "National & International Organizations."

Greyhounds As Pets (GAP)
Springfield, CO
See Colorado for a description of this group and the representative that serves Kansas.

Humane Society of the United States
See Ohio for the regional HSUS office that serves this state.

People for Animal Rights (PAR)
P.O. Box 2928, Olathe, KS 66063-0928, (816) 767-1199
Olathe, KS and Kansas City, MO area. A multi-issue group dedicated to the elimination of animal abuse and exploitation.

KENTUCKY

For additional resources for breed rescue, ferret rescue, wildlife rehabilitation, etc., see "Keeping Up-To-Date" at the front of the chapter.

Animal Refuge Center, Inc. (ARC)
185 Basham Trail, Vine Grove, KY 40175, (502) 877-6064
No-kill shelter and adoption facility for cats, dogs, and some "livestock."

Bluegrass Animal Welfare League
P.O. Box 864, Lexington, KY 40587-0864, (606) 277-8525

The Fund for Animals, Inc.
Field Office: Andrea Reed and Tanya Gilley-Tuell (Kentucky Coordinators), 233 West Broadway, Suite 409, Louisville, KY 40202, (502) 587-0508
See "National & International Organizations."

Humane Society of the United States
See Tennessee for the regional HSUS office that serves this state.

Kentucky Wildlife-Line, Inc. (KWL)
4865 E. Hwy. 22, Smithfield, KY 40068-9303, (502) 222-1853
The largest and most comprehensive wildlife care facility in the state, providing care to injured, orphaned, and distressed wild animals. Feels that for a wild animal who has known nothing but freedom, confinement in a cage is a fate worse than death, so releases when possible and euthanizes when release is not possible. Has the only bobcat facility in the region, successfully returning many former captive bobcats to the wild. All volunteer. "Every dollar donated goes directly to animal care."

Lexington Humane Society
1600 Old Frankfort Pike, Lexington, KY 40504
General Information: (606) 233-0044
Animal Control: (606) 255-9033 or 255-9324
InfoLine: (606) 254-2041
FAX: (606) 259-1598

Sister Julia's Animal Shelter, Inc.
Sister Mary Julia, O.S.B., President, 1278 Basham Road, Fordsville, KY 42343, (502) 276-9537
Shelters homeless animals. Funded solely "by those who care for the animals."

LOUISIANA

For additional resources for breed rescue, ferret rescue, wildlife rehabilitation, etc., see "Keeping Up-To-Date" at the front of the chapter.

Alliance of Louisianians to Protect and Help Animals (ALPHA)
P.O. Box 80275, Baton Rouge, LA 70898-0295, (504) 766-8474
Statewide. Investigates cruelty allegations, rescues endangered animals, distributes educational materials on animal issues, and promotes humane treatment of farm animals and alternative methods to animal research.

Animal Peace
7704 Sycamore, New Orleans, LA 70118, (504) 865-9792
Works to improve the lives of animals.

Capital Area Animal Welfare Society (CAAWS)
P.O. Box 77765, Baton Rouge, LA 70879-7765, (504) 752-5801
Devoted to the prevention of animal suffering. Humane education, cruelty investigations, and adoption days every Saturday. No shelter, but an active foster home program. Requires spay/neuter of all adoptees.

Humane Society of the United States
See Texas for the regional HSUS office that serves this state.

Legislation In Support of Animals (LISA)
P.O. Box 740321, New Orleans, LA 70174, (504) 366-8972
Lobbying, litigation, and investigations. Has 2,000 members.

Louisiana Advocates for Animals, Inc.
P.O. Box 1707, Gretna, LA 70054-1707, (504) 362-5639
Educates whomever they can of the atrocities inflicted on our fellow beings, and motivates people to work together to bring about change.

Protective Animal Welfare Society (P.A.W.S.)
P.O. Box 8641, Alexandria, LA 71306
An animal welfare organization that tries to be active in all local animal issues.

Safe Harbor Rehabilitation
211 Lincoln Street, Haughton, LA 71037, (318) 226-5273
Rehabilitates raptors, especially owls.

Students in Defense of Animals
c/o Dean of Student Life, UC260, Lakefront, New Orleans, LA 70148
University of New Orleans campus. A student organization that meets every 2-3 weeks while school is in session. Interested non-students are also welcome to attend meetings.

Westlake Bird Sanctuary and Rehabilitation Center
2110 Nichols Road, Westlake, LA 70669
Provides care for songbirds and water fowl.

Wildlife in Distress, Inc.
637 Girard Park Drive, Lafayette, LA 70503-2896, (318) 231-1527
Full service wildlife care.

MAINE

For additional resources for breed rescue, ferret rescue, wildlife rehabilitation, etc., see "Keeping Up-To-Date" at the front of the chapter.

Animal Welfare Society, Inc. (AWS)

P.O. Box 43, West Kennebank, ME 04094-0043, (207) 985-3244
An animal shelter that houses and finds homes for unwanted and stray cats and dogs.

Hemlock Hill Farm Sanctuary

North Lebanon, ME
See "National & International Organizations."

Humane Society of the United States

See Connecticut for the regional HSUS office that serves this state.

Maine Animal Coalition (MAC)

P.O. Box 6683, Portland, ME 04101, (207) 442-0156 or (207) 781-7170
Dedicated to the elimination of animal abuse and exploitation through education and example. Advocates the philosophy of animal rights as a natural extension of human rights.

Maine Connection

RR 1, Box 956, Ft. Fairfield, ME 04742-9726, (207) 476-5250 (voice/FAX)

Protectors of Animal Life Society (PALS)

P.O. Box 6, Case Road, East Winthrop, ME 04343-0006, (207) 622-2298 (President, Margaret Fuller), Shelter: (207) 395-4274, FAX: (207) 395-4121
No-kill adoption shelter for 100 stray cats and kittens.

Psychologists for the Ethical Treatment of Animals

New Gloucester, ME
See "National & International Organizations."

Voice for Animals

P.O. Box 513, York, ME 03909, (207) 363-8122
Serves Southern Maine and New Hampshire. Promotes sensitivity and caring for animals through education and other lawful means.

MARYLAND

For additional resources for breed rescue, ferret rescue, wildlife rehabilitation, etc., see "Keeping Up-To-Date" at the front of the chapter.

Alley Animals, Inc.

P.O. Box 27487, Towson, MD 21285-7487
Rescue: (410) 823-0899
Adoption: (410) 515-2594
Baltimore area. A small group that takes as many animals off the streets as they can.

Alley Cat Allies

Mount Rainier, MD
See "National & International Organizations."

American Ferret Association, Inc.

Frederick, MD
See "National & International Organizations."

Animal Rescue, Inc.

P.O. Box 35, Maryland Line, MD 21105, (717) 993-3232
Rescues and finds homes for stray and abandoned dogs and cats. Since the shelter remains full and overflowing, limits activities to truly abandoned companion animals (not those owners want to relinquish).

Animal Rights Coalition, University of Maryland

Box 9, Stamp Union, College Park, MD 20859, (301) 948-2406 (Karen Davis, Faculty Advisor)

Aspin Hill Memorial Park and Animal Sanctuary

13630 Georgia Avenue, Silver Spring, MD 20906, (301) 871-6700
An 8-acre sanctuary owned and operated by People for the Ethical Treatment of Animals (see their description in "National & International Organizations").

Chesapeake Wildlife Sanctuary

17308 Queen Anne Bridge Road, Bowie, MD 20716

- 24-hour Wildlife Hotline (emergencies): (301) 390-7010 (after hours, messages will be returned if a volunteer is available)
- Administration: (301) 390-7011, FAX: (301) 249-3511

A shock-trauma hospital open 365 days/year to administer to sick, injured, orphaned, and otherwise distressed wildlife throughout the Washington, D.C., Chesapeake Bay region, and the state of Maryland.

Companion Animal Resource Exchange, Inc.

P.O. Box 1934, Bethesda, MD 20827, (301) 469-0769

Days End Farm Horse Sanctuary

15856 Frederick Road, Lisbon, MD 21765, (410) 442-1564
- and -
Mt. Airy, (301) 854-5037
Horse rehabilitation and training.

Defenders of Animal Rights, Inc.

14412 Old York Road, Phoenix, MD 21131, (301) 527-1466
Serves the Baltimore Metropolitan area, with a national focus. Operates an animal shelter on a 35.8-acre wildlife sanctuary. Rescues, rehabilitates, and adopts out animals to screened homes.

Farm Animal Reform Movement

Bethesda, MD
See "National & International Organizations."

The Fund for Animals, Inc.

Campaign Office: 850 Sligo Avenue, Suite 300, Silver Spring, MD 20910, (301) 585-2591, FAX: (301) 585-2595
See "National & International Organizations."

Greyhound Rescue, Inc.

c/o John and Denise Davis, 6397 Woodburn Road, Elk Ridge, MD 21227, (410) 796-2803
Greyhound rescue and placement.

Heron Run Refuge, Inc. (HRR)

6565 Belmont Woods Road, Elkridge, MD 21227, (410) 379-0457
"A second chance for large animals." Provides shelter, food, and veterinary care for neglected, abused, or unwanted large animals, including horses, pigs, goats, sheep, etc. You can sponsor the care of an animal through a monthly donation program. "We are definitely animal rights—no apologies!"

Maryland Animal Advocates, Inc. (MAA)

P.O. Box 9184, Baltimore, MD 21222-0184, (410) 825-8714 or 783-0896
Dedicated to the abolition of animal cruelty and all forms of animal exploitation. Primary focus is factory farming.

Maryland Forum for Animals (MFA)

P.O. Box 21166, Catonsville, MD 21228, (301) 536-0643
Statewide. Dedicated to defending the rights of all animals.

Maryland Horse Rescue Center, Inc. (MHRC) / HorseNet

4118 Decatur Avenue, Kensington, MD 20895, (301) 942-4688 (Pam Rutherford, President) or (410) 795-8989 (Elle Powers, Public Relations & Humane Education for HorseNet)
A network of caring people working together for the betterment of horses. Reaches out to horses in need, no matter the reason.

The Order of the Earth

P.O. Box 380, Clarksville, MD 21029, (410) 964-3574
"An invisible community of zealots of all ages, both sexes, all faiths, all ethnic backgrounds, living with reverence for all life." Embraces a return to simple living. Guidelines include a strong animal welfare/rights component. A small, hand-printed booklet (photocopied) on deliberate thoughts and actions for a simpler life available for $1 plus a self-addressed, stamped envelope.

Project BREED, Inc.

Germantown, MD
See "National & International Organizations."

Protect Animal Life (PAL)

P.O. Box 120, Burtonsville, MD 20866-0120, (301) 890-4510 (voice/FAX)
Concerned with all types of animal exploitation and suffering. Works to educate adults and children alike. Many members are junior or senior high school students.

Psychologists for the Ethical Treatment of Animals

Washington Grove, MD
See "National & International Organizations."

Sanders Ferret Halfway House

c/o Judith Sanders, 311 Twin Oaks Road, Linthicum, MD 21090, (410) 850-0143

Ferret rescue and shelter. Ten years experience working with ferrets. Maintains that there would be no need for rescue/shelters if people would stop buying ferrets from pet shops, as those ferrets are unethically bred by large "ferret mills," and are often sold to people lacking the proper knowledge of ferret care. A "daughter" organization of the American Ferret Association, Inc. (see their listing in "National & International Organizations").

Scientists Group for Reform of Animal Experimentation
Washington Grove, MD
See "National & International Organizations."

Spay Neuter All Pets, Inc. (SNAP)
P.O. Box 7555, Baltimore, MD 21207, (410) 484-2020
Statewide (also Delaware and Pennsylvania). Promotes a low-cost spay/neuter program, with over 100 vets who accept their certificates in Maryland and a few cities in nearby Delaware and Pennsylvania.

United Poultry Concerns
Potomac, MD
See "National & International Organizations."

MASSACHUSETTS

For additional resources for breed rescue, ferret rescue, wildlife rehabilitation, etc., see "Keeping Up-To-Date" at the front of the chapter.

Advocates for Animals
c/o Joanne Santella, 96 Fisher Hill Road, Cheshire, MA 01225, (413) 743-1448
Educates the public about vegetarianism, animal rights, and animal welfare.

Alliance for Animals (AfA)
P.O. Box 909, Boston, MA 02103, (617) 265-7577
All-volunteer humane organization concerned with population control, community outreach to poor and elderly caretakers, public education, rescue, shelter, and feral cat sterilization. "When we help animals, we help people."

Animal Legal Defense Fund
Regional Contact: 896 Beacon Street, Suite 303, Boston, MA 02215
See "National & International Organizations."

Animal Rights Coalition
Box 162–Student Union Building, UMASS–Amherst, Amherst, MA 01003, (413) 545-1925
University of MA at Amherst campus. Educates the campus and surrounding community on the many aspects of animal exploitation.

Animal Umbrella
P.O. Box 1324, East Arlington, MA 02174, (617) 731-7267 or (508) 877-1194
Works to prevent animal overpopulation, especially for cats, stray and feral. Operates a rescue program for strays and a neuter/release/management program for feral cat colonies. Advocacy for pet ownership rights of people in rental housing.

Baypath Humane Society of Hopkinton, Inc.
P.O. Box 23, Hopkinton, MA 01748-0023, (508) 435-6938
No-kill adoption shelter for 14 cats and 18 dogs. About 30 minutes west of Boston. Spays/neuters all adoptees.

Bolser Humane Society, Inc.
P.O. Box 520, Barre, MA 01500, (508) 882-3136
The largest no-kill adoption shelter in New England. Spay/neuter services.

Buddy Dog Humane Society, Inc.
- Mailing Address: P.O. Box 296, Sudbury, MA 01776, (617) 237-4747 or (508) 443-6990
- Shelter: 151 Boston Post Road (Rte. 20), Sudbury, MA 01776

No-kill adoption shelter that finds new homes for over 2,000 cats and dogs annually. Humane education, spay/neuter program, and work-study for handicapped adults.

Carver Cat Shelter
13 Fosdick Road, Carver, MA 02330, (508) 866-7238
Provides a no-kill adoption shelter and low-cost spay/neuter for cats.

Citizens Against Pet Shops
10 Walter Street, Lynn, MA 01902

Citizens to End Animal Suffering and Exploitation (CEASE)
Somerville, MA
See "National & International Organizations."

Coalition to Protect Refuge Wildlife
11 Lincoln Street, Newburyport, MA 01950, (508) 463-8103

Concerned Citizens for Animals, Inc. (CCA, Inc.)
P.O. Box 80073, Springfield, MA 01138, (413) 536-0028 or 783-3078
Low-cost spay/neuter service and information on animal-related issues.

Eco-Solar, Inc.
Jamaica Plain, MA
See "National & International Organizations."

Ethical Science Education Coalition
Boston, MA
See "National & International Organizations."

Gaia Institute
South Lynfield, MA
See "National & International Organizations."

The Great Ape Project
Watertown, MA
See "National & International Organizations."

Greyhound Friends, Inc.
Hopkinton, MA
Shelters located in Hopkinton, Falmouth, Great Barrington, and in Skillman, NJ. See "National & International Organizations."

Greyhound Life Line
c/o Irene Milbury, 228 E. Foxboro Street, Sharon, MA 02067, (617) 784-2157
Greyhound rescue and placement.

Homes and Rights for Animals (HRA)
Kathleen Foy, Executive Director, P.O. Box 851, Fall River, MA 02722, (508) 679-8418

Homeward Hound Humane Society
1014 Pearl Street, Brockton, MA 02401, (508) 583-8529
No-kill adoption shelter for dogs.

Humane Society of the United States
See Connecticut for the regional HSUS office that serves this state.

International Fund for Animal Welfare
Yarmouth Port, MA
See "National & International Organizations."

International Wildlife Coalition
North Falmouth, MA
See "National & International Organizations."

Jews for Animal Rights (JAR) / Micah Publications
Marblehead, MA
See "National & International Organizations."

Just Cats, Inc.
P.O. Box 531, Mansfield, MA 02048, (508) 339-6717
No-kill cat shelter. Discount spay/neuter subsidy program. Bimonthly *Feline News* for any donation. Cat merchandise.

The Last Resort
1126 Broadway, Hanover, MA 02339, (617) 826-9560
No-kill adoption and medical services for cats.

Live Elephant, Inc
Canton, MA
See "National & International Organizations."

LivingEarth Learning Project
Boston, MA
See "National & International Organizations."

Massachusetts Society for the Prevention of Cruelty to Animals (MSPCA)
350 South Huntington Avenue, Boston, MA 02130, (617) 541-5000, FAX: (617) 522-4885, Hotline to report suspected animal abuse inside Massachusetts: 1-800-628-5808
State, national, and international. Dedicated to the protection of animals and the advancement of their welfare. Believes that all animals possess intrinsic value, independent of their relationships to or use by human beings. Operates eight animal shelters and one of the most comprehensive animal hospitals in the country, Angell Memorial Animal Hospital in Boston. Publishes *Animals* magazine. (See the Activism: Periodicals section of Chapter 13 for a description of this magazine.)

New England Anti-Vivisection Society
Boston, MA
See "National & International Organizations."

Northeast Animal Shelter
204 Highland Avenue, Salem, MA 01970, (505) 745-9888
The largest no-kill shelter in the area. Never sells animals to research laboratories. Because of the no-kill policy, more selective about the animals accepted in regard to age, temperament, and medical complications.

Orenda Wildlife Trust
P.O. Box 669, West Barnstable, MA 02668, (508) 362-4798, FAX: (508) 362-7478
A land conservation trust committed to re-establishing protected habitat for wildlife. All Orenda wildlife sanctuaries posted against hunting, trapping, and other activities detrimental to flora and fauna, unlike some other land preserves. At this writing, had six sanctuaries in Massachusetts. Deeded their former facility to HSUS for use as a national wildlife rehabilitation training center.

Paw Safe Animal Rescue
167 Derby Road, Melrose, MA 02176, (617) 473-0605

Pet Adoption Welfare Services
Box 1636, Edgartown, MA 02539

Stray Pets in Need of MA, Inc.
485 Washington Street, Wellesley, MA 01281
Cares for strays under the jurisdiction of Animal Control.

University Conversion Project (UCP) Center for Campus Organizing
Cambridge, MA
See "National & International Organizations."

Valley Animal Rights Advocates (V.A.R.A.)
P.O. Box 328, Hadley, MA 01035
Serves Pioneer Valley (Springfield, MA to Brattleboro, VT). A network of activists working to promote animal rights in Western Massachusetts. Welcomes new members and is open to fresh, supportive ideas.

Volunteer Humane Society
505 Center Bridge Road, Lancaster, MA 01523-9502, (508) 365-9470, Animal Emergencies (nights & weekends): 263-1742
No-kill adoption shelter, primarily for cats. Some fostering of dogs who are in desperate need. Low-cost spay/neuter.

WIRES (Wildlife Information, Referral, and Educational Services)
P.O. Box 307, West Barnstable, MA 02668, Hotline: (508) 540-3820, TDD (508) 540-4175
A hotline for the Cape Cod area that answers wildlife-related calls to prevent both wildlife and callers from coming to harm.

World Society for the Protection of Animals
Boston, MA
See "National & International Organizations."

MICHIGAN

For additional resources for breed rescue, ferret rescue, wildlife rehabilitation, etc., see "Keeping Up-To-Date" at the front of the chapter.

Adopt-A-Pet, Inc.
P.O. Box 524, Fenton, MI 48430, (313) 629-0723
No-kill adoption shelter.

Animal's Best Friend
P.O. Box 443, Oshtemo, MI 49077, (616) 624-1090
Spay/neuter organization. No placement. Opposes selling pets to research.

Animal Welfare Society of Southeastern Michigan
29081 Dequindre, Suite E, Madison Heights, MI 48071, (810) 548-1150, FAX: (810) 548-1183
Dedicated to the welfare of animals throughout Southeast Michigan.

Cedar Wildlife Rescue
- Street Address: 2515 Gatzke Road
- Mailing Address: P.O. Box 201, Cedar, MI 49621, (616) 228-6493

Concern for Critters
P.O. Box 990, Battle Creek, MI 49016, (616) 968-1540
Helps raise awareness about animal welfare and animal rights issues. Does not operate a shelter or adopt animals.

Critter Alley Wildlife Care Center
4340 W. St. Joe Highway, Grand Ledge, MI 48837-9447, (517) 627-7758
Cares for sick, injured, and orphaned wildlife.

Defenders of Animal Rights
16420 Rossini Drive, Detroit, MI 48205-2065

For Animals, Inc.
P.O. Box 4555, Traverse City, MI 49685, (616) 334-4122
"The only animal rights organization in Northern Michigan." Committed to the abolition of animal abuse and exploitation. Very willing to work with individuals or other groups to advance the animal rights agenda.

The Fund for Animals, Inc.
Field Offices: Doris Dixon (Michigan Coordinator), 2841 Colony Road, Ann Arbor, MI 48104, (313) 971-4632
- and -
Mike Chiado (Michigan Wildlife Coordinator), P.O. Box 432, Royal Oak, MI 48068, (810) 546-7227
See "National & International Organizations."

Greyhound Rescue and Adoption, Inc.
Local Representative: Nancy Chiesa, Detroit, MI, (313) 593-1043
See Indiana for a description of this group.

Help Orphaned Pets Everywhere (HOPE)
Mailing Address: 112 S. Suffolk Street, Ironwood, MI 49938, (906) 932-5666
A small, no-kill adoption shelter organized by a group of "eternal optimists" who live in an area virtually devoid of any help for stray animals.

H.O.R.S.E. of Michigan, Inc.
P.O. Box 603, Ada, MI 49301, (616) 245-8517

Humane Society of SE Michigan
29081 Dequindre Road, #E, Madison Heights, MI 48071-2657

Humane Society of the United States
See Ohio for the regional HSUS office that serves this state.

Humanitarians for Environmental and Animal Laws PAC (HEAL-PAC)
P.O. Box 14291, Lansing, MI 48901, (810) 887-2184, Contact Person: Eileen Liska (Founder and Treasurer)
Michigan's only Political Action Committee (PAC) dedicated to the passage of environmental and animal laws, and to the support of elected officials who vote to protect animals and their environments.

Kalamazoo Animal Rescue, Inc.
P.O. Box 3295, Kalamazoo, MI 49003, (616) 349-2325

Michigan Humane Society (MHS)
ATTN: Gary W. Tiscornia, Executive Director, 7401 Chrysler Drive, Detroit, MI 48211, (313) 872-3400
Emergency Rescue: (313) 872-0026
Clinic: (313) 872-0004
Rochester Hills Office: (810) 852-7420
Westland Office: (313) 721-7300
Gift Shop (Paw Pourri): 817 N. Main St., Royal Oak, MI 48067, (810) 545-3780
Primary focus is local and statewide, with some national focus. Works for the immediate alleviation or prevention of animal suffering or exploitation, and for the long-term promotion of animal protection and rights. Actively involved in animal rights issues.

Mid-Michigan Society for Animal Protection (MMSAP)
P.O. Box 14264, Lansing, MI 48901-4264, (517) 337-7259
Works to inform the public of animal abuse and to utilize whatever resources available to end animal cruelty. Provides foster homes for all species of needy animals.

People for Animal Liberation
897 Michigan Avenue E., #2, Battle Creek, MI 49017-6264, (616) 968-4345

People for Animal Welfare (P.A.W.)
920 Grant Court, Kalamazoo, MI 49008, (616) 349-4120 or 344-8122
Western Michigan University. Works to educate students and faculty on animal rights issues.

Project Floodlight
P.O. Box 3782, Ann Arbor, MI 48106
Offers a free booklet of anti-fur ads suitable for publication. (See the Activism section of Chapter 12 for more details.)

Sable Peckens Memorial Shelter/ Fheraton Inn
c/o Condie Peckens, 1262 Westlake Woods Drive, Battle Creek, MI 49015, (616) 964-1916
Education, rescue, adoptions, and boarding.

Students Concerned About Animal Welfare
319 Union Building, RSO, Michigan State University, East Lansing, MI 48824

United Students for Animals
3604 Salem, Troy, MI 48084

Washtenaw Citizens for Animal Rights (WCAR)
P.O. Box 2614, Ann Arbor, MI 48106
General Info: (313) 426-1680
Spay/Neuter Program: (313) 426-0637
An educational, peaceful group dedicated to improving the treatment of animals. Operates a no-cost spay/neuter program for those with low income.

The Wyandotte Animal Group
P.O. Box 222, Wyandotte, MI 48192, (313) 753-5252
Furthers the cause of animal rights/welfare. Finds loving homes for needy animals. Conducts public education on spay/neuter, animal care, and animal rights issues. Establishing a building fund for the construction and maintenance of a humane shelter.

MINNESOTA

For additional resources for breed rescue, ferret rescue, wildlife rehabilitation, etc., see "Keeping Up-To-Date" at the front of the chapter.

Animal Rights Coalition, Inc. (ARC)
P.O. Box 20315, Bloomington, MN 55420, (612) 822-6161 or 888-0288, Hotline for details on upcoming events and other information: (612) 866-6604
Statewide. Dedicated to ending the exploitation of all species through public education, special events, direct action, legislation, and grassroots organizing.

Animal Rights Coalition, University of Minnesota Chapter
235D Coffman Memorial Union, 300 Washington Avenue SE, Minneapolis, MN 55455
Statewide. See the above description for Animal Rights Coalition, Inc.

Friends of Animal Adoptions, Inc. ("Animal Ark")
P.O. Box 4444, St. Paul, MN 55104
- Shelter: 2600 Industrial Court, Hastings, MN 55033, (612) 438-9195, FAX: (612) 739-8512
- Thrift & Pet Store: 957 W. 7th Street, St. Paul, MN 55102, (612) 222-4651

No-kill adoption shelter for about 180 dogs, cats, and other small animals. Adoptees receive spay/neuter and vet care. Would like to expand the present shelter and work toward opening more shelters.

Friends of Animals Humane Society of Carlton County (FOAHS)
P.O. Box 107, Cloquet, MN 55720, (218) 879-1655
(*Note*: Not affiliated with the national Friends of Animals.) Conducts cruelty investigations and rescue. Spay/neuter assistance and adoptions. Fights with officials to strengthen animal laws. Conducts campaigns on several issues, including pound seizure, animals in entertainment, fur, factory farming, etc.

Help Our Wolves Live
Minneapolis, MN
See "National & International Organizations."

Humane Society of Ramsey County
1115 Beulah Lane, St. Paul, MN 55108, (612) 645-7387

Humane Society of the United States
See Illinois for the regional HSUS office that serves this state.

Lake Superior Humane Society, Inc.
P.O. Box 244, Knife River, MN 55609, (218) 834-3966, E-mail: LSHSMINN@AOL.COM
"We are small and our resources are limited, but we say in answer to the statement, 'You can't save them all' that 'It is amazing how many you can save *if* you try!'" No-kill adoption shelter for dogs and cats. Emergency medical care.

Minnesota Voters for Animals and the Environment (MVAE)
1471 Barclay Street, St. Paul, MN 55106, (612) 774-4971
Statewide. Works to protect wildlife, domesticated animals, and the environment by educating other citizens as to which city,

county, and state political candidates support these goals.

National Wildlife Rehabilitators Association
St. Cloud, MN
See "National & International Organizations."

Pets Against Laboratories (P.A.L.)
ATTN: Joy Donovan-Mattice, 7100 Brooklyn Blvd., Brooklyn Center, MN 55429, (612) 569-5661
Has lobbied for the last 21 years for repeal of pound seizure in Minnesota. Successful in helping pass bills concerning various animal welfare/rights issues.

S.O.A.R. (Students Organized for Animal Rights)
235 CMU, 300 Washington Avenue SE, Minneapolis, MN 55455, (612) 624-0422, During the summer call: (612) 475-1975
High school students, college students, and community members. Actively pursues a variety of activities.

Students for the Ethical Treatment of Animals
Carleton College, Northfield, MN 55057

MISSISSIPPI

For additional resources for breed rescue, ferret rescue, wildlife rehabilitation, etc., see "Keeping Up-To-Date" at the front of the chapter.

Cedarhill Animal Sanctuary, Inc.
- Street Address: 13572 Hwy 12 East
- Mailing Address: P.O. Box 280, Caledonia, MS 39740, (601) 356-6636, FAX: (601) 356-4707

A sanctuary for abused and neglected exotic and domesticated cats.

Humane Society of the United States
See Florida for the regional HSUS office that serves this state.

In Defense of Animals
Out-of-state representative: Doll Stanley-Branscum, Rte. 1, Box 122-A, Greneda, MS 38901, (601) 237-4382
See "National & International Organizations."

Puerto Rico Street Dog Project
Hattiesburg, MS
See "National & International Organizations."

Wildlife Rehabilitation and Nature Preservation Society
P.O. Box 209, Long Beach, MS 39560, (601) 452-9453

MISSOURI

For additional resources for breed rescue, ferret rescue, wildlife rehabilitation, etc., see "Keeping Up-To-Date" at the front of the chapter.

Amnesty of Animals
A022 Brady Commons, University of Missouri, Columbia, MO 65211

Animal Companion Disaster Reunification Services
Dolores Emily, P.O. Box 414937, Kansas City, MO 64141-4937
Founded by a person whose companion animals were given away/killed during her hospitalization. Seeks others interested in helping reunite people/pets separated due to tragedies, such as hospitalization or war.

Animal Education, Protection, and Information Foundation (A.E.P.I.F.)
Route 1, Box 452, Fordland, MO 65652, (417) 767-2195
No-kill adoption shelter for elephants and (in the future) other exotic animals.

Animal Shelter League of the Ozarks, Inc.
(Also known as Ozarks Animal Shelter)
P.O. Box 989, Nixa, MO 65714, (417) 725-6446
Working to fund, construct, operate, and support an animal shelter for Christian County. (Currently, lost or abandoned animals roam at large.) Current efforts focus on fund-raising and on educating county residents of the unwanted companion animal problem.

Friends of Companion Animals, Inc.
P.O. Box 636, Kearny, MO 64060
Working to establish a cooperative shelter offering a humane approach in an area where there is no animal control, no shelter, and no

low-cost spay/neuter. Appreciates anyone wishing to help.

Humane Society of Southeast Missouri
2536 Boutin Drive, Cape Girardeau, MO 63701, (314) 334-5837
Operates a shelter that averages 4,300 animals annually. Lost/found service. Behavior training and information.

Humane Society of the United States
Midwest Regional Office: Argyle Building, 306 East 12th Street, Suite 625, Kansas City, MO 64106, (816) 474-0888, FAX: (816) 474-0898
Serves MO, KS, NE, and IA. See "National & International Organizations."

Kansas City Ferret Hotline Association
Dr. Bobbi McCanse, 904 E. 28th Street, Kansas City, MO 64109, (816) 842-3707
Rescues, adoptions, give-ups, and info.

Martha's
P.O. Box 22203, St. Louis, MO 63116
No-kill shelter.

National Society for the Protection of Animals
Kansas City, MO
See "National & International Organizations."

People for Animal Rights
P.O. Box 2928, Olathe, KS 66063-0928, (816) 767-1199
Olathe, KS and Kansas City, MO area. See Kansas for a description of this group.

Pet Search
c/o Alice Dodge, 1553 Pond Road, Wildwood, MO 63038, (314) 458-CATS
A licensed spay/neuter group that found homes for 3,768 animals in 1995.

Society for the Treatment of Abandoned Fractured Friends (S.T.A.F.F.)
P.O. Box 1324, Laurie, MO 65038, (314) 374-2629
No-kill foster care, adoption, and spay/neuter.

St. Charles Humane Society
P.O. Box 9, St, Charles, MO 63302, (314) 949-9918
No-kill adoption shelter.

St. Louis Animal Rights Team (START)
P.O. Box 28501, St. Louis, MO 63146, (314) 851-0928 (message phone & info)
An educational and action-oriented group that forces animal issues into the public view.

Universal Great Brotherhood
St. Louis, MO
See "National & International Organizations."

Wildlife Assistance, Inc.
Eureka, MO 63025-0761, (314) 938-4890

Wolf Sanctuary, Wild Canid Survival and Research Center
P.O. Box 760, Eureka, MO 63025, (314) 938-5900
Dedicated to the preservation of the wolf and its natural ecosystem through education, research, and captive breeding.

World Bird Sanctuary
St. Louis, MO
See "National & International Organizations."

MONTANA

For additional resources for breed rescue, ferret rescue, wildlife rehabilitation, etc., see "Keeping Up-To-Date" at the front of the chapter.

Animal Welfare League of Montana
910 6th Avenue, Laurel, MT 59044, (406) 628-7173
- and -
P.O. Box 21427, Billings, MT 59104, (406) 248-7308

Great Bear Foundation
Missoula, MT and Bozeman, MT
See "National & International Organizations."

Greyhounds As Pets (GAP)
Local Representatives: Carol Frank, Belgrade, MT, (406) 388-6593
- and -
Sunny Lewis, Red Lodge, MT, (406) 446-3539
See Colorado for a description of this group.

Grizzly Bear Task Force
P.O. Box 6151, Bozeman, MT 59715, (406) 585-9211

Humane Society of the United States
Northern Rockies Regional Office: Dave Pauli, Director, 490 North 31st Street, Billings, MT 59101, (406) 255-7161, FAX: (406) 255-7162
Serves MT, ID, and WY. See "National & International Organizations."

Montana Animal Rights Coalition
c/o UC 105, University of Montana, Missoula, MT 59801, (406) 243-2628

The Predator Project
Bozeman, MT
See "National & International Organizations."

Wolf Action Group
P.O. Box 9286, Missoula, MT 59807

NEBRASKA

For additional resources for breed rescue, ferret rescue, wildlife rehabilitation, etc., see "Keeping Up-To-Date" at the front of the chapter.

Humane Society of the United States
See Missouri for the regional HSUS office that serves this state.

Midwest Animal Shelter
P.O. Box 286, 608 Q Street, Auburn, NE 68305, (402) 274-3679
No-kill adoption shelter for dogs.

Wildlife Rescue Team, Inc.
2929 Gold Street, Omaha, NE 68105, (402) 345-7985

NEVADA

For additional resources for breed rescue, ferret rescue, wildlife rehabilitation, etc., see "Keeping Up-To-Date" at the front of the chapter.

Greyhounds As Pets (GAP)
Local Representative: Bill Fullerton, Las Vegas, NV, (702) 228-4295
See Colorado for a description of this group.

Humane Society of the United States
See California for the regional HSUS office that serves this state.

Independent Animal Rights Activists
34 Congressional Court, Las Vegas, NV 89113

Nevada SPCA
650 White Drive, Las Vegas, NV 89119, (702) 897-1844 or 897-2045
No-kill adoption shelter for a variety of animals—dogs, cats, rabbits, potbellied pigs, and goats. Cruelty investigations.

United Students for Animals
3380 Iberia, Las Vegas, NV 89102

Wild Horse Organized Assistance
P.O. Box 55, Reno, NV 89504

NEW HAMPSHIRE

For additional resources for breed rescue, ferret rescue, wildlife rehabilitation, etc., see "Keeping Up-To-Date" at the front of the chapter.

Highlands Wildlife Rehabilitation Center, Inc.
9 Adams Street, Milford, NH 03055, (603) 673-9065
Cares for all birds and mammals.

Humane Society of the United States
See Connecticut for the regional HSUS office that serves this state.

Leave It to the Beavers
P.O. Box 40, Plainfield, NH 03781, (603) 675-2555
Humanely traps, sterilizes, and relocates beaver families in need.

National Greyhound Adoption Network
Regional Coordinator: Anne Tepper, RR2, Box 95A, Hinsdale, NH 03451, (603) 336-5997, FAX: (603) 336-5998

New Hampshire Animal Rights League, Inc. (NHARL)
520 Bean Hill Road, Northfield, NH 03276, (603) 286-8477
Statewide. A humane organization that helps the animals, birds, and water creatures of NH, but dedicated to the protection of all animals worldwide. Three-fold approach: dissemination of information, humane education, and legislation. Promotes vegetarianism.

New Hampshire Equine Services, Inc.
Box 954, Memorial Drive, Weare, NH 03281

New Hampshire Spaying and Altering Service (NHSAS)
8 Hutchins Street, Concord, NH 03301-3208, (603) 224-1361 before 2 p.m.
Offers financial help for spaying and altering of dogs and cats.

REGAP (Retired Greyhounds As Pets) of Seabrook, Inc.
Christine Makepeace, Director, P.O. Box 1861, Seabrook, NH 03874, (603) 474-8340
Greyhound rescue and placement.

Voice for Animals
P.O. Box 513, York, ME 03909, (207) 363-8122
Southern Maine and New Hampshire, including Portsmouth and Dover, NH. See Maine for a description of this group.

NEW JERSEY

For additional resources for breed rescue, ferret rescue, wildlife rehabilitation, etc., see "Keeping Up-To-Date" at the front of the chapter.

Advocates for Forgotten Wildlife
68 Mill Road Extension, Woodcliff Lake, NJ 07675, (201) 930-9026 or 930-9432
Works to protect invertebrates, arthropods (insects, crustaceans, etc.), and other cold-blooded vertebrates. Distributes flyers against bug zappers. Welcomes affiliates and local chapters.

American Society for the Welfare of Cats
P.O. Box 487, Bellmar, NJ 08099, (609) 935-2870
No-kill adoption shelter for cats.

Animal Adoption Center
501 N. Berlin Road, Lindenwold, NJ 08021, (609) 435-9116
No-kill adoption shelter. Low-cost spay/neuter services.

Animal Friends for Education and Welfare (AFEW)
P.O. Box 514, Kingston, NJ 08528, (609) 448-5322

Animal Rescue Force (ARF)
P.O. Box 418, East Brunswick, NJ 08816, (908) 257-7559
Central New Jersey. Finds responsible homes for unwanted cats and dogs. Operates two adoption centers, which are open every Saturday and Sunday. Noted for their extensive call-back procedure as a follow-up to adoption. Spay/neuter info, dog crate and humane trap rental, educational material, info and referral.

Animal Watch
WMTR-AM, 1250, 55 Horsehill Road, Cedar Knolls, NJ 07927, Contact: Mary-Kaye Dombrowski (201) 538-1250, ext. 1323, FAX: (201) 538-5744
A weekly 60-second radio feature in the New Jersey/New York area, covering topics ranging from dog grooming to vivisection, and everything in between.

Animal Welfare Association, Inc.
509 Gibbsboro-Marlton Road, Voorhees, NJ 08043, (609) 424-2288
Southern New Jersey area. "Caring for animals...benefiting people." An animal welfare organization that is quickly moving into the animal rights arena. Services include a 24-hour shelter for unwanted, lost, and injured animals.

Animals Need You Kindness Club, Inc.
P.O. Box 65, West New York, NJ 07093

Associated Humane Societies, Inc.
Newark, NJ
See "National & International Organizations."

Balloon Alert Project
12 Pine Fork Drive, Tom's River, NJ 08755-5121

The Beaver Defenders
See Unexpected Wildlife Refuge, Inc. in "National & International Organizations."

Classrooms for Ethical Labs in the Life Sciences
Woodcliff Lake, NJ
See "National & International Organizations."

Closter Animal Welfare Society, Inc.
P.O. Box 172, Closter, NJ 07624, (201) 768-0200
Foster care, screened adoptions, and veterinary care for dogs and cats since 1970.

Coalition For Animals (CFA)
P.O. Box 2422, Edison, NJ 08818-2422, (908) 548-3051, E-mail: NJCFA@aol.com

God's Answering Service
21 Mount Kemble Avenue, #217, Morristown, NJ 07960-5127
Humane education.

Humane Campaign, Inc.
P.O. Box 13001, Jersey City, NJ 07303-4001

Humane Education Committee
Allendale, NJ
See "National & International Organizations."

Humane Society of the United States
Mid-Atlantic Regional Office: Bartley Square, 270 Route 206, Flanders, NJ 07836, (201) 927-5611, FAX: (201) 927-5617
Serves DE, NJ, NY, and PA. See "National & International Organizations."

Hunterdon County SPCA
576 Stamets Road, Milford, NJ 08848, (908) 996-2525
No-kill adoption shelter which is "the only refuge for lost, unwanted, sick, abandoned, or abused animals." Also humane education and a pet therapy program. Never sells animals to research. Requires spay/neuter for adoptees.

Interbeing Partnerships
Rev. Carolyn Carpenter, P.O. Box 1376, Summit, NJ 07901, (201) 829-1967, FAX: (210) 898-6625
National with local events. Audiotapes, lectures, and workshops on healing animal loss, stress relief for animal activists, and healthy diets for animals.

New Jersey Animal Rights Alliance (NJARA)
P.O. Box 174, Englishtown, NJ 07726, (908) 446-6808, FAX: (908) 446-0227, E-mail: njaral@aol.com
Statewide. A community-based educational, activist organization working for the total elimination of animal abuse, oppression, and exploitation, based on a philosophy of reverence for all life. Activities include outreach, citizen empowerment, protests, civil disobedience, advertising, letter-writing, open meetings, and conferences/workshops.

New York Turtle and Tortoise Society
Orange, NJ
See "National & International Organizations."

Paws-N-Claws
725 Elton Road, Freehold, NJ 07728, (908) 462-7958
Rescue, referral, placement, and spay/neuter.

People for Animals
348 Elmwood Avenue, Maplewood, NJ 07040, (201) 763-5732

Pet-Aid
P.O. Box 1402, Blackwood, NJ 08012, (609) 228-4411
Information on low-cost spay/neuter or any animal problem that arises. No shelter.

Pineland Sanctuary for Wildlife
1421 Silverton Road, Toms River, NJ 08755, (708) 341-1209
24-hour information and emergencies.

Ramapo-Bergen Animal Refuge, Inc.
2 Shelter Lane, Oakland, NJ 07436, (201) 337-5180, FAX: (201) 337-2040
Hours: M, W, F, Sat. 10-2, Sun. 11-3
No-kill adoption shelter for 14 dogs and 27 cats. Low-cost spay/neuter info.

Rutgers Animal Rights Law Center
Newark, NJ
See "National & International Organizations."

Save The Animals Rescue Team (S.T.A.R.T.)
P.O. Box 1098, Little Falls, NJ 07424-1652, (201) 785-1245
Dedicated to alleviating the plight of homeless animals. Rescues, rehabilitates, and places abandoned pets, especially cats.

Society in Opposition to Human-Animal Hybridization
Lake Hopatcong, NJ
See "National & International Organizations."

Spay, Neuter And Protect Strays
P.O. Box 92, Oakhurst, NJ 07755, (908) 988-4287

Standardbred Retirement Foundation
Main Office: Blairstown, NJ
See "National & International Organizations."

Thoroughbred Retirement Foundation
1050 Highway 35, Suite 351, Shrewsbury, NJ 07702, (908) 957-0182

Unexpected Wildlife Refuge, Inc.
Newfield, NJ
See "National & International Organizations."

NEW MEXICO

For additional resources for breed rescue, ferret rescue, wildlife rehabilitation, etc., see "Keeping Up-To-Date" at the front of the chapter.

Alliance Against Animal Abuse, Inc. (AAAA)
P.O. Box 90601, Albuquerque, NM 87199, (505) 821-0393
Works with established agencies such as animal control, sheriff's department, etc. to enforce existing animal neglect/abuse laws. Field workers and foster homes (as well as donations) welcome. Low-cost spay/neuter program and adoptions.

Animal Alliance
Santa Fe, NM
See "National & International Organizations."

Animal Ambassadors
P.O. Box 3793, Santa Fe, NM 87501, (505) 455-2945

Animal Humane Association
615 Virginia SE, Albuquerque, NM 87108, (505) 255-5523

Clem and Jethro Lecture Service
Santa Fe, NM
See "National & International Organizations."

Greyhounds As Pets (GAP)
Local Representative: Kay Bird, Santa Fe, NM, (505) 471-4169
See Colorado for a description of this group.

Lost Horse Ranch
Route 10, Box 110B, Santa Fe, NM 87501, (505) 471-8028

Northern New Mexico Animal Protection Society
P.O. Box 428, Santa Cruz, NM 87567

Public Lands Action Network
P.O. Box 712, Placitas, NM 87043

Sangre de Cristo Animal Protection, Inc. (SdeCAP)
P.O. Box 11395, Albuquerque, NM 87192, (505) 281-0032, FAX: (505) 281-0083
Statewide. Provides extensive humane education, pursues animal advocacy, and offers a wide variety of community services to people and their animals.

NEW YORK

For additional resources for breed rescue, ferret rescue, wildlife rehabilitation, etc., see "Keeping Up-To-Date" at the front of the chapter.

American Fund for Alternatives to Animal Research
New York, NY
See "National & International Organizations."

American Society for the Prevention of Cruelty to Animals
National Office: New York, NY
See "National & International Organizations."

Animal Defense League (ADL)
743 Teall Avenue, #6, Syracuse, NY 13206
Anti-fur, etc.

Animal Haven, Inc.
35-22 Prince Street, Flushing, NY 11354, (718) 886-3683
No-kill adoption shelter for abandoned cats and dogs. Lifetime care for elderly cats or those with feline leukemia or brain damage. Also accepts animals whose owners have made arrangements for care after the owner's death.

Animal Liberation
319 West 74th Street, New York, NY 10023, (212) 874-1792
Vegetarians active in animal welfare and anti-vivisection.

Animal News Network
Garrison, NY

See "National & International Organizations."

Animal Protection League
P.O. Box 8, Whitesboro, NY 13492, (315) 724-5374, President: Frances Adams, Spokesperson: Iris Perry
Spay/neuter assistance, help in placing unwanted animals, and pet food and veterinary assistance to indigent owners.

Animal Rights Action League (ARAL)
P.O. Box 1323, Saratoga Springs, NY 12866, (518) 587-6742
Works to raise public awareness about institutionalized animal abuse. Encourages and provides support for vegetarianism/veganism.

Animal Rights Advocates of Upstate New York, Inc.
P.O. Box 18415, Rochester, NY 14618, (716) 461-1332
Educates the general public regarding the various abuses and exploitation of animals. Main areas of concentration are fur, experimentation, and animals in entertainment.

Animal Rights Advocates of Western New York
P.O. Box 475, Amherst, NY 14240

Animal Rights International
New York, NY
See "National & International Organizations." law.

Animal Service League, Inc.
P.O. Box 90737, Rochester, NY 14609-0737, (716) 621-0364
Foster care and adoption for needy companion animals.

Animal Welfare Alliance
P.O. Box 673, Harrison, NY 10528, (914) 232-3204
Fights animal abuses of every type.

Animals and the Environment
(formerly Help The Zoo)
P.O. Box 428, Watertown, NY 13601-0428, (315) 782-1858
Statewide. Works on animal rights/ecology issues not addressed by other groups. Currently trying to get a low-cost spay/neuter program in Jefferson County, and working on a badly needed federal zoo/circus law.

Animals in Politics
P.O. Box 1280, New York, NY 10023

Beauty Without Cruelty USA
New York, NY
See "National & International Organizations."

Binghamton Animal Rights Coalition (B.A.R.C.)
P.O. Box 2000 SA, State University of New York, Binghamton, NY 13901
Focuses on educating the surrounding community as well as students on campus.

The CARING Corps, Inc. (Community of Animal Rescuers In New York's Grassroots)
ATTN: Livi French, Box 319, Gracie Station, New York, NY 10028, (212) 737-9358 (24-hours)
A network and clearinghouse for NYC private companion animal rescuers and activists. Addresses all dog/cat issues, including spay/neuter legislation and assistance, municipal animal control, humane education, domestic violence, and the child abuse/animal abuse connection. Community outreach, including the Store Cat Initiative. Produces "City Kitties, Urban Pups" television show.

Carriage Horse Action Committee (CHAC)
P.O. Box 1280, New York, NY 10023
A coalition of concerned citizens dedicated to ending the abuse of New York City carriage horses.

Christians Helping Animals and People, Inc.
Selden, NY
See "National & International Organizations."

Citizens Committee for Animal Rights
P.O. Box 483, Jackson Heights, NY 11372

Citizens Committee for Laboratory Animal Liberation
New York, NY
See "National & International Organizations."

Citizens for Alternatives to Animal Labs, Inc. (CAAL)
96 Henry Street, #6B, Brooklyn, NY 11201, (718) 522-8274

CIVIS / Civitas
Hartsdale, NY
See "National & International Organizations."

- **Coalition for Non-Violent Food**
- **Coalition to Abolish the LD50 & Draize Tests**
- **Coalition to Abolish Classroom Dissection**

New York, NY
See Animal Rights International in "National & International Organizations."

Coalition to Liberate Animals Worldwide (C.L.A.W.)
P.O. Box 81, Staten Island, NY 10312, (718) 317-5303
New York Metro area, with an international focus. Seeks to effect fundamental societal changes to alleviate suffering by nonhuman and human animals caused by humans.

Coalition to Prevent the Destruction of Canada Geese
P.O. Box 284, Tomkins Cove, NY 10986

Coalition to Protect Animals in Parks and Refuges
Swain, NY
See "National & International Organizations."

The Committee to Abolish Sport Hunting, Inc.
Tomkins Cove, NY
See "National & International Organizations."

Companion Animal Network (C.A.N.)
P.O. Box 05094, Brooklyn, NY 11205, (718) 544-PETS (7387)
Works to stop the needless killing and abandonment of cats and dogs in NYC. At this writing, was about to begin a corporate acquisition attempt of the NYC ASPCA, "in hopes of wresting control away from Wall Street 'parasites' (and even animal hunters) who have for a hundred years 'owned' and ruined this once most noble of all institutions." Already successful in introducing legislation to repeal NYC ASPCA's exclusive animal control contract with NYC and remove a ban on boroughs establishing their own societies. Computerized matchmaking services for people and pets. (*Note*: Allegations against the ASPCA are made by this organization, not by the author.)

Cornell Students for the Ethical Treatment of Animals (CSETA)
Willard Straight Hall Box 39, Cornell University, Ithaca, NY 14853
"One of the most active college animal welfare groups in the country."

The Cousteau Society, Inc.
New York, NY
See "National & International Organizations."

Farm Sanctuary—East
Watkins Glen, NY
See "National & International Organizations."

Feline Rescue, Inc.
P.O. Box A50, Radio City Station, New York, NY 10101, (212) 489-0404
No-kill shelter, adoption, and spay/neuter services for cats. Traps available for loan.

Feminists for Animal Rights
Editorial Office: New York, NY
See "National & International Organizations."

Fight Against Animal Cruelty in Europe
Garrison, NY
See "National & International Organizations."

Friends of Animals
New York Office: 1841 Broadway, #212, New York, NY 10023, (212) 247-8120
See "National & International Organizations."

Friends of Beaversprite
Little Falls, NY
See "National & International Organizations."

The Fund for Animals, Inc.
- National Office: New York, NY
- Field Office: Marion Stark (New York Coordinator), P.O. Box 9029, Albany, NY 12209, (518) 439-2631

See "National & International Organizations."

Hawk Hideaway Wildlife Rehabilitation Center
3086 Haskell Road, Cuba, NY 14727-9402

Henry Bergh Coalition, Inc. (HBC)
ATTN: Livi French, Box 319, Gracie Station, New York, NY 10028, (212) 737-9358 (24-hours)
An open-membership, dues-free "watchdog" coalition of animal activists, NYC taxpayers, and dissatisfied ASPCA members. Striving to restore to the American Society for the Prevention of Cruelty to Animals (ASPCA) founder Henry Bergh's humane vision and to make the ASPCA accountable for "mis-spending donor and taxpayer monies and for years of indifference to animal suffering." Does not accept donations. (*Note*: Allegations against the ASPCA are made by this organization, not by the author.)

Humane Education Committee
New York, NY
See "National & International Organizations."

Humane Society of the United States
See New Jersey for the regional HSUS office that serves this state.

The Institute for the Development of Earth Awareness
New York, NY
See "National & International Organizations."

International League of Doctors for the Abolition of Vivisection
c/o CIVIS/Civitas, Swain, NY
See "National & International Organizations."

Justice For Animals
P.O. Box 4044, Flushing, NY 11360, (718) 225-4103
Sponsors events in the tri-state. Dedicated to the abolition of animal suffering through protests, tabling, concerts, school speaking events, and more. Works all over the country.

Kent Animal Shelter, Inc.
River Road, Calverton, NY 11933, (516) 727-5731
No-kill adoption shelter.

League for Animal Protection of Huntington, Inc. (LAP)
P.O. Box 390, Huntington, NY 11743-0390, Cats: (516) 757-4517, Dogs: (516) 757-9373
Dedicated to the rescue, care, and rehabilitation of cats and dogs.

Learning Alliance
494 Broadway, New York, NY 10012, (212) 226-7171
Works in conjunction with community and social change organizations to bring quality educational programs to the metropolitan area.

The Livestock Liberation Group
P.O. Box 275, Stone Ridge, NY 12484
An animal rights group and sister organization of Noah's Ark—The Horse Rescue Group (see their listing elsewhere in this section).

Medical Research Modernization Committee
New York, NY
See "National & International Organizations."

Mid-Hudson Animal Aid, Inc.
60 Simmons Lane, Beacon, NY 12508, (914) 831-4321
No-kill adoption shelter for cats and foster homes for dogs.

Monroe County Alliance for Wildlife Protection
P.O. Box 90854, Rochester, NY 14609

New York Ferret's Rights Advocacy
David Guthartz (Executive President), 94 Jeffery Lane, Oceanside, NY 11572, (516) 536-6615

New Yorkers for Companion Animals (NYCA)
1324 Lexington Avenue, New York, NY 10128, (212) 427-8273
No-kill animal rescue, adoption, and advocacy. No shelter; only foster homes. Exclusively for strays.

Nine Lives Productions
43-23 Colden Street, Suite 8E, Flushing, NY 11355, (718) 445-4190
Produces half-hour and one-hour talk shows and documentaries intended for cable television. Subjects include health, vegetarian cooking, and fur. (See the Radio & Television Programming section of Chapter 12 for more information.)

Noah's Ark—The Horse Rescue Group
P.O. Box 275, Stone Ridge, NY 12484
A tiny volunteer group whose single purpose is to save horses, mules, and ponies from

slaughter. Attends horse auctions and tries to outbid those buying horses to sell as meat ("meat buyers"). Needs: a working trailer, more volunteers, more funds.

North Shore Animal League International, Inc.
Lewyt Street, Port Washington, NY 11050, (516) 883-7575, FAX: (516) 944-5732
No-kill adoption shelter. Veterinary hospital and emergency medical services.

Panorama Horse Sanctuary
2848 Lynn Road, Branchport, NY 14418, (315) 595-6129

Peace Plantation Animal Sanctuary
Walton, NY
See "National & International Organizations."

People Against Cruelty to Animals
720 Arsenal Street, Watertown, NY 13601

People for Animal Rights
P.O. Box 358, Syracuse, NY 13215, (315) 488-7877 or 488-9338

People for Animals
92 Carriage Court, Farmington, NY 14425

Pet Connection
12935 Williston Road, East Aurora, NY 14052

Pet Pride of New York, Inc.
- Street Address: 3 Mendon-Ionia Road
- Mailing Address: P.O. Box 338, Mendon, NY 14506, (716) 582-1088

Statewide. No-kill shelter and humane society devoted exclusively to cats.

The Pet Savers Foundation, Inc. SPAY/USA
Port Washington, NY
See "National & International Organizations."

Pioneers for Animal Welfare Society (PAWS)
Box 861, Hicksville, NY 11802

Prevention of Cruelty to Animals & Plants
North American Office: Corona, NY
See "National & International Organizations."

Saratoga County Animal Welfare League (SCAWL)
ATTN: Phyllis Shulman, President, P.O. Box 142, Saratoga Springs, NY 12866, (518) 587-8530
No-kill rescue organization.

Save Our Strays, Inc.
P.O. Box 021286, Brooklyn, NY 11202, (718) 332-3956
No-kill adoption shelter.

Sentient Creatures, Inc.
P.O. Box 765, Cathedral Station, New York, NY 10025, (212) 865-5998
Rescues, cares for, and adopts out "junkyard" animals.

Shawangunk Nature Preserve
RD 1, Box 651, Cold Brook, NY 13324, (315) 826-7405
Adirondack State Park. A private 300-acre preserve that cherishes and protects the environment and all living on it. Library, trails, gift shop, canoes, retreat cottage, etc.

Society for the Prevention of Cruelty to Animals (SPCA)
Black River Road, Watertown, NY 13601
Investigates animal abuse cases at the local level. Houses homeless domesticated animals (mostly dogs, cats, and horses, occasionally cows or pigs) in a no-kill shelter.

SPAY/USA
Port Washington, NY
See The Pet Savers Foundation, Inc. in "National & International Organizations."

SPCA Serving Allegany County
P.O. Box 381, Wellsville, NY 14895, (716) 593-2200, FAX: (716) 437-2510
No-kill shelter offering pet care education and consulting, a school humane education program, lost/found service, an aggressive adoption/foster care program, and cruelty investigations. Also active in combating pet theft. Spays/neuters all adoptees.

Students for the Ethical Treatment of Animals
New York University, Student Activities Office, 21 Washington Place—Box 36, New York, NY 10003, (212) 998-4700 (Student Activities Annex—the receptionist will take a message and leave it in the club mailbox)

Educates and activates the New York University community on the many facets of animal suffering and exploitation.

The True Nature Network
New York, NY
See "National & International Organizations."

Total Animal Liberation
P.O. Box 2345, New York, NY 10108, (212) 967-4818 (late evenings)
An independent activist and strong abolitionist who works to educate the public on all areas of animal exploitation and abuse.

Unitarian Universalists For the Ethical Treatment of Animals
New York, NY
See "National & International Organizations."

United Action for Animals, Inc.
New York, NY
See "National & International Organizations."

Volunteers for Animal Welfare
P.O. Box 509, Northport, NY 11768

Volunteers for Wildlife, Inc.
P.O. Box 427, Cold Spring Harbor, NY 11724-0427, (516) 423-0982
Rehabilitates birds and small mammals.

Whiskers Animal Benevolent League
P.O. Box 11190, Albany, NY 12211-0190, (518) 448-9565
No-kill adoption shelter for cats and dogs. Screens potential adopters and requires spay/neuter. Also behavioral advice, food distribution to the needy, and lost/found. Maintains a list of pet-friendly landlords.

Wildlife Rehabilitation and Education Network
ATTN: Sue McDonough, P.O. Box 126, Cropseyville, NY 12052, (518) 279-9768
Cares for wildlife and educates people to see wildlife as something other than "harvestable natural resources." Rehabilitates orphaned and injured wildlife.

Women and Animals—Activist Archive/ Vegetarian Activist Collective
c/o Connie Salamone, 184 Seeley Street, Brooklyn, NY 11201, (718) 435-3998

Woodstock Animal Rights Movement (WARM)
P.O. Box 746, Woodstock, NY 12498, (914) 679-2072
Statewide, with concentration in the Woodstock area. Concerned with all areas of animal rights. Operates The WARM Store, in Woodstock, which offers cruelty-free, environmentally-friendly, and animal rights products.

NORTH CAROLINA

For additional resources for breed rescue, ferret rescue, wildlife rehabilitation, etc., see "Keeping Up-To-Date" at the front of the chapter.

Adopt-A-Rabbit Program
P.O. Box 554, Faith, NC 28041

Corolla Wild Horse Fund
Box 361-PMM, Corolla, NC 27927, (919) 453-8152

Culture and Animals Foundation
Raleigh, NC
See "National & International Organizations."

Feminists for Animal Rights
National Headquarters: Chapel Hill, NC
See "National & International Organizations."

Forsyth Humane Society
P.O. Box 15605, Winston-Salem, NC 27113-5605, (910) 721-1303
No-kill shelter. Spay/neuter and lost/found assistance.

Genesis Animal Sanctuary, Inc.
225 Upper Grouse Ridge Road, Beech Mountain, NC 28604, (704) 387-2979
Wildlife sanctuary. Also picks up injured domesticated animals. Member of The North Carolina Network for Animals (see their listing elsewhere in this state).

Humane Society of Charlotte
P.O. Box 221028, Charlotte, NC 28222, (704) 377-0534, FAX: (704) 525-9353
Dedicated to the promotion of animal welfare, preventing cruelty to animals, providing care for unwanted and distressed animals, and educating the public in proper animal care. Shelters dogs, cats, rabbits, and potbellied pigs.

Humane Society of the United States
See Tennessee for the regional HSUS office that serves this state.

The International Society for Cow Protection
Efland, NC
See "National & International Organizations."

Justice For Animals
P.O. Box 33051, Raleigh, NC 27636
Statewide. Focuses on laws affecting animals.

The North Carolina Network for Animals, Inc. (NCNA)
Home Office: P.O. Box 33565, Raleigh, NC 27636, 1-800-280-NCNA
Computers: Dial into Wilmington 80 BBS and log on to the NCNA area. To get connected, call (910) 763-1850.
Statewide, with chapters in Asheville, Beech Mountain, Charlotte, Durham-Chapel Hill, Fayetteville, Greensboro, Roanoke Rapids, Wake County, and Winston-Salem. Contact the Raleigh office for the chapter nearest you. Works in a variety of ways to stop exploitation of animals. Works closely with animal rights organizations at a number of major colleges and universities in North Carolina.

North Carolina Wildlife Telecommunications Center
(919) 662-4381
24-hour referral to the wildlife rehabilitator closest to you in North Carolina.

NORTH DAKOTA

For additional resources for breed rescue, ferret rescue, wildlife rehabilitation, etc., see "Keeping Up-To-Date" at the front of the chapter.

Humane Society of the United States
See Illinois for the regional HSUS office that serves this state.

Pembina Hills Wildlife Rehabilitation Center
Route 1, Box 3, Mountain, ND 58262, (701) 993-8793
Provides services for raptors and other wildlife, specializing in great horned owls, hawks, and fawns.

OHIO

For additional resources for breed rescue, ferret rescue, wildlife rehabilitation, etc., see "Keeping Up-To-Date" at the front of the chapter.

Animal Liberation Action
Regional Contact: Columbus, OH, (614) 297-7071 (Mark Jacobson)
See "National & International Organizations."

Animal Rights Community (ARC)
P.O. Box 31455, Cincinnati, OH 45231, (513) 542-6810
Greater Cincinnati and Northern Kentucky. Educates the public and creates grassroots awareness in order to stop animal abuse.

Ashtabula County Humane Society
P.O. Box 42, Jefferson, OH 44047

Bide-A-Wee Cat Shelter
8800 Akins Road, North Royalton, OH 44133, (216) 582-4990
No-kill adoption shelter for cats located in a "spacious ranch house nestled in two acres of land." Recognizes cat ownership as a privilege and a significant responsibility, and reserves the right to refuse adoptions.

Cat Welfare Association, Inc.
736 Wetmore Road, Columbus, OH 43214, (614) 268-6096
No-kill adoption shelter for cats.

Ferret Sense—Shelter
c/o Linda Harrah, 128 First Street, Box 61, Buckeye Lake, OH 43008, (614) 929-3392
No-kill shelter for ferrets. Rescues, adoptions, and advice on care and training. All ferrets adopted out are spayed/neutered.

Geauga Humane Society, Inc.
P.O. Box 342, Chardon, OH 44024, (216) 285-3897
No-kill adoption shelter.

Health, Ecology, and Animal Liberation (HEAL)

c/o Randy Shields, 800 East Rose Street, Springfield, OH 45505, (513) 323-3064
Primarily Clark County, but also Greene and Champaign Counties. A small, local, loosely organized group that does "anything and everything."

Helping Our Pets Everywhere (HOPE)

P.O. Box 474, New Albany, OH 43054, (614) 855-2494
"Dedicated to all animals, and to the kind people who find love and truth in the eyes of creatures who speak without words." Provides support and assistance to caretakers who, due to debilitating illness or poverty brought on by disability or age, are unable to keep their pets without help. Has provided foster care for a variety of animals, including dogs, cats, birds, rabbits, and chickens. Some animals are available for adoption, others are placed permanently in foster homes.

Humane Society of Delaware County (HSDC)

4920 State Route 37 East, Delaware, OH 43015, (614) 548-PETS (7387)
Central Ohio. Rescues and attempts to find homes for abandoned dogs and cats. Investigates cruelty cases. Sponsors a low-cost spay/neuter clinic. Serves vegetarian food at fundraisers.

Humane Society of the United States

Great Lakes Regional Office: Sandy Rowland, Director, 745 Haskins Street, Bowling Green, OH 43402-1696, (419) 352-5141, FAX: (419) 354-5351
Serves OH, IN, MI, and WV. See "National & International Organizations."

Medina County Wildlife Rescue

10420 Spencer Lake, Spencer,OH 44275, (216) 667-2386
Assists the game warden in rescuing all species. Specializes in raccoons.

Network for Ohio Animal Action (NOAA)

P.O. Box 21004, Cleveland, OH 44121-0004, (216) 691-0662
Cleveland area and statewide. The largest animal rights group in Ohio. Promotes and protects the rights of all species.

North Coast Humane Society

P.O. Box 09463, Cleveland, OH 44109, (216) 661-2292
Cares for homeless animals through volunteer foster homes. Spay/neuter, cruelty investigations, and public education. Monitors local companion animal activities.

Northlook Wild Bird Rescue

4721 E. Lake Road, Sheffield Lake, OH 44054-1401, (216) 949-7057
Rescues small mammals as well as various types of birds.

Ohio Humane Education Association (OHEA)

P.O. Box 546, Grove City, OH 43123-0546, (614) 875-1810
Statewide. Works to extend humane education and to intercede on behalf of animals to change situations or practices in which cruelty, neglect, or unnecessary suffering exists. Teaching units available on pets, wildlife, and farm animals for grades K-2 and 3-6.

Ohio Legislation for Animal Welfare Coalition (Ohio LAW Coalition)

P.O. Box 21761, Columbus, OH 43221-0761, (614) 491-2069
Statewide. Monitors committee hearings on bills before the Ohio General Assembly.

Our Animal Rights Committee

1501 East McMillan, Cincinnati, OH 45206

People/Animals Network (P/AN)

P.O. Box 70, Dayton, OH 45402, (513) 461-5906
Dayton and surrounding area. Multi-issue organization that works to further the rights of animals to be treated with respect and to live free of exploitation and suffering.

Pet Birth Control Clinics

Box 19143, Cleveland, OH 44119, (216) 531-1512
Convinced city officials to implement the city of Cleveland spay/neuter clinic. Continues to publicize the clinic.

Progressive Animal Welfare Society Adoption Center, Inc. (PAWS)

2790 Cincinnati-Dayton Road, Middletown, OH 45042, (513) 422-7297
A shelter and adoption center for abused, abandoned, or neglected animals.

Protect Our Earth's Treasures (P.O.E.T.)
P.O. Box 10156, Columbus, OH 43201-0656, (614) 224-4598
Central Ohio. Opposes all forms of animal exploitation and abuse. Also monitors state legislation.

SPARE (Save Pets from Abuse, Research, and Euthanasia)
P.O. Box 295, Yellow Springs, OH 45387-0295, (513) 331-0934, FAX: (513) 322-4134
Works on behalf of companion animals in the greater Greene County area. After a four-year battle, succeeded in stopping the sale of Greene County pound animals to Wright State University (Dayton, Ohio). Sued Wright State and achieved two precedent-setting "open records" wins, one gaining access to research records and the other access to research committee meetings. Monitors animal research at the university.

Stand Up For Animal Rights
P.O. Box 4666, Parkersburg, WV 26104-4666, (304) 375-3849
Parkersburg, WV and Marietta, OH. See West Virginia for a description of this group.

S.T.O.P. (Stop The Overpopulation of Pets)
P.O. Box 3865, Mansfield, OH 44907
Low-cost spay/neuter assistance.

Students for Animal Rights
c/o University of Dayton Campus Ministry, 300 College Park, Dayton, OH 45469-2271
Wants to hear from any student animal rights activists interested in forming a network.

Students for Animals
c/o Student Organizations and Leadership Development, Wright State University, Dayton, OH 45435
Campus animal rights group.

Students for the Ethical Treatment of Animals / Student Organization for Animal Rights
Ohio State University, Baker Center Front Desk, 20 East Union, Athens, OH 45701
College and high school students organized to network with others across the nation for the protection of all animals. Wants to hear from any student animal rights activists interested in forming a network.

Toledoans for Animal Rights (T.A.R.)
c/o Hal Hamer, 2655 Calverton, Toledo, OH 43607, (419) 536-4073
Actively involved in issues concerning the welfare of animals.

Wittenberg Animal Rights Club
Mattheis House/Student Activities, Wittenberg University, Springfield, OH 45501
Works to educate the (conservative) University campus and surrounding community.

Wyandot County Humane Society
9640 County Highway 330, Upper Sandusky, OH 43351, (419) 294-4477 (24-hour answering service)
"No animal is ever turned away." Services include cruelty investigations and wildlife rehabilitation.

Youngstown Area Animal Protectionists, Inc. (YAAP)
P.O. Box 11102, Youngstown, OH 44511, (216) 792-4139 (D'Amico) or 743-4300 (business phone)
Active in the areas of fur, factory farming, laboratory animals, product testing, and animals in entertainment.

OKLAHOMA

For additional resources for breed rescue, ferret rescue, wildlife rehabilitation, etc., see "Keeping Up-To-Date" at the front of the chapter.

Council for Animal Awareness
915 Linda, Ada, OK 74820

Free To Live
P.O. Box 130072, Edmond, OK 73013-0072, (405) 282-8617
No-kill adoption shelter.

Greyhounds As Pets (GAP)
Springfield, CO
See Colorado for a description of this group and the representative that serves Oklahoma.

Humane Society of the United States
See Texas for the regional HSUS office that serves this state.
P.O. Box 13190, Oklahoma City, OK 73113, (405) 277-3779

Last Chance for Life, Inc.

P.O. Box 13190, Oklahoma City, OK 73113, (405) 277-3779

A 20-acre, no-kill adoption shelter, currently housing dogs, cats, a potbellied pig, rabbits, and coyotes.

Northeastern Oklahoma Animal Helpers (NOAH)

P.O. Box 0145, Tulsa, OK 74101

Oklahomans for the Ethical Treatment of Animals

P.O. Box 162, Norman, OK 73070, (405) 329-5906

Petfinders Animal Welfare Society, Inc.

P.O. Box 7083, Moore, OK 73153, (405) 794-3332 (voice/FAX)

No-kill adoption shelter.

Save Our Critters

c/o Debbie Smith, Route 1, Box 46, Tipton, OK 73570, (405) 481-6474 (work), (405) 569-2687 (home)

Ferret rescue and a 17-page *Basics to Caring for a Ferret* booklet for $1. Urges anyone with ferret questions or problems to write or call.

Second Chance Animal Sanctuary

P.O. Box 1266, Norman, OK 73070-1266, (405) 321-1915, FAX: (405) 366-8984

No-kill adoption shelter for dogs, cats, and occasional other small animals (birds, rabbits, etc.).

Volunteers for Animal Welfare

P.O. Box 20061, Oklahoma City, OK 73156

Wings Haven

Route 6, Box 61, Stillwater, OK 74074

OREGON

For additional resources for breed rescue, ferret rescue, wildlife rehabilitation, etc., see "Keeping Up-To-Date" at the front of the chapter.

Action for Animals

P.O. Box 5566, Bend, OR 97708-5566, (503) 388-1927

Cascades Raptor Center (CRC) & Environmental Learning Program

P.O. Box 5386, Eugene, OR 97405, (503) 485-1320 (24-hour hotline for injured or orphaned raptors)

Dedicated to preserving a healthy and viable population of birds of prey and other wildlife in their natural habitat. Two primary goals are rehabilitation and release, and public education.

Citizens for Animal Rights, Eugene (CARE)

P.O. Box 1924, Eugene, OR 97440, (503) 485-2237

A strictly educational group that uses tabling, speakers, demonstrations, and a newsletter to alert the community to the exploitation of animals.

Committed Alliance To Strays, Inc. (CATS)

- Mailing Address: P.O. Box 56, Medford, OR 97501, (541) 779-2916
- Shelter: 104 N. Ross Lane, Medford, OR 97501

No-kill adoption shelter and services for cats.

Dogs for the Deaf, Inc.

Central Point, OR

See "National & International Organizations."

Free Flight Bird and Marine Mammal Rehabilitation

1185 Portland Avenue, Bandon, OR 97411, (503) 347-3882

A rehabilitation center for wildlife, specializing in birds of prey and marine mammals. Offers public educational programs.

The Fund for Animals, Inc.

Field Office: Cathy Sue and Roger Anunsen (Oregon Coordinators), 5778 Commercial Street SE, Salem, OR 97306, (503) 588-1175

See "National & International Organizations."

Humane Society of the United States

See California for the regional HSUS office that serves this state.

Honey Foundation

Salem, OR

See "National & International Organizations."

Oregon Greyhound Rescue

8407 NE Fremont, Suite 109, Portland, OR 97220, (503) 257-7220

Works to place retired racing and sometimes AKC greyhounds into loving and lifelong adoptive homes. Accepts greyhounds regardless of condition or age. Program includes rescue and foster care, adoption, pet therapy, and public relations. Their goal is to promote responsible pet ownership through education, support, and example. Adoptions are finalized only after a 90-day probationary period.

People for Animal Rights

3430 SE Belmont Street, P.O. Box 3582, Portland, OR 97208, (503) 230-0892

Dedicated to promoting animal protection through education, legislation, and direct action.

The Rhino Trust

Portland, OR

See "National & International Organizations."

Spay and Neuter Humane Association

333 W. Marine Drive, Astoria, OR 97103, (503) 325-7729

No-kill adoption shelter. Low-income assistance.

World Mission for Animals (WMA)

Glendale, OR

See "National & International Organizations."

PENNSYLVANIA

For additional resources for breed rescue, ferret rescue, wildlife rehabilitation, etc., see "Keeping Up-To-Date" at the front of the chapter.

Adopt-A-Cow

Port Royal, PA

See "National & International Organizations."

Alternatives Research & Development Foundation

Jenkintown, PA

See "National & International Organizations."

The American Anti-Vivisection Society

Jenkintown, PA

See "National & International Organizations."

Animal Advocates, Inc.

P.O. Box 8480, Pittsburgh, PA 15220, (412) 928-9777, Contact Person: Tracey A. Eakin

Statewide; most activities in Southwestern PA. Uses community outreach and education to eliminate animal suffering and exploitation.

Animal Care and Welfare, Inc. / SPCA (AC&W/SPCA)

P.O. Box 8257, Pittsburgh, PA 15218-0257, (412) 244-1372, Hours: 8 a.m.-6 p.m.

Statewide. Educates the public about animal welfare issues and encourages animal owner responsibility. Statewide law enforcement agency.

Animal Care Fund, Inc.

Animal Care Sanctuary, P.O. Box A, East Smithfield, PA 18817, (717) 596-2200

No-kill sanctuary for hundreds of cats and dogs, plus a pig, chickens, rabbits, and ducks. Pets are left to them in wills with money to support the animals' lifetime care.

Animal Friends, Inc.

2643 Penn Avenue, Pittsburgh, PA 15222-4621, (412) 566-2103, FAX: (412) 391-4620

No-kill adoption shelter.

Animal Liberation Action

Regional Contact: Pittsburgh, PA, (412) 521-8231 (Matt Ball)

See "National & International Organizations."

Animal Passion

P.O. Box 22242, Pittsburgh, PA 15222, (412) 734-8997

Conducts theatrical demonstrations and leafleting to educate the public of the exploitation of wildlife and animals in the food, clothing, entertainment, and research industries. Complimentary copy of their newsletter.

ANIPAC

(Political Action Committee for Animals in Pennsylvania)

P.O. Box 6024, Pittsburgh, PA 15211, (412) 381-0104

Statewide. A Political Action Committee (PAC) that politically empowers charitable animal protection organizations prohibited by law from engaging in any political or substantial lobbying activity.

Bird Rescue / York County
125 W. Jackson Street, York, PA 17403-2265, (717) 854-2604
Rehabilitates songbirds and water fowl.

Central Pennsylvanians For Animal Rights (C.P.F.A.R.)
P.O. Box 5228, Harrisburg, PA 17110, (717) 233-0901
Note: C.P.F.A.R. is pronounced "See-Far." Working to eliminate the exploitation of all animals and for laws that will protect animals from exploitation at the hands of humans.

Citizens for Animals
P.O. Box 7, La Plume, PA 18440-0007

Delaware Valley Raptor Center
RD#2, Box 9335, Milford, PA 18337, (717) 296-6025 (relocating to Cumberland Hills Road)
Provides humane, professional care to orphaned, ill, and injured raptors so they can be returned to the wild. Works to foster a greater appreciation and respect for all wildlife.

Francisvale Home for Smaller Animals
P.O. Box 282, Wayne, PA 19087, (215) 688-1018
No-kill adoption shelter.

Fran's Ferret Rescue
Fran Wiles, Director, 870 Barlow Greenmount Road, Gettysburg, PA 17325-8711, (717) 337-0045

The Fund for Animals, Inc.
Field Office: Robin Lord (PA Coordinator), P.O. Box 29445, Philadelphia, PA 19125, (215) 634-5494
See "National & International Organizations."

Green Acres Sanctuary
c/o Carole Morton, RD 2, Box 62, Rockwood, PA 15557
A society for the prevention of cruelty to animals that shelters farm animals removed from abuse/neglect situations. Conducts humane education. Enforces the animal protection statutes through investigation and prosecution. Home to 85 previously abused/neglected animals. You can financially "adopt" an animal for $15.

Harness Horse Retirement and Youth Association, Inc. (HHRYA)
Anne McCloskey, Director, RR 1, Box 81, Loganton, PA 17747, (717) 725-7979
"Horsemen helping horsemen for the betterment of the breed." Places noncompetitive Standardbred Race Horses in loving adoptive homes. Objectives are to promote, foster, and provide for the retired Standardbred's well-being.

Hope for the Animals
P.O. Box 877, Morrisville, PA 19067
A small, no-kill shelter.

Humane Society of the United States
See New Jersey for the regional HSUS office that serves this state.

In Defense of Animal Rights (IDAR)
P.O. Box 1124, Reading, PA 19603, (610) 670-5544

International Network for Religion and Animals
North Wales, PA
See "National & International Organizations."

International Society for Animal Rights, Inc.
Clarks Summit, PA
See "National & International Organizations."

Kitty & K-9 Connection
P.O. Box 312, Drexel Hill, PA 19026, (215) 622-0151
Provides foster homes, rehabilitation, low-cost spay/neuter, and adoption services.

Lehigh Valley Animal Rights Coalition
P.O. Box 3224, Allentown, PA 18106, (610) 821-9552
Works to educate the public about the terrible abuse and exploitation of animals in society today, and opposes the use, abuse, and exploitation of animals whenever and wherever it occurs. Outreach tables, lobbying, letter-writing, demonstrations, etc.

Make Peace With Animals, Inc.
New Hope, PA
See "National & International Organizations."

Mobilization For Animals, Pennsylvania, Inc. (MFA/PA)
- State Office: P.O. Box 688, Harrisburg, PA 17108, (717) 780-1531
- Erie Area Chapter: P.O. Box 10692, Erie, PA 16514, (814) 870-9402
- West Moreland County Chapter: P.O. Box 112, Youngwood, PA 15697, (412) 838-1730

Statewide. Multi-issue group whose main issues include the Hegins Pigeon Shoot, fur, bear wrestling, marine mammal captivity at Hershey Park, and vegetarian/vegan education.

National Greyhound Adoption Program
Philadelphia, PA
See "National & International Organizations."

No More Victims
P.O. Box 56, Dalton, PA 18414-0056
Animal rights with an emphasis on greyhound racing.

Paws, Inc.
P.O. Box 344, Federal Square Station, Harrisburg, PA 17108

Penn State Alliance for Animal Rights
Hetzel Union Building Main Desk, University Park, PA 16802, (814) 234-1474
E-mail: L-AAR@PSUVM.PSU.EDU
Internet: http://www.envirolink.org/fcg/aar
State College and Centre County area, including University Park campus of Penn State. Focuses on education and activism.

Pennsylvania Animal Welfare Society (PAWS)
P.O. Box 16246, Philadelphia, PA 19114-0246, (215) 322-PAWS

People Living Ethically with Animals, Inc. (PLEA, Inc.)
356 Goucher Street, Suite 813, Johnstown, PA 15905
Education, outreach, and legislation to protect all sentient creatures.

Philly Paws
1234 Locust Street, Philadelphia, PA 19107, (215) 985-0206
Helps people with AIDS take care of their companion animals.

PLAN (Pennsylvania Legislative Animal Network)
P.O. Box 12085, Harrisburg, PA 17108, (717) 233-5770, FAX: (717) 233-0611
Lobbies in favor of animal protection issues.

Political Action Committee for Animals in Pennsylvania
See ANIPAC.

Ryers Farm for Aged Equines
Soleil Farm, 1710 Ridge Road, Rt. 23, RD #2, Pottstown, PA 19465, (610) 469-0533

Schuylkill Wildlife Rehabilitation Center
8480 Hagy's Mill Road, Philadelphia, PA 19128-1998, (215) 482-8217, FAX: (215) 482-8158
(A division of the Schuylkill Center for Environmental Education) A fully licensed wildlife rehabilitation and release facility serving both furred and feathered patients free of charge. Also conducts educational programs. The Center is closed to the public.

The Spayed Club
P.O. Box 1145, Frazer, PA 19355, (610) 275-7486 (24-hour hotline)
Delaware Valley. Low-cost dog and cat spay/neuter program. A branch of United Humanitarians. Functions are all vegan.

Spay Neuter All Pets, Inc.
See Maryland for a description of this group.

Stray Cat Blues
P.O. Box 106, Sumneytown, PA 18084, (215) 234-8284
A one-woman barn cat adoption/rescue effort. All cats are neutered and vet checked before placement. "Place Your Pet Yourself Guidelines" available for a self-addressed, stamped envelope.

Students for Animal Protection (SAP)
Marc Freligh, Chairperson, P.O. Box 39, Cochranville, PA 19330
Mostly a resource and referral group for students. Primary issues are vegetarianism, cosmetic testing, and dissection.

United Humanitarians
Philadelphia, PA
See "National & International Organizations."

Wildlife Preservation Trust International
Philadelphia, PA
See "National & International Organizations."

Women's Humane Society
Ben Salem, PA
See "National & International Organizations."

RHODE ISLAND

For additional resources for breed rescue, ferret rescue, wildlife rehabilitation, etc., see "Keeping Up-To-Date" at the front of the chapter.

Defenders of Animals
Box 5634, Weybosset Hill Station, Providence, RI 02903, (401) 738-3710, E-mail: hqng24A@prodigy.com
Legislation, legal action, pet placement, low-cost spay/neuter, and anti-hunting issues.

Elephants in Captivity Fund
166 Everett Avenue, Providence, RI 02906, (401) 521-0767

Friends of Animals
Rhode Island Office: 342 Broadway, Newport, RI 02840, (401) 847-DEER
See "National & International Organizations."

Humane Society of the United States
See Connecticut for the regional HSUS office that serves this state.

Rhode Island Animal Rights Coalition
P.O. Box 3463, Peace Dale, RI 02883, (401) 823-8955 (Linda Leonard)

SOUTH CAROLINA

For additional resources for breed rescue, ferret rescue, wildlife rehabilitation, etc., see "Keeping Up-To-Date" at the front of the chapter.

AWARE (Advocates Working for Animals and Respect for the Earth)
P.O. Box 7424, Hilton Head Island, SC 29938, (803) 842-8090
Works for the rights of animals by promoting respect and compassion for all sentient beings. Educates the public on animal abuse and exploitation, its connection with environmental deprivation, the interdependence of all living things, and on lifestyle alternatives for a more ethical, compassionate, and nonviolent world.

Carolina Wildlife Care
164 Sandhurst Road, Columbia, SC 29210-4101, (803) 772-3994
Specializes in rehabilitating songbirds, water fowl, opossums, cottontails, and squirrels.

Citizens for Responsible Research
1548 Arlene Drive, Columbia, SC 29204

The Fund for Animals Rabbit Sanctuary
P.O. Box 365, Simpsonville, SC 29681, (803) 963-4389
Provides a permanent home for displaced companion rabbits. See the description of The Fund for Animals, Inc. in "National & International Organizations."

Humane Society of the United States
See Florida for the regional HSUS office that serves this state.

Humans for Alternative Research and Testing
P.O. Box 8756, Greenville, SC 29604

International Primate Protection League
Summerville, SC
See "National & International Organizations."

Peaceable Kingdom
Greenville, SC
See "National & International Organizations."

South Carolina Association for Marine Mammal Protection (SCAMMP)
P.O. Box 3233, Myrtle Beach, SC 29578, (803) 238-1674 (voice/FAX), Contact Person: Jim Burton
Statewide. Opposes the public display of dolphins and whales.

SOUTH DAKOTA

For additional resources for breed rescue, ferret rescue, wildlife rehabilitation, etc., see "Keeping Up-To-Date" at the front of the chapter.

Animal Rights Advocates of South Dakota
P.O. Box 90237, Sioux Falls, SD 57105-9062, (605) 330-7902
Statewide. An educational and activist group promoting humane and ethical treatment of all animals, and dedicated to ending cruelty and exploitation.

Humane Society of the United States
See Illinois for the regional HSUS office that serves this state.

Independent Animal Activists' Network (IAAN)
c/o Deb Gibson, P.O. Box 535, Sioux Falls, SD 57101
Currently inactive. (Mail pick-up is every 7-14 days, so please be patient!)

Institute of Range and the American Mustang
P.O. Box 998, Hot Springs, SD 57747
Operates a sanctuary for horses.

TENNESSEE

For additional resources for breed rescue, ferret rescue, wildlife rehabilitation, etc., see "Keeping Up-To-Date" at the front of the chapter.

Alpha Wildlife Awareness through Research and Education
7616 Hall Road, Knoxville, TN 37920

Coalition to Abolish the Fur Trade
Memphis, TN
See "National & International Organizations."

The Elephant Sanctuary
Hohenwald, TN
See "National & International Organizations."

Humane Society of the United States
South Central Regional Office: Phillip Snyder, Director, 109 Northshore Drive, Suite 400, Knoxville, TN 37919, (615) 588-1843, FAX: (615) 588-1862
Serves TN, KY, NC, and VA. See "National & International Organizations."

Knox County Humane Society
P.O. Box 9479, Knoxville, TN 37940, (615) 573-9675

National Foundation to Protect America's Eagles
Pigeon Forge, TN
See "National & International Organizations."

Tennessee Network for Animals
- Knoxville Chapter: 2001 Forest Avenue, Knoxville, TN, 37916-1203, (615) 522-0705 or 436-2861
- Nashville Chapter: P.O. Box 158452, Nashville, TN 37215, (615) 883-6738

Statewide. Informs the public about animal rights issues and ethics. Stopped pound seizure in two East Tennessee counties.

Walden's Puddle
1905 Omohundro Drive, Nashville, TN 37210, (615) 865-7400
Rehabilitates orphaned and abused exotic animals. Specializes in head trauma.

TEXAS

For additional resources for breed rescue, ferret rescue, wildlife rehabilitation, etc., see "Keeping Up-To-Date" at the front of the chapter.

American Bar Association Young Lawyer Division, Committee for Animal Protection
Dallas, TX
See "National & International Organizations."

Animal Adoption Center of Garland
117 N. Garland Avenue, Garland, TX 75040, (214) 494-KIND
No-kill adoption shelter for dogs and cats.

Animal Advocates, Inc.
3503 Arrowhead Drive, Dallas, TX 75204

Animal Connection of Texas (ACT)
P.O. Box 679008-141, Dallas, TX 75367, 24-hour Info Line: (214) 373-7867
Spay/Neuter Your Pet: (214) 349-SNYP
A grassroots group dedicated to ending animal suffering.

Animal Defense League
11300 Nacogdoches Road, San Antonio, TX 78217, (210) 655-4982
No-kill adoption shelter located on 10 acres.

Animal Protection Advisory Network of Texas (A-PANT)
4209 Abbott Avenue, Dallas, TX 75205, (214) 528-4935
Statewide. Addresses various animal cruelty cases throughout the state, and alerts members to problems in the city, state, and nation.

Animal Refuge Foundation (A.R.F.)
Route 3, Box 213A-1, Sherman, TX 75092, (903) 564-7056
No-kill adoption shelter dedicated to improving the lives of animals in N. Central Texas. Cares for more than 130 resident dogs, some of whom will stay for the duration of their lives due to handicaps, the abuse they've suffered, etc. Strict screening for adoptions. Has placed more than 300 animals in homes.

Animal Rehabilitation Center, Inc.
Midlothian, TX
See "National & International Organizations."

Animal Rights Association
4201 Canyon Drive, Amarillo, TX 79110, (806) 353-6697
Texas Panhandle area. Main focus is a low-cost spay/neuter program for companion animals. Also offers affordable vaccines to low-income families.

Animal Rights Kinship, Inc.
Austin, TX
See "National & International Organizations."

Animal Trustees of Austin
405 Westlake Drive, Austin, TX 78746, (512) 327-5487
Adoption program for animals on "death row" and those with disabilities and behavior problems.

The Association Of Sanctuaries, Inc.
Comfort, TX
See "National & International Organizations."

Austin Area Alliance for the Protection of Animals
Austin, TX, (512) 442-8387

Bat Conservation International
Austin, TX
See "National & International Organizations."

Black Beauty Ranch
Murchison, TX
See "National & International Organizations."

Brighter Days Horse Refuge, Inc.
Route 4, Box 4076, Boerne, TX 78006, (210) 755-8782
Dedicated to the care of old, unwanted, and mistreated horses. Refuge for Hill County and surrounding counties.

Center for Marine Conservation
Regional Office: Austin, TX
See "National & International Organizations."

Central Texas Wildlife Institute, Inc. (CTWI)
HRC 64 Box 30, Hamilton, TX 76531, (817) 372-3987
Not an animal rights-oriented organization, but a wildlife rehabilitation and educational facility dedicated to conservation of indigenous species. Primary emphasis is on large mammals, especially large predators.

Citizens for Animal Protection (CAP) Humane Association
11925 Katy Freeway, Houston, TX 77079, (713) 497-0591
"Helping the Animals of Houston Since 1972." Conducts advocacy for animals, provides shelter and care, places homeless animals, provides humane education, and relieves animal suffering by preventing animal cruelty.

Compassion for Animals
P.O. Box 72064, Corpus Christi, TX 78472-2064, (512) 852-6573

Consumers for Animal Rights Education (CARE)
P.O. Box 18331, Austin, TX 78760, (512) 443-7764
Animal rights education group whose goal is to educate the general public about animal rights issues and cruelty-free alternatives.

Engineers and Scientists for Animal Rights
Kyle, TX
See "National & International Organizations."

The Fund for Animals, Inc.
Field Office: Sean Hawkins (Southwest Coordinator), P.O. Box 70286, Houston, TX 77270, (713) 862-FUND
See "National & International Organizations."

Greyhound Pets of America
P.O. Box 200724, Austin, TX 78720-0724, (512) 258-2947

Greyhound Protection League
P.O. Box 160453, San Antonio, TX 78280-2653

Greyhound Racers Recycled, Inc.
Box 270107, Houston, TX 77277-0107, (713) 665-3366

Guardian Animal Rescue, Inc. (GAR)
P.O. Box 65147, San Antonio, TX 78265, (210) 366-6622
Rescues injured, abandoned, and otherwise needy dogs and cats. Volunteers respond to emergency situations and provide information and referrals to the public.

Help for Helpless Animals (HHA)
P.O. Box 797972, Dallas, TX 75379-7972, (214) 424-4860
Provides low-cost and free spay/neuter assistance, pet food, and help with vet bills for injured animals of the needy. Holds mobile pet adoptions. Temporary foster homes needed.

Help Save Animals (H.S.A.)
c/o Amanda Jones, 922 Belvin Street, San Marcos, TX 78666
Founded by a vegetarian youngster (who is now a teenager), this organization provides a way for children to directly participate in helping animal welfare and wildlife projects, and a way to share information with other kids.

Home At Last Animal Haven
P.O. Box 189, Godley, TX 76044, (817) 389-3813

Houston Animal Rights Team
3400 Montrose, Suite 224, Houston, TX 77006, (713) 522-5131, FAX: (712) 529-8759

Humane Enforcement / Legal Protection (H.E.L.P.)
P.O. Box 572, Brownsboro, TX 75756, (214) 852-HELP

Humane Society of the United States
Gulf States Regional Office: 6262 Weber Road, Suite 305, Corpus Christi, TX 78413, (512) 854-3142, FAX: (512) 854-5922
Serves AZ, LA, OK, and TX. See "National & International Organizations."

Mid-Cities Humane Society, Inc.
P.O. Box 540493, Grand Prairie, TX 75054-0493, (214) 263-4567
Rescue, foster care, medical care, spay/neuter, and adoption services.

Non-Releasable Animal Placement Program
P.O. Box 629, Midlothian, TX 76065, (214) 775-6228, FAX: (214) 723-2100

North Texas Rabbit Sanctuary
P.O. Box 295023, Lewisville, TX 75029, (214) 221-5594

Operation Kindness Animal Shelter
- Street Address: 1029 Trend Drive, Carrollton, TX 75006
- Mailing Address: P.O. Box 814452, Dallas, TX 75381-4452, (214) 418-PAWS

No-kill adoption shelter for cats and dogs. "These animals are not merchandise but are living beings entrusted to our care." Reserves the right to deny any adoptions as they see fit. Animals receive spay/neuter and vet care.

Pet Helpers, Inc.
P.O. Box 4104, Austin, TX 78765, (512) 444-PETS
Foster care and adoption for cats and dogs.

Primarily Primates, Inc.
San Antonio, TX
See "National & International Organizations."

Puerto Rico Street Dog Project
Austin, TX
See "National & International Organizations."

Reptile Rescue
Midlothian, TX
See Non-Releasable Animal Placement Program elsewhere in this state.

Society for Texas Animal Rights (STAR)
P.O. Box 595547, Dallas, TX 75359, (214) 821-7047 (24-hour Info Line)
Statewide. Serves as an activist group, a coalition working with all animal-related organizations, and a complete resource center for animal rights. Regional contact for PETA and other national groups.

South Texas Primate Observatory
P.O. Box 702, Dilley, TX 78017, (512) 696-3580

SPCA of Texas
362 South Industrial, Dallas, TX 75207

St. John's Retreat Center
P.O. Box 930, St. Beulah's Lane, Montgomery, TX 77356, (409) 597-5757
A licensed wildlife rehabilitation center.

Students for the Welfare of Animals (SWA)
c/o Office of Student Activities, San Antonio College, 1300 San Pedro, San Antonio, TX 78212, Student Activities Office: (512) 733-2680
San Antonio College community. Primary goal is education. Encourages anyone with any concern about animals to join.

Texas Animal Protection Society (TAPS)
6808 Mesa Drive, Ft. Worth, TX 76180, (817) 281-8607
Serves as a resource center for animal rights information. Works for the elimination of animal suffering through a concerted program of public education.

Texas Humane Legislation Network (THLN)
603 West 13th Street, Suite 1A-287, Austin, TX 78701-1731, (512) 929-9667
Statewide. "The political arm and voice for every animal in Texas." Committed to the passage of animal protection legislation.

Voice for All Animals
Socorro (Sukie) Sargent, Founder, P.O. Box 17894, El Paso, TX 79917, (915) 860-8586, FAX: (915) 860-2665
Informs the community, so people can make conscious choices about how their lifestyles affect the lives of animals.

Voice for Animals, Inc.
P.O. Box 120095, San Antonio, TX 78212, (512) 737-3138
Dedicated to ending animal suffering through grassroots organizing. Networks with other state and national groups. Publishes a local *Cruelty-Free Shopping Guide.*

Volunteers for Animal Protection (VAP)
P.O. Box 5266, Kingwood, TX 77325, (713) 358-9818
Foster homes and adoption services for strays. No shelter. Lost/found hotline.

Wildlife Rescue and Rehabilitation, Inc.
San Antonio, TX
See "National & International Organizations."

UTAH

For additional resources for breed rescue, ferret rescue, wildlife rehabilitation, etc., see "Keeping Up-To-Date" at the front of the chapter.

Best Friends Animal Sanctuary
P.O. Box G, Kanab, UT 84741-5020, (801) 644-2001, FAX: (801) 644-2078
A 100-acre sanctuary for a variety of animals, including dogs, cats, horses, burros, and farm animals. Adoption and spay/neuter services.

Greyhounds As Pets (GAP)
Local Representative: Cathy Slaugh, Salt Lake City, UT, (801) 561-4967
See Colorado for a description of this group.

Hawk Watch International
Salt Lake City, UT
See "National & International Organizations."

Humane Society of Utah
P.O. Box 573659, Salt Lake City, UT 84157-3659, (801) 261-2919
- and -
4242 So. 300 West, Murray, UT 84107-1415
Cares for 14,000 homeless animals each year. Dedicated to the elimination of fear, pain, and suffering in all animals.

Utah Animal Rights Alliance
3245 East 3300 South, Salt Lake City, UT 84109, (801) 461-9032
A "very active" multi-issue group. Successful in getting the USDA to investigate and follow-through on violations at the zoo.

Utahns for Animals
P.O. Box 25661, Salt Lake City, UT 84125

VERMONT

For additional resources for breed rescue, ferret rescue, wildlife rehabilitation, etc., see "Keeping Up-To-Date" at the front of the chapter.

Green Mountain Animal Defenders (GMAD)
61 Industrial Avenue, Williston, VT 05495, (802) 878-2230
Statewide, mainly Northern Vermont. "A strong and effective voice for Vermont's animals." Runs a low-income spay/neuter clinic, traps and rehabilitates feral cats, and sponsors protests, vigils, and humane education tables.

Humane Society of the United States
See Connecticut for the regional HSUS office that serves this state.

Save The Greyhound Dogs! (STGD)
P.O. Box 8981, Essex, VT 05451, (802) 879-8839
Educates the community about the unethical treatment and ongoing suffering of greyhound racing dogs. Happily refers those who wish to adopt greyhounds.

Students Organized for Animal Rights (SOAR)
c/o Emily Fleschner, UVM—SA Office—Billings, Burlington, VT 05405
Educates the University of Vermont community.

Vermont Volunteer Services for Animals
Box 144, Woodstock, VT 05091, (802) 672-5302
- and -
RD1, Box 132, Brattleboro, VT 05301, (802) 254-9010
A humane society focusing on spay/neuter assistance, feral cats, cruelty investigations, and support services for seniors with companions animals. Live-trap lending program. Partial sponsor of Leave It to the Beavers (NH), which humanely traps, sterilizes, and relocates beaver families in need: (603) 675-2555.

VIRGINIA

For additional resources for breed rescue, ferret rescue, wildlife rehabilitation, etc., see "Keeping Up-To-Date" at the front of the chapter.

800 For Animals, Inc. (Animal Referral Hotline)
Richmond, VA
See "National & International Organizations."

Action 81, Inc.
Berryville, VA
See "National & International Organizations."

Animal Allies
P.O. Box 353, Fairfax Station, VA 22039, (703) 250-9584
Serves Northern VA. Promotes the welfare of all animals. Assists homeless companion animals with veterinary care, spay/neuter services, and adoption. Maintains a wildlife refuge, which also houses less-adoptable cats.

Animal Defense League of Washington County, Inc.
P.O. Box 1152, Abingdon, VA 24210, (703) 628-9275 (Weekends)
Inactive until new people and new interests appear. Organized in 1980 as a local humane society in a very rural area. A former member still offers advice and spay/neuter assistance.

Bristol Humane Society (BHS)
P.O. Box 1586, Bristol, VA 24203, (423) 968-9136
Humane education, spay/neuter assistance, lost and found service, adoption help, and legislative efforts. No shelter.

Caring For Creatures (CFC)
Route 2, Box 1009, Palmyra, VA 22963, (804) 842-2404
Operates a 157-acre sanctuary for 150-200 abandoned, abused, neglected, and otherwise homeless dogs and cats. "In addition to expert veterinary care, we offer these animals love, respect, and compassion." Sponsorship program available to help support the sanctuary.

Center for Marine Conservation
Regional Office: Hampton, VA
See "National & International Organizations."

Concern for Helping Animals in Israel
Alexandria, VA
See "National & International Organizations."

The Cousteau Society, Inc.
Chesapeake, VA
See "National & International Organizations."

Dart's Run Wildlife Recovery
Route 1, Box 35-C, Vesuvius, VA 24483, (703) 377-6429
Cares for songbirds, deer, bats, and other small mammals.

Equine Rescue League (ERL)
P.O. Box 4366, Leesburg, VA 22075, (703) 771-1240
Shelter, rehabilitation, and adoption for rescued horses.

The Ferrets of Pet Pals—Ferret Rescue & Adoption Service
John and Pamela Grant, 7402 Joseph Court, Annandale, VA 22003, (703) 354-5073, E-mail: 73613,231@CompuServe.com
Serves Northern Virginia and Washington, D.C. Shelters and places displaced ferrets, including those from the Fairfax County Animal Shelter. Sells equipment and services (including board-ing) to ferret owners. Information and education on ferrets. Free info for a self-addressed, stamped envelope.

Homeless Animals Rescue Team (H.A.R.T.)
P.O. Box 7261, Fairfax Station, VA 22039-7261, (703) 691-HART, Internet: http://www.dolphin.org/sac/dogs/novada.html
No-kill organization that provides adoption assistance while animals stay in the home of the person requesting the assistance. Rescues both cats and dogs, and places them in foster homes. Screens and "home checks" all prospective adopters.

Humane Organization for Retired and Standardbred Equines
Church Road, VA
See "National & International Organizations."

Humane Society of the United States
See Tennessee for the regional HSUS office that serves this state.

In Defense of Animals
State Contact: Betty Lou LaJoy, 8814 Brawner Drive, Richmond, VA 23229, (804) 750-1927
See "National & International Organizations."

Just A Business of Ferrets
P.O. Box 2371, Leesburg, VA 22075, (703) 777-2112, FAX: (703) 771-5037
Ferret rescue and adoption.

Lend-A-Paw Relief Organization
P.O. Box 4864, Falls Church, VA 22044, (703) 536-8809
Rescue, foster homes, and adoption services for cats.

National Humane Education Society
Administrative Headquarters: Leesburg, VA
See "National & International Organizations."

Noah's Friends Unlimited
P.O. Box 36197, Richmond, VA 23235, (804) 320-7090
Improves public awareness and generates media attention to end the suffering, abuse, and exploitation of all our Earth's animal partners. Special interest is the fur industry.

No Kill Cat Shelter, Inc.
27474 Honey Locust Road, Abingdon, VA 24211, (703) 628-9280
Cares for stray cats.

People for the Ethical Treatment of Animals
Norfolk, VA
See "National & International Organizations."

Prevent A Litter Coalition, Inc.
P.O. Box 1412, Centerville, VA 22020, (703) 818-8009
As a coalition, the number one priority is to organize campaigns and involve everyone in ending the needless suffering of animals caused by irresponsible pet ownership and over-population. Offers a directory of spay/neuter groups in Maryland, Virginia, and Washington, D.C.; resource guides (at cost) for humane educators and shelters; information on raffle fundraisers; and a complete package for $30 on organizing a Prevent A Litter Campaign with spay/neuter surgeries donated by area vets, kids' poster contest, billboard and radio participation, etc.

Society for the Study of Ethics and Animals
Blacksburg, VA
See "National & International Organizations."

SPAY, Inc.
4251 Vacation Lane, Arlington, VA 22207-3929

STAR Ferrets (Shelters That Adopt & Rescue Ferrets)
Springfield, VA
See "National & International Organizations."

Virginians for Animal Rights (VAR)
P.O. Box 17265, Richmond, VA 23226, (804) 323-1068
Does whatever it can to protect the rights of all animals: demonstrations, tabling, spay/neuter referral, and humane education and referral.

Voices for Animals
P.O. Box 1324, Charlottesville, VA 22902, (804) 977-8547
Works to end cruelty to animals.

The Wildlife Center of Virginia
P.O. Box 1557, Wayneboro, VA 22980, (703) 942-9453, FAX: (703) 943-9453
One of the nation's leading teaching and research hospitals for native wildlife. Provides injured/orphaned wild animals with care, with the goal of returning them to the wild. Aware that many animals are victims of human-caused problems—cars, pesticides, guns, attacks by companion animals—therefore, works to educate and inspire greater personal responsibility and understanding.

WASHINGTON

For additional resources for breed rescue, ferret rescue, wildlife rehabilitation, etc., see "Keeping Up-To-Date" at the front of the chapter.

Animal Advocates of the Inland Northwest
P.O. Box 4262, Spokane, WA 99202, (509) 459-8502
Focuses on reducing and eliminating animal suffering on factory farms, in classrooms and laboratories, and in the fur trade.

Animal Lovers Society
435 Lake Washington Blvd., Seattle, WA 98122, (206) 325-4587
Raises funds which are then donated to worthy animal organizations.

Concern for Animals
P.O. Box 7306, Olympia, WA 98507, (206) 352-3539
Adoption, spay/neuter, and referral services.

Fashion With Compassion
Burton, WA
See "National & International Organizations."

Friends of Washoe
Ellensburg, WA
See "National & International Organizations."

Harbor Association of Volunteers for Animals (H.A.V.A.)
P.O. Box 1913, Westport, WA 98595, (360) 268-9092, FAX: (360) 268-6320, E-mail: hava@techline.com
HAVA Heart Sanctuary & Thrift Shop: 303 So. Forrest, Westport, WA
"Where love is action, not words." No-kill shelter in the South Beach area of Grays Harbor county, western Washington. Adoptions, 24-hour lost and found registry, and low-cost spay/neuter.

Humane Animal Rescue Team & Muttmatchers Messenger

See California for a description of this group.

Humane Society of the United States

See California for the regional HSUS office that serves this state.

International Foundation for the Protection of the Wolf

Seattle, WA
See "National & International Organizations."

International Snow Leopard Trust

Seattle, WA
See "National & International Organizations."

Northwest Animal Rights Network (NARN)

ATTN: Jerry Esterly, 1704 East Galer Street, Seattle, WA 98112, (206) 323-7301 (hotline for information on upcoming events and activities)
Focus is exposing and opposing animal abuse in the Pacific Northwest.

People for Abandoned Pets

P.O. Box 70025, Bellvue, WA 948007, (206) 453-9222
Main focus is raising money to provide free or reduced rate spay/neuter certificates for dogs and cats. Also works to improve conditions of local shelters, educate the public, and reduce the use of live animals in laboratories.

Progressive Animal Welfare Society (PAWS)

P.O. Box 1037, 15305-44th Avenue W., Lynnwood, WA 98046, (206) 787-2500
24-Hour Emergency Line: ext. 400
Animal Rights: ext. 535
Animal Shelter and Lost & Found: ext. 430
Wildlife Rehabilitation: ext. 485
Membership: ext. 555
Serves Greater Seattle, Bellevue, and Everett. Promotes and protects the rights, interests, and well-being of all animals.

Project Wolf USA

Seattle, WA
See "National & International Organizations."

Spokane People for the Ethical Treatment of Animals (SPETA)

P.O. Box 4262, Spokane, WA 99202, (509) 459-8502
Serves Eastern Washington and Northern Idaho. A local group that believes animals are not ours to eat, wear, or experiment on.

Spokanimal C.A.R.E.

P.O. Box 3151, Spokane, WA 99220-3151, (509) 534-8133, FAX: (509) 535-9630
Adoptions, low-cost veterinary care, and other services for homeless cats and dogs.

Wild Burro Rescue (WBR)

665 Burnt Ridge Road, Onalaska, WA 948570, (360) 985-7282
Dedicated to the rescue, rehabilitation, and preservation of otherwise doomed wild burros.

Wolf Haven International

Terrino, WA
See "National & International Organizations."

Wolf Hollow Wildlife Rehabilitation Center

240 Boyce Road, P.O. Box 391, Friday Harbor, WA 98250, (206) 378-5000

WASHINGTON, D.C.

For additional resources for breed rescue, ferret rescue, wildlife rehabilitation, etc., see "Keeping Up-To-Date" at the front of the chapter.

African Wildlife Foundation

Washington, D.C.
See "National & International Organizations."

American Horse Protection Association

Washington, D.C.
See "National & International Organizations."

American Humane Association

Regional Office: Washington, D.C.
See "National & International Organizations."

American Society for the Prevention of Cruelty to Animals

National Legislative Office: Washington, D.C.
See "National & International Organizations."

Animal Legal Defense Fund
Local Chapter: 900 Second Street NE, Suite 303, Washington, D.C. 20002
See "National & International Organizations."

Animal Welfare Institute
Washington, D.C.
See "National & International Organizations."

Center for Marine Conservation
Headquarters: Washington, D.C.
See "National & International Organizations."

Committee for Humane Legislation
Washington, D.C.
See "National & International Organizations."

Doris Day Animal League
Washington, D.C.
Scc "National & International Organizations."

Elect! For Animals
Washington, D.C.
See "National & International Organizations."

Environmental Investigation Agency
Washington, D.C.
See "National & International Organizations."

Friends of Animals
Washington D.C. Office: 2000 P Street NW, #415, Washington, D.C. 20036, (202) 296-2172
See "National & International Organizations."

Greenpeace
Washington, D.C.
See "National & International Organizations."

Humane Society of the United States
National Office: Washington, D.C.
See "National & International Organizations."

Monitor Consortium
Washington, D.C.
See "National & International Organizations."

National Alliance for Animals
Washington, D.C.
See "National & International Organizations."

Physicians Committee for Responsible Medicine
Washington, D.C.
See "National & International Organizations."

Society for Animal Protective Legislation
Washington, D.C.
See "National & International Organizations."

Student Action Corps for Animals
Washington, D.C.
See "National & International Organizations."

Washington Humane Society / SPCA
7319 Georgia Avenue NW, Washington, D.C. 20012, (202) 333-4010, FAX: (202) 723-1956
Enforces the anti-cruelty laws in D.C.

Wildlife Refuge Reform Coalition
Washington, D.C.
See "National & International Organizations."

WEST VIRGINIA

For additional resources for breed rescue, ferret rescue, wildlife rehabilitation, etc., see "Keeping Up-To-Date" at the front of the chapter.

Equine Rescue and Education
P.O. Box 1504, Shephardstown, WV 25442-1504, (304) 876-3843

Humane Society of the United States
See Ohio for the regional HSUS office that serves this state.

Kanawha Action for Animals, Inc. (KAFA)
P.O. Box 109, Pinch, WV 25156, (304) 342-7297
Public education on companion animal theft, responsible companion animal ownership, spaying/neutering, and humane education.

National Institute for Urban Wildlife
Shepherdstown, WV
See "National & International Organizations."

Potbellied Pig Interest Group and Shelter
Charles Town, WV
See "National & International Organizations."

Southern West Virginia Equine Education and Protection, Inc. (SWEEP)

Box 3, Ramage Hill, Jeffrey, WV 25114, (304) 369-6752

Rescues equines from backyard abuse and neglect. Assists other organizations with horse issues. In the process of setting up foster care and adoption programs.

Stand Up For Animal Rights (SUFAR)

P.O. Box 4666, Parkersburg, WV 26104-4666, (304) 375-3849

Parkersburg, WV and Marietta, OH. Advances the rights of all living, nonhuman species by promoting and exhibiting ethical, nonviolent behavior through education and legislation.

West Virginia Raptor Rehabilitation Center (WVRRC)

P.O. Box 333, Morgantown, WV 26507, 1-800-540-6390

Rehabilitates sick, injured, and orphaned birds of prey, with release if possible. Offers public development and educational programs.

WISCONSIN

For additional resources for breed rescue, ferret rescue, wildlife rehabilitation, etc., see "Keeping Up-To-Date" at the front of the chapter.

Alliance for Animals, Inc.

122 State Street, Suite 309, Madison, WI 53703, (608) 257-6333, E-mail: allanimals@aol.com

Statewide. Contact for affiliates at UW-Madison, UW-Milwaukee, UW-Oshkosh, and Green Bay area. Active on multiple issues to end animal abuse, including formation of a sanctuary for old, ill, or needy Asian elephants.

Animal Liberation Action

Regional Contact: Madison, WI, (608) 251-0093 (Mark McEahern)

See "National & International Organizations."

Animal Protective League

2130 North 106th Street, Milwaukee, WI 53226, (414) 453-7177

Humane Society of the United States

See Illinois for the regional HSUS office that serves this state.

International Crane Foundation

Baraboo, WI

See "National & International Organizations."

JES Exotics Sanctuary

W7593 Town Hall Road, Sharon, WI 53585-9728, (414) 736-9386, FAX: (414) 736-2020

Currently houses over 30 large cats that were created by greed and tossed aside once they were no longer youthful.

NorthEast Wisconsin Voice for Animals (NEWVA)

P.O. Box 549, Denmark, WI 54208, (414) 863-8709

A small but very active multi-issue group.

Orphan Alley

N7458 County Road A, Gresham, WI 54128, (715) 787-4265

Permanent, cageless, no-kill shelter for injured or abused cats (and dogs). Adopt-a-Foster-Kitty program lets you provide financial help to the residents. Public education.

Pine View Wildlife Rehabilitation Center

W4953 Highway 84, Fredonia, WI 53021, (414) 692-9021

Wildlife rehabilitation and education services.

Protective Association of World Species

New Berlin, WI

See "National & International Organizations."

Standardbred Retirement Foundation

Regional Chapter: W4467 Ober Road, Stoddard, WI 54658, (608) 788-8536

Midwest placements. See New Jersey for a description of this group.

Students for Animals

Org Room-UWGB, University of Wisconsin—Green Bay, 2420 Nicolet Drive, Green Bay, WI 54311-7001

Works to stop animal cruelty, especially through protests and demonstrations.

Timber Wolf Preservation Society, Inc. (TWPS)

6669 So. 76th Street, Greendale, WI 53129, (414) 425-6107 or 425-8264

Works to preserve the timber wolf and all other wildlife. Conducts public education on the predator/prey relationship and dispels false notions about "The Big Bad Wolf." Maintains a farm with captive timber wolves, originally raised to research re-introduction of timber wolves into the wild.

WYOMING

For additional resources for breed rescue, ferret rescue, wildlife rehabilitation, etc., see "Keeping Up-To-Date" at the front of the chapter.

Animal Care Center

P.O. Box 299, Laramie, WY 82070, (307) 742-0483

The first no-kill animal organization in Wyoming. Helps abused, sick, and cruelly-treated animals. Sponsors state and local legislation. Active spay/neuter program.

Casper Humane Society

260 Crescent Drive, Mountain View Addition, Casper, WY 82604-2366

No-kill adoption facility for cats and some dogs.

The Fund for Animals, Inc.

Field Office

Contact the National Headquarters of The Fund for Animals, Inc. for this address. See "National & International Organizations."

Greyhounds As Pets (GAP)

Local Representative: Lisa Parsons, Southern Wyoming, (307) 635-6245

See Colorado for a description of this group.

Humane Federation of Wyoming (HFW)

P.O. Box 1073, Laramie, WY 82070

An organization of humane groups whose purpose is to provide assistance to societies wishing to incorporate, uphold anti-cruelty laws, promote education, and further the general well-being of all animals.

Humane Society of the United States

See Montana for the regional HSUS office that serves this state.

Ironside Bird Rescue

49 Road 2DAW, Cody, WY 82414, (307) 587-2747

Care limited to raptors and other birds.

Jackson Hole Animal Rights Network (JHARN)

P.O. Box 8316, Jackson, WY 83001

An educational organization created for local and global concerns. Provides nonprofit graphic arts help to animal rights groups.

Wyoming Advocates For Animals (WAFA)

ATTN: Jeannine R. Stallings, 316 East Pershing Blvd., Cheyenne, WY 82001, (307) 778-4086 (evenings and weekends)

Statewide. Educates aspiring activists on animal issues and the animal rights movement.

Wyoming Humane Federation

P.O. Box 4514, Casper, WY 82604, (307) 234-4658

Chapter 11

Vegetarian Organizations

This listing contains national, international, and local vegetarian contacts. You don't have to be a vegetarian to become involved in a group. In fact, being around vegetarians is an excellent way to learn about cruelty-free eating. Most vegetarian groups happily support those in the exploration or transition stages of vegetarianism.

Groups vary in many respects. Some vegetarian organizations are active in animal rights; others aren't. Many are small, informal groups while others are large and more structured. Some have membership fees, others don't. All groups are presumably not-for-profit. Contact the groups that interest you for details.

But There's No Group in My Area

If you don't see a group listed for your town, you may be able to track one down:

- Check with the vegetarian and animal rights organizations in neighboring communities to see if they know of vegetarians in your area. Check Chapter 10 for animal rights groups near you.
- Contact the Vegetarian Awareness Network (VEGANET), the North American Vegetarian Society (NAVS), or one of the other National/International vegetarian groups and ask if they have any local affiliates in your area. Many keep a list of affiliated groups and individuals nationwide (also in Canada and some overseas).

If there's no vegetarian organization located near you, how about starting one? Contact the National/International organizations for assistance and for literature that you can distribute to members. If you know of an organization missing from the list that should be included, please contact the publisher.

Please Note: A listing is not necessarily an endorsement. The author makes no claims as to the organizations listed herein, which are all believed to operate in good faith.

A Note About Area Codes: A shortage of telephone numbers has prompted the creation of additional area codes for many parts of the country. Because areas codes are still changing, some area codes may be outdated. If you get a "wrong number," check to see whether the area code could be the culprit.

National & International Organizations

American Natural Hygiene Society

P.O. Box 30630, Tampa, FL 33630, (813) 855-6607

Advocates fresh, whole, uncooked foods from nonanimal sources. Helps people overcome the incorrect ways of thinking about health and disease that have become the accepted norm. Publishes *Health Science* magazine.

American Vegan Society (AVS)

56 Dinshah Lane, P.O. Box H, Malaga, NJ 08328, (609) 694-2887 (voice/FAX)

Educates people about the ethical, ecological, healthful, economic, and other benefits of a vegan way of life. Offers mail-order videos, audiotapes, and books. Sponsors meetings and classes, and an annual educational convention. Publishes the quarterly *Ahimsa*.

EarthHeart Foundation

106 N. Wisconsin Street, De Pere, WI 54115, (414) 336-1854

Dedicated to nurturing a peaceful planet through Reverence for Life. Believes in nonviolence through vegetarian food choices, compassion toward all living things, and kindness in thought and action. Provides information, vegetarian cooking classes, discussions, workshops, etc. Along with its other activities, operates the EarthHeart Deli (at the same address).

EarthSave

706 Frederick Street, Santa Cruz, CA 95062-2205, (408) 423-4069, 1-800-362-3648, FAX: (408) 458-0255

Educates people about the cumulative impact of America's food choices and large-scale animal agriculture. Founded by John Robbins, author of *Diet for a New America*. Local Action Groups in many cities nationwide. Quarterly newsletter and merchandise catalog.

Food Not Bombs

3145 Geary Blvd., #12, San Francisco, CA 94118, 1-800-884-1136

An all-volunteer peace network that provides free, hot vegetarian meals and political support to low-income people in North America and Europe. Depends on local volunteers to operate chapters in their communities. For $10 you receive a 128-page book that tells you how to start and maintain a food recovery program, 30 vegan recipes for feeding 100 people, and logos, flyers, and letters you can reproduce.

Friends Vegetarian Society of North America (FVSNA)

P.O. Box 6956, Louisville, KY 40206-0956, (502) 897-9799

Promotes vegetarianism among North American Quakers and familiarizes vegetarians with the values of Quakerism. Publishes a quarterly newsletter, *The Friendly Vegetarian*.

Jewish Vegetarian Society (International)

c/o S. Judah Grosberg (Representative), Box 144, Hurleyville, NY 12747, (914) 434-6335

Information office for the Jewish Vegetarian Society (International) which is headquartered in London, England. Not actively involved in the animal rights movement.

Jewish Vegetarians of North America

6938 Reliance Road, Federalsburg, MD 21632, (410) 754-5550

Promotes the vegetarian viewpoint within the Jewish community, as well as representing Jewish people and values within the vegetarian community. Quarterly newsletter and quarterly *International Jewish Vegetarian Magazine*. Numerous book titles in stock.

Natural Hygiene, Inc.

P.O. Box 2132, Huntington Station, Shelton, CT 06484, (203) 929-1557

An international organization with subscribers in 49 states and 15 countries. Natural Hygiene is a system of healthful living that includes a raw food diet as a component. The research department provides information on over 700 subjects related to Natural Hygiene. Hosts a yearly conference and produces a regular radio program featuring health topics. Offers books, audiotapes, and videotapes. Supports all efforts in animal rights. Publishes the bimonthly *Journal of Natural Hygiene*.

New England Vegetarian Resource Center

Box 38-1068, Cambridge, MA 02238, (617) 625-3790

A resource center for vegetarian information, available to those writing papers, forming groups, requiring guidance on vegetarianism, etc.

North American Vegetarian Society (NAVS)

Box 72, Dolgeville, NY 13329, (518) 568-7970

Dedicated to promoting the vegetarian way of life. Encourages and assists the formation of local vegetarian groups. Originator and organizer of annual World Vegetarian Day (October 1). A member of the International Vegetarian Union. Membership is open to both vegetarians and nonvegetarians. Publishes the quarterly *Vegetarian Voice*, which includes a nationwide list of groups and contacts (plus Canada), as well as extensive merchandise offerings.

Pure Food Campaign (formerly Beyond Beef)

1130-17th Street NW, Suite 630, Washington, DC 20036, (202) 775-1132 or 1-800-253-1681, FAX: (202) 775-0074

Supports an international boycott of genetically engineered foods and a campaign to reform school food programs.

Vegan Action

P.O. Box 4353, Berkeley, CA 94704-0353, (510) 704-4444

Internet: vegan@mellers1.psych.berkeley.edu

A grassroots activist network focused on promoting the vegan diet and lifestyle and inspiring more people to become actively involved in the vegan movement. Works closely with a variety of groups—animal activists, environmentalists, and public health organizations. Membership includes a subscription to *Vegan News*, a stack of pamphlets and information on veganism, and other assistance.

Vegetarian Awareness Network (VEGANET)

- National Headquarters: P.O. Box 3545, Washington, D.C. 20007
- Communications Center: P.O. Box 321, Knoxville, TN 37901, 1-800-USA-VEGE (872-8343), From Canada: 1-800-EAT-VEGE

Networks nationally to advance public awareness of the benefits of a vegetarian lifestyle and to facilitate the formation of local vegetarian groups. Sponsors Vegetarian Awareness Month, a nationwide event celebrated in October. Offers information and referral services, library, speakers bureau, programs, and marketing databases.

Vegetarian Dietitians and Nutrition Educators (VEGEDINE)

c/o George Eisman, 3835 St. Rt. 414, Burdett, NY 14818, (607) 546-2751

A support and referral group for nutrition professionals who are, or service, vegetarians. Publishes the newsletter *Issues in Vegetarian Dietetics*, and maintains a directory of vegetarian dietetic professionals.

Vegetarian Education Network (VE Net)

ATTN: Sally Clinton

- Permanent Address: P.O. Box 3347, West Chester, PA 19381, (610) 696-VNET
- Office Address: P.O. Box 133, Kirkwood, PA 17536, (717) 529-VNET

Devoted to promoting the vegetarian perspective in schools, through education and school lunches. Supports young vegetarians, and advocates compassionate, ecologically-sound living. Serves as a resource for individuals interested in working in schools and provides information for teachers. Supports teens through its publication *How On Earth* (*HOE!*) and through empowerment workshops. Coordinates a National Speakers Network.

The Vegetarian Resource Group (VRG)

P.O. Box 1463, Baltimore, MD 21203, (410) 366-VEGE, FAX: (410) 366-8804

E-mail: VRG@aol.com, Internet: http://www.envirolink.org/arrs/VRG/home.html

Educates others about vegetarianism and the interrelated issues of health, nutrition, ecology, ethics, animal rights, and world hunger. Sponsors numerous outreach projects to the public, students, and professionals such as dietitians and teachers. Sponsors potlucks and other social activities for members. Publishes bimonthly *The Vegetarian Journal*, which contains articles, recipes, merchandise, and nutrition information.

Vegetarian Union of North America (VUNA)

P.O. Box 9710, Washington, DC 20016

A coalition of vegetarian groups and individuals throughout the U.S. and Canada, whose mission is to promote a strong, effective, cooperative vegetarian movement throughout North America. Affiliated with the International Vegetarian Union. Members become automatic members of that larger group. Publishes the 50-page booklet *Guide for Local Vegetarian Groups*, the quarterly *VUNA Views*, and the annual *International Vegetarian Union Newsletter*.

The Vegetarian Youth Network (VYN)
P.O. Box 1141, New Paltz, NY 12561, (914) 255-0671, E-mail: tovahwal@mhv.net
An organization run by and for vegetarian teens who support compassionate and globally-aware living. Provides supportive services to vegetarian teens and helps those who want to become vegetarian. Information: Send a long self-addressed, stamped envelope with *two* 32-cent stamps (instead of one).

Local Vegetarian Organizations

The following list contains not only vegetarian organizations, but also individuals willing to serve as "local contacts" for anyone seeking information on local vegetarian resources. Special thanks to the Vegetarian Awareness Network (VEGANET) and the North American Vegetarian Society (NAVS) for sharing their "local contacts" lists, which appear at the end of each state.

ALABAMA

Vegetarian Society of Alabama
c/o Lesley Johnson, 12102 Greenleaf Drive, Huntsville, AL 35803, (205) 881-0704

Additional Local Contacts
Montgomery: (334) 284-5833
Seale: (205) 855-4764, (334) 855-4781
Wadley: (205) 395-2248

ALASKA

Local Contacts
Anchorage: (907) 272-LIFE, (907) 274-3683

ARIZONA

EarthSave Phoenix
P.O. Box 1811, Tempe, AZ 85281, (602) 280-5558

Jewish Vegetarians of Arizona
ATTN: Jay B. Lavine, M.D., P.O. Box 32842, Phoenix, AZ 85064, (602) 840-7142

Phoenix Area Vegetarians
4232 E. Siesta Lane, Phoenix, AZ 85024, (602) 504-0789

Vegetarian Resource Group of Tucson
6209 N. Chaparral Road, Tucson, AZ 85743, (520) 570-8896

Additional Local Contacts
Glendale: (602) 547-0575
Lake Havasu: (520) 855-3786
Patagonia: (520) 394-2520
Phoenix: (602) 530-8590, 254-1439, 423-1294, 241-9778, 285-3819, 437-2483, 840-9166, 995-2210, 866-2417
Prescott: (520) 776-8364
Sun City: (602) 972-7047 (Lillian Brackett)
Tempe: (602) 831-8688
Tucson: (520) 682-3722 (Nancy Greener), 883-2488, 682-0232, 623-3101, 570-8896

ARKANSAS

Earth! Educate!
Marriane Beasley, 327 West Meadow, Fayetteville, AR 72701, (501) 521-1998

Additional Local Contacts
Fayetteville: (501) 442-4124
Little Rock: (501) 375-5848
Royal: (501) 767-6435

CALIFORNIA

Animal Rights Connection
ATTN: Barbara Pietrowiak, P.O. Box 410862, San Francisco, CA 94141, (415) 441-4245

Association of Veterinarians for Animal Rights
ATTN: Teri Barnato, P.O. Box 6269, Vacaville, CA 95696-6269, (707) 451-1391

Bay Area Jewish Vegetarians
Justin Rosenthal (Animal Rights Spokesperson), 416 Southwind Circle, Richmond, CA 94804

California Vegetarian Association (C.V.A.)
P.O. Box 6213, Thousand Oaks, CA 91359, (818) 377-4090 or (805) 529-7519

Club Veg of San Diego
3716-35th Street, San Diego, CA 92104-3903, (619) 282-3900

Contra Costa Vegetarians
(510) 283-3418

EarthSave
Santa Cruz, CA
See "National & International Organizations."

EarthSave California
- Bay Area: 2130 Fillmore, #135, San Francisco, CA 94115, (415) 765-7665
- Chico: 643 West 11th Avenue, Chico, CA 95926, (916) 896-1240
- Los Angeles: P.O. Box 3326, Los Angeles, CA 90078, (213) 964-4455
- Orange County: 19744 Beach Blvd., #372, Huntington Beach, CA 92705, (714) 239-4699 or 835-1775
- Sacramento: 725 Howe Ave., #93, Sacramento, CA 95825, (916) 920-2889
- San Diego: 652 Mission Blvd., San Diego, CA 92109, (619) 272-7399
- South Bay: P.O. Box 585, Redwood Estates, CA 95044, (408) 353-2145

East Bay Vegetarians
c/o Karen and Richard Karlin, 6037 Claremont Avenue, Oakland, CA 94618, (415) 654-5621

Food Not Bombs
San Francisco, CA
See "National & International Organizations."

Gay and Lesbian Vegetarians of San Diego
(619) 576-0400

Los Angeles Vegetarian Association (LAVA)
505 S. Beverly Drive, Suite 690, Beverly Hills, CA 90212, (213) 964-4FUN

M.A.I.S.—Native American Vegetarian Group
P.O. Box 34427, Los Angeles, CA 90034

Napa Valley Vegetarians
c/o Jennifer Raymond or Steven Avis, 1418 Cedar Street, Calistoga, CA 94515

Orange County Vegetarian Network
12073 Stonegate Lane, Garden Grove, CA 92645, (714) 851-6594

Sacramento Vegetarian Society (SVS)
P.O. Box 163583, 823-28th Street, Sacramento, CA 95816-9583, (916) 689-8897

Salano County Vegetarians
c/o Paul Sheeran, 548 Florance Drive, Vacaville, CA 95688, (707) 451-2156

San Francisco Living Foods Support Group
662-29th Avenue, San Francisco, CA 94121, (415) 751-2806

San Francisco Vegetarian Society (SFVS) & North American Vegetarian Society (NAVS) Western Coordinator
Dixie Mahy, 1450 Broadway, #4, San Francisco, CA 94109, (415) 775-6874

SLO Vegetarian Network
9240 Carmel Road, Atascadero, CA 93422
Meets in late summer or early fall to plan Vegetarian Awareness Month in October.

South Bay Vegetarians
515 Monterey Blvd., Hermosa Beach, CA 90254, (213) 374-5152

South Valley Vegetarians
c/o Diane Blas, 13810 Shelia Avenue, Morgan Hill, CA 95037, (408) 779-2577

Vegan Action
Berkeley, CA 94704
See "National & International Organizations."

Vega Study Center
1511 Robinson Street, Oroville, CA 95965, (916) 533-7702

The Vegetarian Foundation
P.O. Box 9470, Stanford, CA 94309, (415) 917-8786, E-mail: lynn@casbs.stanford.edu
Assists other vegetarian organizations with funds, advice, and information; supports public events and projects promoting vegetarianism; and encourages cooperation, communication, and networking among groups interested in vegetarianism. Publishes the annual *Bay Area Vegetarian* resource guide (see the Vegetarianism & Whole Foods: Guides & Directories section of Chapter 13 for a description).

Vegetarian Friends
Palo Alto, CA , (415) 948-2209

Vegetarian Inclined People (VIP)
Dorothy Gardener, Pres., 383 Walnut Street, Arroyo Grande, CA 93420, (805) 489-5481

Vegetarian Network
c/o Nancy Cohn Burke, 9240 Carmel Road, Atascadero, CA 93422, (805) 461-1212

Vegetarian Singles
c/o San Francisco Vegetarian Society, 1450 Broadway, #4, San Francisco, CA 94109, (415) 775-6874

Vegetarian Society, Inc. (VSI)
- Los Angeles: P.O. Box 34427, Los Angeles, CA 90034, Hotline: (310) 281-1907
- San Diego: P.O. Box 9115, San Diego, CA 92169, (619) 492-8803
- Orange County: P.O. Box 28318, Santa Ana, CA 92799, (714) 647-5590

Vegetarian Special Interest Group (SIG) of American Mensa, Ltd.
c/o Lola Moffitt, P.O. Box 3425, Shell Beach, CA 93448

Vegetarians In Marin
12 Rally Court, Fairfax, CA 94930, (415) 459-4668

Vegetarians of Sonoma County (VSC)
P.O. Box 4003, Santa Rosa, CA 95402, (707) 526-4834

Web of Life / Vegan Resources
P.O. Box 2124, Orange, CA 92669, (714) 639-3791

Additional Local Contacts
Anaheim: (714) 995-1203, 772-8428
Arcata: (707) 822-6846
Berkeley: (510) 843-6343, 562-9934, 653-7966, 704-4444, 548-2220, 649-8746
Beverly Hills: (310) 281-1907
Camarillo: (805) 482-5640
Campbell: (310) 370-0655
Chico: (916) 865-4617
Costa Mesa: (310) 598-0230
Covina: (818) 596-2008, 377-4090
Culver City: (310) 839-6207
Eureka: (707) 445-2290
Fairfield: (707) 451-2156, 434-1609
Forest Knolls: (415) 488-4573
Foster City: (415) 574-3245
Fremont: (510) 490-6974
Half Moon Bay: (415) 726-3505
Irvine: (714) 851-6594
Lafayette: (510) 283-3418
Lancaster: (805) 264-0969
Longmont: Emily Goodin, 3626 Mountain View Avenue, Longmont, CA 80503
Los Angeles: (213) 487-1780 (Randy Ellis), (213) 874-4722 (Andy Mars), 931-7201, 388-4332, (818) 765-8742 (L.A. Singles)
Marina Del Ray: (310) 392-9001

Monterey: (408) 655-2655
Morongo Valley: (714) 360-9310
Nevada City: Tanja Keogh, Box 1950, Nevada City, CA 95959
N. Hollywood: (818) 763-9028, 763-5418
Northridge: (818) 341-6153 (Hans & Coby Siegenthaler), (818) 993-0444
Oakland: (510) 562-9934, 653-7966, 474-4202, 652-5603
Orland: (916) 865-4617
Pacific Grove: (408) 655-2655
Palmdale: (805) 264-4892
Palm Springs: (619) 770-9665
Palo Alto: (415) 948-2209, 369-2779, 599-3320, 949-3115
Paso Robles: (805) 238-2409
Pittsburgh: (510) 458-0507
Redondo Beach: (310) 540-4287
Sacramento: (916) 927-5202, 442-7217, 455-0563
San Anselmo: (415) 459-4668
San Bernardino: (909) 845-7227
San Diego: (619) 693-8272 (Naren Sheth), 634-0192, 464-3346, 454-2024, 755-1411, 229-9200 (Teen), 943-0330 (Teen)
San Francisco: (415) 665-1060, 621-1270
San Jose: (408) 345-7007, 978-9773
San Luis Obispo: (805) 546-9776, 549-8102
San Rafael: (415) 453-9984
Santa Ana: (714) 775-4697, 751-6272
Santa Barbara: (805) 962-7556, 897-9797, 966-6208; and Ann Monihan, 1335 Bath St., #B, Santa Barbara, CA 93101
Santa Clara: (408) 345-7007
Santa Cruz: (408) 423-4069, 427-3211
Santa Monica: (310) 392-7735
Santa Rosa: (707) 527-1734, 576-1415
Seal Beach: (310) 598-0230
Sebastopol: (707) 829-8790
Sherman Oaks: (818) 786-9990
Sonoma: (707) 576-1415
Stanford: (415) 854-8997
Sylmar: (818) 367-5227
Templeton: (805) 434-0790
Thousand Oaks: (805) 378-5098
Topanga: (818) 884-1103
Union City: (510) 429-0855
Vacaville: (707) 449-4814
Ventura: (805) 652-1910

COLORADO

Vegetarian Society of Colorado

- State Headquarters: P.O. Box 6773, Denver, CO 80206, (303) 777-4828
- Sociable Vegetarian Singles: (303) 831-8526

Contact the state headquarters for chapters throughout Colorado, including Metro Denver, Boulder, Durango, Fort Collins, Grand Junction, Mountain, and Pikes Peak.

Additional Local Contacts

Bellvue: (303) 493-7153
Boulder: (303) 665-7844
Colorado Springs: (719) 632-1968
Denver: (303) 744-6530, 329-0316, 421-6193, 779-0439, 986-6245, 680-9011, 777-4761
Durango: (970) 259-3337
Fort Collins: (970) 493-4781
Grand Junction: (970) 243-8184
Loveland: (970) 669-1662
Lyons: (303) 823-5941
Mountain Area: (970) 838-0238
Northglenn: (303) 452-0420

CONNECTICUT

Hartford Vegetarian Society

P.O. Box 271502, West Hartford, CT 06127-1502, (203) 673-6996 or 673-5342

Natural Hygiene, Inc.

Shelton, CT
See "National & International Organizations."

Additional Local Contacts

Bantam: Jane & Larry Sirignano, 191 Bantam Lake Road, Bantam, CT 06750
Darien: (203) 656-1522
Forestville: (203) 584-1442
Hamden: (203) 399-8713
Hartford: (860) 236-4923, 673-6996
Monroe: (203) 452-1619
Norwalk: (203) 656-1522
Quaker Hill: Mark Braunstein (203) 443-1271
Tolland: (203) 871-2315
West Hartford: (860) 537-9271
Westport: (203) 226-3695
Wilton: (203) 762-0294, 866-0523

DELAWARE

Dover Vegetarians
940 Buck Drive, Dover, DE 19901, (302) 734-8976

Additional Local Contacts
New Castle: Dr. Mel Rosenthal (302) 322-3030
Newark: (302) 234-1019

DISTRICT OF COLUMBIA

See Washington, D.C.

FLORIDA

American Natural Hygiene Society
Tampa, FL
See "National & International Organizations."

Black Rhino Vegetarian Society for African-American Women
c/o Marvyne Betsch, Rt. 3, Box 292, American Beach, FL 32034

Environmental Education Center, Miami Dade Community College
Wolfson Campus, David C. Brown, Director, 330 Biscayne Blvd., Room 711, Miami, FL 33132, (305) 237-7593, FAX: (305) 237-7541
An Environmental Education Institute with a Vegetarian Center.

Florida East Coast Vegetarian Society
P.O. Box 1914, Flagler Beach, FL 32136, (904) 427-VEGE

Florida Voices for Animals
P.O. Box 17523, Tampa, FL 33682, (813) 977-2585

G-Jo Institute
P.O. Box 8060, Hollywood, FL 33084, (954) 791-1562
A natural health education organization that offers classes. Introduces the general public to vegetarianism as a healthier, more humane, environmentally-friendly way of eating, and as a means to emotional, mental, and spiritual balance.

Greater Orlando Vegetarian Society
P.O. Box 451071, Kissimmee, FL 34745-1071, (407) 873-0291

Gulf Coast Vegetarian Society
2259 Hawthorne Street, Sarasota, FL 34239, (813) 366-1132

Indian River Vegetarian Society
c/o Muriel Golde, 2435 Tecca Drive, New Smyrna Beach, FL 32168, (904) 427-VEGE (8343)

Life Balancing Center, Inc.
1950 Sandra Drive, Clearwater, FL 34624, (813) 447-6305

Miami Vegetarian Society
Box 41-4256, Miami, FL 33141, (305) 534-2425

Pinellas County Vegetarian Society
3222-20th Street N., St. Petersburg, FL 33713, (813) 822-8359

Shangri-La Natural Hygiene Institute
P.O. Box 2328, Bonita Springs, FL 33959-2328, (813) 992-3811
Practitioners of Natural Hygiene.

Southeast Florida Vegetarian Society
c/o Dr. Richard Berman, Box 8354, Delray Beach, FL 33482, (407) 496-7031

Tampa Bay Vegetarians
c/o Ron Smith, 957 Weatherfield Drive
Dunedin, FL 34698, (813) 736-5129

Vegetarian Gourmet Society
ATTN: Mark Scheinberg, 4101 N.W. Fourth Street, Apt. 309, Plantation, FL 33317, (305) 584-3011

Vegetarian Society of Central Florida
c/o Larry Rumbough, Box 820, Goldenrod, FL 33482, (407) 6472-3723

Vegetarians of South Florida
c/o Cynthia Cowen, Environmental Center, Miami-Dade Community College, 11011 SW 104th St, Miami, FL 33176, (305) 237-2600

Additional Local Contacts
Dania: (305) 926-6420
Ft. Walton Beach: (904) 244-3957
Hollywood: (305) 791-1562

Jacksonville: (904) 771-8136, 781-3304
Lake Buena Vista: (813) 424-1158
Lake Helen: Thomas & Doris Kopko, 416 Norris Lane, Lake Helen, FL 32744
Lecanto: (904) 746-3434
Marco Island: (813) 642-1000
Melbourne: (407) 242-0772
Miami Beach: (305) 865-2176, 673-0771, (305) 673-0771 (Edwin Flatto, M.D.)
N. Miami: (305) 891-3613
N. Palm Beach: (407) 926-6420
Ocala: (904) 351-3993, 732-3516
Orlando: (407) 672-3723
Osprey: (813) 966-4075
Port Orange: (904) 761-6714
Redington Beach: (813) 391-8339
St. Petersburg: (813) 894-2518; and Lucie Ollick, 2901 8th Street N., #2, St. Petersburg, FL 33704
Tallahassee: (904) 878-4075
Tampa: (813) 961-0066
Vero Beach: (407) 231-0159

GEORGIA

Vegetarian Adventures
814 Virgil Street, Atlanta, GA 30307, (404) 798-7978

Vegetarian Society of Georgia
P.O. Box 2164, Norcross, GA 30091, Info Line: (404) 662-4019
Sponsors outings to vegetarian restaurants and events. Member directory (listing only those who give their permission). Newsletter of events: $5.

Additional Local Contacts
Atlanta: (404) 457-7963, 963-0232, 662-6006, 242-4343
Columbus: (706) 323-9194
Fayetteville: (404) 416-4500
Macon: (912) 745-2273
Morrow: Judy Waters, Box 203, Morrow, GA 30260
Norcross: (404) 662-4019
Savannah: (912) 927-4985
Wildwood: (404) 820-1474
Woodstock: (404) 343-8920

HAWAII

Gentle World, Inc.
P.O. Box U, Paia, Maui, HI 96779, (808) 572-1560 or 572-3522
Owns and operates The Vegan Restaurant at 115 Baldwin Avenue in Paia.

Vegetarian Society of Honolulu (VSH)
Box 25233, Honolulu, HI 96825, (808) 395-1499

Additional Local Contacts
Hanalei, Kauai: (808) 826-5120
Honolulu, Oahu: (808) 395-1499, 941-9476
Kaneohe, Oahu: (808) 235-2800
Kailua Kona, Big Island: (808) 324-1704
Paia, Maui: (808) 572-3522, 579-9144

IDAHO

Vegetarian Society of Boise
1810 W. State Street, #310, Boise, ID 83702, (208) 345-0317

Local Contact
Riggins: Thomas Lucas (208) 628-3130

ILLINOIS

Chicago Vegetarian Society, Inc.
P.O. Box 6154, Evanston, IL 60204, (312) 975-VEGY

Fox Valley Vegetarian Society
P.O. Box 1256, Elgin, IL 60121

Govinda's Vegetarian Buffet
1716 Lunt Avenue, Chicago, IL 60626, (312) 973-0901
A vegetarian restaurant located in the Hare Krishna temple.

Heart of Illinois Vegetarian Society
P.O. Box 3583, Peoria, IL 61612-3583, (309) 685-5833

International Non-Violence and Vegetarian Society USA
ATTN: Santokh Singh Saluja, 4039 Enfield Avenue, Skokie, IL 60076

Vegetarians in Motion (VIM)
P.O. Box 6943, Rockford, IL 61125, (815) 399-3357

Additional Local Contacts
Chicago: (312) 975-VEGY, 280-7600, 525-4952, 973-7124, 925-8227, (312) 973-7124 (Rev. Joyce Collins-Maat)
Park Forest: (708) 503-9680
Peoria: (309) 676-3170
Rockford: (815) 397-5579 and 332-5856
St.Charles: (708) 377-1885
Warrenville: (708) 393-2935

INDIANA

Michiana Area Vegetarian Society
P.O. Box 1301, South Bend, IN 46624, (219) 232-5382

Purdue Animal Rights And Diet Information Service (PARADISE)
c/o Ted Zagar, 4216 Tod Avenue, East Chicago, IN 46312

Vegetarian Society of SouthWest Indiana
714 Jefferson, Evansville, IN 47713, (812) 423-6330

Additional Local Contacts
Bloomington: (812) 339-8683
East Chicago: (219) 397-9297
Evansville: (812) 464-1025
Kokomo: (219) 732-1342
South Bend: (219) 288-6995
Valparaiso: (219) 464-2467

IOWA

Cedar Prairie Vegetarians
1710 Walnut Street, Cedar Falls, IA 50613, (319) 266-9727

Des Moines Vegetarian Society
P.O. Box 12, Carlisle, IA 50047, (515) 989-3473 (Ava M. Bothe)

Vegetarian Society of Central Iowa (VSCI)
P.O. Box 761, Ames, IA 50010

Vegetarians Establishing the Greatest Good for Iowa's Environment (V.E.G.G.I.E.)
1535 29th Street, Des Moines, IA 50311, (515) 255-0213

Additional Local Contacts
Ames: (515) 292-0950
Davenport: (319) 326-1606
Humboldt: Frank Zigrang (515) 332-3087
Iowa City (University of Iowa): (319) 337-8403

KANSAS

People for Animal Rights (PAR)
P.O. Box 2928, Olathe, KS 66062-0928, (816) 767-1199

The Vegetarian Society of Kansas
3709 SW Stonybrook Drive, Topeka, KS 66610, (913) 273-3652

Vegetarian Society of Kansas City
P.O. Box 3301, Shawnee Mission, KS 66203, (913) 268-4649

Additional Local Contacts
Lawrence: (913) 749-1330
Overland Park: (913) 362-7439
Wichita: (316) 733-2674

KENTUCKY

EarthSave Louisville
P.O. Box 4396, Louisville, KY 40204, (502) 569-1876
See "National & International Organizations."

Friends Vegetarian Society of North America

Louisville, KY 40206
See "National & International Organizations."

Vegetarian Support Group

c/o Joe Higginbotham, 170 Sherman Avenue, Lexington, KY 40502, (606) 272-0996

Additional Local Contact

Lexington: (606) 269-5622, 299-3074, 269-9850 (Don Mortland)

LOUISIANA

Animal Peace

7704 Sycamore, New Orleans, LA 70118, (504) 865-9792

Jack Sprat's Vegetarian Grill

3240 S. Carrollton, New Orleans, LA 70118, (504) 486-2200
Not an organization, but a restaurant owned and operated by "animal people" involved with the New Orleans-based group Legislation In Support of Animals (see Chapter 10 for a description of that group).

Additional Local Contact

New Orleans: (504) 366-8972; and Brenda Carter,1509 Dublin Street, New Orleans, LA 70118

MAINE

Khadighar Vegan Farm

P.O. Box 1167, Farmington, ME 04938
A vegan family farm that conducts public demonstrations and lectures. Write for schedule of classes which take place every April.

Maine Vegetarian Resource Network

c/o Shari Greenfield, RFD 2, Box 194, Belfast, ME 04915, (207) 338-1861
Statewide. Contact them for the chapter nearest you.

Additional Local Contacts

Bath: (207) 781-7170
Belfast: (207) 338-5675 and 338-6232
Caribou: (207) 496-8091
Center Lovell: Steve Kaplan, c/o Dan Kaplan, Quisisanaon on Lake Kezar, Center Lowell, ME 04016
Fort Fairfield: (207) 476-5250
Hampden: (207) 862-2349
Poland Spring: (207) 998-2795, 998-2894
Portland: (207) 773-6132, 774-7461
Skowhegan: (207) 474-6645
Wayne: (207) 685-4630

MARYLAND

Eclectic Vegetarian Club

c/o Karen A. Boyle, 27 Norman Allen Street, Elkton, MD 21921

Jewish Vegetarian Club

c/o Nina Adler, 2602 Squaw Valley Court, #11, Silver Spring, MD 20906

Vegetarian Resource Group

Baltimore, MD
See "National & International Organizations."

Jewish Vegetarian Society, Inc.

P.O. Box 5722, Baltimore MD 21208-0722, (410) 486-4948 (24-hours, except sundown Friday until sundown Saturday, Eastern Time)

Jewish Vegetarians of North America

Federalsburg, MD
See "National & International Organizations."

The Vegetarian Resource Group

Baltimore, MD
See "National & International Organizations."

Additional Local Contacts

Annapolis: (410) 268-4371, 267-9218
Baltimore: (410) 788-1328; and Eileen Scully, 7 Lodge Road, Baltimore, MD 21228
Bethesda: (301) 530-1737
Bowie: (301) 464-5431
Brentwood: (301) 443-4177
Clarksville: (410) 964-3574
Columbia: (410) 730-1553
Cumberland: John & Amy Shuman, (301) 777-3719
Damascus: (301) 428-0217
Ellicott City: (410) 461-6949
Gaithersburg: (301) 977-3206
Hagerstown: (301) 733-4411

Mt. Ranier: (301) 443-4177
Rockville: (301) 770-0208
Silver Spring: (301) 588-6093, 588-0195

MASSACHUSETTS

Advocates for Animals
c/o Joanne Santella, 96 Fisher Hill Road, Cheshire, MA 01225, (413) 743-1448

Ann Wigmore Foundation
1340 Commonwealth Avenue, Boston, MA 02134, (617) 267-9424
Living Foods Lifestyle. (*Note*: This is not the same as "raw food," which can be hard to digest for people with allergies.)

Berkshire Vegetarian Network
Mary Kelly, Beach Hill Road, New Ashford, MA 01237

Boston Vegetarian Society (BVS)
P.O. Box 38-1071, Cambridge MA 02233-1071, (617) 381-3217 (answered by a human in the evenings and by a machine all other times)

Cape Cod Vegetarians (CCV)
P.O. Box 243, Sagamore Beach, MA 02562

Citizens to End Animal Suffering and Exploitation (CEASE)
P.O. Box 440456, Somerville, MA 02144, (617) 628-9030

Health Valley
Northamtpon, MA, (413) 585-0319

Jews for Animal Rights
Roberta Kalechofsky, 255 Humphrey Street, Marblehead, MA 01945, (617) 631-7601

New England Vegetarian Resource Center
Cambridge, MA
See "National & International Organizations."

North Shore Vegetarians
50 Tracey Street, Peabody, MA 01960, (508) 531-6547 or (508) 777-4312 or (617) 598-0747

Vegetarian Education Group
P.O. Box 1223, Shirley, MA 01464-1223

Additional Local Contacts
Boston: (617) 491-5450, 523-6020, 424-8846, 265-7577, 625-3797
Boylston: (508) 869-2646
Cambridge: (617) 354-0317
Cape Cod: (508) 255-6095
Jamaica Plain: (617) 695-7259
Leicester: Carol Coughlin (508) 892-3164
Marblehead: (617) 631-7601
Medford: (617) 395-1608
New Ashford: (413) 443-4752
Northampton: (413) 585-0319
N. Cambridge: (617) 628-8035
N. Oxford: (508) 892-8432
Orleans: (508) 255-6095
Peabody: (508) 531-6547
Sagamore Beach: (508) 888-2106
South Wellsfleet: Russ Holt (508) 349-6026
Wellesley: Kirsten Chevalier, 4 Cedar Street, #3, Wellesley, MA 02181
Winchester: Daryl Elliot (617) 729-5557
Worchester: (508) 756-5801

MICHIGAN

Health Force Center
Bob Zuraw/Bob Lewanski, 2222 Hempstead Drive, Troy, MI 48083
Not a member organization, but rather vegetarians who conduct lectures, seminars, and workshops.

Michigan Vegetarian Society (MVS)
Liz Morgan (President), P.O. Box 258, Clawson, MI 48017-0258, (313) 435-3514

Vegetarian Information Network & Exchange (VINE)
E-mail: vine-info@umich.edu
- Ann Arbor: P.O. Box 2224, Ann Arbor, MI 48106-2224, (313) 668-9925
- Dexter: (313) 426-8525
- Tecumseh: (517) 423-3226

Washtenaw Citizens for Animal Rights (WCAR)
P.O. Box 2614, Ann Arbor, MI 48106, (313) 426-1680 or 426-2492

Additional Local Contacts

Ann Arbor: (313) 769-2873
Farmington Hills: (810) 478-4455
Perry: (517) 675-5213
Plymouth: (313) 455-1556
Royal Oak: Michael Chiado, Box 432, Royal Oak, MI 480647
Troy: (313) 795-2706

MINNESOTA

EarthSave Minneapolis

277 Brookshire Lane North, Plymouth, MN 55441, (612) 595-8168
See "National & International Organizations."

Vegetarian Information Service of Minnesota

ATTN: John Lowell Simcox, 5049 Thomas Avenue South, Minneapolis, MN 55410, (612) 920-6412

Vegetarian Society for EARTH (Environment, Animal Rights, and Total Health)

721 Second Avenue N., Sauk Rapids, MN 56379, (612) 252-5370

Additional Local Contacts

Bloomington: (612) 822-6161, 866-6604
Minnekonka: Melinda Kjarum-Peterson, 16511 Canterbury Drive, Minnekonka, MN 55345
St. Cloud: (612) 252-0685 (Mary Ahles), 252-8556
St. Paul: (612) 699-5746

MISSISSIPPI

Local Contacts

Grenada: (601) 237-4382
Jackson: (601) 366-1602
Kosciusko: (601) 289-1234
Ocean Springs: (601) 875-8882
Oxford: (601) 236-3757
Ridgeland: Lana Ethridge, Box 1320, Ridgeland, MS 39158

MISSOURI

M.A.I.S. of Missouri

ATTN: Elena Moreno, Rt. 3, Box 560, Fredericktown, MO 63645, (314) 783-6715
Associated with the M.A.I.S.-Native American Vegetarian Group (see California for their description).

Missouri Vegetarian Society

c/o James Betts, P.O. Box 2345, Overland, MO 63114, (314) 429-2786

Solar Yoga Center of St. Louis

6002 Pershing (at Des Peres), St. Louis, MO 63112, (314) 726-5133
Part of the Universal Great Brotherhood, with centers in Los Angeles, Brooklyn, Chicago, and Houston.

St. Louis Animal Rights Team (START)

P.O. Box 28501, St. Louis, MO 63146, (314) 851-0928

Vegetarian Society of Metro St. Louis

P.O. Box 6771, St. Louis, MO 63144, (314) 995-2699

Vegetarians of Kansas City

7643 Holmes, Kansas City, MO 64131-2028

Additional Local Contacts

Kansas City: (816) 363-5767, 331-6783, 767-1199
St. Louis: (314) 961-5096, 863-6321, 773-6373
Springfield: (417) 862-0738, 889-9888

MONTANA

Local Contact

Billings: (406) 322-4231, (406) 656-7416 (Richard Nelson, M.D. & Jerrie Lynn Nelson, R.D.)

NEBRASKA

Nebraska Vegetarian Society (NVS)

- Lincoln Chapter: P.O. Box 30631, Lincoln, NE 68503, (402) 476-7252
- Omaha Chapter: P.O. Box 715, Omaha, NE 68101, (402) 554-1644

Additional Local Contacts

Lincoln: (402) 474-3169
Omaha: (402) 344-2889

NEVADA

Sierra Vegetarian Society

15425 Fawn Lane, Reno, NV 89511, (702) 849-9566

Local Contact

Las Vegas: Nancy Bjornsen (702) 732-1599

NEW HAMPSHIRE

New Hampshire Animal Rights League, Inc. (NHARL)

520 Bean Hill Road, Northfield, NH 03276, (603) 286-8477

Vegetarians of Merrimack Valley

16 Raleigh Drive, Nashua, NH 03062, (603) 888-1450

Additional Local Contacts

Hanover: (603) 643-2667
New Boston: (603) 487-3265

NEW JERSEY

American Vegan Society

Malaga, NJ
See "National & International Organizations."

Animals Need You Kindness Club, Inc.

P.O. Box 65, West New York, NJ 07093

The Beaver Defenders

P.O. Box 765, Newfield, NJ 08344, (609) 697-3541

Cape Atlantic Vegetarians

2018 Rt. 9, Seaville, NJ 08230, Contact: Len Frenkel, (609) 390-9040 (days), 390-0744 (eves)

Central Jersey Vegetarian Group

Stacey Wilder, P.O. Box 952, Manville, NJ 08835

Coalition for Animals

Rose Thiessen, Box 2422, Edison, NJ 08818, (908) 548-3051

Jersey Shore Vegetarian Network

908 Richmond Avenue, Pointe Pleasant Beach, NJ 08742, (908) 892-3588

Jewish Vegetarian Society of Central and Southern New Jersey

c/o Debbie Israel, (908) 846-1972

NE Vegetarian Association (NEVA)

P.O. Box 7116, Sussex, NJ 07461, (201) 875-2068

Two-Fu Vegetarian Singles Connection

P.O. Box 824, Westwood, NJ 07675
A match-making service for vegetarians (fee).

Vegetarian Cycling and Athletic Club

c/o Martin Samelson, 17 Drexel Hill Drive, Kendall Park, NJ 08824, (201) 821-8354

Vegetarian Family Network of the Shore

c/o Maria Hidalgo Dolan, 1138 Concord Drive, Brick, NJ 08724, (908) 458-5435

Vegetarian Lifestyle Institute

P.O. Box 432, Woodridge, NJ 07075, (201) 933-5235

Vegetarian Neighbors

c/o Roshan Dinshah, P.O. Box 385, Malaga, NJ 08328, (609) 694-3025

Vegetarian Society of South Jersey

(Also known as the South Jersey Vegetarian Society)
P.O. Box 272, Marlton, NJ 08053, (609) 354-0909

Additional Local Contacts

Basking Ridge: (908) 953-0060
Belmar: Bill & Pat Griffin (908) 681-1705
Califon: Joan Clifford (908) 832-9612
Denville: (201) 361-0679
Deptford: (609) 853-1847
Elmer: (609) 358-8351
Englishtown: (908) 446-6808
Franklinville: (609) 694-4235
Hamilton: (609) 585-0489
Hoboken: (201) 763-3754
Jersey City: (201) 470-8971
Mahwah: Lorene Cox, 134 Johnson Avenue, Mahwah, NJ 07430
Malaga: (609) 694-2887, 694-3639
Marlton: (609) 354-0909, 983-3964, 768-5140, 768-7281
Mays Landing: (609) 391-9535
Morris Twp: Jeanne Jeffrey, 101-2F Lindsley Drive, Morris Twp, NJ 07960
Newark: (201) 470-8971
Ocean Grove: (908) 775-6242
Ocean View: (609) 390-9040
Oceanville: (609) 927-2473
Piscataway: (908) 752-1629
Plainfield: Susan Gordon (908) 561-6564
Pompton Plains: (210) 839-5919
Princeton: Andrea & Bill Hart, 4414 Sayre Drive, Princeton, NJ 08540
Rockaway: (201) 689-8801
Roselle Park: Sean O'Gara, 200 W. Webster Avenue, #B3, Roselle Park, NJ 07204
St. Cloud: (612) 252-0685
Summit: (908) 273-7762
Sussex: (201) 875-1755
Teaneck: (201) 836-1890
Trenton: (609) 983-3964
Verona: (201) 403-6829
Voorhees: (609) 853-1847, 768-8912
W. New York: (201) 866-8968
West Orange: (201) 731-0792
Willingboro: (609) 877-8923
Woodbridge: (908) 636-2663
Woodstown: (609) 769-1963
Yardville: (609) 585-0489

NEW MEXICO

Santa Fe Rainforest Action

P.O. Box 1171, Santa Fe, NM 87504, (505) 988-1617
See the description for this group in Chapter 10.

Vegetarian Society of New Mexico

P.O. Box 81963, Albuquerque, NM 87198-1963, (505) 266-1293, In Las Cruces: (505) 526-5978

Additional Local Contacts

Albuquerque: (505) 265-1961, 298-5010, 281-0032
Las Cruces: (505) 382-7140
Santa Fe: (505) 983-2200

NEW YORK

Adirondack Foothills Vegetarian Society

RD 1, Box 651, Cold Brook, NY 13324, (315) 826-7405

Afrikan Wholistic Network

P.O. Box 881, New York, NY 10035

Afro-American Vegetarian Society (A.A.V.S.)

P.O. Box 46, Colonial Park Station, New York, NY 10039, (914) 664-2066

Animal Rights Action League (ARAL)

P.O. Box 1323, Saratoga Springs, NY 12866, (518) 587-6742

Big Apple Vegetarians

125 Ocean Parkway, #3A, Brooklyn, NY 11218, (718) 438-1523

Break Bread...For a Change

c/o Tony White, 118 Remsen, Brooklyn, NY 11201, (718) 797-4175

Club Veg—Triple Cities

c/o Amie Hamlin, P.O. Box 625, Westview Station, Binghamton, NY 13905, (607) 724-1691

Corning Vegetarian Society

c/o Margorie Demeo, P.O. Box 302, Painted Post, NY 14870, (607) 936-1239

EarthSave Long Island

P.O. Box 292, Huntington, NY 11743, (516) 421-3791
See "National & International Organizations."

Earthshare—The Vegetarian Alliance (EVA)
(formerly Hudson Valley Vegetarian Society)
P.O. Box 289, Stony Point, NY 10980, (914) 429-1071

Farm Sanctuary's Vegetarian Bed & Breakfast
Farm Sanctuary, P.O. Box 150, Watkins Glen, NY 14891, (607) 583-2225
A sanctuary for farm animals located in the "Finger Lakes Region" of upstate New York.

Feminists for Animal Rights
c/o Batya Bauman, P.O. Box 694, Cathedral Station, New York, NY 10025-0694, (212) 866-6422

Finger Lakes Vegetarian Society
c/o Lars Charles Mazzola, 6919 Old Bald Hill Road South, Springwater, NY 14560, (516) 543-8350

Food Not Bombs
156 Virginia Street, New York, NY 10002, (212) 254-3697

Island Vegetarians
P.O. Box 1146, Huntington, NY 11743, (516) 349-8639

Jewish Vegetarian Society (NY)
5 East 22nd Street, New York, NY 10010, (212) 533-0375

Jewish Vegetarian Society (International)
Hurleyville, NY
See "National & International Organizations."

Long Island Vegetarians
(516) 887-4374

Mid Hudson Vegetarian Society
55 Catskill Avenue, Kingston, NY 12401, (914) 338-8223

Natural Hygiene—New York
(212) 750-5223

New York Vegan Society
c/o Sharon Smithline, 6309 108th Avenue, #3A, Forest Hills, NY 11375, (718) 997-0314

North American Vegetarian Society
Dolgeville, NY
See "National & International Organizations."

RHIO's Living Foods Hotline
(212) 343-1152
Environmental and food-related information—lectures, classes in the NY metro area, books, guides, etc. Message changes once or twice a month.

Rochester Area Vegetarian Society (RAVS)
P.O. Box 20185, Rochester, NY 14602-0185, (716) 381-2208 (Rhoda Sapon or Dr. Stanley M. Sapon, Co-Coordinators)

Shawangunk Nature Preserve
Cold Brook, NY
See the "Local Animal Organizations" section of Chapter 10.

Sephardic Renaissance Society, Inc.—Genesis Project
109-15 Queens Blvd., Forest Hills, NY 11375

Vegan Society of Queens
15039-75th Avenue, #2A, Flushing, NY 113647, (718) 263-7160

Vegetarian Dieticians and Nutrition Educators
Burdett, NY
See "National & International Organizations."

Vegetarian Learning Center
c/o Charray Bryant, 6914 St. Highway 58, Hammond, NY 13646, (315) 578-2715

Vegetarian Society of Chautauqua-Allegheny
c/o John F. Cayer, 701 W. 8th Street, Jamestown, NY 14701, (716) 483-5408

Vegetarian Society of New York
128 E. 83rd, New York, NY 10028, (212) 535-9385

The Vegetarian Youth Network
New Paltz, NY
See "National & International Organizations."

Vegetarians of the Capitol Region
c/o Maria Morato, 111 Acorn Drive, Scotia, NY 12302, (518) 399-9823

VivaVegie Society
P.O. Box 294, Prince Street Station, New York, NY 10012, (212) 966-2060

Whole Life Center
Leonard Burg, E. 181st Street, #7A, Bronx, NY 10457

Women and Animals—Activist Archive/ Vegetarian Activist Collective
c/o Connie Salamone, 184 Seeley Street, Brooklyn, NY 11218, (718) 435-3998

Additional Local Contacts
Amherst: (716) 648-6423
Ardsley: (914) 674-0577
Auburn: (315) 393-1525
Brooklyn: (718) 291-6825
Bronx: (718) 584-5026
Buffalo: (716) 483-5408, 839-0062, 353-4462
Chestnut Ridge: (914) 356-1765
Coram: (516) 696-3685
Dolgeville: (518) 568-7970
E. Berne: (518) 872-2418
Huntington: (516) 549-2545, 887-4374
Jamaica: (718) 291-6825
Little Falls: (518) 568-2077
Manhattan: (718) 438-1523; (212) 724-8782, 873-3674, 978-4338, 535-9385, 750-5223, 334-2355, 662-3787
Montour Falls: (607) 535-6089
New Paltz: (914) 255-2706
New York: (202) 483-8998
Plainview: (516) 349-8639
Pleasantville: (914) 232-3204
Potsdam: (315) 265-9036
Queens: (718) 263-7160
Rego Park: (718) 544-5997
Saratoga Springs: (518) 587-9516
Schenectady: (518) 393-8155
Selkirk: (518) 767-2034
Smithtown: (516) 979-9162
Syracuse: (315) 422-9716, 488-PURR, 425-9362 (SU), 443-9144 (SU)
Vestal: (607) 757-9463
Wantagh: (516) 783-0272
Watertown: (315) 788-2463
Woodridge: (914) 434-5339
Woodstock: (914) 679-4242

NORTH CAROLINA

Mecklenberg Vegetarian Association
P.O. Box 11288, Charlotte, NC 28209, (704) 545-3796

North Carolina Network for Animals (NCNA)
ATTN: D.J. Francis, P.O. Box 7593, Greensboro, NC 27417-0593, (910) 294-NCNA (6262)
- and -
Gastonia/Charlotte Chapter: c/o Rick Williams, 420 Meacham Street, Charlotte, NC 28203
An animal rights group with vegetarian outreach.

Rowan Vegetarians
c/o Molly Carpenter, 4625 US 601 Highway, Salisbury, NC 28147, (704) 633-3866

Triangle Vegetarian Society
P.O. Box 61069, Durham, NC 27705-1069, (919) 682-0309

Vegetarian Society of the Lower Cape Fear
P.O. Box 3411, Wilmington, NC 28406, (919) 791-4907 (JoAnn L. Fogler)

Very Vegetarian Society
620 Bellview Street, Winston-Salem, NC 27103-3502, (919) 756-2614

Western North Carolina Vegetarian Society
P.O. Box 368, Cullowhee, NC 28723

Additional Local Contacts
Asheville: (704) 258-4869, 688-2675, 687-6704, 251-5700, and Miriam Rudow, 9 Reese Road, Asheville, NC 28805
Chapel Hill: (919) 286-1177
Charlotte: (704) 593-3796; and Rick Williams, 420 Meacham Street, Charlotte, NC 28203; Suzanne Havala, R.D., 2933 Robin Road, Charlotte, NC 28211
Durham: (919) 489-3340
Fayetteville: (910) 483-9504
Hendersonville: Frederick Chaffe (704) 692-8937
Raeford: (910) 875-8210

Raleigh: (919) 782-6464
Roanoke Rapids: (919) 537-0695
Wake County: (919) 319-0585

NORTH DAKOTA

Local Contact

Bismark: (701) 258-8280

OHIO

Cincinnati Vegetarian Resource Group (CVRG)

P.O. Box 31455, Cincinnati, OH 45231, (513) 542-6810

Cincinnati Vegetarian Society

ATTN: Charles Francis, 2424 Beekman Street, Cincinnati, OH 45214, (513) 631-4810 or 471-6060

EarthSave Cincinnati

4550 Camberwell Road, #1, Cincinnati, OH 45209-1155, (513) 533-3879
See "National & International Organizations."

Fit for Life Study Group

- West Side Group: Helen Kopp, 12521 Indian Hollow Road, Grafton, OH 44044, (216) 458-5551
- East Side Group: Stanley Alprin, 7711 Dines Road, Novelty, OH 44072, (216) 338-5177

Midwest Macrobiotic Center

840 Central Avenue, Carlisle, OH 45005, (513) 746-4077 (Kathy and Jim Wright) or (513) 625-5240 (Judy Paris)
Vegan macrobiotics.

Network for Ohio Animal Action

P.O. Box 21004, Cleveland, OH 44121-0004, (216) 691-0662

Phoenix Earth Food Coop

1737 Hinsdale, Toledo, OH 43614, (419) 385-0989
A food cooperative.

Protect Our Earth's Treasures

P.O. Box 10156, Columbus, OH 43201-0656, (614) 299-9001

Vegetarian Club of Canton

P.O. Box 9079, Canton, OH 44711, (216) 492-2387

Vegetarian Connection

c/o Donna Corso, 6383 Carolyn Drive, Mentor, OH 44060, (216) 656-4896

Vegetarian Society of Northern Ohio

50 E. Main Street, Norwalk, OH 44857, (419) 668-1010

Vegetarian Society of Toledo (VST)

P.O. Box 12485, Toledo, OH 43606, (419) 536-4073

Vegetarian Society—Greater Dayton Area

P.O. Box 404, Englewood, OH 45322, (513) 429-9163

Vegetarians of the Greater Youngstown Area

c/o Bill and Marianne Whitehouse, 1631 Price Road, Youngstown, OH 44509, (216) 799-7237

Additional Local Contacts

Ashland: Paula Boose, 1414 County Road 1475 Rt. 1, Ashland, OH 44805
Avon Lake: Jeanette Woolsey (216) 933-2590
Brunswick: (216) 225-2862, 888-2224
Cincinnati: (513) 961-5555
Mentor: (216) 257-3093
Norwalk: (419) 668-1010
Parma: Kathleen Green (216) 888-6863
Payne: (419) 263-2371
Reynoldsburg: (614) 861-4859
Springfield: Randy Shields (513) 323-3064
Toledo: (419) 472-6259, 472-2003
Walton Hills: (216) 642-7254
Yellow Springs: (513) 767-7986

OKLAHOMA

Northeast Oklahoma Vegetarian Association (NOVA)

Rt. 1, Box 207, Dewey, OK 74029, (918) 534-3018

Tulsa Vegetarian Society
P.O. Box 14333, Tulsa, OK 74159, (918) 488-0213

Vegetarians for Life
409 NW 33rd Street, Oklahoma City, OK 73118, (405) 524-7989

Vegetarians of Oklahoma City
P.O. Box 57271, Oklahoma City, OK 73157, (405) 598-6742

Additional Local Contacts
Bethany: (405) 789-3506
Midwest City: Padmaja Sundaram, 317 W. Campbell Drive, Midwest City, OK 73110
Oklahoma City: (405) 947-2915, 948-1307

OREGON

EarthSave Oregon
- Bend: c/o Central Oregon Environmental Organization, 16 NW Kansas Street, Bend, OR 97701, (503) 385-7918
- Eugene: P.O. Box 286, Dexter, OR 97431, (503) 998-4970

See "National & International Organizations."

Central Oregon Friends of EarthSave
c/o Cherie Soria, 2119 NW Cascade View Drive, Bend, OR 97701, (503) 388-6806

Corvallis Vegetarians
c/o John Donel, 145 NW 16th Street, #303, Corvallis, OR 97330, (503) 753-2265

Portland Vegetarians
P.O. Box 19521, Portland, OR 97219, (503) 223-5596

Additional Local Contacts
Ashland: (503) 482-1884
Bend: (503) 389-5687, 388-6806, 388-8100
Coos Bay: (503) 267-2223
Eugene: (503) 683-4351, ext. 106
Salem: (503) 364-2448
Seaside: (503) 738-9294

PENNSYLVANIA

Alleghany Foothills Vegetarian Society
RD 3, Box 351, Homer City, PA 15748, (412) 479-3054

Animal Advocates, Inc.
Contact Person: Susan Zdrodowski, P.O. Box 8480, Pittsburgh, PA 15220, (412) 928-9777

Delaware Valley Vegan Society
ATTN: Chris Collins, 1910 Myrtlewood Street, Philadelphia, PA 19121, (215) 765-7207

Go Vegetarian!
P.O. Box 23384, Pittsburgh, PA 15222, (412) 363-2832

Happy Vegetarian's Society
RD1, Box 456, Barto, PA 19504, (215) 845-8289

Lehigh Valley Vegetarians
Gloria M. Perlis, President, 1035 Flexer Avenue, Allentown, PA 18103, (215) 437-3278

Main Line Vegetarian Society
c/o Jim Oswald, 333 Bryn Mawr Avenue, Bala Cynwyd, PA 19004, (610) 667-6876

Pennsylvania Animal Welfare Society (PAWS)
P.O. Box 28599, Philadelphia, PA 19149, (215) 332-PAWS

Pittsburgh Vegetarian Society
106 Cobb Avenue, Pittsburgh, PA 15205-2004, (412) 922-1328

Vegan Outreach
10410 Forbes Road, Pittsburgh, PA 15235, (412) 247-3527

Vegetarian Education Network
Kirkwood, PA
See "National & International Organizations."

Vegetarian Society of Central Pennsylvania, Inc.
P.O. Box 11066, State College, PA 16805-1066, (814) 466-7440

Vegetarian Society of Northeastern Pennsylvania (VSNEPA)
P.O. Box 1724, Wilkes-Barre, PA 18703

Vegetarian Society of Somerset
RD 1, Box 206B, Stoystown, PA 15563, (814) 443-6814

The Vegetarians Of Philadelphia (TVOP)
Contact Person: Andy Lefkowitz, P.O. Box 24353, Philadelphia, PA 19120, (215) 276-3198

Additional Local Contacts
Allentown: (610) 821-9552
Annville: (717) 867-5565
Aston: Anella Izquierdo, 613 Convent Road, Aston, PA 19014
Clarks Summit: (717) 586-2919, 587-3926
Cochranville: (215) 593-2938
Conneaut Lake: Robert Stewart (814) 382-3593
Dalton: David Sickles, Box 56, Dalton, PA 18414
Danville: Steve Dimmick (717) 275-2786
Downington: (215) 873-9985
Harrisburg: (717) 780-1531
Indiana: (412) 349-2192
Jenkintown: (215) 887-0816
N. Wales: (215) 646-2293
Oxford: (717) 529-8638
Philadelphia: (215) 985-1838, 322-1492, 438-1998; and Louise Emma (215) 482-7931
Pittsburgh: (412) 734-5554, 456-7449
Reading: (610) 765-7207
Renfrew: (412) 586-5962
State College: (814) 238-2239
West Chester: (717) 529-8638, (215) 368-7385, 430-3775
York: (717) 845-9683 (Kathryn Wicker), (717) 825-3069

RHODE ISLAND

Rhode Island Animal Rights Coalition
P.O. Box 28514, Providence, RI 02908, (401) 783-1574

Rhode Island Vegetarian Society
P.O. Box 716, N. Scituate, RI 02857, (401) 421-6193

Additional Local Contacts
Newport: (401) 847-DEER
N. Scituate: (401) 647-5664
Woonsocket: (401) 766-2664

SOUTH CAROLINA

Clemson Vegetarian Group
P.O. Box 33131, Clemson, SC 29633, (803) 653-3329

Friends of the Earth Vegetarian Society
P.O. Box 854, Clemson, SC 29631, (803) 868-2402

Greenville Vegetarian Association
10 Terramont Drive, Greenville, SC 29615, (803) 322-0942

Kindred Spirits Vegetarian Collective
c/o JoAnne Shields, 1914 Huntington Place, Rock Hill, SC 29730, (803) 328-5977

South Carolina Vegetarian Society
P.O. Box 1093, Lexington, SC 29071, (803) 957-8155 (Carol H. Cassetti, President)

Additional Local Contacts
Central: (803) 639-6113
Greer: (803) 848-3362
Mt. Pleasant: Elfrida Raly (803) 884-5303

SOUTH DAKOTA

Local Contact
Sioux Falls: (605) 334-8151

TENNESSEE

East Tennessee Vegetarian Society
P.O. Box 1974, Knoxville, TN 37901, (423) 522-5555

Tennessee Vegetarian Society
P.O. Box 854, Knoxville, TN 37901, 1-800-EAT-VEGE (328-8343) (U.S. and Canada)

Vegetarian Association of West Tennessee

c/o Catherine Billings, 787 Ellsworth, Memphis, TN 38111, (901) 454-4975

Vegetarian Awareness Network, Communications Center

Knoxville, TN
See "National & International Organizations."

Additional Local Contacts

Chattanooga: (423) 267-5875
Johnson City: (423) 929-1331
Knoxville: (423) 546-5643
Nashville: (615) 331-0779 (Ton Barron), 385-4047
Sevierville: (615) 436-2861

TEXAS

Animal Connection of Texas (ACT)

P.O. Box 679008-141, Dallas, TX 75367, (214) 373-7867 (24-hour Info Line)
Animal rights group with vegetarian outreach.

Austin Vegetarian Society

c/o Pat Tierra, President, P.O. Box 2335, Cedar Park, TX 78613, (512) 331-5287

Corpus Christi Area Vegetarian Society

c/o Diane Hermansen, 3636 B. South Alameda, #181, Corpus Christi, TX 78411, (512) 884-7929

The Dallas Vegetarians

19 Willow Creek Place, Richardson, TX 75080, (214) 997-1936, For information, write or call: Peggy Vaughan, 4418 Cole, #3, Dallas, TX 75205, (214) 520-7251

Denton Area Vegetarian Organization

2040 W. Oak, Denton, TX 76201, (817) 383-3858

Fort Worth Vegetarian Society

P.O. Box 24008, Ft. Worth, TX 76124, (817) 446-5020 or (817) 588-1826 (Info Line)

Galveston Vegetarian Society

300 Strand, #407, Galveston, TX 77550, (409) 763-2533

I.D.E.A.S. (I Don't Eat Animals Society)

P.O. Box 667, Olmito, TX 78575, (210) 831-0698

International Jewish Vegetarian and Ecological Society

12871 Montfort, #146, Dallas, TX 75230, (214) 991-0123

Lone Star Vegetarian Network

Shirley Wilkes-Johnson (Director) 254 Edgewater Drive, W. Columbia, TX 77486, (409) 345-5453

Rio Grand Valley Vegetarian Society

P.O. Box 667, Olmito, TX 78575, (210) 831-0698

San Antonio Vegetarian Society

P.O. Box 23127, San Antonio, TX 78223, (512) 684-4592

Society for Texas Animal Rights (STAR)

P.O. Box 595547, Dallas, TX 75359, (214) 821-7047 (24-hour Info Line)
Animal rights group with vegetarian outreach.

South Texas Vegetarian Society

P.O. Box 314, W. Columbia, TX 77486, (409) 345-5453 (Shirley Wilkes-Johnson)

Texas Vegetarian Society (TVS)

c/o 5430 Gurley Avenue, Dallas, TX 75223, (214) 823-7264

Valley Vegetarian Society

P.O. Box 102, Boca Chica Star Route, Brownsville, TX 78521, (512) 832-3943

Vegetarian Society of El Paso

Socorro (Sukie) Sargent, Founder, 218 Fresno Drive, El Paso, TX 79915, (915) 860-8585

Vegetarian Society of Houston

P.O. Box 980093, Houston, TX 77098-0093, (713) 880-1055

Vegetarian Society of the Valley

P.O. Box 720598, McAllen, TX 78504, (210) 380-1703

Additional Local Contacts

Austin: (512) 4647-8516 (Michael Bluejay), 454-2355
Brazoria City: (409) 297-0730
Cedar Park: (512) 331-SAVS
College Station: (409) 846-6830
Corpus Christi: (512) 852-6573
Dallas: (214) 823-3078, 821-1048, 239-8678, 233-5025 (SMU)

Denton: Gene Franks (817) 382-3814
El Paso: (915) 859-0037, 860-8586, 526-5919
Fort Worth: (817) 588-1826
Galveston: (409) 762-0008
Garland: (214) 530-8295
Grapevine: (817) 488-5145
Houston: (713) 789-5243, 522-5131, 468-3383
Kyle: (512) 268-2502
Lake Jackson: (409) 297-4296
Montgomery: (713) 298-5665
Richardson: (214) 997-1936
San Antonio: (210) 333-3310
Smithville: (512) 237-4442
Wimberley: Bev Allen, P.O. Box 668, Wimberley, TX 78676

UTAH

EarthSave Salt Lake City
170 St. Moritz Strasse, Park City, UT 84060, (801) 647-0961
See "National & International Organizations."

Vegetarian Society of Utah
3678 East Millcreek Road, Salt Lake City, UT 84109, (801) 277-3585

Additional Local Contacts
Salt Lake City: (801) 268-4237, 943-7664
Spanish Fork: Charv Das, KHQN-1480, 8628 S. State Road, Spanish Fork, UT 84660, (801) 798-3559

VERMONT

Vermont Vegetarian Society (VVS)
RR1, Box 1797, North Ferrisburg, VT 05473, (802) 453-3945

Additional Local Contacts
Milton: Stan Benton, 504 W. Westford Road, Milton, VT 05468
Putney: Steven & Donna Faith Brooks (802) 722-4318

VIRGINIA

Shenandoah Valley Vegetarian Society (SVVS)
c/o Marissa J. Benavente, RR3, Box 163-6, Staunton, VA 24401, (703) 886-7127

Tidewater Vegetarians
Rt. 5, Box 727B, Gloucester, VA 23061, (804) 694-0751

Valley Vegan Society
Rt. 1, Box 343, Port Republic, VA 24471, (703) 249-4801

Vegetarian Society of New River Valley
c/o Linda Ruth Schwab, 117 S. Main Street, Blacksburg, VA 24060, (703) 382-8370 or 552-3622

Virginia Beach Vegetarian Society
c/o Anne Burkey, 2700 Bluebill Drive, Virginia Beach, VA 23456, (804) 721-3980

Virginia Vegetarian Society
c/o Mary Clifford, 6451 Cotton Hill Road, Roanoke, VA 24018, (703) 772-3316

Additional Local Contacts
Ashland: Lois Angeletti (804) 752-4553
Burlington: (802) 865-3492
Newport News: Pam Estelle-Horner (804) 877-2471

WASHINGTON

Bodhi Vegetarian Society
c/o Irl La Grange, Jr., 1411 E. Fir Street, Seattle, WA 98122, (206) 325-6519

EarthSave Seattle
P.O. Box 9422, Seattle, WA 98109, (206) 781-6602
Satellite chapters in Olympia, Tacoma, Bellevue, and Snohomish County, Port Townsend.

North American Vegetarian Society (NAVS) Northwest Coordinator
P.O. Box 13303, Burton, WA 98013
Regional coordinator for the North American Vegetarian Society (see "National & International Organizations").

PAWS ACTION
Farm Animals and Vegetarian Committee, P.O. Box 1037, Lynnwood, WA 98046, (206) 742-4142

Vashon Island Vegan Association
c/o Carol Bodien, 10967-103rd Avenue SW, Vashon, WA 98070, (206) 567-4122

Vegan Network
319 Nickerson Street, Suite 102, Seattle, WA 98109

Vegetus Regime
P.O. Box 22, Mead, WA 99021, (509) 468-9118

Additional Local Contacts
Arlington: (360) 435-5435
Bellvue: Celia Heathcote (206) 453-0577
Eastsound: (360) 376-5642
Everett: (206) 258-0749
Kent: (206) 946-1831
Marysville: (360) 659-0942
Olympia: (360) 943-0893, 352-6716
Orcas Island: (360) 376-5642
Port Townsend: (360) 385-2909
Seattle: (206) 325-8142 (John Yackshaw), 789-2016, 328-0326
Spokane: (509) 459-8502
Tacoma: (206) 925-7035, 759-7984

WASHINGTON, D.C.

Pure Food Campaign
Washington, D.C.
See "National & International Organizations."

Spiritual Peace Center
Nick Kokshis, 1215 O Street NW, Washington, D.C. 20005

Vegetarian Awareness Network (VEGANET)
National Headquarters: Washington, D.C.
See "National & International Organizations."

Vegetarian Society of the District of Columbia (VSDC)
P.O. Box 4921, Washington, D.C. 20008, (301) 589-0722

Vegetarian Union of North America
Washington, D.C.
See "National & International Organizations."

Additional Local Contacts
Contact the North American Vegetarian Society and the Vegetarian Awareness Network (see "National & International Organizations") for possible vegetarian contacts in Washington, D.C.

WEST VIRGINIA

Society of Activist Vegetarians for an Extended Ethic (SAVE)
21 Estill Drive, Charleston, WV 25314

Stand Up For Animal Rights (SUFAR)
P.O. Box 4666, Parkersburg, WV 26104-4666, (304) 375-3849

Additional Local Contacts
Charleston: Patzy Swain, 1210 Virginia Street E., Charleston, WV 25301
Newville: (304) 765-7922

WISCONSIN

EarthHeart Foundation
De Pere, WI
See "National & International Organizations."
Note: Along with its other activities, operates the EarthHeart Deli on 106 N. Wisconsin Street in downtown De Pere, just outside of Green Bay.

No Compromise
173 Jackson Street, Madison, WI 53704, (608) 244-3092
Vegan action.

NorthEast Wisconsin Voice for Animals
P.O. Box 549, Denmark, WI 54208, (414) 863-8709

Platteville Vegetarian Society
c/o Rebecka Larmer, 177 Washington Street, Platteville, WI 53818

Vegetarian Action!
P.O. Box 421, Kenosha, WI 53142

World Deist Society (WDS)
111-9th Avenue, Eau Claire, WI 54703
A religious organization.

Additional Local Contacts
Appleton: (414) 757-6657
Cambridge: Sonja Nikolay, Box 148, Cambridge, WI 53523
Edgerton: (608) 884-9287
Green Bay: (414) 497-1276, 432-8765 (UW)
Madison: (608) 257-6333
Milwaukee: (414) 483-4816, 273-0973, 229-6819 (UW)
Neenah: (414) 722-5730
Ridgeway: (608) 924-3804
Waunakee: (608) 849-5838
Wausau: (715) 848-2784
Wheeler: (715) 658-1042

WYOMING

Vegi Wranglers of the Sheridan Area
32 Redpole Lane, Rt. 3, Sheridan, WY 82801, (307) 674-4795

Wyoming Vegetarians
3251 Brookview Drive, Casper, WY 82604, (307) 237-9676

Additional Local Contact
Cheyenne: (307) 778-4086

Chapter 12

Products and Services

The products and services listed here promote or support animal rights. Unless stated otherwise, companies offer free catalogs and product information.

For new and additional products and services, check the periodicals in Chapter 13. They regularly contain new product announcements or paid product advertisements.

Products and services are listed for the following categories:

- Activist Aids
- Animal Rights Stores
- Audio Tapes & CDs
- Clothing
- Clubs for Kids & Young Adults
- Companion Animal Products & Services
- Computer-Based Communication & Products
- Cruelty-Free Home, Beauty, & Personal Care Products
- Financial Services
- Hotlines
- Humane Education
- Leather Alternatives
- Letter-Writing Services
- Long Distance Telephone Services
- Paints & Stains
- Radio & Television Programming
- Stamps & Stickers
- Toys
- Travel Services
- Vegetarian Supplies & Services
- Videos & Films
- Wildlife Traps, Deterrents, & Attractors

Please Note: The author makes no claims as to the products and services listed herein. They are presumed to be offered in good faith and are taken at face value. Not all products or services have been sampled by the author. Space limitations prevent the listing of all worthy items, but readers who have additional suggestions for listings may contact the publisher.

Prices are subject to change and should be used as approximations only. Contact the distributors for current prices and shipping rates.

Activist Aids

See also the Humane Education section of this chapter. For publications useful to activists, see Chapter 13.

Internships

A number of organizations—such as Farm Sanctuary, The Fund for Animals, and People for the Ethical Treatment of Animals—offer internships to those who want to gain experience (usually for room/board or a stipend). If a particular group or cause interests you, inquire about internships.

Supplies

In addition to the sources listed here, many national groups offer free literature and other supplies to small groups for distribution to the general public. Don't be shy—give them a call and ask if they have free materials to share with you. Also see the publications listed in Chapter 13.

Chicago Animal Rights Coalition
Information on covert (hidden) video equipment and use for the veteran activist willing to make a large investment of time, money, effort, and risk. CHARC has had great success using hidden cameras. Serious inquiries only, please. From: CHARC, P.O. Box 66, Yorkville, IL 60560, (708) 208-0562.

The Fund for Animals, Inc.
Free fact sheets and flyers on animal agriculture, companion animals, fur, hunting, and wildlife. Donation for postage appreciated. From: The Fund for Animals, 850 Sligo Avenue, Suite 300, Silver Spring, MD 20910, (301) 585-2591, FAX: (301) 585-2595.

New England Anti-Vivisection Society
Free anti-vivisection materials for small organizations to use in demonstrations and for public education. Includes flyers on the Draize and LD-50 tests and lists of sources for cruelty-free products. From: NEAVS, 333 Washington Street, Suite 850, Boston, MA 02108, (617) 523-6020.

People for the Ethical Treatment of Animals
Items for sale include *The PETA Guide to Becoming an Activist*, factsheets, a table display, *Cut Out Dissection* info packs, a leaflet holder, literature, posters, stickers, buttons, postcards, books, and videos. From: PETA, 501 Front Street, Norfolk, VA 23501, (757) 622-PETA.

Project Floodlight
Offers a free *Anti-Fur Resource Book,* with anti-fur ads for use on posters, handbills, in newspapers, or any print media. Space is provided for the name and address of your local group. From: Project Floodlight, P.O. Box 3782, Ann Arbor, MI 48106.

RAGE
"Products of protest." Formed by two long-time animal rights activists. T-shirts include slogans such as "Rats Have Rights," "Meat Makes Me Sick," and "Environmental Extremist." Some printed on both front and back. Wholesale prices to organizations for fundraisers. A percentage of proceeds donated to animal rights/environment organizations. From: RAGE, P.O. Box 86837, Portland, OR 97206, (503) 777-6200 or (503) 257-0278.

The Vegetarian Resource Group
Free animal rights/vegetarian literature for tabling. Books at wholesale prices to nonprofit groups. Returns in saleable condition accepted. Other materials (stickers, buttons, T-shirts, etc.) available in quantity. From: VRG, P.O. Box 1463, Baltimore, MD 21203, (410) 366-VEGE, FAX: (410) 366-8804.

Wild Wear
T-shirts, sweatshirts, rubber stamps, magnets, pins, cards, and bumper stickers with animal rights graphics and messages. Wholesale plan with a percentage down and return of undamaged merchandise accepted for activist fundraisers. From: Wild Wear, Box 460477, San Francisco, CA 94146, (415) 647-2125 (in San Francisco), 1-800-428-6947, FAX: (415) 647-3832.

Training & Support

Animals & Culture Studies Program
A 6-course, 21-credit certificate program where students explore the ways people of different cultures perceive and treat other animals, and

how these perceptions/treatments affect the societies. Takes an animal rights perspective by recognizing the inherent value of the lives of individual animals, and is conducive to those who seek to foster this perspective in society. Offered at the Wolfson, South, and North Campuses of Miami-Dade Community College. Info: Animal & Culture Studies Program, c/o Eric Greene, Miami-Dade Community College, Wolfson Campus, Extended Educational Services, 300 NE Second Avenue, Room 2201, Miami, FL 33132, (305) 237-3252, ext. 7363.

DJ&T Foundation

Funds grants for free and low-cost spay neuter clinics. From: DJ&T Foundation, 9201 Wilshire Blvd., #204, Beverly Hills, CA 90210, (310) 278-1160.

Farm Animal Reform Movement

Offers vegetarian and animal advocacy workshops and seminars for activists. From: FARM, P.O. Box 30654, Bethesda, MD 20824, (301) 530-1737.

Good Shepherd Foundation

Offers grants of up to $2,000 to grassroots animal and environmental groups for creative, original, and potentially effective projects. Write for guidelines: Good Shepherd Foundation, P.O. Box 1880, Pahoa, HI 96778 or P.O. Box 1950, Nevada City, CA 95959, (808) 935-5563.

In Defense of Animals

Provides a free list of publications that explain nonviolent theory and strategy. Can help you organize demonstrations, rallies, marches, and nonviolence training workshops. They suggest that those wishing to learn about nonviolent action contact the American Friends Service Committee or a local peace group. From: IDA, 816 West Francisco Blvd., San Rafael, CA 94901, (415) 453-9984.

Last Chance for Animals

Offers for sale *The Civil Disobedience Training Manual* and the video "LCA: Direct Action in Perspective," which explores civil disobedience in historic, contemporary, and strategic perspective. From: LCA, 18653 Ventura Blvd., Suite 356, Tarzana, CA 91356, (818) 760-2075.

New England Anti-Vivisection Society

Offers two-year fellowships to enable activists to devote their full time to anti-vivisection issues. Recipients receive a two-year funding commitment including an annual grant of up to $22,000 and up to $10,000 for expenses. Interested individuals must provide a detailed description of proposed animal rights projects and examples of previous animal rights work and activities, in addition to other information. From: NEAVS, 333 Washington Street, Suite 850, Boston, MA 02108, (617) 523-6020.

Performing Animal Welfare Society

Publications include *The Circus: A New Perspective* which contains instructions on organizing a peaceful, legal protest, as well as information on the problems with circuses and other traveling shows. See the Entertainment: Guides & Directories section of Chapter 13 for ordering info.

Vegetarian / Animal Rights Hotline

A 900 number that costs callers $1.50/minute. Organizations list their events—fundraisers, conferences, demonstrations, marches, social activities, etc.—for free. Listings are updated every two weeks. To place listings contact: P.O. Box 315, N. Cambridge, MA 02140, (617) 628-8035.

The Vegetarian Program

Vegetarian courses with information on cooking, nutrition, international cuisine, pregnancy and child-raising, fast foods, and a beginning nutrition and cooking class conducted in Spanish. Also offers a Thanksgiving Day Vegetarian Feast and hosts on-campus vegetarian luncheons for offices, clubs, and social groups. Info: Cynthia Cowen, Environmental Center, Miami-Dade Community College, 11011 SW 104th Street, Miami, FL 33176-3393, (305) 237-2600.

Animal Rights Stores

This section lists retail stores run by animal rights groups or stores that support animal rights.

Aesop's Earth Store

Nonleather footwear and accessories, other cruelty-free items, ecological products, and clothing. Owned by a vegetarian/animal rights supporter. Mail-order or walk-in. See also their description under Leather Alternatives. From: Aesop's, 285 Washington Street, Somerville, MA, (617) 628-8030.

BodySuite

Donates a portion of the proceeds to People for the Ethical Treatment of Animals. "Cruelty-free products to balance the mind, body and spirit." Specializes in aromatherapy. Owned by a licensed cosmetologist and certified practicing aromatherapist. Products include custom-blended and scented body lotions, oils, shampoos, shower gels, bath salts, skin care products, make-up, books/videos on aromatherapy, etc. From: BodySuite, 1050 Broad Street, San Luis Obispo, CA 93401 and 316 Manhattan Beach Blvd., Manhattan Beach, CA. Mail-order: 1-800-428-2038.

Just In Case

"Cruelty-free bags, cases, art jewelry, and other environmentally conscious gifts." Includes brief cases, diaper packs, fanny packs, knapsacks, etc., bags with the look and feel of leather, and those made from a "silky-like" rubber. From: Just In Case, 2718 Main Street, Santa Monica, CA 90405, (310) 399-3096. Walk-in or mail-order.

The Last White Elephant

Primarily a thrift store, but includes some vegan products. Proceeds donated to animal welfare causes. The owners also operate a vegan mail-order business, Vegan Market, listed elsewhere in this chapter. The thrift store is located at 902-A NE 65th Street, Seattle, WA 98115, (206) 525-0170.

The WARM Store

Proceeds benefit the Woodstock Animal Rights Movement. Entirely cruelty-free. Includes gifts, accessories, jewelry, buttons, stickers, and products for body, kids, healthy homes and gardens, companion animals, reading, viewing, and listening. From: The WARM Store, 12 Tannery Brook Road, Woodstock, NY 12498, (914) 679-GAIA (4242), 1-800-889-WARM.

Audio Tapes & CDs

This section includes cassette tapes and CDs in the following categories: talk, music, and nature recordings.

Talk

Animal Experiments / Diet & Health: Neal Barnard, M.D.

"Beyond Animal Experiments," and "Live Longer, Live Better." Two tapes from the founder of Physicians Committee for Responsible Medicine. Inquiries: PCRM Marketplace, P.O. Box 99, Summertown, TN 38483, 1-800-695-2241.

Comfort & Stress Release: Carolyn Carpenter, MSC, MSTh

"Healing Animal Loss," "Stress Release for Animal Activists and Caretakers," and "Animals as Teachers of Peace, Love, and Forgiveness." A series of audio tapes by a bereavement/stress counselor designed to comfort, support, and enhance the human-animal bond. Includes background music. From: Interbeing Partner-ships, P.O. Box 1376, Summit, NJ 07901, (908) 273-7762.

Diet & Health: John Robbins and Howard Lyman

"John Robbins in Toronto" contains facts and information about health and "the connection between food choices and all of life" from the founder of EarthSave. "John Robbins in Chicago" is billed as the philosophical John Robbins at his best. "Voice for a Viable Future" by Howard Lyman is the story of a fourth generation cattle rancher turned activist, as told in his own words. The two John Robbins tapes are $3.95 each ($3.55 members) and the Howard Lyman tape is $6.95 ($6.25 members). Add $3 shipping per tape ($6 to Canada). From: EarthSave, 706 Frederick Street, Santa Cruz, CA 95062, 1-800-362-3648.

Diet & Health: Michael Klaper, M.D.

"Help Yourself to Health" discusses applications of vegan food to specific medical conditions in a series of ten 30-minute tapes. Different tapes for: nutrition and health, weight loss, heart and arteries, back, arthritis, diabetes, cancer, hypoglycemia, pregnancy, and children's diets. $7 per tape plus $3 shipping ($4 shipping for 2 tapes, $5 shipping for 3-4 tapes, etc.). From: Gentle World, P.O. Box U, Paia, Maui, HI 96779, (808) 572-3522.

Interspecies Communication & Animal Death: Penelope Smith

"Animal Death: A Spiritual Journey" explores the subject of animal death from a spiritual perspective. Intended to be comforting as well as informative, it covers the process of dying, working through guilt and grieving, when to consider euthanasia, contacting animals after they leave their bodies, and reincarnation. *The Interspecies Telepathic Connection Tape Series* is four tapes that may be purchased separately or as a set: 1-"How To Communicate with Animals: The Steps," 2-"Animal Intelligence and Awareness," 3-"Understanding Animals' Viewpoints," 4-"Healing and Counselling with Animals." Pricing and additional information available from: Pegasus Publications, P.O. Box 1060, Point Reyes, CA 94956, (415) 663-1247, Orders: 1-800-356-9315, FAX: 1-800-242-0036.

Interspecies Communication: Samantha Khury

A variety of tapes from Samantha Khury on how to develop your own communication with animals. Samantha is an animal communicator who provides private and long distance consultations, as well as workshops, lectures, and seminars. Single tapes are $15, two-tape sets are $25 (plus shipping). Orders: (310) 374-6812 (voice/FAX).

Vegetarianism, Veganism, and Health

A variety of tapes related to vegetarianism, veganism, and health are available from: The American Vegan Society, 501 Old Harding Highway, P.O. Box H, Malaga, NJ 08328, (609) 694-2887.

Music

"Secrecy" by Karen Goldberg

Although this is not an animal rights collection per se, the song "What If A Cow Ate You?" is worth the pricc of the tape/CD. ("What if a cow ate you? What if a raccoon wore your skin? What if the turkeys had a feast, and used you as their centerpiece?") Also includes a song about a circus. Eclectic style, from Joni Mitchell to blues. From: Corbett Records, P.O. Box 4543, Baltimore, MD 21212, 1-800-473-3138.

"Animal Magnetism" & "Tame Yourself" (various artists)

"Animal Magnetism" is a "compilation of rocking tunes" featuring Linda Ronstadt, Chrissie Hynde, Linda McCartney, Edgar Winter, Leon Russell, and others. CD only. $14 ($12.60 members; VA, CA, and WA addresses add tax) plus $5.95 shipping. Specify item BK900. "Tame Yourself": contains 14 songs with animal themes from Howard Jones, Raw Youth, Indigo Girls and Michael Stipe, k.d. lang, The B-52's, Fetchin Bones, The Pretenders, Nina Hagen and Lene Lovich, Jane Wiedlin, The Goosebumps, Erasure and Lene Lovich, Belinda Carlisle, Aleka's Attic, and Exene Cervenka. CD only. $5 postpaid. Both CDs available from: PETA, 501 Front Street, Norfolk, VA 23501, (757) 622-PETA.

"Animal Tracks" by Dwayne Roberson

Four songs about companion animals: "Bored With Me," "Let Me Live," Friends for Life," and "Why Don't You Love Me?". All proceeds benefit The Spayed Club, which provides spay/neuter assistance. From: The Spayed Club, ATTN: Animal Tracks, P.O. Box 1145, Frazer, PA 19355, (610) 275-7486.

"Counter Revolution" by Larry Brown

Eleven songs in bluegrass/country/blues style. Songs contain animal rights and peace themes, including vegetarianism, factory farming, hunting, and product testing. Humor helps bring attention to serious subjects. Selections include "Hamburger Blues," about a carnivore who unwittingly finds himself in a vegetarian town, "Counter Revolution," an encounter between a carnivore and beings who suddenly come to life in the meat counter at a local grocery store, and "Old McDonald Had a Factory Farm." $7.50 postpaid from: Voices for Peace, 6650 Tipp Cowlesville Road, Tipp City, OH 45371, (513) 667-4024.

Nature Recordings

Various Nature Recordings

Proceeds benefit Woodstock Animal Rights Movement. CDs and cassettes of various nature sounds, including "Howling Harmonies" (wolves howling in concert), "Loon Talk" (the calls of loons), "Songbirds of Spring," "Jungle," "Northwoods Wildlife," "Dawn and Dusk," "Wilderness Thunderstorm," "Frog Talk," "Ocean Encounters," and others. From:

The WARM Store, 12 Tannery Brook Road, Woodstock, NY 12498, (914) 679-GAIA (4242), 1-800-889-WARM.

Clothing

In addition to the clothing sources listed here, many animal rights groups sell T-shirts and sweatshirts to raise money. Check with organizations you want to support. Some of them have great shirts!

People for Animal Rights

T-shirts with the words "People for Animal Rights" and the silhouettes of an elephant, primate, and rabbit. This is a great design suitable for all "people for animal rights." I'm just sorry they don't offer the sweatshirts any more! White with black lettering or black with white lettering. 50/50 sizes M, L, XL, and XXL are $12 each plus shipping. 100% cotton are $13 each plus shipping. Call or write for shipping charges. From: PAR, P.O. Box 2928, Olathe, KS 66062, (816) 767-1199.

RAGE

"Products of protest." Formed by two long-time animal rights activists. T-shirts include slogans such as "Rats Have Rights," "Meat Makes Me Sick," "No More Ivory," "Environmental Extremist," "Think Good Thoughts," "Practice Random Kindness and Senseless Acts of Beauty," "Honor Diversity," and "Walk Your Talk." Some printed on both front and back. Wholesale available to organizations for fundraisers. A percentage of the proceeds donated to animal rights and environmental organizations. From: RAGE, P.O. Box 86837, Portland, OR 97206, (503) 777-6200 or (503) 257-0278.

Wild Wear

T-shirts, sweatshirts, rubber stamps, magnets, pins, cards, and bumper stickers with animal rights graphics and messages. Slogans range from "Be Kind To Animals" and "May All Beings Be Free of Suffering" to "Wear Your Own Skin" and "Animal Liberation" to "There's Plenty to Eat Without Choosing Meat," and more. Offers a wholesale plan with a percentage down and return of undamaged merchandise for activist fundraisers. Free catalog. From: Wild Wear, Box 460477, San Francisco, CA 94146, (415) 647-2125 (in San Francisco), 1-800-428-6947, FAX: (415) 647-3832.

Clubs for Kids & Young Adults

See also the Humane Education section.

Help Save Animals

An organization founded by a vegetarian third grader (who is now a teenager). Lets children directly participate in helping animal welfare and wildlife projects by fundraising for organizations such as Greenpeace, Doris Day Animal League, and The Wilderness Society. The main fundraising activity is collecting recyclables. No membership fees. If you want help in starting a group, write: Amanda Jones, 205 Oakridge Drive, San Marcos, TX 78666.

HSUS Student Action Guide

A guide intended for secondary students, which gives step-by-step instructions for forming an Earth/animal protection club, holding meetings, targeting issues, and planning activities. Free sample copy, but you pay $3 shipping from HSUS.

PETA Kids

A club that promotes animal rights and vegetarianism among young people. Membership includes a PETA Kids magazine twice a year, special mailings, contests, and more. $3 per year (or whatever you can afford) from: PETA, 501 Front Street, Norfolk, VA 23501, (757) 622-PETA.

Roots & Shoots

"An ambitious program dedicated to teaching young members of the Jane Goodall Institute to observe and understand the world around them while becoming actively involved in environmental and humanitarian issues." Regular newsletters connect clubs from around the world. For information on how you can bring Roots & Shoots to your community or school, send $2 to cover postage and handling to: The Jane Goodall Institute, P.O. Box 599, Ridgefield, CT 06877, 1-800-592-JANE.

Sea Shepherd Kids

A group founded, organized, and administered by kids for kids to promote the Sea Shepherd Conservation Society. The group writes and publishes its own newsletter and organizes active campaigns. One of the founders is the youngest person to have ever crewed on a Sea Shepherd voyage. Write to: Sea Shepherd Kids, 3107A Washington Blvd., Marina del Rey, CA 90292.

Youth for Environmental Sanity (YES!)
Educates, inspires, and empowers youth to take positive action for the future of life on earth. Founded by Ocean Robbins, then 16 (whose father is John Robbins of EarthSave) and Ran Eliason, then 18. Organizes and conducts in-depth workshops, summer camps, and school assembly presentations. Members receive updates on YES!'s work and urgent environmental issues through the YES! newsletter. $15 (student), $25 (adult) per year from: YES!, 706 Frederick Street, Santa Cruz, CA 95062, (408) 459-9344, FAX: (408) 458-0255.

Vegetarian Youth Network
Run by and for vegetarian teens who support compassionate and globally-aware living. Provides supportive services to vegetarian teens and helps those who want to become vegetarian. For information, send a self-addressed, stamped envelope with *two* 32-cent stamps (instead of one) to: VYN, P.O. Box 1141, New Paltz, NY 12561, (914) 255-0671, E-mail: tovahwal@mhv.net

Companion Animal Products & Services

This section contains a variety of resources to improve the lives of companion animals.

Boarding & Sitting Services

Critter Sitters
(504) 273-3356 (Louisiana)

National Association of Home Sitting Seniors
(303) 761-1878 (Colorado)

National Association of Professional Pet Sitters
Nationwide Referral Network: 1-800-296-PETS

Pets Are Inn
A franchise that boards pets in private homes rather than kennels. This company is in the business of selling and supporting Pets Are Inn franchise opportunities, but can also tell you if there is a Pets Are Inn service in your area. Info: Pets Are Inn, 27 North 4th Street, Suite 500, Minneapolis, MN 55401, (612) 339-6255, 1-800-248-PETS.

Pet Sitters International
Nationwide Locator Line: 1-800-268-7487

Cat Fences & Enclosures

Alley Cat Allies
Instructions for a do-it-yourself cat fence for a self-addressed, stamped envelope. Donations accepted to help cover costs. From: Alley Cat Allies, P.O. Box 397, Mount Rainier, MD 20712.

Cat Enclosure Kit
A screened enclosure made from redwood and galvanized wire, that allows your cat to be outdoors safely. Includes a door and roof. Assemble with a screw-driver. Additional panels and adjustable shelves available. $195 with free delivery in the San Francisco Bay area. Version that can be shipped anywhere in the U.S. is about $35 higher. Other products include scratching posts and window perches. Info: C&D Pet Products, 1663 Northstar Drive, Petaluma, CA 94954, (707) 763-9205.

Cat Fence-In
A patented system of almost invisible netting barriers to keep cats in or out of your yard. Attaches to existing fencing. Also tree guards to keep cats from climbing up trees. Free brochure from: Cat Fence-In, P.O. Box 795, Sparks, NV 89432, (702) 359-4575.

Cat Litter

Certain types of kitty litter (particularly so-called "scoopable" litter) is considered dangerous—even lethal—by some health care experts. Why? After using the litter box, cats clean their feet by licking them, thereby ingesting particles of litter. The nature of "scoopable" litter is to expand and clump together, which it allegedly does *inside* the cat. This can lead to a plethora of health problems, including a depressed immune system, respiratory distress, irritable bowel syndrome, and/or death. Kittens are particularly susceptible.

Old-fashioned plain clay litter—the kind widely available in stores—is considered acceptable (as long as it doesn't contain deodorizer or other chemicals). If you prefer to try something new, here are some possibilities. (*Note*: All claims are made by the manufacturers; I haven't tested these products.)

Care Fresh

Flushable, biodegradable, dust-free material suitable for use as litter or as bedding for rodents, birds, etc. Made from 100% reclaimed paper mill by-products. Nontoxic; no aromatics. For the location of a distributor near you, contact: Care Fresh, Absorption Corporation, P.O. Box 5667, Bellingham, WA 98277, (360) 734-1370, FAX; (360) 671-1588, Orders only: 1-800-242-2287.

Swheat Scoop

Flushable, scoopable, and utilizes natural enzymes to eliminate nasty litter box odors. Made from 100% wheat. No silica dust (as with clay). Biodegradable. Order through your local store or mail-order available for $5 shipping from: Swheat Scoop, Pet Care Systems, Inc., 717 N. Clinton Street, Grand ledge, MI 48837, (517) 627-2164, FAX: (517) 627-7838, WATS: 1-800-SWHEATS.

Hi-Tor Dust Free Cat Litter

Made from recycled newspaper. Absorbent with superior odor control. From: Triumph Pet Industries, Inc., P.O. Box 100, Hillburn, NY 10931, (914) 357-6666, FAX: (914) 357-6804, 1-800-331-5144.

Doors

Patio Pacific, Inc.

"Pet" doors for installation in walls or sliding glass doors. "Guaranteed lowest prices." 30-day return less shipping cost. From: Patio Pacific, 1931-C North Gaffey Street, San Pedro, CA 90731-1265, 1-800-826-2871.

Petdoors U.S.A.

A variety of doors for installation in walls or sliding patio doors. Also other products. From: Petdoors U.S.A., 4523-30th Street West, Bradenton, FL 34207, 1-800-749-9609.

Foods, Supplements, & Supplies

These resources offer natural "health" foods and supplements that are free from artificial colors, flavors, preservatives, or by-products. Also see the Companion Animals section of Chapter 13 for books that tell you how to make your own natural foods for your animal friends. If you're unfamiliar with flower essences and homeopathic remedies, see the definitions for these healing substances in the Glossary at the back of the book.

A Note About Vegetarian Diets: This section includes information on two products developed for vegetarian cats and dogs, namely Vegecat and Vegedog, as well as several sources for vegetarian foods. Chapter 13 contains some reading on the subject. The controversy over vegetarian diets for companion animals rages on. While some caretakers say they have successfully fed their animal friends vegetarian diets (with the proper supplementation), others claim that a vegetarian diet for dogs and especially cats is harmful over time. Cats, in particular, require supplementation of certain nutrients (taurine is one) if fed a non-meat diet.

In selecting a food for your companion animals, you'll also want to keep allergies in mind. Allergies to corn, soy, wheat, cow's milk, chicken, and beef are common. Symptoms to food allergies may include itchy skin, hot spots, eye discharge, and general lack of energy, as well as more severe symptoms. Some allergic reactions appear only after repeated exposure to the allergen (for instance, eating one or more allergy-producing foods over a period of time).

The key to any healthy diet may well be some diversity. If you are not comfortable feeding your animal friends a 100% vegetarian diet, perhaps you could feed raw meat a couple of times a week for your peace of mind. (If you choose to feed meat, raw is generally preferred over cooked.) Whatever you decide, remember that, like humans, other animals are individuals and each will have her/his own special set of needs and preferences.

IV Trail Products (for Horses)

Ellie Powers, Owner. A portion of the products and services donated to horse rescue. Custom tack, saddlepads and specialties, natural fly wipe and salves, custom hand-drawn/painted sweatshirts, etc. From: IV Trail Products, P.O. Box 1033, Sylesville, MD 21784, (410) 795-8989.

Anaflora: Flower Essence Therapy for Animals

"Both wild animals and pets respond remarkably well to Flower Essence Therapy." Several formulas available for a variety of conditions (fear, shock, depression, relocation anxiety, trauma, abuse, etc.). Sharon Callahan, the owner, is also a holistic healer and animal communication specialist. Free information from: Anaflora, P.O. Box 1056, Mt. Shasta, CA 96067, (916) 926-6424.

Basically Natural

Products "for a healthy and compassionate lifestyle" include PetGuard canned vegetarian dog food and Mr. Barky's vegetarian dog biscuits. From: Basically Natural, 109 East G Street, Brunswick, MD 21716, (301) 834-7923, 1-800-352-7099.

Ellon USA, Inc.

Sells the traditional flower remedies of Dr. Edward Bach (the "Bach flower remedies"). Free information on treating animals with flower essences from: Ellon USA, 644 Merrick Road, Lynbrook, NY 11563, (516) 593-2206, FAX: (516) 593-9668, Orders: 1-800-4-BE-CALM (outside NYC, the five boroughs, and Long Island).

Evolution Diet—Health Food for Dogs, Cats, & Fish

Vegan food (both canned and dry) for cats and dogs, and a vegan powder for fish. From: Evolution Diet, Dr. Eric Weisman & Associates, 1068 So. Robert Street, West St. Paul, MN 55118, (612) 457-5145.

Harbingers of a New Age

Supplies for vegetarian/vegan dogs and cats, including Vegecat and Vegedog supplements, which provide essential nutrients and make it possible for felines and canines to thrive on vegetarian diets. (They are the manufacturer of these VegePet products.) Also an enzyme powder for digestibility, a nutritional yeast with more acid and less magnesium than "regular" nutritional yeast, a newsletter on Vegepet products, and the book *Vegetarian Cats and Dogs* by James A. Peden. From: HOANA, 717 E. Missoula Avenue, Troy, MT 59935-9609, (406) 295-4944, FAX: (406) 295-7603, Orders: 1-800-88-HOANA.

Harvest Direct, Inc.

This is a vegetarian food catalog for people, but it includes Natural Life canned vegetarian dog food. From: Harvest Direct, P.O. Box 4514, Decatur, IL 62525-4514, (217) 422-3324, Orders: 1-800-835-2867.

Holistic Pet Center

"The health food store for pets." Foods include Natural Life, Precise, and Nature's Recipe brands for felines and canines. (Nature's Recipe includes vegetarian dog food.) Also Vegedog and Vegecat supplements, treats (some vegetarian but not vegan), digestive enzymes, herbal products, and food for birds, guinea pigs, rabbits, and hamsters. Also nonfood items. From: Holistic Pet Center, 15599 S.E. 82nd Drive, P.O. Box 1166, Clackamas, OR 97015, (503) 656-5342, 1-800-788-PETS.

Homeopathic Educational Services

Store: 2036 Blake Street (near Shattuck Ave.), Berkeley, CA

Products include veterinary homeopathic remedies and books for the homeopathic treatment of cats, dogs, small domestic animals (including birds, hamsters, mice, and guinea pigs), horses, and cattle. From: Homeopathic Educational Services, 2124 Kittredge Street, Berkeley, CA 94704, (415) 649-0294, FAX: (415) 649-1955, Orders only: 1-800-359-9051.

Morrills' New Directions

Mail-order natural "pet care" products. Their prices are a little high, but they offer a variety of supplements, foods, books, and other products to enhance the health of companion animals. Includes a food and supplement for birds, and a tonic for horses. From: Morrill's New Directions, P.O. Box 30, Orient, ME

04471, Orders: 1-800-368-5057, 24-hour FAX: (207) 532-0895.

The Natural Pet Care Company

Natural supplements, nontoxic flea control and grooming products, meat-based foods (Innova, PetGuard, Wysong, and Precise brands), Fanta bird seed, books, etc. Includes a Chinese herbal deworming powder. (Try to overlook the venison dog treats and the fur toy mice.) From: Natural Pet Care Company, 8050 Lake City Way, Seattle, WA 948115, (206) 522-1667 (inside WA), 1-800-962-8266 (outside WA), FAX: (206) 524-0191.

Nature's Recipe

Vegetarian dry kibble and canned food for dogs. The dry food contains ground whole brown rice, soy flour, barley flour, vegetable oil, carrots, garlic powder, salt, and vitamin/mineral supplements. The canned food contains water, soybean meal, ground whole brown rice, potatoes, carrots, ground whole barley, salt, and vitamin/mineral supplements. Call for the distributor nearest you, or check the other mail-order sources listed in this section. From: Nature's Recipe, Orange, CA 92667, (714) 639-1134.

PetGuard, Inc.

PetGuard brand vegetarian canned dog food, yeast and garlic supplements, and meat-based dog and cat food. From: PetGuard, P.O. Box 728, 165 Industrial Loop S., Orange Park, FL 32073, 1-800-874-3221 (outside FL), 1-800-331-7527 (inside FL), FAX: (904) 264-0802.

Sojourner Farms

Vegetarian, natural foods for dogs and cats. The food is a dry, unrefined, and minimally processed multi-grain cereal that you moisten with liquid. (The main ingredient is oats and the food looks like oatmeal.) The cat food contains buttermilk powder; the dog food is dairy-free. Uses only the finest quality human-grade foods, never animal-grade feed. Organically grown ingredients used whenever possible. Also dog snacks, a cotton garment with velcro closures for female dogs in season, and reference books on homeopathic and natural care for companion animals. From: Sojourner Farms, P.O. Box 8062, Ann Arbor, MI 48107, (313) 994-3974.

Pet Sage

A variety of products for holistic animal care, including books, supplements, skin care, and HomeoPet brand remedies. From: PetSage, 4313 Wheeler Avenue, Alexandria, VA 22304, (703) 823-9711, 1-800-PET-HLTH, FAX: (703) 823-9714.

Solid Gold

Canine, feline, and equine nutrition products. Manufactures an "herbal, holistic pet food" (meat-based) called Hund-N-Flocken (German for "Dog Food Flakes"), which they claim is far superior to other "health" foods. It is free of soybeans, wheat, corn, white rice, animal digest or fats, chicken, or other objectionable ingredients, containing instead amaranth grain, brown rice, organic oils, menhaden herring fish, hormone-free lamb meat (not meal), etc. Also a comparable product for cats. Call for the distributor nearest you, or check the other mail-order sources listed in this section). From: Solid Gold, 1483 N. Cuyamaca, El Cajon, CA 92020, (619) 258-1914 or 258-2780, FAX: (619) 258-3907 (Mon.-Fri., 10 a.m.-5 p.m. Pacific time).

Tasha's Herbs for Dogs

Alcohol-free formulas designed specifically for dogs. These liquid formulas contain flower essences along with herbal components. Includes formulas for seniors, skin and hair, motion sickness, arthritis, and nervousness. From: Tasha's Herbs for Dogs, Coyote Springs Company, P.O. Box 1175, Jackson, WY 83001, (307) 734-0142, FAX: (307) 734-0144.

Whiskers

"Holistic products for pets." This catalog isn't vegetarian-minded, but it contains some hard-to-find products: super blue green algae, herbal remedies, wheat grass powder, and seeds and supplements for companion birds. It also contains the widest selection of dog and cat foods I've seen in a single catalog. Brand names include Solid Gold, Wysong, Cornucopia, Nature's Recipe, Nutro, Fromm, Natural Life, Pet Guard, Natural Life, Triumph, and Sojourner Farms. Separate catalog for horse products. From: Whiskers, 235 East 9th Street, New York, NY 10003, 1-800-WHISKERS, FAX: (718) 423-3504.

The Whole Animal Catalog

Vitamins, homeopathic remedies, enzymes, oils, dog biscuits, and catnip. Non-food items include nail clippers, a pill gun, Gentle Leader head harness for dogs, and products for fleas, grooming, oral hygiene, and fun. From: The Whole Animal Catalog, A Division of the Uptown Vet, 3131 Hennepin Avenue South, Minneapolis, MN 55408, 1-800-377-6369,

FAX: (612) 824-6436, E-mail: pangia@imaginet.com:80/uptownvet.com/

Wow-Bow Distributors Ltd.

Health food for animals. Includes vegetarian, non-vegetarian but "humanely-raised," and meat-based foods for dogs; meat-based cat food; supplements; grooming products; all-natural treats for dogs, cats, and horses, including vegan dog biscuits; and books. Brand names include Nature's Recipe and Solid Gold. From: Wow-Bow, 309 Burr Road, East Northport, NY 11731, (516) 499-8572, 1-800-326-0203 (outside NY state).

Wysong Corporation

A vegan kibble (dry food) for dogs or cats (meets all NRC recommendations for canine maintenance and all for feline except protein, which is 22% compared to NRC's recommended 28%). Also meat-based dog and cat food, health treatment aids for animals, other companion animal supplies, and healthy products for people. From: Wysong, 1880 North Eastman Road, Midland, MI 48640, (517) 631-0009, FAX: (517) 631-8801.

Gates

Indoor security gates can be used to keep dogs in or out of certain areas of your home. (The gates aren't a solution for cats; they simply climb over them!)

You can find both removable, pressure-held gates and those that attach to the wall in the infant department of discount stores or department stores. The mail-order sources I know of all carry objectionable items (such as shock collars), so I can't recommend them in good conscience, but if you can't find the gate you need elsewhere, you may want to send for their catalogs. They are:

Discount Master, (Humboldt Industries, Inc.), Lake Road, P.O. Box 3333, Mountaintop, PA 18707, (717) 384-3600, 1-800-346-0749, FAX: (717) 384-2500

Doctors Foster & Smith, 2253 Air Park Road, P.O. Box 100, Rhinelander, WI 54501-0100, 1-800-826-7206, FAX: (715) 369-2821

R.C. Steele, 1989 Transit Way, Box 910, Brockport, NY 14420-0910, 1-800-872-3773.

I.D. Tags

Every companion animal should *always* wear an I.D. tag! You can purchase them at hardware or "pet" supply stores, or from the mail-order sources below.

Ethic

Custom-engraved, stainless steel tags. "Because life itself is far more precious than money, Ethic will provide an I.D. tag for your dog or cat for any price you choose to pay—even free." Donations are optional and support Ethic's I.D. and education programs. Send clearly printed information for tag: your or your companion animal's name and phone number are suggested; additional information such as address or medical alert optional. From: Ethic, P.O. Box 1234, Capitola, CA 95010, (408) 423-1156.

PAWS

Proceeds benefit the Progressive Animal Welfare Society. Stainless steel tags with an "O" ring for attachment. Send $3 per tag and the printed information as you want it to appear on the tag, including: your name, address, city, state, zip code, phone number, and alternate phone number (your work number or the number of a friend or relative who will take responsibility for your companion animal in the event you can't be reached). Make checks payable to: PAWS, P.O. Box 1037, Lynnwood, WA 98046.

Holistic Health Practitioners

Association of Veterinarians for Animal Rights (AVAR)

Veterinarians oriented toward animal rights. AVAR, P.O. Box 6269, Vacaville, CA 95696-6269, (707) 451-1391.

The American Holistic Veterinary Medical Association (AHVMA)

Veterinarians with a nutritional, holistic approach to health. Send a long, self-addressed, stamped envelope for a list of the holistic veterinarians nearest you. AHVMA, 2214 Old Emmorton Road, Bel Air, MD 21015, (410) 569-0795, FAX: (410) 515-7774.

American Veterinary Chiropractic Association (AVCA)
A certification program for veterinarians and chiropractors. Also information on animal chiropractic and practitioners in your area. AVCA, P.O. Box 249, Port Byron, IL 61275, (309) 523-3995.

International Veterinary Acupuncture Society (IVAS)
Veterinarians that offer acupuncture services. Send a self-addressed, stamped envelope for a list of certified practitioners in your area. You can also request a brochure on veterinary acupuncture from: IVAS, 2140 Conestoga Road, Chester Springs, PA 19425, (215) 827-7245.

National Center for Homeopathy
Contact them for a directory of classical homeopaths, which includes veterinarians: National Center for Homeopathy, 801 N. Fairfax, Suite 306, Alexandria, VA 22314, (703) 548-7790.

TTouch (TTEAM) Practitioners
TTouch is a hands-on technique developed by Linda Tellington-Jones that has been proven effective in communicating with, teaching, training, and healing animals. A list of certified practitioners for horses, companion animals, and llamas is available as well as a list of instructors, books, videos, and other information on TTouch from: TTEAM Training International, P.O. Box 3793, Santa Fe, NM 87501-0793, 1-800-854-TEAM, (505) 455-2945, FAX: (505) 455-7233.

Interspecies Communicators

Dr. Dolittle was right—humans and animals can talk to each other! More and more people are discovering the very real existence of telepathic communication between human and nonhuman animals. I use an interspecies communicator regularly for my companion animals' health care needs.

Animal communicators vary widely according to abilities and styles. If you're interested in this service, you may want to check out more than one practitioner. The following publications include resource lists of interspecies communicators.

Wolf Clan magazine contains paid ads for interspecies communicators: *Wolf Clan*, 3952 N. Southport Ave., Suite 122, Chicago, IL 60613, (312) 935-1000.

Species Link newsletter, published by communicator Penelope Smith for other interspecies communicators, contains a list of subscribers who request their names be listed: Pegasus Publications, P.O. Box 1060, Point Reyes, CA 94956, (415) 663-1247, Orders: 1-800-356-9315.

Or, send a self-addressed, stamped envelope to this publisher for an informal list of communicators compiled from various sources.

Poison Control

National Animal Poison Control Center
1-900-680-0000 ($20 for the first 5 minutes, then $2.95 each additional minute, billed by your telephone company)
- or -
1-800-548-2423 ($30 per case charged to a major credit card)
24 hours a day, 7 days a week. Staffed by veterinarians from the College of Veterinary Medicine, University of Illinois at Urbana-Champaign. For both numbers, the center will make free follow-up calls on critical cases.

Sierra Anti-Freeze & Coolant
"Safety Freeze." At last, an alternative to poisonous anti-freeze that is lethal to animals! (They are attracted to the sweet flavor.) This formula contains propylene glycol (instead of ethylene glycol), which is classified by the FDA as "generally accepted as safe." Available at discount or auto part stores, or contact: Safe Brands Corporation, P.O. Box 3007, Omaha, NE 68103, 1-800-289-7234.

Ramps & Carts

These products provide assistance for older or injured animals.

K-9 Cart Company
Mobility for animals that have lost the use of their back legs, or require special support in order to walk. These carts support the hind quarters and let the animal use her/his forelimbs to walk. Carts have been fitted to dogs, cats, rabbits, sheep, and goats. Free information from: K-9 Cart Company, P.O.

Box 160639, Big Sky, MT 59716, (406) 995-3111, FAX: (406) 995-3113, M-F, 9 a.m.-5 p.m.

Pet Inclinations
Indoor and outdoor adjustable ramps for companion animals who need help in and out of cars, up and down stairs, etc. Prices range from $50 to $125 from: Pet Inclinations, 2415 Royal Drive, Lombard, IL 60148, (708) 932-1860. *Note*: You might also check with a local carpenter and see what it would cost to have a ramp custom built, or rig one up yourself with a board and some carpet.

Spay/Neuter Referrals

For low-cost spay/neuter services in your area, also check with your local humane society, shelter, or animal rights group.

Friends of Animals Low-Cost Spay/Neuter Information
Referrals to veterinarians participating in a low-cost spay/neuter program. Over 1300 vets in 47 states. From: FoA, P.O. Box 1244, Norwalk, CT 06856, 1-800-321-PETS. *Note*: In many areas of the country, their prices will not be considered "low-cost."

Prevent A Litter Coalition, Inc.
Referrals in the Maryland, Virginia, and Washington, D.C. area from: Prevent a Litter Coalition, P.O. Box 1412, Centerville, VA 22020, (703) 818-8009.

Spay/Neuter USA!
National referrals from: Spay/Neuter USA!, 14 Vanderventer Avenue, Port Washington, NY 11050, 1-800-248-SPAY (in CT, call 375-6627).

Tattoo & Registry Services

These are for-profit businesses that allow you to tattoo and register your animals for a fee. They will refer you to a representative near you.

National Dog Registry
(914) 679-BELL or 1-800-NDR-DOGS

Tattoo-A-Pet
1-800-828-8667

Computer-Based Communication & Products

Bulletin Boards

These Computer Bulletin Boards contain information on vegetarianism, animal issues, and/or the environment. Note that the phone numbers listed are the numbers you have your computer dial; they are not for voice calls. You pay regular long-distance charges.

Environmental Worldwide Connection
(913) 897-1040 (Kansas)

Environet (Greenpeace)
(415) 512-9120 (California)

SALATA
(310) 543-0439 (California)

SKATEboard
(508) 788-1603 (Massachusetts)

Internet Provider Forums

America Online
Voice calls for information: 1-800-827-6364 or (703) 448-8700

- *Keyword:* Cooking Club or Vegetarian takes you to the cooking Club, where you can select Vegetarians Online
- *Keyword*: Environment or EForum takes you to EForum, where you can search for Animal Rights, Animal Welfare, or Vegetarian

CompuServe
Voice calls for information: 1-800-848-8199 or (614) 457-8600

- Cooks' Online Forum (Vegetarianism)
- Earth Forum (Animal Rights, Farm Animal Welfare, Fur, etc.)
- Pets Forum (The Association of Veterinarians for Animal Rights uploads its newsletter and articles by AVAR members to this forum)
- Vegetarian Forum (Recipes, Nutrition & Health, etc.)

Internet Sites

Animal Welfare Act
http://netvet.wustl.edu/awa.htm

Animal Rights Resource Site
http://www.envirolink.org/arrs/

Vegetarian Pages
http://www.veg.org/veg/
"Intended to be a definitive guide to what is available on the Internet for vegetarians, vegans, and others." Includes a World Guide to Vegetarianism (listings of restaurants, organizations, etc.).

Veggies Unite!
http://www.honors.indiana.edu/~veggie/recipes.cgi/
"Your on-line guide to vegetarianism."

Software

Alternatives in Education Database
Designed for use with Windows software on a PC. "Thousands of alternatives to the harmful/fatal use of nonhuman animals in education," including dissection. $5 includes disks and postage. From Association of Veterinarians for Animal Rights, P.O. Box 6269, Vacaville, CA 95696-6269, (707) 451-1391.

The Vegetarian Game
An IBM-compatible game for three levels: ages 5-9, 10 and up, and individuals with advanced knowledge. Players test their knowledge by answering questions on vegetarianism, nutrition, famous vegetarians, animal and ethical issues, and ecology. Requirements: MS DOS 2.0 or higher, CGA or better, or Hercules graphics. Specify 5.25" or 3.5" disk. $20 from: The Vegetarian Resource Group, P.O. Box 1463, Baltimore, MD 21203, (410) 366-VEGE, FAX: (410) 366-8804.

VegieCard
A Hypercard 2.0 stack for Macs with a hard drive and at least 2 megabytes of RAM. Over 200 screens show you how to change your diet. Topics include cravings, snack foods, cooking, etc. Newly revised edition (1994). $6 ($5.40 to members; CA addresses add 8.25% tax) plus $3 shipping ($6 to Canada). From: EarthSave, 706 Frederick Street, Santa Cruz, CA 95062-2205, 1-800-362-3648.

Cruelty-Free Home, Beauty, & Personal Care Products

"Cruelty-free" means that products were not tested on animals. Some products billed as "cruelty-free" may contain animal ingredients such as lanolin, honey, or beeswax. Be sure to ask!

Cruelty-Free Lists & Contacts

Cruelty-free lists tell you the names of companies that sell cruelty-free home and personal care products. Carry these lists with you when you shop and use them to determine which companies test on animals and which don't.

The American Vegan Society
Maintains a list of "Vegan Information Points (VIPs)," individuals and groups who have volunteered to provide information on the vegan lifestyle and local sources of cruelty-free products: AVS, 501 Old Harding Highway, P.O. Box H, Malaga, NJ 08328, (609) 694-2887.

The Compassionate Shopper
A newsletter published three times a year that contains information on animal-friendly products and companies. Fees support the dissemination of information on cruelty-free products to the public. For subscription info: Beauty Without Cruelty USA, 175 W. 12th Street, Suite 16G, New York, NY 10011.

Cruelty-Free Shopping Guide (pocket-size)
Fold-up guide that easily fits into a wallet. Also offers a list of retailers who offer cruelty-free products and a list of safe do-it-yourself cleaning formulas. Free from: New England Anti-Vivisection Society, 333 Washington Street, Suite 850, Boston, MA 02108, (617) 523-6020.

- **Cruelty-Free Shopping Guide**
- **Cruelty-Free Products Suppliers**

The *Shopping Guide* contains 638 entries. The *Products Suppliers* guide contains 516 product listings, 313 publications, formulas to make some products, and 166 companies that sell nonanimal products. Both are 5-1/2" by 8-1/2" spiral bound editions. $9.95 (CA addresses add 7% tax) plus $2 shipping ($3 in Canada) for each guide from: Web of Life, P.O. Box 2124, Orange, CA 92669.

Personal Care for People Who Care

Over 150 pages list companies alphabetically and indicate which companies test on animals or contract out animal testing, which do not test on animals, whether or not their products contain animal-derived ingredients, and which offer mail-order services. Includes a product list to help you locate which cruelty-free companies sell what products (for example, you can look up which companies sell air freshener, companion animal products, etc.). Also contains a list of ingredients derived from animals, questions and answers about animal testing, and other information. The 1996 edition is $4.95 or free with membership to NAVS ($25). From: The National Anti-Vivisection Society, 53 W. Jackson Blvd., Suite 1550, Chicago, IL 60604, (312) 427-6065, FAX: (312) 427-6524.

•PETA Cruelty-Free Shopping Guide
•Shopping Guide for Caring Consumers

The *PETA Cruelty-Free Shopping Guide* is a free, pocket-size, fold-up guide containing the names of companies that do and do not test their products on animals, and companies whose products may contain animal ingredients or by-products. The *Shopping Guide for Caring Consumers* lists more than 500 cruelty-free companies, the types of products they carry, and where to buy the products. The 1996 edition was $7.95 (members $7.15; VA, CA, and WA addresses add tax) plus $3.95 shipping. The *Shopping Guide* is also on the Internet at http://www.envirolink.org/arrs/peta/shopguid/shopguid.htm
From: People for the Ethical Treatment of Animals, 501 Front Street, Norfolk, VA 23501, (757) 622-PETA.

Shopping For A Better World

Rates a variety of companies and products on "socially responsible" criteria, such as minority advancement, charitable giving, etc. The ratings do not necessarily reflect the sentiments of the animal rights community, but there's some good, easily-accessible information here. Although not part of the rating criteria, indicates if a company tests on animals or participates in factory farming, and the list includes companies that manufacture drugs and/or surgical equipment (another way of saying "we test our products on animals"). The products listed represent the food and nonfood items typically lining supermarket shelves. Updated regularly. 394 pages. Sierra Club Books. $7.49 postpaid from: Council on Economic Priorities, 30 Irving Place, New York, NY 10003, 1-800-729-4237.

Mail-Order Sources

There are dozens (more likely hundreds) of mail-order catalogs that carry cruelty-free products. This listing is confined to organizations or companies that have the welfare of animals at heart and/or who contribute to their welfare. For additional mail-order sources, see the cruelty-free lists in the previous section.

Amberwood

Proceeds help provide a sanctuary for wild burros who would otherwise be slaughtered by the government. Includes personal care products, cosmetics, fragrances, home care products, companion animal products, adult and children's books, stickers, rubber stamps, vegetarian "gelatin" and marshmallows, cloth wallets, and more. From: Amberwood, Route 2, Box 300, Milford Road, Baker County, Leary, GA 31762, (912) 792-6246.

Animals Love Us!

$5 for a 113-page catalog. The catalog can be returned for a full refund, no questions asked. Free annual updates for all customers. Large print makes this computer-printed catalog easy to read. Products appear alphabetically by manufacturer under descriptive categories (for instance, the "cosmetics" section lists all Bare Escentuals cosmetics first, followed by Beauty Without Cruelty cosmetics, and so on). From: Animals Love Us!, 1053 Rainier Avenue, Pacifica, CA 94044-3829, (415) 355-5557.

Basically Natural

"All-vegetarian, non-animal tested products for a healthy and compassionate lifestyle." Includes products for companion animals (PetGuard canned vegetarian dog food, Mr. Barky's vegetarian dog biscuits, flea powder, and shampoo), body and hair care, Beauty Without Cruelty skin care and cosmetics, selected Paul Penders products, and household cleaners from Shaklee USA. From: Basically Natural, 109 East G Street, Brunswick, MD 21716, (301) 834-7923, 1-800-352-7099.

BodySuite

Donates a portion of the proceeds to People for the Ethical Treatment of Animals. "Cruelty-free products to balance the mind, body and spirit." Specializes in aromatherapy. For a fuller description, see their listing under Animal Rights Stores or call (301) 834-7923 or 1-800-352-7099.

The Compassionate Consumer

Donates 5% of your purchase cost to the animal rights group, animal shelter, or environmental group of your choice. Some products contain beeswax, honey, or lanolin; these are noted in the descriptions. No product has been tested on animals. Products include those for skin, body, bath, hair, personal hygiene, babies, companion animals, as well as household cleaners, fragrances, books, shoes, nonleather products, and more. Brand names include Aubrey Organics, Paul Penders, Kiss My Face, Mountain Fresh, and more. From: The Compassionate Consumer, P.O. Box 27, Jericho, NY 11753, (718) 445-4134.

Karen's Nontoxic Products

Donates a percentage (usually 10%) of certain product purchases to the Whale Adoption Project to study whales in their natural habitats. Includes products for household, companion animals, cosmetics, organic foods, personal care, aromatherapy, herbs, toys, notecards, an array of cotton products, and more. From: Karen's Nontoxic Products, 1839 Dr. Jack Road, Conowingo, MD 21918, Info: (410) 378-4939, Orders: 1-800-KARENS-4 (1-800-527-3674).

The Vegan Market

Founded by folks who "wanted to devote our full time and attention to working for animal rights." Personal care and household products, organic clothing, and books. From: The Vegan Market, 8512-12th Avenue NW, Seattle, WA 98117, (206) 789-2016, FAX: (206) 781-9435.

Financial Services

Bank Cards

Many animal groups now offer VISA or MasterCards through various banks, because the groups receive a small percentage of the purchase transactions or a set amount each time the card is used. The donations are paid by the bank and don't cost you anything. Most cards contain a photo of an animal. These are just a few of the groups that offer cards. If your favorite group isn't listed, give them a call to see if they have a similar offer.

VISA Cards

American Society for the Prevention of Cruelty to Animals receives $6 of the initial annual fee and one-half percent of all purchases. From: MBNA America, P.O. Box 15464, Wilmington, DE 19885-9440, 1-800-847-7378 (ext. 5000).

International Wildlife Coalition's Whale Adoption Project. Minimum annual income of $12,000 required. From: IWC Credit Card Program, Monogram Bank USA, P.O. Box 429417, Cincinnati, OH 45242-8876.

Working Assets VISA and VISA GOLD cards. No annual fee. Benefits Working Assets Funding Service, a socially responsible organization that contributes to a changing pool of nonprofit organizations working for peace, human rights, environment, or economic justice. Cardholders nominate nonprofit groups and vote on where the money goes. Some groups supported in the past are Earth Day 1990, Environmental Defense Fund, Greenpeace, and African Wildlife Foundation. From: MBNA America, Working Assets Funding Service, 230 California Street, San Francisco, CA 94111, 1-800-522-7759.

MasterCards

Associated Humane Societies. Issued by Steel Valley Bank. Request application forms from: Associated Humane Societies, 124 Evergreen Avenue, Newark, NJ 07114 or call 1-800-556-4029.

International Wildlife Coalition. Minimum annual income of $12,000 required. Info: IWC Credit Card Program, Monogram Bank USA, P.O. Box 429417, Cincinnati, OH 45242-8876.

The Fund for Animals, Inc. Info: The Fund for Animals, c/o Piedmont Trust Bank, P.O. Box 4751, Martinsville, VA 24115.

Last Chance for Animals. Issued by Capital One Bank. Info: 1-800-367-7297, ext. 259.

Letters for Animals. Issued by Capital One Bank. $15,000 minimum income required. Info: Card Center, P.O. Box 85651, Richmond, VA 23286-9029.

Santa Cruz SPCA. Issued Through Signet Bank, VA. Info: 1-800-367-7297, ext. 120.

Checks

The Fund for Animals, Inc.

Personal checks with The Fund for Animals' name and logo and four different wildlife scenes. Checks carry all the same banking and personal information that's on your present checks. Call or write for details on designs and prices. From: Affinity Products, P.O. Box 59165, Minneapolis, MN 44559-0165, 1-800-327-7123.

PETA, ARM!, IDA, VRG, PAWS...

"Checks With A Conscience." Personal checks customized for a number of organizations, including People for the Ethical Treatment of Animals, Animal Rights Mobilization, In Defense of Animals, The Vegetarian Resource Group, Progressive Animal Welfare Society, and others. A minimum of 7% is returned to the organization. Checks carry all the same banking and personal information that's on your present checks. Call or write for details on specific designs and prices: Message! Products, P.O. Box 64800, St. Paul, MN 55164-0800, 1-800-243-2565, Internet: http://www.envirolink.org/products/message

Investments

Good Money Publications, Inc.

Offers an Animal Rights Investor Package that discusses the common concerns in animal rights issues, provides screens for investors, and notes tactics people can take to ensure appropriate use of their money. This is not an investment firm, but rather a publisher of resource materials for socially concerned investors. Doesn't accept advertising. Info and cost: Good Money Publications, Inc., Box 363, Calais Road, Worcester, VT 05682, 1-800-535-3551, FAX: (802) 223-8949.

Cindie Kessler (PaineWebber)

Socially-conscious, cruelty-free investing in companies that do not use animal tests, do not sponsor inhumane animal-related events, and whose parent companies and subsidiaries also adhere to those guidelines. Recommended by the manager of PETA's Cruelty-Free Products Campaign. Contact: Cindie Kessler, Paine-Webber, 7700 Wisconsin Avenue, #300, Bethesda, MD 20814, (301) 718-5062, 1-800-638-2909.

Brad Pappas (Rocky Mountain Humane Investing Corporation)

Cruelty-free investing from: Brad Pappas, President, Rocky Mountain Humane Investing Corporation (affiliated with D.E. Frey & Co.), One Norwest Center, 1700 Lincoln-Sherman Level, Denver, CO 80203, 1-800-678-3739, (303) 839-2592.

Hotlines

Abuse Hotlines

PETA Laboratory Abuse Reporting

(757) 622-PETA (ask for the Research & Investigation Department)

For whistle blowers who want to report laboratory abuse of animals (anonymously, if preferred). $500 reward for information leading to sanctions against a lab.

Laboratory Use of Greyhounds

Greyhound Protection League

1-800-G-HOUNDS (1-800-446-8637)

To report information about greyhounds in research laboratories (calls are held in the strictest confidence). This is also the number you call to adopt a greyhound.

SPCA Tip Line

1-800-540-SPCA

A national hotline for reporting animal abuse.

Dissection Hotlines

National Dissection Hotline

National Anti-Vivisection Society)

1-800-922-FROG

Help for students seeking alternatives to animal dissection.

New Mexico Dissection Hotline

1-800-479-7223

Local support for New Mexico students.

Help Lines

Animal Referral Hotline

1-800-8-ANIMAL (or in Richmond, VA (804) 798-5957)
Provides free referrals and information on animal-related services.

Pet Information Hotline

Tree House Animal Foundation
(312) 784-5605 (Voice/TDD)
A counselor will listen to your questions and provide advice regarding dog/cat behaviors.

Pet Loss Support Hotline

UC Davis, School of Veterinary Medicine
(916) 752-4200 (Voice/TDD)
M-F 6:30 p.m.-9:30 p.m. (Pacific time)
Summer: T, W, Th only
For those struggling with grief and recovery from sad feelings related to companion animal loss. Callers pay normal long-distance phone charges (if applicable).

Low-Cost Spay/Neuter

See Companion Animals: Spay/Neuter Referrals, earlier in this Chapter.

Political Updates

Project VoteSmart

1-800-622-SMAR(T)
Information on how federal representatives or senators voted on particular bills, who they have received donations from, etc. A free service.

Poison Control

National Animal Poison Control Center

1-900-680-0000 ($20 for the first 5 minutes, then $2.95 each additional minute, billed by your telephone company)
- or -
1-800-548-2423 ($30 per case charged to a major credit card)
24 hours a day, 7 days a week. Staffed by veterinarians from the College of Veterinary Medicine, University of Illinois at Urbana-Champaign. For both numbers, the center will make free follow-up calls on critical cases.

Wildlife Help Lines (Local)

Connecticut

Fund for Animals Wildlife Hotline, (203) 393-1050

Maryland

Chesapeake Wildlife Sanctuary, (301) 390-7010 (24-hours)

Massachusetts

WIRES, (508) 540-3820, TDD (508) 540-4175

North Carolina

N.C. Wildlife Telecommunications Center, (919) 662-4381 (24-hour referral to rehabilitators)

Oregon

Cascades Raptor Center, (503) 485-1320 (24-hour line for raptors)

Humane Education

See also the Children & Young Adults section of Chapter 13 for recommended publications.

ANIMALEARN (AAVS)

An internal department of The American Anti-Vivisection Society. Educates teachers and secondary school students about animal rights and related issues. Offers a packet of teaching materials. From: Director of Education, AAVS, 801 Old York Road, Suite 204, Jenkintown, PA 19046-1685, (215) 887-0816.

American Humane Association

Materials for teachers, including lesson plans and activities, a magazine, activities designed specifically for Be Kind to Animals Week, etc. Request a catalog from: AHA, 63 Inverness Drive East, Englewood, CO 80112, (303) 792-9900, FAX: (303) 792-5333.

Animal Awareness Club (SF SPCA)

Five Theme Packets, totaling more than 300 pages of educational materials in a three-ring binder, newsletter, coloring books, and other materials. Teachers receive field trips to the SPCA, classroom visits, training seminars, and access to a humane library. Free to San Francisco teachers, one-time $35 fee to other teachers. Write or call: The San Francisco SPCA, 2500 16th Street, San Francisco, CA 94103, (415) 554-3000.

Animal Protection Educators

Prepares and disseminates curricula, video and audio tapes, slides, and literature to animal rights groups, schools, individuals, and the community at large. Also offers lectures, classes, and training. From: Animal Protection Educators, 8503 East Davies Avenue, Englewood, CO 80112, (303) 773-2571.

Animal Welfare Institute

Free and inexpensive books, films, and other educational materials for research institutions, libraries, humane societies, and school teachers from: Animal Welfare Institute, P.O. Box 3650, Washington, D.C. 20007, (202) 337-2332.

Animals & Culture Studies Program

See the description for this college course in the Activist Aids: Training & Support section.

Clem and Jethro Lecture Service

A traveling program that teaches school children and others about wolves, and encourages respect for the connectedness of life and environmental involvement. Intent is to heighten the public's awareness and thus help the survival of wolves. Program includes a film, a live wolf "ambassador" (when available), and a question and answer period. Geared to all age levels. Fee negotiable from: Pamela Brown, P.O. Box 5817, Santa Fe, NM 87502, (505) 983-8602.

Focus on Animals

See Videos & Films for a description of this group.

Helen Woodward Animal Center

A large, nationally-recognized center for animal care, education, and treatment located in San Diego county. Offers a teacher's packet called "Sharing the Earth." From: Helen Woodward Animal Center, 6461 El Apajo Road, P.O. Box 64, Rancho Santa Fe, CA 92067, (619) 756-4117.

Humane Education Committee

Offers Humane Education Conferences and a free copy of the *Humane Education Resource Guide* to NYC public school educators who teach grades K through 6. Please send request on school letterhead. $6 to educators outside of New York City. From: HEC, P.O. Box 445, New York, NY 10028, (212) 410-3095.

Humane Education Programs (NEAVS)

Offers a variety of 45-60 minute programs free of charge, presented by New England Anti-Vivisection Society regional instructors to students from third grade through college. Sessions include titles such as: "Introduction to Animal Rights," "Medical Experimentation," "Cruelty-Free Living," "The Pros and Cons of a Meat-Based Diet," etc. From: NEAVS, 333 Washington Street, Suite 850, Boston, MA 02108, (617) 523-6020.

Humane Society of the United States

Several publications and guides, including a four-page student newspaper published monthly September through May, with a teaching guide and two reproducible worksheets. Produced for three levels: primary (grades K-2), junior (grades 3-4), and senior (grades 5-6). Subscription can start at any time and includes a free teaching aid, classroom poster, and KIND ID for students. Free sample available with a self-addressed, stamped envelope (specify level). $25/year, $37 outside U.S. from: HSUS, 2100 L Street NW, Washington, D.C. 20037.

International Wildlife Coalition

Free elementary teacher's kit on whales from: IWC, 634 North Falmouth Highway, P.O. Box 388, North Falmouth, MA 02556, (508) 564-9980.

Kids and Critters Humane Education Materials

Hand-lettered and hand-illustrated humane education materials. The samples I've seen are delightful—really impressive. All prices include permission for an individual or nonprofit organization to make copies for their own noncommercial use. A variety of packets are available and include games, worksheets, projects, patterns, and ideas. Make checks payable to Charlotte Moore (no purchase orders). For information and pricing: Kids and Critters, 518 Lorraine Avenue, Santa Barbara, CA 93110.

List of Medical Schools Without Animal Labs

A free list of medical schools with no animal labs from: Physicians Committee for Responsible Medicine, P.O. Box 6322, Washington, D.C. 20015, (202) 686-2210.

Live Elephant, Inc.

The Live Elephant Book, a fully-illustrated, cross-cultural teaching program about the African elephant and its recent decline. For grades 4-6. Over 30 student activities. Topics include sound transmission, marketing principles, memory, ethics, and current international laws. Word problems, graphing exercises, a scent lab, and writing exercises related to the elephant. Priced around $12.50. For details, contact: Live Elephant, Inc., P.O. Box 10, Canton, MA 02021, (617) 821-1521.

LivingEarth Learning Project

Instructors who present a series of dynamic, interactive educational programs about animal and environmental issues for grades 3-college level throughout New England and New York. Informative presentations, lively classroom discussions, short videos, and group activities. Also speakers for teacher in-service training and conferences, a video loaning library, and lesson plans. All presentations free of charge thanks to the financial support of New England Anti-Vivisection Society. From: LivingEarth Project, P.O. Box 2160, Boston, MA 02106, (617) 367-8687.

Massachusetts Society for the Prevention of Cruelty to Animals

A variety of teaching aids, including three issues of a poster-style magazine, badges, and activity sheets to help children help animals; curriculum-oriented activities and discussion material for elementary and secondary students; an illustrated book with questions and activities, designed as a community living unit for intermediate grades; and the benefits and consequences of keeping pets in the classroom. From: MSPCA, 350 South Huntington Avenue, Boston, MA 02130, (617) 541-5000, FAX: (617) 522-4885.

National Association for Humane and Environmental Education

An Adopt-A-Teacher program that provides each student in a classroom with a monthly issue of *KIND News* (up to grade 6). Cost of the program is $20 from: NAHEE, P.O. Box 362, East Haddam, CT 06423-0362, (203) 434-9579.

PETA's Education Program

A Humane Education Kit that includes lesson plans, handouts, etc. for schools or public libraries. Classroom presentations also available. From: People for the Ethical Treatment of Animals, 501 Front Street, Norfolk, VA 23501, (757) 622-PETA.

Ohio Humane Education Association

Humane education teaching units from: OHEA, P.O. Box 546, Grove City, OH 43123-0546, (614) 875-1810.

Student Action Corps for Animals

Writes literature directly for student use, such as a "Say No to Dissection" pamphlet and a "Their Eyes Don't Lie" farm animal rights poster. Materials are geared toward empowering student activists to take responsibility for their own activism. From: SACA, P.O. Box 15588, Washington, D.C. 20003-0588, (202) 543-8983.

The True Nature Network, Inc.

See the description for this organization under Radio & Television Programming.

Vegetarian Education Network

Promotes the vegetarian perspective in schools, primarily through direct education and school lunch programs. Helps individuals pursue such changes in their local schools. Provides curricular materials for teachers, recipes and menu guidelines for food service personnel, resources especially for teens, and action packets for students, parents, and activists. Coordinates a National Speakers Network on issues related to vegetarianism. From: Vegetarian Education Network, ATTN: Sally Clinton, P.O. Box 3347, West Chester, PA 19381, (215) 696-VNET.

The Vegetarian Program

See the description for this college course in the Activist Aids: Training & Support section.

The Wild Ones (Wildlife Preservation Trust International)

A classroom-based, interactive, international children's program of the Wildlife Preservation Trust International. *The Wild Thing* (published three times yearly; includes a teacher's guide) contains kids' writing and artwork, as well as book excerpts and research activities. Specify 7-9 year-old version or 10-13 year-old version. Contact: The Wild Ones Membership, WPTI, 3400 West Girard Avenue, Philadelphia, PA 19104, (215) 222-3636, FAX: (215) 222-2191, Internet: http://www.columbia.edu/cu/cerc/WildOnes

Leather Alternatives

This section includes sources for nonleather sports gear, footwear, bags, and other accessories. In addition to these mail-order sources, check your local discount stores and discount shoe stores for nonleather shoes, purses, and belts. For an additional guide to nonleather product sources, contact: The Vegetarian Resource Group, P.O. Box 1463, Baltimore, MD 21203, (410) 366-VEGE, FAX: (410) 366-8804.

Aesop Unlimited

"Let live, Be free, Don't wear animal skins." Leather-free accessories, including shoes and boots for men and women, handbags, a brief case, and wallets. Nonleather Birkenstock sandals and Etonic running shoes, as well as men's wingtips and oxfords. From: Aesop Unlimited, 55 Fenno Street, P.O. Box 315, N. Cambridge, MA 02140, (617) 492-6165.

Atlas Fitness Products

Nonleather weight-lifting belts and gloves from: Atlas Fitness Products, 1721 Commercial Park Drive, Knoxville, TN 37918.

The Compassionate Consumer

Donates 5% of purchases to the animal rights, animal shelter, or environmental group of your choice. Wallets, handbags, attaché, shoes, and belts. $1 for catalog with photographs (credited toward purchase). From: The Compassionate Consumer, P.O. Box 27, Jericho, NY 11753, (718) 445-4134.

Creatureless Comforts

"Creatureless accessories for the style conscious individual with a conscience," including bags, belts, and wallets. From: Creatureless Comforts, 702 Page Street, Stroughton, MA 02072, (617) 344-7496.

Footprints—The Birkenstock Store

A full line of Birkenstock sandals, including some made from the synthetic, "Birko-Flor." Returns and exchanges accepted. From: Footprints, 1339 Massachusetts, Lawrence, KS 66044, 1-800-488-8316.

Heartland Products, Ltd.

Shoes for men and women (including cowboy boots, workboots, dress, casual, and sport shoes), baseball/softball fielder's glove, jackets, etc. $1 for flyer, to be credited toward purchase. From: Heartland Products, Box 218, Dakota City, IA 50529, (515) 332-3087, FAX: 1-800-441-4692.

Just In Case

"Cruelty-free bags, cases, art jewelry, and other environmentally conscious gifts." Includes brief cases, diaper packs, fanny packs, knapsacks, etc., bags with the look and feel of leather, and those made from a "silky-like" rubber. From: Just In Case, 2718 Main Street, Santa Monica, CA 90405, (310) 399-3096. Walk-in or mail-order.

The Natural Choice Catalog

A catalog with lots of different "natural" products, one of which is hemp shoes for men and women. Different styles available. From: The Natural Choice Catalog, Eco Design Company, 1365 Rufina Circle, Santa Fe, NM 87505, (505) 438-3448.

Nike, Inc.

Nonleather sports footwear for men, women, and children, including shoes for running, racing, track and field, basketball, tennis, cross training, cheerleading, walking, hiking, cycling, aqua sports, golf, football, soccer, baseball, wrestling, and multi-purpose. Call the Brochure Hotline for a list (be sure to specify your interest in *nonleather* shoes): Nike, Brochure Hotline: 1-800-462-7363 (24-hour answering machine takes your name and mailing address for brochure), Consumer Services: 1-800-344-0453.

People for the Ethical Treatment of Animals

PETA's catalog now includes "upscale" items such as shoes, belts, hats, a tapestry purse, and faux fur coats, as well as an assortment of other animal-friendly products for people and animals. From: PETA, 501 Front Street, Norfolk, VA 23501, (757) 622-PETA.

Real Goods

Nonleather Dega Shoe footwear for men and women. Various styles in hemp and leather-free material which looks like leather but is stronger. From: Real Goods, 966 Mazzoni Street, Ukiah, CA 95482-3471, (707) 468-9214, Orders: 1-800-762-7325, FAX: (707) 468-9486.

Spalding

Nonleather softball. From: Spalding, 1-800-642-5004 (for the store nearest you).

Letter-Writing Services

Note: See the Resources section of Chapter 9, "Activism," for addresses of politicians, television networks, and movie companies.

Letters do make a difference! If you don't have time to write your own, if putting words together isn't your strong point, or if you don't know who to write to, one of the following services can help.

Animail
"A voice for the animals." Members receive a newsletter from which they can choose to write their own letters or can receive pre-written letters with stamped/addressed envelopes to sign and send. Starts at $15/year for newsletter only. Prices and details: Animail, P.O. Box 7119, Corte Madera, CA 94976, (415) 924-2551.

Animal Letters
Writes free letters for people with busy lifestyles. Send a self-addressed, stamped envelope for every four letters (for eight letters, put two stamps on the envelope). From: Jill Schechter, P.O. Box 340022, Boca Raton, FL 33434, (407) 487-1084.

Animal Rights Lobbying Network
At this writing, scope limited to California only, but expanding to other states. "With the stroke of your pen, you can help save animals' lives and end their suffering..." Monthly newsletter from which you choose three issues and receive three personalized, persuasive letters with stamped, pre-addressed envelopes to sign and send. Starts at $20 for 9 letters (3/month for 3 months). From: Animal Rights Lobbying Network, P.O. Box 4518, Foster City, CA 94404, (415) 574-3245.

Humane Society of the United States Action Alert Team
Note: Because of IRS restrictions, only voting members of The Humane Society of the United States may participate in the Action Alert Program (annual membership, payable to HSUS, is $10 Individual, $18 Family). Members receive alerts whenever critical animal issues arise so that they can write timely, effective letters to key people. Alerts are sent only when it is believed that immediate action will measurably affect the outcome of a critical concern, therefore there is no way to predict when or how often alerts are issued. Members also receive a quarterly newsletter, regular HSUS publications and benefits, may join the Activist Telephone Network, and may elect to receive the *Student Network News*, an activist guide for junior and senior high school students. Only people willing to respond with letters or telegrams when asked to do so are requested to join the team. From: HSUS, Action Alert Team, 2100 L Street NW, Washington, D.C. 20037.

Joan W. Jenrich
An independent activist who offers brief letters on animal rights concerns that you can use as a guide or copy word-for-word. A number of different letters every month on a variety of concerns. Joan is retired and offers this service for free. She says, "I'm just trying to help the animals by helping people write letters." (Although she hasn't requested it, I'm sure she could use donations for postage if you feel like contributing!) From: Joan W. Jenrich, P.O. Box 7251, St. Petersburg, FL 33734-7251.

Letters for Animals
Prewritten, sign-and-send letters of praise or censure regarding the addressee's treatment of animals. You are encouraged to freely copy and distribute the letters. A one month subscription ranges from $3.05 to $11.30, depending on the number of letters and other options. For info and sample letters, send a self-addressed, stamped envelope with two stamps on it to: Letters for Animals, P.O. Box 29, Factoryville, PA 18419, (717) 945-5312 (long distance calls cannot be returned; please call in the evening). *Note*: Letters for Animals' founder writes a weekly newspaper column which she is trying to syndicate. To help in the syndication effort, send a long, self-addressed, stamped envelope for information and copies of several columns.

Lots O' Letters
Quarterly, you receive 40 to 100 letters per year to sign and send. (You are encouraged to photocopy and distribute them to others.) Letters also available on Macintosh disk, if you prefer. $60/year. Check or money order payable to Darlene Boord. For sample letter, send a self-addressed, stamped envelope to: Darlene Boord, P.O. Box 2124, Orange, CA 92669.

What We Can Do

A monthly packet of letters on behalf of animals, ready to sign and mail. Send a self-addressed, stamped envelope for information or enclose $10 for a current packet of letters to: What We Can Do, P.O. Box 4724, Westlake Village, CA 91359.

The Write Cause

Promotes animal and environmental rights. You receive personalized letters on recycled stationery to sign and send, and stamped, addressed envelopes. A monthly newsletter describes five animal rights/environmental rights issues, from which you choose two or more. Info and prices: The Write Cause, P.O. Box 2524, Petaluma, CA 94953-2524, (707) 769-0116.

Long Distance Telephone Services

Affinity Fund—Long Distance with a Purpose

Contributes 5% of your total bill to the nonprofit group you signed up with (among them, Alliance for Animals (WI), EarthSave (CA), or the Predator Project (MT); other groups may also offer this service). Guarantees you 10% savings over any residential program you currently have. Affinity buys discounted blocks of phone service from America's foremost carriers, provides its own customer service and billing, and doesn't advertise. That's how they do it. For more information, check with your favorite groups to see if they offer this service, or call: 1-800-670-0008.

TransNational Communications

Long-distance telephone service through U.S. Sprint. A percentage of your long distance charges benefit the Whale Adoption Project of the International Wildlife Coalition. Call: 1-800-888-8940.

Working Assets Long Distance

Donates 1% of your long-distance telephone charges to a fund for selected nonprofit groups. Some groups supported in the past are Earth Day 1990, Natural Resources Defense Council, Rainforest Action Network, Environmental Defense Fund, Trust for Public Land, Citizen's Clearinghouse for Hazardous Wastes, Clean Water Fund, and African Wildlife Foundation. The carrier is U.S. Sprint. Info: Working Assets Long Distance, 230 California Street, San Francisco, CA 94111, 1-800-877-2100, ext. 222.

Paints & Stains

Auro Organic Paints

Art supplies, house paints, and natural building supplies from: Auro Organic Paints, P.O. Box 857, Davis, CA 95617, (916) 753-3104.

Livos Plant Chemistry

Nontoxic products that are harmless to humans, animals, and plants. All products made entirely of plant ingredients. No petroleum products. Includes paints, primers, thinners, stains, waxes, oil finishes, varnishes, spackles, adhesives, cleaners, and natural arts materials. *Note:* You'll want to avoid the oil-based finishes, which do contain an ingredient that has been tested on animals. From: Eco Design Company, 1365 Rufina Circle, Santa Fe, NM 87505, (505) 438-3745, 1-800-621-2591.

Radio & Television Programming

Radio

Animal Watch (WMTR-AM, 1250)

A weekly 60-second radio feature in the New Jersey/New York area, covering topics ranging from dog grooming to vivisection, and everything in between. From: WMTR-AM, 1250, 55 Horsehill Road, Cedar Knolls, NJ 07927, Contact: Mary-Kaye Dombrowski (201) 538-1250, ext. 1323, FAX: (201) 538-5744.

Humane Society of the United States

30-second Public Service Announcements on audio cassette by Candice Bergen and Ana-Alicia on fur, ivory, chimpanzees, and cruelty-free cosmetics. For prices and details contact: HSUS, 2100 L Street NW, Washington, D.C. 20037.

Speaking of Animals (KSCO-AM 1080)
A call-in show airing in the Santa Cruz area which "celebrates the animals in our lives." Hosts are Marilee Geyer (Santa Cruz SPCA) and J.P. Novic (Center for Animal Protection and Education).

Television

This category includes Public Service Announcements (PSAs) and programs designed for cable television. For information on how to get this programming onto your local stations, contact one of the distributors in this section or your local cable access station.

American Humane Association
30-second Public Service Announcements on adopting an adult cat, adopting an adult dog, and spay/neuter. All three just $10 for VHS versions or $30 for 3/4" broadcast versions, postpaid from: AHA, 63 Inverness Drive East, Englewood, CO 80112, (303) 792-9900, FAX: (303) 792-5333.

The Animal News Network
"A new concept in television programming." A loose confederation of individuals and organizations consisting of producers, directors, and writers of environmental video materials with a special emphasis on animal issues. Provides members with the information needed to get started as a public access television producer. Also provides access to a catalog of animal rights/welfare/protectionist programming, access to unedited animal-related footage for use in your program, and a networking list. From: ANN, P.O. Box 439, Old Albany Post Road, Garrison, NY 10524, (914) 424-3005, FAX: (914) 424-4132.

Animal Protection Institute
30-second Public Service Announcement in which "unsuspecting animals approach an open steel-jaw leghold trap. Just as a kitten seems doomed to become the trap's latest victim, the shot cuts away to a trap slamming closed in slow motion, dramatically shattering a ballpoint pen." One of two slogans then appears: "Traps Have No Conscience...Do You?" or "Feel The Impact? In the U.S. 12 to 22 million animals a year do!" It closes with API's logo, telephone number, and a message that a disabled trap was used for the shots. From: API, Humane Education Director, P.O. Box 22505, Sacramento, CA 95822, (916) 731-5521.

Animal Rights Information Service
Produces and distributes to dozens of cities in the U.S. and Canada a weekly cable television program called "Speaking of Animals...," a series of documentary and interview programs that stimulates viewers to examine their relationships with animals. Sample program titles are "Fur Crimes," "Ivory: Digging the Elephant's Graveyard," "From Mice to Men? (The Use of Animals in Experimental Psychology)," "Animals Used as Entertainment," and "Teach Your Children Well." Information on how to put "Speaking of Animals..." on TV in your community, and a catalog of videotapes for rent or purchase, or for loan to schools. Contributions and purchases are tax-deductible from: ARIS, P.O. Box 20672, Columbus Circle Station, New York, NY 10023.

Focus on Animals
See the description for this group under Videos & Films.

Gaia Institute
Produces and distributes a series of 55 programs called "Animal Rights," which has aired in over 500 cities and towns in 28 states. Available to activists willing to make the necessary arrangements with their cable companies. Annually brings to cable television "Festival for the Earth and the Animals," a collection of internationally-solicited videos. Currently producing a series for mainstream television called "ANIMALWATCH." From: Gaia Institute, P.O. Box 852, South Lynfield, MA 01940, (508) 535-8980.

Humane Society of the United States
30-second Public Service Announcements by celebrities on various subjects. Also a Spanish language spay/neuter PSA. For prices and details contact: HSUS, 2100 L Street NW, Washington, D.C. 20037.

New England Anti-Vivisection Society
Offers for rent the video "A Medical Turning Point," designed for broadcast over cable television. This is not a "horror show," but rather a "balanced argument aimed at the excesses of animal research." Features three prominent physicians: Dr. Neal Barnard (PCRM), Dr. John McDougall (*The McDougall Plan*), and Dr. Henry Heimlich (the Heimlich Maneuver). "Entertaining, yet informative." Includes step-by-step procedures for requesting

broadcast time from your local cable network. From: NEAVS, 333 Washington Street, Suite 850, Boston, MA 02108-5100, (617) 523-6020.

Nine Lives Productions

Produces half-hour and one-hour talk shows and documentaries intended for cable television. Subjects include health, vegetarian cooking, and fur. Programs currently aired in New York and Massachusetts. Also produces Public Service Announcements on animal concerns. From: Nine Lives Productions, 43-23 Colden Street, Suite 8E, Flushing, NY 11355, (718) 445-4190.

The True Nature Network, Inc.

Animal protection/ecology group that produces and actively distributes cable television programs. Also sends educational materials to schools, universities, and libraries. Videos (3/4" broadcast and VHS) available on loan basis to television stations, schools, and libraries. Each 28-minute video sells for $20 postpaid. Titles include: "Born to be Betrayed," "Fur Crimes," "Elephants on the Edge," "The Politics of Medicine and You," "Teach Your Children Well," "From Mice to Men?," "Show Business Is No Business for Animals," "The Plights of Pigeons," "Probing the Mind of the Vivisector," "A Conversation with Bob Barker," and "Is Animal Research Necessary for Human Health?" From: TTNN, P.O. Box 20672, Columbus Circle Station, New York, NY 10023-1487.

Voices for Animals

Produces "The Animals' Advocate," an award-winning news magazine format television series. From: Voices for Animals, ATTN: Lisa Markkula, P.O. Box 1405, Tucson, AZ 85702, (602) 791-2946.

Stamps & Stickers

Rubber Stamps

Amberwood

Proceeds help a sanctuary for wild burros. Rubber stamps with vegetarian messages, including "Be Kind To Animals, Don't Eat Them," "Happiness Is...Reverence for Life — Be a Vegetarian," and "Vegetarianism...The Humane Alternative." Catalog: Amberwood, Route 2, Box 300, Milford Road, Baker County, Leary, GA 31762, (912) 792-6246.

Justice For Animals

A variety of self-inking stamps. You can also order a customized stamp of your choice (up to 65 letters/spaces). Catalog: Justice for Animals, P.O. Box 4044, Flushing, NY 11360.

Stamper Hans

"Stamp out cruelty to animals!" These are really great stamps and I highly recommend them! Rubber stamps with hand-drawn animal images and messages that promote animal welfare and environmental responsibility. Original designs and designs from other companies. Messages include: "Ban Animal Testing," "Boycott Veal," "My Coat Is Not For Sale," "Buy Cruelty Free," "Prevent a Litter, Spay and Neuter," "Love Animals, Don't Eat Them," "Hunting, Sport of Cowards," Don't Support Animals in Entertainment," "Greyhound Racing, A Cruel Bloodsport," "Be Kind To Animals," "There's No Excuse for Animal Abuse," etc.! Ink pads available. Stamps are around $6 each. Catalog: Stamper Hans, P.O. Box 8846, Scottsdale, AZ 85252, (602) 994-3555, FAX: (602) 947-6469.

Stickers

Amberwood

Proceeds help a sanctuary for wild burros. Animal rights stickers perfect for placing on correspondence. Some stickers have drawings as well as text. Messages include "Cruelty, Not Sport! Boycott Rodeo," "The question is not, Can they reason? nor Can they talk? but, Can they suffer?, Jeremy Bentham," "Man's Inhumanity to Man is Only Surpassed by His Cruelty to Animals," "Animal Liberation, Human Liberation," and "They pity and they eat the objects of their compassion, Oliver Goldsmith." Catalog: Amberwood, Route 2, Box 300, Milford Road, Baker County, Leary, GA 31762, (912) 792-6246.

Vegetarian Resource Group

"Be Kind To Animals—Don't Eat Them" and "Vegetarians Have Good Hearts" envelope stickers. 40 of one style for $5 from: VRG, P.O. Box 1463, Baltimore, MD 21203, (410) 366-VEGE, FAX: (410) 366-8804.

Toys

Animal Town
Offers a catalog of toys, some of which have animal themes. (*Note*: Despite its name, this catalog isn't geared toward animals. Alongside animal-friendly toys, sells a fishing game!) Board games include "Dam Builders, " which teaches about beavers ($26), and "Save the Whales," a cooperative game where players work together to save eight different types of whales ($37). Also other animal-friendly toys, games, books, and puzzles. From: Animal Town, P.O. Box 485, Healdsburg, CA 95448, 1-800-445-8642, FAX: (707) 837-9737.

PETA Factsheet: "Toy Companies & Animal Testing"
A list of toy companies that do and do not test their toys on animals. From: People for the Ethical Treatment of Animals, 501 Front Street, Norfolk, VA 23501, (757) 622-PETA.

The Vegetarian Game
See Computer-Based Communication & Products for a description of this IBM-compatible game.

Travel Services

See also the Vegetarianism & Whole Foods section of Chapter 13 for guides to vegetarian vacation spots. For additional listings of tour operators and travel agencies, check your library or bookstore for eco-travel books such as *Ecotours and Nature Getaways* by Alice M. Geffen and Carole Berglie (Clarkson Potter Publishers, 1993) and *A Guide to Earthtrips* by Dwight Holing, Conservation International (Living Planet Press, 1991). *Note*: Ironically, many ecotours are *not* vegetarian-oriented, so be sure to make your needs known.

Ancient Forest Adventures
Guided trips explore the Cascade Mountains of the Pacific Northwest. Learn about plants, forest ecology, and management issues. Hot springs soaks, yoga, meditation, and massage optional. Vegetarian meals (vegan option). Offers six-day, resort-based trips, lower-priced backpacking trips, and day trips. From: Ancient Forest Adventures, 16 NW Kansas Avenue, Bend, OR 97701-1202, Applications: 1-800-551-1043, Questions: (503) 385-8633.

Earthwatch
A member organization that sponsors scientific expeditions to "improve human understanding of the planet, the diversity of its inhabitants, and the processes that affect the quality of life on Earth." Members pay to help with studies of animal behavior, coral reefs, endangered species, etc. For those who want a "working vacation." Membership ($35) includes six issues of a 64-page color magazine. From: Earthwatch, 680 Mount Auburn Street, P.O. Box 403, Watertown, MA 02272-9924.

Environmental Travel, Inc.
Committed to the support of animal rights organizations. Offers the *Catalogue of Worldwide Vegetarian & Vegan Vacation Spots* for $2 postpaid. Provides to clients who book airline reservations with them information on vegetarian restaurants at their destination. From: Environmental Travel, 119-66 80th Road, Kew Gardens, NY 11415, 1-800-929-3005 (outside New York City), (718) 263-0048, FAX: 1-800-580-8630.

Farm Sanctuary's Vegetarian Bed & Breakfast
A bed & breakfast located at a sanctuary for farm animals. Located in the "Finger Lakes Region" of upstate New York. From: Farm Sanctuary, P.O. Box 150, Watkins Glen, NY 14891, (607) 583-2225.

Grateful Bed & Breakfast Luquillo, Puerto Rico
"A tranquil hide-away nestled in the foothills of the Luquillo Mountains with an inspiring panoramic view of the ocean, rolling hills, and El Yunque National Rainforest." Will help you plan a custom-designed vacation experience. Serves vegetarian meals and uses recycled products. "Dead head" theme to their literature. From: Grateful Bed & Breakfast, P.O. Box 568, Luquillo, PR 00773, (809) 889-4919. (*Note*: Some activists are boycotting Puerto Rico because of the neglect and subsequent suffering of dogs and cats there, but these bed & breakfast folks can't be blamed for the entire country's neglect of companion animals.)

Natural Habitat Adventures
"See the Wild World." Excursions to watch whales, dolphins, polar bears, harp seals, wolves, etc. Led a "seal watch" trip in

conjunction with the International Fund for Animal Welfare, designed to boost ecotourism in efforts to curb the clubbing of baby seals. From: Natural Habitat Adventures, 2945 Center Green Court South, Boulder, CO 80301, 1-800-543-8917.

Newport-Mesa Travel

Services include travel arrangements geared toward vegetarians and environmentalists. Call: 1-800-223-0915 or (714) 650-8818.

Oceanic Society Expeditions

Worldwide environmental trips, including non-invasive whale watching and wildlife encounters, low-impact rainforest and reef exploration, and research expeditions. (*Note*: I recently participated in their dolphin research efforts in Belize. I advise vegetarians, particularly vegans, to take along your own food, or at least supplemental food!) From: Oceanic Society Expeditions, Fort Mason Center, Building E, Suite 230, San Francisco, CA 94123, 1-800-326-7491, FAX: (415) 474-3395.

Working Assets Travel Service

A full-service travel agency that donates 2% of total sales to a pool of socially responsible nonprofit groups, such as Rainforest Action Network, Environmental Defense Fund, etc. From: Working Assets Travel Service, 230 California Street, San Francisco, CA 94111, 1-800-332-3637.

Vegetarian Supplies & Services

See also the Companion Animal Products & Services section of this chapter for vegetarian food for companion animals, and the Travel Services section for vegetarian vacations. See Chapter 13 for vegetarian publications. For services not listed here, contact The Vegetarian Resource Group — they are a storehouse of information!

School Lunches & Quantity Recipes

School lunches traditionally not only taste bad, they're also bad for you! The meat and dairy industries have been feeding school children their propaganda for years. Now health-conscious individuals are successfully instituting vegetarian and vegan alternatives to the traditional school lunch menus. Here are some resources for those interested in instituting such change and telling children the truth about nutrition.

The American Vegan Society

127 recipes by Freya Dinsha, each for 100 portions. No sugar, spices, or refined foods. 3" by 5" cards in a file box. $24.95 (revised edition) postpaid from: AVS, 56 Dinshah Lane, P.O. Box H, Malaga, NJ 08328-0908, (609) 694-2887 (voice/FAX).

CHOICE (Consumers for Healthy Options In Children's Education)

"Promoting informed choice of wholesome plant-based foods in school." Their three-step strategy is: (1) to review and select accredited plant-based nutrition education curricula and supporting materials, (2) motivate local consumer advocates and parent-teacher groups to request use of the curricula, and (3) assist food service personnel in meeting the demand for wholesome, plant-based foods. From: Farm Animal Reform Movement, P.O. Box 30654, Bethesda, MD 20824, (301) 530-1737.

EarthSave Healthy School Lunch Program

Offers the *Healthy School Lunch Action Guide* to promote plant-based diets in schools. (See the Vegetarianism & Whole Foods: Guides & Directories section of Chapter 13 for a description of that publication.) Also a four-minute video introducing the program. From: EarthSave, 706 Frederick Street, Santa Cruz, CA 95062, 1-800-362-3648.

Food Not Bombs

Offers a 128-page book that tells you how to start and maintain a vegetarian food recovery program for low-income people, 30 vegan recipes for feeding 100 people, and logos, flyers, and letters you can reproduce for a Food Not Bombs campaign. $10 from: Food Not Bombs, 3145 Geary Blvd., #12, San Francisco, CA 94118, 1-800-884-1136.

Healthy Transitions School Catering & Consulting

Fresh and natural school meals. Vegetarian entree daily; vegan also available. Info:

Healthy Transitions, P.O. Box 2262, Morristown, NJ 07962, (201) 829-19647, FAX: (201) 898-6625.

Physicians Committee for Responsible Medicine
Vegetarian recipes for institutions from: PCRM, P.O. Box 6322, Washington, D.C. 20015.

Vegetarian Education Network
Curricular materials for teachers, recipe and menu guidelines for food service personnel, resources especially for teens, action packets for students, parents, and activists, and a National Speakers Network from: Vegetarian Education Network, P.O. Box 3347, West Chester, PA 19381, (215) 696-VNET.

The Vegetarian Resource Group
Offers a packet which includes 28 vegan recipes to serve 25-50 people and sources for institution-sized vegetarian food. From: VRG, P.O. Box 1463, Baltimore, MD 21203, (410) 366-VEGE, FAX: (410) 366-8804.

Introduction & Correspondence

At The Gate (Hetero)
An international "contact network for socially responsible singles interested in the many aspects of green living." Shares 5% of profits with groups like Greenpeace, Amnesty International, Oxfam America, and People for the Ethical Treatment of Animals. Info: At The Gate, P.O. Box 09506, Columbus, OH 43209.

Two-Fu Vegetarian Singles Connection
National profiles of vegetarian singles who want to meet other vegetarian singles. Info: 1-800-241-5798.

Vegetarian International Pen (V.I.P.) Club
"A magazine where vegetarians and those who have an interest share ideas, recipes, and friendship." Includes personal ads for pen pals and those seeking romantic relationships. For information, send a self-addressed, stamped envelope to: V.I.P. Club, P.O. Box 2036, Tempe, AZ 85281, Voice mail: (602) 352-4383, E-mail: Ocatilla@mail.hvs.com

Veggie Social News (Hetero, Same Sex, Just Friends)
"Helping vegetarian singles meet & eat." Offers nonprofit animal groups one-third off on all advertising. A national publication featuring personal ads; announcements of places and events where vegetarians meet and socialize; articles on dating, food, animal rights, etc.; recipes; restaurant reviews; and more. 1 year (6 issues) for $18 from: *Veggie Social News*, P.O. Box 300412, Brooklyn, NY 11230-0412.

Food & Supplies

Beano
"Beano" comes in pill or liquid form and prevents the gas that forms from eating beans, peas, cabbage, broccoli, eggplant, soy, and other foods. It contains an enzyme that helps break down the complex sugars in these foods, making them digestible. (*Note*: Diabetics should note that Beano makes vegetable sugars available. People allergic to molds and/or penicillin should also exercise caution.) Widely available over-the-counter from drug stores, or contact the manufacturer: AkPharma, Inc., P.O. Box 111, Pleasantville, NJ 08232, 1-800-257-8650.

Amberwood
Profits benefit a wild burro sanctuary. Animal-free "gelatin" and marshmallows, and a variety of nonfood products from: Amberwood, Route 2, Box 300, Milford Road, Baker County, Leary, GA 31762, (912) 792-6246.

Beehive Botanicals
(*Note*: I do not recommend the use of bee products. This information is included for those who may currently be using bee products and wish to lessen the harmful impacts of such products on the bees.) All products contain ingredients produced by bees and "gathered without harm to the bees." Items include chewing gum and nutritional supplements of Bee Propolis and Royal Jelly. From: Ogren Road, P.O. Box 8258, Hayward, WI 54843, 1-800-283-4274.

Carr's Specialty Foods
Organic and natural foods, including granolas and cereals, dried fruits, nuts, seeds, legumes, grains, flours, snacks, and condiments. Also home appliances and books from: Carr's Specialty Foods, P.O. Box 1016, Manachaca, TX 78652, (512) 282-9056.

Diamond Organics
Fresh, organically grown vegetables (including gourmet greens and mushrooms),

fruits, sprouts, herbs, and flowers (both edible and not). Also breads, pasta, organic olive oil, nuts, and dried fruits. Next day, year-round delivery via Federal Express. "No minimum—no order too small." From: Diamond Organics, Freedom, CA 95019, 1-800-922-2396.

Dixie USA, Inc.

Vegetarian Burger'n Loaf mixes, Beef (Not!) and Fat (Not!) mixes, Wonderslim egg and fat substitute, a fat-free chocolate fudge sauce sweetened with fruit juice, FruitSweet natural sugar replacement, and several other food and nonfood items. (*Note*: Vegans be careful—whether or not a product is vegan is not evident from the catalog descriptions.) From: Dixie USA, P.O. Box 55549, Houston, TX 77255, Orders: 1-800-347-3494, Info: (713) 688-4993, FAX: (713) 688-5932.

Gold Mine Natural Food Company

A large selection of natural foods, organically grown foods, macrobiotic foods (including umeboshi products, tamari, unpasteurized miso, sea vegetables, seitan, etc.), and a variety of other products (including unyeasted breads, dried foods, and pickled foods). Also nonfood products from: Gold Mine Natural Food Company, 1947-30th Street, San Diego, CA 92102, Info: (619) 234-9711, Orders: 1-800-475-FOOD (3663).

Gracious Living Organic Farms

Organically grown fruits and vegetables. Sells to both members and nonmembers, but annual $25 membership fee gets you greatly reduced prices on a variety of vegetables, fruits, popcorn, and assorted other items. Will also "raise anything upon member's request." Shipped UPS. Started and operated by a person sprayed with poisons in Vietnam who maintains his health through exercise and organic foods. From: Gracious Living Organic Farms, c/o Paul Patton, 101 Mountain Parkway East, Insko, KY 41443, (606) 662-6245.

Harvest Direct, Inc.

A wide variety of vegetarian products, including meat substitutes, beans, grains, broths and gravies, soups, pasta, salad dressings, condiments, milk alternatives, cereals, baking mixes, egg replacers, baby food, kitchen helpers, books, and more. From: Harvest Direct, P.O. Box 4514, Decatur, IL 62525-4514, (217) 422-3324, Orders: 1-800-835-2867.

Jaffe Bros., Inc.

Organically grown natural foods. Many items have a five-pound minimum. Foods include dried fruits, peas, beans, seeds, grains and grain products, pasta, low-salt sauerkraut, low-salt dill pickles, dehydrated vegetables, oils, nut butters, nuts, olives, herb teas, juices, jams, carob confections, syrup, and baby food. From: Jaffe Bros., P.O. Box 636, Valley Center, CA 92082-0636, (619) 749-1133, FAX: (619) 749-1282.

Maine Coast Sea Vegetables

Nourishing products from the sea, including dulse, kelp, alaria, laver/nori, and digitata. Also low-sodium sea seasonings, sea chips, sea sweets, and nonfood items. From: Maine Coast Sea Vegetables, Franklin, ME 04634, (207) 565-2907.

Mountain Ark Trading Company

Natural macrobiotic foods (including umeboshi products and sea vegetables) and organic foods (including a nondairy Alfredo sauce). Also grains, cereals, breads, beans, noodles, nuts, seeds, snacks, oils, vinegars, dried foods, teas, and nonfood products. From: Mountain Ark Trading Co., 120 South East Avenue, Fayetteville, AR 72701, 1-800-643-8909.

Natural Lifestyle Supplies

Natural, organic, and macrobiotic specialties, including baby food, supplements, miso, sea vegetables, condiments, seitan, specialty foods, soy beverages, fruit juices, spreads, cookies, chips, sweeteners, candy sweetened with malt syrup, teas, and organic coffee. Also kitchenware, water filters, toys, recycled paper products, books, and products for body, baby, and companion animals. From: Natural Lifestyle Supplies, 16 Lookout Drive, Asheville, NC 28804, 1-800-752-2775.

Organic Foods Express, Inc.

Organically grown and natural products, including produce, pasta, snacks, sweeteners, oil, dairy products, juices, sodas, baked goods, grains, seeds, beans, flour, nuts, dried fruit, cereal, soups, nut butters, soy products, coffee, and miscellaneous items. From: Organic Foods Express, 11003 Emack Road, Beltsville, MD 20705, (301) 937-8608.

Quality Health Foods

A wide variety of canned, dry, and frozen meat substitutes from Worthington, La Loma, Cedar Lakes, and Morningstar Farms. Also soy products, vegetarian kosher "gelatin," broths, pickles, other miscellaneous foods, and cookbooks. From: Quality Health Foods, P.O. Box 1230, Mt. Vernon, OH 43050, (614) 392-0111, 1-800-643-5714.

Simply Good

Juicers and appliances for healthy living, including Acme juicers, Champion juicers, wheatgrass juicers, sprouters, coffee mills, steamer pressure cookers, and others. From: Simply Good, Kitchen Corner, P.O. Box 148, Brewster, NY 10509, (914) 279-4273 (call mornings or early afternoons to reach a person; call anytime to leave a message).

Vermont Country Maple Mixes, Inc.

Organic, low-fat mixes made from maple syrup powder. Cake, cookie, and frosting mixes. From: Vermont Country Maple Mixes, 76 Ethan Allen Drive, South Burlington, VT 05403, 1-800-528-7021.

Vegan Treats

Christopher's Chewies

These yummy treats are reminiscent of a healthy version of "Rice Krispie Squares." Made with puffed brown rice, sweetened with barley malt (no refined sugar), and relatively low fat, these are a sensible way to satisfy your sweet tooth. Many varieties, including Chocolate Peanut Butter Crunch, Apricot Almond, Cinnamon Raisin Walnut, Carob Chip Almond, and many others. Free samples available by calling their 800 #! Ask your health food store to order some, or you can order for yourself (one dozen minimum). From: Home Again Foods, Inc., 20-G Mountainview Avenue, Orangeburg, NY 10962, (914) 359-6356 or 1-800-800-0208, FAX: (914) 359-5288.

Frankly Natural Bakers

A variety of vegan goodies, including cookies, rice crunchies, squares, and a "wickedly rich" brownie called Vegan Decadence. Ask your local health food store to order some or send for a free flyer and order for yourself (one dozen minimum). From: Frankly Natural Bakers, 4901 Morena Blvd., Suite 403, San Diego, CA 92117, 1-800-727-7229.

From the Rain Forest

Unsalted cashews and Tropical Mix (cashews, coconut, banana chips, Brazil nuts, papaya, and pineapple chunks). Dedicated to preserving living tropical forests and rainforests, and their original inhabitants, by creating a market for indigenous products from these forests with sustainable agroforestry systems. Donates 5% of net profits, and 5% from every pound of fruits and nuts purchased, to Cultural Survival, a nonprofit organization working with the forest inhabitants. From: From the Rain Forest, 8 East 12th Street, #5, New York, NY 10003, 1-800-327-8496 (1-800-EARTH 96), FAX: (212) 675-5020.

Rapunzel Premium Dairy-Free Organic Swiss Chocolate Bars

Made in Switzerland. Organic and dairy-free, but high in saturated fat! An occasional indulgence for the chocolate addict. Ask your health food store to order some, or contact: Cloud Nine, Inc., Hoboken, NJ 07030.

Pueblo to People

Dry roasted cashews (no salt or oil). Cultivated and processed by poor peasants to achieve economic progress and social justice by nonviolent means. Nonprofit marketing, training, and financing provided by: Pueblo to People, 1616 Montrose Blvd., Houston, TX 77006, (713) 523-1197, 1-800-843-5257.

Tropical Source Dairy-Free Rainforest Chocolate Bars

Donates 10% of profits to help local communities, tribes, and organizations produce ecologically sustainable tropical food products. These chocolate bars come in a variety of flavors, from wild rice crisp to hazelnut espresso crunch to maple almond granola. Manufactured by Tropical Source. Ask your health food store to order some. At the time of this writing, they were also available from the following mail-order catalog: EarthCare, Ukiah, CA 95482-8507, 1-800-347-0070, FAX: (707) 468-9486.

Videos & Films

See also Radio & Television Programming for videos, films, and PSAs designed for television broadcast.

The American Vegan Society

A variety of videotapes related to vegetarianism, veganism, and health from: AVS, 501 Old Harding Highway, P.O. Box H, Malaga, NJ 08328, (609) 694-2887.

Animal Rights Information Service
Write for a catalog of videotapes for rent or purchase. Contributions and purchases are tax-deductible. From: ARIS, P.O. Box 20672, Columbus Circle Station, New York, NY 10023.

Bullfrog Films, Inc.
A variety of videos for sale and rental. From: Bullfrog Films, Inc., Oley, PA 19547, 1-800-543-FROG or (215) 779-8226, FAX: (215) 370-1978.

Dedication & Everlasting Love To Animals
"Safe House," finding a safe new home for a companion animal. 80 minutes. $29.95 plus $4 shipping. No rental. From: D.E.L.T.A., P.O. Box 9, Glendale, CA 91209-9832.

EarthSave
Offerings include "Diet for a New America," a 60-minute PBS documentary hosted by John Robbins; "Your Diet and the Future of Life," a John Robbins lecture; "The McDougall Video," the best segments of the television show, "McDougall's Medicine" with John McDougall, M.D.; "A Diet for All Reasons," with Michael Klaper, M.D.; and "Healthy School Lunch Program," a four-minute introduction to EarthSave's school lunch program. Catalog: EarthSave, 706 Frederick St., Santa Cruz, CA 95062, 1-800-362-3648.

Focus on Animals
$3 (applied toward video/film purchase) for a 35-page catalog that includes photographs, descriptions, age levels, running times, prices, and instructions for getting programming on local cable television. Approximately 60 films, videotapes, and slide shows for rent or purchase. A variety of subjects including companion animal loss, vegetarianism, zoos, animal overpopulation, hunting, wildlife, greyhound racing, fur, animals in research, product testing, and classroom dissection. Many award-winning documentaries. Suitable for use on cable television and in classrooms. Works with teachers and administrators nationwide, and provides teaching guides for classroom use with the videotapes. From: Focus on Animals, P.O. Box 150, Trumbull, CT 06611, (203) 377-1116.

Friends of Animals
"The Face of Fur: Fur Ranching in America" and "Caught in a Snare," about wolf snaring in Alaska. $15 each from: FoA, 777 Post Road, Suite 205, Darien, CT 06820, (203) 656-1522, 1-800-321-PETS, ext. 110, FAX: (203) 656-0267.

Humane Farming Association
"The Pig Picture," an 18-minute video documentary that "traces the development of commercial pig rearing in America," the natural behavior of pigs, factory farm-raised pigs, drug use, environmental impacts, etc. No scenes of slaughter. Appropriate for all audiences. $15 (CA addresses add 7.25% tax) plus $3.50 shipping from: HFA, P.O. Box 3577, San Rafael, CA 94912, (415) 771-CALF.

Humane Society of the United States
Videos on various subjects, including footage of rodeos and of the transportation and slaughter of horses for human consumption abroad. Catalog: HSUS, 2100 L Street NW, Washington, D.C. 20037.

International Society for Animal Rights, Inc.
Videos for $15 rental. Subjects include a trip to a humane society, the life and death of pigs on a farm, vegetarianism, hunting, and a trip to New York City's old Central Park Zoo. From: ISAR, 421 South State Street, Clarks Summit, PA 18411, (717) 586-2200, FAX: (717) 586-9580.

LivingEarth Learning Project
Video loaning library for the New York/New England area from: LivingEarth Learning Project, P.O. Box 2160, Boston, MA 02106, (617) 367-8687.

North American Vegetarian Society
Free rental of VHS videos on vegetarianism and animal rights for a deposit and postage/handling costs. The deposit is returned upon return of the video. Limit of two videos per order. For titles and deposit information: NAVS, Box 72, Dolgeville, NY 13329, (518) 568-7970.

People for the Ethical Treatment of Animals
A variety of videos, mostly on laboratory animals. Also one on a fur farm and a music video. VHS, Beta, and U-matic or V-8. VHS and Beta available on loan for $15. Free to libraries and the media. (Please make your request on library or company stationary.) Write or call for descriptions and ordering information: PETA, 501 Front Street, Norfolk,

VA 23501, (757) 622-PETA.

Performing Animal Welfare Society

Actual footage of abused elephants, interviews, and more. $5 (covers duplication cost only; does not produce any profit). From: PAWS, P.O. Box 849, Galt, CA 95632, (209) 745-2606.

Student Organization for Animal Rights

"Angels of Mercy," a 25-minute documentary on the Animal Liberation Front, which shows actual footage of raids, interviews, etc. Professionally produced for British television. $9 postpaid from: SOAR, 235 CMU, 300 Washington Avenue SE, Minneapolis, MN 55455.

SUPRESS, Inc.

"Hidden Crimes," a 78-minute documentary on the devastation to human health caused by the fraud of vivisection. Available in English or French. $27 postpaid (U.S.), $35 (Canada), $40 (Other). "Controversy," a 30-minute interview by Michele Dabney with Javier Burgos, the founder of SUPRESS, on topics which include reasons for the existence of vivisection, why vivisection is medical and scientific fraud, experimental versus clinical research, transplantation and heart disease, dissection, and animal rights versus anti-vivisection. $17 postpaid (U.S.), $25 (Canada), $30 (Other). U.S. funds only. From: SUPRESS, P.O. Box 1062, Pasadena, CA 91102, (818) 584-0446 or 1-800-KILL-VIV.

TTouch Videos

"Practical, solid, and informative advice for common problems and concerns shared by dog and cat owners everywhere." Cat video (1 hour) covers aloofness, biting, scratching, fear, emergency care, and "much, much more." Dog video (1-1/2 hours) covers barking, chewing, fear of the vet's office, car sickness, etc. Also a number of different videos for horses (riding, handling, etc.) Each video is $29.95 plus $5.95 shipping from: TTEAM Training International, P.O. Box 3793, Santa Fe, NM 87501-0793, 1-800-854-TEAM, (505) 455-2945, FAX: (505) 455-7233.

Varied Directions Educational Videos, Inc.

"The Other Side of the Fence" discusses farm animals in general and veal calves in specific. 10 minutes. Suitable for junior high through adult. "A Question of Respect" is about having respect for all animal life. Touches on dissection in schools and product testing. 12 minutes. Suitable for junior high through adult. $69.95 for either tape or $99.95 for both (3/4" U-matic is more), plus shipping. 30 Day Preview is $15 per tape (VHS only) plus shipping from: Varied Directions Educational Videos, 69 Elm Street, P.O. Box 1957, Camden, ME 04843-9972, 1-800-888-5236, FAX: (207) 236-4512.

The Vegetarian Resource Group

Will loan out the following videos for a $4 mailing charge: "Healthy, Wealthy, and Wise" and "Food Without Fear." From: VRG, P.O. Box 1463, Baltimore, MD 21203, (410) 366-VEGE, FAX: (410) 366-8804.

Wildlife Traps, Deterrents, & Attractors

Bat & Bird Houses

It's obvious why you might want to attract birds to your yard, but bats...? A single bat can consume up to 600 mosquitos in an hour and also eats insects that feast on agricultural crops. (Bats "swoop" to catch night-flying insects, not to get *you*. The fear of rabid bats is unfounded; the percentage of bats that contract rabies is no more than for other animals, less than one-half of a percent.) Nearly 40% of bat species in the U.S. are endangered. For further information, contact Bat Conservation International, Inc. (see Chapter 10 for their address).

Karen's Nontoxic Products

Wooden birdhouse and bathouse kits, ready to assemble. You supply the hammer. Bird house styles include bluebird, chickadee, and wren. $9 plus shipping. Bathouse measures approximately 6" by 15" by 8". $17.50 plus shipping from: Karen's Nontoxic Products, 1839 Dr. Jack Road, Conowingo, MD 21918, Info: (410) 378-4939, Orders: 1-800-KARENS-4 (1-800-527-3674).

The Plow & Hearth

Ready-to-mount or easy-assemble-yourself bathouse endorsed by Bat Conservation

International, Inc. Large is 19" by 6" by 25" ($79.95 plus shipping); small pre-assembled and assemble-it-yourself are 15-1/2" by 3" by 25" ($49.95 plus shipping for pre-assembled, $39.95 plus shipping for assemble-it-yourself). Also bat books, squirrel feeders, and a variety of bird feeders from: Plow & Hearth, P.O. Box 5000, Madison, VA 22727-1500, Orders: 1-800-627-1712, Customer Service: 1-800-866-6072, FAX: 1-800-843-2509.

Real Goods
A ready-made, 24-1/2" by 16" bat house for up to 40 bats ($45 plus shipping). Also the book *America's Neighborhood Bats* by Merlin Tuttle ($10 plus shipping). From: Real Goods, 555 Leslie Street, Ukiah, CA 95482-5576, (707) 468-9214, Orders: 1-800-762-7325, FAX: (707) 468-9486.

Deer Warning Devices

"Deer warning devices" are small, wind-activated plastic devices that mount on the front bumper of your car and make a high-pitched sound audible to deer and other wildlife when your car reaches a certain speed. I found these devices at K-Mart, or you can mail-order them from one of the following sources.

Heartland Products, Ltd.
Products include a deer warning device. $1 for flyer, to be credited toward purchase. Heartland Products, Box 218, Dakota City, IA 50529, (515) 332-3087, FAX: (515) 332-2179.

Sav-A-Life, Inc.
Deer Alert, used on state trooper vehicles for years. From: Sav-A-Life, P.O. Box 1226, New York, NY 10025, (212) 826-6611 or 1-800-OK-4-DEER (1-800-654-3337), FAX: (212) 593-1801.

Mousetraps

Note: Victor Havahart mousetraps—humane traps available in many hardware and discount stores—are manufactured by the Wood Stream Corporation. This company also sells grossly inhumane traps, such as one that spears live gophers with sharp stakes, and steel-jaw leghold traps. If possible, select a different brand of humane trap and write Wood Stream Corporation to register your disgust with their inhumane line: Wood Stream Corporation, P.O. Box 327, Lititz, PA 17543 or 5781 Ellen Avenue, Niagara Falls, Ontario L2E 6T3. This company is a subsidiary of Ekco Group, Inc., which manufactures housewares, so you may also want to boycott Ekco products.

The traps listed here are reusable and capture mice without harm to them. After capture, you release the mice to a suitable habitat.

The Mouse House
Humane mousetrap. $6.95 plus $2 shipping. Inquire about special sales and discounts on quantities from: The Mouse House, 2401 West Turner Road, #360-410, Lodi, CA 95242.

PETA Catalog
"Smart Mouse Trap" for humane capture and release. Lets you view occupant. $11.50 ($10.35 members; VA, CA, and WA addresses add tax) plus $5.95 shipping from: PETA, 501 Front Street, Norfolk, VA 23501, (757) 622-PETA. Specify item HP200.

Real Goods
See-through, ventilated, green plastic mouse trap for humane capture and release. $10 plus shipping from: Real Goods, 555 Leslie Street, Ukiah, CA 95482-5576, (707) 468-9214, Orders: 1-800-762-7325, FAX: (707) 468-9486.

Other Traps & Solutions

This section lists live-catch traps, which allow you to humanely capture and relocate animals to a suitable habitat. For other devices, such as electronic alarms, distress calls, flashing lights, barriers, etc., see the *Pocket Guide to the Humane Control of Wildlife in Cities and Towns*, available from HSUS (see the Hunting & Wildlife section of Chapter 13 for ordering information). *Note*: Your local animal shelter, humane society, or hardware store may have humane traps available for rent or loan.

Friends of Beaversprite
Nonlethal, effective solutions to beaver/

human conflicts from: Friends of Beaversprite, P.O. Box 591, Little Falls, NY 13365, (518) 568-2077.

Gardener's Supply Company

A variety of solutions, including copper tape to repel slugs, a solar vibrational device to humanely ward off voles and moles, an inexpensive mesh fence, garlic concentrate to spray on plants, a fake "flying" hawk, and ultrasonic devices. Free catalog from: Gardener's Supply, 128 Intervale Road, Burlington, VT 05401-2850, (802) 863-1700.

H.B. Sherman Traps, Inc.

P.O. Box 202647, Tallahassee, FL 32316, (904) 562-5566.

Ketch-All Company

2537 University Avenue, San Diego, CA 92104, (619) 297-1953.

Morrison Manufacturing Corporation

Highway 175, Box 52, Morrison, IA 50657, (319) 345-6406, 1-800-648-CAGE.

MSI Tru-Catch

P.O. Box 816, Belle Fourche, SD 57717, 1-800-247-6132.

Mustang Manufacturing Company

P.O. Box 920947, Houston, TX 77292, (713) 453-2249.

National Live Trap Corporation

P.O. Box 302, Tomahawk, WI 54487, (715) 453-2249.

The Plow & Hearth

Humane traps for chipmunks, rats, squirrels, muskrats, rabbits, cats, raccoons, and woodchucks. Prices range from $25.95 to $54.95. Also humane devices for keeping birds and animals out of your garden, including a heat- and motion-triggered sound alarm and a balloon that deters birds. Other products include feeders for birds, squirrels, and other animals, and the book *How to Be Smarter Than Squirrels* which contains strategies for dealing with "those cute but annoying seed-stealers." From: Plow & Hearth, P.O. Box 5000, Madison, VA 22727-1500, Orders: 1-800-627-1712, Customer Service: 1-800-866-6072, FAX: 1-800-843-2509.

Reed-Joseph International

Cage traps, balloons, electronic alarms, etc. from: Reed-Joseph International, P.O. Box 894, Greenville, MS 38702, 1-800-647-5554.

Stendal Products, Inc.

9486 East Laurel Road, Bellingham, WA 98226, (206) 398-2353.

Tomahawk Live Trap Company

P.O. Box 323, Tomahawk, WI 54487, (715) 453-3550.

Chapter 13

Further Reading

These books, guides, periodicals, reports, and booklets represent a small sampling of the many animal rights and vegetarian publications available for sale or for free. A large number of animal rights and vegetarian organizations offer a variety of publications, ranging from pamphlets on selected topics to newsletters and magazines. By joining a variety of groups, you can stay informed on current issues of interest.

Publications listed here are grouped into the following categories. Since many of the categories overlap, you may want to scan them all to see what's available:

- Activism
- Animals, Rights, & Ethics
- Children & Young Adults
- Companion Animals
- Entertainment (Performing Animals)
- Factory Farming
- Hunting & Wildlife
- Interspecies Communication
- Research, Education, & Product Testing
- Vegetarianism & Whole Foods

Finding What You Need

This chapter includes only a tiny fraction of existing animal rights/vegetarian books. To locate additional titles, try the following sources:

- **The Reference Guide *Books in Print***
  Available at your local library, this is a handy way to find contemporary books. Look under the subject headings "Animals, Treatment of," "Animals, Rights," "Vegetarian Cookery," and "Vegetarianism."

- **The Reference Guide *Ulrich's International Periodicals Directory***
  Available at your local library, this guide contains magazines and other periodicals currently in print. Look under the subject headings "Animal Welfare," and "Physical Fitness/Hygiene" (for vegetarian magazines).

- **Animal Rights and Vegetarian Organizations (Both National and Local)**
  Many groups sell books to raise funds, so buying books from them is one way to show your support. Be sure to check with your favorite groups for their offerings.

Ordering Information for the Publications

Many of the publications listed here can be purchased from a core group of organizations. Instead of repeating the ordering information over and over, I've listed it here. Simply refer to this section to find ordering addresses, shipping costs, and so forth, if not included with the publication's description.

- **AHA** (American Humane Association), 63 Inverness Drive East, Englewood, CO 80112, (303) 792-9900, FAX: (303) 792-5333. Minimum order $2. Postpaid (no additional for shipping). Street addresses only; no P.O. boxes.
- **AAVS** (The American Anti-Vivisection Society), 801 Old York Road, Suite 204, Jenkintown, PA 19046-1685, 1-800-SAY-AAVS. Sales tax: PA 6%. Shipping: Add $1 for orders $2-$5; $2 for $5.01-$10; $3 for $10.01-$20; $4 for $20.01+. Street addresses only; no P.O. boxes.
- **ALDF** (Animal Legal Defense Fund), 1363 Lincoln Avenue, San Rafael, CA 94901.
- **AVAR** (Association of Veterinarians for Animal Rights), P.O. Box 6269, Vacaville, CA 94696-6269.
- **American Vegan Society**, 56 Dinshah Lane, P.O. Box H, Malaga, NJ 08328-0908, (609) 694-2887 (voice/FAX). Shipping: Add $1 if total under $5. AVS pays shipping for orders $5+. Check, Money Order, MC, VISA, Discover ($10 minimum for credit cards).
- **EarthSave**, 706 Frederick Street, Santa Cruz, CA 95062, 1-800-362-3648, FAX: (408) 458-0255. Minimum order $5. Sales tax: CA 8.25%. Shipping: Add $3 for orders of $10 or less; $4 for $10.01-$20; $5 for $20.01-$30; $6 for $30.01-$40; etc. Canadian orders add $3. Check, MC, VISA ($10 minimum for charge cards).
- **Farm Sanctuary**, P.O. Box 150, Watkins Glen, NY 14891, (607) 583-2225. Shipping: $3 for orders of $10 or less; $4 for $11-$25; $5 for $26-$50; $7 for $76-$100; $8 for $101+. Check, Money Order.
- **HSUS** (Humane Society of the United States), 2100 L Street NW, Washington, D.C. 20037. Sales tax: AL 4%, CA 7.25%, CT 6%, DC 6%, FL 6%, MD 5%, MO 5.725%, NJ 6% (except periodicals), OH 5%, TN 8.25%, VT 5%. Shipping: $3 on all orders. Check, MC, VISA.
- **ISAR** (International Society for Animal Rights, Inc.), 421 South State Street, Clarks Summit, PA 18411, (717) 586-2200, FAX: (717) 586-9580. Shipping: $1 for orders up to $2.50; $1.65 for $2.51-$5; $2.15 for $5.01-$10; $2.75 for $10.01-$20; $3.75 for $20.01-$50; $5 for $50.01-$75. Check, Money Order, MC, VISA.
- **National Anti-Vivisection Society**, Dept. 530-0110W, P.O. Box 94020, Palatine, IL 60094-4020. Shipping: $1.50 for orders up to $5.99; $2.50 for $6-$11.99; $3.50 for $12-$17.99; $1.50 each additional $6. Check, Money Order, MC, VISA.
- **North American Vegetarian Society**, P.O. Box 72, Dolgeville, NY 13329, (518) 568-7970. Shipping: Add $1 for orders under $3; $3 for $3.01-$45; $4 for $45.01+.
- **PETA Catalog**, 501 Front Street, Norfolk, VA 23501, (757) 622-PETA. Sales tax: VA 4.5%, CA 7.25%, WA 8.25%. Shipping: $3.95 for orders up to $9.99; $5.95 for $10-$24.99; $7.95 for $25-$49.99; $9.95 for $50-$74.99; $12.95 for $75+. Check, Money Order, MC, VISA.

- **PCRM Marketplace**, P.O. Box 99, Summertown, TN 38483, 1-800-695-2241. Sales tax: TN 7.5%. Shipping: $3.50 for first item ($5 UPS); 75 cents each additional item. Check, Money Order, MC, VISA.
- **VRG** (The Vegetarian Resource Group), P.O. Box 1463, Baltimore, MD 21203, (410) 366-VEGE, FAX: (410) 366-8804. Postpaid (no additional for shipping). Check (payable to "Vegetarians"), MC, VISA.
- **UPC** (United Poultry Concerns), P.O. Box 59367, Potomac, MD 20859, (301) 948-2406.

Please Note: The author makes no claims as to the publications listed herein. Many, but not all, of the publications were previewed by the author. Space limitations prevent the listing of all worthy publications, but readers who have additional suggestions for listings may contact the publisher.

Prices and sources for books are subject to change. Contact the distributors for current prices, shipping rates, and availability. Most books are available from sources other than the one listed. Remember to check your public library if you want to "try before you buy"!

Activism

These publications are useful to those who want to keep up-to-date on animal rights activities or engage in activism for animals. See also the Activist Aids section of Chapter 12.

Activism: *Books*

The Animal Rights Movement in America: From Compassion to Respect
by Lawrence Finsen and Susan Finsen
An overview of the history and philosophies of the animal rights movement in the U.S. through the eyes of two animal rights advocates. Photos. Paperback. 309 pages. Twayne Publishers, 1994. $15.95 plus shipping from Farm Sanctuary. Specify item BK3.

Animals and Their Legal Rights
U.S. legislation with appendices on important foreign laws. Fourth edition, 1990. 441 pages. One copy free to libraries, police, and humane societies. $8 postpaid to others from: Animal Welfare Institute, P.O. Box 3650, Washington, D.C. 20007, (202) 337-2332.

Animalscam: The Beastly Abuse of Human Rights
by Kathleen Marquardt, founder and chair, Putting People First!
Limbaugh-style animal rights-bashing at its best! If you're unfamiliar with the speciesist line and want a taste of true extremism, this book will be educational. From the founder of an anti-animal rights group whose slogans include, "Save an animal; Road kill an activist," "Save an animal; Dissect an activist," etc. This author claims that the American Farm Bureau, Circus Fans of America, and the Foundation for Biomedical Research are "animal welfare" organizations (no kidding!). If your library has this book, check it out (literally!). Whatever you do, don't buy this book—in any sense of the phrase!

Animals, Property, and the Law
by Gary L. Francione, Professor of Law, Rutgers University Law School
Discusses the question, "How can we establish rights for animals and treat them humanely when we continue to view them as property?" Includes a historical perspective and discusses anti-cruelty laws, as well as citing specific examples. 349 pages. Temple Press. Paperback is $22.95 postpaid from the American Vegan Society.

Circles of Compassion: A Collection of Humane Words and Work
Edited by Elaine Sichel, photos by Sumner W. Fowler
This one's a tear-jerker. Forty-six stories by and about animals and people in the animal welfare system. Although many of these short profiles do not have happy endings, they are touching and compelling; I had to keep reading. These accounts are well-written and insightful. They renewed my commitment to get in there and offer what little I can to the unfortunates caught in this system. 226 pages. Paperback. Photos. $12 (CA addresses add 7.5% tax) plus $2.50 shipping (75 cents each additional book) from: Voice & Vision Publishing, 12005 Green Valley Road, Sebastopol, CA 95472, (707) 823-1306.

Free the Animals!
by Ingrid Newkirk, National Director, People for the Ethical Treatment of Animals
A "behind-the-scenes" look at real Animal Liberation Front (ALF) rescues, as told to Ingrid Newkirk by "Valerie," founder of the U.S. ALF. An easy read, written in the style of a novel. Photos. Paperback. 372 pages. The Noble Press, Inc., 1992. $13.95 (members $12.50) from PETA Catalog. Specify item BK601.

Save the Animals! 101 Easy Things You Can Do
by Ingrid Newkirk, National Director, People for the Ethical Treatment of Animals
A book of solutions to 50 problems animals face. Warner Books, Inc. $4.95 ($4.40 members) from: PETA Catalog. Specify item BK590.

The Struggle for Animal Rights
by Dr. Tom Regan
A series of essays on various animal rights topics—vegetarianism, vivisection, etc.—from a professional philosopher and long-time animal rights advocate who is well-established in the movement. Includes an autobiographical sketch. $5.95 (NC residents add tax; members subtract 10%) plus $1.50 shipping from: The Culture and Animals Foundation, 3509 Eden Croft Drive, Raleigh, NC 27612, (919) 782-3739.

You Can Save the Animals: 50 Things to Do Right Now
by Dr. Michael W. Fox, Vice President, Humane Society of the United States, and Pamela Weintraub
Very accessible information in 50 small, easy-to-digest portions. Includes the animal bill of rights and useful resources, such as sources for cruelty-free toys, companies that don't test on animals, etc. Also pointers for "in-betweeners" such as, if you *must* fish, use artificial lures. 201 pages. St. Martins Paperbacks, 1991. Available from your local bookstore or library.

Activism: *Guides & Directories*

For laws related to animals, see the Activism: Laws section, immediately following this one.

Activists Guide to Defeating the Fur Trade
$2 from Coalition to Abolish the Fur Trade, P.O. Box 40641, Memphis, TN 38174.

Animal Rights Resources Catalog
A collection of merchandise flyers from various animal rights sources. A handy way to see some of what's out there. $10 postpaid from: The Fund for Animals, Fort Mason Center, San Francisco, CA 94123, (415) 474-4020, FAX: (415) 474-5323.

Investigating Animal Abuse Information Packet
Free information on how to investigate animal abuse from ALDF.

Animals Under the Law: The Pathway to Animal Rights
An information packet designed to help you start a successful Political Action Committee (PAC) to support animal-friendly candidates. Published by the Animal Legislative Action Network, which has been successful at practicing what they preach. $5 covers printing and mailing. Also publishes a quarterly newsletter on significant animal legislation nationwide for $5. From: ALAN, 2379 Panorama Terrace, Los Angeles, CA 90039, (213) 662-6728.

•***Animal Welfare: List of Licensed Dealers (APHIS 41-35-029)***

•***Animal Welfare: List of Registered Research Facilities (APHIS 41-35-030)***

•***Animal Welfare: List of Registered Carriers and Intermediate Handlers (APHIS 41-35-032)***

•***Animal Welfare: List of Licensed Exhibitors (APHIS 41-35-033)***
The names and addresses of current animal exhibitors, dealers, transporters, and research facilities (by state) registered with or licensed by the federal government. Find out who is doing what in your area and elsewhere. Free from: U.S. Dept. of Agriculture, 6505 Belcrest Road, Room 269AC, Hyattsville, MD 20782.

Avoiding Defamation Lawsuits
A 21-page guide on libel/slander cases. Free from: Animal Legal Defense Fund, 1363 Lincoln Avenue, San Rafael, CA 94901.

Bunny Hugger's Gazette Directory of Organizations
An annually-updated list of approximately 1,000 animal protection and vegetarian groups. $10 from: Directory, BHG, P.O. Box 601, Temple, TX 76503. (See the description for *Bunny Hugger's Gazette* in Activism: Periodicals, below.)

Campus Organizing Guide for Peace & Justice Groups
A 16-page newsprint guide on how to start a group, conduct meetings, plan an event or campaign, conduct nonviolent direct action, etc. $1 each postpaid (50 for $15) from: Center for Campus Organizing, P.O. Box 748, Cambridge, MA 02142, (617) 354-9363. Also available: assistance with starting your own alternative campus newspaper, a quarterly bulletin for campus activists, training for campus activists, a publications list, and more.

Consumer's Resource Handbook
Names, addresses, and telephone numbers of corporations, trade associations, and selected federal agencies. A handy guide for registering consumer complaints (for example, if you know of a company that uses animals in product testing, sponsors rodeos, etc., you can find its address and phone number here). Free from: Handbook, Consumer Information Center, Pueblo, CO 81009.

Guide for Local Vegetarian Groups
Keith Akers, editor
A 50-page booklet designed to help you form a local vegetarian group. Includes advice on organizing a group or conference; sample Articles of Incorporation, by-laws, and constitution; lists of organizations, cookbooks, and books; and vegetarian fact sheets. $3 postpaid from: Vegetarian Union of North America, P.O. Box 9710, Washington, D.C. 20016.

How to Use the Freedom of Information Act
A booklet on understanding and using the Freedom of Information Act to obtain federal records that can be used to help animals. $1 postpaid from ISAR.

The PETA Guide to Action for Animals
Real actions that people across the country have taken for animals. This will give you lots of ideas and start those creative juices flowing. $4 postpaid from PETA Catalog. Specify item 5113.

The PETA Guide to Becoming an Activist
A very useful guide that includes advice on table displays, making/distributing leaflets, starting a group, speaking in public, organizing public meetings, lobbying, using the Freedom of Information Act, working with the media, fundraising, applying for tax-exempt status, answers to frequently asked questions, etc. 70 pages. Illustrated. At the time of this writing, it was being updated and was unavailable. Inquire to PETA Catalog.

Report on the Summit on Violence to Children and Animals
A summary of the 1991 American Humane Association Summit discussions on the link between animal abuse and child abuse. 22 pages. $5 from AHA. Specify item AVL103. Also available: brochures on the *Cycle of Violence to Children and Animals* for 60 cents each, 100 for $15 (item AVL102).

Tell It To Washington: A Guide to Citizen Action
A directory of important names and telephone numbers for the executive, legislative, and judicial branches of government. Also information and etiquette on communicating effectively with officials. Includes the White House, cabinet secretaries and executive officers, congressional party leaders, Supreme Court justices, Senators and Representatives, Senate committees, and House committees. $3.30 postpaid from: League of Women Voters, 1730 M Street NW, Washington, D.C. 20036, (202) 429-1965. Specify Pub. 349. Discounts on quantities.

U.S. Congress Handbook
A useful guide that includes information on federal senators and representatives with photos, addresses, phone and FAX numbers, committee assignments, etc.; presidential cabinet members; the White House staff; Supreme Court justices; Congressional committees and subcommittees; selected federal agencies; a glossary of legislative terms; how a bill moves; how committees function; how Congress is organized; how to write a Congressional member; etc. Updated annually. 1996 edition $10.95 plus $3 shipping from: *U.S. Congress Handbook*, Box 566, McLean, VA 22101, (703) 356-3572, FAX: (703) 760-0942.

Voter's Self-Defense Manual
Lists addresses, phone numbers, FAX numbers, and E-mail addresses for federal representatives and senators, along with information on the sources and amounts of their finances, their voting records on key issues, and their ratings by selected organizations. You can also call Project Vote Smart's hotline at 1-800-622-SMAR(T) for more detailed information. (Key issues monitored include "environment" and "agriculture," but unfortunately not "animals.") Free from Project Vote Smart, or you can support them by joining for a minimum contribution of $35. From: Project Vote Smart, Center for National Independence in Politics, 129 NW Fourth Street, #204, Corvallis, OR 97330, (541) 754-2746, 1-800-662-SMAR(T), FAX: (541) 754-2747, E-mail: comments@vote-smart.org, Internet: http://www.votesmart.org

Washington Information Directory
A useful guide that contains the names, addresses, contact persons, and brief descriptions for federal agencies, Congress, and private nonprofit organizations in the Washington D.C. area. Includes hierarchy charts for government agencies, Congressional committees and subcommittees and their members, agency and department contacts in Freedom of Information Act requests, regional offices for federal agencies, etc. Published by Congressional Quarterly, Inc., 1414-22nd Street NW, Washington, D.C. 20037. Available in the reference section of public libraries.

Zero Tolerance for Cruelty
An information packet for those working to encourage stricter enforcement of animal protection laws in their neighborhoods. Free from ALDF. *Note*: ALDF also offers free assistance to District Attorneys prosecuting animal cruelty cases.

Activism: *Laws*

For help in finding local or federal laws, consult your reference librarian.

Animal Welfare Act and Regulations
A copy of the federal law and accompanying regulations that address the standards for the care and treatment of animals by animal dealers, exhibitors, and research facilities. Free from: USDA Docket Reprints, VS/REAC, Room 266/Federal Building, 6505 Belcrest Road, Room 269, Hyattsville, MD 20782, (301) 436-7833.

Cruelty Statutes—United States and Canada
A chart comparing animal cruelty penalties and classifications for each U.S. state, D.C., and Canada. Updated regularly. $5 from AHA.

Endangered Species Act of 1973
A copy of the Endangered Species Act and a list of endangered species is free from: U.S. Fish and Wildlife Service, Publications Unit, ARLSQ Room 130, Washington, D.C. 20240.

Model Legislation
Copies of model state laws on three topics: anti-cruelty statutes, endangered species, and leghold trap bans. For use in strengthening your own state laws. Donation appreciated but not mandatory. From ALDF.

U.S. Code
The complete listing of federal laws. Available at your local library. Ask your reference librarian for help with locating specific laws you wish to review.

Activism: *Periodicals*

See also the periodicals in the Children & Young Adults section, and in other sections of this chapter.

ADVANCE (Activists of Delaware Valley Animal Network Calendar of Events)
A regional calendar of events on animal, environmental, and other grassroots topics for NJ, PA, DE, NY, and D.C. Includes some national/international events. 12 pages. Subscriptions: Payable to Maureen Koplow, 476 Warwick Road, Deptford, NJ 08096, (609) 853-1847. 1 year (12 issues) for $10. Sample calendar free on request.

The Animals' Agenda
"Helping people help animals." A magazine covering the full range of animal rights issues. Tries to inspire a deep regard for, and greater activism on behalf of, animals and nature. 45 pages. Published by Animal Rights Network, Inc. Subscriptions: *The Animals' Agenda*, Subscription Dept., P.O. Box 6809, Syracuse, NY 13217-7923, 1-800-825-0061. 1 year (6 issues) for $22/U.S, $28/Canada & Mexico, $35/Other (U.S. funds).

Animal Citizens

A quarterly newsletter on significant animal legislation nationwide. $5 from: Animal Legislative Action Network, 2379 Panorama Terrace, Los Angeles, CA 90039, (213) 662-6728.

Animal People

"News for people who care about animals," including humane workers, animal control officers, veterinarians, activists, and wildlife rehabilitators. Routinely exposes those within the animal protection movement as well as animal exploiters. I don't always agree with what they choose to cover or how they cover it, but there is definitely information here you won't see elsewhere. No lack of controversy! Annually publishes the top salaries of animal protection employees and other financial data on the largest animal protection groups. Newsprint. 20 newspaper-sized pages. Published by Animal People, Inc. Subscriptions: *Animal People*, P.O. Box 205, Shushan, NY 12873. 1 year (10 issues) for $18 (U.S. funds).

Animals

A more mainstream magazine that still hits the issues. Written to the general public rather than to activists. Interesting articles and exceptional photography. 40 pages. Published by Massachusetts Society for the Prevention of Cruelty to Animals. Subscriptions: 1-800-998-0797. 1 year (6 issues) for $19.94 to nonmembers.

The Animals' Voice Magazine

An award-winning color magazine that offers "in-depth news coverage, timely articles, and uncompromising photography" of how humans treat other animals. 36 pages. Published by the Compassion for Animals Foundation, Inc. Subscriptions: *The Animal's Voice Magazine*, 12190-1/2 Ventura Blvd., #392, Studio City, CA 91604, 1-800-82-VOICE. 1 year (4 issues) for $23/U.S., $28/Canada, $32/Other.

Bunny Huggers' Gazette

A must for every activist. A comprehensive source of current information. Tells you what's going on and what you can do. Includes animal rights and vegetarian events, publications, groups, legislation, campaigns...enough to keep an activist busy till the next issue! Contains addresses for selected newspapers, broadcast stations, radio and television programs, and federal agencies. Also publishes an annual directory of animal-protection and vegetarian organizations. Newsprint. Approximately 16 pages. Subscriptions: *Bunny Hugger's Gazette*, P.O. Box 601, Temple, TX 76503-0601. 1 year (6 issues) for $14/U.S., $18.50/Canada, $28/Overseas.

College AnimaLife: The College Animal Rights Publication

A national magazine published annually by Cornell Students for the Ethical Treatment of Animals (CSETA). Written by college students for college students. Welcomes contributions. Newsprint. 24 pages. For a subscription, contact: CSETA, Cornell University, Willard Straight Hall Box 39, Ithaca, NY 14850.

E: The Environmental Magazine

Primarily an environmental magazine, but it strives to unite the environmental and animal rights movements. Contains news and articles about animals, their habitats, the impact of a meat-based diet on the environment, endangered species, etc. A nonprofit endeavor and a good magazine! Published by Earth Action Network. Subscriptions: Payable to *E: The Environmental Magazine*, Subscription Department, P.O. Box 699, Mt. Morris, IL 61054-7590, (212) 674-0952. 1 year (6 issues) for $19.95. Free trial issue available.

No Compromise

"The Militant, Direct Action Newsletter of Grassroots Animal Liberationists & Their Supporters." A publication by and for activists actively engaged in animal liberation via protests, civil disobedience, etc. The goal is to network and share tactics and success stories. Also news on Animal Liberation Front activities and addresses for incarcerated activists. $15 for 6 issues, $10 students/low-income from: Student Organization for Animal Rights (S.O.A.R.), 235 CMU, 300 Washington Avenue SE, Minneapolis, MN 55455, (612) 626-5566 or National Activist Network, P.O. Box 19515, Sacramento, CA 95819, (916) 452-7179.

Satya: A Magazine for Vegetarianism, Environmentalism, and Animal Advocacy

An informative and interesting publication of nonviolent social change. Distributed free of charge at places of learning and business all over New York City. Appropriate for national/international subscribers as well as locals. "Satya" is the sanskrit word for "truth."

Includes articles, interviews with international activists, book and restaurant reviews, recipes, and a calendar of events. Newsprint. 24 pages. Subscriptions: Payable to Voice News, Inc., P.O. Box 1771, New York, NY 10159, (212) 674-0952. 1 year (12 issues) for $5. (What a deal!)

VRG's Tips for Vegetarian Activists
Pointers and ideas for spreading the vegetarian message. 4-8 pages. Free from VRG.

Animals, Rights, & Ethics

These publications address the ethics, philosophy, and theory of animal rights. See also the publications in the Interspecies Communication section, later in this chapter.

Animals, Rights, & Ethics: *Books*

Animal Liberation: A New Ethics for Our Treatment of Animals
By Peter Singer
This was the first widely read book on animal rights philosophy. Includes discussions of speciesism, animals in research, factory farms, and vegetarianism. Photos. 320 pages. Second edition. $9.95 from the American Vegan Society.

Animal Revolution: Changing Attitudes Towards Speciesism
by Richard D. Ryder
A historical perspective of animal welfare and attitudes towards animals. Hardbound. 385 pages. Basil Blackwell Inc., 1989. $22.95 from AAVS. Specify item 16-B.

Animal Rights and Human Morality
by Bernard E. Rollin
A thorough and very readable text that debunks Immanuel Kant's philosophical basis for excluding nonhuman animals from moral concern, a mode of thought that still underlies the thought processes of many people. Lays a sound philosophical argument for including animals in our moral framework. Devotes an entire chapter to the use and abuse of animals in research. Includes personal anecdotes. Published by Prometheus Books, 1992. 248 pages. $18.95 from bookstores or check with your local library.

Animals, Nature, and Albert Schweitzer
Editing and commentary by Ann Cottrell Free
A lovely, personal account of Albert Schweitzer and his ethic of compassion, as told in his own words and those of the author. Follows Schweitzer's life from early boyhood, when he struggled with the conflict of his own feelings versus those of the larger society. Many photos. Suitable for all ages. 82 pages. Flying Fox Press. $3.30 from HSUS. Specify item GR3071. ($7.95 from bookstores.)

Animals' Rights Considered in Relation to Social Progress
by Henry S. Salt
A work originally published in 1892, that espouses a philosophy of animal rights as a natural extension of human rights. Preface by Peter Singer. Published by Society for Animal Rights, Inc., 1980. $6.95 from AAVS.

The Case for Animal Rights
by Dr. Tom Regan
A scholarly, philosophical treatise justifying the "rights" view in regard to nonhuman animals. Nominated for a Pulitzer Prize. $10.95 (NC residents add tax; members subtract 10%) plus $2.75 shipping from: The Culture and Animals Foundation, 3509 Eden Croft Drive, Raleigh, NC 27612, (919) 782-3739.

The Dreaded Comparison: Human and Animal Slavery
by Marjorie Spiegel
A powerful book that discusses parallels between the enslavement of black people and the enslavement of animals. Preface by Alice Walker. Graphic photos and illustrations. Highly recommended. Paperback. 105 pages. New Society Publishers. Revised edition $12.95 plus $3 shipping from: Institute for the Development of Earth Awareness, P.O. Box 124, Prince Street Station, New York, NY 10012, (212) 741-0338.

The Extended Circle: A Commonplace Book of Animal Rights
by Jon Wynne-Tyson
Mostly historical (but some contemporary) quotes about animals, their treatment, and the rights they deserve. Listed alphabetically by

the speaker, from George Abraham to Emile Zola. Includes quotes from well-knowns such as Abraham Lincoln, Paul Harvey, Mark Twain, Aldous Huxley, and others. Paragon House Publishers. 650 pages (revised edition). $14.95 from the American Vegan Society.

The Great Ape Project: Equality Beyond Humanity

Edited by Paola Cavalieri and Peter Singer

The Great Ape Project is an undertaking by several scholarly individuals to extend to all great apes those rights which we have thus far reserved only for the great apes known as human beings. This book contains several essays by several experts, covering topics such as ethics, similarities and differences, language, personhood, etc. St. Martin's Press, 1993. 312 pages. $11.85 (members subtract 10%) from the National Anti-Vivisection Society.

The Human Nature of Birds: A Scientific Discovery with Startling Implications

by Theodore Xeenophon Barber, Ph.D.

Written by a behavioral scientist, this book challenges the dominant misconception that nonhuman animals are mere creatures of instinct and reflex. By summarizing a body of scientific evidence, the author shows that birds—and other nonhuman animals—are intelligent, conscious, willful, sensitively aware, emotional, distinct individuals. Highly recommended. Color photos. Hardbound. 226 pages. St. Martins Press, 1993. $19.95 from bookstores or check with your local library.

In Defense of Animals

Edited by Peter Singer

A collection of essays by various animal rights proponents on various subjects. Paperback. 224 pages. Basil Blackwell, 1985. $7.95 from AAVS. Specify item 6-B.

Ishmael

by Daniel Quinn

While not an animal rights book, this is an artfully crafted piece of fiction that, step by step, reveals how humans came to be at conflict with and alienated from nature. Uses the very effective technique of a dialogue between a wise gorilla and his student, a human. From the book: "The people of your culture cling with fanatical tenacity to the specialness of man. They want desperately to perceive a vast gulf between man and the rest of creation. This mythology of human superiority justifies their doing whatever they please with the world..." 266 pages. Bantam Books, 1992. From your local bookstore or library.

Replenish the Earth

by Lewis G. Regenstein

"A history of organized religion's treatment of animals and nature—including the *Bible*'s message of conservation and kindness toward animals." $13 postpaid from the Interfaith Council for the Protection of Animals, 4290 Raintree Lane, NW, Atlanta, GA 30327. Booklets based on this text are also available for $2 each (discounts on quantities).

- ***The Sexual Politics of Meat: A Feminist-Vegetarian Critical Theory***

  by Carol J. Adams (256 pages, 1991, $14.95)
- ***Neither Man Nor Beast: Feminism and the Defense of Animals***

  by Carol J. Adams (272 pages, 1994, $15.95)
- ***Beyond Animal Rights: A Feminist Caring Ethic for the Treatment of Animals***

  edited by Josephine Donovan and Carol J. Adams (228 pages, 1996, $22.95 hardcover)

Books that examine the connections between male control, animal oppression, and women's oppression. Continuum Publishing Group. Order from your bookstore or *The Sexual Politics of Meat* is available for $14.95 plus $2 shipping from: Feminists for Animal Rights, P.O. Box 694, Cathedral Station, New York, NY 10025-0694.

An Unnatural Order: Uncovering the Roots of Our Domination of Nature and Each Other

by Jim Mason

From the jacket: "A provocative search for the basic beliefs of western culture that feed racism, sexism, animal cruelty, and other forms of subjugation." Describes how our cultural heritage changed from one of respect for nature to one of domination and a belief in human superiority. A friend of mine claims that this book changed her life! 320 pages. Simon & Schuster, 1993. Hardbound. $15 ($13.50 members) from EarthSave.

When Elephants Weep: The Emotional Lives of Animals

by Jeffrey Moussaieff Masson and Susan McCarthy

Explores the vast emotional capacities of

nonhuman animals, and makes a strong case for the reevaluation of our treatment of animals based on the fact that, like humans, they *feel*. From the prologue: "We are horrified when we read, even in fiction, of people who kill other people in order to sell parts of their bodies. But every day elephants are slaughtered for their tusks, rhinos for their horns, gorillas for their hands. My hope is that as it begins to dawn on people what feeling creatures these animals are, it will be increasingly difficult to justify these cruel acts." Hardcover. 291 pages. Delacorte Press, 1995. $23.95 postpaid from the American Vegan Society.

Animals, Rights, & Ethics: *Booklets*

The Philosophy of Animal Rights
by Dr. Tom Regan
States the animal rights position, gives ten reasons for animal rights and their explanations, and ten reasons against animal rights and their replies. Very nicely done, with quotes and photos. $2 postpaid (bulk rate for 100 or more) from: Culture and Animals Foundation, 3509 Eden Croft Drive, Raleigh, NC 27612, (919) 782-3739.

Replenish the Earth
by Lewis G. Regenstein
"A history of organized religion's treatment of animals and nature—including the *Bible*'s message of conservation and kindness toward animals." Booklets are based on the book of the same name. Booklets are $2 each (discounts on quantities). The book is $13 postpaid from: Interfaith Council for the Protection of Animals, 4290 Raintree Lane, NW, Atlanta, GA 30327.

Animals, Rights, & Ethics: *Guides & Directories*

Feminists for Animal Rights Bibliography
"A bibliography of books and articles related to feminism and animal liberation." 1993-94 edition is $7.50 plus $2 shipping from: Feminists for Animal Rights, P.O. Box 694, Cathedral Station, New York, NY 10025-0694.

Animals, Rights, & Ethics: *Periodicals*

See also the periodicals in the Activism section.

Between the Species: A Journal of Ethics
A forum for the discussion of animal ethics issues. Includes philosophy, psychology, critical reviews, interviews, fiction, and poetry. Also publishes papers and commentaries presented at the meeting of the Society for the Study of Ethics and Animals. Illustrated. 60 pages. Published by the Albert Schweitzer Center. Subscriptions/inquiries: *Between the Species,* P.O. Box 8496, Berkeley, CA 94707, (510) 526-5346. Make checks payable to San Francisco Bay Institute. 1 year (4 issues) for $15 (Individuals), $25 (Institutions). 40% discount on institutional price for humane societies, animal protection, and welfare organizations (direct order). Single copies $4.

la Joie (Joy): The Journal In Appreciation of All Animals
This little (4-1/4" by 5-1/2") journal has essays and poems by people who love animals, book reviews, and "support team" listings (people who listen and help with emotional distress experienced because of companion animal death, illness, etc.). A portion of funds donated to assist animals, both wild and domesticated. Welcomes unsolicited manuscripts. 60 pages. 1 year (4 issues) for $12.50 from: la Joie & Co., P.O. Box 145, Batesville, VA 22924.

Society and Animals: Social Scientific Studies of the Human Experience of Other Animals
A journal of studies that describe and analyze the human experience of nonhuman animals. The journal's goal is to stimulate and support an emerging content area within the social sciences consisting of studies of the ways in which animals figure into our lives. Currently accepting manuscripts. (Priority is given to manuscripts that contain significant new results of empirical investigations, but other types of papers are also considered. Contact Psychologists for the Ethical Treatment of Animals for guidelines.) Published twice per year. Subscriptions: PSYeta, P.O. Box 1297, Washington Grove, MD 20880-1297. 1 year (2 issues) for $30 (Individuals), $55 (Institutions), $20 (Students), within the U.S.

Children & Young Adults

These are just a few of the many animal-friendly publications geared toward children or young adults. Check your local library or humane education office for even more!

Children & Young Adults: *Activity Books*

Animaze!: A Collection of Amazing Nature Mazes
by Wendy Madgwick, illustrated by Lorna Hussey
Colorful and educational scenes of 12 different ecosystems and several creatures which inhabit them. Each scene is a maze, and it is the reader's task to find safe passage through the maze. Facts about each animal shown are located at the back of the book, along with the solutions to the mazes. Intended for preschoolers, but appropriate for much older children, I think. Published by Alfred A Knopf, 1992. Hardbound. $13 plus $3.75 shipping from: Animal Town, P.O. Box 485, Healdsburg, CA 95448, 1-800-445-8642, FAX: (707) 837-9737.

The Associated Humane Societies Coloring Book
Drawings of different animals for a young person to color. A variety of drawing styles by different artists adds interest. Commentary or poetry, and sometimes a photo, accompanies each drawing. Many of the animals depicted live at Popcorn Park, a special zoo for animals with special needs. Over 120 pictures to color. $5 postpaid from: Associated Humane Societies, 124 Evergreen Avenue, Newark, NJ 07114, (201) 824-7080.

Be Kind To One And All
An 11" by 14" poster of whimsical animals, suitable for coloring. 25 cents each, $2.20 for 10 from: Massachusetts Society for the Prevention of Cruelty to Animals (MSPCA), 350 South Huntington Avenue, Boston, MA 02130, (617) 541-5000, FAX: (617) 522-4885.

Best Friends Animal Coloring & Activity Book
Includes connect-the-dots, picture stories, color by number, a maze, and more. $3.50 plus $1.50 shipping from: Best Friends Animal Sanctuary, Kanab, UT 84741.

The Circus Elephant Coloring Book
This little 7-page book tells the sad story of a baby elephant stolen from her family and sold to a circus. No happy ending here, but it will educate kids about the plights of elephants used in entertainment. This would be a great handout to kids at circus protests. For prices contact: The Elephant Alliance, 6265 Cardeno Drive, La Jolla, CA 92037.

•Color & Activity Book, Level I (ages 3-10)
•Story & Activity Book, Level II (ages 6-14)
$3 each plus $2.50 shipping (on orders up to $9.99) from: The Humane Farming Association, P.O. Box 3577, San Rafael, CA 94912, (415) 771-CALF. (*Note*: Please use this address for merchandise rather than their office address.)

•Earth Quiz
•Food for Everyone
Earth Quiz is a handout illustrating the environmental impacts of a meat-based diet for ages 7-12. Includes solutions. Suitable for coloring. *Food for Everyone* describes how the foods people eat affect world hunger. Intended for grades K-8. Both publications are made out of recycled paper and are 50 cents each plus a self-addressed, stamped envelope for up to 4 copies. 5 or more, add $3 shipping instead of SASE. From: EarthSave.

Gypsy and You: How to Avoid Dog Bites
A coloring booklet that explains why some dogs bite and how to avoid being bitten. For elementary age children. 60 cents each or 100 for $15 (minimum order is $2) from AHA. Specify item AHE703.

Learning/Activity Sheets for Kids
Three different sets: fact sheets, crossword puzzles, and word search puzzles. Each set includes chickens, pigs, and cows. $1 per set plus $1 shipping (for orders under $3; $2 shipping for orders $3-$10) from: Animal Place, 3448 Laguna Creek Trail, Vacaville, CA 95688.

•Leprechaun Cake and Other Tales: A Vegetarian Story-Cookbook
•I Love Animals and Broccoli Activity Book
•The Soup to Nuts Natural Foods Coloring Book
Leprechaun Cake and Other Tales is written by Vonnie Winslow Crist with recipes by Debra Wasserman. It contains four stories, each culminating with multi-cultural characters preparing and eating foods from around the world. Includes recipes, glossary, and safety tips. Ages 8-11. $11 postpaid. *I Love Animals*

and Broccoli is a children's activity book of nutrition and animal rights. For all ages that read. (Some activities require adult interaction.) 40 pages. $5 postpaid. *The Soup to Nuts Natural Foods Coloring Book* contains poems by Ellen Sue Spivack and illustrations by Ann Barlow. 46 pages. $3 postpaid. All of these books are available from VRG.

Manatee Coloring and Activity Book

Free to elementary-level educators from: Save the Manatee Club, 500 N. Maitland Ave., Suite 210, Maitland, FL 32751, 1-800 432-JOIN.

Nature Coloring Books

Separate coloring books for butterflies, birds, coral reefs, whales and dolphins, tropical fish, horses, wild animals, dogs, cats, small animals of North America, etc. Each approximately $2.95 plus $4 shipping per total order. Catalog: Dover Publications, Inc., 31 East 2nd Street, Mineola, NY 11501-3582.

- ***Nature Hide and Seek: Oceans***
- ***Nature Hide and Seek: Woods and Forests***
- ***Nature Hide and Seek: Rivers and Lakes***

by John Norris Wood

"Seek and find" scenes with an abundance of animals hiding beneath fold-over flaps of natural wilderness camouflage. Facts about the animals provided on accompanying pages. Fun and educational. Ages 5-9. The *Oceans* version is $12.95 plus $3.95 shipping from: Whale Gifts, Center for Marine Conservation, P.O. Box 388, Centerbrook, CT 06409-0388, 1-800-227-1929, FAX: (203) 767-4381. The *Woods and Forests* and *Rivers and Lakes* versions are $13 each plus $3.75 shipping ($4.75 covers both books) from: Animal Town, P.O. Box 485, Healdsburg, CA 95448, 1-800-445-8643, FAX: (707) 837-9737.

We're All Animals Coloring Book

Kids learn about animals while they color. 16 pages. Order as part of a 4-book set (bundled with *The Lady and the Spider*, *The Gnats of Knotty Pine*, and *Perfect the Pig*) for $15 ($13.50 members) from PETA Catalog. (What a deal!) Specify item BK201. Or you can order a single copy of the coloring book for $3.95 (TN addresses add 8% tax) plus $3.50 shipping ($4.50 UPS) from: The Mail Order Catalog, P.O. Box 180, Summertown, TN 38483, 1-800-695-2241 or (615) 964-2241.

Children & Young Adults: *Books*

This section contains both "how-to" books for young activists and story books that inspire kindness toward animals.

Books for Young Activists

Students may also want to see the books on dissection in the Research, Education, & Product Testing section.

Animal Rights

by Charles Patterson

A concise look at some animal rights issues, including animals as companions, food, research specimens, hunting targets, and entertainers. Geared toward young adults. 112 pages. Photos. Hardbound. Enslow Publishers, Inc. $17.95 (members subtract 10%) plus $3 shipping from the National Anti-Vivisection Society.

Animals in Society: Facts and Perspectives on Our Treatment of Animals

by Zoe Weil, Director of Animalearn, American Anti-Vivisection Society

This book is packed with photos and information. It's attractively designed to appeal to secondary level students. Each chapter ends with a conclusion and suggested projects and questions. 126 pages. Photos. 1991. $4.95 from AAVS. Specify item 1-B. Bulk rates available.

Choices For Our Future: A Generation Rising for Life on Earth

by Ocean Robbins and Sol Solomon

"A perfect introduction for people of any age who want to learn the environmental basics." Written by two founders of YES! (Youth for Environmental Sanity). One of the authors is the son of EarthSave founder John Robbins. Includes a history of YES! and lifestyle choices for a "healthier, happier, saner world." The book got a thumb's up from singer John Denver! $9.95 ($8.95 members) from EarthSave.

Kids Can Save the Animals: 101 Easy Things To Do

by Ingrid Newkirk, National Director, People for the Ethical Treatment of Animals

A book of animal facts, drawings, projects, and ideas for how kids can help animals. Ages 8-13. New edition is $8 postpaid from: Kids Can Save the Animals, c/o PETA, 501 Front Street, Norfolk, VA 23501, (757) 622-PETA.

So, You Love Animals: An Action-Packed, Fun-Filled Book to Help Kids Help Animals

by Zoe Weil, Director of Animalearn, American Anti-Vivisection Society; illustrated by John R. Gibson

A highly-accessible resource for teachers, parents, and children alike. Full of information and activities. Covers a wide range of topics, from animals we eat, wear, or care for to those we consider pests. Especially geared toward ages 7-12. Paperback (8-1/2" by 11"). 190 pages. 1993. $12.95 (PA addresses add 6% tax) plus $2 shipping for first book, 50 cents for additional books from AAVS. Specify item 2-B. Five or more copies, call for special rates.

A Teen's Guide to Going Vegetarian

by Judy Krizmanic

By a former editor of *Vegetarian Times* magazine. Includes the definition of a vegetarian, a list of well-known vegetarians, reasons for being a vegetarian, myths about vegetarianism, what to eat, how to handle particular situations (such as your first meatless Thanksgiving), and recipes to get you started. 219 pages. Penguin Books USA, Inc., 1994. $6.99 (members subtract 10%) from North American Vegetarian Society.

Story Books for Fun & Education

A Boy, A Chicken, and The Lion of Judah: How Ari Became a Vegetarian

by Roberta Kalechovsky

A rather complex story of a nine-year-old boy who doesn't feel right eating meat, and the inner and outer conflicts that result. Examines the inner turmoil of a young boy struggling with his feelings, peer pressure, family relationships, and societal norms. Particular attention given to contrasting the lives of battery chickens with free roaming chickens. Takes place in Israel and includes Jewish references. Intended for ages 7-10 (although contains words such as "environmentalist" and "Byzantine"). This is not a picture book. 50 pages. Micah Publications, Inc., 1995. $8 postpaid from the American Vegan Society.

Among the Orangutans

by Evelyn Gallardo

The story of Biruté Galdikas, who has devoted her life to living among and studying orangutans in Borneo. As well as a close-up look at orangutans, includes difficult life decisions Biruté made to follow her heart (such as choosing to let her son go live with his father instead of with her). Ages 8-12. Hardbound. 45 pages. Color photos. Byron Preiss Visual Publications, Inc., 1993. $15 postpaid for hardcover, or $8 postpaid for softcover (overseas, $20 and $12) from: International Primate Protection League, P.O. Box 766, Summerville, SC 29484. Also available: *Apes* and *Baboon Orphan*.

Animal Place: Where Magical Things Happen

by Kim Sturla, illustrated by Eric Sakach

Vegetarian theme, told through the eyes of a young girl, who experiences a transformation while visiting the animals at her aunt and uncle's home. The setting is a real California animal sanctuary called Animal Place for abused and unwanted animals. Illustrated. $8.99 plus $2 shipping from: Animal Place, 3448 Laguna Creek Trail, Vacaville, CA 95688.

The Benefactory Collection

Sets consisting of stuffed toys, story books with rhyming verse, and story cassettes by musician Tom Chapin. These are true stories about real animals, designed to "encourage, and empower children, to show them how to focus their love and concern in a meaningful way." Includes stories and accompanying stuffed toys about Jasmine the cat, Bentley and Blueberry the dogs, and parrots Ruffle and Coo and owl Hoo Doo. Donates at least 3% of all sales to the Humane Society of the United States. Catalog available from: The Benefactory, Inc., One Post Road, Fairfield, CT 06430, 1-800-PAWPAL-1.

Can I Be Good?

by Livingston Taylor, illustrated by Ted Rand

A light-hearted look at life from a golden retriever's point of view. Rhyming text (by musician Livingston Taylor) is accompanied by colorful watercolor illustrations. The opening page reads: "I'm a big dog, But I'm not very old, I try very hard, To do just as I'm told. I wish all the time, I could do what I should, But it's awfully hard to be good." Hardbound. Gulliver Books, 1993. $14.95 from bookstores or check with your local library.

The Chimpanzee Family Book
by Jane Goodall, photos by Michael Neugebaur
The shining, brown eyes of the baby chimp featured in this story are absolutely irresistible! This book chronicles in words and color photos a single day in the life of chimpanzees in Tanzania, East Africa, as observed by Jane Goodall. Readers get to know the chimpanzees by name as individuals, and learn about food gathering, family ties, playing, fighting, protecting, grooming, etc. The close-up photography really makes this book. Highly recommended. 72 pages. Published by Picture Book Studio, 1991. $17.95 from bookstores or check with your local library.

Cows are Vegetarians
by Ann Bradley, illustrated by Elsie Huffman
"A book for vegetarian kids." Educates vegetarian children about the environmental wisdom of their diet, particularly on how being vegetarian helps save the rainforests. Heavy on text with black and white drawings. 15 pages. Healthways Press, 1992. $7.95 plus $4 shipping from: *Vegetarian Times* Bookshelf, P.O. Box 446, Mt. Morris, IL 60154, 1-800-435-9610.

D Is For Dolphin
by Cami Berg, illustrations by Janet Biondi
An unusual and beautiful swim through the alphabet with dolphins. Each letter stands for a dolphin trait or behavior, and all of the pages are blue, depicting dolphins in various underwater poses. Visually compelling. A glossary at the back explains more about dolphin traits and behavior. Hardbound. Windham Books, 1991. A portion of the proceeds benefit The Marine Mammal Fund. $18.95 from bookstores or check with your local library.

Koko's Kitten
by Dr. Francine Patterson, photos by Ronald H. Cohn
A true story in photos and text about Koko, a captive gorilla, who began learning American Sign Language as a baby. For her twelfth birthday, Koko said she wanted a kitten, and picked out one she named "All Ball." This is the fascinating story of the relationship between a "talking" gorilla and her pet kitten. From your local bookstore or library. *Note:* Some activists may be offended by Koko's captive status, while others will regard her as an ambassador who is helping to educate humans.

The Lady and the Spider
by Faith McNulty, illustrated by Bob Marstall
A touching and beautifully-written story about the "tiny, very important life" of a small green spider living in a head of lettuce and the woman who picks the lettuce for lunch. Highly recommended. Intended for ages 4-8, but appropriate for any age (including adults!). Hardbound is $12.95 plus shipping (varies with destination) from: Amberwood, Route 2, Box 300, Milford Road, Baker County, Leary, GA 31762, (912) 792-6246. Paperback bundled with three other books (*Perfect the Pig*, *The Gnats of Knotty Pine*, and *We're All Animals Coloring Book)* is $15 ($13.50 members) from PETA Catalog. Specify item BK201.

Leprechaun Cake and Other Tales: A Vegetarian Story-Cookbook
by Vonnie Winslow Crist, recipes by Debra Wasserman
Four culturally diverse fantasy tales, each followed by recipes related to the story (over 40 recipes in all). Includes cooking terms and safety tips. Recipes vary from very simple to more complex. A fun and healthy cookbook! 128 pages. Illustrated. 1995. $9.95 postpaid from VRG.

Marlin Justice
by Eugene D. Wheeler
See Entertainment: Books for a description of this book.

My Greyhound Friend
by Nora Star
The story of a young boy who learns about greyhounds and greyhound racing when he visits his grandmother in Florida. Told from the boy's perspective. Has a happy ending! 12-page booklet. Photos. Proceeds benefit Greyhound Friends for Life, which places greyhounds into homes. California Publishing Company, 1995. $5.95 postpaid from Greyhound Friends for Life, 9728 Tenaya Way, Kelseyille, CA 95451.

Nature's Chicken: The Story of Today's Chicken Farms
by Nigel Burroughs
Despite a bit of propaganda-laden terminology (the chemists' "dark and terrible laboratories"), this cartoon booklet effectively tells the sad but true story of what happens to chickens in factory farms. Includes information about becoming a vegan. The Book Publishing Company. $5.95 postpaid from UPC.

Pole Dog

by Tres Seymour, illustrated by David Soman

A simple but moving story of an old dog dumped by a telephone pole, who waits in vain through rain and hunger for his family's return. (But there is a happy ending.) Sparse, rhyming, repetitive text make this appropriate for beginning readers or pre-readers who are being read to, but the message is appropriate for any age. I was very moved by this book. Pastel chalk drawings. Orchard Books, 1993. $14.99 from bookstores or check with your local library.

Prince Siddhartha

by Jonathan Landaw and Janet Brooke

The gentle and powerful story of the life and teachings of Buddha, broken down into digestible chapters of 1-5 pages (many stories within a story). Teaches kindness and compassion toward all beings, including animals, as the way to happiness. Colorful illustrations. Recommended for grades 1-8, but suitable for any age (including adults). Paperback. 144 pages. Published by Wisdom, 1984. $15.95 from bookstores or check with your local library.

Sam the Sea Cow

by Francine Jacobs, illustrated by Laura Kelly

A "Reading Rainbow" book that follows the adventures of a manatee, commonly known as a "sea cow." Ages 4-8. $7.95 plus shipping ($3.95 for orders up to $19.99) from: Whale Gifts, Center for Marine Conservation, P.O. Box 388, Centerbrook, CT 06409-0388, 1-800-227-1929, FAX: (203) 767-4381.

She's Wearing a Dead Bird on Her Head!

by Kathryn Lasky, illustrated by David Catrow

Winner of the 1995 New York Times Choice of Best Illustrated Children's Books award. A lavishly illustrated tale, based on the true story of how the Massachusetts Audubon Society came into being when two proper Boston ladies took action to change the "senseless murdering for fashion" of millions of the world's birds, whose feathers and bodies were being used to adorn hats. Occurring at a time in history when women lacked political power, this is also a book about women's empowerment. An inspiring story that shows how an individual can make a difference! Recommended for ages 5-9, but appropriate for any age, including (and maybe especially!) adults. Hardbound. Hyperion Books for Children, 1995. $14.95 from bookstores or check with your local library.

Twas the Night Before Thanksgiving

written and illustrated by Dav Pilkey

A delightful and colorful book with rhyming text that loosely follows the well-known "'Twas the Night Before Christmas." Children on a school field trip liberate turkeys from the Thanksgiving axe. Recommended for all ages. Hardbound. $15.95 from Farm Sanctuary. Specify item BK8.

Victor, the Vegetarian: Saving the Little Lambs

by Radha Vignola, illustrated by Julia Bauer

The story of a young boy who makes the connection between the lambs he dearly loves and the lamb chops he likes to eat. Has a happy ending! Large print suitable for young or elderly readers. 50 pages. Published by AVIVA!, 1994. $6.95 (members subtract 10%) from: North American Vegetarian Society.

Wild Fox: A True Story

by Cherie Mason, illustrated by Ellen McAllister Stammen

The touching, gentle, firsthand account of the friendship between a young woman and a wild fox—the victim of a steel-jaw leghold trap. Full of respect. A true story! Highly recommended. Hardbound. 32 pages. Color illustrations. $15.95 plus $4.50 shipping from: Chosen for Children, P.O. Box 185, Merion Station, PA 19066, Orders: 1-800-554-4414, Info: (610) 664-6595.

Wildlife Rescue: The Work of Dr. Kathleen Ramsey

by Jennifer Owen Dewey, photos by Dan MacCarter

A riveting, close-up look at a New Mexico vet who has dedicated her life to rehabilitating wild animals so they can be returned to the wild. Some disturbing incidents (a woman who kills a beaver in self-defense, and the feeding of live mice to some recuperating birds of prey), but mostly fascinating accounts of rehabilitation, release, and animal advocacy (in one instance, the doctor refuses to return an obviously neglected parrot to his "owners"). Many color photos and lots of text. 64 pages. Boyds Mill Press. $16.95 from bookstores or check with your local library.

Children & Young Adults: *Guides & Directories*

Animals, Kids & Books
by Barbara Freedman
A 40-page guide for adults seeking humane books for children up to about age seven. Reviews over 125 story books and classifies them into one of three categories: Kind, Nice, or Cruel. $3.50 plus shipping (varies with destination) from: Amberwood, Route 2, Box 300, Milford Road, Baker County, Leary, GA 31762, (912) 792-6246.

Children's Books on Kindness to Animals
compiled by Nancy Hargrave
A list of 21 books that teach kindness. Includes a summary of the storyline and suggested ages. Free for a self-addressed, stamped envelope from: Animal Rights Coalition, P.O. Box 20315, Bloomington, MN 55420.

HSUS Student Action Guide
Intended for secondary students. A step-by-step guide to forming an Earth/animal protection club, holding meetings, targeting issues, and planning activities. Free sample copy, but you pay $3 shipping from HSUS.

Think Like the Animal: Questions to Ask Before You Kill
See the Hunting & Wildlife: Guides & Directories section for a description of this booklet.

Children & Young Adults: *Periodicals*

See also the periodicals in the Activism section.

Animalearn: The Magazine for Kids Who Love Animals
Quarterly magazine for kids 8-12 years old. Each issue focuses on a different topic, such as wildlife in your neighborhood or dolphins and whales. Published by the American Anti-Vivisection Society (make checks payable to AAVS/Animalearn). Free copy available. 1 year (4 issues) for $10 ($13 in Canada) from *Animalearn Magazine,* AAVS.

GRRR!
"The 'zine that bites back!" 8 pages. Celebrity news, what activists are doing, what you can do to help animals. Very colorful! 1 year (3 issues) free from PETA.

How On Earth! (HOE!)
Quarterly newsletter written by, for, and about youths who value compassionate, ecologically-sound living. Encourages activism and empowerment. Covers a variety of environmental, animal, and global issues. Submissions from youths ages 13-24 accepted in the form of articles, poetry, personal essays, vegetarian recipes, photography, and advice on everything from current issues, to activism and boycotts, to dealing with parents or peers who just don't understand. Send a self-addressed, stamped envelope for writer's guidelines and volunteer info. Published by the Vegetarian Education Network. 1 year (4 issues) for $18 ($21 Canada; postal money order, please). Sample issue $6 from: *HOE!,* P.O. Box 339, Oxford, PA 19363-0339, (717) 529-8638.

HSUS Student Network News
A newsletter for junior and senior high school students who want to protect animals and the environment. Published every fall. Designed to help students share ideas and information with other student activists or clubs. Free to students ages 12-18 with HSUS student membership. 25 cents each, 50 for $5, or 100 for $9 from HSUS. Specify item HE1078.

Companion Animals

Additional publications are available from the organizations listed in Chapter 3, "Companion Animals" and from the many humane organizations listed in Chapter 10, "Animal Advocacy Organizations."

Companion Animals: *Books*

See also *Stolen for Profit* (Research, Education, & Product Testing), *Circles of Compassion: A Collection of Humane Words and Work* (Activism), and various books in the Children & Young Adults section.

Behavior & Training

•The Art of Raising a Puppy

•How to Be Your Dog's Best Friend: A Training Manual for Dog Owners

by the Monks of New Skete

Advice and instruction to help you develop a respectful and affectionate relationship with your canine friend, while providing the proper care and training that prevents problem behaviors. The foundation for their training is "understanding canine behavior and enhancing the bond between dog and owner." *Note*: Uses the training collar correction method (recommends a soft, braided nylon training collar for most breeds), but with this reminder: "Correction is not punishment; it is communication between you and your pup. It carries with it no anger, and it is just unpleasant enough to help her change her behavior." Both books are published by Little, Brown & Company, and are available from your local bookstore or library. *The Art of Raising a Puppy* is $19.95 plus $3.55 shipping from: The Whole Animal Catalog, 3131 Hennepin Avenue South, Minneapolis, MN 55408, 1-800-377-6369, FAX: (612) 824-6436.

Big Lick Walking Horses

by Ms. Maxwell Dickinson

See the Entertainment: Books section for a description of this book.

Good Owners, Great Dogs: A Training Manual for Humans and Their Canine Companions

by Brian Kilcommons with Sarah Wilson

Written by the only American to study and work with the legendary Barbara Woodhouse. This book is designed to be pleasing to the eye with numerous photos, anecdotes, sidebars, and information partitioned into easily digestible chunks. The author devotes a great deal of the book to simply teaching the reader about dogs and puppies. Addresses problem behaviors as well as basic training. Although he advocates use of the choke-chain collar, he does emphasize the *correct* way to employ it, something most people don't know. 276 pages. Warner Books, Inc., 1992. Order through bookstores or check with your local library.

Just Say "Good Dog"

by Linda Goodman with Marlene Trunnell

A new approach to teaching dogs using only positive reinforcement, *without* choke-chain collars. Addresses "problem" behaviors such as barking, digging, chewing, etc. (*Note:* The author told me she takes exception to some of the cartoon drawings included in the book, but could not persuade the publisher to withdraw them. She feels that some of the drawings, intended to be humorous, depict negative rather than positive images.) 188 pages. Paperback. Illustrated. TFH Publications, Inc., 1993. $13.50 postpaid from: P.O.R.G.I.E. (Pet Ownership Requires Getting Involved and Educated), 2023 Chicago Ave., B22, Riverside, CA 92507, (909) 784-9070.

•Mother Knows Best: The Natural Way to Train Your Dog

•Dog Problems

•Second-Hand Dog: How to Turn Yours into a First-Rate Pet

•The Chosen Puppy

by Carol Lea Benjamin

Good books on understanding and educating your dog. An entertaining, witty writing style and cartoon drawings make these books fun to read. Although this author still advises the use of "punishment" as well as praise, by "punishment" she means a collar shake, a leash correction, or "a surprising assist into a sit or down," immediately followed by praise. *Second-Hand Dog* particularly teaches patience and understanding with "a dog with a bad history." *The Chosen Puppy* is about getting a puppy from an animal shelter. Order through bookstores or check with your local library.

Superdog: Raising the Perfect Canine Companion

by Dr. Michael W. Fox, Vice President, The Humane Society of the United States

This is not so much a "training" guide as it is a book on understanding who dogs are. This author admonishes the use of choke-chains. A look at the chapter titles clues you in to the tone of this book: "Do Animals Think? Can They Reason?," "Know How Your Dog Communicates," "Supernature and Psychic Abilities of Dogs and Other Friends," "How to Decode Dog Behavior," "IQ Tests (Games and Exercises) for Dogs," etc. 210 pages. Photos. Howell Book House, 1990. From your local bookstore or library.

•The Tellington TTouch: A Breakthrough Technique to Train and Care for Your Favorite Animal

by Linda Tellington-Jones with Sybil Taylor

•TTEAM Approach to Problem Free Training

by Linda Tellington-Jones with Ursula Bruns

- ***TTEAM Workbook for Dogs, Cats, Wildlife, and Humans***
  by Linda Tellington-Jones with Robyn Hood
- ***Getting In TTouch: Understand and Influence Your Horse's Personality***
  by Linda Tellington-Jones with Sybil Taylor
- ***Llama Handling and Training: The TTEAM Approach***
  by Marty McGee with Linda Tellington-Jones

TTouch is a proven, hands-on technique that soothes and assists in the healing and training of animals, as well as humans. It is not massage therapy, but rather is more similar to the Feldenkrais therapy developed for humans, which uses nonhabitual movement to activate new neurological pathways to the brain. The author has developed this technique over a number of years and is very well known. From: TTEAM, P.O. Box 3793, Santa Fe, NM 87501, 1-800-854-TEAM, (505) 455-2945, FAX: (505) 455-7233.

Diet & Health

The Healing Touch: The Proven Massage Program for Dogs and Cats
by Dr. Michael W. Fox, Vice President, The Humane Society of the United States

A do-it-yourself manual for massaging cats and dogs. Photos and illustrations. 151 pages. Newmarket Press, 1990. $10.95 (CA addresses add 7.25% tax) plus $3 shipping from: Alternatives, P.O. Box 2845, Chino, CA 91708-2845, 1-800-860-9422.

Healing Your Horse: Alternative Therapies
by Meredith Snader, Sharon Willoughby, and others

Written by holistic veterinarians who are experts in their specialties. Discusses a variety of alternative therapies for horses. $25 (CA addresses add 7.25% tax) plus $3 shipping from: Alternatives, P.O. Box 2845, Chino, CA 91708-2845, 1-800-860-9422.

Dr. Pitcairn's Complete Guide to Natural Health for Dogs and Cats
by Richard H. Pitcairn, DVM, PhD and Susan Hubble Pitcairn

Still the definitive guide on humane and holistic animal care. Includes information on commercial pet food, recipes for cats and dogs (including vegetarian recipes), natural remedies, successful instances of treating animals with nutritional therapy, and an encyclopedia of ailments and remedies. This book also explores psychological reasons behind some health problems, and discusses how companion animals mirror their human caretakers. Paperback. 287 pages. Rodale Press. Second edition, 1995. $12.95 plus $3.25 shipping from: The Whole Animal Catalog, 3131 Hennepin Avenue South, Minneapolis, MN 55408, 1-800-377-6369, FAX: (612) 824-6436.

Flower Essences: Reordering Our Understanding and Approach to Illness and Health
by Machaelle Small Wright

Explains what flower essences are and how to select and use them, especially Perelandra essences. Though mostly about the use of essences with humans, includes sections on using essences with animals, including during the death process. (I used this book to assist a raccoon in the death process.) Published by Perelandra, Ltd., 1988. 260 pages. $10.95 plus $4 shipping from: Perelandra, P.O. Box 3603, Warrenton, VA 22186, (703) 937-2153 (answering machine), FAX: (703) 937-3360.

Love, Miracles, and Animal Healing: A Veterinarian's Journey from Physical Medicine to Spiritual Understanding
by Allen M. Schoen, DVM and Pam Proctor

The story of one veterinarian's journey into holistic medicine and his recognition of animals as spiritual beings. Lots of anecdotes. This is not a do-it-yourself guide, although the last half of the book discusses some specific acupressure points, homeopathic remedies, and food (the recipes are meat-based). A good overall introduction into holistic veterinary practices and a touching personal account. 239 pages. Hardbound. Simon & Schuster, 1995. $22 plus $5 shipping from: Homeopathic Educational Services, 2124 Kittredge Street, Berkeley, CA 94704, Orders: 1-800-359-9051, Inquiries: (510) 649-0294, FAX: (510) 649-1955.

Natural Healing for Dogs and Cats
by Diane Stein

For the very open-minded, this book presents an overview of holistic healing modalities for companion animals. Includes discussions of psychic healing and communication, nutrition, herbs, homeopathy, acupressure, massage, TTouch, flower essences (both Bach flower and Perelandra remedies), death and reincarnation, and more. A comprehensive overview of possibilities. 192 pages. Paperback. Illustrated. The Crossing Press, 1993. $16.95

(CA addresses add 7.25% tax) plus $3 shipping from: Alternatives, P.O. Box 2845, Chino, CA 91708-2845, 1-800-860-9422.

The Natural Remedy Book for Dogs and Cats
by Diane Stein
A do-it-yourself guide that lists natural remedies for 50 common ailments. Treatments include nutrition, herbs, homeopathy, flower essences, accupressure, and more. 350 pages. $16.95 from bookstores or check with your local library.

The New Natural Cat: A Complete Guide for Finicky Owners
by Anitra Frazier with Norma Eckroate
This is considered the definitive guide on natural cat care. Includes diet, grooming, the litter box, special situations (for example, when a new baby arrives), the scratching post, home health care, common health problems, etc. Published by Plume, 1990. 448 pages. $14.95 plus $4.95 shipping from: The Natural Pet Care Company, 8050 Lake City Way, Seattle, WA 948115, 1-800-962-8266 M-F, 10-5 Pacific Time (outside Washington), (206) 522-1667 (inside Washington), FAX: (206) 522-1132, or save shipping charges by ordering through your local bookstore.

TTouch Books
by Linda Tellington-Jones, et. al.
See the TTouch and TTEAM books listed under Behavior & Training, above.

Vegetarian Dogs and Cats
by James A. Peden
The resource book for those who wish to feed their dog or cat a vegetarian diet. Includes an explanation of the nutritional needs of cats and dogs, recipes for both species, testimonials, and a variety of other information, such as discussions on health and healing and commercial pet foods. A vegetarian diet for cats is possible because of a vegetarian nutritional product developed by the author (Vegecat) that supplies the nutrients required by cats. A vegetarian nutritional product for dogs (Vegedog) is also available. Paperback. 236 pages. Photos. 1992. $13.95 plus $2 shipping from: Harbingers of a New Age, 717 E. Missoula Avenue, Troy, MT 59935, 1-800-884-6262, FAX: (406) 295-7603.

Companion Animals: *Guides & Directories*

Canine Consumer Report: A Guide to Hereditary Diseases in Purebred Dogs
From the introduction: "Pedigreed dogs are subject to more than 300 genetically transmitted abnormalities...This brochure can make people aware of the problems they might be acquiring when they buy a pedigreed dog...Adopting a dog from an animal shelter will save a life and will not contribute to an industry that perpetuates genetic diseases." 28 pages. $1 from AVAR. Also available: *Surgical Claw Removal: A Radical Solution* (argues against cat declawing) and *Cosmetic Surgeries: Standards of Cruelty* (argues against tail docking and ear cropping in dogs).

Dog & Cat Book Catalog: Your Complete Source for Dog and Cat Books & Videos
This free 48-page catalog is a mixed bag, to say the least. It offers some truly offensive and irresponsible books (*Hijacking the Humane Movement* ("An expose of the 'animal rights' movement, showing how extremists have used defamation and sensationalism to create public outrage and raise money"), *Basic Gun Dog Training*, *Last Great Race: The Iditarod*, etc.), but it is balanced by other books and videos on subjects such as ending undesirable behavior through "affection training," competitive obedience without force, telepathic communication with your dog or cat, and books on health and healing for companion animals. It's free, so why not get it and see what's out there. After all, you don't have to buy the books from them; you can order them through your local bookstore. From: Direct Book Service, P.O. Box 2778, Wenatchee, WA 98807-2778, 1-800-776-2665, FAX: (509) 662-7233.

House Rabbit Handbook: How to Live with an Urban Rabbit
by Marinell Harriman
Various people share their experiences and insights on living with companion rabbits. "Advice on health care, housetraining, and bunny proofing." 96 pages. Photos. Drollery Press, 1991 (revised edition). $8.95 from bookstores or check with your local library.

Preventing Overpopulation

A Guide to the TTVAR-M Method of Feral Cat Control

A working manual for the "trap, test, vaccinate, alter, release, and maintain (TTVAR-M)" method of feral cat control. Sections include "Feral Cat Colony Management," "Veterinary Participation," and "Encouraging Community Support." Proceeds applied to helping feral cats. $30 postpaid from: Forgotten Felines of Sonoma County, 1275 Fourth Street, #366, Santa Rosa, CA 95404, (707) 576-7999.

Humane Society of the United States Publications

Various publications on pet overpopulation, including *How to Establish Spay/Neuter Programs and Clinics* ($2), *Information on Selected Spay/Neuter Clinics and Programs* ($2), *Breeding Moratorium Packet* ($4), *52 Simple Things You Can Do to Help End Pet Overpopulation* ($2.95), and *Pet Overpopulation Fact Sheet* (35 cents, 25 for $3.50). They also offer posters and bumper stickers on this subject. From HSUS.

Killing the Crisis, Not the Animals: A Blueprint for Passing a Lifesaving Ordinance

By Kim Sturla

A manual for passing legislation to regulate the breeding of dogs and cats. The legislation requires people to either spay/neuter their companions or apply for a breeding permit. Topics include everything you ever wanted to know about spaying and neutering, researching other laws, building a coalition, planning your strategy, communicating with the news media, mobilizing your supporters, etc. 89 pages. Photos. $5 plus 15% shipping (members subtract 10% from total) from: The Fund for Animals, 850 Sligo Avenue, Suite 300, Silver Spring, MD 20910, (301) 585-2591, FAX: (301) 585-2595. Specify item B-6.

Making It Happen! Networking to End Companion Animal Overpopulation

Edited by Esther Mechler

A collection of ideas by different people in the "spay/neuter movement." Topics include starting a program or clinic; statewide, government, private, and combination programs; working with animal control and veterinarians; legislation; marketing; fund-raising; etc. 1994. 240 pages. $19.95 plus $3 shipping from: North Shore Animal League, Lewyt Street, Port Washington, NY 11050, (516) 883-7575, FAX: (516) 944-5732.

Prevent A Litter Campaign Package

A package containing instructions on how to organize a Prevent A Litter campaign, complete with spay/neuter surgeries donated by area vets, kids' poster contest, billboard and radio participation, etc. $30 from: Prevent A Litter Coalition, Inc., P.O. Box 1412, Centerville, VA 22020.

Rescue & Adoption

Adopting the Racing Greyhound

by Cynthia A. Branigan

A "must read" for anyone thinking about adopting a racing greyhound. Covers all aspects of introducing a greyhound into your family. My only disappointment with this book is the failure to implicate the greyhound racing industry for its blatant cruelty toward these dogs. The author is president of Make Peace With Animals, Inc. 148 pages. Photos. Macmillan/Howell Book House, 1992. Order through your local bookstore or inquire at Make Peace With Animals, Inc., P.O. Box 488, New Hope, PA 18938, (215) 862-0605, FAX: (215) 862-2733.

Adoption Programs

A 47-page guide to creating your own adoption program. Includes forms, guidelines, interviewing tips, staff/volunteer training tips, and a list of free sources for pet care materials. $4.50 postpaid from AHA. Also available: additional guides on shelter administration and cruelty investigations.

How to Find a Loving Home for Your Pet or Rescued Animals

Free booklet from Dedications & Everlasting Love To Animals (D.E.L.T.A.), P.O. Box 9, Glendale, CA 91209, (818) 241-6282, FAX: (805) 269-5049.

Muttmatchers Breed Rescue List

Names and telephone numbers of breed rescuers (those who save homeless dogs of a particular breed) for specific geographic areas. List is organized by breed. Subscriptions: Humane Animal Rescue Team, P.O. Box 920, Fillmore, CA 93016, (805) 524-4542. Published quarterly. $5 per issue.

Muttmatchers Messenger Pet Rescue and Placement Publication

A bimonthly newspaper that advertises companion animals needing homes in Southern CA (Bakersfield to San Diego) and Washington state. Ads are placed and paid for by animal protection shelters. Different editions published for specific geographic areas. Includes animals generally considered "unadoptable" such as old or handicapped animals and those rescued from medical research. Photos. Can help you set up an edition of *Muttmatchers Messenger* for your geographic area. Subscriptions: Humane Animal Rescue Team, P.O. Box 920, Fillmore, CA 93016, (805) 524-4542. 2 years (12 issues) for $22.50. Free sample available.

No-Kill Directory

Compiled by Lynda J. Foro

A list of 250 "non-euthanizing" humane organizations that provide rescue, sanctuary, and rehabilitation to animals. Listed by state and also alphabetically. 48 pages. 1996 (updated annually). $15 postpaid from: Doing Things for Animals, Inc., P.O. Box 2165, Sun City, AZ 85372-2165.

Project BREED (Breed Rescue Efforts & EDucation) Directory, Volumes 1 & 2

"Breed rescuers" save homeless dogs of a particular breed. Combined, these directories contain information on nearly 3,000 volunteers rescuing over 100 breeds of dogs, rabbits, ferrets, and wild bats nationwide (including Hawaii and Alaska) and in Canada. Directory buyers also get access to 7,000 more contacts through the Project Breed Hotline.

- *Red Book Edition (Volume 2),* 1993, 168 pages of nearly 1,400 rescue contacts for 32 breeds of dogs and three other animal species. Paperback. $25 plus $3.05 shipping (MD addresses add 5% tax or provide tax exemption information).
- *Yellow Book Edition (Volume 1)*, 1989, 291 pages providing nearly 1,500 rescue contacts for 72 breeds of dogs. Paperback. $15.95 plus $3.05 shipping (MD addresses add 5% tax or provide tax exemption information).
- *Set of both editions*: $35 plus $5.05 shipping (MD addresses add 5% tax or provide tax exemption information).

Both directories compiled by and available from: Project BREED, Inc., P.O. Box 15888, Chevy Chase, MD 20825-5888.

Traveling with Animals

See also *DogGone: Fun Places to Go and Cool Stuff to Do with Your Dog* in the Periodicals section.

Pets-R-Permitted Directory

A yellow pages (literally) of almost 10,000 hotels, motels, and campgrounds that allow pets. Also lists kennels, petsitters, and other useful information. Information is well-organized and easy to find. 300+ pages. Updated regularly. Published by The Annenberg Communications Institute. $9.95 plus $3 shipping from: Doris Day Animal League, 227 Massachusetts Avenue NE, Suite 100, Washington, D.C. 20002.

Eileen's Directory of Pet-Friendly Lodging

by Eileen Barish, illustrated by Gregg Nyers

Over 20,000 hotels, bed and breakfasts, and other lodgings in the U.S. and Canada that welcome your animal companions. Paperback. 688 pages. $19.95 ($17.95 members) from PETA Catalog. Specify item BK550.

Frommer's On the Road Again with Man's Best Friend

by Dawn Habgood and Robert Habgood

"A selective guide to bed and breakfasts, inns, hotels, and resorts that welcome you and your dog." Different editions for different areas of the country: Mid-Atlantic, Southeast, New England, California, and Northwest. Published by Howell Book House/Macmillan Publishing. $14.95 plus shipping from the publisher (1-800-428-5331) or order through your local bookstore.

Wills & Companion Animals

Good Intentions Gone Astray: Thwarted Gifts for the Benefit of Animals

An essay illustrating how to write your will to ensure that it will benefit animals. Includes several principles to follow and examples of complications due to poorly drafted wills. 50 cents each plus $1 shipping (covers up to $2.50 in purchases) from ISAR. Specify item 222.

Providing for Your Pets in the Event of Your Death or Hospitalization

by Frances B. Carlisle and Paul L. Franken

A pamphlet by two estate attorneys which discusses a too-often neglected subject. Includes sample provisions that can be added to your will. Some information is specific to New York state law, but this information will still be helpful to you and your attorney. $2 payable to "Association of the Bar" from: Association of the Bar of the City of New York, Office of

Communications, 42 West 44th Street, New York, NY 10036-6690, (212) 382-6695.

Companion Animals: *Periodicals*

See also the periodicals in the Interspecies Communication section.

DogGone: Fun Places to Go and Cool Stuff to Do with Your Dog
"A unique blend of travel features and activity articles in a newsletter just for dog owners." This 12-page newsletter is a delight! It's pleasing to the eye and contains interesting tidbits for those of us smitten with canines, whether or not we travel with them. 1 year (6 issues) for $24/U.S. (FL addresses add $1.44 sales tax), $30/Canada (U.S. funds) from: *DogGone*, P.O Box 651155, Vero Beach, FL 32965.

Love of Animals: Natural Care and Healing for Your Pets
At 52 cents per page, this is a very expensive newsletter! Still, it is thoughtfully composed and contains tested information on natural health care for companion animals. Written by Bob and Susan Goldstein, a holistic veterinarian and an "expert" on animal nutrition and the emotions of dogs and cats, respectively. 8 pages. 1 year (12 issues) for $49.95 (!). (Perhaps you and some friends could go together on a subscription and then share the newsletter. Or, for this price, you could buy Dr. Pitcairn's book and a couple of other books on holistic health for animals.) From: Phillips Publishing, Inc., 7811 Montrose Road, Potomac, MD 20854, (301) 340-2100, FAX: (301) 424-6228.

Muttmatchers Breed Rescue List
See the Rescue & Adoption section, above.

Muttmatchers Messenger
Pet Rescue and Placement Publication
See the Rescue & Adoption section, above.

Natural Pet Magazine
If you can get past the amateurish appearance and production quality of this publication, you'll find some useful information on holistic health care for dogs, cats, horses, birds, etc. 80 pages per issue. Sample issue $5. 1 year (6 issues) for $20/U.S. from: *Natural Pet Magazine*, Pet Publications, Inc., Box 351, Trilby, FL 33593, (352) 583-2770, FAX: (352) 583-4667. Canada: $30 plus GST from: Alive Books Div. of Canadian Health Reform Prod., (604) 435-1919, FAX: (604) 435-4888.

TTEAM News International
A 30-page quarterly journal of news, training techniques, and case studies on the Tellington TTouch for horses, dogs, cats, llamas, or other animals. (See the Companion Animals: Books section for a description of TTouch.) Subscription includes a 10% discount on all books, videos, or other TTEAM purchases. Published and edited by Robyn Hood (Tellington-Jones' sister). 1 year (4 issues) for $25/U.S., $35/Overseas from: TTEAM, P.O. Box 3793, Santa Fe, NM 87501, 1-800-854-TEAM, (505) 455-2945, FAX: (505) 455-7233.

Wolf Clan
"A guardian's guide to holistic health for dogs." These publishers are convinced that a raw meat-based diet for dogs is the only way to go, but don't let that stop you from accessing the other information in this magazine. These folks obviously care deeply about the well-being of dogs. (If you have had success feeding your dog a vegetarian diet, perhaps you could write them a letter, or offer to do an article on vegetarian dogs.) This is a new magazine and has the "down-home" feel of a newsletter. 36 pages. Subscriptions: *Wolf Clan*, 3952 N. Southport Ave., Suite 122, Chicago, IL 60613, (312) 935-1000, FAX: (312) 935-1083. 1 year (6 issues) for $18 (U.S.), $26 (Canada/Mexico), $36 (Overseas).

Entertainment (Performing Animals)

See also the publications listed under Hunting & Wildlife. Additional publications are available from the organizations listed in the Resources section of Chapter 8, "Animals in Entertainment."

Entertainment: *Books*

Behind the Dolphin Smile
by Richard O'Barry with Keith Coulbourn
A former dolphin trainer for the television show "Flipper" describes his work with dolphins and his transition from the exploitive arena of

using dolphins for commercial exploitation into activism on behalf of dolphins. O'Barry now heads the International Dolphin Project in California. 259 pages. Published by Algonquin Books of Chapel Hill, 1989. From your local bookstore or library.

Beyond the Bars: The Zoo Dilemma
Edited by Virginia McKenna, Will Travers, and Jonathan Wray
An informative collection of writings by different authors on zoos, endangered species, and the impact of keeping wild animals in captivity. Photos. Paperback. 208 pages. Borgo Press, 1988. Order through your local bookstore or check with your local library.

Big Lick Walking Horses
by Ms. Maxwell Dickinson
A novel based on documented facts. This book is a prime example of the pervasive "old school" welfare mindset. It does a superb job of exposing the cruelty of a dirty business—mutilating Tennessee Walking Horses to obtain the artificial high-stepping gait known as "The Big Lick"—but it unblinkingly accepts the cruelty inherent in the consumption of animals for food, clothing, and other "sports" (fishing). It's included here because it does a good job of showing the type of personality, culture, and corruption that allows (even condones) violence towards animals. The dog and horse racing industries particularly came to mind. The author is a former owner and exhibitor of Walking Horses, and is the daughter of a founder of the breed, General J.M. Dickinson. The characters in the book are composites of actual people. Rated "R" for sexual content. $11.95 postpaid from: Maxwell Dickinson, P.O. Box 5739, Santa Barbara, CA 93150-5739.

The Case Against Marine Mammals in Captivity
by Naomi A. Rose and Richard Farinato for the Humane Society of the United States
A concise, strong narrative that scientifically refutes claims of marine mammal captivity being harmless. Includes a discussion of "swim with dolphin" programs. Very well done. 46 pages. $3 from HSUS. Specify item GR3197.

The Lady and Her Tiger
"The first exposé of animals in entertainment." The story of Pat Derby, former animal trainer and co-founder of the Performing Animal Welfare Society, a sanctuary for animals rescued or retired from the entertainment industry. $7.50 plus $2.50 shipping from: PAWS, P.O. Box 849, Galt, CA 95632-9979, (916) 393-3340 (Office), (209) 745-2606 (Shelter), FAX: (209) 745-1809.

Marlin Justice
by Eugene D. Wheeler
Despite its shortcomings (a few grammatical errors, and the inclusion of animal and alcohol consumption), I think the pros outweigh the cons. This fictional account doesn't speak against eating animals, but it does crusade against sport fishing (fishing for "fun"). It shows how one person can make a difference, and creates some vivid images of what it might be like if the "tables were turned" and humans were tried for murder by fish. In my opinion, the reading level is young adult, although I think it's intended for adults (as stated, lots of references to social alcohol consumption.) 180 pages. Illustrated. Pathfinder Publishing, 1990. Paperback $9.95 (CA addresses add 7.25% tax) plus $2.75 shipping from: Pathfinder Publishing, 458 Dorothy Avenue, Ventura, CA 93003-1723, (805) 642-9278, FAX: (805) 650-3656, Credit Card Orders: (805) 650-3440.

My Greyhound Friend
by Nora Star
See Children & Young Adults: Books for a description of this book.

Orca—A Family Story
by Peter Hamilton
A fictional account based on the true story of an 18-member orca whale family—including the well-known "Corky"—torn apart for use in the aquarium industry. Historic and scientific facts reveal the "horrors of the live-capture industry." "Proceeds from this book of hope will be used in Lifeforce conservation projects and to distribute the book to public and school libraries." $17.99 from: Lifeforce, Box 210354, San Francisco, CA 94121, (415) 441-3339.

Entertainment: *Guides & Directories*

•***Animal Welfare: List of Licensed Dealers (APHIS 41-35-029)***
•***Animal Welfare: List of Licensed Exhibitors (APHIS 41-35-033)***
These lists show the names and addresses of current animal exhibitors and dealers (by state) registered with or licensed by the federal government. Some of these are "exotic animal" dealers/exhibitors. Free from: U. S. Department

of Agriculture, 6505 Belcrest Road, Room 269AC, Hyattsville, MD 20782.

The Circus Elephant Coloring Book
See Children & Young Adults: Activity Books for a description of this coloring book.

•***The Circus: A New Perspective***
•***Everything You Should Know About Elephants***
The Circus is a booklet detailing the problems with circuses and other traveling shows. Tells you how to organize a peaceful, legal protest, and alternatives to the use of animals as fundraisers. $4 plus $2.50 shipping (covers any size order). *Everything You Should Know About Elephants* contrasts the lives of elephants in the wild with those in captivity. Describes life in circuses and zoos, including disciplinary techniques, stereotypic behaviors, chaining, etc. Also introduces proposed legislation to protect elephants. A revealing look at a cruel industry. $3.50 postpaid. Both publications are available from: Performing Animal Welfare Society, P.O. Box 849, Galt, CA 95632, (916) 393-3340 (Office), (209) 745-2606 (Shelter), FAX: (209) 745-1809.

Entertainment: *Periodicals*

For additional periodicals on entertainment-related issues, check with groups who work against the use of animals in entertainment.

Greyhound Network News
"A quarterly newsletter of general information and state-by-state news items intended to serve as a communications link for the many groups and individuals concerned about the plight of the American racing greyhound." This newsletter is a must for anyone who wants to monitor racing greyhound updates. It is published independently from any specific greyhound group. 8 pages per issue. Subscription is by voluntary donation, which is tax-deductible. From: *Greyhound Network News*, P.O. Box 44272, Phoenix, AZ 85064-4272.

Factory Farming

See also Vegetarianism & Whole Foods. Additional publications are available from the organizations listed in Chapter 5.

Factory Farming: *Books*

Animal Factories
by Jim Mason and Peter Singer
Examines the consequences of intensive confinement methods of factory farming. Many photos. This is the updated version of the popular 1980 edition. Highly recommended. Paperback. 240 pages. Crown Publishers, Inc. $12.95 from AAVS. Specify item 7-B.

Beyond Beef: The Rise and Fall of the Cattle Culture
by Jeremy Rifkin
A fascinating look at humanity's perceptions of cattle and the influence of the cattle industry in western civilization. Provides not only insightful background information regarding how the present cattle industry evolved, but also examines the ramifications of this industry on the earth and its inhabitants. 353 pages. Dutton (The Penguin Group), 1992. $11 ($9.90 members) from EarthSave.

Diet for a New America: How Your Food Choices Affect Your Health, Happiness, and the Future of Life on Earth
by John Robbins
A "must read" Pulitzer Prize-nominated book that addresses the disease, poison, and suffering inherent in animal food products today. This is *the* book that prompted me to take the final step to change my carnivorous habits—and my life. Thoroughly researched and footnoted with an easy reading style. This book does not preach, it just presents the facts. Written by a former heir to the Baskin-Robbins ice cream empire turned vegan. Everyone should read this book. Paperback. 423 pages. Stillpoint Publishing. $13.95 ($12.55 members) from EarthSave. Discounts on 2 or more.

Pulling the Wool: A New Look at the Australian Wool Industry
by Christine Townsend
For anyone who has ever needed to answer the question, "But what's wrong with wearing wool?" From the preface: "Although this book is about the mistreatment and abuse of livestock in Australia, it is also about much more than that...The history of Australia's pastoral development involves not only exploitation of animals, but of humans as well." 157 pages. Photos. Hale & Iremonger (Australia). Order through your local bookstore or check with your library.

Factory Farming: *Booklets & Handouts*

Additional booklets and handouts are available from organizations that work against factory farming (see the Resources section of Chapter 5, "Factory Farms.").

Realities for the 90's
134 statistics and facts excerpted from the Pulitzer Prize-nominated book *Diet For a New America* by John Robbins, the founder of EarthSave. 16 pages. $1 postpaid (90 cents members) from EarthSave. Discounts on 10 or more.

Factory Farming: *Periodicals*

Check with groups who work against factory farming for newsletters that update members on current factory farming issues.

Hunting & Wildlife

See also the publications listed under Entertainment. Additional publications are available from the organizations listed in the Resources section of Chapter 7, "Wildlife in Crisis."

Hunting & Wildlife: *Books*

The American Hunting Myth
by Ron Baker, Committee to Abolish Sport Hunting
Exposes the truth behind hunting and the state and federal agencies that perpetuate the "sport." A must-read for anyone who wants to be able to stand his/her ground in discussions with hunters. Hardbound. 287 pages. Vantage Press. Autographed copies are $14.95 plus $2.50 shipping from: The Committee to Abolish Sport Hunting, P.O. Box 44, Tomkins Cove, NY 10986, (914) 429-8733, FAX: (914) 429-1545.

Animals in Peril: How "Sustainable Use" is Wiping Out the World's Wildlife
Edited by John A. Hoyt, Chief Executive, Humane Society of the United States
The inside story of the widely-used animal "mismanagement" technique called "sustainable use," which has devastated populations of endangered species. Includes background, case studies, poaching, the role of the U.S. and the World Bank, ecotourism as a partial solution, and more. 257 pages. Avery Publishing Group, 1994. $6.95 from HSUS. Specify item GR3220.

Balancing on the Brink of Extinction
Edited by Kathryn A. Kohm
A collection of essays on the Endangered Species Act. A good resource for those interested in the Act and its effectiveness or ineffectiveness. 315 pages. Island Press. Available from your local bookstore or library.

The Bowhunting Alternative
by Adrian Benke
This is by a bowhunter for bowhunters. It does not argue against bowhunting, but rather argues in favor of using a poison called succomy-choline chloride (SCC) on the tips of arrows, thereby guaranteeing a more timely death for wounded animals. This book will acquaint those unfamiliar with bowhunting with this barbaric activity and it points out many of the inherent failings of bowhunting. Some disturbing photos of wounded animals. Not for everyone. Paperback. 110 pages. B. Todd Press, 1989. $7.95 from bookstores or $9.50 postpaid from the publisher: B. Todd Press, 8480 Fredericksburg Road, #350, San Antonio, TX 78229.

Earth Warrior: Overboard with Paul Watson and the Sea Shepherd Conservation Society
by David B. Morris
A non-glamorized, behind-the-scenes look at a Sea Shepherd campaign as reported by an outsider who accompanied the crew on a 3-week mission to stop illegal driftnetters in the Pacific Ocean. An adventure story that chronicles events, personalities, and personal feelings. Photos. Published by Fulcrum Publishing, 1995. 212 pages. Photos. $14.95 from bookstores or check with your local library.

Jaws of Steel
by Thomas Eveland
Written by a former trapper who came to see that so-called "wildlife management" practices were based on nothing more than politics and economics, rather than on scientific facts. This book refutes the arguments set forth by trappers to condone trapping, including disease control,

population control, predator control, etc. Diagrams, but no photos of trapped animals. An easy reading style. 160 pages. Published by The Fund for Animals, Inc., 1991. $3 plus $1.50 shipping from: The Fund for Animals, ATTN: Merchandise Dept., 850 Sligo Avenue, Suite 300, Silver Spring, MD 20910, (301) 585-2591.

Marlin Justice
by Eugene D. Wheeler

See Entertainment: Books for a description of this book.

Waste of the West: Public Lands Ranching
by (Mr.) Lynn Jacobs

In the words of John Robbins: "...an extraordinarily important work. It is a thorough and poignant description of the destruction of an entire ecosystem by a single industry. Not only does it show us who and what is doing the damage, it shows us the way to restoration." Paperback. 602 pages (8-1/2" by 11"). Heavily illustrated with photos and drawings. Signed copies for $28 postpaid from: Lynn Jacobs, P.O. Box 5784, Tucson, AZ 85703, (602) 578-3173.

Wildlife Poaching
by Laura Offenhartz Greene

Not a pro-animal book (doesn't speak against legal hunting), but a decent discussion of the consequences of illegal hunting ("poaching") in North America, Africa, and Asia. A "conservation" viewpoint. 142 pages. Hardcover. Published by Franklin Watts, 1994. $19.95 from bookstores or check with your local library.

Hunting & Wildlife: *Guides & Directories*

Living with Wildlife: How to Enjoy, Cope with, and Protect North America's Wild Creatures Around Your Home and Theirs
by The California Center for Wildlife with Diana Landau and Shelley Stump

Discusses the range, habitat, enemies, defenses, and other characteristics of a wide variety of wildlife, as well as possible problematic human-wildlife situations and solutions. Includes tips for living with backyard wildlife and "wildlife-proofing" your home and garden. Covers a comprehensive list of animals, including small land mammals, rodents, large carnivores, ungulates, marine mammals, birds, reptiles, and amphibians. Includes a list of state wildlife agencies and some local wildlife centers. Illustrated. 341 pages. Sierra Club Books, 1994. $15 plus $3 shipping from: Sierra Club Store, 730 Polk St., San Francisco, CA 94109, 1-800-935-1056.

Pocket Guide to the Humane Control of Wildlife in Cities and Towns
Edited by Guy R. Hodge

A guide to humanely coexisting with wildlife, from armadillos to woodpeckers. Gives background information on each species and suggests humane deterrents. Includes a list of companies that sell wildlife control products, including cage traps, electronic alarms, pyrotechnic devices, recorded alarm or distress calls, flashing lights, and various barriers. Paperback. 112 pages (4-1/4" by 7-1/2"). $6.95 from bookstores or $4.95 plus $3 shipping (and appropriate state tax) from HSUS. Specify item GR3141.

Think Like the Animal: Questions to Ask Before You Kill

A booklet aimed at potential young sport hunters. From: The Fund for Animals, ATTN: Merchandise Dept., 850 Sligo Avenue, Suite 300, Silver Spring, MD 20910, (301) 585-2591. Also available: wallet-sized "Young Person's Pledge to Respect Wildlife" card.

Hunting & Wildlife: *Periodicals*

Also check with anti-hunting groups for newsletters that update members on hunting, trapping, and other wildlife issues.

Wildlife Rehabilitation Today

This little (8-1/2" by 5-1/2") magazine is for people who care *for* as well as *about* wildlife. Specializes in coverage of wildlife rehabilitation. "Provides important information through concise articles in layman's terms." (*Note*: Beware the inevitable "live food" ads of crickets, mice, etc.) 64 pages. Subscriptions: Coconut Creek Publishing Co., 2201 NW 40th Terrace, Coconut Creek, FL 33066-2032, (305) 972-6092. 1 year (4 issues) for $15.

Hunting & Wildlife: *Special Reports*

Animal Damage Control: How Your Tax Dollars Subsidize Agri-Business by Killing and Harassing America's Wildlife

by Ben D. Deeble and Felice Stadler, Environmental Clinic Program, University of Montana, Missoula for Predator Project

A guide for understanding the funding of the federal Animal Damage Control program and those areas in the appropriations processes where citizens have an opportunity to influence the budget. December 1993. 72 pages. Illustrated. $10 postpaid from: Predator Project, P.O. Box 64733, Bozeman, MT 59771, (406) 587-3389 (voice/FAX).

Waste, Fraud, and Abuse in the U. S. Animal Damage Control Program

by Pat Wolff for Wildlife Damage Review

Documents evidence to support the view of Wildlife Damage Review that the federal Animal Damage Control program should be abolished. 31 pages. Photos. $10 postpaid from: Wildlife Damage Review, P.O. Box 85218, Tucson, AZ 85754, (602) 884-0883. (A reference packet containing copies of studies, news articles, and other documents referred to in the report can be obtained for $25 from New West Research, P.O. Box 401, Santa Fe, NM 87504.)

Interspecies Communication

These publications are devoted to telepathic communication between humans and other species. While many people are skeptical when it comes to telepathic communication, animals don't seem to have any problem whatsoever with the practice! Many people use telepathic communication effectively to relay messages to and receive messages from nonhuman species, as well as to "see" into animals' bodies and emotional states. It can be very helpful in problem-solving and understanding behaviors, emotions, and physical conditions.

See also the Audio Tapes & CDs section of Chapter 12 for more on interspecies communication.

Interspecies Communication: *Books*

Animals: Our Return to Wholeness

by Penelope Smith

Full of firsthand accounts of communication between human and nonhuman animals, this book covers a plethora of subjects, including: who animals really are, how to develop telepathic communication with animals, living with animals, animals as guides and healers, reincarnation, and communicating with nature spirits. Paperback. 355 pages. Illustrations/ photos. 1993. $19.95 (CA addresses add 7.25% tax) plus $2.50 shipping from: Pegasus Publications, P.O. Box 1060, Point Reyes, CA 94956, (415) 663-1247, Orders: 1-800-356-9315, FAX: 1-800-242-0036.

Animal Talk: Interspecies Telepathic Communication

by Penelope Smith

A "how-to" book for those who want to develop their mind-to-mind connection with animals. Includes other useful information on human-nonhuman interactions. Paperback. 100 pages. $8.95 (CA addresses add 7.25% tax) plus $2.50 shipping from: Pegasus Publications, P.O. Box 1060, Point Reyes, CA 94956, (415) 663-1247, Orders: 1-800-356-9315, FAX: 1-800-242-0036.

Kinship With All Life

by J. Allen Boone

A personal account of one man's experience with the silent communication that can exist between animals and humans. An interesting, inspiring, and very special glimpse into the worlds of animals. Paperback. 157 pages. Harper and Row. $.8.95 postpaid from the American Vegan Society.

Talking with Nature

by Michael J. Roads

From the cover: "Michael Roads had always been close to nature, but one day when a river started talking to him, he began to doubt his sanity...After reading this book, you will never again wonder if nature can speak. It can and does..." A profound, firsthand experience of the intelligence that is the essence of all being, and the ignorance and arrogance that keep most of humankind from knowing this truth. In response to the question, "Why does man kill such beauty for so little gain?" a kangaroo replies, "Our pain is the sickness of man. This will only end when man heals himself. He is sick, for he has no knowing of himself or the part he plays in life. Man stands alone—and very afraid." Highly recommended. 154 pages. H.J. Kramer, Inc., 1987. $9.95 from bookstores or check with your local library.

Interspecies Communication: *Periodicals*

Species Link: The Journal of Interspecies Telepathic Communication

Written by and for interspecies telepathic communicators, this newsletter provides a forum "to share experiences, helpful hints, insights, humor, the joy of deep understanding and heightened awareness with all beings." Includes a brief list of interspecies telepathic communicators. 24 pages. 1 year (4 issues) for $20, single copies for $6 from: Pegasus Publications, P.O. Box 1060, Point Reyes, CA 94956, (415) 663-1247, Orders: 1-800-356-9315, FAX: 1-800-242-0036.

Research, Education, & Product Testing

See also the publications listed under Activism for information on laws, conducting investigations, and facilities that use animals. For sources of cruelty-free products (products not tested on animals), see the Cruelty-Free Home, Beauty, and Personal Care Products section of Chapter 12.

Research, Education, & Product Testing: *Books*

Books on dissection are listed apart from the other books for easy reference.

Dissection & Student Rights

Also see the Guides & Directories section for catalogs of alternatives to dissection.

Animals in Education: The Facts, Issues, and Implications

by Lisa Ann Hepner

A guide for empowering high school and college-level students and teachers who wish to implement alternatives to dissection into the classroom. Written by a biology graduate who successfully implemented alternatives to dissection on a wide scale at the University of New Mexico. Includes the author's firsthand experience, as well as facts and considerations about dissection and alternatives to dissection. Paperback. 303 pages. $12.95 plus $2 shipping from: Richmond Publishers, P.O. Box 91683, Albuquerque, NM 87199-1683.

Vivisection and Dissection in the Classroom: A Guide to Conscientious Objection

by Professor Gary Francione and Anna Charlton

Provides the legal basis for conscientious objection to dissection. Written by two attorneys. Includes sample wording for letters students may have to write to teachers and suggested strategies for defending your rights. 136 pages. 1992. Published by and available for $6.95 from AAVS. Specify item 3-B.

Vivisection

1000 Doctors (and Many More) Against Vivisection

Compiled by Hans Ruesch

A collection of expert testimonies on vivisection from a variety of medical doctors through the years 1824 to 1989. Paperback. 280 pages. Published by and available for $19.95 (an additional donation for postage appreciated) from: CIVIS, P.O. Box 491, Hartsdale, NY, 10530, (607) 545-6213.

The Cruel Deception: The Use of Animals in Medical Research

by Dr. Robert Sharpe

A convincing argument against the use of animals in medical research from both an ethical and scientific perspective. Contains many facts that speak for themselves regarding the unreliability of using animals as research subjects. Paperback. 228 pages. Thorsons Publishers Limited. $12 (members subtract 10%) from the National Anti-Vivisection Society.

Monkey Business: The Disturbing Case That Launched the Animal Rights Movement

by Kathy Snow Guillermo, Education Coordinator, People for the Ethical Treatment of Animals

The true saga of the now famous "Silver Spring Monkeys," seized from researcher Edward Taub, who became the first researcher criminally prosecuted for animal cruelty. This is the decade-long story of the undercover investigation and subsequent actions by People for the Ethical Treatment of Animals (PETA), which exposed Taub, pursued his conviction, and attempted to gain sanctuary for the primates. Foreword by Oliver Stone. Hardbound. 254 pages. Photos. National Press Books, Inc., 1993. $23.95 from bookstores or check with your local library.

The Monkey Wars

by Deborah Blum

Explores the battle between animal advocates and animal researchers over the use of primates. The author, who is a science journalist, won a Pulitzer Prize in 1992 for a series of articles about this subject. Considered to be an objective perspective, free of rhetoric. 306 pages. Oxford University Press, 1994. $15 (members subtract 10%) from the National Anti-Vivisection Society.

Slaughter of the Innocent

by Hans Ruesch

The first book to expose the scientific fraud of vivisection. Answers the who, what, and why of vivisection and its dangers to human health. Paperback. 446 pages. Published by and available for $4.95 (an additional donation for postage appreciated) from: CIVIS, P.O. Box 491, Hartsdale, NY, 10530, (607) 545-6213.

Stolen for Profit

by Judith Reitman

The shocking, must-read story of the pet theft industry and how animal researchers and the USDA support this lucrative criminal network. This is a powerful, disturbing book that will move you to tears and enrage you. Written like a novel, but true to fact. Everyone who shares their home with a dog or cat should read this! 307 pages. Photos. Kensington Books, 1995 (second edition). Paperback version $12 from bookstores or check with your local library.

Superpigs and Wondercorn: The Brave New Worlds of Biotechnology...And Where It All May Lead

by Dr. Michael W. Fox, Vice President, The Humane Society of the United States

An exploration of biogenetics—the manipulation of genes to produce new life forms or "improve on" existing life—and its implications. This is indeed a science-fiction-come-to-life topic with very frightening possibilities. Like atomic power, this may well be another example of technology existing outside of the moral and ethical environment needed to use it wisely. 209 pages. Lyons & Burford, 1992. $19.95 from AAVS. Specify item 8-B.

Research, Education, & Product Testing: *Guides & Directories*

See also the cruelty-free shopping guides in the Cruelty-Free Home, Beauty, and Personal Care Products section of Chapter 12.

101 Non-Animal Biology Lab Methods

Contains over 100 non-animal biology lab alternatives. Includes sources and prices. $2 postpaid (discounts on quantities) from: Student Action Corps for Animals, P.O. Box 15588, Washington, D.C. 20003-0588, (202) 543-8983.

Alternatives in Medical Education

Describes some of the alternatives currently available for training medical doctors. Includes sources and prices. Free from: Physicians Committee for Responsible Medicine, P.O. Box 6322, Washington, D.C. 20015, (202) 686-2210.

Alternatives to the Harmful Use of Nonhuman Animals in Veterinary Medical Education

Compiled by Eric Dunayer, DVM

A 37-page booklet listing and describing dozens of alternatives for physiology, pharmacology, toxicology, surgery, anesthesia, and other veterinary courses. Includes sources and prices. $3 postpaid from AVAR.

- ***Animal Welfare: List of Licensed Dealers (APHIS 41-35-029)***
- ***Animal Welfare: List of Registered Research Facilities (APHIS 41-35-030)***
- ***Animal Welfare: List of Registered Carriers and Intermediate Handlers (APHIS 41-35-0332)***

These lists show the names and addresses of current animal dealers, transporters, and research facilities (by state) registered with or licensed by the federal government. These lists will help you know who is doing what in your area and elsewhere. Free from: U.S. Dept. of Agriculture, 6505 Belcrest Road, Room 269AC, Hyattsville, MD 20782.

The Argument for Abolition
by Steven Tiger, PA-C (Physician Assistant-Certified)
Summarizes the humane, ethical, and scientific arguments for the abolition of vivisection. 50 cents plus $1 shipping (covers up to $2.50 in purchases) from ISAR.

Beyond Dissection: Innovative Teaching Tools for Biology Education
A 63-page catalog of nearly 400 products for the study of whole animal dissections, human anatomy, comparative anatomy, organ or system anatomy/physiology, biotechnology, embryology, and genetics. For elementary through college levels. March 1995. Newsprint. 11" by 14". Illustrated. $2 postpaid (check payable to NEAVS) from: Ethical Science Education Coalition, 167 Milk Street, #423, Boston, MA 02109-4315, (617) 367-9143 or (203) 872-8877.

A Critique of the American Medical Association's White Paper: Use of Animals in Biomedical Research, The Challenge and Response
by Dean Smith
An excellent response to the "White Paper" published by the American Medical Association in 1989 and again in 1992. The White Paper argues in favor of the use of animals in research and against animal rights efforts to counter vivisection. Responds to direct quotes from the AMA document. 18 pages. $3 postpaid from AAVS. (To obtain a copy of the White Paper, request the document titled "Use of Animals in Biomedical Research: The Challenge and Response" from The American Medical Association, ATTN: Department of Science & Medical Education, 515 North State Street, Chicago, IL 60610.)

Replacing School Hatching Projects: Alternative Resources & How to Order Them
Humane alternatives to hatching projects for educators. 11 pages. $3.50 postpaid from UPC.

Point/Counterpoint: Responses to Typical Pro-Vivisection Arguments
Presents the realities behind ten common myths about vivisection. 25 cents each (minimum order $2) plus $1 shipping from AAVS. Specify item 2-BR.

Research, Education, & Product Testing: *Periodicals*

Also check with anti-vivisection groups for newsletters that update members on issues related to animals used in research, education, and product testing.

Beauty Without Cruelty USA
For $15, you receive an annual membership in the organization Beauty Without Cruelty and information on sources of cruelty-free products which is updated three times a year. Subscriptions: BWC, 175 West 12th Street, Suite 16G, New York, NY 10011, (212) 989-8073.

Vegetarianism & Whole Foods

See also the publications listed under Factory Farming. Contact the national and international vegetarian organizations listed in Chapter 11 for additional books, periodicals, and other publications.

Vegetarianism & Whole Foods: *Books*

For cookbooks, see the separate list of recipes and cookbooks later in this section. Also see the Children & Young Adults: Books section for children's books about vegetarianism.

Beyond Beef: The Rise and Fall of the Cattle Culture
by Jeremy Rifkin
See Factory Farming: Books for a description of this book.

Diet for a New America: How Your Food Choices Affect Your Health, Happiness, and the Future of Life on Earth
by John Robbins
See Factory Farming: Books for a description of this book.

Dr. Dean Ornish's Program for Reversing Heart Disease
by Dean Ornish, M.D.
"The only system scientifically proven to reverse heart disease without drugs or surgery." Includes diet (including recipes), exercise, how to quit smoking, and less commonly addressed topics such as opening your heart to others and to a higher self. In the author's words, "This is a book about healing your heart: physically, emotionally, and spiritually." Illustrated. 631 pages. Random House, 1990. $14.95 postpaid from the American Vegan Society.

Food for Life: How the New Four Food Groups Can Save Your Life
by Neal D. Barnard, M.D., recipes and menus by Jennifer Raymond
Presents a system of eating that addresses some of today's most pressing general health concerns—aging, heart disease, cancer, weight control, and others. Includes menus and recipes for 21 days. 334 pages. Harmony Books, 1993. $13 from PCRM Marketplace.

Good Food Today, Great Kids Tomorrow
by Jay Gordon, M.D.
A pediatrician with special training in nutrition tells you "50 things you can do for healthy, happy children" by providing them with a whole foods, vegan diet. 212 pages. $17.95 postpaid from the American Vegan Society.

May All Be Fed: Diet for a New World
by John Robbins, recipes by Jia Patton and friends
Sequel to the landmark *Diet for a New America.* From the Introduction: "*May All Be Fed* exposes the commercially motivated programming that has shaped and continues to shape much of the prevailing food consciousness in our society...[It] exposes some of the forces at work in our world that cause the affluent to be burdened with unnecessary disease, and also cause poorer people to be deprived of the right to ample and wholesome food." Includes 175 vegan recipes. Illustrated. 415 pages. Avon Books, 1992. $12 ($10.80 members) from EarthSave.

The McDougall Program: 12 Days to Dynamic Health
by John A. McDougall, M.D., recipes by Mary McDougall
A nationally renowned, medically-sound, low-fat, starch-based diet and exercise plan that will help you lose weight, lower your cholesterol and blood pressure, and reverse serious illness. Discusses the McDougall program versus standard treatments for a variety of medical conditions, from acne to cancer to multiple sclerosis. By the authors of *The McDougall Plan* and other books. Includes 130 recipes. Paperback. 436 pages. Nal Books (The Penguin Group), 1990. $12 (members subtract 10%) from the North American Vegetarian Society. Or for further information, contact: The McDougalls, P.O. Box 14039, Santa Rosa, CA 95402, (707) 576-1654.

Pregnancy, Children, and the Vegan Diet
by Michael Klaper, M.D.
Information and advice on a diet free of animal flesh, dairy, and other animal products for pregnant or nursing women and children. Includes testimonies from vegan parents, meal suggestions, and recipes. Photos/illustrations. Paperback. 109 pages. Published by and available for $9.95 plus $3 shipping from: Gentle World, Inc., P.O. Box U, Paia, Maui, HI 96779, (808) 572-3522.

The Power of Your Plate
by Neal D. Barnard, M.D.
A portion of the proceeds from this book goes to support the work of Physicians Committee for Responsible Medicine (PCRM). Examines the role of nutrition in health and illness. Includes information on weight control, preventing heart problems and cancer, the role of foods in mental acuity and other brain functions, and the evolution of the human diet. Written for the lay person. Tips on making diet changes easy and fun. Includes recipes. "The book for people who care about healthful eating. For skeptics. Or for people who just want to try new and delicious foods." Paperback. 240 pages. Book Publishing Company. $12.95 from PCRM Marketplace.

The Sexual Politics of Meat: A Feminist-Vegetarian Critical Theory
by Carol J. Adams
See Animals, Rights, & Ethics: Books for a description of this book.

Vegetarian Baby: A Sensible Guide for Parents
by Sharon Yntema, illustrated by Tom Parker
By the mother of a vegetarian baby. Topics include nutrition, food preparation, recipes, vegetarian child-rearing in other cultures, pregnancy and lactation, and more. Illustrated. 224 pages. McBook Press, 1980. $10.95 from PCRM Marketplace.

Vegetarian Children
by Sharon Yntema
From the introduction: "Raising a child on a health vegetarian diet is one of the most concrete actions of love a parent can make." Topics include child development, your child's health, moral development and social responsibility, and more. Includes comments and advice from parents of vegetarian children. Covers infants through the school-age years. 169 pages. McBook Press. $8.95 from PCRM Marketplace.

Vegetarian Dogs and Cats
by James A. Peden
See Companion Animals: Books for a description of this book.

A Vegetarian Sourcebook: The Nutrition, Ecology, and Ethics of a Natural Foods Diet
by Keith Akers
Examines the nutritional, ecological, and ethical aspects of a vegetarian diet. Includes a discussion of vegetarianism from the perspective of different religions and philosophers, and an extensive list of vegetarian cookbooks and books on vegetarianism. Vegetarian Press, 1989. Paperback. 240 pages. $11.45 postpaid (Denver and Colorado addresses add tax) from: Vegetarian Press, P.O. Box 61273, Denver, CO 80206.

What's Wrong with Eating Meat?
by Vistara Parham, illustrated by Andrea Carmen
A pocket-sized book that presents historical, health, and political reasons for becoming vegetarian. Includes facts supporting the design of the human body for a vegetarian diet, the dangers of eating meat, meat consumption and world starvation, a list of famous vegetarians, and more. Friendly, easy reading in a pleasant format. $3.50 from the American Vegan Society.

Vegetarianism & Whole Foods: *Booklets & Handouts*

101 Reasons Why I'm a Vegetarian
A flyer containing—you guessed it—101 facts obtained from a variety of sources. $1 plus a self-addressed, stamped envelope (50 cents for additional copies; $20 for 50) from: The VivaVeggie Society, Prince Street Station, P.O. Box 294, New York, NY 10012.

Don't Plants Have Feelings Too?: Responding Effectively to 13 Frequently Asked Questions About Food, Fiber, Farm Animals, and the Ethics of Diet
Answers for questions such as, "What will we do with all the animals if we stop eating them?" and "Why concentrate on animals when so many suffering people need help?" 6 pages. Free for a long self-addressed, stamped envelope from UPC.

Good Eating: The Vegetarian Alternative
by Walter Simpson and Nan Lampka Simpson, RN
Questions and answers about vegetarianism in an easy-to-read style. A nice booklet for introducing someone, including yourself, to the ethical reasons for a vegetarian lifestyle. 16 pages (sized to fit in an envelope). 50 cents plus a long self-addressed, stamped envelope from: Walter and Nan Simpson, P.O. Box 43, Amherst, NY, 14226.

Our Food Our World: Realities of an Animal-Based Diet
Fully footnoted statistics and facts exposing the connections between our personal food choices and global issues, including resources, health, the environment, and the future of the farmer. 22 pages. $2.50 ($2.25 members) from EarthSave. Discounts on 10 or more.

Realities for the 90's
See Factory Farming: Booklets for a description of this publication.

The Vegetarian's Self-Defense Manual
The scientific basis for vegetarianism. Includes discussions of pregnancy, vegetarian kids, protein, vitamin B-12, and more. $6 postpaid from VRG.

Vegetarian Starter Kit
"The whys and hows of a healthier diet." Topics include protein, calcium, children, pregnancy, the new four food groups, recipes, reading list, and more. 16 pages. $2 from PCRM Marketplace.

Vegetarianism & Whole Foods: *Cookbooks*

There are literally hundreds of vegan/ vegetarian cookbooks to chose from today! I've listed some favorites and some "specialty" books here. To see more of what's out there, visit a large bookstore or request booklists from the national and international groups listed in Chapter 11. For quantity recipes (for 25-100 people), see the Vegetarian Supplies & Services: School Lunches & Quantity Recipes section of Chapter 12.

Free vegetarian recipe cards from People for the Ethical Treatment of Animals

Send a long self-addressed, stamped envelope to: Recipe Cards, PETA, 501 Front Street, Norfolk, VA 23501.

The American Vegetarian Cookbook from the Fit for Life Kitchen

by Marilyn Diamond

This over-sized book contains information on healthful eating habits as well as over 500 meat-free, dairy-free recipes. New twists on old favorites help make this book extra special. For example, there are recipes for quiche and crepes (without dairy), "fish" and "chicken" fillets (without meat), and "cheese" sauce (without cheese). From the co-author of *Fit for Life*. Hardbound. 422 pages. Warner Books, Inc. $26.95 from the North American Vegetarian Society.

The Cookbook for People Who Love Animals

Meat-free, dairy-free recipes for people, and also for cats and dogs. Includes a glossary of ingredients and a discussion of vegan philosophy. Paperback. 192 pages. $9.95 plus $3 shipping from: Gentle World, Inc., P.O. Box U, Paia, Maui, HI 96779, (808) 672-3522.

Delights of the Garden: Vegetarian Cuisine Prepared without Heat from Delights of the Garden Restaurants

by Imar Hutchins

A "no cook" cookbook with over 100 recipes served in Delights of the Garden restaurants (currently open in Atlanta and Washington, D.C., and soon to offer franchises). From appetizers, soups, and salads through entrees and desserts. Includes a food nutrient index, a vitamin and mineral index (including food sources, function, therapeutic uses, and depletors), a discussion of what's wrong with meat and dairy, and more. Eye-catching, contemporary style. Published by Main Street Books (Doubleday), 1996. 212 pages. $15.95 from bookstores or order through BookMasters at 1-800-247-6553.

Dr. Dean Ornish's Program for Reversing Heart Disease

by Dean Ornish, M.D.

See Vegetarianism & Whole Foods: Books for a description of this book.

Ecological Cooking: Recipes to Save the Planet

by Joanne Stepaniak and Kathy Hecker

More than 500 vegan recipes, from dips to desserts. 228 pages. $10.95 postpaid from the American Vegan Society.

Food for Life: How the New Four Food Groups Can Save Your Life

by Neal D. Barnard, M.D., recipes and menus by Jennifer Raymond

See Vegetarianism & Whole Foods: Books for a description of this book.

Good Time Eatin' in Cajun Country: Cajun Vegetarian Cooking

by Donna Simon

Vegetarian versions of favorite Cajun recipes, from breakfast through dessert. Includes mail-order sources for ingredients. The author is of Cajun-French descent. Vegan, except for a few recipes that call for honey (vegans can simply substitute a non-animal sweetener). 107 pages. Book Publishing Company, 1995. $9.95 (members $8.96) from the North American Vegetarian Society.

Instead of Chicken, Instead of Turkey: A Poultryless "Poultry" Potpourri

By Karen Davis

Over 100 "egg- and dairy-free vegetarian recipes that duplicate and convert traditional poultry and egg dishes to satisfy the taste buds without destroying the birds." In addition to the usual fare, includes grilled dishes and holiday menus. Vegan, except for a few recipes that call for honey (vegans can simply substitute a non-animal sweetener). Paperback. 159 pages. Book Publishing Company. $11.95 postpaid from UPC.

Leprechaun Cake and Other Tales

See Children & Young Adults: Books for a description of this book.

May All Be Fed: Diet for a New World

by John Robbins, recipes by Jia Patton and friends

See Vegetarianism & Whole Foods: Books for a description of this book.

The New McDougall Cookbook
by John A. McDougall, M.D. and Mary McDougall
300 low-fat recipes from the authors of *The McDougall Program: 12 Days to Dynamic Health* (see Vegetarianism & Whole Foods: Books). Includes helpful tips for "making the change," such as how to handle resistance from friends and family. Also includes a list of name brand packaged food products for healthy living. 405 pages. Dutton (The Penguin Group), 1993. $24 (members subtract 10%) from the North American Vegetarian Society.

Simply Vegan: Quick Vegetarian Meals
by Debra Wasserman, Nutrition section by Reed Mangels, PhD, RD
This book contains vegan recipes, including a separate section for soy products, but its real strength is the nutritional information. It talks about protein, fat, calcium, iron, zinc, vitamin D, riboflavin, B-6, and B-12, including food sources for these nutrients. Also includes sections on pregnancy, vegan kids, sources for cruelty-free products, and a bibliography. 224 pages. Published by The Vegetarian Resource Group, 1995 (second edition). $13 postpaid from VRG.

A Teen's Guide to Going Vegetarian
See Children & Young Adults: Books for a description of this book.

The Uncheese Cookbook
by Joanne Stepaniak
Innovative recipes for creating dairy-free (vegan) cheese substitutes (from "Gee Whiz Spread" to "Betta Feta"). Also recipes for uncheese soups, pestos, dips, breads, main dishes, and desserts. 191 pages. Book Publishing Company, 1994. $11.95 postpaid from the American Vegan Society.

The Vegetarian No-Cholesterol Barbecue Cookbook
by Kate Schumann and Virginia Messina, M.P.H., R.D.
No need to miss out on backyard barbecues just because you're a vegetarian. Includes recipes for grilling and other dishes to complete the picnic. 116 pages. $9.95 postpaid from the American Vegan Society.

Vegetarianism & Whole Foods: *Guides & Directories*

Bay Area Vegetarian
by The Vegetarian Foundation
A comprehensive guide to vegetarian resources in the San Francisco Bay Area and Northern California. Includes catering, restaurants, markets, cooking instruction, etc., as well as recipes and articles on health and nutrition, good food, ecology, and ethics. Published annually. $5 from: The Vegetarian Foundation, P.O. Box 9470, Stanford, CA 94309.

Canadian Vegetarian Dining Guide
by Lynne Tomlinson
"Your passport to healthy eating in Canada." $9.95 (members subtract 10%) from the North American Vegetarian Society.

Catalogue of Worldwide Vegetarian and Vegan Vacation Spots
$2 postpaid from: Environmental Travel, Inc., 119-66 80th Road, Kew Gardens, NY 11415, Outside NYC: 1-800-929-3005, Inside NYC: (718) 263-0048, FAX: 1-800-580-8630.

Colorado Vegetarian Dining
A restaurant guide to vegetarian dining around Colorado. From: Vegetarian Society of Colorado, State Headquarters, P.O. Box 6773, Denver, CO 80206, (303) 777-4828.

Cruelty-Free Guide to London
Restaurants and more. 246 pages. $8.50 postpaid from the American Vegan Society.

A directory of vegetarian dietetic professionals
From: Vegetarian Dietitians and Nutrition Educators, c/o George Eisman, 3835 St. Rt. 414, Burdett, NY 14818, (607) 546-2751.

Guide for Local Vegetarian Groups
Keith Akers, Editor
See Activism: Guides & Directories for a description of this book.

Transformative Adventures, Vacations, & Retreats
by John Benson
A directory of resorts, spas, etc. for those seeking "personal growth" vacations. Indicates which sites accommodate vegetarians/vegans. Clear and complete information. Nicely done. Published by New Millennium Publishing, 1993. 300 pages. $14.95 plus $3.50 shipping ($4 Canada) payable to: New Millennium

Publishing, P.O. Box 3065, Portland, OR 97208.

The Healthy School Lunch Action Guide
by Susan Campbell and Todd Winant
Provides everything you need to coordinate a healthy meal program in your local schools. Contains over 60 low-fat, cholesterol-free recipes for volume cooking, resources for food service training and healthy food suppliers, the structure and politics of the federal government's food program, advice on how to approach individuals and give a presentation, and a resource list of books, organizations, and curriculum. 180 pages. $19.95 ($17.95 members) from EarthSave.

Restaurants Serving Vegetarian and Vegan Food in California
$7.25 postpaid from: Web of Life, P.O. Box 2124, Orange, CA 92669.

Restaurants Serving Vegetarian and Vegan Food in Southern California
$6 postpaid from: Web of Life, P.O. Box 2124, Orange, CA 92669.

Vegan Guide to Amsterdam
36 pages, stapled. $6 postpaid from the American Vegan Society.

Vegan Guide to New York City
by Max Friedman and Dan Mills
Includes sources for vegan food, including restaurants, grocers, etc. $4 (members subtract 10%) from the North American Vegetarian Society.

Vegan Guide to Paris
by Alex Bourke
A vegan shopping guide. 32 pages. $6 from the American Vegan Society.

Vegetarian Asia: A Travel Guide
by Teresa Bergen
Includes food customs and other tips for those traveling in Asia. $9.95 (members subtract 10%) from the North American Vegetarian Society.

Vegetarian Dining Guide for Albuquerque
A list of restaurants and food stores that accommodate vegetarians in the Albuquerque area. (They don't request this, but you can save them funds if you send a long self-addressed, stamped envelope which they can use to send the dining guide to you.) From: Sangre de Cristo Animal Protection, Inc., P.O. Box 5179, Albuquerque, NM 87185, (505) 265-1961.

Vegetarian Dining Guide—Southern New Jersey and Greater Philadelphia
by the Vegetarian Society of South Jersey
A leaflet available for 10 cents plus $1 shipping from the American Vegan Society, or contact the Vegetarian Society of South Jersey, P.O. Box 272, Marlton, NJ 08053, (609) 354-0909.

Vegetarian Dining L.A. Style
by Marla Friedler
A guide to vegetarian restaurants and other restaurants that serve vegetarian food in Los Angeles, the San Fernando Valley, San Gabriel Valley, Orange County, San Diego County, and Santa Barbara. $8 plus $2 shipping from: Los Angeles Vegetarian Association, 505 S. Beverly Drive, #690, Beverly Hills, CA 90212, (213) 964-4FUN.

Vegetarian Journal's Guide to Natural Food Restaurants in the U.S. and Canada
2,000 restaurants, vacation spots, camps, and local vegetarian group contacts. $14 postpaid from VRG.

Vegetarian Vacation Guide
by The Vegetarian Resource Group
Vegetarian camps, resorts, etc. 12 pages, stapled. $3 plus $1 shipping from the American Vegan Society.

Vegetarianism & Whole Foods: *Periodicals*

Also check with the national & international vegetarian groups in Chapter 11 for newsletters and magazines that update members on vegetarian-related issues.

Good Medicine
A quarterly magazine of the Physicians Committee for Responsible Medicine (PCRM). Articles and news updates on nutrition, health, and animal research. Also recipes, actions you can take, and additional reading. 22 pages. Distributed to PCRM members ($20/year basic membership) from: PCRM, 5100 Wisconsin Avenue NW, Washington, D.C. 20016, (202) 686-2210.

How On Earth! (HOE!)
See Children & Young Adults: Periodicals for a description of this periodical.

The New Vegetarian News
A bimonthly newsletter designed to educate, provide a focus for vegetarians and environmentalists in the San Francisco Bay area, and just be good reading for everyone. Sample issue available. 8 pages per issue. Subscriptions: Sally K. Ravenwood, Editor and Publisher, 131 Maureen Circle, Pittsburg, CA 94565, (510) 458-0507. 1 year (6 issues) for $7.

A Real Life: A Reminder of How Good It Can Be
This creative, artistically-designed "green" publication contains exceptionally high-quality writing on healthy, nontoxic lifestyle choices, including whole vegetarian foods. "We consistently support a vegetarian lifestyle, by offering nutrition and recipe information to show people how to drop animal products from their diet." Single copy for $6. 1 year (6 issues) for $30 ("Let's see — I can handle $2.50/month—that's the cost of a bag of chips, a cappucino, I can't even rent a video for that") from: A Real Life, Box 400, 245 Eighth Avenue, New York, NY 10114-1142.

Vegetarian Journal
Contains articles on food and health, letters from members, meal plans, recipes, book reviews, product reviews, event announcements, poetry, and more. While not as glossy as magazines that carry advertising, this friendly journal is a wonderful medium for exchanges of information. 36 pages. 1 year (6 issues) for $20 (includes membership) from: The Vegetarian Resource Group, P.O. Box 1463, Baltimore, MD 21203, (410) 366-VEGE, FAX: (410) 366-8804.

Vegetarian Times
A monthly magazine that includes vegetarian recipes, dietary information, updates on animal rights issues, advice on buying and preparing whole foods, articles on nutritional approaches to disease, information for travelers, and profiles of prominent vegetarians. 120 pages. Subscriptions: *Vegetarian Times*, P.O. Box 446, Mt. Morris, IL 61054-9894, 1-800-435-9610 (outside Illinois), 1-800-435-0715 (inside Illinois), (815) 734-5824 (outside the U.S.). 1 year (12 issues) for $29.95/U.S., $41.95/Canada, $54.95/Other.

Veggie Life
A bimonthly magazine that includes vegetarian recipes, advice on buying and preparing whole foods, and other articles of interest to vegetarians. The emphasis is on cooking. 82 pages. Subscriptions: *Veggie Life*, P.O. Box 412, Mt. Morris, IL 61054-8163. 1 year (6 issues) for $17.70 ($23.70 outside the U.S.).

Veggie Social News
"Helping vegetarian singles meet & eat." A nice publication even if you aren't looking for "that special someone." See the Vegetarian Supplies & Services section of Chapter 12 for a description of this publication.

Dates to Remember

DATE	EVENT
JANUARY	Check with your local organizations for events.

FEBRUARY

DATE	EVENT
Entire month	Responsible Pet Owner Month (coordinated by the American Society for the Prevention of Cruelty to Animals)
Varies	Animal Care Expo: Trade Show & Educational Conference for Animal-Care Professionals (hosted by The Humane Society of the United States)
14th (Valentine's Day)	National Pet Theft Awareness Day (coordinated by Last Chance for Animals)
Last Tuesday of the month	Spay Day USA (coordinated by the Doris Day Animal League)

MARCH

DATE	EVENT
Varies	Genesis Awards presentation, honoring individuals in the media who have increased understanding of animal issues (sponsored by The Ark Trust, Inc.)
20th (first day of spring)	Great American Meatout, a day to "Kick the meat habit" (coordinated by Farm Animals Reform Movement)

APRIL

DATE	EVENT
Entire month	Prevent-A-Litter month (coordinated by The Humane Society of the United States)
Entire month	Prevention of Animal Cruelty Month (coordinated by the American Society for the Prevention of Cruelty to Animals)
22nd	Earth Day (activities often held on the weekend nearest to the 22nd)

continued...

DATE	EVENT

APRIL (continued)

DATE	EVENT
24th	World Laboratory Animal Liberation Day (coordinated by In Defense of Animals)
Week containing April 24th (varies)	World Laboratory Animal Liberation Week (coordinated by In Defense of Animals)

MAY

DATE	EVENT
Varies	New England Vegetarian Conference (coordinated by the Hartford Vegetarian Society)
Varies	Annual Spring Mourning Vigil for Chickens (coordinated by United Poultry Concerns)
First full week of May, starting on the first Sunday	Be Kind to Animals Week (coordinated by the American Humane Association)
Mother's Day (second Sunday in May)	National Veal Ban Action (coordinated by Farm Animals Reform Movement)
Varies	Lobby Day (coordinated by Humanitarians for Environmental and Animal Laws PAC and the Michigan Humane Society)

JUNE

DATE	EVENT
Entire month	Adopt-A-Shelter-Cat Month (coordinated by the American Society for the Prevention of Cruelty to Animals)
Varies	Annual Animal Rights Symposium (hosted by the National Alliance for Animals)
First week in June	International Animals Rights Awareness Week (coordinated by In Defense of Animals)
3rd	Memorial Day for Animals killed in wars or experimented on by the military (coordinated by Animal Rights Connection, San Francisco, CA)
10th-17th	Animal Rights Awareness Week (coordinated by In Defense of Animals)
22nd	National Veal Boycott Day

DATE	EVENT

JULY

NOTE: Many conferences take place over the summer months. Here are just a few. Check the periodicals listed in Chapter 13 and local groups for details.	Vegetarian Summerfest (coordinated by the North American Vegetarian Society) International Animal Rights Symposium (coordinated by National Alliance for Animals, organizer of the historic 1990 and 1996 March for the Animals in Washington, D.C.) Vegetarian Vacation (coordinated by the Vegetarian Resource Group)

AUGUST

Varies	Annual Vegetarian Beach Gathering (coordinated by The Vegetarian Resource Group)
Varies	Farm Sanctuary's Country Hoe Down (hosted by Farm Sanctuary)
3rd Saturday in August	Annual Candlelight Vigil for National Homeless Animals Day (coordinated by International Society for Animal Rights, Inc.)

SEPTEMBER

Labor Day (the first Monday in September)	Hegins, Pennsylvania Annual Pigeon Shoot Protest (coordinated by The Fund for Animals, Inc.)
Varies	Animals in Entertainment conference to discuss solutions to the many problems created by the use of animals in entertainment (coordinated by the Performing Animal Welfare Society)
Varies; always on a Sunday in September	Annual Greyhound Walk (hosted by Save the Greyhound Dogs!, Vermont)
End of September, beginning of Oct.	National Farm Animal Awareness Week (coordinated by the Humane Society of the United States)

continued...

DATE	EVENT

OCTOBER

Entire month	Adopt-A-Shelter-Dog Month (coordinated by the American Society for the Prevention of Cruelty to Animals)
Entire month	Cut Out Dissection month (coordinated by People for the Ethical Treatment of Animals)
Entire month	Vegetarian Awareness Month (coordinated by the Vegetarian Awareness Network)
First week	World Week of Prayer for Animals (coordinated by International Network for Religion & Animals)
1st	World Vegetarian Day (coordinated by North American Vegetarian Society)
2nd	• World Farm Animal Day (Ghandhi's birthday) • Annual Walk for the Animals (fundraiser for Farm Sanctuary)
4th	World Animals Day (Feast of St. Francis)
Varies	PIGS Annual Open House (hosted by Potbellied Pig Interest Group and Shelter)
Last Saturday in October	National Wildlife Ecology Day (coordinated by Committee to Abolish Sport Hunting and In Defense of Animals), designed to counteract National Hunting and Fishing Day
Last Sunday in October	Greyhound Homecoming and Make Peace Picnic (hosted by Make Peace With Animals, Inc.)

NOVEMBER

Entire month	Adopt-A-Turkey Project (coordinated by Farm Sanctuary)
First week	International Orangutan Awareness Week (coordinated by Orangutan Foundation International)
Day after Thanksgiving	Fur-Free Friday, a day to protest the killing of animals for their fur (coordinated by Animals Rights Mobilization)

DECEMBER Check with your local organizations for events.

Endnotes

Chapter 1: Animal Rights

(1) Kim Bartlett, "Page Two: Means and Ends," *The Animal's Agenda,* May 1990, pg. 2.

(2) Robert Wright, "Are Animals People Too?," *The New Republic*, March 12, 1990, pg. 20.

(3) Jeremy Bentham, *An Introduction to the Principles of Morals and Legislation* (New York: Hafner Publishing Company, 1963), pg. 311. Reprinted with the permission of Hafner Press, a Division of Macmillan Publishing Company.

(4) Dr. Tom Regan, *The Philosophy of Animal Rights*, Culture and Animals Foundation.

(5) Dr. Tom Regan, see note 4.

(6) From *Supersenses* by John Downer. Copyright 1988 by John Downer. Reprinted by courtesy of Henry Holt and Company, Inc.

(7) Alice Walker, "Am I Blue?," *Living By The Word* (New York: Harcourt Brace Jovanovich, Publishers, 1988), pg. 5.

(8) J. Allen Boone, *Kinship With All Life* (New York: Harper and Row, Publishers, 1976), pp. 53 and 52, respectively.

(9) The Gorilla Foundation, *Gorilla*, December 1990, Vol. 14, No. 1, pg. 2.

(10) Dennis Bardens, *Psychic Animals: A Fascinating Investigation of Paranormal Behavior* (New York: Henry Holt and Company, 1987), pg.23. Copyright 1987 by Dennis Bardens. Reprinted by courtesy of Henry Holt and Company, Inc.

(11) Peter Singer, *Animal Liberation: A New Ethics for Our Treatment of Animals* (New York: Avon, 1975), pp. 3 and 6.

(12) American Fund for Alternatives to Animal Research, *News Abstracts*, Spring 1991.

(13) *Encyclopedia of Associations*, Volume 1, edited by Deborah M. Burek, Karin E. Koek, and Annette Novallo (Detroit: Gale Research Inc., 1990), pg. 481.

Chapter 2: Violence

(1) Tom Heymann, *On An Average Day* (New York: Fawcett Columbine, 1989), pp. 36-38 and 139.

(2) *Webster's Ninth New Collegiate Dictionary* (Springfield, MA: Merriam-Webster, Inc., 1985).

(3) Andrew Linzey, *Christianity and the Rights of Animals* (New York: Crossroads, 1987), pg. 56.

(4) Richard D. Ryder, *Animal Revolution: Changing Attitudes Towards Speciesism* (Cambridge: Basil Blackwell, 1989), pg. 39.

(5) Andrew Linzey, see note 3, pg. 64.

(6) Paul Nussbaum, *Knight-Ridder Newspapers*, as reprinted in *The Fund for Animals, Inc.*, Vol. 23, No. 2.

(7) *The American Heritage Dictionary*, Second College Edition (Boston: Houghton Mifflin Company, 1985).

(8) Jeff Cox, "The Three Phases of Health," *SelfCare Catalog & Journal*, March/April 1990, pg. 24.

(9) Marian Breland Bailey, "Every Animal is the Smartest: Intelligence and the Ecological Niche," *Animal Intelligence: Insights into the Animal Mind*, edited by R. J. Hoage and Larry Goldman (Washington, D.C.: Smithsonian Institution Press, 1986), pg. 106.

(10) *New York Post*, November 28, 1972, as quoted in *The Extended Circle*, edited by Jon Wynne-Tyson (New York: Paragon House, 1989), pg. 76.

Chapter 3: Companion Animals

(1) Lynn Lohmeier, Ph.D., "The Healing Power of Pets," *EastWest*, June 1988, pg. 52.

(2) John Sedgwick, "The Doberman Case," *Wigwag*, June 1990, pg. 32.

(3) Gary Francione, "The Paradigm of Property," *The Animals' Voice Magazine*, Vol. 3, No. 2, pg. 68.

(4) National Society for the Protection of Animals, *NSPA Report*, Winter 1987.

(5) Denis Horgan, "Animal Protectors Seek Humane Ways to Fight Cruelty," *The Hartford Courant*, as reprinted by Animal Friends of Connecticut, Inc., undated.

(6) Mary Clifford, "The Case Against Purebreds," *The Animals' Voice Magazine*, Vol. 3, No. 2, pg. 30.

(7) *Cat Fancy* as reported by Animal Protection Institute of America, letter, undated.

(8) National Society for Animal Protection, *Silent Voice*, Winter 1990, as reported by *The ARIES Newsletter*, Vol. 2, No. 5., May 1990, pg. 5.

(9) International Society for Animal Rights, Inc. pamphlet, undated.

(10) American Humane Association, Animal Protection Division, letter.

(11) People for the Ethical Treatment of Animals, *Pet Shops & Puppy Mills*, brochure, undated.

(12) Massachusetts Society for the Prevention of Cruelty to Animals, "Animals and the Earth," *Animals*, March/April 1990, pg. 26.

(13) American Society for the Prevention of Cruelty to Animals, *ASPCA Quarterly Report*, Vol. 8, No. 3, Fall 1988, pg. 7.

(14) People for the Ethical Treatment of Animals, see note 11.

(15) The Humane Society of the United States, *HSUS News*, Vol. 35, No. 4, Fall 1990, pg. 30.

(16) *The Animals' Agenda,* as reported in *Bunny Hugger's Gazette*, No. 4, August 1990, pg. 10.

(17) "Behind the Pet Store Window," *The Animals' Voice Magazine*, Vol. 3, No. 2, pg. 33. Information for the article was provided by The Humane Society of the United States.

(18) The Monks of New Skete, *How to Be Your Dog's Best Friend: A Training Manual for Dog Owners* (Boston: Little, Brown and Company, 1978), pg. 18.

(19) The Animal Welfare Association, Inc. newsletter, Summer 1990, pg. 1.

(20) Terry Jenkins, "How High the Price?," *HSUS News*, Vol. 36, No. 1, Winter 1991, pg. 21.

(21) United Animal Nations - USA, *Journal of the United Animal Nations*, Vol. 4, No. 4, Fall 1990, pg. 2.

(22) Terry Jenkins, see note 20.

(23) From an article appearing in the *Los Angeles Times*, as excerpted in a newsletter of the Doris Day Animal League and paraphrased in a newsletter of the American Humane Association.

(24) Coalition of Municipalities to Ban Animal Trafficking, *COMBAT's Guide to Pet Theft Prevention Fact Sheet.*

(25) Coalition of Municipalities to Ban Animal Trafficking, see note 24.

(26) Coalition of Municipalities to Ban Animal Trafficking, *Network News*, Vol. 1, No. 2, Spring 1989, pg. 1.

(27) Coalition of Municipalities to Ban Animal Trafficking, see note 26, pg. 2.

(28) John Sedgwick, see note 2.

(29) Sandra Lewis, "Seal of Approval: How the American Kennel Club Sanctions Abuse," *Action Line*, April/May 1991, Friends of Animals, pg. 6.

(30) Mary Clifford, see note 6.

(31) Ann Hodgman, "Rare Breeds," *Connoisseur*, September 1990, pg. 86.

(32) Ann Hodgman, see note 31, pg. 90.

(33) The Monks of New Skete, see note 18, pg. 23.

(34) Massachusetts Society for the Prevention of Cruelty to Animals, *Statements of Belief.*

(35) Mercy Crusade, Inc., "'Helping Hands' Not Helpful," newsletter, Winter 1989, pg. 4.

(36) "Lancaster Shelter Investigated for Abuses," *The Animals' Voice Magazine*, Vol. 3, No. 2, pg. 56.

(37) "Shelter Cited," *The Animals' Voice Magazine*, Vol. 2, No. 6, pg. 63.

(38) Animal Rights Information and Education Service, Inc., *The AIRES Newsletter*, Vol. 3, No. 1, January 1991, pg. 12.

(39) The Humane Society of the United States, *HSUS News*, Vol. 36, No. 1, Winter 1991, pg. 27.

(40) "More No-Kill Shelter Scandals," *The Animals' Agenda*, Vol. X, No. 9, November 1990, pg. 37.

(41) "More No-Kill Shelter Scandals," see note 40, pg. 38.

(42) Merritt Clifton, editor, "News Shorts," *The Animals' Agenda*, September 1990, pg. 40.

(43) Animal Rights Information and Education Service, Inc., *The ARIES Newsletter*, Vol. 2, No. 9, September 1990, pg. 1.

(44) Dr. Lemmon, DVM, *Animal Guardian*, Vol. 2, No. 3, 1989, Doris Day Animal League, pg. 11.

(45) Mark Sunlin, "Inside the American Pet Food Industry," *The Animals' Agenda*, December 1990, pg. 16.

(46) Frank Kuznik, "Animal Feed: Render Unto Salmonella," *Nutrition Action Healthletter,* April 1992, pg. 9.

Chapter 4: Vegetarianism

(1) Associated Press, "Restaurant Poll Shows Demand for Veggies," *Dayton Daily News*, September 1, 1991, pg. 17-A.

(2) Living Planet Press, *The Animal Rights Handbook* (Venice, CA: Living Planet Press, 1990), pg. 42.

(3) Farm Animal Reform Movement, *Meat Facts*, brochure, undated.

(4) As quoted by Jane E. Brody, "China's Blockbuster Diet Study," *The Saturday Evening Post,* October 1990, pg. 32.

(5) Much of the diet-disease relationship information presented was extracted from John Robbins' *Diet for a New America* (New Hampshire: Stillpoint Publishing, 1987), Part Two (Chapters 6 - 10). Please see this excellent book for more detail on the link between meat, dairy products, eggs, and health. (See Chapter 13 for ordering information.)

(6) David C. Nieman, OHSc, MPH, FACSM, and others, "Dietary Status of Seventh-Day Adventist Vegetarian and Non-vegetarian Elderly Women," *Journal of the American Dietetic Association,* December 1989, pg. 1768.

(7) The Humane Farming Association, *Consumer Alert: The Dangers of Factory Farming*, undated.

(8) The Humane Farming Association, "USDA Findings Confirm HFA Warnings," *Watchdog*, Fall 1989, pg. 2.

(9) John Robbins, *Diet for a New America* (New Hampshire: Stillpoint Publishing, 1987), pp. 315-318.

(10) Center for Science in the Public Interest, "Is It Safe?," *Nutrition Action Newsletter*, October 1990, pp. 5 and 6.

(11) Orville Schell, *Modern Meat: Antibiotics, Hormones, and the Pharmaceutical Farm* (New York: Random House, 1984), pp. 281-285.

(12) Earth Works Group, *50 Simple Things You Can Do To Save The Earth* (Berkeley: Earthworks Press, 1989), pg. 42.

(13) Center for Science in the Public Interest, see note 10.

(14) Neal D. Barnard, M.D., *The Power of Your Plate* (Summertown, TN: Book Publishing Company, 1990), pg. 103.

(15) Scott Bronstein, "Critics Call Chicken Unsafe," *Dayton Daily News*, June 23, 1991, pg. 6-A.

(16) Public Citizen Foundation, *Public Citizen*, July/August 1990, pg. 8.

(17) As quoted by Scott Bronstein, see note 15.

(18) People for the Ethical Treatment of Animals, *Vegetarian Living*, brochure, undated.

(19) Warren Belasco, "The Two Taste Cultures," *Psychology Today*, December 1989, pg. 33.
(20) Harvey and Marilyn Diamond, *Fit for Life* (New York: Warner Books, 1985), pg. 81.
(21) Earth Works Group, see note 12, pp. 26-27.
(22) The Humane Society of the United States, "Intensive Confinement: Cruel to Animals, Destroyer of the Environment," *Close-Up Report*, February 1990.
(23) Earth Works Group, see note 12, pp. 88, 87, 91, and 32, respectively.
(24) The Humane Society of the United States, see note 22.
(25) The Humane Society of the United States, see note 22.
(26) North American Vegetarian Society, *Meat – Destroying the Planet with a Knife and Fork*, booklet, undated.
(27) Rainforest Action Network, brochure, undated.
(28) "Beefs About Beef," *Consumer Reports*, Vol. 55, No. 8, August 1990, pg. 509.
(29) Rainforest Action Network, see note 27.
(30) *EastWest*, February 1990, as reported in *The ARIES Newsletter,* Vol. 2, No. 5, May 1990, pg. 5.
(31) Earth First! Wolf Action Network, as reported in *The ARIES Newsletter*, Vol. 2, No. 8, August 1990, pp. 3-4.
(32) The Humane Society of the United States, *Personal Action Guide* (Friends of the United Nations, 1990), pg. 4.
(33) John Robbins, see note 9, pg. 351.
(34) Frances Moore Lappé, *Diet for a Small Planet*, First Edition (New York: Friends of the Earth/Ballantine Books, 1974), pp. 6-8.
(35) Frances Moore Lappé, *Diet for a Small Planet*, Tenth Anniversary Edition (New York: Ballantine Books, 1982), pg. 92.
(36) People for the Ethical Treatment of Animals, see note 18.
(37) The Earth Works Group, see note 12, pg. 90.
(38) Sally Clinton, "The Vegetarian Perspective: An Examination of Nutrition Education in the American Diet," *Vegetarian Journal*, May/June 1990, pg. 15.
(39) Physicians Committee for Responsible Medicine, "The New Four Food Groups," *PCRM Update*, May/June 1991, pg. 1.
(40) Sea Shepherd Conservation Society, "Can I Eat Tuna Now?," *Sea Shepherd Log*, Autumn 1990, pg. 3.
(41) Tom Heymann, *On An Average Day* (New York: Fawcett Columbine, 1989), pg. 122.
(42) John McDougall, *McDougall's Medicine*, as reported by EarthSave in *Realities 1990* (facts excerpted from *Diet for a New America* by John Robbins).
(43) Dr. T. Colin Campbell, as quoted by Jane E. Brody, see note 4.
(44) Tufts University Diet & Nutrition Letter, as reported by EarthSave in *EarthSave*, Spring/Summer 1991, Vol. 2, Nos. 2 and 3, pg. 3.
(45) Neal D. Barnard, M.D., see note 14, pp. 128-129.
(46) Jane E. Brody, see note 4.

Chapter 5: Factory Farming

(1) People for the Ethical Treatment of Animals, *Factory Farming*, pamphlet, undated.
(2) Edward F. Dolan, Jr., *Animal Rights* (New York: Franklin Watts, Inc., 1986), pg. 67.
(3) The Humane Society of the United States, "Intensive Confinement: Cruel to Animals, Destroyer of the Environment," *Close-Up Report*, February 1990.
(4) Gene Logsdon, "Maybe the Animal Rights Movement is Good for Us," *Farm Journal*, January 1989, pg. 26-D.
(5) The Humane Farming Association, *Consumer Alert: The Dangers of Factory Farming,* 1985.
(6) The Vegetarian Resource Group, "A Day at the Kansas City Stockyard," *Vegetarian Journal*, March/April 1990, pg. 8.

(7) Scott Bronstein, "Critics Call Chicken Unsafe," *Dayton Daily News*, June 23, 1991, pg. 6-A.
(8) For information on how to order these books, see Chapter 13.
(9) "Hatchery Horror Exposed!," Farm Sanctuary, letter, undated.
(10) People for the Ethical Treatment of Animals, "Stopping Cruelty to Chickens," *PETA News*, Vol. 5, No. 2, March/April 1990, pg. 10.
(11) The Humane Farming Association, see note 5.
(12) "Pigs Die of Stress," *The Animals' Voice Magazine*, Vol. 2, No. 6, pg. 62.
(13) Jim Mason and Peter Singer, *Animal Factories* (New York: Crown Publishers, Inc., 1980), pg. 24.
(14) Jim Mason and Peter Singer, see note 13, pg 25.
(15) The Vegetarian Resource Group, see note 6.
(16) People for the Ethical Treatment of Animals, *PETA News*, Vol. 5, No. 3, May/June 1990, pg. 9.
(17) John Robbins, *Diet for a New America* (New Hampshire: Stillpoint Publishing, 1987), pg. 105.
(18) John Robbins, see note 17, pg. 111.
(19) *The Stall Street Journal*, April 1973, as reported by Peter Singer in *Animal Liberation* (New York: Avon Books, 1975), pg. 126.
(20) Food Animal Concerns Trust, *FACT Acts*, Spring 1990.
(21) Animal Rights International, advertisement about Frank Perdue in *The New York Times,* October 20, 1989, pg. A-17.
(22) John Robbins, see note 17, pp. 141-142.
(23) American Society for the Prevention of Cruelty to Animals, "Sweden's Farm Animals Get New Lease On Life," *ASPCA Quarterly Report*, Vol. 8, No. 4, Winter 1988/Spring 1989, pg. 16.
(24) People for the Ethical Treatment of Animals, *PETA News*, Vol. 5, No. 2, March/April 1990, pg. 11.
(25) The Humane Society of the United States, see note 3.
(26) The Humane Farming Association, *Watchdog*, Fall 1989, insert.

Chapter 6: Research, Education, and Testing

(1) Alice Steinbach, "Whose Life is More Important: An Animal's or a Child's?," *Glamour*, January 1990, pg. 170.
(2) Hans Ruesch, *1000 Doctors (and Many More) Against Vivisection* (CIVIS, 1989), pg. 1.
(3) Ron Karpati, "A Scientist: 'I am the Enemy'," *Newsweek*, December 18, 1989, pg. 12.
(4) Murry Cohen, M.D., "It Should Come As No Surprise," *In Defense of Animals*, undated, pg. 13.
(5) *Science*, August 21, 1987, as reported by Dr. Tom Regan in "A Question of Honor," *The Animals' Voice Magazine*, Vol. 3, No. 2, pg. 61.
(6) John Belleme, "Animal Research Under Fire," *EastWest,* March 1989, pg. 61.
(7) Physicians Committee for Responsible Medicine, "NIH: Science or Public Relations?," *PCRM Update*, March/April 1990, pp. 2-3.
(8) Joyce Tischler, letter to Animal Legal Defense Fund members, May 1991.
(9) Animal Protection Institute, *Taking Animals Out of the Labs*, brochure, November 1988.
(10) Physicians Committee for Responsible Medicine, "Law in the Lab," *PCRM Update*, September/October 1987, pp. 1 and 4.
(11) Barnaby J. Feder, "Pressuring Perdue," *The New York Times Magazine*, November 26, 1989, pg. 60. Copyright 1989 by The New York Times Company. Reprinted by permission.
(12) New England Anti-Vivisection Society, *Through the Laboratory Door*, booklet, undated, pg. 28.
(13) United Action for Animals, Inc., *Animal Welfare Act: Unreported Crimes*, brochure, undated.
(14) New England Anti-Vivisection Society, see note 12, pg. 31.
(15) Physicians Committee for Responsible Medicine, "Inspections: Infrequent at Best," *PCRM Update*, September/October 1987, pg. 2.

(16) National Humane Education Society, *On Animal Experimentation*, brochure, undated.
(17) Physicians Committee for Responsible Medicine, see note 15, pp. 2 and 4.
(18) New England Anti-Vivisection Society, see note 12, pg. 37.
(19) Physicians Committee for Responsible Medicine, see note 7, pg. 2.
(20) National Humane Education Society, see note 16.
(21) Both quotes are from the American Medical Association, *AMA Animal Research Action Plan*, June 1989, as provided by the Animal Liberation Front Support Group.
(22) The American Anti-Vivisection Society, "Cancer Researchers Switching Tactics," *The AV Magazine*, March 1991, pg. 2.
(23) NEAVS, reprint from *The New York Times*, "Reading the Truth About Animal Testing Will Take 5 Minutes. And a Very Strong Stomach.," undated.
(24) The American Anti-Vivisection Society, *Point/Counterpoint: Responses to Typical Pro-Vivisection Arguments*, undated, pg. 6.
(25) Steven Tiger, PA-C, *The Argument for Abolition*, International Society for Animal Rights, Inc., pg. 8.
(26) Physicians Committee for Responsible Medicine, *Research on the Major Killers of Americans*, brochure, undated.
(27) Susan Fowler, "Industry Takes the Long View: Companies Plan for a Future Without Lab Animals," *Animal Rights Coalitions Coordinator's Report '88*, November 1988, Animal Rights International, pg. 27.
(28) Citizen's Committee for Laboratory Animal Liberation, *Tell Congress to End Animal Agony*, flyer, undated.
(29) In Defense of Animals, *Animal Addiction Studies: Focus on Yale*, and *Animal Addiction Studies: Focus on Harvard* fact sheets, undated.
(30) In Defense of Animals, *Animal Addiction Studies: Focus on Harvard*, fact sheet, undated.
(31) Lise Giraud, "University Thievery Exposed! Stanford University First to Fall," *In Defense of Animals Magazine*, Winter/Spring 1991, pp. 7-9.
(32) Disabled and Incurably Ill for Alternatives to Animal Research, *Advancing Medical Research Without Cruelty to Animals*, brochure, undated.
(33) Dr. Robert Sharpe, *Health and Humane Research*, American Anti-Vivisection Society, undated, pg. 9.
(34) Julie Lytle, *PCRM Update*, Special Edition, undated, pg. 8.
(35) Disabled and Incurably Ill for Alternatives to Animal Research, see note 32.
(36) Martin L. Stephens, *Alternatives to Current Uses of Animals in Research, Safety Testing, and Education* (Washington, D.C.: The Humane Society of the United States, 1986), pg. 51.
(37) New England Anti-Vivisection Society, see note 12, pg. 6.
(38) "Animal Testing for Reproductive Harm," *NRDC Newsline*, Vol. 8, No. 3, July/August 1990, National Resources Defense Council, pg. 11.
(39) Deepak Chopra, M.D., as excerpted from *Longevity Magazine* in "Another Cholesterol Cure," *SelfCare Journal*, November/December 1989.
(40) Patrick Cooke, "A Rat is a Pig is a Dog is a Boy," *In Health*, July/August 1991, pg. 60.
(41) The American Anti-Vivisection Society, see note 24, pg. 5.
(42) 48 Hours transcript #45, February 2, 1989, Journal Graphics, Inc., pp. 5-6.
(43) Physicians Committee for Responsible Medicine, *PCRM Update*, Special Edition, undated, pg. 6.
(44) Lynda Dickinson, *Victims of Vanity* (Toronto: Summerhill Press, 1989), pg. 20.
(45) Janet Grady Sullivan, "New Research Without Animals," *The West Side Spirit*, July 3, 1988.
(46) Dr. Robert Sharpe, *The Cruel Deception* (England: Thorsons Publishing Group, 1988), pg. 114.
(47) Physicians Committee for Responsible Medicine, *Beyond the Draize Test*, pg. 1.
(48) Lynda Dickinson, see note 44, pg. 31.
(49) Physicians Committee for Responsible Medicine, letter to Henry Waxman, House

Subcommittee on Health and the Environment Committee on Energy and Commerce, May 5, 1988.

(50) This information, and much of the information in this section, is from Joel S. Newman and Neal D. Barnard, M.D., "The Military's Animal Experiments," *PCRM Update*, January/February 1991, pp. 1-9.

(51) "Victory at Sea: Flipper Fidelis," *The Economist,* January 14, 1989, pg. 30.

(52) Jan Polon, as quoted by Joel S. Newman and Neal D. Barnard, M.D., see note 50, pg. 8.

(53) Physicians Committee for Responsible Medicine, "Pentagon Cancels Cat Experiments," *PCRM Update*, March/April 1991, pg. 1.

(54) Physicians Committee for Responsible Medicine, see note 50, pg. 7.

(55) Bruce Max Feldman, DVM, in a letter to the Midwest Coordinator of In Defense of Animals, December 8, 1989.

(56) Bernard F. Feldman, DVM, in a letter to the Midwest Coordinator of In Defense of Animals, February 14, 1990.

(57) Associated Press,"Wright-Pat Attacked for Animal Abuse," *Springfield News-Sun,* April 20, 1990, pg. 4.

(58) Joel S. Newman and Neal D. Barnard, M.D., "The Military's Animal Experiments, Part II," *PCRM Update*, March/April 1991, pg. 6.

(59) Kenneth Shapiro and John Carr, "The Politics of Psychology," *The Animals' Agenda*, May 1991, pg. 42.

(60) Alan D. Bowd, "Ethical Reservations About Psychological Research with Animals," *The Psychological Record*, 1980, pg. 203. The study quoted by Bowd is by M. Sidman in *Tactics of Scientific Research* (New York: Basic Books, 1960), pg. 11.

(61) New England Anti-Vivisection Society, see note 12, pp. 15-16.

(62) In Defense of Animals, *Just Say No! to the Alcohol, Drug Abuse, and Mental Health Administration*, brochure, undated.

(63) Studies and costs from United Action for Animals, Inc., *Science Gone Insane*, brochure, undated.

(64) The American Society for the Prevention of Cruelty to Animals, *ASPCA Update: Animals in Education*, flyer, undated.

(65) Chris DeRose, letter to Last Chance for Animals supporters, undated.

(66) Merritt Clifton, "Dissection Lab Animal Dealers Exposed," *The Animals' Agenda*, November 1990, pg. 37.

(67) "PETA Asks for Your Help to Rescue Animals from the Dissection Industry," *The Animals Voice Magazine*, Vol. 4, No. 1, pg. 62 and "Special R&I Case Report: High School Cut-Ups," *PETA News*, Vol. 5, No. 5, September/October 1990, pg. 3.

(68) People for the Ethical Treatment of Animals, *PETA Annual Review*, December 1990, pg. 6.

(69) American Fund for Alternatives to Animal Research, *News Abstracts*, Spring 1990, pg. 2.

(70) Lena Williams, "Influence of Pets Reaches New High," *The New York Times*, August 17, 1988, as reported in *Animal Rights Coalitions Coordinator's Report '88*, November 1988, Animal Rights International, pg. 20.

(71) The American Society for the Prevention of Cruelty to Animals, see note 64.

(72) People for the Ethical Treatment of Animals, *Dissection: Your Rights to Refuse*, brochure, undated.

(73) Eight schools are named by the Association of Veterinarians for Animal Rights in "Update on Non-Harmful Use of Live Animals at U.S. Veterinary Schools," *AVAR Directions*, No. 26, November/December 1990, pg. 1. Since that article was published, Ohio State University has joined the list.

(74) The American Anti-Vivisection Society, "Buyukmihci v. University of California," *The AV Magazine*, October 1991, pp. 10-11.

(75) Alternatives to Animals brochure, undated.

(76) Eric Dunayer, DVM, "Learning Veterinary Surgery Without Harming Healthy Animals," *Alternatives to the Harmful Use of Nonhuman Animals* (Vacaville, CA: Association of

Veterinarians for Animal Rights, 1990), pg. 22.

(77) Physicians Committee for Responsible Medicine, list of Medical Schools with No Animal Labs, Medical Schools with Optional Animal Labs, and Schools with Mandatory Animal Labs, September 10, 1990, and Compassion for Animals Foundation, "World Laboratory Animal Liberation Week," *The Activists' Voice Newsletter*, Issue 1.

(78) Sangre de Cristo Animal Protection, Inc., *Pound Seizure Facts,* brochure, undated.

(79) Abram Ber, as quoted by Hans Ruesch, see note 2, pg. 50.

(80) Physicians Committee for Responsible Medicine, "Private Health Foundations Which Do Not Fund Animal Experiments and Private Health Foundations Which Still Fund Animal Experiments" listing, 10-1-95.

Chapter 7: Wildlife

(1) Kenneth Brower, "The Destruction of Dolphins," *The Atlantic Monthly,* July 1989, pg. 37.

(2) *U.S. Code,* Title 16, Chapter 31, Subchapter II, Section 1371(a)((2).

(3) Kenneth Brower, see note 1, pg. 58.

(4) Andrew Davis, "Can We Save Marine Mammals? The Deadly Decline of the Marine Mammal Protection Act," *Greenpeace*, January/February 1988, pp. 11-15.

(5) Andrew Davis, see note 4.

(6) Mark Silberman, "Driftnets: Trouble At Sea," *Not Man Apart*, Friends of the Earth, May/June 1986, pg. 14.

(7) Richard O'Barry, "Dolphins in Captivity: Wasted Lives,Wasted Minds," *The Animals' Agenda*, March 1989, pp. 12+.

(8) Bill Hewitt and Linda Marx, "Flipper's Ex-Trainer Wants His Favorite Mammals Free to Swim with the Fishes," *People Weekly*, September 4, 1989, pg. 41.

(9) *U.S. Code*, Title 16, Chapter 35, Section 1531(a)(3).

(10) *U.S. Code*, Title 16, Chapter 35, Section 1536(a)(2).

(11) *The Hour*, October 19, 1990, as reported in *The ARIES Newsletter*, Vol. 2, No. 12, December 1990, pg. 2.

(12) "Lujan's Views on Wildlife Act Are Dead Squirrelly," *National Catholic Reporter*, June 1, 1990, pg. 24.

(13) Dr. Robert Witzeman as quoted by Frank Graham, Jr., "Talk of the Trail," *Audubon*, March 1990, pg. 10.

(14) Defenders of Wildlife, "Just When You Thought They'd Be Safe On a Refuge...," brochure, undated.

(15) The Humane Society of the United States, "National Wildlife Refuges: A Cruel Hoax," *HSUS Close-Up Report,* undated.

(16) Wildlife Refuge Reform Coalition, brochure, undated.

(17) John. G. Mitchell, "You Call This A Refuge?," *Wildlife Conservation*, March/April 1991, pp. 82-83.

(18) John G. Mitchell, see note 17, pg. 76.

(19) John G. Mitchell, see note 17, pg. 76.

(20) Paul and Anne Ehrlich, *Extinction: The Causes and Consequences of the Disappearance of Species* (New York: Random House, 1981), pg. 147.

(21) Massachusetts Society for the Prevention of Cruelty to Animals, "Animals and the Earth," *Animals*, March/April 1990, pg. 25.

(22) Michael Milstein, "Slaughter in Our National Parks," as condensed from *National Parks* magazine, May/June 1989, appearing in *Reader's Digest*, April 1990, pg. 124.

(23) Roland Boyes, "Lobbying For Parliament," *Beyond the Bars*, edited by Virginia McKenna, Will Travers, and Jonathan Wray, (Rochester, VT: Thorsons Publishing Group, 1987), pg. 90.

(24) As concluded by the Senate Commerce Committee Report on the Endangered Species Act of 1973, as reported by Lewis Regenstein, "The Truth About Sport Hunting," brochure, published

by The Fund for Animals, undated.

(25) John P. Wiley, Jr., "Phenomena Comment and Notes," *Smithsonian*, Vol. 1, No. 1, February 1990, pg. 30.

(26) "No Quiet on the Hunting Front," *The Animals' Agenda*, September 1990, pg. 32.

(27) Lynn Jacobs, "Raping the Land," *The Animals' Voice Magazine*, Vol. 3, No. 3, pg. 43.

(28) Randall Hayes, "Gone With the Trees," *The Animals' Voice Magazine*, Vol. 3, No. 3, pg. 32.

(29) Jacqueline Domac, "And Then There Were None," *The Animals' Voice Magazine*, Vol. 3, No. 3, pg. 35.

(30) Massachusetts Society for the Prevention of Cruelty to Animals, see note 21, pg. 22.

(31) The American Anti-Vivisection Society, "Thousands of Dolphins Die," *The AV Magazine*, January 1991, pg. 5.

(32) Michael Bowker, "Caught in a Plastic Trap," *International Wildlife*, May/June 1986, pg. 22.

(33) Kate Patterson, "Plastic Everywhere," *The Animals' Voice Magazine*, Vol. 3, No. 3, pg. 44.

(34) The Fund for Animals, "An Overview of Killing for Sport," *Hunting Fact Sheet #1*, undated.

(35) *U.S. News & World Report*, February 5, 1990, with data compiled by The Fund for Animals, Inc.

(36) Merritt Clifton, "Killing the Female: The Psychology of the Hunt," *The Animals' Agenda*, September 1990, pg. 30.

(37) Jim Jones, F.E. "Bud" Eyman, Frank Disbrow, and Homer Moe, "Hunter Education: Safety and Responsibility," *Restoring America's Wildlife*, Harmon Kallman, Chief Editor, (U.S. Department of Interior, Fish and Wildlife Service, 1987), pg. 209.

(38) *Deer and Deer Hunting*, September 1991, pp. 49 and 98.

(39) Michael Satchell, "The American Hunter Under Fire," Copyright 1990 by *U.S. News and World Report*, February 5, 1990, pg. 34.

(40) Ted Williams, "Open Season on Endangered Species," *Audubon*, January 1991, pg. 30.

(41) Ted Williams, see note 40, pg. 33.

(42) Friends of Animals, *A Time to Choose* as quoted by Edward F. Dolan, Jr. in *Animal Rights* (New York: Franklin Watts, 1986), pg. 98.

(43) Michael Satchell, see note 39, pg. 33.

(44) Tony J. Peterle, "Substituting Facts for Myths," *Restoring America's Wildlife* (U.S. Department of the Interior, Fish and Wildlife Service, 1987), pg. 60.

(45) Animal Legal Defense Fund, "Taking Aim at Fish and Game Boards," *The Animals' Advocate*, Winter 1990, pg. 1.

(46) Luke Dommer, "Legacy of a Killer," *The Animals' Voice Magazine*, Vol. 2, No. 1, pg. 90.

(47) People for Animal Rights, *Animal Rights: A Natural Extension*, March 1990.

(48) Joy Williams, "The Killing Game," *Esquire*, October 1990, pg. 128.

(49) "Trapping Outrages," *The Animals' Agenda*, November 1990, pg. 35.

(50) "Trapping Outrages," see note 49.

(51) Orange County People for Animals, *Member Update*, January 31, 1990, pp. 3-5.

(52) Ron Baker, *The American Hunting Myth* (New York: Vantage Press, Inc., 1985), pg. 11.

(53) Douglas Chadwick, as quoted by Lewis Regenstein, see note 24.

(54) Animal Legal Defense Fund, see note 45, pg. 6.

(55) Michael Satchell, see note 39, pg. 35.

(56) Vanessa Kelling, "Modern Day Cowboys," *The Animals' Voice Magazine*, Vol. 4, No. 1, pg. 18.

(57) Roger A. Gurner, as quoted in an ad for People for the Ethical Treatment of Animals.

(58) The Fund for Animals, see note 34.

(59) Bill Burton, *The Fund for Animals, Inc.*, Vol. 23, No. 2, pg. 6, reprinted from *The Baltimore Sun*.

(60) Merritt Clifton, see note 36, pg. 26.

(61) F. Reed Johnson, "Wildlife Benefits and Economic Values," *Restoring America's Wildlife* (U.S.

Department of the Interior, Fish and Wildlife Service, 1987), pg. 220.

(62) Joy Williams, see note 48, pg. 124.

(63) Jim Jones and others, see note 37, pg. 215.

(64) The Fund for Animals, "The Destruction of Our Nation's Waterfowl," *Hunting Fact Sheet #3*, undated.

(65) Daniel Glick, "The New Killing Fields," *Newsweek*, July 23, 1990, pg. 54.

(66) Lewis Regenstein, see note 24.

(67) U.S. Fish and Wildlife Service, *Endangered and Threatened Wildlife and Plants*, 50 CRF 17.11 & 17.12, July 15, 1991.

(68) Michael Satchell, see note 39, pg. 35.

(69) Dr. Aaron N. Moen, "Crippling Losses," *Deer and Deer Hunting*, June 1989 as reported by James I. McKee, "The Wounded Whitetail: Built to Survive," *Deer and Deer Hunting*, September 1990, pg. 87.

(70) Adrian Benke, *The Bowhunting Alternative* (San Antonio: B. Todd Press, 1989), pg. 18.

(71) Wayne Pacelle, "Bow Hunting: A Most Primitive Sport," *The Animals' Agenda*, May, 1990, pg. 16.

(72) Adrian Benke, see note 70, pp. 39-40.

(73) James I. McKee, "The Wounded Whitetail: Built to Survive," *Deer and Deer Hunting Magazine*, September 1990, pg. 91.

(74) Adrian Benke, see note 70, pg. 39.

(75) Ted Williams, see note 40, pp. 26-35.

(76) Jim Zumbo, "Going, Going, Gone!," *Outdoor Life*, April 1981, pg. 36.

(77) Cole McFarland, "A Killing on the African Plains of Texas," *The Animals' Voice Magazine*, Vol. 3, No. 3, pg. 18.

(78) *Animal Welfare Institute Quarterly*, Fall/Winter 1989-90, as reported in *The ARIES Newsletter*, Vol. 2, No. 5., May 1990, pg. 6.

(79) African Wildlife Foundation, letter, undated.

(80) Dee Dunheim, "Africa's Poaching Wars," *The Animals' Voice Magazine*, Vol. 3, No. 3, pg. 40.

(81) Michael Milstein, see note 22, pg. 124.

(82) Michael Milstein, see note 22, pg. 124.

(83) Sea Shepherd Conservation Society, "Canadian Seals Go to Hollywood," *Sea Shepherd Log*, Spring 1991, pg. 4.

(84) The American Anti-Vivisection Society, "Sea Turtles Threatened in Japan," *The AV Magazine*, June 1991, pg. 15.

(85) Sarah Fitzgerald, *International Wildlife Trade: Whose Business Is It?* (Washington, D.C.: World Wildlife Fund, 1989), pg. 5.

(86) Mark C. Trexler and Laura H. Kosloff, "International Implementation: The Longest Arm of the Law?," *Balancing on the Brink of Extinction*, edited by Kathryn A. Kohm (Covelo, CA: Island Press, 1991), pg. 117.

(87) Ted Williams, see note 40, pg. 32.

(88) Frank Graham, Jr., "A Bird in the Hand is Worth...Plenty!," *Audubon*, March 1988, pg. 98.

(89) Merritt Clifton, "Eco-Tourism: Making Animals Worth More Alive," *The Animals' Agenda*, November 1990, pg. 39.

(90) Julie Winokur, "Access and Conservation: The Paradox of Ecotourism," *The San Francisco Examiner*, March 18, 1990, pg. T-10.

(91) Joan Dunayer, "Fish: Sensitivity Beyond the Captor's Grasp," *The Animals' Agenda*, July/August 1991, pp. 12-18.

(92) Captain Paul Watson, "Sea Shepherd Rams Mexican Dolphin Killer," *Sea Shepherd Log*, Spring 1991, pg. 6.

(93) Susan Woldenberg, "Walls of Death," *The Animals' Voice Magazine*, Vol. 3, No. 3, pg. 36.

(94) Jack and Anne Rudloe, "Shrimpers and Lawmakers Collide Over a Move to Save the Sea Turtles,"

Smithsonian, December 1989, pp. 47 and 49.

(95) Scott Trimingham, "Killing Cetaceans," *The Animals' Voice Magazine*, Vol. 3, No. 3, pg. 39.

(96) The Humane Society of the United States, "Crisis in the Oceans," *HSUS Close-Up Report*, May 1990.

(97) Beauty Without Cruelty USA, *Action Alert*, Fall 1990, pg. 1.

(98) "Furriers on the Defensive," *The Animals' Agenda*, April 1990, pg. 39.

(99) Beauty Without Cruelty USA, "Say No to Furs — They Did," flyer, undated.

(100) International Society for Animal Rights, Inc., *Peace on Earth Goodwill to All*, flyer, undated.

(101) The Humane Society of the United States, "The Hidden Canadian Seal Hunt," *HSUS News*, Fall 1989, pg. 9.

(102) Captain Paul Watson and Scott Trimingham, "Protecting the South African Seals" and "Canadian Seals Go to Hollywood," *Sea Shepherd Log*, Spring 1991, pp. 5 and 4, respectively.

(103) Association of Veterinarians for Animal Rights, member letter, December 18, 1989.

(104) Aspen Society for Animal Rights, *What's Wrong with Trapping?*, undated.

(105) Association of Veterinarians for Animal Rights, see note 103.

(106) Society for Animal Rights, *This Coat Is Too Expensive At Any Price*, brochure, undated.

(107) Aspen Society for Animals Rights, see note 104.

(108) *Get Set to Trap*, California Department of Fish and Game, excerpts provided by Orange County People for Animals, *Member Update*, January 31, 1990, pg. 5.

(109) Association of Veterinarians for Animal Rights, see note 103.

(110) "Why Lynx is Campaigning Against the Fur Trade," *Lynx Magazine*, undated.

(111) "Trapping Outrages," *The Animals' Agenda*, November 1990, pg. 35.

(112) Association of Veterinarians for Animal Rights, see note 103.

(113) Aspen Society for Animal Rights, *Fact Sheet on Ranch-Raised Furbearing Animals*, undated.

(114) People for the Ethical Treatment of Animals, "Exporting Cruelty," *PETA News*, September/October 1989, pg. 5.

(115) Rod Coronado, Coalition Against Fur Farms letter, undated.

(116) Vanessa Kelling, see note 56.

(117) Merritt Clifton, "The Wiley Coyote," *The Animals' Agenda*, May 1990, pg. 50.

(118) Greenpeace, *Greenpeace Magazine*, January/February 1991, pg. 6.

(119) Earth First! Wolf Action Network, as reprinted in *The ARIES Newsletter*, Vol. 2, No. 8, August 1990, pp. 3-4.

(120) The Humane Society of the United States, member letter, September 1990.

(121) The Humane Society of the United States, see note 120.

(122) Lynn Jacobs, see note 27.

(123) Merritt Clifton, see note 117, pg. 51.

(124) Jay D. Kirkpatrick, Ph.D., "Animals on the Pill: Pipe Dream or Promise?," *The Animals' Agenda*, March 1989, pg. 57.

(125) The Humane Society of the United States, see note 120.

(126) Michael Satchell with Joannie M. Schrof, "Uncle Sam's War on Wildlife," Copyright 1990 by *U.S. News and World Report*, February 5, 1990, pg. 37.

(127) Dr. Tony Povilitis, "Living With Deer," *HSUS News*, Fall 1989, pg. 27.

(128) Sea Shepherd Conservation Society, "Boycott Files," *Sea Shepherd Log*, Spring 1991, pg. 7.

(129) Richard D. Ryder, *Animal Revolution: Changing Attitudes Toward Speciesism* (Cambridge: Basil Blackwell, 1989), pg. 35.

Chapter 8: Entertainment

(1) J. Allen Boone, *Kinship With All Life* (New York: Harper and Row, Publishers, 1976), pg. 86.

(2) Jill Schensul, "Investigating The Making of The Movie Message," *ASPCA Quarterly Report*, Vol. 7, No. 2, Fall 1987, pg. 14.

(3) "Ringling Brothers Circus Picketed," *The Animals' Voice Magazine*, Vol. 3, No. 2, pg. 57.

(4) Animal Advocates, Inc., "Good-bye Gunther and Good Riddance!," *Animal Advocates Newsletter*, Winter 1990, pg. 7.

(5) Animal Rights Community, circus flyer, undated.

(6) *The Christian Science Monitor*, September 14, 1988, as reported by the Animal Rights Front, *Why We Protest The Circus*, fact sheet, undated.

(7) Network for Ohio Animal Action, *News Release*, November 3, 1988.

(8) "Tyrone the Terrible," Primarily Primates, Inc., flyer, undated.

(9) Mercy Crusade, Inc., "AFTRA Acts Against Animal Abuse On Union TV Stages" and "American Humane Association's $10 Million Lawsuit Against Humanitarian Bob Barker," newsletter, Winter 1989, pg. 2.

(10) Jill Schensul, see note 2.

(11) Dr. Cindy Bauman, as quoted by Defenders of Animal Rights (Maryland) in *Defenders of Animal Rights Bans Calf Roping in Baltimore County*, flyer, undated.

(12) As quoted by Barbara Boyer, "Animal Rights Groups Target Rodeos," *The Tampa Tribune*, Friday, March 8, 1991, pg. 1-Florida/Metro.

(13) "Cockfighting: Fun and Profit?," *The Animals' Voice Magazine*, Vol. 3, No. 2, pg. 55.

(14) Daniel Chu and Tom Nugent, *People Magazine*, as reprinted by The Fund for Animals in "They Shoot Pigeons, Don't They?," *The Fund for Animals*, Vol. 24, No. 2.

(15) Doris Day Animal League, "Greyhounds Racing for Their Lives," *Animal Guardian*, Vol. 3, No. 1, 1990, pp. 5-6.

(16) Physicians Committee for Responsible Medicine, "Army Drafts Stolen Dogs for Bone-Breaking Experiments" and "A Race to the Death," *PCRM Update*, July-August 1990, pp. 1-6.

(17) In Defense of Animals, "IDA Pursues Black Market Dog Ring: Successfully Sues USDA," *In Defense of Animals*, Spring 1990, pg. 6.

(18) The Humane Society of the United States, "Hounding Racing in Its Stronghold," *HSUS News*, Winter 1990, pg. 8.

(19) Doris Day Animal League, see note 15, pg. 6.

(20) Jack Rosenberger, "Iditarod: Extreme or Extreme Cruelty?," *Animals*, March/April 1996, pg. 19.

(21) Cynthia A. Branigan, "The Dark Side of Horse Racing," *The AV*, January 1991, The American Anti-Vivisection Society, pg. 16.

(22) Dale Marcellini, as quoted by Robert M. Andrews, "Zoo Animals Confused, Befuddled by Behavior of Friendly Visitors," Associated Press, *Dayton Daily News*, September 20, 1991, pg. 3-C.

(23) Mark Glover, "Can the Earth Survive Man?," *Beyond the Bars*, edited by Virginia McKenna, Will Travers, and Jonathan Wray (Rochester, VT: Thorsons Publishing Group, 1987), pg. 100.

(24) Network for Ohio Animal Action, "Zoo Doo," *Winter 90 Update*, pg. 5.

(25) Peter Batten, *Living Trophies* (New York: Thomas Y. Crowell Company, 1976), pg. ix.

(26) Lifeforce, "Editorial: Lifeforce Study Proves Abuse," *Lifeforce Ecology News,* Vol. 2, No. 2, Summer 1992, pg. 2.

(27) Animal Rights Front (Connecticut), *Mystic Marinelife Aquarium: A Prison for the Innocent,* fact sheet, undated.

(28) Animal Rights Front (Connecticut), see note 26.

(29) Richard O'Barry, "Dolphins in Captivity: Wasted Lives, Wasted Minds," *The Animals' Agenda*, March 1989, pp. 12+.

(30) Network for Ohio Animal Action, see note 23.

(31) "San Francisco Zoo Elephant Beaten," *The Animals' Voice Magazine*, Vol. 3, No. 3, pg. 57.

(32) Doris Day Animal League, "Member Spotlight: Florence L. Lambert," *Animal Guardian*, Vol. 3, No. 2, 1990, pg. 7.

(33) International Primate Protection League, newsletter, October 1990.

(34) "Detroit Zoo Kills Sheep," *The Animals' Voice Magazine*, Vol. 3, No. 2, pg. 55.

(35) Massachusetts Society for the Prevention of Cruelty to Animals, "Animals and the Earth," *Animals*, March/April 1990, pg. 27.

(36) Primarily Primates, Inc., *Survivors of the Snake Farm,* undated.

(37) Massachusetts Society for the Prevention of Cruelty to Animals, see note 34.

(38) Network for Ohio Animal Action, *Winter 90 Update* and *Summer 1991 Up-Dates*, pp. 5 and 7.

(39) Massachusetts Society for the Prevention of Cruelty to Animals, *Statements of Belief.*

(40) National Society for the Protection of Animals, "Pulling Passengers Profitable, Precarious," *NSPA Report*, Fall 1988, pp. 1-2.

(41) "Pulling for Horses," *The Animals' Agenda*, March 1990, pg. 36.

(42) *Maine Animal Coalition Newsletter*, Vol. 3, No. 3, Summer 1990.

Chapter 9: Getting into the Act

(1) Mark Glover, "Can the Earth Survive Man?," *Beyond the Bars*, edited by Virginia McKenna, Will Travers, and Jonathan Wray (Rochester, VT: Thorsons Publishing Group, 1987), pp. 108 and 109.

(2) League of Women Voters Education Fund, *Tell It To Washington*, March 1991-1992, pg. 6.

(3) Paul Obis, "Learning to Love the Hunter," *Vegetarian Times*, January 1991, pg. 4.

(4) Michael Klaper, M.D., "Happy Holidays? Avoiding Disagreements Over Food," *EarthSave*, Vol. 2, No. 1, Winter 1991, pg. 2.

(5) G. Thomas Morgan, "Nothing to be Ashamed Of," *Deer and Deer Hunting*, September 1990, pg. 49.

(6) The American Anti-Vivisection Society, *Point/Counterpoint: Responses to Typical pro-Vivisection Arguments*, undated, pg. 9.

Chapter 10: Animal Advocacy Organizations

(1) "Who Gets the Money?," *Animal People*, December 1995, pg. 13.

Glossary

Note: Words that appear in *italics* are defined elsewhere in the glossary.

American Association for Accreditation of Laboratory Animal Care (AAALAC)
A private accreditation organization for research facilities which is funded by the research community. AAALAC accreditation is not required by the federal government and does not affect a research facility's eligibility for federal funding.

American Association of Zoological Parks and Aquariums (AAZPA)
The standard-setting accreditation organization for zoos and aquariums. Certification by AAZPA is not a requirement for zoos or aquariums and AAZPA approval is no guarantee of humane or competent supervision of animals.

Animal and Plant Health Inspection Services (APHIS)
The division of the *United States Department of Agriculture* responsible for inspecting research facilities registered with the federal government to verify their compliance with the *Animal Welfare Act.*

Animal Care and Use Committee
A committee required to exist at each research facility that uses animals covered by the *Animal Welfare Act.* The committee consists of at least three members appointed by the Chief Executive Officer of the research facility. One of the members is supposed to represent "general community interests in the proper care and treatment of animals." The committee may be called different names by different institutions, such as the "Laboratory Animal Use Committee."

Animal Damage Control (ADC) program
A federal program operated by the *United States Department of Agriculture* designed to control "nuisance" wildlife, such as those animals that eat farmers' crops or kill livestock. Most of ADC's budget is directed toward the trapping, poisoning, shooting, burning, and clubbing of predators, with unintentional victims including birds, dogs, cats, and other animals.

animal dealer
A person who buys, sells, transports, or delivers animals for profit. Dealers obtain animals from a variety of sources, including pounds, shelters, and from individuals called *bunchers,* who sometimes obtain animals illegally. Clients of animal dealers include research laboratories.

animal research
See *vivisection.*

Animal Research Action Plan
The title of the plan developed by the American Medical Association (AMA) and sent to each of its U.S. members, which outlines the AMA's strategy for countering what the AMA calls the "problem" of "animal rights groups who are dedicated to the elimination of the use of animals in biomedical and other scientific research."

animal rights

The assertion that animals are *sentient* expressions of life with *intrinsic value*, and as such are entitled to certain privileges, which include living as natural a life as possible and not being exploited for human gain.

animal supply house

A commercial enterprise that acquires, prepares, and supplies animals dead or alive to clients such as schools and laboratories.

animal welfare

The assertion that animals should be treated kindly. Animal welfare is not traditionally the same as *animal rights*.

Animal Welfare Act (AWA)

Federal legislation which specifies minimum care standards for animals used in research facilities, by animal dealers, and by exhibitors. The AWA is largely a "housekeeping" bill which specifies minimum standards for things such as cage size, temperature, ventilation, and transportation. The Act applies only to the care and handling of animals before and after experiments. It does not limit what is done to an animal during an experiment, including how much or what type of pain may be inflicted. The specific regulations of the Act are determined and administered by the *United States Department of Agriculture*. The Act itself excludes cold-blooded animals and all animals "used or intended for use as food or fiber" (all farm animals). The regulations established by the Secretary of Agriculture exclude mice and rats from the Act (70% to 90% of all research animals).

Animal Welfare Caucus (AWC)

A group formed by congressional members who support legislation benefiting the interests of animal users such as farmers and researchers. Formed in response to the pro-animal *Congressional Friends of Animals*.

anti-vivisectionist

A person who opposes *vivisection,* the invasive use of animals for research, testing, or education.

battery cage

A wire cage approximately one-foot square which is used to house four to five chickens simultaneously. Battery cages have been outlawed as inhumane in many European countries, but continue to be legal in the United States.

bucking strap

A belt secured around a horse's middle and over his genitals, which is pulled tight to cause pain and make the horse buck in rodeo performances.

buncher

An individual who collects animals, mostly cats and dogs, and sells them to an *animal dealer*, who in turn sells them to research laboratories and other clients. Some bunchers steal animals or obtain them from pounds or by answering "free to good home" ads.

companion animals

Those animals who live with us in our homes and serve as our companions ("pets").

Congressional Friends of Animals (CFA)
A group formed by congressional members who support legislation benefiting animals.

Conibear trap
A "whole body" trap designed to snap shut around the neck of an animal, strangling her to death, but often resulting in a prolonged, agonizing death for unsuspecting animals. The trap is named after its inventor.

cruelty-free products
Products not tested on animals. "Cruelty-free" may or may not include products that contain animal ingredients.

dead pile
A collection of animals at a stockyard, too sick or injured to move under their own power, who are left in a pile to die.

debeaking
A standard procedure practiced by the chicken industry which involves slicing off approximately one-third of a chick's upper beak with a hot blade, without anesthetic. Debeaking is employed to prevent factory farm chickens, who peck at each other out of stress, from mutilating each other.

declawing
The practice of surgically removing a cat's claws, a common but psychologically and physically harmful procedure.

Draize Eye Irritancy Test
A product test that involves introducing substances, from lipstick to oven cleaner, into the eyes of animals to observe the degree of irritation caused by the substances. White albino rabbits are the animal of choice because their eyes are very sensitive and because the structure of their tear ducts prevents tears from washing away the foreign substances.

endangered species
Species in danger of extinction.

Endangered Species Act
Federal legislation passed in 1973 to protect plant and animal species threatened with extinction. The Act has been grossly undermined by commercial interests.

ethical vegetarian
A person who is a vegetarian because s/he believes that it is morally wrong to kill animals for use as "food."

exotic game ranches
Private, commercial sport hunting preserves that provide nonnative animals such as jaguars, leopards, antelope, giraffes, and gazelle as targets for *trophy hunters*. Animals on game ranches include tame animals from zoos and endangered species.

factory farming
The most prevalent method of commercial meat, egg, and milk production today. Factory farms employ *intensive confinement* methods of production, focusing solely on quantity without regard to the quality of animals' lives. In factory farming, animals are treated as products, not as beings.

flanking strap

See *bucking strap.*

flower essences

Liquid solutions made from a sun infusion of blossoms in water, most well known for addressing emotional imbalances. Flower essences work on a vibrational level, that is, on the energy fields of living beings. They were first developed in the 1930s by Dr. Edward Bach, an English physician, thus many people commonly refer to flower essences as "Bach Flower Remedies."

four food groups

A widely-publicized concept that categorized "essential" foods into four groups — meat, dairy, bread/cereal, and fruits/vegetables. A recent redefinition of the four food groups by the Physicians Committee for Responsible Medicine names the following food groups as the basis for a nutritionally sound diet: whole grains, legumes, vegetables, and fruits.

fruitarian

A person who eats only the fruits of plants, including nuts and seeds, thereby sparing the plant itself.

fur farm

A commercial enterprise that subjects foxes, minks, and other undomesticated, fur-bearing animals to lifelong confinement in cages and then kills them for their pelts in order to fill the demand for fur products. Fur farming is similar to *factory farming* in that animals are treated simply as commodities without regard for their needs or instincts.

homeopathy (*home-me-AH-pathy*)
homeopathic (*home-me-oh-PATH-ic*) remedies

Homeopathy is a branch of medicine that helps the body cure itself based on the "law of similars" or "like cures like." That is, a substance that produces "disease" symptoms in a healthy person will produce a "cure" in a person exhibiting those same symptoms, if the substance is first prepared according to the rules of homeopathic preparation—a series of highly controlled dilutions and "shakings." Ironically, the more diluted the substance when prepared in this manner, the higher its potency. A German physician, Samuel Hahnemann, is credited with developing homeopathy in the early 1800s. Like flower essences, homeopathic remedies work on a vibrational level, that is, on the energy fields of living beings. A certain level of knowledge is required to know which homeopathic remedies are appropriate and in what doses, as the effects can be quite profound.

institutional cruelty

Cruelty that is tolerated, or is not acknowledged as cruelty, because it is interwoven into our culture and has become an accepted custom.

intensive confinement

A method of animal agriculture utilized in *factory farming* that involves confining as many animals as possible in as small a space as possible.

interspecies communication

An exchange of understanding between members of differing species. As used in this book, the term "interspecies communication" means "telepathic interspecies communication," the exchange of information on a "mind-to-mind" level. While people unfamiliar with telepathic communication may be skeptical of its existence, several people successfully employ this type of communication to relate with nonhuman species. While some people come by this ability without effort, it can be developed by anyone with a sincere desire to do so.

intrinsic value
Considered valuable in and of itself, for no reason other than the fact that it exists.

lacto-ovo (*lack-toe-OH-voe*) vegetarian
A person who does not eat any form of animal flesh, but does eat dairy products (lacto) and eggs (ovo).

LD50
An abbreviation for "Legal Dose 50," a product test that determines the amount of a substance required to kill 50% of the animals to whom the substance is administered.

leghold trap
See *steel-jaw leghold trap.*

macrobiotics
A set of principles for living a healthy, happy life based on helping the body regain and maintain proper balance. A standard macrobiotic diet consists of the proper balance of "yin" and "yang" — about 50-60% grains, 25% vegetables, 10% sea vegetables and beans, and 5% soup. Special macrobiotic diets are recommended for helping the body recover from specific illnesses.

Marine Mammal Protection Act
Federal legislation passed in 1972 to protect depleted populations of marine mammals, primarily in response to the slaughter of dolphins by tuna fishers.

"milk-fed" veal
The tender, white muscle of a calf, produced by keeping the calf on an iron-deficient, liquid diet and denying him even minimal exercise, such as walking. "Milk-fed" veal is misnamed because the largest U.S. producer of the formula fed to veal calves does not include any cow's milk in the formula.

National Institutes of Health (NIH)
The federal government's primary funding agency for animal research. NIH is a division of the Department of Health and Human Services.

National Wildlife Refuge System
A collection of separate acreages across the country officially designated as federal refuges for wildlife and managed by the *United States Fish and Wildlife Service*. Although the original intent in 1903 was to set aside safe habitat for wildlife, animals in today's refuges are legally hunted and trapped, and are exposed to water pollution, military exercises, and a host of commercial enterprises including oil drilling, logging, mining, and ranching.

Natural Hygiene
A set of principles for living in harmony with natural laws as they apply to humans and all animals. Natural Hygiene emphasizes the roles of air, water, food, sunshine, activity, exercise, rest, sleep, fasting, and mental and emotional factors in health and well-being. A Natural Hygiene diet emphasizes eating foods compatible with our digestive systems and compatible with each other from a digestion standpoint.

pet theft
The practice of stealing companion animals out of backyards, from cars, and off of streets by individuals who often sell them to research laboratories or to animal dealers who in turn sell

them to research laboratories. Animals are also stolen by impostors answering "found" ads or "free to good home" ads.

pound seizure
The practice of releasing live pound or shelter animals to research or teaching facilities for use in laboratories or classrooms. Pound seizure has been outlawed by some states and many communities.

product testing
The practice of subjecting animals to various consumer products, from nail polish to lawn care chemicals, in an attempt to determine whether or not substances are harmful to people. A product test may involve force-feeding substances to animals, applying substances to the raw, scraped skins of animals, or forcing animals to inhale substances. Product tests on animals do not guarantee consumer safety.

puller
A person employed by the egg industry who sorts baby chickens by sex, keeping the females and discarding (killing) the males. Also called a "sexer."

puppy mill
A low-budget commercial enterprise that breeds dogs for sale to pet shops and other buyers. Puppy mills are often backyard operations that expose animals to filthy, overcrowded conditions with no veterinary care or socialization. Dogs from puppy mills often exhibit physical and psychological problems as they grow up.

purse seining (*SAY-ning*)
A method of fishing where a large net called a "seine" is used to encircle fish, and the bottom of the net is then closed to form a large bag or "purse." Dolphins and other marine animals are often mutilated and killed during purse seining by tuna fishers.

right
A just claim or entitlement.

selective compassion
An emotional distancing that allows us to reserve our empathy for a chosen few.

sentient
Capable of experiencing sensation or feeling.

sexer
See *puller*.

speciesism (*SPEE-she-izm*)
Prejudice or discrimination based on species. Speciesism is the "us" and "them" rationalization that allows human animals to exploit other animals.

steel-jaw leghold trap
A spring-loaded trap designed to clamp around the paw or leg of an animal and hold the animal until the trapper can return to kill him or her, usually by clubbing or suffocation. Some animals gnaw their paws off in an attempt to escape the trap.

strict vegetarian
A person who does not eat any form of animal flesh, and also does not eat dairy products or

eggs. Sometimes called a "total vegetarian" or "dietary vegan."

tabling
Setting up literature and information tables at places such as local fairs or shopping malls.

tail-biting
A stress-induced behavior in which a crazed pig bites off the tail of another pig. Common in *factory farming* (*intensive confinement*) settings.

tail-docking
The practice of cutting off an animal's tail. Routinely implemented by factory farmers to prevent *tail-biting* in pigs and by breeders to make dogs fit American Kennel Club standards.

threatened species
Species likely to become *endangered species.*

trophy hunter
A hunter who kills "big game" animals and collects their body parts for display as symbols of conquest.

United States Department of Agriculture (USDA)
The department of the federal government responsible for establishing and enforcing the regulations mandated by the *Animal Welfare Act,* and for operating the *Animal Damage Control program.*

United States Department of the Interior
The department of the federal government responsible for overseeing a variety of functions related to U.S. territories and properties. Includes the *United States Fish and Wildlife Service* and the National Parks Services.

United States Fish and Wildlife Service (USFWS)
The agency of the *United States Department of the Interior* that manages fish, wildlife, and endangered species and their habitats, and oversees hunting and fishing practices.

veal crate
A stall in which a veal calf is isolated for his entire lifetime. The stall is just big enough for the calf to stand up in, but is too small for him to comfortably lie down in. Veal crates are still legal in the U.S., but have been banned as inhumane in Great Britain.

vegan (*VEE-gun*)
A person who abstains from all animal-derived foods, including meat, dairy products, and eggs, and all animal products that could have been gained through exploitation or harm to an animal, including leather, wool, and silk. Some vegans include honey as an animal product.

vegetarian
A person who does not eat any form of animal flesh, including mammals, fish, and fowl. The true vegetarian does not eat any food that contains ingredients from a dead animal, including gelatin (obtained from boiling animal tissues) and lard (animal fat). Contrary to popular belief, a person who eats fish or fowl is not a vegetarian.

vivisection
The injurious use of animals in laboratories and classrooms, whether for experimentation, product testing, training, or demonstration. Also called "animal research" or "animal

experimentation."

wildlife conservation

The preservation of animal species in their natural habitats. In general, conservationists are concerned with preserving species as a whole and not with individual animals. Conservation of selected species is often practiced by hunters at the expense of other species.

Index

A

B

C

F

G

H

N

O

P

Q

R

S

W

X-Z

Order & Update Form

(Please Photocopy This Form — Leave This Page Intact)

Name (Please Print): ______________________________

Address: ______________________________

City: ____________________ State: __________ Zip: __________

Phone (in case there is a question about your order): (_____)____________________

❐ Please send me _____ copies of *Animal Rights: A Beginner's Guide (second edition)* at $19.95 each (includes free shipping). I am enclosing a check or money order *payable to WriteWare, Inc.*

❐ I am having the book(s) shipped to an Ohio address, therefore I am adding the mandatory $1.20 per book Ohio sales tax ($19.95 + $1.20 = $21.15 per book).

(Please allow 4-6 weeks for delivery, although shipment is usually much faster.)

❐ I have enclosed information about an organization, product, or service that I think readers of *Animal Rights: A Beginner's Guide* would like to know about.

Send orders, updates, and inquiries to:

WriteWare, Inc.
P.O. Box 51
Yellow Springs, Ohio 45387

Thank-you!